The Measurement of Capital

Studies in Income and Wealth
Volume 45

National Bureau of Economic Research
Conference on Research in Income and Wealth

The Measurement of Capital

Edited by Dan Usher

The University of Chicago Press

Chicago and London

DAN USHER teaches in the Department of Economics at Queen's University, Kingston, Ontario. He is the author of *The Price Mechanism and Meaning of National Income Statistics* and *The Measurement of Economic Growth.*

The University of Chicago Press, Chicago 60637
The University of Chicago Press, Ltd., London

Printed in the United States of America
84 83 82 81 80 5 4 3 2 1

Library of Congress Cataloging in Publication Data

Conference on the Measurement of Capital, Toronto, Ont.
1976.
The measurement of capital.

(Studies in income and wealth ; v. 45)
Includes bibliographical references and index.
1. Capital—United States. 2. Capital—Statistical methods. I. Usher, Dan, 1934– II. Title.
III. Series: Conference on Research in Income and Wealth. Studies in income and wealth ; v. 45.
HC106.3.C714 vol. 45 [HC110.C3] 330'.08s 79–18893
ISBN 0–226–84300–9 [332'.041]

Since this volume is a record of conference proceedings, it has been exempted from the rules governing critical review of manuscripts by the Board of Directors of the National Bureau (resolution adopted 6 July 1948, as revised 21 November 1949 and 20 April 1968).

Contents

Prefatory Note

This volume contains the papers presented at the Conference on the Measurement of Capital held in Toronto on 14 and 15 October 1976. Funds for the Conference on Research in Income and Wealth are provided to the National Bureau of Economic Research by the National Science Foundation; we are indebted for its support. We also thank Dan Usher, who served as chairman of the conference and editor of this volume.

Executive Committee, October 1976
Dorothy Projector, chairman
Clopper Almon
Robert M. Coen
Stanley Lebergott
Jack A. Sawyer
Dan Usher
Dorothy A. Walters
Burton A. Weisbrod
Allan H. Young
Geoffrey H. Moore, NBER representative

Introduction

Dan Usher

This volume is a collection of papers all related in one way or another to the general problem of how to construct a time series of capital in real terms. Capital in real terms is also referred to as "real capital," "aggregate capital stock," "capital in its own units," or just plain "capital," the term I shall employ in this Introduction. Capital in this sense must be distinguished from the "value of capital in current dollars," a related but nonetheless distinct concept. In introducing problems in the measurement of capital it is useful to begin with a case where these problems do not arise at all. This is where all capital goods are constructed from uniform and indestructible blocks, like the blocks children play with, where the quantity of capital per unit of each type of capital good is the number of blocks it contains, and where capital goods can be assembled or disassembled costlessly. The quantity of capital is simply the total number of blocks. Specifically, if there were n distinct types of capital goods, if each type, i, of capital good consisted of P^o_i blocks, and if there were K^t_i units of the i type of capital goods in the economy in the year t, the total capital stock K^t in the year t could be measured unambiguously according to the formula

$$(1) \qquad K^t = P^o_1 K^t_1 + P^o_2 K^t_2 + \ldots + P^o_n K^t_n.$$

The papers can be divided into two distinct groups. The first group, the papers by Young and Musgrave, Coen, Hulten and Wykoff, Engerman and Rosen, Soladay, and to some extent Eisner, start with the working premise that the object in measuring capital is to construct a measure of capital in accordance with equation (1), where the P^o_i are

Dan Usher is associated with Queen's University, Kingston, Ontario.

interpreted not as numbers of blocks, but as prices of capital goods in some chosen base year. The central problem in all these papers is to deal with complexities of the world, notably the diverse patterns of depreciation of capital goods and the changes over time in the nature of capital goods themselves, which are abstracted away in the model where equation (1) is unambiguously defined. Allan Young and John Musgrave discuss the assumptions and methods in the United States Department of Commerce time series of real capital stock in the United States. Other papers in this group can be looked upon as studies of how the series might be improved or modified. Robert Coen, and Charles Hulten and Frank Wykoff, derive alternative ways of measuring depreciation. Stanley Engerman and Sherwin Rosen review two new books with implications for the measurement of capital—a volume by John Kendrick on how to extend the definition of capital, with special emphasis on human capital, and a volume by Robert J. Gordon on new methods of constructing price indexes for capital goods. John Soladay's paper extends the definition of capital to include reserves of oil and gas. Robert Eisner's paper introduces an imputation for capital gains or losses as indicated by, for instance, changes in the value of shares traded on the stock market.

The second group of papers, those by Murray Brown and W. E. Diewert, examine the premise that capital in real terms can be measured in accordance with equation (1). Can time series of quantities of capital goods be combined into a single number that may be interpreted as "the" measure of real capital in the economy as a whole? Can it be said that the capital stock in one industry is greater than the capital stock in another? Does equation (1) provide an adequate representation of real capital? Can a better index number be devised? These papers contain extensive discussions of index number and aggregation problems in capital measurement.

To introduce this volume I shall discuss the papers briefly, not one by one, but in the context of a summary of what I take to be the main problems of capital measurement. I have chosen this format to give the reader a sense of how each paper relates to the other papers in this volume and contributes to the overall problem of capital measurement. I begin by reviewing the purposes of capital measurement, for we cannot evaluate techniques of measuring capital until we know what the measurements are for. Then, following the order of the papers in this book, I consider a series of problems in measuring capital defined in accordance with equation (1). Next I list and compare the different meanings of the term "real capital" in economic analysis. And, finally, there is a brief discussion of index numbers and aggregation.

The Purposes of Capital Measurement

We can conveniently identify five purposes, though these are not entirely distinct.

1. *The investment function.* We want a measure of capital in real terms to serve as an argument in the investment function

$$I = f(K,p, \ldots), \tag{2}$$

where I is the amount of investment over some period of time, K is the capital stock at the outset of the period, p is the relative price of capital goods in terms of consumption goods, and the blanks in the function indicate that other factors are also important. This function may be studied on its own or in conjunction with other functions in a large econometric model designed to forecast the progress of the economy.

2. *The consumption function.* As an important component of wealth, real capital appears implicitly as an argument in the consumption function

$$C = g(Y,W, \ldots), \tag{3}$$

where C is real consumption, Y is real income, and W is real wealth, which includes title to physical assets, financial assets, and whatever extra items are required to take account of liabilities, title to foreign assets, and so on. Once again, the function can be studied by itself or in the context of a large econometric model.

3. *The production function.* Among the many uses of the production function in economic analysis, three should be mentioned here because the role of the time series of capital is different in each case, and these differences might be reflected in the design of the time series themselves. The production function is

$$Q = f(K,L), \tag{4}$$

where Q is output, L is labor, and K is capital. The first use of the production function is to measure the elasticity of substitution between labor and capital. This elasticity is, of course, essential for predicting the effects upon the distribution of the national income of changes in technology, tax rates, or factor supplies. Typically, when we measure elasticities of substitution, we are exclusively concerned with the shape of the isoquants today. The second use of the production function is to apportion observed economic growth into that which can reasonably be attributed to the replication of factors of production such as were available at the outset of the time period over which growth is observed and that which has to be attributed to technical change between the initial and final year of the time period. In this case, the emphasis of the analysis is upon the technology in the base period. The third use is really a miscellaneous collection. Over the last twenty years or so, the two-sector, two-factor model of the economy has been growing in importance as the basis for much of the analysis in economic history, economic development, public finance, and international trade. We want time series of capital in real terms to enable us to estimate production functions as a way to test theories and quantify their predictions.

Here, however, we must be on our guard against an elementary fallacy that can crop up in several ways. In the course of this Introduction, I shall present a list of difficulties with the concept of capital. Most of these are well known, and some authors consider them so serious that no reasonably satisfactory time series of capital in real terms can ever be devised. In general, the fallacy is to say that, because capital does not exist, the theories normally formulated by means of a model with capital and labor as the only primary factors of production must be either wrong or useless. The baldest and crudest variant of this fallacy is the assertion that the nonexistence of capital indicates a fundamental contradiction in capitalism itself. If there is no capital, then it cannot have a marginal product. If capital's marginal product is undefined, so too must be the marginal product of labor. Thus the allocation of the national product of labor among factors cannot be determined by economic forces and must be the outcome of political forces, class power, and exploitation. This conclusion may or may not be true, but the argument is surely false in the sense that the conclusion is independent of the existence or nonexistence of an aggregate called real capital. To decide whether and under what conditions wages of labor and returns of capital goods are endogenous to the competitive economy, one should examine not the two-sector model, but the full general equilibrium model as perfected by Arrow, Debreu, and many others. It is clear from these models that the existence or nonexistence of a general equilibrium solution, including an allocation of the national income among factors of production, does not in any way depend upon whether quantities of capital goods can be aggregated into a measure of the total capital stock.

We use the two-sector model in international trade and public finance as a kind of shorthand for the full general equilibrium model with many kinds of capital goods, products, and labor. It would of course be a pity if measures of capital were so unsatisfactory from a theoretical point of view that it would be wrong to estimate production functions at all. But that would not detract from the relevance or usefulness of propositions about conditions under which free trade is best or the burden of tax is shifted onto an untaxed sector of the population.

4. *Budgeting and planning.* Statistics on the size of the capital stock are used in budgeting, planning, and forecasting. The simplest and perhaps still most commonly employed technique in this area is to predict income in the near or intermediate future from actual or expected investment by postulating constant capital-output ratios or constant incremental capital-output ratios. Time series of capital in real terms are used in more complex and subtle ways in budgeting and forcasting to predict the effect of changes in the tax rates or public expenditure upon income and employment.

5. *Connections with the rest of the national accounts.* Real capital has acquired a bad name in that it is alleged to be particularly fraught with theoretical and statistical difficulties. It may be that real capital does not altogether deserve its reputation, for many of these difficulties are present in other elements of the national accounts, especially investment in real terms, depreciation, capital gains, and wealth, all of which are closely connected to real capital itself. In particular, depreciation is the loss of value in the course of the year of that part of the capital stock that was in existence when the year began. Statistics of depreciation can of course be thrown together in some rough and ready way, but an accurate and well-grounded measure can be obtained if and only if we can measure real capital as well.

The Measurement of Capital in Accordance with Equation (1)

Capital is usually measured by the "perpetual inventory" method[1] in which the time series of the stock of capital is built up step by step from time series of dollar values of investment and prices of capital goods.

To compute a time series of real capital according to the perpetual inventory method, one needs time series of gross investment in current dollars, I^t_i, where the superscript t refers to the year and the subscript i refers to the type of capital goods, time series of capital goods prices, P^t_i, and a rule connecting values of new and old capital goods from which one can compute time series of depreciation D^t_i. Then, for each type of capital goods, the increase in real capital in the year t is

$$\Delta K^t_i = \frac{I^t_i - D^t_i}{P^t_i} \tag{5}$$

and the value of each K^t_i in equation (1) can be estimated as

(6) $$K^t_i = K^o_i + \sum_{\tau=0}^{t-1} \Delta K^\tau_i,$$

where the initial value of capital K^o_i can be computed in a straightforward manner by a variant of the perpetual inventory method itself. The measure of total capital can now be computed by summing up the K^t_i for each year t weighted by the base year prices of capital goods.

This, broadly speaking, is the method of measuring real capital employed by national statistical agencies throughout the world and, in particular, by the Bureau of Economic Analysis of the United States Department of Commerce as described by Young and Musgrave. Two features of their methods are worth emphasizing in view of the discussion of these matters in other papers: their handling of depreciation and their notion of the price of capital goods.

The problem of depreciation is to decide what proportion of capital produced in a given year is deemed to be still available t years later. There are four elements to consider: (1) Part of the capital stock has been *retired*; it is out of the capital stock entirely. (2) Some of the remaining capital stock may have deteriorated; its marginal product in a physical sense is less than when it was new, or it requires more maintenance and repair. (3) The capital stock is *older*; it has fewer years of service left than when it was new. (4) It has become *obsolete*; its marginal value product is less than when it was new because of changing tastes, the availability of more efficient capital goods, or increases in the rents of cooperating factors of production.

Young and Musgrave hold the view that, all things considered, the joint effect of the last three elements of depreciation can best be accounted for by straight-line depreciation; that is to say, if a piece of capital equipment lasts T years and is counted as one unit of capital when new, it should be counted as $(T - t)/T$ units of equipment when it is t years old, for all $t \leq T$. They recognize that this is less than ideal as a measure of depreciation, but they argue that our information about true economic depreciation is so skimpy and imprecise that one cannot do better in practice. Lives of capital equipment are taken from the tax schedule of the Department of the Treasury, with adjustments to approximate actual average economic lives and to account for variability in the lives of the different units of the same kind of capital equipment.

In measuring prices of capital goods, Young and Musgrave follow Denison's lead (1957) in that they avoid on principle treating costless quality change in capital goods as a reduction in price. They state that "deflation of gross fixed investment . . . counts only cost-associated quality change as a change in real capital," and they go on to argue that, viewed in this light, the often-heard criticism of the official price indexes of capital goods—that they overstate the amount of price increase—may be misplaced.

The papers of Coen, Hulten and Wykoff, Engerman and Rosen, Soladay, and Eisner, and of course the comments by Rymes and Faucett can all be thought as developments of themes introduced in the Young and Musgrave paper:

Alternatives to the Perpetual Inventory Method

It is important for us to take a critical and skeptical stance toward the perpetual inventory method, precisely because of its popularity and the apparent ease with which it lets us compile time series of real capital stock. Most of the difficulties with the measurement of capital pertain to the perpetual inventory method to some extent, but two general issues are worth considering now. The first is that the perpetual inventory method is very theoretical in the pejorative sense of the term. At no point in the perpetual inventory method is it necessary to compare quantities of captial goods directly—to make inventories of the capital goods available in the year 0 and the capital goods available in the year *t*, and to decide which inventory constitutes the larger capital stock. This decision is avoided by treating the total stock each year as the sum of the increments in every preceding year. Even the increments are not quantities that may be compared directly from one year to the next. They are ratios of values and prices, and any errors in these data—or more precisely any misjudgment, for there is no unambiguous way of deciding which price index is appropriate—reverberate throughout the time series. A second difficulty with the perpetual inventory method is, as it were, the reverse side of its principal advantage. The perpetual inventory method never fails to yield us a time series of real capital, no matter how long the time series in question or how radically the technology and the nature of capital goods have changed between the first and final years. The perpetual inventory always works as long as there are data on gross investment, depreciation, and price indexes of capital goods. There is no red light that flashes, no internal check that tells us when the whole process becomes absurd. This is, of course, a difficulty with all aggregate time series in real terms—real consumption, real gross national product, and so on. But between real capital and, for instance, real consumption there is a difference in degree, if not in kind. Statistics of real consumption are intended to serve as indicators of the heights of the indifference curves attained in each of the years of the time series, the underlying assumptions being that the indifference curves themselves are stable over time and that the constancy of taste permits us to compare quantities of food, clothing, housing, and so on, from the present day right back to medieval or ancient times. But the continual change in the technology of production brings forth new processes and new machines every year, depriving us of a reference point from which real capital stock can be compared forward and backward in time.

There are several possible alternatives to the perpetual inventory method. The aggregate capital stock might be estimated from book values of companies, insurance records, or direct surveys of capital goods in existence. Faucett suggests in his comment that book values might be preferable to the perpetual inventory method for measuring the industrial composition of the capital stock because book values automatically take account of transfers among industries of secondhand equipment. Survey methods have been employed to measure capital in the Soviet Union. They are said to be very expensive and to involve virtually intractable problems of classifying the myriad types of capital goods employed at different times into standard categories that can play the role of K_1, K_2, and so forth, in the definition of real capital in equation (1) above.[2] Alternatively, it has been found possible to construct time series of real capital from statistics of fire insurance (see Barna 1957). This would be much cheaper than a survey of all capital goods, but there are of course great problems with the compatability and reliability of the data.

Alternative Ways of Measuring Depreciation

Rymes and Faucett's principal criticism of the Young and Musgrave paper is that their measure of depreciation fails to reflect the time pattern of the fall in the market value of capital equipment as it ages—fails, that is, to reflect what is commonly called "economic depreciation." The criticism has to do with the conversion from service prices to stock prices and with the reasons a piece of capital might become less productive over time. Faucett and Rymes argue that if, for instance, a capital good yields a constant flow of services over its life, its depreciation ought to be small at first and then progressively larger to reflect the time path of the present value of the capital good. They also argue that all sources of decline in present value should be accounted for—not only physical deterioration of the capital good, but obsolescence owing to increased cost of cooperating factors of production or to competition with new and better machines. Coen's paper and Hulten and Wykoff's paper are attempts to estimate economic depreciation from two quite different sorts of data.

Hulten and Wykoff base their estimates on a United States Treasury sample of prices of new and used structures. Broadly speaking, their findings are that economic depreciation is less than allowed for in the tax code and in the national accounts (so that the measure of the capital stock in real terms is correspondingly larger), and that the time pattern of depreciation that provides the best fit to the data is not straight line but geometric or something even more accelerated, the distinction being that under straight-line depreciation the value of capital declines by a constant amount each year of its life, while under geometric depreciation the value declines by constant proportion. Geometric depreciation is made consistent with a finite lifetime of capital goods by eliminating all remaining value at the terminal date.

An important theoretical point emerges from Hulten and Wykoff's analysis—economic depreciation depends upon the tax laws. The value of secondhand equipment declines more or less rapidly with age according to the rate of depreciation for tax purposes; the more rapidly a firm may depreciate a piece of equipment, the more rapidly it declines in value, for part of the value of any piece of equipment is the present value of the remaining depreciation allowances. The existing rate of economic depreciation is therefore different from what it would be if economic depreciation were chosen as the basis for depreciation in the tax code. The relation between tax and economic depreciation is not an infinite regress but more like a set of equations that need to be solved simultaneously.

The dependence of economic depreciation on the tax laws has similar implications for the measurement of capital in accordance with equation (1). Ideally, we would like a measure of real capital to reflect a property of the technology of the economy exclusively. We might like the measure of K^t in equation (1) to play the role of K in the production function, so that any increase in K^t reflects a capacity of the economy to produce more in some sense, regardless of the tax laws or of the tastes of consumers. We now see that the measure of capital constructed by the perpetual inventory method need not have that property, because the size of the capital stock in each category K^t_i depends on the rate of depreciation, which in turn depends on the tax laws in force in the year t. One might try to get around this problem by estimating K^t "as though" the tax laws remained invariant, by treating base year tax laws analogously to base year prices. Or one might argue that K^t obtained by the perpetual inventory method, though less than ideal, is adequate for some purposes. In fact, Hulten and Wykoff's evidence shows that rates of economic depreciation were virtually constant over the period they studied, despite the substantial changes in the tax laws.

Coen's paper is based on the idea that one can infer the rate of economic depreciation from time series of investment. Firms invest to maintain a proportion between productive capacity and output, but the productive capacity at any moment depends upon the prior rates of deterioration and obsolescence of its capital equipment. Consequently, the time path of deterioration and obsolescence can be inferred by observing which among a variety of possible paths provides the best fit in an equation linking investment to output, productive capacity, and other economic variables. This procedure leads Coen to an exact specification of the relation between economic depreciation and loss of efficiency of capital goods, for it is the latter alone that affects the rate of investment in his model. There is also a discussion of the relation between economic depreciation and the accuracy of expectations about inflation; there are circumstances where past errors in estimating the rate of inflation can affect the rate of depreciation today.

The Pricing of Capital Goods

The pricing of capital goods may prove to be the Achilles' heel in the measurement of capital in real terms. Equation (1), which is our working definition of real capital, contains the terms K^t_i. To write such terms is to assume, albeit implicitly, that the nature of each type i of capital goods persists unchanged through time. To measure the output of newly produced capital goods, we divide their value (which can be measured with tolerable accuracy) by a price index. But if our implicit assumption is false, if new capital goods are materially different from old capital goods, then we have no sure basis for choosing a price index; and whatever price index we choose reflects, whether we like it or not, an assumption about the equivalence of new and old types of capital goods. How, to take the prime example of this difficulty, do we construct a price index to convert the Marchant calculator on which the older generation of economists used to run its regressions and the computing facilities now available into amounts of a single type of capital?

There are two main schools of thought on this issue. One school, represented in this volume by Young and Musgrave, would measure real capital on the *supply* side, comparing new and old machines according to their cost of production and thereby excluding costless improvements in capital goods from the measure of the size of the capital stock. The other view, represented in a new book by Robert J. Gordon, reviewed here by Engerman and Rosen, would measure real capital on the *demand* side, comparing new and old machines according to their usefulness as assessed by performance characteristics such as speed, size, and safety of automobiles or number of additions per second of calculators. The difference is empirically important; Gordon's preliminary estimate of the growth rate of real investment in the United States, presented in Engerman and Rosen's table 4.3, is literally twice the rate in the official United States national accounts.[3]

There is no general consensus among economists and statisticians on which concept of the price index is preferable, but there is a recognition on all sides that there are major conceptual and theoretical problems with each. Capital could be measured precisely and unambiguously on the demand side if there were a finite number of performance characteristics in the economy as a whole, if the nature of performance characteristics were invariant over time, if the value of each type of capital good were an invariant function of the amounts of the performance characteristics it contained, and if we could always determine the amounts of the different performance characteristics in any capital good. But the world is not like that. Changes over time in the nature of capital goods cannot be entirely represented as different amounts of invariant characteristics; technical change causes prices of capital goods to rise or fall over time in ways that do not conform to any stable function of amounts of characteristics; prices of characteristics vary greatly over time as characteristics become scarce or plentiful; and, as Denison pointed out long ago, it is difficult to see how machines that embody laborsaving technical change can be compared on a common scale with machines that have no effect upon labor productivity. Capital could be measured precisely and unambiguously on the supply side if the relative prices of machines within any category (such as computers) remained constant over time. We could then say that, for instance, if a Marchant calculator costing $200 in the year when the SR 50 appears on the market counts as two units of capital and if the SR 50 costs $50 in that year, then the SR 50 is always to be counted as one-half a unit of capital regardless of the characteristics of the two machines. But the world is not like that either. Relative prices of capital goods within any category are constantly changing, newly discovered types of capital goods are typically more expensive when they first appear on the market than they become later on when the market is more nearly saturated and when their cost of production has been reduced by further technical change.

The debate over the choice of a price index of capital goods reminds one of the question posed by Joan Robinson (1953–54) in the opening shot in recent round of debate on capital theory. "In what units," it was asked, "is capital to be measured?" Young and Musgrave's answer is, "In Marchant calculator equivalents where other machines are equated to Marchant calculators according to their cost of production." Gordon's answer is, "In additions per second and other characteristics evaluated at prices in a base year."

The Scope of Real Capital

Capital may be defined narrowly as produced means of production, or it may be defined broadly to include all or a large part of the factors of production in the economy. Young and Musgrave, adopting the narrower definition, measure capital as the sum at base-year prices of equipment, structures, inventories, and residences, as is the practice in the national accounts of many countries. Kendrick, Soladay, and Eisner are in different ways attempting to account for a wider range of factors of production.

In the volume reviewed here by Engerman and Rosen, Kendrick extends the definition of capital to include land, consumer durables, human capital (the accumulated cost of education treated as investment), and accumulated expenditure on research and development. He does this to provide a test for the hypothesis that growth in real output per head in the United States can be explained by the growth of real capital per head. Clearly, if a large part of capital formation is in human capital, then human capital has to be accounted for in any comparison of growth rates of inputs and outputs. Although the residual that must be attributed to something like aggregate technical change is reduced by Kendrick's extension of the scope of capital, it is still not eliminated.

Soladay adds an imputation for stocks of oil and gas. It is rather queer, when one thinks of it, that the stock of subsoil assets is excluded from the measure of capital, and the depletion of subsoil assets is excluded from the measure of depreciation, though their exclusion is required by the formal definition of capital as produced means of production. Excluding subsoil assets from capital means that Saudi Arabia, despite its oil reserves, must be counted as a capital-poor country. Excluding the wastage of subsoil assets from depreciation means, for instance, that the abandonment of an oil rig is treated as a reduction in the capital stock while the loss of the oil field that led to its abandonment is not. Similarly, a country rapidly using up its oil reserves would be counted as having a net investment in the oil industry if it is devoting resources to drilling new wells to discover what is left of the ever-smaller stock of oil underground. The situation can be rectified by expanding the definition of capital.

The stock of subsoil assets and the corresponding capital consumption allowance might be measured according to assumptions that lie along a continuum. At one extreme, the stock of subsoil assets is looked upon as given at the beginning of time, and all production represents a kind of depreciation. On this assumption, net investment in oil is the expenditure over the year on discovery of oil, drilling, and plant and equipment minus the sum of depreciation of existing facilities and the production of oil evaluated at a shadow price equal to the difference between the world price of oil and the current cost of extraction. At the other extreme, one might identify the stock of capital in oil with the quantity of proved reserves; net investment is positive on this assumption if proved reserves are larger at the end of the year than they were at the beginning. The in-between cases would involve recognizing both proved and unproved reserves as part of the capital stock, but unproved reserves would have a lower shadow price, so that discovery increases the quantity of capital. Soladay chooses the second extreme case, including only proved reserves in the capital stock.

Eisner adds an imputation to the capital stock for accumulated capital gains, permitting him to compare capital stocks among the different sectors of the economy with measures corresponding to their own valuations of their assets at different periods of time. The imputation for capital gains is intrinsically different from the other extensions to the definition of capital and is best discussed in the next section.

The Definition of Capital

There is widespread agreement that the working definition of real capital in equation (1) is only an approximation, but there is less than full agreement on what the definition is supposed to approximate. There seem to be four main contenders for the definition of capital in real terms: instantaneous productive capacity, long-run productive capacity, cumulated consumption forgone, and real wealth. Because these concepts are logically distinct, it is entirely possible that each of them is preferable to the others for a certain range of purposes. I shall discuss them in turn.

1. *Instantaneous productive capacity.* According to this definition of capital, one lot of capital goods constitutes more capital than another lot of capital goods if more output can be produced this year with the first lot than with the second lot when the production function and the labor force are the same in each case. For simplicity, suppose one good is produced with two kinds of capital and two kinds of labor,

$$Q^t = f^t(K^t{}_1, K^t{}_2, L^t{}_1, L^t{}_2), \tag{7}$$

where the superscript t indicates that the production function represents the technology available in the year t, and where $Q^t, K^t{}_1$ . . . are quantities of output and input in the year t.

Let us choose the year 0 as the base year and arbitrarily set the index of real capital associated with the capital goods employed in that year at 1; we designate the index as K, and we say that $K = 1$ for the stocks of capital goods $K^0{}_1$ and $K^0{}_2$. We must now attach a value of K to the mix of capital goods, $K^t{}_1$ and $K^t{}_2$, employed in the year t. We can proceed as follows: the basic idea is to choose a definition of capital such that the amount of capital associated with the pair $K^t{}_1$ and $K^t{}_2$ is at least as large as the amount of capital associated with the pair $K^0{}_1$ and $K^0{}_2$ if $K^t{}_1$ and $K^t{}_2$ can replace $K^0{}_1$ and $K^0{}_2$ in the production function without loss of output. Let us say that $K^t{}_1$ and $K^t{}_2$ constitutes an amount of capital γ, that $K^t = \gamma$, if $K^t{}_1$ and $K^1{}_2$ can be reduced by a factor γ and still do the same job as $K^0{}_1$ and $K^0{}_2$. (This is what Diewert calls a Malmquist index.) In other words, the value of K associated with $K^t{}_1$ and $K^t{}_0$ is equal to γ if

$$(8) \qquad f^0\left(\frac{K^t{}_1}{\gamma}, \frac{K^t{}_2}{\gamma}, L^0{}_1, L^0{}_2\right) = f_0\left(K^0{}_1, K^0{}_2, L^0{}_1, L^0{}_2\right).$$

This definition of capital has in common with the usual definition of real consumption in the economic theory of index numbers that it is dependent on a functional form and certain base-year values. Real consumption is dependent on the utility function. Real capital is dependent on the production function f^0 and on the supplies of labor $L^0{}_1$ and $L^0{}_2$. The definition could be modified in several ways. In particular, we could weaken the requirement that all bundles of capital goods must be combined with precisely $L^0{}_1$ and $L^0{}_2$ by allowing a choice among equal values of labor at base-year prices. I do not think that would affect the essence of any of the problems we discuss here.

This definition of real capital is—so far as I can tell—internally consistent and free from any hint of paradox. But that desirable quality is purchased at no small cost. For most of the purposes of real capital listed above, we would like real capital to be a unique concept. We would like a definition such that if the mix of capital goods K_1 and K_2 is more real capital than the mix of capital goods K'_1 and K'_2 within the production function f^0 and for supplies of labor $L^0{}_1$ and $L^0{}_2$, then the mix K_1 and K_2 is more real capital than the mix K'_1 and K'_2 for all functions f and all supplies of labor L_1 and L_2. Normally—almost invariably—this is not so. Real capital is a family of concepts, one member for each set of f, L_1 and L_2.

The study of the conditions under which the separate definitions of real capital give rise to the same time series—what unfortunately (for the terminology is off-putting) has come to be known as the problem of existence—constitutes a major part of the papers by Diewert and Brown, both of which are primarily concerned with capital as instantaneous productive capacity as defined here. The conditions under which real capital exists in this sense turn out to be disappointingly restrictive. On one hand, it is sufficient for existence of an aggregate capital stock if the process by which capital goods are produced is such that relative service prices of the different capital goods remain constant over time, for in that case a greater value (again at service prices) of capital goods represents a more productive bundle regardless of the form of the production function, as long as an optimal mix of capital goods is chosen at any given time. This is the Hicks's aggregation theorem; unfortunately, it amounts to saying that there is only one capital good in the system, for many goods with invariant relative prices are just like one good with a variety of uses. On the other hand, capital exists for a particular production function if that function displays "homogeneous weak separability"—that is, if the production function takes the form $f^t(k(K^t{}_1, K^t{}_2), L^t{}_1, L^t{}_2)$, where the interior function k is homogeneous in degree one with respect to $K^t{}_1$ and $K^t{}_2$. If the function k exists, then the value of the function is itself the measure of the aggregate capital stock. Otherwise, the combined productive capacity of $K^t{}_1$ and $K^t{}_2$ depends on the mix of $L^t{}_1$ and $L^t{}_2$ employed. Similarly, their combined productive capacity depends on which production function they are employed in, unless the interior function k is the same in every function f.

These problems of the existence of capital are important in practice because there is always some technical change between the first year and the final year of any time series. Suppose we want a time series of capital beginning in the year t and ending in the year T, and suppose that technical change is gradually shifting the production function from f^t to f^{t+1} to f^{t+2} and so on until f^T. Which year's production function is to be taken as the basis for constructing the time series? If a measure of capital "exists" in the sense of that word used by index number theorists, then all production functions generate the same time series. If capital almost exists in the sense that the production functions are very similar or that they give rise to very similar time series of real capital, we can be content with a measure of the capital stock based on any one of the set of production functions. But if capital does not exist, then a time series of capital based on the production function and stocks of labor of the year t may well show capital to be increasing from one year to the next when, in fact, the productive capacity of the capital goods available is diminishing.

Long-run productive capacity. In our first definition of capital,[4] the quantities of the capital goods K_1 and K_2 were aggregated according to their capacity to produce output today, but their durability was not taken into account. It made no difference whether the existing stock of K_1, for instance, will wear out next year, in two years, or in a hundred years. Only its effectiveness today was considered. A measure of capital as an indicator of long-run productive capacity incorporates both durability and productivity of capital goods. It can be defined analogously to the first measure, except that the production function would need to be generalized to take account of the flow of consumption goods in every future year. A mix of capital goods K_1 and K_2 would then constitute more real capital than a mix K'_1 and K'_2 if people are better off with the first mix than they are with the second, where "better off" incorporates potential output tomorrow as well as potential output today.

The empirical measure of capital defined in equation (1) and discussed by Young and Musgrave, Coen, Hulten and Wykoff, Soladay, and Engerman and Rosen seems to approximate a measure of long-run productive capacity because the durability of capital is taken into account and, what amounts to the same thing, because quantities of capital goods are weighted by market prices rather than by service prices. All of the problems of existence and aggregation we encounter in trying to define capital as instantaneous productive capacity carry over into the definition of capital as long-run productive capacity, and there is the additional problem that the mix of captial goods K_1 and K_2 may count as more or less capital than the mix K'_1 and K'_2, depending upon the rate of interest. Here once again the issue is not whether capital exists in the special technical sense we are giving to the word "exists"—for in practice capital never exists—but whether it comes close enough to existing for the time series we construct to tell us something useful about the economy.

Accumulated consumption forgone. Both of the preceding definitions of real capital—instantaneous productive capacity and long-run productive capacity—are aggregations of capital goods according to what we can do with them in certain circumstances. One might also measure real capital according to its opportunity cost. Capital in this sense is measured as the amount of consumption forgone in the process of acquiring the stocks of capital goods in existence. Suppose the only consumption good is potatoes, the only capital good is tractors, and tractors last forever (so we need not distinguish between instantaneous and long-run productive capacity). In the year 1 the output of tractors was 100 and the relative price of tractors and potatoes was 20 tons of potatoes per tractor. At the beginning of the year 2, there occurs a technical change in the tractor industry such that the alternative cost of producing tractors falls to half what it was in year 1. The relative price of tractors falls from 20 tons of potatoes to 10 tons of potatoes. Then in the year 2 the output of tractors increases to 200. According to the use definitions discussed above, the output of new capital goods has increased from 100 in the year 1 to 200 in the year 2. According to the opportunity cost definition, based on consumption forgone, the addition to capital is the same in both years because 2,000 tons of potatoes was sacrificed in the process of investment in each year. From a statistical point of view, the main difference between these measures of real capital is that the value of capital goods is deflated by a price index of capital goods in one case and a price index of consumption in the other.

This definition of capital is in a sense the logical conclusion of the attempt to price capital on the supply side according to their cost of production. For cost is only definable with respect to a numeraire, and the only numeraire that presents itself—if we exclude money and if we exclude capital goods themselves (since that is what we want to measure the cost of)—is consumption goods. This definition of capital is that employed by Kendrick in his measures of human capital; the forgone earnings of students and the alternative cost of research and development can be assessed in no other way. A straightforward implication of this definition of capital in real terms is that maintenance and repair should be treated as part of gross investment.

Real wealth. Real wealth is the present value, at some given time series of interest rates, of the stream of consumption goods earned by the existing stock of capital goods. Real wealth differs from the other measures of capital in real terms in a number of respects, the most interesting of which from our point of view is that any technical change that enhances the productivity of capital goods increases the quantity of real wealth as well. A given mix of capital goods K_1 and K_2 should count as the same amount of instantaneous productive capacity or long-run productive capacity at all times, but it represents more real wealth at a time when the current technology has endowed it with a high present and future marginal product than it does at a time when it is less favored by the existing technique.

The statistical implication of this feature of the concept of real wealth is that the measure of capital should include capital gains in addition to the original cost of equipment. It is for this reason that I hesitated to classify Eisner's imputation of capital gains to Young and Musgrave's measure of capital as an attempt to make the measure of real capital conform more closely to the definition of real capital in equation (1). That is not what Eisner is doing at all. Eisner starts out with a conventional estimate of capital in real terms, but he modifies that estimate for the purpose of measuring real wealth, which is in some sense independent of the stocks of capital goods.

Real wealth and accumulated consumption forgone are sometimes called the "forward-looking" and "backward-looking" measures of capital, while instantaneous productive capacity and long-run productive capacity are measures of capital "in their own units." One of the interesting theoretical issues that was touched upon but certainly not resolved at this conference was whether any price index can be constructed to reflect the quantity of capital in its own units, for it is at least arguable that the demand concept of price indexes advocated by Gordon leads inevitably to a measure of real wealth, whereas the supply concept advocated by Young and Musgrave leads to a measure of accumulated consumption forgone, leaving capital in its own units in a sort of theoretical limbo whenever technical change alters the nature of capital goods to a significant extent.

This issue was at least peripheral to the old debates over capital theory between Irving Fisher and Böhm-Bawerk[5] and, later on, between Hayek and Knight,[6] and it crops up again in the more recent controversy over the reswitching of techniques (Samuelson 1966) discussed in Brown's paper.

Ideally, our choice among these concepts of real capital ought to be governed by the purpose of the time series. It would be very convenient if we could go through our list of purposes of real capital and show that one particular concept of capital is preferable to the rest in every case. Unfortunately, this appears not to be so. I think that long-run productive capacity is the most appropriate concept of capital for inclusion in an investment function, because firms assess the need for new capital goods in accordance with their plans for the future and not just in accordance with their capacity to produce today. The concept of capital as wealth may be more appropriate as an argument in the consumption function. On the other hand, instantaneous productive capacity seems to be the appropriate species of capital for estimating production functions because the productivity of capital next year is irrelevant when we are concerned, for instance, to discover the elasticity of substitution between labor and capital today.[7] Views differ on which concept of capital is appropriate for computing the proportion of observed economic growth that can be attributed to technical change. My own view on the matter is that we want a measure of cumulative consumption forgone, because the essense of the problem is to estimate what national income would be today if technical change had not occurred and because change in the relative price of consumption goods and capital goods is one of several forms technical change can take. It is difficult to say which concept of capital is most appropriate for planning and budgeting until we have specified what methods of planning and budgeting are being employed. Presumably, instantaneous productive capacity would be the appropriate concept for the computation of capital-output ratios.

Index Numbers and Aggregation

Once we have decided why we want to measure capital and which among the many possible definitions is appropriate for our purpose, we must set about building a time series of capital with the information at hand. The working assumption in Young and Musgrave's paper is that, as an indicator of long-run productive capacity, capital can be adequately represented by the Laspeyres index of equation (1). Diewert and Brown scrutinize this assumption carefully. They investigate the accuracy of the Laspeyres index as an indicator of the size of the capital stock, they consider alternative index number formulas, and they raise the question whether it is reasonable to postulate an aggregate production function to represent what is in effect the interaction of many production processes in which many capital goods are employed.

Problems in this area can be classified under two main headings. There are index number problems having to do with the measurability of capital with the available data, and there are aggregation problems having to do with the existence of summary measures of the capital stock. As a simple example of the index number problem, suppose we know there is a function $K = g\ (K_1, K_2)$ and we have time series of quantities of capital goods available, K_1 and K_2, and of prices of capital goods, P_1 and P_2, where P_1 and P_2 are proportional to first derivatives of g with respect to K_1 and K_2; but we do not know the functional form g and we do not have a time series of the values of K. The problem is to infer the time series of K from the time series of K_1,K_2,P_1, and P_2. As a simple example of the aggregation problem, suppose there exists, not a function $g(K_1,K_2)$, but a pair of production functions $Q^A = f^A(K^A{}_1,K^A{}_2)$ and $Q^B = f^B(K^B{}_1,K^B{}_2)$ for each of two industries, A and B, where Q^A and Q^B are outputs, and total supplies of the two capital goods are $K_1 = K^A{}_1 + K^B{}_1$ and $K_2 = K^A{}_2 + K^B{}_2$. The problem is to determine whether and in what circumstances one can derive a function $K = g(K_1,K_2)$ from the production functions f^A and f^B, where g has the property that $g(K_1,K_2) = T(Q^A,Q^B)$ and where the function T is the production possibility curve for the economy as a whole.

It is difficult to assess the importance of the aggregation problem. On the one hand, one might argue that all models falsify reality to some extent, that a simple model such as that in which real capital is defined cannot as a rule be derived from richer and more complex models of the economy, and that one must accept the inevitable discrepancy if one is to describe the economy at all. The aggregation problem in capital measurement is not different in principle from the aggregation problem in deriving a community demand curve from the demand curves of the people within the community. On the other hand, it is arguable that if we cannot solve the aggregation problem and if we cannot imagine a variable in a function that our statistics of capital are intended to represent, then we lose all sense of what it is we are supposed to be measuring, we have no basis for choosing among alternative measures of capital, and we do not know what, if anything, the resulting time series of capital tells us about the economy.

Both Brown and Diewert discuss the aggregation problem in detail. They show that aggregation is not normally possible except by stringent and unrealistic restrictions on the form of the production function or on the organization of the market. Diewert also conducts a systematic study of the properties of several alternatives to the Laspeyres index of equation (1). He investigates Fisher's ideal index, the Divisia index, and the Vartia index, which is an approximation to the Divisia index for use on time series data. He considers a class of indexes, which he calls superlative, with the property that they all yield particularly good approximations to the unknown time series *K* for a wide class of functional forms of *g*. He assesses the usefulness of the different indexes in the measurement of technical change by sector and for the economy as a whole, and he considers some of the problems in incorporating new goods into the index number formulas.

Notes

1. The classic statement is Goldsmith (1951), followed in 1956 by the three volumes of *A Study of Savings in the United States.*

2. *Measuring the Nation's Wealth* (Joint Economic Committee of the Congress of the United States, 1964), a study directed by J. W. Kendrick. The study contains a great deal of information on many aspects of the measurement of capital. The survey of capital goods in the USSR is discussed in a paper by A. Kaufman.

3. For a useful discussion of this issue, see Griliches (1964), together with comments in the same volume by G. Jaszi, E. Denison, and E. Grove. See also Stigler and Kindahl (1970); Gordon (1971); and the comment on Gordon's paper by J. Popkin and R. Gillingham in the September 1971 issue of *Review of Income and Wealth.*

4. For an early and still very instructive account of the distinction between instantaneous and long-run production capacity, see Griliches (1963).

5. See the section on Böhm-Bawerk entitled "Technical Superiority of Present Goods" in Fisher (1930, pp. 473–85).

6. The controversy is reviewed and the relevant articles by Hayek, Knight, and others are listed in Hayek (1941).

7. In their study of aggregate technical change, Jorgenson and Griliches (1967) have constructed special time series of capital, weighting quantities by rents rather than by capital goods prices to reflect instantaneous productive capacity. Note particularly that the appropriate rate of depreciation on capital as instantaneous productive capacity is different from that on capital as long-run productive capacity, and that it is the latter that is estimated in the studies by Young and Musgrave, Coen, and Hulten and Wykoff. Consider two machines, *A* and *B*, for which the value of services decline at 10% per year in each year of their lives, and that differ only in that *A* disintegrates after five years while *B* disintegrates after twenty. If both machines are two years old, their rates of depreciation as instantaneous productive capacity are the same, but the rate of depreciation of the long-run productive capacity is greater for *A* than for *B* because a larger portion of the lifetime services of *A* is used up in the second year of its life.

References

Barna, T. 1957. The replacement cost of fixed assets in British manufacturing industry in 1955. *Journal of the Royal Statistical Society,* ser. A, part 1.

Denison, Edward F. 1957. Theoretical aspects of quality change, capital consumption, and net capital formation. In *Capital formation*. Studies in Income and Wealth, vol. 19. New York: National Bureau of Economic Research.

Fisher, I. 1930. *The theory of interest*. New York: Macmillan.

Goldsmith, R. W. 1951. *A perpetual inventory of national wealth*. Studies in Income and Wealth, vol. 14. New York: National Bureau of Economic Research.

Gordon, R. J. 1971. Measurement bias in price indexes for capital goods. *Review of Income and Wealth*, ser. 17, no. 2, pp. 121–74.

Griliches, Z. 1963. Capital stock in investment functions: Some problems of concept and measurement. In *Measurement in economics*, ed. C. Christ et al. Stanford: Stanford University Press.

———. 1964. Notes on the measurement of price and quality changes. In *Models in income distribution*, ed. I. Friend, pp. 381–418. Studies in Income and Wealth, vol. 28. New York: National Bureau of Economic Research.

Hayek, F. 1941. *The pure theory of capital*. London: Routledge and Kegan Paul.

Jorgenson, D. W., and Griliches, Z. 1967. The explanation of productivity change. *Review of Economic Studies* 34:249–83.

Robinson, J. V. 1953–54. The production function and the theory of capital. *Review of Economic Studies* 21 (2), no. 55: 81–106.

Samuelson, P. 1966. A summing up. *Quarterly Journal of Economics* 80, no. 4 (November): 568–83.

Stigler, G. J., and Kindahl, J. 1970. *The behavior of industrial prices*. New York: National Bureau of Economic Research.

1 Estimation of Capital Stock in the United States

Allan H. Young and John C. Musgrave

There are essentially two methods for estimating stocks of fixed capital—direct measurement of the stock and perpetual inventory calculations. Only limited use has been made of direct measurement in the United States because the existing data are incomplete and because there are problems in valuation of the assets in the stock. Extending the coverage and obtaining the information needed to assign the desired valuation to assets would require a substantial statistical program.

With the exception of stocks of autos, the United States Bureau of Economic Analysis (BEA) estimates are based on the perpetual inventory method. Section 1.1 of this chapter briefly reviews BEA's application of the perpetual inventory method and the resulting estimates of capital stocks and related estimates of capital consumption allowances in the national income and product accounts (NIPAs). Section 1.2 discusses concepts, definitions, and statistical problems involved in estimating capital stocks; considers direct measurement of stocks (under which we subsume the derivation of stocks from information carried on balance sheets of businesses); and takes note of capital stock estimates prepared by other researchers. A statistical appendix provides BEA's estimates of capital stocks valued in constant 1972 dollars for selected major aggregates.

1.1. The Bureau of Economic Analysis Estimates

The perpetual inventory method derives gross capital stock for a given year by cumulating past investment and deducting the cumulated value

Allan H. Young is deputy director, Bureau of Economic Analysis, U.S. Department of Commerce. John C. Musgrave is an economist with the National Income and Wealth Division, Bureau of Economic Analysis, U.S. Department of Commerce.

Jerry Silverstein assisted in preparing this paper. The views expressed are those of the authors and not necessarily those of the Bureau of Economic Analysis.

of the investment that has been discarded. Net capital stock is obtained in a similar manner by deducting the cumulated value of depreciation.

Estimates of fixed nonresidential business capital have been prepared in varying detail by BEA since the mid-1950s, and estimates of residential capital have been prepared since 1970. The latest BEA capital stock publication[1] contains annual estimates for the years since 1925 of gross and net stocks, depreciation, discards, ratios of net to gross stocks, and average ages of gross and net stocks in historical, constant, and current cost valuations by legal form of organization (financial corporations, nonfinancial corporations, sole proprietorships and partnerships, other private business). The fixed nonresidential business capital estimates are also available within each legal form by major industry group (farm, manufacturing, nonfarm nonmanufacturing), and the residential estimates are also available by tenure group (owner-occupied and tenant-occupied). Estimates of capital stocks and related measures by detailed types of assets are also available. Gross and net stocks of fixed nonresidential business and residential capital for selected aggregates are provided in the Appendix to this paper.

In addition to the published estimates of stocks of fixed nonresidential business and stocks of residential capital, preliminary estimates of stocks of durable goods owned by consumers[2] and stocks of fixed nonresidential capital owned by the federal government[3] and by state and local governments are also presented here. Final estimates of stocks of consumer durables and government capital will be published later in the *Survey of Current Business*. The stocks of fixed capital owned by governments include assets owned by government enterprises. Future research will include the compilation of separate estimates of capital stocks owned by government enterprises.

Although this paper deals primarily with the fixed capital portion of total tangible wealth, estimates of stocks of business inventories have also been developed by BEA, and these estimates are given in the Appendix for selected aggregates. The methodology and annual estimates back to 1928 were published in an article in the December 1972 *Survey of Current Business* (Loftus 1972); revised estimates for the years since 1947 were given in part II of the January 1976 *Survey* and are updated in the regular national income and product tables in the *Survey*.

1.1.1 Derivation of the BEA Estimates

The NIPA investment flows used to implement the perpetual inventory method for the years since 1929 are: for fixed business capital—gross private domestic fixed investment; for consumer durables—personal consumption expenditures for durable goods; and for government-owned capital—government purchases of durable goods and structures. These flows are extended back into the nineteenth century using data from public and private sources. The NIPA flows are modified in the case of transfers of secondhand assets among sectors. They are also disaggregated to provide detail by legal form of organization and by major industry group (fixed nonresidential business capital) and tenure group (residential capital).

The service lives used to derive the stock estimates are given in table 1.1. For nonresidential business equipment, the service lives are 85% of the lives specified in the 1942 edition of Bulletin F, issued by the Internal Revenue Service (IRS). The service lives for nonresidential structures are based on 85% of Bulletin F lives for new structures, with an allowance for shorter lives for additions and alterations. The average service life for nonresidential structures including additions and alterations is 20% shorter than that for new structures in manufacturing industries and 7% shorter in nonmanufacturing industries. Alternative estimates of stocks of fixed nonresidential business capital based on service lives equal to 100% of Bulletin F, 75% of Bulletin F, and

Table 1.1 Service Life Assumptions Used in BEA Capital Stock Study

Type of Asset	Life (Years)
Fixed nonresidential business capital[a]	
Furniture and fixtures	15
Fabricated metal products	18
Engines and turbines	21
Tractors	8
Agricultural machinery (except tractors)	17
Construction machinery (except tractors)	9
Mining and oil field machinery	10
Metalworking machinery	16
Special-industry machinery, n.e.c.	16
General industrial, including materials handling, equipment	14
Office, computing, and accounting machinery	8
Service-industry machines	10
Electrical machinery	14
Trucks, buses, and truck trailers	9
Autos	10[b]
Aircraft	9
Ships and boats	22
Railroad equipment	25
Instruments	11
Other equipment	11
Industrial buildings	27
Commercial buildings	36
Religious buildings	48
Educational buildings	48
Hospital and institutional buildings	48
Other nonfarm nonresidential buildings	31
Railroad structures	51

Table 1.1 (continued)

Type of Asset	Life (Years)
Fixed nonresidential business capital[a] (continued)	
Telephone and telegraph structures	27
Electric light and power structures	30
Gas structures	30
Other public utility structures	26
Farm nonresidential buildings	38
Petroleum, gas, and other mineral construction and exploration	16
All other private nonresidential structures	31
Residential capital	
1-to-4 unit structures	
New	80
Additions and alterations	40
5-or-more unit structures	
New	65
Additions and alterations	32
Mobile homes	16
Nonhousekeeping	40
Equipment	11
Consumer durables	
Furniture, including mattresses and bedsprings	14
Kitchen and other household appliances	11
China, glassware, tableware, and utensils	10
Other durable house furnishings	10
Radio and television receivers, records, and musical instruments	9
Jewelry and watches	11
Ophthalmic products and orthopedic appliances	6
Books and maps	10
Wheel goods, durable toys, sports equipment, boats, and pleasure aircraft	10
Trucks, trailers, and recreational vehicles, and parts and accessories	8
Autos	10[b]
Fixed nonresidential government-owned capital	
Equipment	15
Industrial buildings	27
Educational buildings	50
Hospital buildings	50
Other nonfarm nonresidential buildings	50
Highways and streets	60
Conservation and development structures	60
Sewer structures	60
Water structures	60
Other nonresidential structures	50

[a]85% of Bulletin F lives.

[b]As explained in the text, the estimation of the gross stocks of autos does not depend on an explicit service life assumption. The unit values used to derive net stocks are depreciated according to a ten-year life, and a nominal net unit value is assigned to autos over ten years old.

100% of Bulletin F through 1940 with a gradual decline to 75% of Bulletin F by 1960 are given in Bureau of Economic Analysis (1976*b*).

For residential structures, the service lives are those used by Goldsmith and Lipsey (1963, chap. 3). For mobile homes, the service life is based on trade association data. For residential equipment, the service life is based on the lives for similar types of nonresidential equipment. For government-owned capital and consumer durables, the service lives are based on expert opinions, evidence from direct measurement of the stock, and comparisons with similar assets in business capital stocks.

The service lives are averages. Underlying the average service life for a given type of asset is a distribution of discards. To take into account that assets of a given type are discarded at different ages, patterns of retirements are used. The patterns of retirements are based on modifications of the following curves developed by Winfrey (1935): fixed nonresidential capital, the Winfrey S-3 modified so that retirements start at 45% and end at 155% of the average life; residential capital, the Winfrey S-3 modified so that retirements start at 5% and end at 195% of the average life; consumer durables, the Winfrey L-2 modified so that retirements start at 25% and end at 215% of the average life. These retirement patterns are given in table 1.2. The S-3 curves are bell-shaped distributions centered on the average service life of the asset. The L-2 curve is an asymmetrical distribution with heavy discards before the average service life is reached and a tapering pattern thereafter. This curve was selected for consumer durables because it appears that many of these goods are discarded after a few years, while others remain in use far beyond the average life.

The BEA capital stock estimates are available in historical, constant, and current cost valuations. Historical cost and constant cost stocks are derived by cumulating current-dollar and constant-dollar investment flows, respectively. Current cost stocks are derived by revaluing the constant cost stocks, using the price indexes employed in the NIPAs to deflate the investment flows.

Assets are carried in gross capital stocks at their undepreciated value during the entire time they remain in the stock. The value of these assets is depreciated to obtain net stocks, which equal the difference between the cumulative value of gross investment and cumulative depreciation. The BEA estimates of net stocks are based on the straight-line depreciation formula, which assumes equal dollar depreciation each year over the life of the asset. Discounting of anticipated future services is not used in computing depreciation and net stocks.

Alternative estimates of depreciation and net stocks based on the double-declining balance formula (which assumes an annual percentage

Table 1.2 **Modified Winfrey Retirement Patterns Used in BEA Capital Stock Study**

Nonresidential S-3		Residential S-3		Consumer Durables L-2	
Percentage of Average Service Life	Percentage of Original Expenditure Discarded	Percentage of Average Service Life	Percentage of Original Expenditure Discarded	Percentage of Average Service Life	Percentage of Original Expenditure Discarded
Less than 45	0	Less than 5	0	Less than 25	0
45	1.2	5	.1	25	1.5
50	1.2	10	.2	35	2.1
55	1.7	15	.2	45	3.6
60	2.4	20	.2	55	6.0
65	3.2	25	.3	65	8.4
70	4.0	30	.3	75	9.8
75	5.0	35	.4	85	10.2
80	5.9	40	.4	95	9.6
85	6.6	45	.6	105	8.6
90	7.2	50	.8	115	7.5
95	7.7	55	1.5	125	6.4
100	7.8	60	2.2	135	5.5
105	7.7	65	3.0	145	4.7
110	7.2	70	3.9	155	4.0
115	6.6	75	4.9	165	3.2
120	5.9	80	5.8	175	2.6
125	5.0	85	6.5	185	2.0
130	4.0	90	7.1	195	1.5
135	3.2	95	7.7	205	1.0
140	2.4	100	7.8	215	1.8
145	1.7	105	7.7	More than 215	0
150	1.2	110	7.1		

Table 1.2 (continued)

Nonresidential S-3		Residential S-3		Consumer Durables L-2	
Percentage of Average Service Life	Percentage of Original Expenditure Discarded	Percentage of Average Service Life	Percentage of Original Expenditure Discarded	Percentage of Average Service Life	Percentage of Original Expenditure Discarded
155	1.2	115	6.5		
More than 155	0	120	5.8		
		125	4.9		
		130	3.9		
		135	3.0		
		140	2.2		
		145	1.5		
		150	.8		
		155	.6		
		160	.4		
		165	.4		
		170	.3		
		175	.3		
		180	.2		
		185	.2		
		190	.2		
		195	.1		
		More than 195	0		

rate of depreciation that is equal to twice the first-year straight-line rate) are given in Bureau of Economic Analysis (1976*b*).

Stocks of autos are an exception to the use of the perpetual inventory procedure described above. The numbers of cars in use, by age of car, are available each year through state registration data tabulated by the R. L. Polk Company. Gross stocks of cars are derived by multiplying the number of cars of each age by the average unit value in the year of original registration. Net stocks are derived similarly by using depreciated unit value figures based on the straight-line formula. Alternative estimates based on the double-declining balance formula are also calculated.

1.1.2 Capital Consumption Allowances in the NIPAs

A major feature of the recently completed benchmark revision of the NIPAs was the introduction of measures of economic depreciation obtained from BEA's capital stock calculations. In the revised NIPAs, capital consumption allowances are based on depreciation computed with the straight-line formula and the service lives for fixed nonresidential and residential business capital shown in table 1.1. The new capital consumption allowances are shown in current and constant dollars.

Previously, capital consumption allowances had included primarily depreciation as tabulated by the IRS from tax returns filed by businesses. The major exceptions were depreciation for the farm sector and for housing that is owned either by owner-occupants or by landlords who file individual tax returns rather than business returns. For the farm sector, BEA used United States Department of Agriculture perpetual inventory estimates valued in current prices. For housing, BEA prepared perpetual inventory estimates valued at historical costs.

Business income in the revised NIPAs is calculated net of capital consumption allowances valued in current prices. The revised presentation shows the new measures of income as the sum of before-tax book income, the inventory valuation adjustment, and a new item, the capital consumption adjustment, which is equal to the tax return–based measure of depreciation less the new measure. The new measure of capital consumption allowances also results in an improved measure in the NIPAs of current-dollar net national product and the introduction of its constant-dollar counterpart.[4]

Capital consumption allowances in the NIPAs are identical to depreciation in the capital stock calculations with a minor exception. Depreciation in the capital stock calculations assumes that accidental damage occurs at the same rate each year. The capital consumption allowances in the NIPAs are adjusted so as to reflect the generally small year-to-year variations in the rate of accidental damage. This refinement has not been carried back into the capital stock calculations.

1.2 Conceptual and Statistical Considerations

1.2.1 Gross Stocks

The concept of capital on which BEA's stock estimates rest is that of capital measured by its cost. Capital defined and measured on this basis is useful in the measurement of productivity. Measured by its cost, capital provides a basis for determining if the use of factors of production is becoming more or less efficient over time. Cost-based measures of capital are not appropriate for determining industrial capacity, or for analyzing the determinants of investment or production, because identical amounts of real capital will represent different capacities to produce goods and services. For such analyses, capital should be measured in terms of its ability to contribute to production. It has been considered difficult to implement such measures statistically. The basic problem is that of measuring the contribution of different types of capital to production. In lieu of such measures, rough allowances for embodied technological change—the costless quality change referred to later—are sometimes added to the cost-based measures.

The concept of capital measured by its cost evolved relatively early in the development of national economic accounting. The standard reference has become a paper by Edward F. Denison (1957) presented at an earlier meeting of this conference. The definition of gross stocks as stated by Denison in that paper is as follows:

> The method, if generalized, leads to the following definitions. The value, in base period prices, of the stock of durable capital goods (before allowance for capital consumption) measures the amount it would have cost in the base period to produce the *actual* stock of capital goods existing in the given year (not its equivalent in ability to contribute to production). Similarly, gross additions to the capital stock and capital consumption are valued in terms of base year costs for the *particular* types of capital goods added or consumed. This must be modified immediately, in the case of durable capital goods not actually produced in the base year, to substitute the amount it would have cost to produce them if they had been known and actually produced. But a similar modification is required in all deflation or index number problems. [p. 222]

Basic to this definition of the quantity of capital is that only cost-associated quality change of capital goods is counted as quantity change. Quality change (e.g., a larger motor) that results in a change in cost is counted as a change in quantity. Quality change that results in no change in cost (e.g., a more efficient motor that costs the same as an older model) is not counted as a change in quantity.

1.2.2 Depreciation

Economists apparently do not fully agree on a single definition of depreciation for allocating the cost of the asset over its service life. Nowadays the field is usually limited to two contenders. We shall refer to these as the NIPA definition and the discounted value definition. The information necessary for implementing either definition is imprecise and incomplete, and simplifying assumptions play major roles. With some oversimplification, we shall describe the two approaches.[5]

The NIPA definition of depreciation, which provides the basis for BEA's net stock estimates and for the estimates of capital consumption allowances and net national product in the NIPAs, can be stated as follows: Depreciation is the cost of the asset allocated over its service life in proportion to its estimated service at each date. The services are net of maintenance and repair expenses. In theory, the service life used in determining the allocation is the physical life—the length of time it is physically possible to use the asset. In some instances this is longer than the economic life—the length of time it is economically feasible to use the asset. The services are not discounted and they do not reflect the effect of obsolescence. Obsolescence is charged when the asset is retired. The reason for this treatment is that obsolescence has little if any effect on the time pattern of services provided by the asset before retirement, even though it is a determinant of the timing of retirement. The charge for obsolescence at retirement writes off the remainder of the asset as a component of capital consumption and in effect replaces the physical life with the economic service life.

Given the available information, the depreciation curve that best implements the definition cannot be determined precisely. In the BEA estimates, the asset is written off by straight-line depreciation over its estimated economic life. BEA's judgment is that straight-line depreciation provides a close approximation to the desired measure. For a single asset, the straight-line formulation has the following properties:

1. If services are constant over the service life and no obsolescence occurs, straight-line depreciation is the correct measure.

2. If services decline over the service life and no obsolescence occurs, straight-line depreciation is too low in the early years of the service life and too high in the later years.

3. If services are constant over the service life and obsolescence occurs, straight-line depreciation is too high in all years of the service life except in the last year, when it is too low.

4. If services decline over the service life and obsolescence occurs, the types of errors in properties 2 and 3 arising from straight-line depreciation tend to be offsetting, depending on the amount and pattern of the decline in services and the amount of obsolescence.

Figure 1.1 compares the pattern of depreciation in each of the four cases enumerated above with that which results from the straight-line formulation. In each case, the original cost of the asset is 100 and the economic service life is ten years. In cases 1 and 2, the physical service life is equal to the economic service life; in cases 3 and 4, the physical life is fifteen years, but the asset is retired after ten years because of obsolescence. In cases 1 and 3, services are constant; in cases 2 and 4, services decline linearly to zero at the end of the physical life. It should be noted that when the depreciation pattern with the parameters specified in case 4 is applied against an increasing or decreasing investment stream, the errors would be further offsetting.

We do not know the relative weights to assign to the four cases. In addition, the illustrations suggest that the effect of obsolescence on the retirement of an asset from the stock is sudden and complete. In practice, retirement is often not well defined and sometimes is viewed as occurring more gradually than in the example. Nevertheless, the four cases point up the general applicability of the straight-line formulation as an approximation to the NIPA definition.

The discounted value definition of depreciation can be stated as follows: Depreciation is the decline in the value of the sum of the remaining anticipated services discounted to the present. The anticipated services are net of maintenance and repair expenses and net of the reduction in value occasioned by obsolescence. The effect of obsolescence is probably best viewed as occurring at a constant rate. The total of the depreciation charges under the discounted value definition, as with the NIPA definition, equals the cost of the asset. The time path of the charges, however, can vary from that based on the NIPA definition.

Depreciation based on the discounted value definition can be either more or less than straight-line depreciation in the early years of an asset's service life, with the reverse occurring in later years. A decline over time in the services provided by an asset because of either deterioration or constant-rate obsolescence contributes to a more rapid write-off than straight-line depreciation. The effect of discounting works in the opposite direction.

The NIPA definition arises from the view that depreciation represents the quantity of capital, as measured by its cost, that is expended in production and that net national product represents output after allowance for this quantity. Also, the view is that such flows for the year in question do not reflect past or present expectations of future returns. This approach is consistent with the basic design of the NIPAs, which

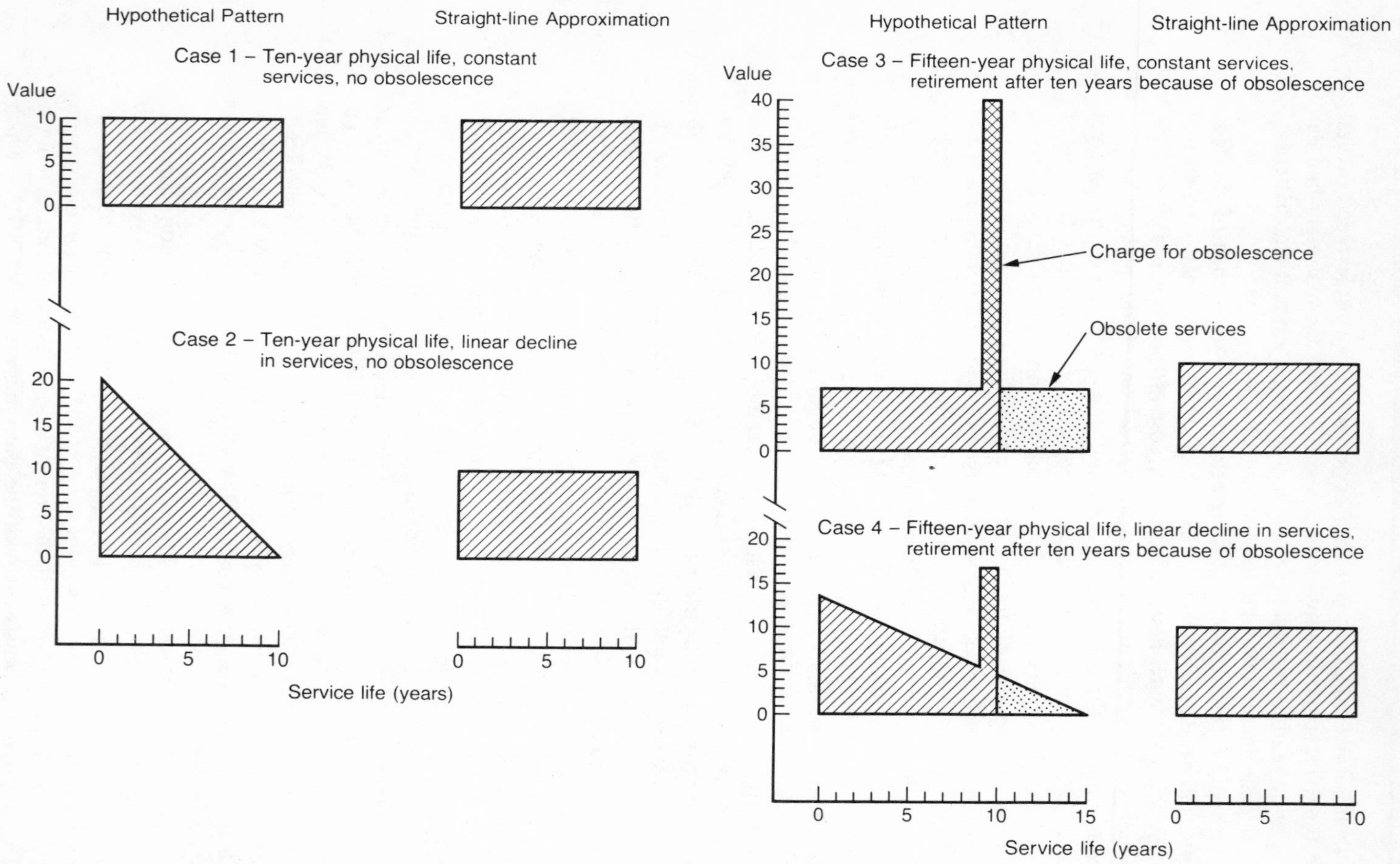

Fig. 1.1 Hypothetical depreciation patterns and straight-line approximation.

measure flows of goods and services—including the services of the factors of production—and with the use of the NIPAs to analyze production and productivity.

Does the discounted valued definition also have a place within the context of national economic accounting? In the most general terms, this question amounts to whether the definition is useful in defining or analyzing aggregate flows of business income. The discounted value definition is frequently described as appropriate for accounting for profits by the individual firm and in studies carried out at the aggregate level that are concerned with the behavior of the firm. Examples of such studies are the examination of the basis for investment decisions and the assessment of the adequacy of depreciation taken on tax returns. For these types of studies, it seems that national economic accounts based on the discounted value definition would be useful. Some investigators apparently go beyond this position and consider the discounted value definition to be the only appropriate measure (for example, Christensen and Jorgenson 1973; Mendelowitz 1971). To some extent the question is academic, however, if the difference between the two statistical measures is small. This is the subject we shall now take up.

Taubman and Rasche (1969) estimated that the decline in the value of discounted future services of office buildings is less rapid than straight-line depreciation in the early years of the service life. They believe this finding can be extended to apartment buildings and factories. The depreciation curve obtained by Taubman and Rasche shows a somewhat more rapid write-off than straight-line depreciation when the discounting calculation is removed. An allowance for some degree of obsolescence, which is called for with the NIPA definition, would move the curve back toward straight-line depreciation. Various evidence suggests that housing is also approximated by the straight-line formulation.

There are several studies of depreciation patterns for equipment (for example, Wykoff 1970; Terborgh 1954). They almost all show that the decline in the value of discounted future services is more rapid than straight-line depreciation in the early years of the service life. However, most of these studies are of motor vehicles and are based on prices observed in secondhand markets. Such studies probably understate the services provided by assets that are retained by their original owners and therefore indicate too rapid a decline in value.[6]

Other than secondhand market prices, there is evidence for some types of equipment, such as that in Terborgh's studies, that indicates decreasing services over the life of the asset because of increasing maintenance and repair expense and changes in the intensity of use. It seems reasonable to conclude that for some types of equipment the effect of maintenance and repair coupled with obsolescence outweighs the effect of discounting, and consequently the decline in the value of discounted future services is more rapid than straight-line depreciation in the early years of the service life. (Such findings probably should not be extrapolated, however, to all types of equipment. For example, furniture may have a pattern similar to that of buildings.)

A study by Coen (1975) estimated the decline in service provided over the service life by plant and by equipment separately for twenty-one two-digit SIC manufacturing industries. Discounting was not reflected in the pattern of decline. However, obsolescence was taken as occurring at a constant rate. In this respect the specification was not consistent with the NIPA definition. Because of the treatment of obsolescence, the service declines estimated by Coen are overstated in terms of the NIPA definition. It is possible that they are also overstated because Coen preselected only a few patterns of decline with no graduation between the one-horse-shay pattern and the pattern showing a linear decline to zero over the service life.

Coen's results indicate that services provided by about 50% of plant and 12% of equipment in manufacturing resemble those of a one-horse shay.[7] Services of another 28% of plant and 44% of equipment decline linearly to zero over the service life. With respect to the NIPA definition, a revised treatment of obsolescence and a finer graduation might provide a pattern of services for assets in this latter category that would be roughly consistent with straight-line depreciation. With respect to the discounted value definition, the introduction of discounting would also shift Coen's results toward less rapid write-offs.

Mendelowitz (1971) estimated that the decline in value of discounted future services for the aggregate of plant and equipment owned by manufacturers was less rapid than straight-line depreciation in the early years of the service life. His estimate of depreciation was less than that provided by the straight-line formula for 1962 to 1969.

The empirical results are imprecise, and one hopes they can be improved in the future. In particular it may be worthwhile to conduct empirical studies that take explicit account of the NIPA definition.

Our reading of the empirical results is as follows: (1) For broad aggregates, straight-line depreciation comes reasonably close to the measure called for by either definition. (2) This judgment relies partly on the presence of offsetting errors. For the discounted value definition, straight-line depreciation may provide too slow a write-off for certain types of equipment. However, such understatement tends to be offset by the use of straight-line depreciation for buildings. For the NIPA definition, errors arising from the use of straight-line depreciation for types of equipment where services decline over the service life tend to be offset by errors arising from the treatment of obsolescence. (3) For the discounted value definition, the offsets between structures and equipment noted in point 2 do not apply to separate estimates for housing (virtually all structures) or consumer durables (all equipment).

1.2.3 Net Stocks

Given the NIPA definition of depreciation, net stocks are the sum of unused capital as measured by its cost. The discounted value definition of depreciation ties into a definition of net stocks measured by their market values. It is this latter definition that is consistent with a market valuation of balance sheets and wealth accounts. To the extent that the two definitions of depreciation can be distinguished statistically, investigators who construct balance sheets and wealth accounts based on market valuations can achieve consistently between net stocks in these accounts and the stock-related flows in the NIPAs with an adjustment item in the revaluation account.

1.2.4 Capital Services

The state of the art is such that many economists do not use the estimates of gross or net stocks as a measure of capital services without some modification. We will touch on some of the major aspects of this subject here.

Estimates of capital services have typically involved one or two modifications to aggregate gross stocks. One modification is the weighting by rates of return of the detailed gross stock estimates by sector and legal form of organization and also sometimes by industry. The other modification is that the one-horse-shay assumption of capital services inherent in BEA's gross stocks is not always considered to provide an appropriate measure of capital services. For example, in his recent work, Denison weights gross and net stocks in the ratio of three to one to obtain a rough allowance for declining services over an asset's service life. Other investigators have used a rapid geometric decline to describe the write-off in services (for example, Jorgenson and Griliches 1967).

With more evidence concerning the pattern of capital services provided by an asset over its service life, some investigators think it would be appropriate for BEA to introduce indexes of capital services by sector, legal form of organization, and industry. Such evidence would also improve the basis for the depreciation estimates, although for the reasons noted previously the straight-line formulation might very well remain the appropriate choice for an aggregate measure.

1.2.5 Gross Fixed Investment

For the estimation of the capital stocks presented in this paper, gross fixed investment is defined as the value of acquisitions of fixed capital assets by private business and nonprofit institutions, government (including government enterprises), and households. This definition is more inclusive than that used in the NIPAs, where fixed investment is limited to fixed capital assets purchased by private business and nonprofit institutions. Fixed capital assets include equipment and structures located in the United States. Land is excluded. Military assets are also excluded. For business and government, equipment is defined as durable goods with an average service life of more than one year. For households, equipment (consumer durables) is defined as durable goods having an average service life of at least three years. In practice, the effect of the difference in the average service lives is small.

Gross fixed investment consists of both the acquisition of new assets and the net acquisition (purchases less sales) of used assets. It includes costs of installation and margins and commissions of dealers and brokers on transactions in both new and used assets. Also included in investment are additions, alterations, and major replacements of parts of assets such as a new furnace installed in a building or an engine in an airplane.

Replacements of small parts and repairs are not included in investment, and it is necessary to establish a boundary between these items and major replacements. For business, the boundary is based on whether the item is capitalized under IRS regulations. For government, the boundary is based on that established for business. An examination currently under way at BEA indicates that a substantial proportion of major replacements in private structures is probably being missed in the present NIPA estimates. We expect this investigation to result in an upward revision in gross fixed business investment in the next benchmark revision of GNP.

Fixed investment by the business sector in the NIPAs differs in several respects from that capitalized under IRS regulations. The major difference is the inclusion of owner-occupied housing in fixed investment in the NIPAs. Other items included in the NIPA measure but not capitalized under IRS regulations include assets owned by nonprofit institutions, expenditures for mining exploration, mine shafts and petroleum and natural gas wells, and autos of employees reimbursed for travel expenses.

For the total of the business, government, and household sectors, the net acquisition of used assets is a minor item in gross fixed investment. It consists of the net flow of used equipment to the rest of the world and the net flow of used equipment to dealers' inventories. All other flows of used assets are among the three sectors and sum to zero. When the total is disaggregated into the three sectors, especially when these sectors are further disaggregated, the net acquisition of used assets becomes an important aspect of the definition of investment. Not only are there transactions among sectors or more detailed groupings of transactors, but there are transfers of used assets that result from changes in the classification of transactors. For example, the incorporation of an unincorporated business firm moves capital from the noncorporate stock to the corporate stock.

The largest intersector flows of used assets in the NIPAs are the sales of used plant and equipment by the federal government to other sectors after World Wars I and II and the sale of used autos by business to households. Another flow of some size is the acquisition of private structures by state and local governments for demolition in conjunction with highway construction and urban renewal. Since these structures are purchased for demolition, they are treated as discards from total stocks. There are two important flows that are inadequately accounted for in the NIPAs because of lack of information—takeovers of privately owned transit systems and other public utilities by state and local governments, and donations of streets and other improvements to municipalities by developers.

In general, an accounting of transfers of used assets at more disaggregated levels than the three sectors mentioned above is not necessary in the NIPAs. Such an accounting, however, is necessary for detailed estimates of stocks. Unfortunately, it is missing in the detailed stock estimates, with the exception of the disaggregation by legal form of organization and industry of the flows of used assets between business and the other two sectors, which are available in the NIPAs. Probably the most important flows not explicitly accounted for in the detailed estimates are those between corporate and noncorporate business. The lack of explicit estimates implies that increases in corporate stock due to incorporations of unincorporated businesses are offset by sales of used assets by corporations to unincorporated business.

The transfers of used assets among sectors in the NIPAs are valued at the market price at the time of transfer. In estimating gross and net stocks it is necessary to modify the market valuation. The modification consists of valuing the asset at its original acquisition (when new) price for purposes of moving it from the gross stock of the seller to the gross stock of the buyer. For net stocks the modification consists of valuing the asset at the straight-line depreciated value of the original acquisition price. An exception to these procedures is for assets purchased new by the government during periods of war and subsequently sold secondhand to business that contained characteristics of no use to their postwar business purchaser. The valuation of these transfers is based on an estimate of the value that business would have paid for new assets of equal productivity.

The procedure for valuing transfers of used assets requires information on the length of time the asset is held by its original owner and its original acquisition price. Reasonably good estimates of such information are available to value the intersector flows described above. It is apparent that the lack of this type of information is a serious limitation on the use of the perpetual inventory method to obtain estimates for more detailed groups of transactors.

Margins and commissions include those on transactions among sectors and within sectors. The inclusion of margins and commissions in investment is based largely on their treatment in IRS regulations that require that these items be capitalized. For purposes of estimating capital stock, it is not clear that it is desirable to treat margins and commissions on used assets as investment, since this implies an increase in the stock when a used asset is tranferred between owners and a margin or commission is earned by a broker. This seems inconsistent with the treatment of assets that do not change ownership during their lives. If an alternative procedure were adopted that treated margins and commissions on used assets as a business expense, capital consumption allowances and profits in the NIPAs would also be affected. In 1975, margins and commissions on used assets accounted for about $5.6 billion in business investment, mostly on housing, and $6.0 billion in purchases of consumer durables, mostly on autos.)

1.2.6 Deflation and Price Indexes

Constant-dollar investment in the NIPAs is generally derived by deflating current-dollar investment flows by price indexes. Thus, implementation of the NIPA definition of real capital depends crucially on the treatment of quality change in the price indexes BEA uses to separate current-dollar flows into prices and quantities. The approach taken by the Bureau of Labor Statistics (BLS) and other compilers of the price indexes is essentially to attempt to remove from the reported price change the change in costs associated with quality change. Deflation of gross fixed investment by the resulting price indexes counts only cost-associated quality change as a change in real capital.

Deflation is particularly difficult when new products are introduced, since there is no obvious way to value these products at base period prices if they did not exist in the base period. The method generally used considers the new product equivalent to one unit of the old product multiplied by the ratio of the cost of the new product to that of the old product in an overlap period. If an overlap period does not exist, a hypothetical comparison must be undertaken by estimating what it would have cost to produce the new product in a period when the old one still existed.

Many presume that the compiled price indexes overstate the amount of price increase. If so, the growth in constant-dollar capital stock is understated. However, a recent review by Jack Triplett (1975) of several components of the consumer and wholesale price indexes suggests that one should not jump to conclusions on this subject. He indicates that editing procedures designed to detect and adjust for quality change could introduce biases in either direction and that findings of several emprical studies are mixed as to the direction of bias.

In the recently completed benchmark revision of GNP, improved deflation procedures were adopted for structures (see Bureau of Economic Analysis 1974). These improvements came as a result of an extensive review of available price data by BEA and the Bureau of the Census and resulted in a significant reduction in the dollar value of structures deflated by the prices of construction inputs. In the present deflation of structures, price indexes based on construction outputs are available for housing, office buildings, road building, petroleum pipelines, and dams and reclamation projects. Price indexes based on construction outputs are not available for other types of structures. These latter types of structure are deflated either by price indexes of construction inputs or by weighted averages of the available price indexes of construction outputs. For example, all expenditures on construction of nonresidential buildings are deflated by an average of the price indexes for housing, office buildings, and highway structures. This procedure is considered reasonably accurate, although it is difficult to judge the extent of any bias until additional price indexes for specific types of nonresidential structures are available.

As has been discussed many times at this conference, much else remains to be done on the price front. We single out three areas where more work is needed: (1) Further assessment of the statistical treatment of quality change in the BLS-compiled and other price indexes is needed. (2) The pricing coverage by BLS is deficient or nonexistent for certain types of equipment and should be extended, particularly for ships, aircraft, and computers; (3) Price information is needed for new types of capital assets entering the stock. One such type of asset that is increasing in importance is nuclear generating plant and equipment.

1.2.7 Service Lives and Retirement Patterns

The success of the perpetual inventory method in measuring the stock of fixed capital depends, to a large extent, on the accuracy of the service lives assigned to different types of assets. Unfortunately, only fragmentary information is available on actual or economic service lives of assets.

Service lives on which depreciation of fixed nonresidential business capital is computed for tax purposes declined substantially between the issuance of IRS Bulletin F in 1942 and the adoption of the asset depreciation range (ADR) in 1971.[8] Studies conducted by IRS showed that tax service lives for new investment in 1954–59 were approximately

75% of Bulletin F lives (0.75F). The 1962 IRS guidelines permitted a reduction in tax service lives for new and existing equipment to about 0.6F or 0.7F. The 1971 ADR allowed businesses to depreciate new equipment with lives up to 20% shorter than the guideline lives. However, the actual service lives probably were not as long as Bulletin F lives during the 1940s, and the decline, if any, in actual lives has not matched by change in tax service lives. Thus the BEA estimates for fixed nonresidential business capital are based on the assumption that actual lives are about 15% shorter than Bulletin F lives over the entire period of the stock calculations. For housing, the service lives used for tax purposes are forty years for apartments and forty-five years for houses. The service lives for residential capital given in table 1.1 are considerably longer than these, since evidence from the census of housing and other studies of the housing stock indicates that actual lives are longer than tax lives.

Several studies have provided indirect evidence of actual service lives for fixed nonresidential business capital. The Jack Faucett Associates studies cited later in this paper suggested that actual service lives for manufacturing industries were equal to or longer than Bulletin F lives. Studies by Coen (1975) indicated that actual service lives for equipment for the period 1947–66 were in the same range as the 1962 guideline lives. Because of data limitations, it is difficult to attach much precision to these empirical studies. Surveys of actual service lives used by businesses are needed for assessing the accuracy of the service lives used in the BEA study.

With the exception of automobiles, the Winfrey retirement patterns given in table 1.2 are applied uniformly to all types of investment. While this undoubtedly introduces an artificial smoothness into the stock numbers, it seems to be the best procedure available considering the lack of information on actual retirements. The Winfrey patterns may be viewed as representing two different phenomena: within each asset group in the study, there are a number of different types of assets with different service lives; for each type of asset, there is a distribution of retirements about the average service life.

1.2.8 Direct Measurement

As noted earlier, stocks of autos are the only type of asset for which the BEA estimates are based on direct measurement. Because capital stock estimates based on the perpetual inventory method are subject to considerable error if the investment data and service lives used are not accurate, there is a need for estimates based on direct measurement to supplement and serve as a check on the perpetual inventory estimates.

In 1964, the Wealth Inventory Planning Study (WIPS) (see Kendrick 1964) reviewed the available data and made a detailed series of recommendations for developing estimates of wealth in the United States by sector and industry. An important part of the WIPS recommendations centered on the need for detailed, periodic censuses of tangible wealth. These recommendations have not been implemented in the federal statistical program. If implemented, they could provide the same sort of benchmark check on the levels of national wealth that are now provided by the sources used to benchmark the NIPAs.

The WIPS sector recommendations call for two basic types of data: census and survey data where data on physical units are available; and balance sheet data where data on physical units are generally not available.

The census and survey method involves a periodic counting and valuing of all assets in the stock, updated by sample surveys. Some data of this type are already available, and the WIPS proposals call for upgrading and expanding such data. Housing is an example of an asset where a periodic census type of data is available (every ten years), updated with survey data.[9] However, for stock estimation the problem is valuation. Homeowners are asked to estimate the present value of their house and lot, which may be difficult for those who have not bought or sold a house recently. Also, there are problems in separating the value of the land from that of the structure. These problems are not insurmountable, but careful attention needs to be paid to correct valuation in such estimates.

Other types of assets for which stock estimates based on census and survey information may be feasible are trucks and other types of transportation equipment. It may be possible to derive stocks of trucks by utilizing registration data as is done for autos. Stocks of buses, ships, aircraft, and railroad equipment might be developed from data contained in the periodic reports to federal regulatory agencies. Here again the valuation of the assets may prove difficult.

Balance sheet data on gross book value of depreciable assets are available for some industries at five-year intervals from the Census Bureau's economic censuses (establishment-based) and annually from IRS Statistics of Income (company-based). A considerable upgrading of this type of data is proposed by the WIPS, with more detail by type of asset, industry, and geographic area. The WIPS also proposes collecting more data on accounting practices, age distributions, and actual service lives of assets. Balance sheet data, expressed at historical costs, can be converted to constant or current costs if data on the age of the assets in the stock are known. Historical cost balance sheet data can also be used to derive benchmarks for perpetual inventory estimates.[10]

One important aspect of balance sheet data is the valuation of used assets acquired by an establishment. These assets are carried on the books at their secondhand purchase prices, and a revaluation is necessary to derive estimates of their acquisition prices when new. This would require collection of information that would permit the estimation of the dates when these assets were acquired new and their original acquisition prices.

An area where balance sheet data would be particularly useful is rented capital. The BEA stock estimates are based on ownership rather than on use. Alternative estimates classified by user would clearly be desirable and could be made possible by collecting a balance sheet type of data on the value and age of rented capital.

In summary, implementation of the WIPS proposals could provide the basis for substantially upgrading the accuracy and available detail of estimates of capital stock in the United States.

1.2.9 Other Estimates

Several studies have produced estimates of capital stock in the United States other than those prepared by BEA. Some of these include industry detail not available in the BEA study. In some cases the industry detail is controlled to the BEA aggregates. There also are cases where the researcher utilized some aspects of BEA's work, particularly the investment flows and service lives, and chose to measure or define other aspects differently. A partial list follows. Consult the reference list for full facts of publication.

Raford Boddy and Michael Gort, "The Estimation of Capital Stocks by Industry, 1947–63" (1968); and their "Obsolescence, Embodiment, and the Explanation of Productivity Change" (1974). Boddy and Gort derived estimates of gross and net fixed capital stocks for thirty industries using the perpetual inventory method, with investment flows developed from IRS tabulations of balance sheets by taking changes in year-end net assets and adding depreciation charges.

Laurits R. Christensen and Dale W. Jorgenson, "Measuring Economic Performance in the Private Sector" (1973). Christensen and Jorgenson used the perpetual inventory method and the BEA investment data to develop annual estimates of capital input for three sectors (corporate business, noncorporate business, households and institutions) for the years since 1929. The decline in services provided by an asset was assumed to follow the pattern provided by the double-declining balance depreciation formula.

Daniel Creamer, *Capital Expansion and Capacity in Postwar Manufacturing* (1961). Creamer's estimates of gross fixed capital stocks for twenty-three manufacturing industries were developed by revaluing book value stocks from IRS tabulations of balance sheets, using assumptions on the average age of capital for each industry. His work also includes separate estimates of the value of rented capital.

Edward F. Denison, *Accounting for United States Economic Growth 1929–1969* (1974). Denison used the BEA estimates of gross and net fixed capital stocks based on Bulletin F service lives to derive measures of capital input. Gross and net stocks were weighted three to one as an allowance for the decline in capital services over the service life.

Jack Faucett Associates, Inc. (JFA), *Development of Capital Stock Series by Industry Sector* (1973); and their *Fixed Capital Stocks by Industry Sector, 1947–70 (71)* (1975). The JFA studies derived estimates of gross and net fixed capital stocks for about 170 industry groups, with separate estimates of government-owned, contractor-operated stocks. These estimates were derived by the perpetual inventory method, utilizing detailed investment flows back to 1890 that JFA dveloped using data from the economic census where available and the Boddy/Gort approach for most other industries, and controlling to aggregate investment flows in the BEA capital stock study.

Raymond W. Goldsmith, *The National Wealth of the United States in the Postwar Period* (1962); and his *Institutional Investors and Corporate Stock: A Background Study* (1973). The Goldsmith studies derived estimates of total gross and net wealth by sector. The fixed capital estimates were derived by the perpetual inventory method. The 1973 study used BEA stock estimates where available. These are updatings of Goldsmith's earlier pioneering studies in the estimation of capital stock by the perpetual inventory method.

Frank Gollop and Dale W. Jorgenson, "U.S. Total Factor Productivity by Industry, 1947–1973" (1975). Gollop and Jorgenson derived capital input estimates for sixty-seven industries using the perpetual inventory method and the JFA industry investment series controlled to the BEA structures and equipment totals. The decline in services provided by an asset was assumed to follow the pattern provided by the double-declining balance depreciation formula.

Bert G. Hickman, *Investment Demand and U.S. Economic Growth* (1965). Hickman derived annual estimates of net capital stocks for the years 1945–62 for twenty-one industry groups, using the perpetual inventory method and industry investment series from the BEA Plant and Equipment Expenditures Survey, supplemented by data from trade associations and other researchers. Declining balance depreciation rates were assigned by industry, ranging from 1.5 to 2.0 times the straight-line rate.

John W. Kendrick, with Kyu Sik Lee and Jean Lomask, *The National Wealth of the United States by Major Sector and Industry* (1976); and John W. Kendrick, assisted by Yvonne Lethem and Jennifer Rowley, *The Formation and Stocks of Total Capital* (1976). Kendrick derived annual and quarterly estimates of total capital stocks and total wealth in the United States. He also derived annual and quarterly estimates of gross and net fixed capital stocks for thirty-two industry groups, based primarily on the perpetual inventory method and utilizing the work of Boddy and Gort, Creamer, and JFA, and controlling to the BEA stock estimates for the farm, manufacturing, and nonfarm nonmanufacturing totals.

Helen Stone Tice, "Depreciation, Obsolescence, and the Measurement of the Aggregate Capital Stock of the United States, 1900–1961" (1967). Tice developed annual estimates of gross and net stocks of residential structures, nonresidential structures, producers' durable equipment, and consumer durables, using the investment flows from Goldsmith's earlier work and assumptions about embodied technological change.

Also of interest is another BEA study concerned with projections of capital stock and investment: United States Bureau of Economic Analysis, *A Study of Fixed Capital Requirements in the U.S. Business Economy 1971–1980* (1975). This study derived estimates of gross fixed capital stock for eighty-five industry groups in 1980, implied by projected estimates of output and projected capital-output ratios in 1980, and also provided estimates of the investment by industry for 1971–80 necessary to derive these stocks. The 1970 capital stock estimates that served as a starting point for these projections were based on the JFA stocks by industry, controlled separately for equipment and structures to the BEA industry totals for farm, manufacturing, and nonfarm nonmanufacturing.

Appendix

Estimates of constant-dollar gross and net stocks of reproducible tangible capital for selected years in the period 1925–75 are presented in the following tables:

Totals, by sector and legal form of organization, Table 1.A.1
Business, by type of capital, 1.A.2
  Corporate, 1.A.3
    Nonfinancial, 1.A.4
  Noncorporate, 1.A.5
Government, by type of capital, 1.A.6
  Federal, 1.A.7
  State and local, 1.A.8

Sectors consist of business, government, and households. Within the business sector, legal forms of organization are corporate and noncorporate, with estimates also presented for nonfinancial corporations. Types of capital consist of nonresidential equipment, nonresidential structures, residential, and business inventories. Estimates for the government sector exclude inventories and military assets.

Table 1.A.1 Constant-Dollar Gross and Net Stocks of Reproducible Tangible Capital, by Sector and Legal Form of Organization, Selected Years, 1925–75 (Billions of 1972 Dollars)

	Gross Stocks							
		Business			Government[a]			
End of Year	Total	Total	Corporate	Noncorporate	Total	Federal	State and Local	Households[b]
1925	1,326.2[c]	1,052.0[c]	445.2[c]	606.8[c]	143.3	14.3	129.1	130.8
1930	1,646.6	1,286.1	557.9	728.2	189.8	15.8	174.0	170.7
1935	1,626.4	1,233.6	512.7	720.9	228.5	23.2	205.2	164.3
1940	1,717.0	1,261.7	510.0	751.7	281.6	38.8	242.8	173.7
1945	1,828.9	1,265.5	503.0	762.5	384.8	135.0	249.7	178.7
1950	2,192.9	1,517.3	614.2	903.1	420.9	132.7	288.2	254.7
1955	2,634.4	1,795.4	729.5	1,065.8	491.8	139.8	352.0	347.2
1960	3,068.0	2,075.2	841.6	1,233.6	564.3	122.9	441.4	428.6
1965	3,652.7	2,441.4	1,006.6	1,434.8	683.5	127.1	556.4	527.8
1970	4,469.2	2,932.8	1,284.6	1,648.2	837.6	138.2	699.5	698.8
1975	5,350.8	3,434.7	1,544.2	1,890.4	962.6	144.3	818.3	953.6
	Net Stocks							
		Business			Government[a]			
End of Year	Total	Total	Corporate	Noncorporate	Total	Federal	State and Local	Households[b]
1925	784.5[c]	612.3[c]	235.9[c]	376.4[c]	100.4	9.1	91.4	71.8
1930	1,020.1	792.0	326.9	465.1	134.6	9.6	125.0	93.5
1935	935.7	699.4	270.2	429.2	157.2	16.0	141.3	79.1
1940	990.8	710.1	271.8	438.3	190.9	28.3	162.6	89.7
1945	1,034.4	694.7	268.2	426.6	259.9	106.6	153.3	79.7
1950	1,283.3	900.1	361.1	539.0	253.0	77.8	175.2	130.3
1955	1,564.5	1,098.1	439.9	658.2	292.8	73.5	219.4	173.6
1960	1,844.1	1,292.1	510.7	781.5	351.1	67.9	283.1	200.9
1965	2,260.0	1,558.8	630.1	928.7	445.4	79.1	366.3	255.8
1970	2,803.5	1,900.5	831.9	1,068.6	554.2	84.6	469.5	348.9
1975	3,286.7	2,206.0	986.8	1,219.2	623.4	83.9	539.5	457.4

[a]Government sector stocks exclude inventories and military assets.
[b]Household sector stocks consist of durable goods owned by consumers.
[c]Excludes business inventories.

Table 1.A.2 **Constant-Dollar Gross and Net Stocks of Reproducible Tangible Capital, Business, by Type of Capital, Selected Years, 1925–75 (Billions of 1972 Dollars)**

	Gross Stocks					Net Stocks				
		Nonresidential					Nonresidential			
End of Year	Total	Equipment	Structures	Residential	Inventories	Total	Equipment	Structures	Residential	Inventories
1925	1,052.0[a]	169.3	395.4	487.2	n.a.[b]	612.3[a]	89.7	209.0	313.6	n.a.[b]
1930	1,286.1	188.8	444.4	557.5	95.4	792.0	97.3	241.3	358.0	95.4
1935	1,233.6	166.1	424.4	563.1	80.0	699.4	71.5	209.6	338.4	80.0
1940	1,261.7	164.9	411.5	589.9	95.3	710.1	79.3	193.2	342.2	95.3
1945	1,265.5	174.9	386.3	597.6	106.7	694.7	89.2	170.6	328.2	106.7
1950	1,517.3	274.0	419.6	693.5	130.2	900.1	162.1	205.4	402.4	130.2
1955	1,795.4	363.4	466.8	810.0	155.3	1,098.1	201.7	249.6	491.6	155.3
1960	2,075.2	426.0	537.9	939.7	171.6	1,292.1	225.9	307.1	587.6	171.6
1965	2,441.4	500.6	634.6	1,097.3	209.0	1,558.8	269.7	376.2	703.9	209.0
1970	2,932.8	651.4	770.1	1,249.9	261.3	1,900.5	364.4	469.3	805.5	261.3
1975	3,434.7	805.5	895.7	1,443.2	290.3	2,206.0	440.9	540.0	934.8	290.3

[a]Excludes inventories.
[b]n.a. = not available.

Table 1.A.3 **Constant-Dollar Gross and Net Stocks of Reproducible Tangible Capital, Corporate Business, by Type of Capital, Selected Years, 1925–75 (Billions of 1972 Dollars)**

	Gross Stocks					Net Stocks				
		Nonresidential					Nonresidential			
End of Year	Total	Equipment	Structures	Residential	Inventories	Total	Equipment	Structures	Residential	Inventories
1925	445.2[a]	128.1	304.9	12.2	n.a.[b]	235.9[a]	67.8	159.4	8.6	n.a.[b]
1930	557.9	138.8	339.9	16.8	62.4	326.9	70.7	181.8	12.0	62.4
1935	512.7	121.7	322.9	17.1	51.0	270.2	52.0	156.1	11.0	51.0
1940	510.0	118.3	311.8	17.9	61.9	271.8	55.8	143.4	10.7	61.9
1945	503.0	125.6	292.9	17.7	66.8	268.2	64.4	127.5	9.5	66.8
1950	614.2	194.2	314.8	18.4	86.8	361.1	113.9	151.0	9.4	86.8
1955	729.6	262.1	341.9	18.9	106.8	439.9	147.0	176.7	9.5	106.8
1960	841.6	318.8	380.4	21.8	120.5	510.7	171.4	206.9	11.9	120.5
1965	1,006.6	385.0	434.1	31.9	155.6	630.1	209.8	243.6	21.0	155.6
1970	1,284.6	514.1	520.6	42.8	207.0	831.9	290.6	304.5	29.9	207.0
1975	1,544.2	653.4	604.6	53.9	232.3	986.8	361.1	355.4	38.0	232.3

[a]Excludes inventories.
[b]n.a. = not available.

Table 1.A.4 **Constant-Dollar Gross and Net Stocks of Reproducible Tangible Capital, Nonfinancial Corporate Business, by Type of Capital, Selected Years, 1925–75 (Billions of 1972 Dollars)**

	Gross Stocks					Net Stocks				
		Nonresidential					Nonresidential			
End of Year	Total	Equipment	Structures	Residential	Inventories	Total	Equipment	Structures	Residential	Inventories
1925	436.5[a]	126.8	298.2	11.5	n.a.[b]	230.7[a]	67.2	155.4	8.1	n.a.[b]
1930	547.3	137.3	331.7	16.0	62.4	320.4	69.9	176.7	11.4	62.4
1935	502.3	120.3	314.7	16.3	51.0	264.6	51.4	151.7	10.5	51.0
1940	500.0	116.8	304.2	17.0	61.9	267.0	55.1	139.9	10.2	61.9
1945	494.3	124.5	286.2	16.8	66.8	264.7	64.0	124.9	9.0	66.8
1950	605.0	192.2	308.5	17.4	86.8	357.0	112.6	148.6	8.9	86.8
1955	718.5	258.9	334.8	17.9	106.8	434.1	145.1	173.3	8.9	106.8
1960	827.7	314.4	372.1	20.7	120.5	502.6	168.8	201.9	11.3	120.5
1965	987.0	378.2	422.7	30.5	155.6	617.2	205.7	235.7	20.1	155.6
1970	1,248.1	499.4	500.6	41.1	207.0	806.0	281.1	289.3	28.7	207.0
1975	1,486.6	628.6	573.9	51.9	232.3	947.6	346.2	332.4	36.7	232.3

[a]Excludes inventories.
[b]n.a. = not available.

Table 1.A.5 **Constant-Dollar Gross and Net Stocks of Reproducible Tangible Capital, Noncorporate Business, by Type of Capital, Selected Years, 1925–75 (Billions of 1972 Dollars)**

	Gross Stocks					Net Stocks				
		Nonresidential					Nonresidential			
End of Year	Total	Equipment	Structures	Residential	Inventories	Total	Equipment	Structures	Residential	Inventories
1925	606.8[a]	41.2	90.6	475.0	n.a.[b]	376.4[a]	21.9	49.6	305.0	n.a.[b]
1930	728.2	50.0	104.4	540.7	33.0	465.1	26.6	59.5	346.0	33.0
1935	720.9	44.4	101.6	545.9	29.0	429.2	19.5	53.4	327.3	29.0
1940	751.7	46.6	99.8	571.9	33.4	438.3	23.5	49.8	331.5	33.4
1945	762.5	49.4	93.4	579.8	39.9	426.6	24.9	43.1	318.7	39.9
1950	903.1	79.8	104.8	675.2	43.4	539.0	48.2	54.4	393.0	43.4
1955	1,065.8	101.3	125.0	791.0	48.5	658.2	54.7	72.9	482.1	48.5
1960	1,233.6	107.1	157.5	917.9	51.1	781.5	54.5	100.2	575.7	51.1
1965	1,434.8	115.6	200.4	1,065.4	53.3	928.7	59.9	132.6	682.9	53.3
1970	1,648.2	137.3	249.5	1,207.1	54.3	1,068.6	73.7	164.8	775.7	54.3
1975	1,890.4	152.1	291.1	1,389.2	58.0	1,219.2	79.8	184.6	896.8	58.0

[a]Excludes inventories.
[b]n.a. = not available.

Table 1.A.6 **Constant-Dollar Gross and Net Stocks of Reproducible Tangible Capital, Government, by Type of Capital, Selected Years, 1925–75 (Billions of 1972 Dollars)**

End of Year	Gross Stocks				Net Stocks			
		Nonresidential				Nonresidential		
	Total	Equipment	Structures	Residential	Total	Equipment	Structures	Residential
1925	143.3	4.3	138.8	.2	100.4	2.6	97.6	.2
1930	189.8	6.7	182.9	.2	134.6	4.4	130.1	.1
1935	228.5	9.9	218.3	.3	157.2	6.1	150.9	.2
1940	281.6	18.8	259.5	3.3	190.9	12.3	175.6	3.0
1945	384.8	84.0	292.6	8.2	259.9	63.9	188.6	7.4
1950	420.9	87.5	324.8	8.5	253.0	43.9	201.8	7.3
1955	491.8	83.7	396.3	11.8	292.8	32.8	250.3	9.7
1960	564.3	62.5	485.0	16.8	351.1	26.4	311.1	13.6
1965	683.5	59.5	601.6	22.3	445.4	32.2	395.7	17.5
1970	837.6	69.7	740.4	27.5	554.2	38.9	494.5	20.7
1975	962.6	78.0	851.6	33.0	623.4	41.1	558.5	23.8

Note: Excludes inventories and military assets.

Table 1.A.7 **Constant-Dollar Gross and Net Stocks of Reproducible Tangible Capital, Federal Government, by Type of Capital, Selected Years, 1925–75 (Billions of 1972 Dollars)**

	Gross Stocks				Net Stocks			
		Nonresidential				Nonresidential		
End of Year	Total	Equipment	Structures	Residential	Total	Equipment	Structures	Residential
1925	14.3	1.3	12.8	.2	9.1	.7	8.2	.2
1930	15.8	1.2	14.4	.2	9.6	.5	9.0	.1
1935	23.2	1.7	21.3	.3	16.0	1.1	14.7	.2
1940	38.8	8.1	28.3	2.4	28.3	6.1	20.1	2.1
1945	135.0	74.4	54.9	5.7	106.6	59.4	42.1	5.2
1950	132.7	74.2	54.4	4.1	77.8	36.2	38.2	3.4
1955	139.8	64.0	72.1	3.8	73.5	20.7	50.0	2.7
1960	122.9	34.7	82.4	5.8	67.9	10.4	53.1	4.5
1965	127.1	22.3	97.0	7.7	79.1	11.3	62.1	5.8
1970	138.2	22.9	107.0	8.3	84.6	12.3	66.6	5.7
1975	144.3	18.4	115.8	10.0	83.9	7.2	70.0	6.7

Note: Excludes inventories and military assets.

Table 1.A.8 **Constant-Dollar Gross and Net Stocks of Reproducible Tangible Capital, State and Local Government, by Type of Capital, Selected Years, 1925–75 (Billions of 1972 Dollars)**

	Gross Stocks				Net Stocks			
		Nonresidential				Nonresidential		
End of Year	Total	Equipment	Structures	Residential	Total	Equipment	Structures	Residential
1925	129.1	3.0	126.0	0	91.4	2.0	89.4	0
1930	174.0	5.5	168.5	0	125.0	3.9	121.1	0
1935	205.2	8.3	197.0	0	141.3	5.0	136.3	0
1940	242.8	10.7	231.1	1.0	162.6	6.2	155.5	1.0
1945	249.7	9.6	237.7	2.4	153.3	4.5	146.6	2.2
1950	288.2	13.3	270.5	4.4	175.2	7.7	163.5	3.9
1955	352.0	19.7	324.2	8.0	219.4	12.1	200.3	7.0
1960	441.4	27.9	402.6	10.9	283.1	16.0	258.0	9.1
1965	556.4	37.3	504.6	14.6	366.3	20.9	333.6	11.7
1970	699.5	46.9	633.4	19.2	469.5	26.6	427.8	15.1
1975	818.3	59.6	735.8	23.0	539.5	33.9	488.5	17.1

Note: Excludes inventories.

Notes

1. Bureau of Economic Analysis (1976*b*). A summary of the tabulations and method in this volume is given in Musgrave (1976*a*). Revised estimates for 1973–75 are given in Musgrave (1976*b*).

2. Earlier estimates of stocks of consumer durables were given in Shavell (1971).

3. Estimates of the value of capital owned by the federal government and operated by private contractors are given in Bureau of Economic Analysis (1976*b*).

4. The revised NIPAs are described in Bureau of Economic Analysis (1976*a*).

5. In the first approach, there is room for some latitude in the treatment of obsolescence depending on one's view of whether foreseen obsolescence should be treated differently from unforeseen obsolescence. What we are calling the NIPA definition represents the view that the two types of obsolescence should be treated in the same manner. The most complete discussion of the NIPA definition and the discounted value definition of which we are aware is that by Denison (1972, pp. 101–8).

6. We like the way Eisner states one aspect of this point. "In the case of automobiles there is as well a substantial element of 'moral hazard.' A disproportionate number of cars put on the market may be offered for sale because they have proved to be 'lemons.'" See his "Comment" on Christensen and Jorgenson (1973).

7. The percentages were obtained by combining Coen's industry results with weights based on book values of fixed assets from the 1970 Annual Survey of Manufactures.

8. For a review of the tax service lives, see Young (1975).

9. For estimates of housing stocks based on the census and survey techniques, see Young, Musgrave, and Harkins (1971).

10. Examples of these uses of balance sheet data are given in the works by Creamer and Jack Faucett Associates cited in the next section.

References

Boddy, Raford, and Gort, Michael. 1968. The estimation of capital stocks by industry, 1947–63. Mimeographed.

———. 1974. Obsolescence, embodiment, and the explanation of productivity change. *Southern Economic Journal* 40 (April): 553–62.

Bureau of Economic Analysis (U.S. Department of Commerce). 1974. Revised deflators for new construction, 1947–63. *Survey of Current Business* 54 (August, part 1): 18–27.

———. 1975. *A study of fixed capital requirements in the U.S. business economy 1971–1980*. Washington, D.C.: U.S. Department of Commerce, National Technical Information Service.

———. 1976*a*. The national income and product accounts of the United States: Revised estimates, 1929–74. *Survey of Current Business* 56 (January, part I).

———. 1976*b*. *Fixed nonresidential business and residential capital in the United States, 1925–75*. Washington, D.C.: U.S. Department of Commerce, National Technical Information Service.

Christensen, Laurits R., and Jorgenson, Dale W. 1973. Measuring economic performance in the private sector. In *The measurement of economic and social performance*, ed. Milton Moss. Studies in Income and Wealth, vol. 38. New York: National Bureau of Economic Research.

Coen, Robert M. 1975. Investment behavior, the measurement of depreciation, and tax policy. *American Economic Review* 65 (March): 59–74.

Creamer, Daniel. 1961. *Capital expansion and capacity in postwar manufacturing*. Studies in Business Economics, no. 72. Washington, D.C.: National Industrial Conference Board.

Denison, Edward F. 1957. Theoretical aspects of quality change, capital consumption, and net capital formation. In *Problems of capital formation*. Studies in Income and Wealth, vol. 19. New York: National Bureau of Economic Research.

———. 1972. Final comments. *Survey of Current Business* 52 (May, part 2): 95–110.

———. 1974. *Accounting for United States economic growth, 1929–1969*. Washington, D.C.: Brookings Institution.

Goldsmith, Raymond W. 1962. *The national wealth of the United States in the postwar period*. New York: National Bureau of Economic Research.

———. 1973. *Institutional investors and corporate stock: A background study*. New York: National Bureau of Economic Research.

Goldsmith, Raymond W., and Lipsey, Robert E. 1963. *Studies in the national balance sheet of the United States*. Vol. 1. New York: National Bureau of Economic Research.

Gollop, Frank, and Jorgenson, Dale W. 1975. U.S. total factor productivity by industry, 1947–1973. Paper presented at the Conference on New Developments in Productivity Measurement, November 1975, sponsored by the Conference on Research in Income and Wealth.

Hickman, Bert G. 1965. *Investment demand and U.S. economic growth*. Washington, D.C.: Brookings Institution.

Jack Faucett Associates, Inc. 1973. *Development of capital stock series by industry sector*. Washington, D.C.: Office of Emergency Preparedness.

———. 1975. *Fixed capital stocks by industry sector, 1947–1970 (71)*. Washington, D.C.: U.S. Department of Labor, Bureau of Labor Statistics.

Jorgenson, Dale W., and Griliches, Zvi. 1967. The explanation of productivity change. *Review of Economic Studies* 34 (July): 249–83. Reprinted in *Survey of Current Business* 52, (May 1972, part 2).

Kendrick, John W. 1964. *Measuring the nation's wealth.* Studies in Income and Wealth, vol. 29. New York: National Bureau of Economic Research.

Kendrick, John W., with Lee, Kyu Sik, and Lomask, Jean. 1976. *The national wealth of the United States by major sector and industry.* New York: Conference Board.

Kendrick, John W., with Lethem, Yvonne, and Rowley, Jennifer. 1976. *The formation and stocks of total capital.* New York: National Bureau of Economic Research.

Loftus, Shirley F. 1972. Stocks of business inventories in the United States, 1928–71. *Survey of Current Business* 52 (December): 29–32.

Mendelowitz, Allan I. 1971. The measurement of economic depreciation. *Proceedings of the Business and Economic Section of the American Statistical Association, 1970.*

Musgrave, John C. 1976*a*. Fixed nonresidential business and residential capital in the United States, 1925–75. *Survey of Current Business* 56 (April): 46–52.

———. 1976*b*. Fixed nonresidential business and residential capital in the United States, 1973–75. *Survey of Current Business* 56 (August): 64.

Shavell, Henry. 1971. The stock of durable goods in the hands of consumers, 1946–69. *Proceedings of the Business and Economic Section of the American Statistical Association, 1970.*

Taubman, Paul, and Rasche, Robert. 1969. Economic and tax depreciation of office buildings. *National Tax Journal* 22 (September): 334–46.

Terbough, George. 1954. *Realistic depreciation policy.* Washington, D.C.: Machinery and Allied Products Institute.

Tice, Helen Stone. 1967. Depreciation, obsolescence, and the measurement of the aggregate capital stock of the United States, 1900–1961. *Review of Income and Wealth* 13 (June): 119–54.

Triplett, Jack E. 1975. The measurement of inflation. In *The analysis of inflation*, ed. Paul Earl. Lexington, Mass.: Lexington Books.

Winfrey, Robley. 1935. *Statistical analyses of industrial property retirements.* Iowa Engineering Experiment Station, Bulletin 125. Ames, Iowa: Iowa State College.

Wykoff, Frank C. 1970. Capital depreciation in the postwar period: Automobiles. *Review of Economics and Statistics* 52 (May): 168–72.

Young, Allan H. 1975. New estimates of capital consumption allowances in the benchmark revision of GNP. *Survey of Current Business* 55 (October): 14–16, 33.

Young, Allan H.; Musgrave, John A.; and Harkins, Claudia. 1971. Residential capital in the United States, 1925–70. *Survey of Current Business* 51 (November): 16–27.

Comment Thomas K. Rymes

Though it has been some time since I "measured capital" by the perpetual inventory method,[1] I recognize a job well done, and I congratulate the authors of this paper. They not only present some of the latest BEA estimates of the gross and net stock of capital and capital consumption allowances in current, constant, and historical dollars at various sectoral levels, but they also survey a number of alternative estimates with clarity and succinctness. At this conference one need not recite the usual litany of problems associated with the perpetual inventory method, but it is useful, as the authors commendably do, to remind ourselves how limited is our knowledge of intersectoral transactions in existing fixed capital, survival and depreciation functions, average economic lives, and biases in capital good price indexes. As the authors say, some of these questions are academic, since trends and cyclical swings in gross capital formation data may swamp the effects of even substantial variations in life estimates and in survival and depreciation functions on the resulting gross and net stock and capital consumption allowance estimates.

Academic or not, though, I confess I am somewhat puzzled by the conceptual discussion. It has always been my understanding that, while recognizing that "chops and changes" of non–steady-state real economic life prevent one from attaching precision to capital flow and stock estimates, however produced, one wants those estimates to come as close as possible to those the price system would generate. Thus, in case 1 of Young and Musgrave's paper, where a single capital good lasts a number of years with its stream of services (its gross marginal product) remaining intact, and where there is no obsolescence, the authors state that straight-line depreciation is the correct answer—correct, I presume, in relation to what they call the discounted value definition of depreciation. Yet in such a case, so long as some positive rate of profit is being earned by such assets, surely the discounted value definition is different and correct. A single asset, halfway through its life, under straight-line depreciation, would have a net stock value half that of its gross stock value, while under the discounted value definition its net

Thomas K. Rymes is associated with the Department of Economics at Carleton University.

stock value would stand at more than half its gross stock value. The time pattern of the value of the net stock of the asset generated by the discounted value definition, with its correspondingly different time pattern of depreciation, would be that generated by the market value of the asset—assuming, of course, that the usual tranquillity conditions hold. That, it seems to me, is what we want, and so I strongly support the discounted value definition. Of course, for a balanced stationary stock of such assets the net stock estimates will differ while the estimates of capital consumption allowances will be the same, but for a growing stock they will not.[2] For total factor productivity calculations this will be important, since a *partial* component of such calculations will be $\ldots \beta k_n + \gamma k_d \ldots$, where β is the share of the net returns to capital, k_n is the growth rate of the net stock of capital, and γ is the share and k_d is the growth rate of capital consumption allowances; and it will evidently matter, conceptually at least, particularly for estimated shares, whether the net stock and capital consumption allowances estimates are calculated in the manner the authors suggest or by adherence to the discounted value or economic criterion.

Similarly, if one deflated current-dollar *net* returns to the asset in question by a capital services price index to obtain constant-dollar *net* services estimates (or constant-dollar value of the *net* marginal product of the asset), it would be the discounted value criterion one would want.[3] Thus, whether we measure capital inputs in terms of constant-dollar net stocks and capital consumption allowances, constant-dollar gross service flows, constant-dollar net service flows and capital consumption allowances, it is the economic or discounted value definition of capital consumption allowances that is desired.[4]

The same considerations apply, with much elaboration required, to the authors' position on the measurement of "depreciation by obsolescence." I do not see any theoretical force to the argument of excluding obsolescence from measures of depreciation. A capital good, requiring a fixed amount of labor throughout its life, may continue to produce an unchanging flow of gross services (their third case) until its associated wages bill rises to snuff out any positive net returns to capital. Once again, the price of the *net* marginal product will decline by the economic or discounted value definition.

All this seems to me to follow from the obvious fact that when the capital good first enters the stock it appears at its new economic or discounted or gross stock value. I do not see why the same concept is not applied when estimating its net stock value (and associated capital consumption allowances) simply because it has aged or has become by obsolescence closer to the end of its economic life.[5]

Of course I realize that in the case of "depreciation by obsolescence" I am touching upon the vexed question of how one constructs a price index of capital goods subject to "depreciation by obsolescence" or "embodied technical progress" or "quality improvements," but I would observe that where (*a*) price-relative overlap information for new capital goods exists and is used, the discounted value criterion is in fact being employed; where (*b*) price-relative overlap information is constructed by the "characteristics price" approach, once again the discounted value criterion is being employed; and where (*c*) the "characteristics price" approach is given up because a new characteristic is involved without overlap and the comparative cost construction is used, then once again it seems to me that the discounted value criterion is being used—*unless* it is assumed that the ex ante rate of return on capital involved in producing the new good is higher than on the old so that all advances in knowledge are embedded in costly additions to constant-dollar outputs and inputs and, with respect to total factor productivity, we can all go home, since it is definitionally always unity.

(Parenthetically, I agree with the authors when they refer to evidence, and the need for more careful empirical work, that suggests that price indexes may not be so badly biased upward as is commonly assumed because of their supposed failure to account adequately for "quality improvements," and I would note the existence of similar evidence in Canada [Asimakopolos 1962].)

My argument applies, I think, with much force when one takes into account "intersectoral transactions" in existing fixed capital goods. Consider, for example, a case where the capital stock of an unincorporated enterprise is sold to an incorporated enterprise. I recognize, of course, that some "backtracking" of data will be necessary to adjust the gross stocks, and, assuming that the authors' remarks about revaluation are not just related to general inflation, I think it would be a mistake if the net stock estimates of the unincorporated enterprise were constructed so as not to be the market value of the capital stock sold to the corporate enterprise sector. In short, use of the discounted value criterion would, ceteris paribus, obviate the necessity of a formidable number of adjustments associated with intersectoral transactions in existing fixed capital goods. There appears to me, then, to be a very practical objection to the valuation procedures the authors advocate at least conceptually. In addition, the position I advocate would support the authors' inclusion of the costs of transactions in existing capital goods in gross fixed capital formation and would resolve the difficulties they see involved.

If one accepts my argument, it seems that, with respect to rented capital goods, the fact that the BEA estimates are based on ownership rather than on user is a strength, not a weakness to be corrected by alternative estimates. Rents paid by the user sector should be treated as intermediate inputs of the using sector and as gross outputs of the owning sector.

The price indexes needed for expressing such flows in constant dollars will be approximated by the gross rental prices discussed above and in the Appendix and, for total factor productivity estimates, the net stocks and capital consumption allowances are hence correctly allocated to the sector in which the net returns and depreciation on the discounted value criterion are originating.

Finally, while I believe the discount value criterion is correct, particularly in the preparation of capital input data for total factor productivity estimates, I hasten to note that, for such estimates, one must also remember that capital goods (or capital goods services—no issue of substance is really involved in this distinction) are reproducible inputs; and I am pleased to say that Denison (1974) and Hulten (1975) at least begin to see the point. That capital inputs are reproducible is clear, and the point has nothing to do with "aggregation and all that."[6] One needs nonetheless to obtain estimates of capital outputs and inputs in constant dollars and their respective prices that are as meaningful as possible, and this is why I am puzzled by the conceptual discussion in this otherwise workmanlike and informative paper.

Appendix

In this appendix, the relationships between gross and net stocks of capital, capital consumption allowances, and gross and net market rentals for capital goods are set out in a world of tranquillity and lucidity (Robinson 1969, p. 59)—a world of long-period competitive semistationary equilibrium where expectations and outcomes are such that "today" is exactly like "yesterday," and "tomorrow" is confidently expected to be exactly like "today." The devices of tranquillity and lucidity are used simply to isolate the logic of the problems; the analysis says nothing about events in historical time; and, in particular, though money is used as a numeraire, the monetary aspect of the economy is completely without significance. I wish to reiterate that nothing substantive is involved in this appendix—in particular, it does not tell us what are the best empirical approximations to average economic lives and patterns of depreciation for capital goods. It merely indicates the logical relationships between stocks and flows of capital goods and their services and the corresponding prices when it is assumed that lives and depreciation rates are known.[7]

Consider, then, a capital good where gross marginal product is constant over its economic life. The ith vintage of such a capital good will have a value equal to

$$Pk_i = \int_{t=0}^{t=(T-i)} \overline{P}\frac{\partial \overline{Q}}{\partial K} e^{-Rt} dt = \frac{\overline{P}}{R}\frac{\partial \overline{Q}}{\partial K}\left[1 - \frac{1}{e^{R(T-i)}}\right],$$

where $\frac{\partial \overline{Q}}{\partial K}$ is the constant gross marginal physical product of the capital good, $\overline{P}$ is the price of the product produced by the capital good, T is the economic life, and R is the ruling equilibrium net rate of return or rate of profit on capital.

If the capital good is new, $i =$ zero, P_{K_0} is the gross price, whereas P_{K_i} $(T \geq i > 0)$ is the net price of the ith vintage.

For the ith vintage, its value declines as it ages by

$$\frac{\partial P_{K_i}}{\partial i} = -\overline{P}\frac{\partial \overline{Q}}{\partial K} \cdot \frac{1}{e^{R(T-i)}}$$

and by the proportionate rate

$$\frac{1}{P_{K_i}} \cdot \frac{\partial P_{K_i}}{\partial i} = \frac{-R}{e^{R(T-i)} - 1},$$

where $\frac{\partial P_{K_i}}{\partial i}$ is the value of the depreciation experienced by the ith vintage

and $\frac{1}{P_{K_i}} \frac{\partial P_{K_i}}{\partial i}$ is the proportionate rate of depreciation.[8]

What are the prices of the services of such capital goods? The gross rental for a capital good of the ith vintage will be the gross rate of return on the vintage multiplied by the net price of the vintage. The gross rate of return is the prevailing net rate of return or rate of profit plus the rate of depreciation (or the rate of profit minus the proportionate rate of change in the price of the vintage). Thus,

$$GV_i = \left(R - \frac{1}{P_{K_i}} \frac{\partial P_{K_i}}{\partial i}\right) P_{K_i}$$

$$= \left(\mathrm{R} - \frac{-R}{e^{R(T-i)} - 1}\right) \frac{\overline{P}}{R} \frac{\partial \overline{Q}}{\partial K}\left(1 - \frac{1}{e^{R(T-i)}}\right)$$

$$= \left(\frac{Re^{R(T-i)}}{e^{R(T-i)} - 1}\right) \frac{\overline{P}}{R} \frac{\partial \overline{Q}}{\partial K}\left(\frac{e^{R(T-i)} - 1}{e^{R(T-i)}}\right)$$

Cancelation yields

$$GV_i = \overline{P} \cdot \frac{\partial \overline{Q}}{\partial K}.$$

Thus the gross rental for a capital good of the ith vintage, GV_i, whose gross marginal product is constant over its life will be also unchanged over its life—as a competitively determined rental would indicate. The net rental for the ith vintage, NV_i will be

$$NV_i = RP_{K_i} = \bar{P}\frac{\partial Q}{\partial K}\left[1 - \frac{1}{e^{R(T-i)}}\right],$$

which will, of course, be affected by its vintage. Thus the net rental for a capital good will reflect the fact that the value of its net marginal product will be lower the greater its age. For *new* capital goods with very long economic lives, the net rental will approximate the gross rental.

If the gross marginal product of a capital good declines as it ages, then the formulas are adjusted to that the net price of the ith vintage will be

$$PK_i = \int_0^{T-i} \bar{P}\frac{\partial Q}{\partial K_0} e^{-(R+\delta)}\, dt = \frac{\bar{P}}{R+\delta}\frac{\partial Q}{\partial K_0} \times \left[1 - \frac{1}{e^{(R+\delta)\,(T-i)}}\right],$$

where δ is the proportionate rate at which the gross marginal physical product of the capital good declines as it ages. Other functions depicting the decline of the gross marginal physical product of the capital good could, of course, be considered. Again, if the capital good is new, $i = 0$, P_{K_0} is the gross price, whereas P_{K_i} is the net price of the ith vintage. For that vintage, its net price declines as it ages by

$$\frac{\partial P_{K_i}}{\partial i} = -\bar{P}\frac{\partial Q}{\partial K_0}\frac{1}{e^{(R+\delta)\,(T-i)}}$$

and by the proportionate rate

$$\frac{1}{P_{K_i}}\frac{\partial P_{K_i}}{\partial i} = \frac{-(\mathrm{R}+\delta)}{e^{(R+\delta)\,(T-i)} - 1}.$$

The gross rental of the ith vintage would be

$$GV_i = \left(R - \frac{1}{P_{K_i}}\frac{\partial P_{K_i}}{\partial i}\right) P_{K_i}$$

$$= \left\{\frac{R}{R+\delta} + \frac{\delta}{(R+\delta)\, e^{(R+\delta)\,(T-i)}}\right\} \bar{P}\frac{\partial Q}{\partial K_0}.$$

In this case the gross rental is lower the older the capital good, reflecting the decline in its gross marginal physical product as it ages. The net rental of the ith vintage would be

$$NV_i = RP_{K_i} = \frac{R}{R+\delta}\bar{P}\frac{\partial Q}{\partial K_0}\left[1 - \frac{1}{e^{R+\delta)\,(T-i)}}\right].$$

As a third case to consider, one might think of a capital good whose gross marginal physical product is maintained over its economic life only by rising expenditures on labor for maintenance purposes. In this case, while the gross *gross* rental of the capital good would be constant over its life (gross, that is, of the wage payments associated with maintenance), its net price and gross and net rentals would have the time profiles exhibited by the second case, with δ being interpreted as the proportionate rate of increase in wage payments associated with the capital good for maintenance purposes.

Consider now "depreciation by obsolescence." As a fourth case, then, one might consider a captial good requiring for its operation a fixed amount of labor that, in a world where newer capital goods require steadily less labor to produce the same output and consequently steadily rising own-product real wage rates, has an economic life determined by the length of time the net rentals remain positive.[9] In such a fixed coefficients case, one has for the *i*th vintage

$$P_{K_i} = \int_0^{T^*-i} (\overline{PQ} - W_0 e^{\delta t}\bar{L}) e^{-Rt} dt,$$

where δ is the rate at which money wage rates are confidently expected to rise relative to the prices of the products and T^* is the economic life of the capital good determined by the number of periods required to reduce $(PQ - W_0 e^{\ t}\mathrm{L})$ to zero. If $R \geq \delta$ (the rate of return exceeds or equals the rate of technical progress), then

$$P_{K_i} = \frac{\overline{PQ}}{R}\left[1 - \frac{1}{e^{R(T^*-1)}}\right] - \frac{W_0 L}{\mathrm{R} - \delta} \times \left[1 - \frac{1}{e^{(R-\delta)\ (T^*-i)}}\right],$$

where the first term on the right-hand side depicts the present value of the stream of gross rentals $\overline{PQ}$ and the second term the present value of the stream of wage payments with money wage rates rising at the rate δ, the rate of technical progress.

Then,

$$\frac{\partial P_{K_i}}{\partial i} = -\left[\frac{\overline{PQ}e^{(R-\delta)\ (T^*-1)} - W_0\bar{L}e^{R(T^*-i)}}{e^{R(T^*-1)}e^{(R-\delta)(T^*-i)}}\right]$$

and

$$\frac{1}{P_{K_i}}\frac{\partial P_{K_i}}{\partial^i} = \frac{-R(R-\delta)[\overline{PQ}e^{(R-\delta)\ (T^*-i)} - W_0\bar{L}e^{R(T^*-i)}]}{(e^{R(T^*-1)} - 1)[\overline{PQ}(R-\delta)e^{(R-\delta)(T^*\_1)} - W_0\bar{L}\cdot R\cdot e^{R(T^*-1)}]}$$

A fifth case, "depreciation by obsolescence" with variable coefficients, would take into account the reduction in labor because of rising own-product wage rates associated with this ith vintage capital good as it aged and the consequent diminution in the gross marginal physical product associated with any ith vintage capital good as it aged. In the fourth case, it is clear that the gross gross rental on the capital good, as it ages, remains unchanged, its gross rental declines as the associated wages bill rises, and its net rental declines more rapidly because a diminishing stream of gross rentals is being discounted. In the fifth case even the gross gross rental is declining as the ith vintage ages. Cases 4 and 5, then, are seen as similar to cases 1 and 2.

Return to case 1. If one had steadily growing gross capital formation in such capital goods, then, at any moment of time t_0, the value of the gross stock of capital at t_0 in t_0 dollars would be

$$K_G = \frac{\bar{P}}{R}\frac{\partial \bar{Q}}{\partial K}\bar{K}\left(1 - \frac{1}{e^{RT}}\right)\frac{1}{g}\left(1 - \frac{1}{e^{gT}}\right),$$

where K is the number of new capital goods installed at t_0 and g is the rate of growth of gross capital formation. The total gross rentals accruing to such a stock would be $\bar{P}\frac{\partial \bar{Q}}{\partial K}\frac{\bar{K}}{g}\left[1 - \frac{1}{e^{gt}}\right]$, so that the ratio of the total gross rentals to the total gross stock would be

$$\frac{R}{\left(1 - \frac{1}{e^{RT}}\right)}.$$

The value of the net stock of capital would be

$$K_N = \frac{\bar{P}}{R}\frac{\partial \bar{Q}}{\partial K}\bar{K}\left\{\frac{1}{g}\left[1 - \frac{1}{e^{gT}}\right] + \frac{1}{e^{RT}(R-g)}\left[1 - \frac{1}{e^{-(R-g)T}}\right]\right\}.$$

The total value of capital consumption allowances, or depreciation, would be

$$-\bar{P}\frac{\partial \bar{Q}}{\partial K}\bar{K}\frac{1}{e^{RT}(R-g)}\left[1 - \frac{1}{e^{-(R-g)T}}\right].$$

The total net returns to the net capital stock would then be

$$\bar{P}\frac{\partial \bar{Q}}{\partial K}\bar{K}\left\{\frac{1}{g}\left[1 - \frac{1}{e^{gT}}\right] + \frac{1}{e^{RT}(R-g)}\left[1 - \frac{1}{e^{-(R-g)T}}\right]\right\},$$

and the ratio of the net returns to the net capital stock would then be R as desired. In the first case, only if capital consumption allowances or depreciation were calculated on the economic or discounted value definition would the ratio of capital consumption allowances to the net value of the stock of capital reflect the unchanging net rate of return to capital and would the weights attached to the steadily growing net stock of capital and capital consumption allowances in constant prices in total factor productivity measurement be correct. Similarly, if a current-dollar flow of gross rentals were deflated by a gross rental price index, then only if the gross rental price index were calculated on the basis outlined in this appendix would the constant-dollar gross service flows be obtained correctly. For the gross rental price relative for the ith vintage would be

$$GV_{i_{01}} = \frac{R_1 - \left(\frac{1}{P_{K_{i1}}}\frac{\partial P_{K_{i1}}}{\partial i}\right)P_{K_{i1}}}{R_0 - \left(\frac{1}{P_{K_{i0}}}\frac{\partial P_{K_{i0}}}{\partial i}\right)P_{K_{i0}}},$$

which, when summed over all vintages with correct vintage weights derived from the foregoing analysis, yields a price index of gross rentals. Such an index, when divided into an index of the value of gross rentals, would show constant-dollar gross services flows growing at the rate g.

Furthermore, if current-dollar net rentals and capital consumption allowances were deflated by price indexes to obtain constant-dollar net service flows and capital consumption allowances, then the price indexes would have to be derived from the price relatives based on the formulas outlined here to get the correct results. The price relative for the net rentals on the ith vintage would be

$$\frac{R_1 P_{K_{i1}}}{R_0 P_{K_{i0}}},$$

and for capital consumption on the ith vintage would be

$$\frac{\frac{1}{P_{K_{i1}}}\frac{\partial P_{K_{i1}}}{\partial i} \cdot P_{K_{i1}}}{\frac{1}{P_{K_{i0}}}\frac{\partial P_{K_{i0}}}{\partial i} \cdot P_{K_{i0}}},$$

which would be combined with the appropriate vintage weights and based on the economic or discounted value definition of depreciation.

Thus, in case one, concepts such as the constant-dollar gross and net stocks of capital and capital consumption allowance, constant-dollar gross and net service flows, and their various current-dollar counterparts and weights in the national accounts and total factor productivity measurement are seen to be cogently related only when the economic or discounted value definition of depreciation is employed.

Since the same arguments can be made with respect to the other cases covered in this appendix, it can be seen that, if economic lives and depreciation functions of capital goods are known, such arbitrary variants of depreciation measures as straight-line or double-declining balance methods are at least conceptually seen to be unsatisfactory as compared with the economic or discounted value definitions. Again, it is always recognized that such arbitrary measures are merely least-cost approximations to what is desired in the real world of non–steady-state accumulation; but, as this appendix shows, there is no a priori reason to expect such arbitrary variants to be satisfactory from a conceptual point of view. How close such variants come to what would be conceptually desired in a world where precision of measurement is not possible is a moot question. Only much additional empirical research can shed light on it.

Notes

1. See Statistics Canada, *Fixed Capital Flows and Stocks, Manufacturing, Canada, 1926–1960: Methodology*. My early estimates are, of course, now replaced by Statistics Canada, *Fixed Capital Flows and Stocks 1926–1973* and *1970–1974*, and experimental work is being carried on with alternate survival and depreciation functions and regional estimates. (cf. P. Koumanakos, Statistics Canada, "Alternative Estimates of Nonresidential Capital in Canada, 1926–1975" and "Provincial Capital Stocks in Manufacturing [1947–1971] and Non-Manufacturing sectors [1959–1971]").

2. The formulas underlying these cases are well known. See, for example, Robinson (1960*a*, *b*) and Rymes (1971), especially chapter 4.

3. The gross service price of the asset would be $(R - \Delta P_k/P_k)P_k$ (where R is the prevailing rate of profit, $\Delta P_k/P_k$ is the decline of the value of the asset owing to "depreciation by sudden death," and P_k is the market or discounted value measure of its remaining stream of services) and though (ignoring general inflation), older assets would have a lowerP_k, the higher rates of depreciation on the economic criterion would result in offsettingly larger negative values of $\Delta P_k/P_k$ so that gross rental prices would be unchanged over the life of any asset. These gross service prices would exactly measure the unchanging gross marginal product of the asset in question. The *net* service price of the asset would be RP_k, and older assets would have, of course, a lower service price, reflecting the fact that older assets, though yielding the same *gross* marginal product, would not be yielding the same *net* marginal product. On all this, see the Appendix to these comments.

4. The same arguments apply, mutatis matandis, to the author's second case.

5. H. Barger, in his comments from the floor, made the same points, and my Appendix covers much the same ground as an unpublished note he has written—

a copy of which Barger was kind enough to give me. As his oral and written comments, and mine as well, indicate, it seems that the arguments are common and well known. Thus it is difficult to understand the opposition to the discounted value or economic definition of depreciation.

6. In my *On Concepts of Capital and Technical Change* (Rymes 1971), I pointed out that aggregation problems, reswitching debates, and so forth, were not central to criticisms I advanced against standard measures of total factor productivity. Cambridge criticisms of traditional theory run deeper than aggregation difficulties.

7. More substantive issues *may* be involved. See Denison (1972).

8. This is the "depreciation by sudden death" case.

9. The case mentioned under "depreciation by obsolescence" in the comments.

References

Asimakopulos, A. 1962. *The reliability of selected price indexes for measuring price trends*. Ottawa: Queen's Printer for the Royal Commission on Banking and Finance.

Denison, Edward F. 1972. Final comments. *Survey of Current Business* 52 (May):95–110.

———. 1974. *Accounting for United States economic growth, 1929–1969*. Washington, D.C.: Brookings Institution.

Hulten, C. R. 1975. Technical change and the reproducibility of capital. *American Economic Review* 65 (December):956–65.

Robinson, J. 1960*a*. Some problems of definition and measurement of capital. In *Collected economic papers*, vol. 2. Oxford: Blackwell.

———. 1960*b*. Depreciation. In *Collected economic papers*, vol. 2. Oxford: Blackwell.

———. 1969. *The accumulation of capital*. 3d ed. London: Macmillan.

Rymes, T. K. 1971. *On concepts of capital and technical change*. Cambridge: Cambridge University Press.

Comment Jack G. Faucett

We are indebted to Allan Young and John Musgrave for giving us a good description of the procedures employed in constructing the BEA capital stock series and for pointing out the weaknesses and limitations of the data. The procedures used are probably the best available in view of the data limitations. I wish, however, to discuss some of the issues involved in capital stocks measurement and particularly the problems with measures for more disaggregated sectors. In addition, I agree with those who contend that a discount factor should be applied in the calculation of economic depreciation.

Jack G. Faucett is president of Jack Faucett Associates, Chevy Chase, Maryland.

I wish to discuss the four following issues and problems in current measures of capital stocks:

(1) perpetual inventory method versus deflation of book value measures; (2) accounting for assets furnished to private business by the government; (3) owned versus rented assets; and (4) economic depreciation.

Perpetual Inventory Method versus Deflation of Book Value Measures

The perpetual inventory method involves the accumulation of measures of prior investment by year (adjusted to prices of a common year). Each yearly investment stream is depreciated over time and is finally reduced to zero at the estimated end of the useful life of the asset. The measures of stocks for each year are obtained by summing the remaining values of past investment streams—either the gross as undepreciated values to derive gross stock measures or the depreciated values to derive net stock measures.

There are several major problems with this procedure:

1. There are no good estimates of lives of plant and equipment.
2. There is shifting over time of the industrial classification of establishments holding the stocks.
3. The investment data are weak before 1947 and are woefully lacking in the early years needed to establish stock measures beginning with 1925.
4. Transfers of assets between industries, between industry and government, and exports of used equipment are extremely difficult to identify and properly value.

Estimates of lives are generally based on lives used by companies for tax depreciation, adjusted by estimate to reflect best guesses on actual lives. The adjustments are based on fragmentary evidence and observation of actual lives. No comprehensive measures of actual lives exist. This lack of data on actual lives can introduce substantial error in the stock estimates.

The industrial classification of establishments changes when the major production of a establishment shifts to products classified in other industries. This is a major problem at the three- and four-digit SIC classification levels for manufacturing industries, and, to some extent, at the two-digit level. It is a much small problem at the three-sector economy levels at which the BEA stock measures are tabulated.

The shifting of assets between industries owing to the reclassification of establishments cannot be accommodated in the perpetual inventory method. As a result, the time series of stock measures are not consistent with output measures, which are tabulated on the current classification of establishments. This is a serious problem in most applications of stocks data for disaggregated sector detail.

In view of these problems, it appears that some way must be found to use book value measures to serve the need for stocks data at the detailed industry level, as well as to avoid measurement error resulting from poor data on asset lives. Book value is not subject to the limitations and problems discussed above. Unfortunately book values have not been available generally except at the company level and, further, unknown vintage distribution in these values has made accurate deflation impossible.

Book value data on stocks held by manufacturing establishments are now reported by the census, first in 1957 and annually beginning in 1962, with the exception of one or two years that were missed. However, separate data on plant and equipment were collected starting only in 1967. Within a few years these series should provide enough observations for use in econometric analysis.

For nonmanufacturing industries, book value data are available generally only by company from the IRS *Statistics of Income* and from regulatory agency reports for regulated industries. In nonmanufacturing, company data may be satisfactory since there is less diversity in the operations of companies than in manufacturing, except for financial conglomerates, which generally file separate IRS returns by type of business through their subsidiary companies. Also, the IRS data represent a principal source for sales or output measures for these industries in lieu of other census-type sources, and therefore consistency is maintained between the stock measures and associated output measures.

I propose that the two approaches—perpetual inventory and book value deflation—be combined to provide better measures than are now available. The perpetual inventory method would be used to develop reasonably good stock deflators, and these deflators would be applied to book values to derive stock measures in constant dollars. The deflators are subject to some error, of course, owing to the same problems inherent in the perpetual inventory method. However, the distortion effect is much less on a deflator series, since the error only affects the weights in the development of the deflators.

Accounting for Assets Furnished to Private Business by the Government

These assets account for 6 to 8% of stocks used by the private business sector but are concentrated in a relatively few industries, mainly in defense production. They contribute to the output of these sectors, but the value of this contribution is not reflected in sales measures, since the equipment is furnished without charge by the government and contract prices for the output, sold to the government, are negotiated to reflect this.

This situation creates a problem in use of the stock measures, since the output measures are not consistent with stock input measures when these stocks are added to contractor-owned stocks; on the other hand, if these stocks are not included, the production function relationship (e.g., the capital/labor ratio) is distorted for the industries that use these government-furnished stocks.

One way to resolve the problem would be to adjust the output measures to reflect the contribution of this capital. This of course would be difficult to do, and the adjustment would necessarily be made on the basis of the value of the capital input, rather than on any direct measure of its contribution to output, and therefore would in fact specify productivity change. This specification of productivity change would considerably reduce the value of the data for productivity measurement.

There appears to be no satisfactory solution to this problem. However, its importance is small when one considers the general problem of assets used but not owned by the industry—that is, the large amounts of rented and leased equipment and structures.

Owned versus Rented Assets

Young and Musgrave contend that there is a need to develop capital stocks data by using industry rather than by owning industries. The ultimate in this procedure would lead to trying to impute the value of a vast amount of rented and leased equipment and buildings to the using industries, probably an impossible and frustrating task. Extending this concept could conceivably imply the imputation of capital owned by industries supplying services to each industry; the differing degrees of vertical integration among plants in each industry would require this to make the stocks/output ratios comparable.

Rather than adjusting the stocks data, perhaps an easier way is to make the adjustment in the cost of capital services, the proper measure for the capital input in production function analyses. If the capital input is measured by the cost of its services (explicit or implicit), then the measurement problem is reduced. The values of owned assets are converted to implicit rental costs, and the rental costs for rented or leased assets are added to derive the total capital costs, after subtracting the value of rental receipts.

For this procedure, data are needed on rental payments and receipts. Some data are now collected by the Bureau of the Census and the Internal Revenue Service. I suggest that efforts to collect better and more complete data on rental payments and receipts are of high priority in improving the measurement of real capital input by detailed sectors of the economy.

Economic Depreciation

I agree with those who contend that economic depreciation should be calculated with a discount factor; that is, it should involve a calculation of the present value of the future stream of services from the capital assets. The discussion on economic depreciation below is taken from some work I did a few years ago, and I believe it sheds some further light on the proper method for calculating economic depreciation and its use in capital analysis.

Differences between accounting and economic depreciation cause a divergence between book values of stocks (after adjustment for price change) and market values. Market values reflect economic depreciation, whereas book values reflect accounting depreciation methods that are often arbitrary and are not good approximations to economic depreciation. Economic depreciation reflects the loss in the current and future service value of the stock, which, by definition, affects the price a purchaser is willing to pay for the stock—the market value. As a stock increases in age, its current service value may decrease because of physical deterioration, which renders it less efficient in production. Its future service value also declines with age because its remaining life or stored-up value is reduced. There is no reason the sum of these two effects should be linear (straight-line depreciation) or exponential (declining-balance depreciation). Under the assumption of no less in efficiency over the life of the stock, the shape is quite different from either of these methods as shown in figure C1.1.

Economic depreciation is calculated as the loss in the value of the stock during a specified period of time, usually calculated annually. The value of the stock by definition is the sum of the time-discounted values of its future flow of services. Thus, each year it loses one year of remaining life; that is, the final year, which is distant and therefore worth less than the current year's service because of the discount factor. (Economic depreciation increases steadily over the life of the stock under the assumption of no decline in productive services over its life.) The calculation for depreciation in time period, a to $a + 1$, is:

$$a^{d}a + 1 = \sum_{t=1}^{n-a} [1 + r]^{-t}\, CS_t - \sum_{t=1}^{n-(a+1)} [1 + r]^{-t}\, CS_t,$$

where $a =$ age of stock

$n =$ expected economic life of stock

$r =$ discount factor

$CS_t =$ index of capital services at time t normalized so that

$$\sum_{t=1}^{n} [1 + r]^{-t}\, CS_t = \text{original cost of the stock.}$$

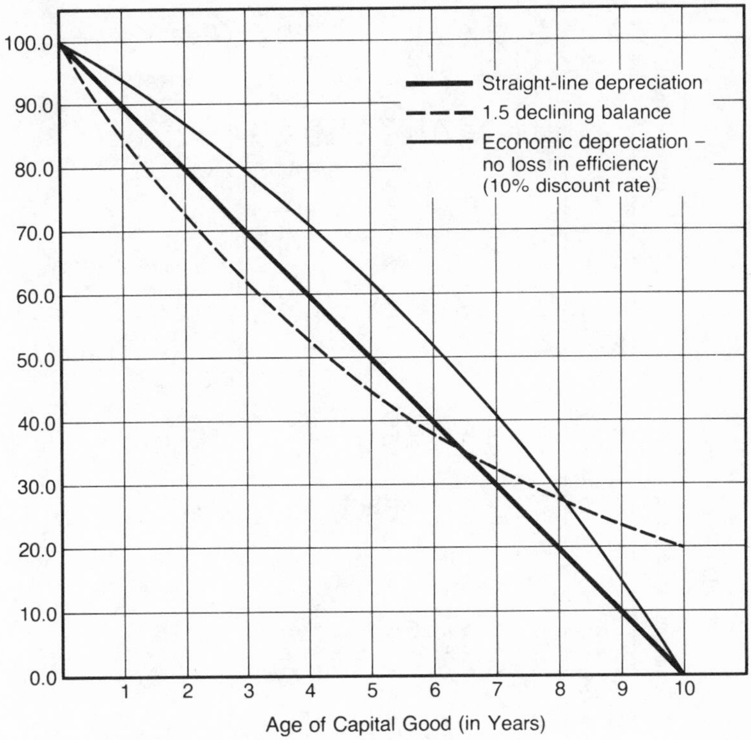

Fig. C1.1 Asset value under different depreciation methods, ten-year life, in percentage of original cost.

To explain further, depreciation in any period is equal to the change during that period in the value of discounted future services of the stock over its remaining life. *CS* is an abstract measure of the flow of those services, the discounted sum of which is equal to the original cost of the stock.

Straight-line and declining-balance depreciation are contrasted with economic depreciation in table C1.1. Economic depreciation is calculated under two different assumptions: no loss in productivity (efficiency) over the life of the asset; and productivity decline according to the formula

Table C1.1 **Depreciation, Depreciated Value, and Cost of Capital Services**

$10,000 Original Cost
Ten-year Life
10% Discount Factor

	Straight-line Depreciation		1.5 Declining Balance Depreciation		Economic Depreciation: No Decline in Productivity		Economic Depreciation: Decline in Productivity		Cost of Capital Services: No Decline in Productivity			Cost of Capital Services: Decline in Productivity		
Year[a]	Depr.	Value	Depr.	Value	Depr.	Value	Depr.	Value	Depr.	Int.	Total	Depr.	Int.	Total
1	1,000	9,000	1,500	8,500	627	9,373	804	9,196	627	1,000	1,627	804	1,000	1,804
2	1,000	8,000	1,275	7,225	691	8,682	867	8,329	691	937	1,628	867	920	1,787
3	1,000	7,000	1,084	6,141	759	7,923	929	7,400	759	868	1,627	929	833	1,762
4	1,000	6,000	921	5,220	835	7,088	992	6,408	835	792	1,627	992	740	1,732
5	1,000	5,000	783	4,437	919	6,169	1,051	5,357	919	709	1,628	1,051	641	1,692
6	1,000	4,000	666	3,771	1,011	5,158	1,104	4,253	1,011	617	1,628	1,104	536	1,640
7	1,000	3,000	565	3,206	1,111	4,047	1,147	3,106	1,111	516	1,627	1,147	425	1,572
8	1,000	2,000	481	2,725	1,222	2,825	1,153	1,953	1,222	405	1,627	1,153	311	1,464
9	1,000	1,000	409	2,316	1,345	1,480	1,091	862	1,345	283	1,628	1,091	195	1,286
10	1,000	0	347	1,969	1,480	0	862	0	1,480	148	1,628	862	86	948

[a]Stock values are end-of-year values.

$$D(a) = \frac{A - a}{A - .9a} \qquad 0 \leq a \leq A,$$
$$= 0 \qquad a \geq A$$

where $D(a)$ = index of service units of asset (efficiency index) at age (a)
A = economic life of asset in years
a = age of asset in years.

Economic depreciation increases steadily over the life of the asset under the assumption that there is no decline in efficiency over the life of the asset (this assumption implies uniform maintenance costs over the life of the asset—see later section). This is directly opposite to declining-balance depreciation, which starts out much higher and declines steadily over the asset life. Under the assumption of no efficiency decline, economic depreciation is lower than straight-line depreciation initially and higher near the end of the life of the asset.

Under the assumption of a decline in productivity or efficiency over the life of the asset, economic depreciation is higher in the beginning and lower near the end (relative to the assumption of no decline in efficiency). The steeper the decline in efficiency, the more the depreciation schedule is tilted toward high initial values (in the extreme case, where efficiency declines linearly with age, it starts out nearly equal to double declining-balance depreciation but decreases more slowly with age). Within the range of realistic assumptions on the rate of efficiency decline and discount rate, surprisingly, straight-line depreciation is a fair approximation of economic depreciation over most of the life of the asset.

Cost of Capital Services

The cost of capital services is the sum of economic depreciation and the interest cost of capital (ignoring gains or losses from revaluation of assets for the time being). This cost should be proportional to the units of capital services at any point in time—the marketplace will adjust the prices of used assets so that units of capital services from used assets will cost the same as from new assets. Economic depreciation reflects this adjustment in market prices.

The costs of capital services are calculated in the last section of table C1.1. Note that under the assumption of no decline in productivity or efficiency, the cost of capital services remains constant over the life of the asset. This is true only under economic depreciation; under arbitrary accounting methods of depreciation this is not true. Under both straight-line and declining-balance depreciation, the sum of depreciation and interest cost declines steadily over the life of the asset.

Under the assumption of a decline in productivity, the cost of capital services decreases in proportion to the loss in capital service units. This may be seen by comparing the annual costs (table C1.1) with the annual service units inherent in the efficiency decline function (fig. C1.2). The cost per service unit remains constant at approximately 0.1805 per unit over the life of the asset.

Revaluation owing to price changes also affects changes in the market prices of capital goods and the implicit costs of capital services. Changes owing to revaluation are not predictable and therefore cannot be built into the depreciation schedule. Revaluations can be handled separately and need not lead to revisions in the depreciation base unless the asset is sold. This is so whether or not the investment base is revaluated for rate-of-return calculations.

Relationship of Efficiency Decline to Maintenance and Repair Costs

Efficiency decline as reflected in economic depreciation is essentially the complement of *rising* maintenance and repair costs (M&R costs) needed to keep the asset at 100% efficiency (if it is cost-effective to do so). (A uniform level of maintenance and repair costs over the life of the asset is consistent with the assumption of no efficiency decline in the calculation of economic depreciation—economic depreciation is not affected by the level but only the distribution of maintenance and repair costs over the life of the asset.) There are very few data on the distribution of M&R costs over the life of assets. It is certain that these costs generally increase with the age of the asset, if the productive efficiency of the asset is maintained at 100%. We have assumed a decline in efficiency (i.e., increasing M&R costs required for 100% efficiency over the life) at an increasing rate over the life of the asset by the following equation:

$$D(a) = \frac{A - a}{A - Ba} \qquad 0 \leq a \leq A.$$

$$= 0 \qquad a \geq A$$

$D(a)$, A, and a have been defined earlier. B is a parameter to be estimated; I have assumed a value of 0.9 in the calculations in this report. The lower the value of B, the more rapid the decline in efficiency.

As indicated above, the equation specifying decline in efficiency has a dual interpretation: it represents either: the decline in efficiency (in terms of productive service units of the capital) with any uniform level of maintenance over the life of the capital; or the increasing costs of M&R required to maintain 100% efficiency measured at age a as follows:

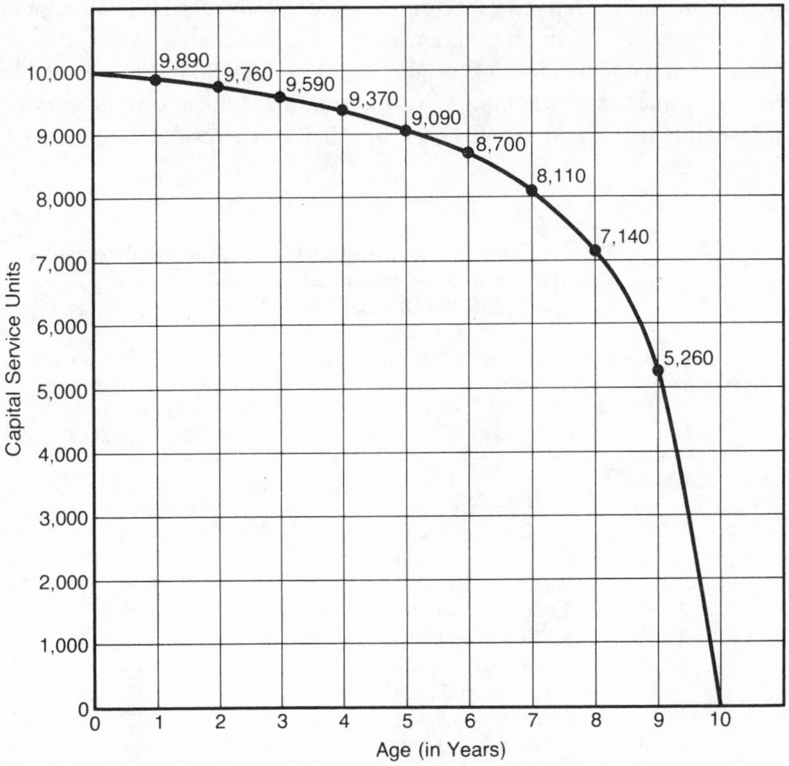

Fig. C1.2 Efficiency decline function (B = 0.9).

$$\left[1 - \frac{A - a}{A - Ba}\right] \cdot \frac{\textit{Original Cost}}{A}.$$

This formula simply states M&R cost or efficiency loss as a fraction of amortized original cost. A loss in productive service (expressed as a fraction of service units) or a maintenance cost equal to the same fraction of amortized original cost (assuming constant prices) has exactly the same effect on the market value of the asset (and therefore on economic depreciation). It does not matter to the market value whether future maintenance is actually performed; it is assumed that it will be performed if it is cost-effective and is not performed otherwise.

The distribution of maintenance and repair costs over the life of the assets can affect market value and depreciation very significantly. To illustrate the range of this effect I have calculated market values and depreciation for a $10,000 asset (original cost) under three different assumptions with respect to the distribution of maintenance and repair costs: (1) increases annually by a constant amount; (2) constant amount annually; and (3) decreases annually by a constant amount. In each case, the sum of maintenance and repair costs over the life of the asset equals 55% of original cost, or $5,500. Present values (market value) are calculated by discounting future capital services (and maintenance and repair cost) by 10%. The results are shown in table C1.2.

Table C1.2 **Present Value of Assets and Depreciation under Alternative Distributions of Maintenance and Repair**
$10,000 Original Cost
Ten-Year Life
10% Discount Factor

	Present (Market) Value (End of Year)			Depreciation (During Year)		
Year	Case 1	Case 2	Case 3	Case 1	Case 2	Case 3
1	8,223	9,372	11,000	1,777	628	−1,000
2	6,578	8,682	11,633	1,645	690	− 663
3	5,078	7,923	11,957	1,500	759	− 294
4	3,733	7,088	11,884	1,345	835	113
5	2,562	6,170	11,283	1,171	918	561
6	1,585	5,160	10,223	977	1,010	1,060
7	820	4,049	8,628	765	1,111	1,595
8	283	2,826	6,434	537	1,223	2,194
9	0	1,480	3,580	283	1,346	2,854
10	0	0	0	0	1,480	3,580

Note:
Case 1: Maintenance and repair costs are $100 in first year and increase by $100 each year.
Case 2. M&R costs are $550 each year.
Case 3. M&R costs are $1,000 in first year and decrease by $100 each year.

These extreme cases dramatize the effect of the distribution of maintenance costs over the life of the asset. Note that in the first case the market value declines not unlike double declining-balance depreciation initially, and less rapidly after the midpoint of its life. Note further that the market value has declined to zero after nine years, since in the last year the M&R costs are equal to the value of the capital services (based on amortized original cost). In this case the assumed rate of increase in M&R is unrealistically high (M&R increases by tenfold over the life of the equipment).

The second case illustrates the effect of constant M&R costs over the life of the asset. Note that the market values and depreciation are identical with those in table C1.1 for the assumption of no decline in productivity (economic depreciation is affected only by the time distribution and not by the *level* of M&R).

The third case requires some interpretation. In this case M&R costs are heavy initially and decline to one-tenth of the first-year amount by the tenth year—admittedly, not a very likely case. (As a possible example, some machinery requires an extensive breaking-in period as well as initial adjustments and does not reach full productivity until after a few years). The heavy initial costs (either for costs of adjustments or for loss in output) result in increases in the value of the machine (negative depreciation) over the first few years.

The assumption we have made with respect to the distribution of M&R over the life of the asset is embodied in our efficiency decline function, previously described. It is plotted to scale in figure C1.2. The units represent capital service units, arbitrarily normalized to the initial purchase price for convenience in exposition. M&R in a given year necessary to maintain 100% efficiency is, then, the area between the 100% efficiency line and the efficiency curve for that year expressed as a fraction of the total area over all years, times the original purchase price ($10,000). However, this M&R may be increased by a constant amount each year and still be consistent with the annual market values and depreciation derived by applying this function. Hence, our function establishes only the distribution and not the level of M&R.

The annual market values and depreciation consistent with this efficiency decline/M&R assumption are plotted in figure C1.3 from data in table C1.1. The approximation to straight-line depreciation is remarkable. It is somewhat ironic that simple straight-line depreciation is a fair approximation of economic depreciation. We must keep in mind that the assumptions made on M&R and the discount factor both influence the distribution of depreciation over the life of the asset. The effect of the M&R distribution has been discussed above. As for the effect of the discount factor, a higher discount factor results in a lowering of economic depreciation in the early years and an increase in later years. Consequently, market values tend to be higher, the higher the discount factor. The effect of the discount factor is illustrated in table C1.3 for three rates; 6%, 10%, and 14%. It can be seen that these differences in rates yield significant differences in market values (and the distribution of depreciation over the life of the assets).

Caution on Market Value

"Market value" as used in this paper refers to the depreciated original cost of the asset with a proportionate adjustment—that is, revaluation—for price change in equivalent new assets. Thus it is an estimate of reproduction cost adjusted for depreciation. This measure will differ from observed market values if the asset is obsolete and no longer being

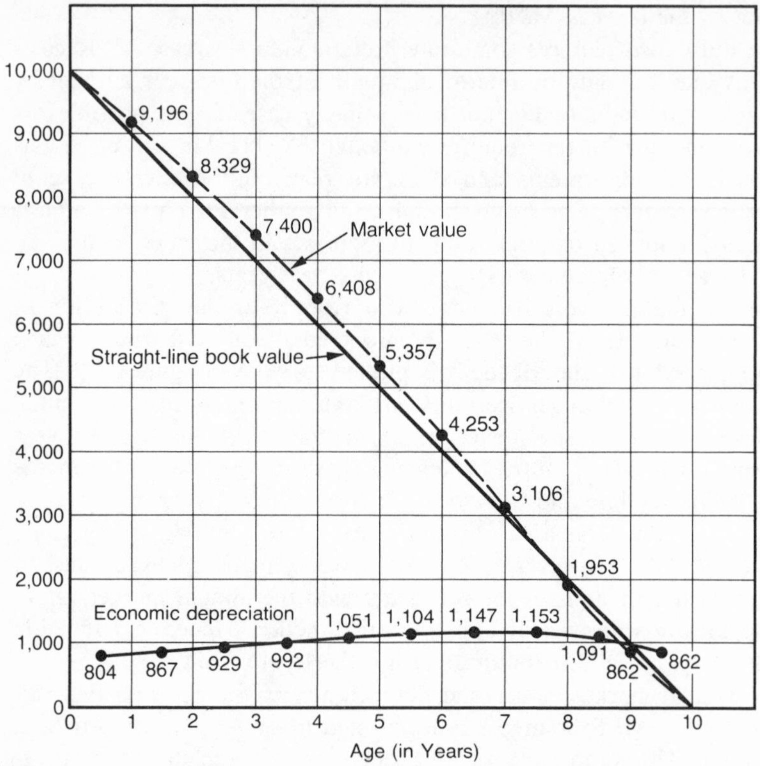

Fig. C1.3 Market value and economic depreciation, in constant dollars. From table C1.1 (efficiency decline, B = 0.9; discount factor, 10%).

produced. It also will differ from net sales value due to transfer costs—that is, sales commissions, moving costs, and so forth. It may also differ from market value owing to imperfections and uncertainties in the marketplace; for example, a new car drops significantly in value with the first few miles because of the potential buyer's uncertainty and suspicion about its condition.

For all these reasons—apart from any errors owing to the assumptions with respect to average life, M&R costs, or the discount factor—the market values discussed in this paper must be interpreted with caution.

Table C1.3 **Market Value and Depreciation for Selected Discount Assumptions**

$10,000 Original Cost
Ten-year Life

	Market Value (End of Year)			Depreciation (During Year)		
Year	6%	10%	14%	6%	10%	14%
1	9,073	9,196	9,299	927	804	701
2	8,107	8,329	8,524	966	867	775
3	7,102	7,400	7,665	1,005	929	859
4	6,063	6,408	6,725	1,039	992	940
5	4,996	5,357	5,697	1,067	1,051	1,028
6	3,908	4,253	4,584	1,088	1,104	1,113
7	2,815	3,106	3,396	1,093	1,147	1,188
8	1,746	1,953	2,169	1,069	1,153	1,227
9	758	862	968	988	1,091	1,201
10	0	0	0	758	862	968

Note: Efficiency decline as in table C1.1.

Reply by Young and Musgrave

We endorse the comments of both Faucett and Rymes on the need for more information, particularly better empirical evidence on service lives and depreciation. Perhaps we should have stressed our position on this point more strongly.

We agree with Rymes on his exposition of the time pattern of the value of the net stock of an asset using the discounted value definition of depreciation. However, our four examples were based on what we have considered to be the NIPA definition, not on the discounted value definition. In our paper, we attempted to contrast these two approaches to depreciation, both of which have received considerable attention in the past by this conference.

Two additional pieces of evidence seem to support the use of straight-line depreciation. First, Faucett's judgment approach yields a depreciation pattern that is close to straight-line. Second, BEA's stocks and depreciation estimates fall about halfway between those presented by Coen and those presented by Hulten and Wycoff in their chapters in this volume. While the empirical studies by Coen and by Hulten and Wycoff are based on limited data and may involve considerable statistical difficulties, it is interesting that these independently derived estimates bracket the BEA estimates. In this connection we note that the results in Coen's chapter in this volume imply a greater incidence of accelerated depreciation than the results in his 1975 article that we cited.

2 Economic Depreciation and the Taxation of Structures in United States Manufacturing Industries: An Empirical Analysis

Charles R. Hulten and Frank C. Wykoff

A vigorous controversy has been taking place in recent years over the appropriate specification of the neoclassical investment function. One of the central disputes concerns the extensive use of geometric depreciation, which produces a relatively straightforward, consistent model of replacement demand.[1] The conflict has generated considerable interest among econometricians in the rate and pattern of economic depreciation.[2] Recently, the United States Bureau of Economic Analysis (BEA) introduced imputed economic depreciation, based upon specific a priori rates and patterns, into the national income and product accounts.[3] Meanwhile, repeated attempts at tax reform have been focusing much attention upon the depreciation allowances permitted taxpayers. Samuelson (1964), Eisner (1973), and Coen (1975) all suggest that the tax allowances should conform to actual economic depreciation.

Of course economic depreciation, unlike an engineering production function, is not a technological datum: economic depreciation, the loss in its value as an asset ages, is a price concept. Feldstein and Rothschild (1974) point out that economic depreciation will depend upon, among other things, the tax treatment of assets. The Feldstein-Rothschild results, based upon theoretical argument and hypothetical illustration, suggest that the relation between tax and economic depreciation is very complex.[4]

In this paper we have four objectives: (1) to compare tax depreciation deductions with economic depreciation estimates, produced by

Charles R. Hulten is senior research associate at the Urban Institute. Frank C. Wykoff is associate professor of economics at Pomona College.

This research was funded by the Office of Tax Analysis under Treasury contract #TOS-74-27. We wish to thank Dennis Cox, Seymour Fiekowsky, Harvey Galper, Gary Robbins, and Emil Sunley for helpful suggestions. Valuable assistance was provided by Flint Brayton and Mary Simpson. Opinions and errors are our sole responsibility.

Hulten and Wykoff (1976), for sixteen classes of commercial and industrial structures, including apartments, factories, office buildings, retail stores, and warehouses; (2) to estimate the instantaneous effect upon asset values and tax liabilities, for each asset class, of possible changes in the tax code; (3) to construct capital stock estimates of structures, employing the mortality function derived from the dual to economic depreciation, for the twenty-one two-digit level Standard Industrial Classification (SIC) manufacturing industries; and (4) to determine the rate of tax subsidy per capital dollar by industry grouping.

The economic depreciation estimates of Hulten and Wykoff (1976) are based upon observed market acquisition prices of new and used structures. These prices are reported in a 1972 United States Treasury sample survey of more than seven thousand owners of structures.[5] Tax regulations pertaining to the depreciation of structures are in section 1250 of the Federal Tax Code. Briefly, taxpayers may deduct a "reasonable allowance" for the wear, tear, and obsolescence on capital assets used to generate income. The Internal Revenue Service publishes acceptable accounting methods for calculating depreciation on each asset class. The tax life of an asset, the parameter that, combined with the accounting method, determines the stream of tax deductions, may be selected in one of two ways. The taxpayer may either use the life for his asset's class published in Revenue Procedure 62-21, Internal Revenue Service or, if warranted by his own "facts and circumstances," he may use a shorter life. A shorter tax life will usually result in lower tax liability. The 1972 Treasury survey indicated that considerable use must have been made of the "facts and circumstances" clause, because actual tax lives were far shorter than those published in Revenue Procedure 62-21. The United States Treasury announced in 1976 that only lives published in Revenue Procedure 62-21 would be allowed on structures.

Because we employ several different economic depreciation estimates and because two sets of tax depreciation practices are in use, summary information about differences between tax and economic depreciation is difficult to provide. Nonetheless, the following observations provide a general overview of our results: (1) The present value at asset acquisition of tax depreciation exceeds that of economic depreciation, for all large asset classes, apartments, factories, offices, retail stores, and warehouses, regardless of the economic depreciation estimation method employed. (2) For all asset classes, except one, actual tax depreciation deductions reported by taxpayers in the 1972 survey exceed "guideline" tax depreciation deductions.[6] However, the difference between actual tax and guideline deductions is relatively small in comparison with the difference between tax and economic depreciation. (3) The magnitude of the subsidy, assuming a corporate tax rate of 48%, varies considerably across asset classes. Unfortunately, the rank ordering of assets by class is not stationary across depreciation estimation methods. Larger subsidies do appear to be received by owners of apartments, offices, and retail trade buildings, and smaller subsidies, perhaps even surcharges, are incurred by owners of banks, recreational facilities, and medical buildings. (4) Changes in tax regulations to require that deductions be based upon guideline lives, rather than shorter lives actually used, would have only modest effect upon removing tax subsidies. Return to Bulletin F lives and to straight-line depreciation (see below for details) would remove most of the tax subsidies. (5) The magnitude of the annual subsidies per dollar of capital stock (of industrial and commercial buildings) are different for different industries in manufacturing, ranging from —2¢ on the dollar for SIC group 19 to 1.1¢ for SIC group 27.

In section 2.1, we present the theory of tax and economic depreciation to be used in this paper. In the second and third sections, we summarize the measurement of depreciation from Hulten and Wykoff (1976) and the tax regulations that pertain to industrial and commercial structures. Section 2.4 contains a comparison of tax and economic depreciation estimates and an examination of several possible changes in the tax laws. In section 2.5 the stocks of industrial and commercial structures in United States manufacturing are calculated, and in the final section we give estimates of the depreciation subsidy per dollar by two-digit manufacturing industry.

2.1 The Theory of Economic and Tax Depreciation

In efficient, competitive capital markets, the acquisition price of an asset equals the present value of the future flow of user costs on the asset throughout its economic life.[7] If $q(s,t)$ is the acquisition price of an age-s asset in time t, $c(s,t)$ is the user cost of an age-s asset at time t, r is the rate of interest, and L is the asset's life, then

$$(1) \qquad q(s,t) = \sum_{x=0}^{L} \frac{c(s+x, t+x)}{(1+r)^{x+1}}.$$

Equation (1) can be modified to allow for capital taxation:[8] let u be the marginal effective tax rate, and let $d_T(s)$ be the deduction for depreciation allowed on an asset at age s, whose original acquisition price was \$1. At age s the present value of the future tax depreciation deductions can be written as $z(s)$ where:

$$(2) \qquad z(s) = \sum_{x=s}^{T} \frac{d_T(x)}{(1+r)^{x-s+1}},$$

where T is the tax life over which the deductions are allowed. The competitive asset price is the present value of the after-tax flow of income from the asset plus the tax not paid owing to the depreciation deduction allowed on the original price of the asset. Equation (1) thus modified to allow for a constant tax rate, u, becomes:

$$q(s,t) = (1 - u) \sum_{x=0}^{L} \frac{c(s + x, t + x)}{(1 + r)^{x+1}} + uz(s)q(0, t - s). \tag{3}$$

One may take first differences of (3) and simplify to derive:

$$(1 - u)c(s,t) = rq(s,t) + [q(s,t) - q(s + 1, t + 1)] - ud_T(s)q(0, t - s). \tag{4}$$

From equation (4) one may compute $c(s,t)$, the before-tax service flow, and $(1 - u)c(s,t)$, the after-tax service flow, from $q(s,t)$, observed acquisition prices, r, the rate of return, u the marginal tax rate, and $d_T(s)$ the tax depreciation deduction.

Economic depreciation is defined as the change in the price of the asset from aging:[9]

$$D(s,t) = q(s,t) - q(s + 1,t). \tag{5}$$

If in equation (4) we add and subtract $q(s + 1,t)$ to the term in square brackets, we have:

$$(1 - u)c(s,t) = rq(s,t) + D(s,t) - [q(s + 1,t + 1) - q(s + 1,t)] - ud_T(s)q(0,t - s). \tag{6}$$

Let $[q(s + 1,t + 1) - q(s + 1,t)] = \rho(s,t)$; ρ measures the change over time in a fixed-age asset and is therefore the degree of asset inflation. Equation (6) becomes:

$$(1 - u)c(s,t) = rq(s,t) + D(s,t) - \rho(s,t) - ud_T(s)q(0,t - s). \tag{7}$$

The after-tax user cost of a unit of age-s capital over time t is thus seen to consist of four terms: (1) $rq(s,t)$, the opportunity cost of holding resources in the asset over period t; (2) $D(s,t)$, economic depreciation on the asset; (3) $\rho(s,t)$; capital gains on the asset; and (4) $ud_T(s)q(0, t - s)$, the tax saving from taking depreciation deductions on the asset. The last two terms are subtracted from the after-tax user cost. The greater are capital gains, the lower is the cost of capital, and, similarly, the larger are tax depreciation deductions, the smaller will be the cost of capital.[10]

The second and fourth terms on the right side of equation (7) indicate that the after-tax cost of capital depends upon both economic depreciation and the tax deduction for depreciation. The difference between economic and tax depreciation is

$$\Delta(s,t) = D(s,t) - d_T(s)q(0, t - s). \tag{8}$$

In the absence of inflation, the sum over the life of the asset of the difference between economic and tax depreciation, $\sum_{s=0}^{L} \Delta(s,t+s)$, equals zero; when economic and tax depreciation are congruent, $\Delta(s,t+s) = 0$, for all s. If, however, taxpayers are allowed to accelerate tax deductions relative to actual depreciation, the present value of the stream $\Delta(s,t+s)$ is, given a positive discount rate, negative. Therefore, given sufficient income to absorb the deduction, the taxpayer receives a subsidy that conceptually is equivalent to an interest-free loan from the Treasury.[11]

Equation (5) can be used to estimate economic depreciation from market prices. Since the observed prices reflect actual market conditions, depreciation estimates will reflect prevailing rates of return and prevailing tax laws. Consequently, one may directly compare existing tax depreciation with economic depreciation estimates based upon these prices. However, the problem of assessing the effect of hypothetical alternative tax regimes is more complicated, because, as equations (3) and (7) indicate, asset prices depend upon the tax treatment of capital, and one cannot therefore assume that asset prices and economic depreciation are given. One must account for the effect upon economic depreciation of changes in tax depreciation.

We shall assume that the physical durability of capital is not altered by the tax laws, so that the relative productive efficiencies of new and used assets are stationary across tax regimes. We also assume that the ratio of the marginal product of an age-s asset to a new one is a function of age alone, $\phi(s)$: then, under competitive conditions:

$$\phi(s) = c(s,t)/c(0,t). \tag{9}$$

$\phi(s)$, $s = 0,1,2, \ldots, L$ is the relative efficiency function of vintage capital. Of course, the owners of capital assets can in fact alter the durability of their assets in response to changes in tax treatment of capital by varying maintenance and repair, capacity utilization, and so on. However, these effects are extremely difficult to deal with empirically, and we are forced to treat the exogeneity of $\phi(s)$ as a maintained hypothesis. Using equation (9) we may write the acquisition price of an age-s asset, equation (3), as:

$$q(s,t) = (1-u) \sum_{x=0}^{L} \frac{c(0,t+x)\phi(s+x)}{(1+r)^{x+1}} + uz(s)q(0, t-s). \tag{10}$$

If $c(0,t)$ is also stationary over time, we have:

$$q(s,t) = (1-u)c(0) \sum_{x=0}^{L} \frac{\phi(s+x)}{(1+r)^{x+1}} + uz(s)q(0, t-s). \tag{11}$$

Equation (11) is useful for investigating the *short run* effect of alternative tax depreciation policies. Assuming that $c(0)$ and $\phi(s)$ are not affected in the short run by changes in tax policy, (11) can be used to generate a new sequence of acquisition prices that capture the effect of the policy change. In other words, the ceteris paribus assumption permits the calculation of the change in economic depreciation resulting from a change in tax depreciation.

2.2 Measurement of Economic Depreciation

In 1972 the United States Treasury's Office of Industrial Economics (OIE) undertook a survey of more than seven thousand taxpayers to determine the tax treatment of twenty-two classes of commercial and industrial structures. In addition to questions about their actual tax practices, respondents were asked the acquisition price of the building, the year the building was constructed, and the year they acquired it. From the responses, one can compile a cross section of acquisition prices on buildings by age and date. Distinguishing physical characteristics of buildings, square footage, construction quality, primary material, and location were also reported. Hulten and Wykoff (1976) employ this data to estimate economic depreciation and asset revaluation for sixteen classes of structures.[12] Sample size was rather large for major classes: apartments (203 usable observations), factories (526), offices (1,654), retail trade buildings (1,666) and warehouses (580). Other classes had fewer data: hotels (42), motels (65), and recreational buildings (58) were the smallest. Except for the service station and terminal building classes, considerable variations in price, age, and date were observed within each class.

To determine an asset's depreciation pattern, one must determine both the speed of depreciation and the path. Consequently, nonlinear, flexible estimation methods are needed. We used two basic approaches: a polynomial power series and a Box-Cox power transformation. Both approaches are flexible in that they admit a variety of shapes for the estimated path. The polynomial method is intrinsically linear, and additional variables could be easily introduced. The Box-Cox form includes both linear and geometric decay as special cases. In both approaches comparison was made between the best estimated form and geometric depreciation. The latter is easy to work with and, as noted above, has received considerable attention in the literature.

With the polynomial equations, comparisons to the geometric were undertaken with a modified statistic for sums of square residuals adjusted for degrees of freedom suggested by Theil (1971). Neither form consistently outperformed the other. Furthermore, the optimal polynomial forms tended to be nearly U-shaped and therefore to closely approximate the geometric form. Since the geometric is so convenient, much of the analysis in this chapter is based upon the geometric depreciation estimates.

The constant geometric depreciation form is a special case of the flexible Box-Cox depreciation estimation method. However, for most classes the depreciation rate was not constant. Nevertheless, the actual rates produced were approximately geometric. We estimated the closest geometric rate to the actual estimated Box-Cox rates and found that in most cases the constant geometric rate was very close to the actual Box-Cox rates in all but the earliest years of the assets' lives. Therefore, again, we adopt the geometric approximations here, because using actual Box-Cox estimates is more costly to their complexity, and because the Box-Cox estimates vary over both vintage and time, and a summary measure of the rate of depreciation is useful.

Because the data consist of a cross-sectional sample taken at a point in time, only assets that survived to the date of the survey were included in the study. If our depreciation estimates are to reflect the performance of typical assets of each vintage, then some allowance is needed for the nonsurvivors—assets that were scrapped or retired before the sample was collected. To compensate for the exclusion of nonsurvivors, we modified our data by reducing each observed vintage asset price by the probability that the old asset survived to the date of the cross-sectional study. This compensation amounts to adding back into the sample all assets that were retired and valuing them at zero. The retirement pattern is taken from the study by Winfrey (1935), and the resultant estimates are called Winfrey-transformed estimates.

The Winfrey retirement distribution is not based upon actual structure retirement. Rather, Winfrey studied an obscure set of assets, such as railroad ties and telephone poles. One cannot be sure, therefore, that the Winfrey distribution accurately reflects the true distribution of structures. However, the distribution is centered at the Bulletin F (1942) average lives of structures, so that only the shape of the distribution, not the location, is based upon Winfrey's study.

A case can be made that asset values are not actually zero at retirement but rather are valued the same as nonretired assets, and, because the Winfrey pattern may be unreliable in any case, we maintain depreciation estimates both for Winfrey-transformed price data and for untransformed prices. We do prefer the Winfrey transformed prices because, despite arguments to the contrary, we believe assets, when scrapped, are near zero in price. Thus we will present the Winfrey-transformed results in the text and only make general reference to other results.

Table 2.1 contains the geometric depreciation rates employed in this study. Four sets of rates are used: the geometric rates estimated directly on observed market prices, both transformed and untransformed for retirement; and the geometric approximations to the best Box-Cox patterns both transformed and untransformed. Only the details of the direct geometric on transformed prices are presented here.

Table 2.1 Rates of Depreciation by Asset Class

	Direct Geometric Estimates		Box-Cox Approximations	
Class	Transformed	Untransformed	Transformed	Untransformed
Apartment	3.90	1.46	3.36	2.22
Bank	3.48	2.15	5.07	1.12
Factory	4.09	1.45	3.61	1.28
Hotel	3.93	.26	—	.95
Machine shop	2.02	1.40	—	—
Medical building	3.65	1.55	8.48	7.05
Motel	4.44	1.39	4.92	.26
Office	2.97	1.26	2.47	1.05
Recreational	6.31	2.42	4.87	3.19
Repair garage	3.28	2.07	4.00	2.54
Restaurant/bar	3.36	1.32	4.34	.88
Retail trade	2.73	1.11	2.20	.82
Service station	4.01	2.67	10.80	9.55
Shopping center	2.14	.40	3.36	1.24
Terminal	2.43	1.31	5.63	1.70
Warehouse	2.95	1.76	2.73	1.22

2.3 Tax Depreciation Statutes and Practice

Taxpayers use accounting depreciation schemes allowed by the Internal Revenue Service and compute their actual tax deductions by applying a tax-life parameter to these formulas.[13] As of 1976, owners of new structures other than apartments are allowed to use the 1.5 declining-balance formula and may switch to the straight-line formula when they choose. Let $d_T(s)$ be the tax depreciation rate calculated at age s on the original acquisition price of the asset, then

$$(12) \qquad d_T(s) = \begin{cases} \dfrac{1.5}{T}\left(1 - \dfrac{1.5}{T}\right)^{s-1} & s = 1, \ldots, \tau \\ \dfrac{3}{T}\left(1 - \dfrac{1.5}{T}\right)^{\tau-1} & s = \tau, \ldots, T \end{cases},$$

where T is the tax life of the asset, and τ, the age for switching to straight-line depreciation is $2T/3$. The taxpayer is seen to use the 1.5 declining-balance formula through the first two-thirds of tax life. After $2T/3$ years, straight-line depreciation exceeds 1.5 declining-balance depreciation, and the rational owner would switch to the straight-line method.

Taxpayers have some discretion in choosing the tax life they are to apply to equation (12). They may use the lives published by the Treasury in Revenue Procedure 62-21, amended in 1971, or they may use shorter lives if the latter can be justified by the owner's "facts and circumstances." In the OIE sample, the taxpayers reported the actual tax lives they use on their assets, and the results were published by the Treasury in *Business Building Statistics*, August 1975. The actual tax lives reported were quite a bit lower than the guideline lives published in Revenue Procedure 62-21. In table 2.2, we report three sets of tax lives: Bulletin F lives, Revenue Procedure 62-21 lives, and the average tax lives reported by the taxpayer survey. Hereafter, for convenience, we refer to the Revenue Procedure 62-21 lives as "guidline" lives and the reported lives as "actual" tax lives.

Table 2.2 Asset Lives Used for Tax Purposes

Asset Class	Bulletin F	Revenue Procedure 16–21[a]	OIE Survey 1975
Apartment	50	40	32
Bank	67	50	43
Factory	50	45	36
Hotel	50	40	41
Machine shop	60	45	32
Medical building	67	—	34
Motel	40	40	31
Office	67	45	41
Recreational	40	—	30
Repair garage	60	45	29
Restaurant/bar	60	50	31
Retail trade	67	50	34
Service station	50	16	19
Shopping center	50	50	36
Terminal	75	—	27
Warehouse	75	60	37

[a]The 1975 OIE report indicates that these lives (updated in December 1971) are now used by taxpayers. No lives are reported for medical, recreational, and terminal buildings, so we have substituted Bulletin F lives in our analysis.

To illustrate the application of table 2.2 to formula (12), consider a factory, the original basis of which is $1,000. The guideline tax life is forty-five years. Thus, the guideline deduction at age ten is

$$d_T(10) = \frac{1.5}{45}\left(1 - \frac{1.5}{45}\right)^9 = .02457. \tag{13}$$

In dollar terms the deduction is $24.57.

The tax treatment of apartments is unique for Code 1250 property. Apartment owners may depreciate their property according to the double-declining balance formula and switch to straight-line when desired. For apartment owners, equation (12) is modified so that the depreciation rate is 2 over the tax life rather than $1.5/T$, so that τ is $T/2$, not $(2/3)T$. No allowance was made for the recapture provisions.

2.4 Tax versus Economic Depreciation

2.4.1 Comparisons of Economic Depreciation to Existing Tax Depreciation Rules

For each asset class, we calculate the economic depreciation on an hypothetical asset that has a new acquisition price of $1,000. The depreciation rates employed are those from table 2.1. To translate an economic depreciation rate, $d(s)$, into actual economic depreciation value, we assume the initial acquisition price of an asset to be $1,000, and we assume the cost to depreciate at rate $d(s)$ at age s, *and that there is no inflation*:

$$\begin{aligned} q(0) &= \$1{,}000.00 \\ q(s) &= q(s-1)\,[1 - d(s)] \end{aligned} \tag{14}$$

and

$$D(s) = q(s) - q(s+1). \tag{15}$$

The asset is depreciated according to (14) up to age $L - 1$, where L is the economic life calculated by Hulten and Wykoff (1976) from the straight-line depreciation estimates. The remainder of the asset is then fully depreciated at age L.

As a detailed example of comparisons between economic and tax depreciation streams, table 2.3 contains the economic, guideline tax, and actual tax depreciation values of apartment buildings computed for selected years of an asset's life. The economic depreciation values are based upon semilog least-squares estimates from Winfrey-transformed prices.

Row 1 of table 2.3 indicates that, in the first year of an apartment's life, economic depreciation is $39.00, while the guidelines allow tax deductions of $50.00 and actual tax practice consists of deductions of $62.50. For apartments, tax deductions continue to exceed economic depreciation through the first thirty years of economic life. Of course, eventually these larger tax deductions are offset by large economic de-

Table 2.3 Apartment Buildings: Economic and Tax Depreciation by Age
(Geometric Economic Depreciation on Winfrey-Transformed Prices)

Age in Years	Economic Depreciation	Tax Depreciation	
		Guideline	Actual
1	39	50	62.50
2	37.48	47.5	58.59
3	36.02	45.13	54.93
4	34.61	42.87	51.50
5	33.26	40.73	48.28
6	31.97	38.69	45.26
7	30.72	36.75	42.43
8	29.52	34.92	39.78
9	28.37	33.17	37.295
10	27.26	31.51	34.96
15	22.35	24.38	25.32
20	18.32	18.87	22.25
30	12.30	17.92	22.25
50	5.55	0	0
100	0.76	0	0

preciation in later years. However, in present value terms, tax exceeds the economic depreciation stream, as we will shortly see. Tables, like table 2.3, have been prepared for each asset class and are available on request from the authors. Furthermore, similar tables have been prepared for each method of measuring economic depreciation.

Let us now summarize the findings. Economic depreciation when using transformed prices is as large as actual tax depreciation in early years only for banks, hotels, and recreational buildings; thus, subsidies were received by owners for all other new structures. Compared with the depreciation rates in the guidelines, Revenue Procedure 62-21, economic loss of value is greater for medical buildings, motels, repair garages, restaurants, factories, and warehouses as well. But, for the large classes of office buildings and retail stores, economic depreciation is small compared with early deductions allowed for tax purposes, both according to the guidelines and in actual practice.

When nontransformed prices form the basis of empirical estimation, geometric economic depreciation is slower than when transformed prices were used. In every case, economic depreciation in early years is less than guidelines and actual tax depreciation practice. Furthermore, the gap between economic depreciation and guidelines is usually far greater than the distance between the latter and actual tax practice. When the geometric approximation to Box-Cox estimates of economic depreciation are compared with tax depreciation, the rankings of assets by depreciation comparison are changed. But this change has a smaller effect upon the levels of depreciation than does the Winfrey transformation for retirement.

A convenient summary picture of the differences between tax and economic depreciation can be obtained by computing the present value at acquisition of a new asset of economic depreciation and the two tax depreciation streams.[14] Table 2.4 contains the present-value calculations, for each asset class, using the direct geometric estimates on transformed prices and assuming a constant rate of time discount of 10%.

Table 2.4 **Present Value of Economic and Tax Depreciation Streams** (Direct Geometric Winfrey Depreciation Rates)

Class	Economic Depreciation	Tax Depreciation	
		Guideline	Actual
1. Apartment	308.63	372.08	431.97
2. Bank	285.21	261.53	295.89
3. Factory	319.31	285.17	340.41
4. Hotel	308.63	313.52	307.42
5. Machine shop	183.68	285.17	372.16
6. Medical building	291.18	204.21	355.64
7. Motel	336.11	313.52	380.97
8. Office	251.89	285.17	307.42
9. Recreation	425.19	313.52	390.12
10. Repair garage	272.98	285.17	399.81
11. Restaurant/bar	279.11	261.53	380.97
12. Retail trade	233.86	261.53	355.64
13. Service station	315.10	577.41	525.63
14. Shopping center	190.91	261.53	340.41
15. Terminal	212.93	185.27	420.33
16. Warehouse	253.85	224.38	333.30

The same calculations were undertaken for the other sets of economic depreciation estimates. When the present value of tax depreciation exceeds that of economic depreciation, the purchase price of the asset includes the purchase of a tax rate below the statutory tax rate for that taxpayer's adjusted gross income.

Consider the five large asset classes—apartments, factories, offices, retail trade stores, and warehouses. For apartments, both the tax depreciation streams exceed the economic depreciation stream present value at acquisition, and this result holds up regardless of economic depreciation method used. On an apartment class asset valued at $1,000 when new, actual tax deductions are worth $60 more than the guidelines suggest. The guideline deduction's value itself exceeds economic deductions by between $60 and $230, depending upon the estimation method used. Recall that apartment owners compute deductions on a double-declining balance formula rather than on the 1.5 declining-balance scheme.

Factory, office building, and retail trade store owners appear to receive considerable net subsidies as well. Economic is nearly the same as tax depreciation for only one set of depreciation estimates and only for factories. Otherwise actual tax depreciation streams are valued higher at acquisition than the corresponding economic depreciation streams, regardless of estimation method for all three large classes. Warehouse results are ambiguous when we compare economic with guideline tax depreciation. The warehouse economic depreciation estimates vary from \$130 to \$253, and guideline deductions are valued at \$224.

An additional exercise that should shed light upon the implications to taxpayers of these depreciation regulations is to compute the reduction in tax liability as a result of large tax depreciation deductions. For this purpose we assume the marginal corporate tax rate of 48%.[15] The marginal tax rate times tax minus economic depreciation yields the "tax saving." Table 2.5 contains the tax savings according to both actual and guideline tax practice. In some cases taxpayer savings are negative, because economic depreciation is more rapid than the tax deduction. For the larger classes, however, we have subsidies rather than surcharges. For factories and warehouses, if guideline lives were used we would have surcharges. In short, even if one uses the Winfrey retirement distribution to modify prices and to increase economic depreciation, sub-

Table 2.5 **Present Value of Tax Saving over Asset Life**
(Direct Geometric on Winfrey Prices)

	Tax Saving		Difference
	Guideline	Actual	Actual − Statute
1. Apartment	63.45	123.34	59.89
2. Bank	−23.68	10.69	34.36
3. Factory	−34.13	21.10	55.24
4. Hotel	4.38	−1.22	−6.10
5. Machine shop	101.49	183.48	86.99
6. Medical building	−86.97	64.46	151.43
7. Motel	−22.60	44.86	67.46
8. Office	33.28	55.53	22.25
9. Recreation	−111.67	−35.07	76.60
10. Repair garage	12.20	126.83	114.64
11. Restaurant/bar	−17.58	101.87	119.45
12. Retail trade	27.67	121.78	94.11
13. Service station	262.30	210.52	−51.78
14. Shopping center	70.62	149.50	78.88
15. Terminal	−27.66	207.39	235.06
16. Warehouse	−29.47	79.45	108.92

sidies are received by asset holders in large classes. The third column of the table contains the difference between actual and guideline tax depreciation methods. Except for hotels and service stations, actual deductions exceed guideline deductions. However, large differences still tend to maintain between guideline tax and economic depreciation. Although subsidies would be reduced by movement toward guideline deductions, the greater portion of the subsidies would remain.

One concluding point must be emphasized. The question of who benefits from the subsidies implied by the divergence of tax and economic depreciation is similar to the question of who pays the corporation income tax. If a depreciation subsidy is unexpectedly given to a certain type of asset, the after-tax rate of return to that asset will rise. Since after-tax rates of return (in each risk class) tend to be equated in a competitive capital market, investment will flow toward the subsidized asset. The rates of return of other assets will therefore tend to rise (assuming a fixed amount of capital), and the subsidy will be diffused to these assets. This is, of course, the same mechanism underlying the Harberger model of the incidence of the corporation income tax.[16] Our findings must therefore be interpreted as short run, or impact, rates of subsidy.

2.4.2 Consideration of New Tax Depreciation Rules

Since actual tax practice over the sample period appears to have resulted in potential subsidies to holders of most commercial and industrial structures, one may wish to consider changes in the tax laws. In fact, the United States Treasury has already announced that taxpayers are to use the Revenue Procedure 62-21 lives rather than the shorter lives reported in *Business Building Statistics*, August, 1975. Up to now we have treated tax and economic depreciation as given, but, as is shown in section 2.1, changes in the tax treatment of assets can alter the economic depreciation stream. We now consider the problem of measuring the short-run effect of several plausible alternatives to existing actual tax practice and recompute economic and tax depreciation for each new tax regime before comparing the two streams.

For comparison, we select a hypothetical asset that, when new, provides a service flow of $1,000 and that loses productive efficiency according to the geometric decay rates in table 2.1. For each tax regime, a new sequence of acquisition prices $q(0)$, $q(1)$, $q(2)$, . . . over age is calculated using equation (11) in section 2.1. Economic depreciation is calculated from the new sequence, and the present value of economic depreciation, as measured, is calculated. The "tax saving" is the corporate tax rate times the difference between tax and economic depreciation. Because asset values are also changed by the tax laws, we report the present values of the hypothetical asset in each class under each tax regime.[17]

Table 2.6 contains the present value of the hypothetical asset, with the characteristics discussed above, in each class, given current actual taxpayer practice. Column 2 contains the tax saving τ. (All results in this section are for the direct geometric estimate based on transformed prices.) The magnitude of the tax subsidies is large, amounting to about 10% of asset value.

Table 2.6 **Tax Savings and Asset Values under Existing Tax Practice**

Class	New Asset Acquisition Price	Tax Saving
Apartment	$5,191.56	$272.23
Bank	4,945.62	53.89
Factory	4,942.54	148.56
Hotel	4,817.05	25.51
Machine shop	5,791.50	479.44
Medical building	5,053.06	167.18
Motel	4,847.70	127.33
Office	5,173.60	151.69
Recreation	4,314.83	19.91
Repair garage	5,329.82	321.09
Restaurant/bar	5,239.58	265.59
Retail trade	5,418.24	305.61
Service station	5,454.47	499.13
Shopping center	5,631.93	376.93
Terminal	5,764.68	519.71
Warehouse	5,258.20	216.04

Assumptions: Relative efficiency functions are based upon geometric estimates of Winfrey-transformed prices. All assets, except apartments, are depreciated for tax purposes at 1.5 declining-balance. Apartment tax depreciation is double declining-balance. Tax lives are taken from *Business Building Statistics* (1975) and the lives by which geometric decay is computed are from Hulten and Wykoff (1976). See eq. (11) (section 2.1) for the formula used to obtain column 2.

Four hypothetical tax regimes, in addition to actual practice, are considered. Regime 1: The adoption of Revenue Procedure 62-21 guideline lives rather than the shorter actual lives now used. Regime 2: The adoption of straight-line depreciation, rather than 1.5 declining-balance, and the return to early Bulletin F lives, which are even longer than Revenue Procedure 62-21 lives. Regime 3: A more liberal tax package—the adoption of the double declining-balance depreciation method, more accelerated than 1.5 declining balance, with maintenance of the actual lives now used. Regime 4: Adoption of our economic depreciation estimates for tax depreciation so as to eliminate subsidies.

Table 2.7 contains the asset values and tax savings that would prevail under each of the alternative sets of tax regulations. Regime 1, the new

Table 2.7 **New Asset Prices and Tax Savings under Alternative Tax Regimes**

	I		II		III		IV
Class	q(0) (1)	τ (2)	q(0) (3)	τ (4)	q(0) (5)	τ (6)	q(0) (7)
Apartment	$5,009.86	$143.38	$4,596.34	−$137.61	$5,191.56	$272.23	$4,115.11
Bank	4,852.33	− 23.92	4,605.53	− 218.34	5,110.87	157.76	4,243.20
Factory	4,778.76	20.87	4,534.36	− 156.59	5,121.55	247.54	4,059.61
Hotel	4,883.65	38.89	4,586.45	− 140.67	4,980.65	126.29	4,106.25
Machine shop	5,511.32	256.18	5,214.26	25.92	6,001.26	595.42	4,756.92
Medical building	4,645.86	−170.47	4,548.31	− 235.67	5,233.76	269.80	4,190.48
Motel	4,662.93	− 15.83	4,548.33	− 79.15	5,024.45	223.78	3,961.22
Office	5,109.59	99.14	4,786.77	− 158.56	5,349.30	259.93	4,410.18
Recreational	4,128.08	−162.32	4,026.63	− 218.38	4,473.07	65.20	3,506.85
Repair garage	4,990.03	55.21	4,721.08	− 152.00	5,526.26	425.19	4,306.99
Restaurant/bar	4,896.06	− 8.73	4,693.07	− 160.57	5,430.63	369.84	4,281.44
Retail trade	5,138.35	78.87	4,877.00	− 127.08	5,612.00	415.65	4,493.31
Service station	5,642.02	622.53	4,555.24	− 160.02	5,659.13	589.82	4,078.30
Shopping center	5,388.08	177.83	5,262.70	102.38	5,830.69	492.72	4,711.70
Terminal	5,050.78	− 58.23	4,949.81	− 128.29	5,979.40	630.14	4,601.62
Warehouse	4,950.11	− 40.65	4,751.18	− 198.04	5,442.39	324.63	4,416.96

Treasury regulations of Revenue Procedure 62-21 lives and 1.5 declining-balance on all asset classes except apartments, which use double declining-balance, has the effect of reducing the tax subsidies by about one-third. If the tax regulations were to return to old Bulletin F lives and the original straight-line depreciation method, regime 2, then the subsidies would be converted into surcharges. Columns 3 and 4 contain these latter results. Regime 3 liberalizes depreciation regulations by allowing double declining-balance over the short lives now reported by taxpayers. The consequence is, of course, to increase the subsidy by further reducing the liability. The last column of table 2.7 contains asset values if tax is congruent with economic depreciation.

2.5 Capital Stock Estimation

We turn now to the construction of capital stock estimates based upon the Hulten-Wykoff economic depreciation estimates. These capital stock figures will be used to determine the tax subsidies, under existing practice, by industry groups in manufacturing. However, these stock estimates are useful in their own right. As we indicated in our introduction, BEA recently introduced imputed economic depreciation into the United States National Income and Product Accounts. The BEA imputations are based upon straight-line and double declining-balance formulas, Bulletin F lifetimes, and a modified Winfrey S_3 retirement distribution. The next step logically would be to replace these accounting-based imputations with those based upon actual empirical estimates.

The dual problem to measuring asset prices is that of measuring the quantity of capital. As Jorgenson has shown (1973), the quantity and price figures, to be internally consistent, must both be based upon the same relative efficiency function. In this section we discuss and employ this theory of replacement and depreciation.

In a competitive capital market, economic depreciation is the dual of physical deterioration. This can be shown by substituting equation (1) into the definition of economic depreciation, equation (5), which yields

$$D(s,t) = \sum_{x=0}^{L} \frac{c(s+x, t+x) - c(s+1+x, t+x)}{(1+r)^{x+1}}. \tag{16}$$

Applying the basic duality relationships from equation (9), we have:

$$D(s,t) = \sum_{x=0}^{L} \frac{c(0, t+x)\,[\phi(s+x) - \phi(s+1+x)]}{(1+r)^{x+1}}. \tag{17}$$

The term in square brackets is the one-period loss in relative economic efficiency, called the "mortality sequence," in Jorgenson (1973). Equation (17) indicates that economic depreciation is equivalent to the present value of the income lost by shifting the relative efficiency profile by one year. Equation (17) explicates the relationship between the decline in asset value, $D(s,t)$, and the decline in asset efficiency, $\phi(s+x) - \phi(s+1+x)$.

The basic conclusion of this analysis is that the decline in asset value owing to aging cannot be estimated independently of the corresponding decline in asset quantity. For example, if economic depreciation occurs at a constant (geometric) rate, then the relative efficiency sequence must also be geometric, that is,

$$(18) \qquad \phi(s) = (1-\delta)^s,$$

where δ is the constant rate of economic depreciation. The geometric case is, however, the only one in which both depreciation and the efficiency functions are of the same form. Straight-line depreciation does not imply that $\phi(s)$ declines linearly, nor does a linear decline in $\phi(s)$ imply straight-line economic depreciation.

The stock of capital at any point in time depends upon $\phi(s)$, the relative efficiency function. Letting $K(t)$ and $I(t)$ denote the stock of capital and flow of gross investment respectively,

$$(19) \qquad K(t) = \sum_{s=0}^{\infty} \phi(s) I(t-s);$$

that is, the capital stock is the efficiency-weighted sum of past investments. Taking first differences yields the recursive equation widely used in estimating capital stock:

$$(20) \qquad K(t) = I(t) - R(t) + K(t-1).$$

$R(t)$ denotes the cumulative replacement requirements on the existing capital stock:

$$(21) \qquad R(t) = \sum_{s=1}^{\infty} [\phi(s-1) - \phi(s)] I(t-s).$$

In the case of geometric depreciation, equation (21) reduces to the familiar

$$(22) \qquad K(t) = I(t) + (1-\delta)K(t-1),$$

which provides a convenient method for estimating the capital stock, since the relative efficiency profile is summarized by the one parameter δ.

A modified version of equation (19) forms the basis for the capital stock estimates of this chapter.[18] Investment by input-output sector is taken from the capital stock study of Jack Faucett Associates (1973), and the relative efficiency sequence is derived from the Box-Cox estimates of Hulten and Wykoff (1976). Table 2.8 summarizes the Box-

Table 2.8 **Transformed Box-Cox Estimates of Economic Depreciation on a $1,000 Asset, by Asset Class for the Year 1966**

Age in Years	Asset Class[a] 1	2	3	4	5	6	7	8	9	10	11	12	13	14	15	16
1	$36.94	$67.91	$30.23	−$531.56	$1.22	$25.67	$34.64	$43.20	$52.71	$ 7.53	$33.09	$35.36	$21.63	$93.43	$108.93	$55.68
2	33.70	50.61	29.14	− 433.74	1.19	23.99	31.94	35.97	47.61	9.38	30.27	30.90	22.79	60.25	64.82	44.48
3	31.44	41.55	28.20	− 380.37	1.19	22.82	30.11	31.70	43.89	10.82	28.32	28.09	23.42	45.24	46.24	38.11
4	29.66	35.71	27.32	− 345.04	1.19	21.88	28.69	28.71	40.88	11.97	26.80	26.00	23.79	36.49	35.90	33.75
5	28.17	31.54	26.50	− 319.26	1.19	21.10	27.50	26.42	38.30	12.95	25.33	24.36	23.98	30.69	29.31	30.51
6	26.87	28.37	25.71	− 299.32	1.19	20.40	26.47	24.59	36.04	13.78	24.42	22.98	24.05	26.55	24.73	27.95
7	25.71	25.85	24.97	− 283.23	1.19	19.78	25.56	23.06	34.01	14.52	23.46	21.81	24.04	23.42	21.36	25.84
8	24.65	23.79	24.23	− 269.88	1.19	19.20	24.72	21.75	32.17	15.13	22.55	20.78	23.96	20.97	18.78	24.09
9	23.69	22.06	23.54	− 258.56	1.19	18.68	23.96	20.62	30.48	15.68	21.75	19.87	23.82	19.00	16.75	22.56
10	22.80	20.58	22.86	− 248.77	1.19	18.18	23.25	19.61	28.93	16.16	20.99	19.04	23.64	17.37	15.09	21.24
15	19.10	15.50	19.79	− 214.12	1.19	16.07	20.23	15.87	22.57	17.70	17.88	15.81	22.27	12.19	10.03	16.46
20	16.24	12.43	17.15	− 192.25	1.19	14.35	17.79	13.33	17.87	18.16	15.44	13.50	20.46	9.39	7.44	13.38
30	11.99	8.78	12.83	− 164.97	1.16	11.61	13.82	9.97	11.42	17.12	11.77	10.27	16.33	6.40	4.84	9.53
50	6.70	5.21	7.05	− 135.87	1.12	7.69	7.92	6.20	4.77	11.30	7.04	6.43	8.32	3.83	2.76	5.54
99	1.51	1.98	1.36	− 104.65	1.06	2.58	0.08	2.31	0.51	0.64	1.92	2.37	0.02	1.78	1.26	1.91

[a]See table 2.5 for the asset classes corresponding to the class number codes.

Cox depreciation rates on transformed prices for one year, 1966. The BEA's 1967 capital flow matrix provides the link between the efficiency estimates by asset type and investment by I-0 sector.[19] The steps in the capital stock construction can be briefly outlined. First, the Box-Cox estimates for each asset class are used to generate "fitted" acquisition prices, $q(s,t)$, for each vintage and year. These prices are then used to impute service prices, $c(s,t)$, using the conceptual framework of section 2.1.[20] The imputed service prices were then used to calculate the relative efficiency function: $\phi(s,t) = c(s,t)/c(0,t)$. This function differs from $\phi(s)$, equation (9) in that efficiency sequence is not now assumed to be stationary.

As indicated above, the investment series, in constant prices, used here are obtained from the 1973 Faucett study of capital stocks. The Faucett estimates have the following properties: (1) they cover the period 1890–1966; (2) they are reconciled to the 1957 Standard Industrial Classification; (3) they are based on establishment; (4) investment in nonresidential structures is net of land values; (5) they include investment in establishments not in operation; (6) they include expenditures for administrative facilities; (7) they cover both corporate and noncorporate sectors; and (8) they include government-owned–contractor-operated capital. The estimates are of lower quality in the early years, as Faucett himself points out. However, these early years receive the smallest weight in the perpetual inventory calculation, so that the effect of an increasing measurement error, backward over time, is minimized. BEA control totals were used to improve the accuracy of the estimates.

The allocation of real investment data by sector between the various types of nonresidential business structures is based upon BEA's 1967 capital flow matrix. Although twenty-six types of structures are identified and allocated across I-0 sectors, the only asset types relevant for our purpose are the nonresidential buildings. These classes of structures account for 32% of total new investment in all structures in 1967. The asset types for which the estimated relative efficiencies are available account for 80% of total investment in nonresidential buildings in 1967. The 1967 proportions of these asset types in each I-0 sector are used to allocate Faucett investment in all years; the resulting allocation separates annual gross investment by I-0 sector between categories for which $\phi(s,t)$ is available. A residual category for which capital stocks were not calculated is included in the allocation of gross investment.

In this chapter we are focusing on the manufacturing sector. Approximately 93% of the 1967 investment in all manufacturing structures is classed as "industrial structures and office buildings," a class for which Box-Cox relative efficiencies have been produced.[21] An apparent enigma about the resultant capital stock figures requires comment. When acquisition prices are transformed to allow for asset retirement, using Winfrey's L_0 transformation, the average rate of depreciation tends to be larger than estimates of depreciation derived from untransformed prices. Naturally one would expect, therefore, that stock estimates based upon transformed data would be smaller than their untransformed counterparts. However, in some classes transformed prices produced larger capital stock estimates than those of untransformed prices. The reason for this unexpected result is that transformed prices often produced large relative efficiency values, $\phi(s,t)$, for young assets, and consequently, a high rate of investment in such classes led to comparatively larger stocks for transformed data.

The total stocks of nonresidential structures in manufacturing are given in table 2.9. The last two columns do not include the unallocated investment, but this amounted to only 7% of new investment in manufacturing structures in 1967. For comparison, we include recent BEA estimates based on Musgrave (1976). The BEA net stocks are calculated using straight-line depreciation and a modified Winfrey S_3 distribution centered on 85% of the 1942 Bulletin F asset lives. These BEA assumptions produce stock estimates that are quite a bit lower than either

Table 2.9 **Stock of Nonresidential Structures in United States Manufacturing (Billions of 1958 Dollars)**

Year	BEA[a] Net Stocks	Box-Cox, Transformed[b]	Box-Cox, Untransformed[b]
1948	31.8	51.9	48.6
1949	32.3	52.5	49.0
1950	32.5	52.6	49.0
1951	33.3	53.8	50.0
1952	33.4	54.7	50.9
1953	34.6	55.8	52.0
1954	35.1	56.7	52.9
1955	36.0	57.7	53.8
1956	37.1	59.3	55.4
1957	38.3	61.0	57.1
1958	39.1	62.1	58.2
1959	39.1	62.3	58.5
1960	39.5	63.0	59.3
1961	39.8	63.5	60.0
1962	39.9	64.0	60.7
1963	40.2	64.7	61.6
1964	40.6	65.5	62.6
1965	41.8	66.9	64.3
1966	43.6	69.0	66.7

[a]Table 4 of Musgrave (1976), converted to 1958 dollars.
[b]Totals for industrial buildings and office buildings, which constitute 93% of net investment in all structures in manufacturing in 1967.

version of our Box-Cox estimates. The reason for such low BEA estimates is the higher implicit rate of replacement under the BEA method. Equation (22) was used to calculate an implied constant rate of depreciation, δ, given the stock estimates of table 2.9 and Faucett's gross investment data for manufacturing structures. The average rate of depreciation is approximately 6.5% for the BEA stocks, and 3.7% and 3.9% respectively for the transformed and untransformed Box-Cox stocks. These last two numbers differ sharply from the average geometric rates for the factory class (which dominates the manufacturing calculation) given in table 2.1—3.6% for the transformed data and 1.3% for the untransformed. The reason for this difference is explained above: the rate of depreciation is not constant in the early years of asset life and is actually slower with the transformed data than with the untransformed. Given a higher rate of investment, the result is a larger stock of capital with the L_0 retirement transformation than without it.

2.6 Economic and Tax Depreciation in Manufacturing Industries

We have so far considered the depreciation subsidy problem and the capital stock estimation problem separately. We now combine the two in order to ask how much subsidy is received by the various industries in manufacturing. First, we compute $\phi(s,t)$ (the difference between economic and tax depreciation), as defined in equation (8) of section 2.1, for $t = 1966$ and for s varying between one and one hundred. When the result is divided by the value of allocated structures in each manufacturing industry in 1966, the rate of subsidy per dollar of capital is obtained. This index is a rough measure of the distribution of the depreciation subsidy across manufacturing industries. The actual value of the subsidy to each producer would depend upon his marginal tax rate. The annual rates of subsidy per dollar of capital in each two-digit SIC group in 1966 are given in table 2.10.[22] It is evident that the rate of subsidy varies across industries, from —2 cents to 1.1 cents per year per dollar of capital stock. In assessing these results, one must recall the caveat above that to determine who benefits from these subsidies and to determine their precise allocative effect requires a tax incidence analysis well beyond our scope here. At the same time, considerable economic research indicates that divergence between tax and economic depreciation can lead to distortions in economic decisions, and thus to excess burdens and to reductions (increases) in business tax liabilities.

Table 2.10 **Economic and Tax Depreciation in Manufacturing Industries, 1966 (Millions of 1966 Dollars)**

Two-digit SIC Industry	Economic Depreciation (ED)	Tax Depreciation: Statute (TD_S)	Tax Depreciation: Actual (TD_A)	$ED-TD_A$ ÷ Value of Structures
19	54.8	54.1	89.3	−0.020
20	242.5	300.8	272.2	−0.004
21	7.4	7.9	8.4	−0.004
22	68.3	67.0	57.8	−0.005
23	33.2	35.0	35.4	−0.002
24	67.5	70.8	58.6	0.004
25	23.8	25.5	27.5	−0.005
26	93.0	98.3	102.5	−0.003
27	181.2	211.7	120.8	0.011
28	231.8	238.2	310.7	−0.011
29	309.7	339.0	326.4	−0.002
30	30.7	32.4	35.0	−0.004
31	10.3	11.6	10.1	0.001
32	95.9	102.8	109.9	−0.005
33	433.6	494.3	422.0	0.001
34	94.9	100.1	109.3	−0.005
35	143.5	150.4	171.7	−0.006
36	115.0	122.4	121.1	−0.002
371	94.1	100.3	105.5	−0.004
37–371	132.4	137.8	175.9	−0.011
38	28.7	29.8	35.4	−0.007
39	22.7	23.8	24.9	−0.001

Notes

1. Jorgenson (1971) reviews the literature on geometric depreciation in investment studies. Jorgenson (1973) discusses his model of replacement and depreciation. A contrary position on depreciation is contained in Eisner (1974). Feldstein and Rothschild (1974) question a number of the assumptions of the Jorgenson model.

2. Since Jorgenson's 1971 review, empirical analysis of vintage asset prices has been undertaken by Ackerman (1973) and Ramm (1971) of automobiles and by Wykoff (1974) and Hulten and Wykoff (1976) of structures. Robert Coen (1975) has studied depreciation in investment models.

3. See Young (1975) and the *Survey of Current Business*, January and March 1976.

4. Feldstein and Rothschild (1974) analyze the endogeneity of economic depreciation in detail. Their analysis raises the possibility that built-in physical durability, as well as in-use productive efficiency, will change with changes in the tax laws and rates of return. Our analysis treats asset productivity, that is, the relative efficiency function, as given. We have been unable to detect, in our

empirical analysis, changes in relative efficiencies as a result of variations in tax parameters and rates of return.

5. The survey results are summarized in *Business Building Statistics*, August, 1975, Office of Industrial Economics, Department of the Treasury, Washington, D.C.

6. "Actual" practice refers to depreciation practices reported to the Treasury in the 1972 survey. Tax deductions calculated on the basis of Revenue Procedure 62-21 lives are referred to as "guideline" deductions. See section 2.3 for details. Both methods were, of course, quite legal.

7. The fundamental relation between asset and service prices is contained in Hotelling (1925) and discussed in detail in Hall (1968), Jorgenson (1973), and Wykoff (1970, 1973). Hulten and Wykoff analyze the depreciation term derived from equation (1) in "Empirical Evidence of Economic Depreciation of Structures," *Conference on Taxation*, August 1975, U.S. Treasury Department, forthcoming.

8. Modification of the user cost of capital to allow for various tax regulations is undertaken by Hall and Jorgenson (1967) and by Christensen and Jorgenson (1969).

9. See Wykoff (1970), Hall (1968), and Jorgenson (1973).

10. Arguments for accelerating tax depreciation have been advanced to the effect that inflation slows investment through increased replacement costs at retirement. This view is in part valid: inflation does indeed raise the value of capital services lost through wear and tear and through obsolescence. However, for this to justify a change in tax policy, part of the increased value of existing assets should be treated as a capital gain and included as an item of taxable income. The issue of depreciation and inflation is discussed in the testimony of Tax Treatment of Capital Recovery, Committee on Ways and Means, 93d Congress, February 1973 (cf. Eisner 1973). Also, the publication *Essays on Inflation and Indexation*, American Enterprise Institute for Public Policy Research, Washington, D.C., contains several articles (Giersch et al. 1974) on inflation finance. John B. Shoven and Jeremy I. Bulow (1975) suggest new accounting methods under inflation.

11. If, of course, tax depreciation is decelerated with respect to economic depreciation, the taxpayer is in effect assessed a surcharge. The use of the terms subsidy and surcharge is taken from Taubman and Rasche (1969).

12. The six classes excluded had too few observations, or were too ill defined, for analysis. Excluded were theaters, stadiums, parking garages, supermarkets, and several catchall categories; 90% of the data was in the remaining sixteen classes.

13. These tax methods are discussed in the 1971 IRS publication *The Asset Depreciation Range System*.

14. These formulas are derived in Wykoff (1974).

15. The statutory marginal rate 48% is used for illustration only. The effective marginal tax rate varies from taxpayer to taxpayer and is less than the statutory rate, since not all business taxpayers are taxed as larger corporations, interest payments are deductible, and so on.

16. Harberger (1962). For a recent review of the literature on excess burden and tax incidence, see Break (1974). Distortions due to differences between tax and economic depreciation are discussed by Smith (1963) and Samuelson (1964).

17. Calculations of asset prices and subsidies will now differ from those recorded earlier, because we are now undertaking a different experiment. Rather

than taking depreciation based directly on estimated acquisition prices, we treat the estimation process as yielding only in-use relative efficiencies of assets as they age. From these efficiency functions, Φ (s), we then compute new prices. Thus the entire economic depreciation stream will be computed. Consequently, different subsidies and asset values are now calculated.

18. The actual capital stock calculation is based upon a revision of equation (19), in which there is an initial capital benchmark. Because of the length of the investment series, however, the benchmark value is assumed to be zero.

19. Specifically, the link is based on table 1 of *Interindustry Transactions in New Structures and Equipment,* 1963 and 1967, vol. 1, United States Department of Commerce, Bureau of Economic Analysis.

20. In these calculations, the rate of return, r_{ts} for the period 1937 to 1970 was taken to be the four- to six-month prime commercial paper rate published in the *Survey of Current Business.* For the period 1890 to 1936, the commercial paper rate calculated by Macaulay (1938) was used.

21. See Hulten and Wykoff (1976).

22. The calculations are based on the formulas:

$$\sum_s D(s,1966)I(1966-s)$$

$$\sum_s d_T(s)I(1966-s).$$

References

Ackerman, Susan Rose. 1973. Used cars as a depreciating asset. *Western Economic Journal* 11 (December): 463–74.

Break, George F. 1974. The incidence and economic effects of taxation. In *The economics of public finance; Studies in government finance.* Washington, D.C.: Brookings Institution.

Christensen, Laurits, and Jorgenson, Dale W. 1969. The measurement of U.S. real capital input, 1929–1967. *Review of Income and Wealth* 16 (December): 19–50.

Coen, Robert. 1975. Investment behaviour, the measurement of depreciation, and tax policy. *American Economic Review,* March, pp. 59–74.

Eisner, Robert. 1972. Components of capital expenditures: Replacement and modernization. *Review of Economics and Statistics* 54 (August): 297–305.

———. 1974. Econometric studies of investment behaviour. *Economic Inquiry* (March).

———. 1973. Testimony on tax treatment of capital recovery (investment credit, accelerated depreciation and amortization). Committee on Ways and Means, 93d Congress. Part 3 of 11. February 1, 1973, pp. 370–91.

Faucett, J. 1973. *Development of capital stock series by industry sector.* Washington, D.C.: Office of Emergency Preparedness.

Feldstein, Martin, and Rothschild, Michael. 1974. Towards an economic theory of replacement and investment. *Econometrica* 42 (May): 393–423.

Giersch, Herbert, et al. 1974. *Essays on inflation and indexation.* Washington, D.C.: American Enterprise Institute for Public Policy Research.

Hall, Robert. 1968. Technical change and capital from the point of view of the dual. *Review of Economic Studies* 35 (January): 35–46.

Hall, Robert E., and Jorgenson, Dale W. 1967. Tax policy and investment behaviour. *American Economic Review* 57 (June): 391–414.

Harberger, Arnold C. 1962. The incidence of the corporation income tax. *Journal of Political Economy* 70 (June): 215–40.

Hotelling, Harold S. 1925. A general mathematical theory of depreciation. *Journal of the American Statistical Society* 20 (September): 340–53.

Hulten, Charles R., and Wykoff, Frank C. 1975. *Empirical evidence on economic depreciation of structures.* In *Conference on Tax Research.* Washington, D.C.: U.S. Department of the Treasury.

———. 1977. *The economic depreciation of non-residential structures.* Working Papers in Economics, no. 16. Baltimore: Johns Hopkins University.

———. 1978. On the feasibility of equating tax and economic depreciation. In *Compendium of tax research*, pp. 91–120. Washington, D.C.: U.S. Department of the Treasury.

Jorgenson, Dale W. 1971. A survey of econometric investigation of investment behaviour. *Journal of Economic Literature* 9 (December): 1111–47.

———. 1973. The economic theory of replacement and depreciation. In *Essays in Honor of Jan Tinbergen*, ed. W. Sellykaerts.

Macaulay, Fredrich R. 1938. *The movements of interest rates, bond-yields, and stock prices in the U.S. since 1856.* New York: National Bureau of Economic Research.

Musgrave, John C. 1976. Fixed nonresidential business and residential capital in the United States, 1925–75. *Survey of Current Business* 56 (April): 46–52.

Ramm, Wolfhaard. 1971. Measuring the services of household durables: The case of automobiles. *Proceedings of the American Statistical Association, 1970*. Washington, D.C.: American Statistical Association.

Samuelson, Paul A. 1964. Tax deductibility of economic depreciation to insure invariant valuations. *Journal of Political Economy* 72 (December): 604–6.

Shoven, John B., and Bulow, Jeremy I. 1975. Inflation accounting and nonfinancial corporate profits: Physical assets. *Brookings Papers on Economic Activity*, no. 3, pp. 557–98.

Smith, Vernon L. 1963. Tax depreciation policy and investment theory. *International Economic Review* 4 (January): 80–91.

Taubman, Paul, and Rasche, Robert. 1969. Economic and tax depreciation of office buildings. *National Tax Journal* 22 (September): 334–46.

Theil, Henri. 1971. *Principles of econometrics.* New York: John Wiley.

U.S. Bureau of the Budget. Office of Statistical Standards. 1957. *Standard industrial classification manual.* Washington, D.C.: Government Printing Office.

U.S. Department of Commerce. Bureau of Economic Analysis. *Survey of Current Business.* Selected issues.

———. 1975. *Interindustry transactions in new structures and equipment, 1963 and 1967.* Vol. 1. A supplement to the *Survey of Current Business,* September.

U.S. Department of Commerce. Office of Business Economics. 1966. *The national income and product accounts of the United States, 1929–1965: A Supplement to the survey of current business.* Washington, D.C.

U.S. Treasury. Bureau of Internal Revenue. 1942. *Income tax depreciation and obsolescence estimated useful lives and depreciation Rates.* Bulletin F (revised), January.

U.S. Treasury. Internal Revenue Service. 1964. *Depreciation guidelines and rules, revenue procedure 62-21.* Revised.

———. 1971. *Asset depreciation range* (ADR) system. July 1971.

U.S. Treasury. Office of Industrial Economics. 1975. *Business building statistics* (August).

Winfrey, R. 1935. *Statistical analyses of industrial property retirements.* Iowa Engineering Experiment Station, Bulletin 125.

Wykoff, Frank C. 1970. Capital depreciation in the postwar period: Automobiles. *Review of Economics and Statistics* 52 (May): 168–72.

———. 1973. A user cost approach to new automobile purchases. *Review of Economic Studies* 40 (July): 377–90.

———. 1974. Economic depreciation of relatively new apartments in the U.S. *Claremont Economics Papers.*

Young, Allan H. 1975. New estimates of capital consumption allowances in the benchmark revision of GNP. *Survey of Current Business* 55 (October): 14–16, 35.

Comment Paul Taubman

Hulton and Wykoff are to be congratulated on working on two extremely important and, as they point out, interrelated problems. They are also to be applauded for bringing to light the issue of the treatment of retirements and disappearances. And while I am still praising, I might as well mention the Congress and Treasury, who initiated a study to try to resolve an important empirical issue.

The object of this paper is to measure economic depreciation, which is then compared with tax depreciation and used to generate new estimates of industry capital stock. The basic data used in this study are from a survey of building owners conducted by the Treasury. The survey contains information on various classes of structures for example, office buildings and shopping centers. The data on each building include date of construction, date of acquisition, price of acquisition, square footage, and other characteristics.

Hulten and Wykoff divide the sample into classes of building, then run equations of the following form

$$P_t = F(Age_t, t, x), \quad (1)$$

where P_t is the acquisition price in year acquired, denoted by t. The price is not deflated.

Age_t is the age of the building, or date of acquisition
t is year of acquisition
x is a vector of characteristics, such as square footage.

In parts of the analysis they adjust for previous retirements of assets of a particular age cohort. In estimating this equation they employ Box-Cox and polynominal forms to try to determine the age price profiles.

They use the derivative of these profiles with respect to age to calculate economic depreciation, assuming there is no adjustment to the taxes. They then compare the annual estimates of economic depreciation with the charges contained in the tax statutes and with actual tax depreciation, which can differ from the statutory amount if nonstatutory lives are used. They generally find that in the early years economic depreciation is less than statutory depreciation, which is less than actual tax depreciation. The present discounted value of the three depreciation series are ranked in the same order, and the tax depreciation allowances confer a tax subsidy.

Using an input-output approach, they can allocate investment flows to various industries and then calculate total investment in each in-

Paul Taubman is professor of economics at the University of Pennsylvania and a research associate of the National Bureau of Economic Research.

dustry. Then, using perpetual inventory methods, estimates of economic depreciation and assumptions on retirement patterns, they can calculate capital stock by industry. Since they estimate depreciation to be lower than straight-line, which is used by BEA, and since investment has an upward trend, they find higher capital stocks than BEA.

After this brief outline of their paper, let me begin my critique. I think I can assert that Bob Rasche and I were the first persons to try to examine the pattern of economic depreciation of structures. Since we based our results on net rent for only four or five broad age groups, I can say without fear of contradiction that the data used in the current study are better than those previously available. I am not sure, however, whether the results are better or worse or more or less believable.

How can we measure the way the value of a given asset would vary over time, all else being equal? Ideally, we want data on the sales price of the same or homogeneous assets throughout the lifetime of the asset during a steady-state period when relative and absolute market prices and tax regimes and their future expectations remain constant. We could, of course, use data when there were only random deviations from these conditions—a situation probably met in the eight markets for secondhand machinery and equipment examined by Terborgh or the markets for automobiles examined by Wykoff. Since we do not live in this world, or in one that deviates only randomly from it, we must be more ingenious. The first step in this direction is to use theory to obtain an equation.

In a competitive market, in equilibrium and with no uncertainty, the price of an asset should be equal to the present discounted value (PDV) of its after-tax income stream, discounted at the appropriate interest rate, which I will assume is the after-tax interest rate at which the investor can borrow or lend. Hulton and Wykoff following the lead of Jorgenson and others, then express this equilibrium price in terms of the construction price and tax law features. I have several complaints about the formula they use. First, they call it a "user cost" price, the term Jorgenson originally used in his pioneering work on investment functions but subsequently changed to "rental" price. I believe Jorgenson made this change because the term he and they derive differs from what Keynes earlier meant by "user" cost. To avoid confusion I would hope the authors would also switch to "rental" price. Second, their formula assumes that the whole complex of the tax law can be written so the tax base equals revenues minus the sum of wage, repair, other money costs, and the tax allowance for depreciation. That is, they use Jorgenson's standard formula with the investment tax credit set equal to zero. Tax lawyers, tax reformers, and the people I have known at the Treasury's Office of Tax Analysis would double up with laughter at the idea that that formula captures the essence of the situation *for structures*.

I will not try to be exhaustive but will only point out a few highlights. I will also restrict my comments primarily to office and apartment buildings—the two major categories of structures I have studied, though I suspect they apply to many other major categories of structures. One particular feature of the tax laws that increases the profitability of such investment and has been the subject of much debate is the conversion of ordinary income to tax-preferred capital gains. Everyone agrees with Hulton and Wykoff that, for structures, tax depreciation is greater than economic depreciation in the early years of the assets' lives. Since the tax base is original purchase price minus accumulated depreciation, the tax base is less than the current selling price with the difference taxable as a capital gains, subject to a holding-period rule. This rule states that, for the first eight years, all the excess tax depreciation above straight-line is taxed as ordinary income, and that for each additional month the percentage of this excess taxed as ordinary income decreases. This conversion to capital gains is not in their formula, though it is very important, especially since the recapture applies only to excess depreciation above that granted by the straight-line methods. Nor is there any provision for the treatment of interest payments. Most purchases of office and apartment buildings are financed by mortgages that are often 90% of purchase price, and 100% mortgages are not unknown. Most of the mortgage payments in the early years are interest payments, which are deductions against the *owners'* income tax. These owners are the ones who determine the asset's market price, and they should make the price calculation on income after taxes. Second, in this market, the interest payments and tax depreciation decline as the building ages. With the decrease in expenses, eventually taxable income appears, but then tax-sheltered investors sell and obtain capital gains.

These might be considered nitpicking comments for the calculation of economic depreciation, since the authors are using market prices that should incorporate all relevant market and the real world phenomena, as perceived through the eyes of tax lawyers and investors. There are two problems with this response. First, my comments do apply to the calculation of the value of the tax subsidies, which is a part of the paper. Second, as far as I can tell, the market prices the authors are using are those at *date of acquisition*, which must be no later than 1972. During the preceding decade, there were many changes in the tax laws, some of which pertained directly to structures. For example, some of the assets must have been purchased when double declining-balance was available for structures or before the imposition of the previously described partial recapture rule. The change in tax rules here would have lowered current market prices but not *recorded acquisition prices* on previously purchased structures. Also, some of these acquisition prices were recorded before the introduction of shorter lives under Asset Depreciation Range System (ADR). The tax laws indirectly affect the market price of structures through the tax rate schedule and the treatment of all other incomes. The value of the tax subsidies depends upon the taxpayer's marginal tax rate. Decreases in this rate such as occurred in 1964 and 1965 decrease the value of tax subsidies. Closing or creating loopholes also affects the supply of investors for a given loophole. The recorded prices are also inappropriate because they reflect the mortgage conditions then current.

Finally, these recorded prices depend on the prevailing price level. The only adjustment made for inflation is the introduction of a polynominal in time. They find that this variable is not very important, probably because inflation did not proceed smoothly and tax changes with positive and negative effects occurred at various points in time.

For all these reasons, the recorded prices on past acquisitions are not appropriate to measure economic depreciation unless you assume that the future changes were expected and incorporated into the acquisition price (and that inflation is unimportant). But, I repeat, as far as I can determine, and I think note 20 bears this out, the authors have not adjusted the past market prices for the tax law and mortgage changes or inflation. The tax law and mortgage features can be calculated at least roughly, as Rasche and I have done, and inflation can be handled by better means than a time trend.

Incidentally, there is another potential problem with these data that I am less certain how to handle. Presumably, some of these buildings underwent major repairs and modernization that show up in the prices and thus reduce their calculated economic depreciation.

For these reasons I do not think Hulton and Wykoff have measured even the short-run effects of tax laws on tax subsidies. I suppose I would be less concerned with this if their numbers were in accord with what I believe and have published. Rasche and I, using a bit of information on profit age profiles, have calculated that for office and apartment buildings the rate of depreciation was very low for the first fifteen years and that in each of the first forty years or so true depreciation was less than the tax depreciation then allowed. (Allowances for the early years have been increased since then.)

In the early years we did not have depreciation rates nearly as large as the ones cited in this paper. Ours began at less than half of 1% and generally rose steadily. Thus what we found was not a constant geometric decay but a pattern that was approximately the reverse sum of the years' digits. There is some other evidence that we are in the correct ballpark when we say there is little depreciation in early years. In the early sixties, when there was little or no inflation for several years, you could get fifteen-year, 100% mortgages. Banks must have expected little depreciation if they felt the mortgage was secured. Second, I once saw a draft of a paper by Wykoff on apartment buildings, in which he concluded there was appreciation for the first fifteen years of the asset's life. If this is so, why use a constant depreciation rate, which I must add Hulton and Wykoff say does not work well for the first fifteen years —the very years that naturally receive the highest weight in a PDV calculation.

The authors have calculated the PDV of economic and tax depreciation rules. They find that most structures are subsidized. I think this is true, but I do not think their numbers are correct. For this calculation they do need to use the correct formula and, as I noted, they do not have it. Moreover, they assume that the marginal tax rate is the corporate rate of 48%. But, for much of this market, the investors are individuals in higher marginal tax brackets.

Finally, let me turn to the capital stock calculation. The authors are absolutely right that one should integrate the economic depreciation series into the capital stock series. They are also right that something has to be done about retired, abandoned, and destroyed assets. I do not fault them for using the Winfrey estimates, since nothing else is available. But I think the Winfrey Study is far out of date, and the patterns found for a few assets need not apply to all structures. I would like to see a study done on survival rates—perhaps by drawing a random sample of permits from fifty to seventy-five years ago and then periodically seeing if the buildings are still in use and what major innovations, if any, they have undergone.

I do think there is at least one problem in the authors' capital stock accounting. Essentially, their paper focuses on the calculation of economic depreciation. They do not try to examine responses of the structure industry to tax law provisions. If in the adjustment process all that happens is that rental prices change, there is no difficulty, since they or the census use market information on construction costs. But there is every reason to suspect that one result of the tax law is a reduction in quality of the building. This occurs because the tax law encourages fairly frequent sales to convert ordinary income to capital gains. Initial and subsequent owners have an incentive to cut corners on construction and maintenance of hard-to-observe characteristics of the building, whose defects will not be noticed until the building has been disposed of. Moreover, and perhaps more germane, Rasche and I demonstrated in another paper that nearly every tax subsidy scheme would cause buildings to be destroyed earlier than with no subsidy. Thus the useful life of the assets should have changed with tax laws—a modification it would be well to incorporate in perpetual inventory methods.

As I said in the beginning, the authors are working on important problems. I think what they have done provides a useful starting point.

It may be that the numbers would not change much if they made the adjustments I suggested, but I would like to see the authors try to incorporate them.

Reply by Hulten and Wykoff

We wish to thank Professor Taubman for his detailed assessment of our work. That he does not believe our numbers is no doubt the result of his (1969) work with Rasche on the depreciation of office buildings. Taubman and Rasche report an age-price pattern in which the price declines very little in the early years of asset life and accelerates rapidly toward the end. This pattern is consistent with the conventional view that the relative efficiency of buildings declines very little with age; that is, physical depreciation is acts like the one-horse shay. Our results are quite different. We estimate an age-price pattern that is convex with respect to the origin rather than concave. Our prices thus decline more rapidly in the early years of asset life than in the later years. We wish to stress Taubman's assertion that "the data used in [our] study is better than that available [to him and Rasche]," for the main thrust of our reply will be to show that the fundamental conclusion of convex depreciation, rather than concave, follows from the basic data rather than from our treatment of inflation, taxes, or user costs.

First, let us begin by illustrating the age-price pattern of our *raw* data.[1] In figure C2.1 we have plotted the *average* acquisition price per square foot in each five-year age interval against age for each of our four largest building classes (offices, retail trade, factories, and warehouses).[2] No adjustment is made for asset retirement or for the differing average date of purchase within each age interval. For example, the average date of purchase for new office buildings is 1957, and the average for the age interval six to ten years is 1965. The resulting age-price pattern is somewhat variable and shows some tendency for the average price to remain high in the first fifteen to twenty years of asset life. However, the general shape is distinctly convex and provides little support for the concave, "one-horse-shay" age-price pattern.

This point is made even clearer by figure C2.2. Here the mean acquisition price in each age interval has been adjusted for asset retirement using the Winfrey L_0 distribution and deflated to constant (1967) dollars using a "Boeckh" construction price index.[3] The adjusted data are unmistakably convex, and introducing the business tax code is unlikely to alter the evident conclusion.

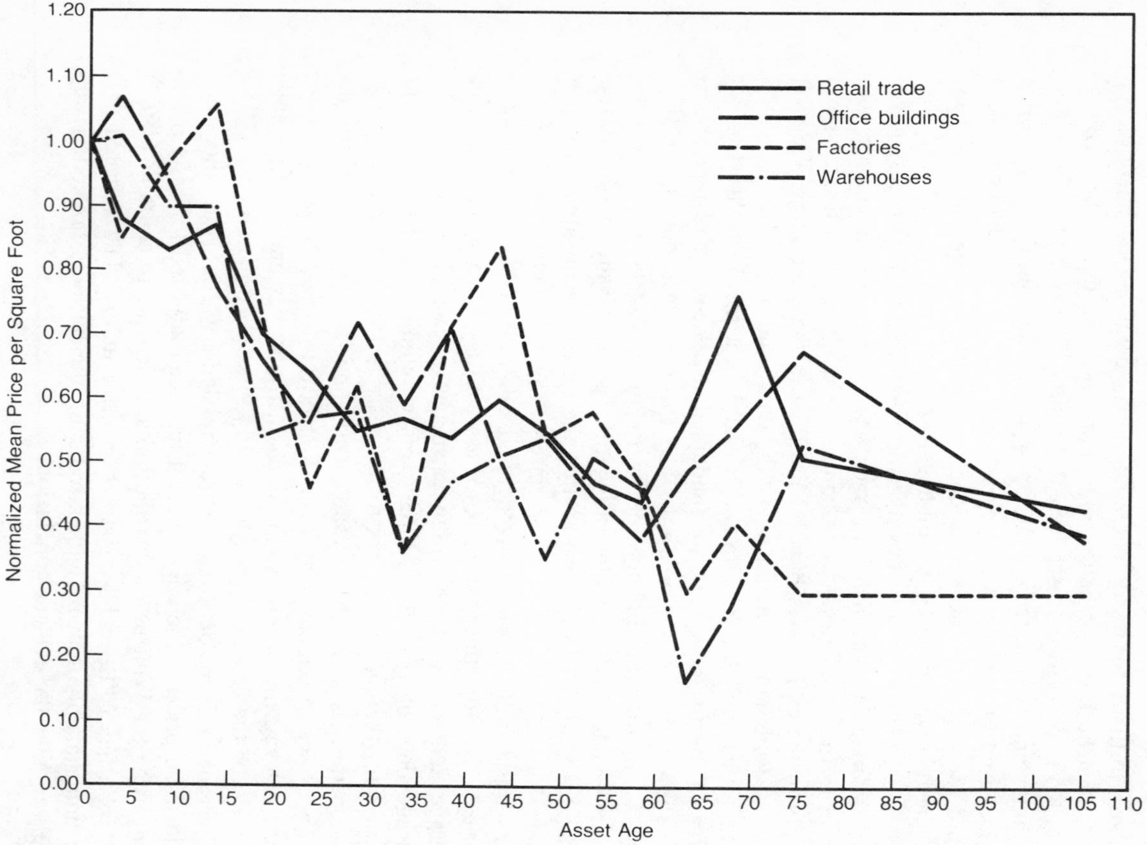

Fig. C2.1 Mean asset price by age interval, untransformed/undeflated.

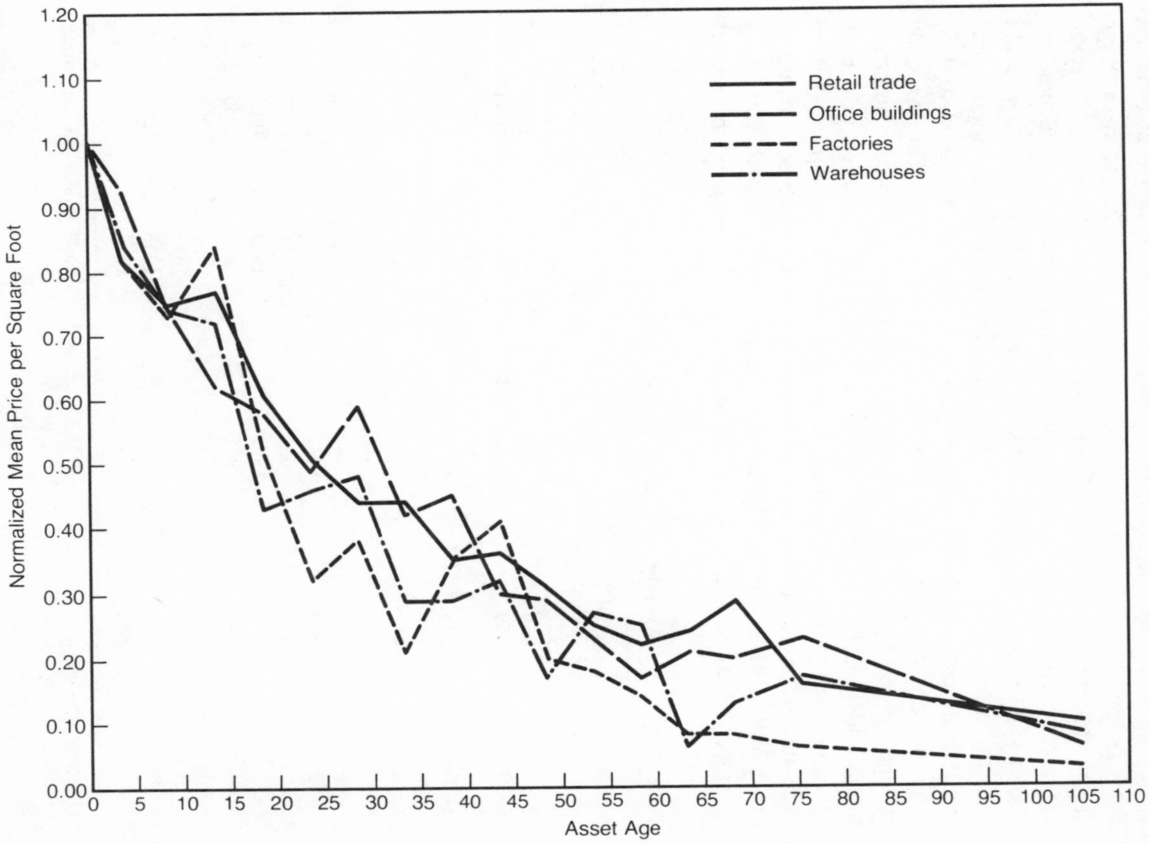

Fig. C2.2 Mean asset price by age interval, transformed/deflated.

We wish to emphasize that the data underlying figures C2.1 and C2.2 refer to market transactions of new and used buildings. Economic depreciation is usually thought of as the rate of change of an asset's market value, implicit or explicit, owing to the process of aging.[4] The data in figures C2.1 and C2.2 thus provides a basis for the *direct* measurement of economic depreciation. We would certainly agree with Taubman that changes in the tax code will in general change the market value of new and used buildings.[5] Assets with the same relative efficiency patterns can therefore have different market values at different dates of purchase. The data in figures C2.1 and C2.2 is an average across different dates of purchase, and, as noted above, the average date of purchase varies across age intervals. It is therefore possible that a systematic relationship between date of purchase and age could bias the age-price patterns of these figures. Table C2.1 does reveal some relationship between age and date.[6] It is therefore useful to consider the direction and magnitude of the possible bias. The tax code changes of 1954 and 1962 liberalized depreciation allowances on structures, and thus they exert an upward bias in the observed prices. A correction for this bias would thus tend to make the age-price pattern even more convex. Depreciation allowances were tightened starting in the middle 1960s by such provisions as recapture, and this exerts a downward bias in the observed prices that tends to offset the earlier

Table C2.1 **Average Date of Purchase, by Age Interval**

Age Interval	Retail Trade	Office Buildings	Factories	Warehouses
New	1957	1957	1954	1957
0–5	1959	1962	1955	1963
6–10	1959	1965	1962	1964
11–15	1959	1963	1958	1964
16–20	1958	1958	1958	1961
21–25	1958	1956	1959	1960
26–30	1957	1957	1961	1957
31–35	1956	1960	1957	1956
36–40	1960	1962	1961	1965
41–45	1960	1962	1961	1963
46–50	1961	1963	1956	1967
51–55	1960	1962	1964	1965
56–60	1960	1962	1964	1959
61–65	1963	1962	1961	1968
66–70	1963	1966	1966	1963
71–80	1969	1963	1958	1968
81–115[a]	1961	1961	1957	1964

[a]The average age in the last interval is 99 years for retail trade, 110 for office buildings, 100 for factories, and 113 for warehouses.

effects. The net bias will depend on the relative strengths of the bias and—more importantly—on the lag with which the effects take place.

It is important to recognize that while the tax code indicates large, discrete changes in the treatment of corporate capital, Ture and others point out that businesses adopted new procedures gradually and with some skepticism. Built-in durability changes probably require rather substantial procedural changes in durable goods and construction industries. Producers are unlikely to undergo such disruptions unless they are reasonably certain that the tax environment mandating these changes is likely to persist. The numerous code changes and tax debates have not provided such a stable environment. Furthermore, major changes in asset valuations are not likely to occur as a result of changes in a fluid tax code subject to different interpretations. The effect of changes in the tax code is therefore likely to be spread over a considerable period of time.

In view of the ambiguous direction of the bias, we are inclined to stand by the conclusions reached in our statistical analysis and reinforced by figures C2.1 and C2.2.

We would also like to point out that we attempted to estimate the effect on asset prices of a term reflecting the business tax code from 1954 to 1972 and of a rate of return term. These new terms contributed nothing to the regressions. Their coefficients were small, insignificant, and often perverse in sign. In view of the lags discussed above, this is not particularly surprising.

Notes

1. We emphasize the use of raw data rather than data weighted by sampling probabilities. We rejected the weighted data because the weights showed extreme variability and because of certain technical problems associated with their construction. Hulten and Wykoff (1978) contains a more detailed discussion of the weighting problem. We note here that the use of the unweighted data results in an unbiased estimate of the age-price pattern.

2. Average prices have been normalized on the average price of new assets for purposes of comparison. Furthermore, the end points of the curves in figures C2.1 and C2.2 differ among the classes. The footnote to table C2.1 gives the actual terminal points.

3. The Boeckh indexes were taken from the *Construction Review*, Bureau of Domestic Commerce, United States Department of Commerce.

4. Or, in other words, depreciation is the dollar amount that must be "put back" in order to keep capital intact, holding asset inflation constant.

5. This is, in fact, one of the main points of our paper.

6. The simple correlation between age and date is 0.14 for retail trade and 0.13 for office buildings in the underlying sample.

3 Alternative Measures of Capital and Its Rate of Return in United States Manufacturing

Robert M. Coen

3.1 Introduction

The recent benchmark revisions of the national income accounts of the United States incorporate new measures of capital consumption that depart substantially from the old.[1] The prior estimates were based largely on tax return data on depreciation and thus were subject to capricious variations associated with changes in tax depreciation policy and enforcement practices. They had the further shortcoming of embodying valuations reflecting original acquisition prices (historical costs) of capital goods rather than the current prices employed in valuing other flows in the accounts. The new measures, by contrast, make use of current capital goods prices to value "real depreciation," the latter being obtained by consistently applying given depreciation formulas to real capital expenditures over time.

Users of the accounts will no doubt welcome these changes, since many had already been following similar procedures in their own work involving measures of capital, capital consumption, and income. Indeed, the Commerce Department has for some time been inconsistent in its behavior, maintaining the tax return measures of capital consumption in the national accounts while rejecting them in its own computations of capital stocks (U.S. Department of Commerce, OBE 1971). Perhaps all of us can now enjoy a less complicated existence—keeping one set of books instead of two.

I say perhaps, because there are aspects of the new approach that merit close scrutiny. The first is largely a factual matter: Are the asset

Robert M. Coen is professor of economics at Northwestern University.

The author is indebted to Mark Wilson and David Small for their careful work on the calculations underlying this paper and to Molly Fabian for her expeditious typing of the manuscript. This research has been supported by the United States Treasury Department under contract numbers OS-570 and OS-1543.

service lives and depreciation patterns employed in deriving the new series reasonable? The second is largely methodological: Is the approach founded upon a measure of income to which economists would generally subscribe? A major purpose of this paper is to examine these questions. Since my answers are in part negative, I construct alternative measures of capital consumption that, though basically in the same spirit as the new Commerce approach, embody different assumptions. I then compare my own estimates with those of the Commerce Department to determine whether the different constructs have substantially different implications regarding matters of ultimate concern to economic analysts—the growth of capital and fluctuations in profits and rates of return. The empirical results to be reported pertain to total manufacturing over the period 1947–74.

I should emphasize that my intention is *not* to establish whether the new Commerce approach is right or wrong. To point out weaknesses or problems in the application of the approach is not necessarily to condemn it, especially in the difficult area of capital and income measurement. As Hicks has so aptly stated and carefully demonstrated: "At bottom, they [capital and income] are not logical categories at all; they are rough approximations, used by the business man to steer himself through the bewildering changes of situation which confront him" (1946, p. 171). I hope to clarify some issues raised by the Commerce approach and to establish whether the businessman (or the economist) would perceive the situation differently and therefore be likely to steer a different course (recommend a different policy) if he were to use approximations other than the Commerce Department's.

3.2 A Critique of the Commerce Approach

The new Commerce method of estimating capital consumption can be stated in simplified form as follows. Let I_τ be capital expenditures at date τ (end of period), w_i be the depreciation rate of capital in the ith period of its service life, and n be the service life. Then capital consumption in period t arising from capital acquired in period τ is

$$(1) \qquad \begin{cases} D_{t\tau} = 0, & t > \tau + n. \\ D_{t\tau} = w_{t-\tau} I_\tau, & \tau < t \leq \tau + n \end{cases}$$

The contribution of vintage τ acquisitions to capital stock at the end of period t is

$$(2) \qquad K_{t\tau} = I_\tau - \sum_{j=\tau+1}^{t} D_{j\tau}.$$

Total capital consumption and capital stock for period t are obtained by summing the above expressions over all vintages.

In Commerce's latest capital stock study (U.S. Department of Commerce 1976*a*), these calculations are performed in two ways. The first uses I_τ in nominal terms, valuation being at the original acquisition price. This leads to what are referred to as historical-cost measures of capital consumption and capital stock. The second uses I_τ in real terms, obtained by deflating nominal expenditures in period τ by an index of capital goods prices for that period. This leads to what are referred to as constant-cost measures of capital consumption and captial stock, which when multiplied by the capital goods price index for period t, yield the so-called current-cost variants of the variables. It is this current-cost variant of capital consumption that now enters the national income accounts. The service life and depreciation pattern are the same in both sets of calculations.

Applying this approach requires information on service lives and depreciation patterns of various types of capital goods, but little appears to be known about these key parameters. The Treasury Department has occasionally conducted surveys of company (usually company engineers') estimates of service lives, the most noteworthy of these occurring in the 1930s and resulting in the detailed, prescribed lives of the Treasury's Bulletin F. After weighing other fragmentary evidence, Commerce decided to use service lives that are 85% of those appearing in Bulletin F. Since shorter lives are assumed for alterations and additions to structures, the average lives applied to structures expenditures are about 68% of the Bulletin F lives for new buildings. On the matter of depreciation patterns, even more guesswork was necessary, the final decision being to assume straight-line depreciation of all capital goods ($w_i = 1/n$ for $i = 1, n$).

In my own recent research (Coen 1974, 1975) I have explored a new method of inferring service lives and depreciation patterns of capital goods from the historical behavior of capital expenditures. Adopting a neoclassical, capital-stock-adjustment formulation of the investment decision that links net investment to changes in output and the real implicit rental price of capital, I experimented with alternative specifications of service lives and depreciation patterns in measuring both net investment and the rental price to determine which specification best accounted, on the average, for observed fluctuations in gross capital expenditures. The best-fitting alternatives may be viewed as the service life and depreciation pattern revealed or indicated by investment behavior.

It is important to note that the capital stock concept appropriate to the study of investment decisions is not market value of fixed assets but current productive capacity of fixed assets. By the same token, the appropriate depreciation concept is not loss of market value but loss of productive capacity or efficiency of fixed assets. A rather farfetched but simple example might help illustrate this point. Suppose we wished to explain the investment behavior of a firm producing light, the desired output of light being the amount emitted by one light bulb (the firm's capital asset). Investment would take place only intermittently, as the bulb burned out. If we knew the average life of a bulb, we could accurately predict the firm's capital expenditures. Put another way, we should be able to infer from the firm's capital expenditures over time that its capital asset has a certain average service life and does not lose efficiency during the service life. Furthermore, the firm's capital stock measured in terms of current productive capacity never changes. Nonetheless, its capital stock in value terms does change through time. A used light bulb, though equivalent to a new one in ability to emit light, will be worth less because it embodies a smaller stream of future services. Depreciation in an economic sense occurs even though depreciation in a loss-of-efficiency sense does not.

Thus, we must clearly distinguish between loss of efficiency and economic depreciation and recognize that analyses of investment behavior can tell us about the former but not the latter. But if our ultimate objective is to measure income, then we must find some way to translate loss of efficiency into economic depreciation—a problem I shall take up in a moment.

My empirical investigations of service lives and loss-of-efficiency patterns covered equipment and structures used in the manufacturing sector, disaggregated into twenty-one subindustries. The revealed lives and patterns are shown in table 3.1.[2] Table 3.2 indicates the industrial breakdown. The weighted-average equipment life for total manufacturing is about twelve years, while that for structures is about thirty-two years.[3] The Bulletin F average lives are about sixteen years for equipment and forty to fifty years for structures. Thus, the revealed life for equipment is about 75% of that in Bulletin F, significantly shorter than the life assumed by the Commerce Department. On the other hand, the revealed life for structures is about 65–70% of that in Bulletin F, in line with that assumed by Commerce.

The predominant loss-of-efficiency pattern in table 3.1 is the one denoted as GD-FIN, which is characterized by geometrically decaying weights truncated at the end of the service life, the rate of decay being twice the reciprocal of the service life. The straight-line (SL) loss-of-efficiency pattern did, however, yield superior results in many instances. Although there is, of course, no way of aggregating the loss-of-efficiency patterns, it seems fair to say that something approximating geometric decay rather than straight-line loss of efficiency is typical of capital used in manufacturing, particularly since the SYD and GD-FIN patterns both suggest greater loss of efficiency in the early years of the service life than in the later years. Hence, if Commerce's choice of a straight-

Table 3.1 Service Lives and Loss-of-Efficiency Patterns Revealed by Investment Behavior

	Equipment		Structures	
SIC Industry Code[a]	Service Life (in Years)	Capacity Depreciation Pattern	Service Life (in Years)	Capacity Depreciation Pattern
20	12	SL	20	SL
21	10	SL	20	SYD
22	18	GD-FIN	20	OHS
23	10	SYD	40	GD-FIN
24	8	SL	50	GD-FIN
25	20	GD-FIN	50	OHS
26	10	GD-FIN	30	SL
27	22	SL	20	SYD
28	14	GD-FIN	25	SL
29	10	SL	45	GD-FIN
30	10	SYD	40	GD-FIN
31	10	GD-FIN	20	GD-FIN
32	10	GD-FIN	35	GD-FIN
33	16	GD-FIN	40	GD-FIN
34	10	GD-FIN	45	SL
35	10	GD-FIN	20	GD-FIN
36	6	SL	30	SL
37+19–371	8	SYD	40	GD-FIN
371	8	GD-FIN	45	GD-FIN
38	10	GD-FIN	20	GD-FIN
39	20	SL	25	SYD

Note: A capacity depreciation pattern is defined by a set of parameters d_j, $j = 1, \ldots, n$, where d_j is the loss of productive capacity of an asset in year j of its service life, relative to its productive capacity when new, and n is the service life. The patterns appearing in this table have the following characteristics:

for SL, $d_j = 1/n$.

for GD-FIN, $d_j = (2/n)[1 - (2/n)]^{j-1}$

for SYD, $d_j = (n + 1 - j) \sum_{i=1}^{n} i$.

for OHS, $d_j = 0$, for $j = 1, \ldots, n - 1$, and $d_n = 1$.

[a]See table 3.2 for identification of SIC (standard industrial classification) industry codes.

line formula is meant to refer to loss of efficiency, it appears to be wide of the mark.

Commerce's treatment of the depreciation formula is confusing, however, since the very same formula is alternatively applied to nominal and real capital expenditures. If the formula refers to loss of efficiency, then it makes sense to apply it to real expenditures, but the resulting "depreciation" measures the real replacement expenditures needed to maintain the productive capacity of the capital stock. Multiplying real replacement requirements by current prices of capital goods yields an estimate of current-dollar replacement, which is not an appropriate concept to use in measuring income. If the formula refers to economic depreciation (loss of value), then it makes sense to apply it to nominal expenditures, giving a historical-cost measure of economic depreciation that would be appropriate to the measurement of income provided prices of capital goods are not changing over time. The point is that one formula cannot serve both purposes. Because the Commerce approach fails to distinguish between loss of efficiency and loss of value, or replacement requirements and economic depreciation, it is difficult to interpret the resulting estimates. Moreover, the approach lacks an articulated concept of income, without which economic depreciation cannot be defined and made operational. The following section presents an explicit and consistent framework for measuring economic depreciation, income, and capital.

3.3 Historical-Cost and Current-Cost Concepts of Economic Depreciation

3.3.1 The Historical-Cost Concept

In my earlier papers (Coen 1974, 1975) I showed how a loss-of-efficiency pattern of a capital good can be translated into a pattern of economic depreciation, depicting the loss in value of the capital good as it ages. To illustrate, let us consider an asset whose service life is three years. Let d_j be the loss of productive capacity of the asset in year j of its life relative to its efficiency when new. Suppose that the asset, when new, adds X units to real net output (net of materials costs, labor, etc.) and that the price, P, at which output may be sold remains constant through time. The asset will then give rise to the following stream of net money returns:

Year of Service Life	*Net Money Return*
1	PX
2	$PX(1-d_1)$
3	$PX(1-d_1-d_2)$

The value of the asset at the end of each year is given by the present value of the stream of net money returns from that year to the end of the service life. If r is the discount rate (assumed constant over time), then for the asset being considered we have

$$C_0 = \frac{PX}{1+r} + \frac{PX(1-d_1)}{(1+r)^2} + \frac{PX(1-d_1-d_2)}{(1+r)^3} \tag{3}$$

$$Z_1 = \frac{PX(1-d_1)}{1+r} + \frac{PX(1-d_1-d_2)}{(1+r)^2} \tag{4}$$

Table 3.2 Standard Industrial Classification Codes and Descriptions of Industries Referred to in table 3.1

SIC Code	Description
20	Food and kindred products
21	Tobacco manufactures
22	Textile mill products
23	Apparel and related products
24	Lumber and wood products, except furniture
25	Furniture and fixtures
26	Paper and allied products
27	Printing and publishing
28	Chemical and allied products
29	Petroleum and related industries
30	Rubber and miscellaneous plastic products
31	Leather and leather products
32	Stone, clay, and glass products
33	Primary metal industries
34	Fabricated metal products
35	Machinery, except electrical
36	Electrical machinery
37+19–371	Transportation equipment and ordnance, except motor vehicles
371	Motor vehicles and equipment
38	Instruments and related products
39	Miscellaneous manufacturing industries

(5) $$Z_2 = \frac{PX(1 - d_1 - d_2)}{1 + r}$$

(6) $$Z_3 = 0,$$

where C_0 is the original cost of the asset, Z_1 is the value of the asset at the end of its first year of service, and so forth. Depreciation each year, that is, the loss in value of the asset, is given by

(7) $$D_1 = C_0 - Z_1$$

(8) $$D_2 = Z_1 - Z_2$$

(9) $$D_3 = Z_2 - Z_3,$$

and depreciation charges summed over the service life equal the eventual replacement cost of the asset.

What property do these measures of depreciation possess? The fundamental point is as follows. In each year of the asset's life, it generates a certain amount of money receipts. The problem of depreciation accounting is to decompose these receipts into two components, of which we call one income, the other depreciation. If we define income as the portion of receipts that *could be* consumed (or withdrawn for some other purpose) and still leave the owner with the same real wealth at the end of the year as he possessed at the beginning of the year, then the depreciation method proposed here is the appropriate one, *provided that the price of a comparable new asset is not changing over time.*

To establish that this proposition is correct, let us examine the situation in the first year of the asset's life. Suppose we denote income in year 1, as income was defined above, by Y_1. The owner's nominal wealth at the beginning of year 1 is simply C_0, and his real wealth is one (one capital good). If the price of new capital goods of this type is constant through time, then we require that the owner's wealth at the end of year 1 be C_0, so that his real wealth will not have changed. He will, of course, have a used asset worth Z_1 at that time, and he will have $PX - Y_1$ in cash. Thus, if his wealth at the end of year 1 is to be C_0, we must have

$$PX - Y_1 + Z_1 = C_0. \tag{10}$$

But $PX - Y_1$ is what we would identify as depreciation in year 1, D_1, so that

$$D_1 = C_0 - Z_1. \tag{11}$$

Receipts in the second year are composed of two flows: the net money return generated by the asset, $PX(1 - d_1)$, and interest on depreciation set aside in year 1, rD_1. Also, the owner's wealth at the end of year 2 is composed of two items: the two-year-old asset worth Z_2, and the amount of cash set aside for depreciation in year 1, D_1. Again assuming that the price of a new capital good similar to the used one has not changed, we require that the owner's wealth at the end of year 2 be C_0. Thus income in year 2 is implicitly defined by

$$PX(1 - d_1) + rD_1 - Y_2 + Z_2 + D_1 = C_0. \tag{12}$$

Since D_2 is $PX(1 - d_1) + rD_1 - Y_2$, that is, total receipts minus income, we have

$$D_2 = C_0 - Z_2 - D_1 = C_0 - Z_2 - C_0 + Z_1 = Z_1 - Z_2. \tag{13}$$

Similar reasoning would lead to the conclusion that $D_3 = Z_2 - Z_3$.

With depreciation in each year defined by these expressions, it can easily be shown that income in each year of the asset's life is the same and equal to rC_0 and that the rate of return is the same each year and equal to r.

Thus, under the assumption of constant prices the calculation of depreciation is straightforward. For our purposes it is convenient to normalize the depreciation flows in the above example on the initial value of the asset. This gives us a set of parameters v_j, defined as

(14) $$v_1 = \frac{C_0 - Z_1}{C_0}$$

(15) $$v_2 = \frac{Z_1 - Z_2}{C_0}$$

(16) $$v_3 = \frac{Z_2 - Z_3}{C_0},$$

which characterize the pattern of economic depreciation on the asset. In other words, the v_j depict the pattern of economic depreciation on an asset of this type costing one dollar when new. Note that under this normalization, the term PX will not appear in the v_j. They will depend only on the parameters characterizing capacity depreciation and on the discount rate. Depreciation in each year and the value of the asset at the end of each year can then be expressed in terms of the original cost of the asset:

(17) $$D_1 = v_1 C_0 \qquad Z_1 = (1 - v_1)C_0$$

(18) $$D_2 = v_2 C_0 \qquad Z_2 = (1 - v_1 - v_2)C_0$$

(19) $$D_3 = v_3 C_0 \qquad Z_3 = 0.$$

This approach, based as it is on the assumption of constant prices, is certainly rather unrealistic. Its implementation results in depreciation measures reflecting the historical, or original, cost of assets. In times of changing prices, historical-cost depreciation will be incorrect in the sense that the measure of income associated with it will not properly indicate how much of current receipts can be consumed and still leave real wealth intact. Nonetheless, the simplicity of historical-cost depreciation and its conceptual similarity to tax accounting practices in the United States are notable features.

These results can be stated in a more general way. If d_j is the fraction of an asset's original productive capacity that is lost in period j of its service life (with $d_0 = 0$), and if the asset has a productive capacity of unity when new, then the value of the asset at the end of period j of its service life is

(20) $$V_j = \sum_{k=j}^{n} \left(1 - \sum_{i=0}^{k} d_i\right) (1 + r)^{-k+j-1}, \quad j = 0,n.$$

The fraction of the asset's original value, V_0, lost in period j of its service life—economic depreciation in period j—is

(21) $$v_j = (V_{j-1} - V_j)/V_0, \quad j = 1,n.$$ [4]

By the nature of these definitions, the sum of the economic depreciation weights, the v_js, over the life of the asset must be unity. Then historical-cost economic depreciation on vintage τ capital goods in period t is given by

$$(22) \qquad \begin{cases} D_{t\tau} = v_{t-\tau} I_\tau, & \tau < t \leq \tau + n \\ D_{t\tau} = 0, & \tau > \tau + n, \end{cases}$$

where I_τ is measured in nominal terms at the original acquisition price.

The contribution of vintage τ capital goods to what I shall call the book value of capital at the end of period t is

$$(23) \qquad B_{t\tau} = I_\tau - \sum_{j=\tau+1}^{t} D_{j\tau}.$$

Equations (22) and (23) are identical in form to those used by the Commerce Department in calculating historical-cost depreciation and capital stock. But here the depreciation rates are explicitly related to the underlying loss-of-efficiency pattern and service life, and the "capital stock" is explicitly referred to as "book value of capital" to distinguish it from a physical measure of productive capacity.

3.3.2 The Current-Cost Concepts

Capital goods prices commonly change over time, raising serious difficulties in the measurement of depreciation and income. While knowledge of the causes of these changes, as well as whether they are foreseen or unforeseen, is required to take proper account of them, we can do little but speculate about such matters. Consequently, any approach to depreciation measurement under conditions of changing prices is necessarily somewhat arbitrary. We can formulate a set of assumptions and examine their implications, but we must recognize that a different, and perhaps equally plausible, set of assumptions may lead to different results.

Here I shall examine the implications of three assumptions regarding price expectations:

Case A: Firms expect last period's price level to prevail indefinitely, so that any change in the price level is a surprise.

Case B: Firms expect last period's rate of inflation to prevail indefinitely, so that any change in the rate of inflation is a surprise.

Case C: Firms can perfectly predict the rate of inflation.

In each case I shall assume that these expectations pertain to product prices, that changes in capital goods prices result solely from changes in prices of the outputs they produce, and that the value of a capital good is equal to the present value of the expected stream of net money returns it will produce.

Before proceeding, it is worth noting that cases A and C might be viewed as two ends of a continuum running from complete inability to predict prices to perfect foresight, while B lies somewhere between these extremes. As we shall see, one of the extremes—Case C—gives rise to current-cost accounting procedures that are analogous to those adopted by the Commerce Department.

The depreciation measures appropriate to these special cases are most easily derived from a general accounting framework incorporating changing prices. Suppose an individual purchases a new capital good at the end of year 0 for C_0 dollars. The capital good has a three-year life, and its capacity depreciation in year j of its life is d_j. We shall assume that the purchase price equals the present value of the stream of expected future net money returns. In addition, we shall assume that at the time of purchase the asset's owner expects the rate of inflation to be $\gamma^e{}_1$ and expects the nominal rate of interest to adjust so as to keep the real rate of interest constant at r. Thus,

$$(24) \qquad C_0 = \frac{(1+\gamma^e{}_1)P_0X}{(1+r)(1+\gamma^e{}_1)} + \frac{(1+\gamma^e{}_1)^2\, P_0X(1-d_1)}{[(1+r)(1+\gamma^e{}_1)]^2} + \frac{(1+\gamma^e{}_1)^3\, P_0X(1-d_1-d_2)}{[(1+r)(1+\gamma^e{}_1)]^3}$$
$$= \frac{P_0X}{1+r} + \frac{P_0X(1-d_1)}{(1+r)^2} + \frac{P_0X(1-d_1-d_2)}{(1+r)^3},$$

the same as in equation (3).

If the price level in the first year of the asset's life turns out to be $P_1 = (1+\gamma_1)P_0 \neq (1+\gamma^e{}_1)P_0$, and if the owner changes his expected rate of inflation to $\gamma^e{}_2$, then the value of the used asset at the end of the first year will be

$$(25) \qquad Z_1 = \frac{(1+\gamma^e{}_2)\, P_1X(1-d_1)}{(1+r)(1+\gamma^e{}_2)} + \frac{(1+\gamma^e{}_2)^2\, P_1X(1-d_1-d_2)}{[(1+r)(1+\gamma^e{}_2)]^2} = \frac{P_1X(1-d_1)}{1+r}$$
$$+ \frac{P_1X(1-d_1-d_2)}{(1+r)^2} = (1+\gamma_1)(1-v_1)C_0,$$

where v_1 is defined as in equation (14); that is, v_1 is the first-year historical-cost depreciation rate.

A new asset of the same type should sell at the end of year 1 for

$$(26) \qquad C_1 = \frac{(1+\gamma^e{}_2)P_1X}{(1+r)(1+\gamma^e{}_2)} + \frac{(1+\gamma^e{}_2)^2\, P_1X(1-d_1)}{[(1+r)(1+\gamma^e{}_2)]^2} + \frac{(1+\gamma^e{}_3)^3\, P_1X(1-d_1-d_2)}{[(1+r)(1+\gamma^e{}_2)]^3} = (1+\gamma_1)C_0.$$

We see then that under our assumptions the price of new capital goods and the value of used capital goods should rise or fall at the same rate as the output price level.

Nominal ex post income in the first year of the asset's life is implicitly given by

$$P_1X - Y_1 + Z_1 = C_1; \tag{27}$$

so depreciation in that year is

$$\begin{aligned} D_1 = C_1 - Z_1 &= (1 + \gamma_1)C_0 - (1 - v_1)\ (1 + \gamma_1)C_0 \\ &= (1 + \gamma_1)v_1C_0. \end{aligned} \tag{28}$$

Thus, first-year current-cost depreciation is the first-year historical-cost depreciation, v_1C_0, multiplied by one plus the actual rate of inflation. This result, which is evidently independent of the manner in which price expectations are formed, is in accord with a frequently recommended change in tax depreciation policy, namely, that firms be permitted to inflate their historical-cost depreciation by a factor reflecting the rate of change of the price level. When we move on to the second year, however, we see that the situation is not quite so simple.

Suppose that the price level in the second year is $P_2 = (1 + \gamma_2)P_1 \neq (1 + \gamma^e{}_2)P_1$, and suppose that the owner once again revises his expected rate of inflation to $\gamma^e{}_3$. The value of the used asset at the end of the second year should then be $Z_2 = (1 - v_1 - v_2)(1 + \gamma_2)(1 + \gamma_1)C_0$, and a new asset of the same type should sell for $C_2 = (1 + \gamma_2)(1 + \gamma_1)C_0$. Since the owner anticipated an inflation rate of $\gamma^e{}_2$ in the second year, it seems reasonable to assume that he would have held his depreciation reserve in a form that (*a*) would yield a nominal rate of return of $(1 + \gamma^e{}_2)r$ and thus a real rate of return of r and (*b*) would have appreciated at the rate of $\gamma^e{}_2$. Hence, receipts in the second year consist of $P_2X(1 - d_1)$ from production and $(1 + \gamma^e{}_2)r\ D_1$ in interest on the depreciation reserve; and at the end of the second year the owner has a used asset worth Z_2 and a depreciation reserve amounting to $(1 + \gamma^e{}_2)D_1$. Nominal ex post income in the second year is implicitly given by

$$\begin{aligned} &P_2X(1 - d_1) + (1 + \gamma^e{}_2)rD_1 - Y_2 + Z_2 \\ &\quad + (1 + \gamma^e{}_2)D_1 = C_2; \end{aligned} \tag{29}$$

so depreciation in that year is

$$\begin{aligned} D_2 &= C_2 - Z_2 - (1 + \gamma^e{}_2)D_1 \\ &= (1 + \gamma_2)(1 + \gamma_1)C_0 \\ &\quad - (1 - v_1 - v_2)(1 + \gamma_2)(1 + \gamma_1)C_0 \\ &\quad - (1 + \gamma^e{}_2)(1 + \gamma_1)v_1\ C_0 \\ &= (1 + \gamma_2)(1 + \gamma_1)v_2C_0 + \\ &\quad (\gamma_2 - \gamma^e{}_2)(1 + \gamma_1)v_1C_0. \end{aligned} \tag{30}$$

The first term in the final expression for D_2 is the second-year historical-cost depreciation inflated to the price level of year 2, but to this we must add an adjustment of the first-year current-cost depreciation, marking it up by the excess of the actual over the expected rate of inflation in year 2.

The key assumption here is that the depreciation reserve (in this case the first-year current-cost depreciation) does not appreciate pari passu with the price level in year 2; instead, it appreciates at the *expected* rate of inflation in year 2. Hence, insofar as the actual price increase in year 2 exceeds the expected increase, additional depreciation must be claimed, so that the total reserve at the end of year 2, when added to the value of the used asset, equals the purchase price of a new asset of the same type. This assumption would be incorrect if the depreciation reserve were held in the form of commodities or capital goods whose value automatically rose at the actual rate of inflation; but it would be correct if, for example, the reserve were held in the form of financial assets whose terms were fixed contractually at the end of the first year. It is nearly impossible, of course, to identify in practice the form or forms in which firms hold their depreciation reserves, since these reserves are often mere accounting entries. Lacking clear evidence one way or the other, I am inclined to follow a more conservative course and presume that firms are at best able to earn nominal capital gains on their depreciation reserves at a rate equal to the expected rate of inflation, in which case the real value of reserves would be maintained only if the expected and actual rates of inflation were the same.

A similar result holds for current-cost depreciation in the third year. If at the end of year 2 the owner expects the inflation rate to be $\gamma^e{}_3$ in the third year and beyond, he should hold his total depreciation reserve, $(1+\gamma^e{}_2)D_1 + D_2 = (1+\gamma_2)(1+\gamma_1)(v_2+v_1)C_0$, in a form that yields a nominal rate of return of $(1+\gamma^e{}_3)r$ and that appreciates at the rate $\gamma^e{}_3$. The used asset should be worth $(1+\gamma_3)(1+\gamma_2)(1+\gamma_1)\cdot(1-v_1-v_2-v_3)C_0 = 0$ at the end of year 3, and a comparable new asset should sell for $(1+\gamma_3)(1+\gamma_2)(1+\gamma_1)C_0$, where γ_3 is the actual rate of inflation in year 3. Nominal ex post income in year 3 is given by

$$
\begin{aligned}
(31)\qquad & P_3X(1-d_1-d_2) + (1+\gamma^e{}_3)r \\
& [(1+\gamma^e{}_2)D_1 + D_2] - Y_3 \\
& + (1+\gamma^e{}_3)[(1+\gamma^e{}_2)D_1 + D_2] + Z_2 = C_3,
\end{aligned}
$$

from which it follows that

$$
\begin{aligned}
(32)\qquad D_3 &= C_3 - Z_3 - (1+\gamma^e{}_3)\,[(1+\gamma^e{}_2)D_1 + D_2] \\
&= (1+\gamma_3)(1+\gamma_2)(1+\gamma_1)v_3C_0 \\
&\quad + (\gamma_3-\gamma^e{}_3)(1+\gamma_2)(1+\gamma_1)(v_2+v_1)C_0.
\end{aligned}
$$

The first term in the final expression for D_3 is the third-year historical-cost depreciation inflated to the price level of the third year, and to this we must again add an adjustment of the depreciation reserve accumulated at the end of the previous year, marking it up by the excess of the actual over the expected rate of inflation in year 3.

Making use of these expressions for current-cost depreciation, we can derive the following measures of income over the life of the asset:

(33) $$Y_1 = (1 + \gamma_1) r C_0$$

(34) $$Y_2 = (1 + \gamma_2)(1 + \gamma_1) r C_0 - (\gamma_2 - \gamma^e_2)(1 + r)(1 + \gamma_1) v_1 C_0$$

(35) $$Y_3 = (1 + \gamma_3)(1 + \gamma_2)(1 + \gamma_1) r C_0 - (\gamma_3 - \gamma^e_3)(1 + r)(1 + \gamma_2)(1 + \gamma_1)(v_2 + v_1) C_0.$$

If the actual rate of inflation were always perfectly foreseen, the second terms of Y_2 and Y_3 would be zero, nominal income would rise pari passu with the price level, and the real rate of return on the asset would be constant at r. Should the actual rate of inflation continually exceed (fall below) the expected rate, however, nominal income will rise less (more) rapidly than the price level and the real rate of return on the asset will decline (rise) over the service life.

Perfect foresight regarding inflation corresponds to case C above, whereas for case A we have $\gamma^e_i = 0$ and for case B we have $\gamma^e_i = \gamma_{i-1}$. Thus, only case C results in measures of depreciation that imply constant real income over the life of an asset. On the other hand, only case A results in depreciation allowances that sum over an asset's life to its eventual replacement cost; in an inflationary environment, total depreciation allowances associated with cases B and C will fall short of replacement cost, although the depreciation reserves accumulated by the end of an asset's life, which include capital gains on the reserves held during the life of the asset, will equal the replacement cost.

We can now illustrate how these current-cost measures of depreciation will be applied to firms that invest year after year. Let I_τ once again be nominal gross capital expenditures in year τ; let c_t be an index of capital goods prices in year t; and let $D_{t\tau}$ be current-cost depreciation in year t on vintage τ capital goods. Noting that prices of new capital goods rise or fall at the same rate as product rises, according to our assumptions, and that for $t > \tau$, $c_t = (1 + \gamma_t)(1 + \gamma_{t-1}) \ldots (1 + \gamma_{\tau+1}) c_\tau$, we have:

$$(36)\quad \text{Case } A\text{: } D_{t\tau} = \frac{c_t}{c_\tau} v_{t-\tau} I_\tau + \frac{c_t - c_{t-1}}{c_\tau} \left(\sum_{j=1}^{t-\tau-1} v_{t-\tau-j} \right) I_\tau$$

$$(37)\quad \text{Case } B\text{: } D_{t\tau} = \frac{c_t}{c_\tau} v_{t-\tau} I_\tau + \left(\frac{c_t}{c_{t-1}} - \frac{c_{t-1}}{c_{t-2}} \right) \frac{c_{t-1}}{c_\tau} \left(\sum_{j=1}^{t-\tau-1} v_{t-\tau-j} \right) I_\tau$$

$$(38)\quad \text{Case } C\text{: } D_{t\tau} = \frac{c_t}{c_\tau} v_{t-\tau} \mathrm{I}_\tau,$$

all of which hold for $\tau < t \leq \tau + n$, where n is the service life. Since our assumptions also imply that the values of used capital goods rise or fall at the same rate as product prices, the contribution of vintage τ capital goods to the book value of capital at the end of period t does not depend on the expectations hypothesis and can be expressed in each case as:

$$(39)\qquad B_{t\tau} = \frac{c_t}{c_\tau} \left[1 - \sum_{j=\tau+1}^{t} v_j \right] I_\tau .$$

In case A, calculating $B_{t\tau}$ in this way is the same as subtracting accumulated depreciation charges from real vintage τ capital expenditures valued at current prices. But this is not true of cases B and C; in these latter cases, $B_{t\tau}$ is real vintage τ capital expenditures valued at current prices less the depreciation reserve at the end of year t, which includes capital gains on previous depreciation charges.

Comparing these measures with the Commerce procedures, we see that there is a close parallel between equation (38) and what Commerce calls current-cost depreciation. According to equation (38), we should calculate current-cost depreciation by applying a given depreciation schedule to real capital expenditures (I_τ / c_τ) and valuing the result at current prices, which is what Commerce does. The only difference in our approaches lies in the choice of a depreciation schedule; while Commerce assumes a straight-line formula with lives 15% shorter than Bulletin F, I base my vs on the loss-of-efficiency patterns and service lives revealed by investment behavior. Like equation (38), however, the Commerce procedure is now seen to be appropriate only if firms are able to predict perfectly the rate of inflation (and if all the other assumptions we have made hold). That expectations are so accurate is doubtful, I believe, and it therefore seems worthwhile to compare the implications of this extreme hypothesis with those associated with imperfect foresight (cases A and B).

Although equation (38) does not appear to resemble equation (2), in fact it does. In computing its current-cost capital stock, Commerce first computes a constant-cost measure of capital stock using equation

(2), with I_τ defined as *real* vintage τ capital expenditures and $D_{j\tau}$ defined as *real* depreciation in period j on vintage τ capital. Real depreciation is obtained by applying the depreciation rate w to real capital expenditures. Multiplying the constant-cost capital stock, $K_{t\tau}$, by the capital goods price index in period t, c_t, Commerce arrives at its current-cost capital stock. Thus, differences between my current-cost book value and Commerce's current-cost capital stock result solely from differences in the service lives and depreciation patterns employed, and we see that Commerce's procedure is equivalent to subtracting the depreciation reserve (*not* accumulated depreciation charges) at the end of year t from vintage τ capital expenditures valued at current prices.

Finally, Commerce's so-called constant-cost measures of depreciation and capital stock appear to have no obvious parallels in these results. We could, of course, deflate my measures for $D_{t\tau}$ and $B_{t\tau}$, and the associated nominal income estimates, by c_t to obtain constant-dollar variants of them, but this would provide little additional information; indeed, it would have no effect on my estimates of rates of return. What can be of interest, however, are estimates of real replacement requirements, which differ conceptually from constant-dollar depreciation. The real capital expenditure, $R_{t\tau}$, required in year t to maintain the productive capacity (*not* the real value) of vintage τ capital goods is found by applying the appropriate loss-of-efficiency pattern to real capital expenditures of year τ:

$$(40) \qquad R_{t\tau} = d_{t-\tau} I_\tau / c_\tau.^5$$

Current-dollar replacement is then given by

$$(41) \qquad c_t R_{t\tau} = c_t \, d_{t-\tau} \, I_\tau / c_\tau.$$

Equations (40) and (41) resemble Commerce's formulas for calculating constant-cost and current-cost depreciation, but here the d_js explicitly refer to loss of efficiency. Because Commerce fails to make any distinction between loss of efficiency and loss of value, the concepts of depreciation and replacement, as well as the related notions of value of capital and of productive capacity, are obscured. If the depreciation schedule Commerce adopts is meant to depict loss of efficiency, then what Commerce calls constant-cost depreciation ought to be called constant-cost replacement, and what Commerce calls current-cost depreciation ought to be called current-cost replacement.

3.4 Empirical Comparisons of Alternative Measures of Depreciation and Their Implications

Table 3.3 presents annual estimates of historical-cost and current-cost depreciation in total manufacturing for 1947–74, prepared accord-

Table 3.3 **Alternative Estimates of Capital Consumption, Total Manufacturing, 1947–74 (in Billions of Dollars)**

		BEA		Coen				
				Economic Depreciation				Current-Cost Replacement
					Current Cost			
Year	Tax	Historical Cost	Current Cost	Historical Cost	A	B	C	
1947	2.422	2.286	3.276	2.513	8.817	4.471	3.413	3.371
1948	2.859	2.666	3.923	3.217	5.535	−0.947	4.232	4.060
1949	3.246	2.991	4.216	3.737	4.983	3.504	4.743	4.479
1950	3.497	3.287	4.562	3.990	7.934	7.585	5.124	4.823
1951	4.049	3.651	5.390	4.255	10.679	7.599	5.798	5.512
1952	4.703	4.055	5.794	4.802	7.989	2.415	6.287	5.938
1953	5.573	4.437	6.166	5.284	7.553	5.728	6.702	6.367
1954	6.378	4.828	6.449	5.756	7.288	6.374	7.082	6.721
1955	7.177	5.220	6.932	6.228	8.840	8.576	7.565	7.157
1956	7.747	5.679	7.858	6.643	14.106	12.715	8.463	8.116
1957	8.558	6.208	8.668	7.399	14.008	7.639	9.515	9.267
1958	9.110	6.659	9.003	8.076	10.373	5.477	9.995	9.665
1959	9.136	6.989	9.280	8.239	10.986	10.556	10.036	9.748
1960	9.680	7.364	9.517	8.407	10.650	9.637	10.069	9.733
1961	10.162	7.730	9.721	8.697	10.616	9.964	10.151	9.889
1962	11.998	8.082	9.951	8.890	11.525	11.037	10.252	9.867
1963	12.771	8.484	10.251	9.193	11.963	10.624	10.509	10.185
1964	13.688	8.948	10.659	9.589	13.053	11.531	10.917	10.666
1965	14.856	9.578	11.316	10.212	13.767	11.539	11.561	11.368

Table 3.3 (continued)

				Coen				
				Economic Depreciation				
		BEA			Current Cost			
Year	Tax	Historical Cost	Current Cost	Historical Cost	A	B	C	Current Cost Replacement
1966	16.127	10.448	12.378	11.244	15.782	13.493	12.745	12.748
1967	17.661	11.436	13.655	12.635	19.049	15.934	14.423	14.312
1968	19.393	12.413	14.835	13.939	20.770	15.926	16.052	15.692
1969	20.921	13.443	16.471	14.960	26.217	21.181	17.607	17.059
1970	22.099	14.459	18.162	16.138	29.276	19.716	19.474	18.784
1971	23.320	15.328	19.587	17.065	33.005	22.091	21.136	20.420
1972	24.813	16.255	20.716	17.629	27.865	14.597	21.786	21.097
1973	25.840	17.401	22.402	18.568	34.760	28.249	23.224	22.537
1974	27.364	18.791	25.416	20.165	45.959	33.138	26.535	25.733

ing to the procedures described in sections 3.2 and 3.3. The Commerce Department, or Bureau of Economic Analysis (BEA), estimates (from 1976*a*) appear in columns 2 and 3. My estimates, appearing in columns 4 through 7, represent aggregates of separately calculated equipment and structures estimates for the twenty-one subindustries shown in table 3.2. For comparative purposes, two additional series are included in the table—the BEA's tax-return measure of depreciation and my measure of current-cost replacement.

My historical-cost series exceeds the BEA's in every year, being about 10% higher in 1947 and 7% higher in 1974. Since my service lives for equipment are shorter on average than those assumed by Commerce and my depreciation patterns are generally more accelerated, this outcome was to be expected. Both historical-cost series display smoother growth over time than does the tax-return measure, since the latter is influenced by accelerated amortization during World War II and the Korean period, by the introduction of accelerated tax write-off methods in 1954, and by reductions in tax service lives in 1962 and 1971. According to either the BEA's estimates or my own, depreciation allowances for tax purposes began to substantially exceed consistently measured historical-cost depreciation about 1954, the excess growing to 36–46% by 1974.

As we saw above, the formula used by the BEA to calculate current-cost depreciation resembles the one that emerges in my case C, and we see in table 3.3 that these two measures of current-cost depreciation are empirically very similar. My case C current-cost depreciation somewhat exceeds the BEA's for the same reasons that my historical-cost depreciation exceeds the BEA's—shorter service lives for equipment and higher depreciation rates in the early years of the service lives.

On the other hand, variants A and B of my current-cost estimates differ radically from the BEA's, with the possible exception of the period of relatively stable prices from 1959 to 1964. For these cases of imperfect foresight, the rate of inflation of capital goods prices has a much more pronounced influence on measured depreciation. Inflation enlarges measured depreciation not only by raising proportionately the amount that would otherwise have been claimed in a given year, as in case C, but also by adjusting upward the depreciation claimed in prior years. In case A this latter adjustment is larger the higher the current inflation rate and will be negative when prices fall; in case B the adjustment is larger the larger the excess of the current over the lagged rate of inflation and will be negative when the rate of inflation declines. These adjustments result in wide fluctuations in measured depreciation, with variant B actually turning negative in 1948 because of the sharp decline in the rate of change of structures prices from 21% in 1947 to only 1% in 1948. Recall that by the assumptions of case B, the depreciation reserve at the end of 1947 would appreciate during 1948 at a rate equal to the 1947 rate of inflation; and given this substantial appreciation of the reserve, a negative addition to the reserve would be called for in 1948.

Although variant A exceeds the other current-cost measures in every year, there is no consistent relation between variants B and C. When the rate of inflation changes little from year to year, variants B and C are roughly the same; and when the inflation rate rises at a steady pace, variant B exceeds variant C. But when the inflation rate undergoes marked year-to-year changes, variant B is sometimes above and sometimes below variant C.

How do tax depreciation allowances measure up when compared with these consistent current-cost estimates of depreciation? It is often claimed that depreciation permitted for tax purposes has been inadequate in the inflationary environment of recent years, because tax regulations allow only the original cost of an asset to be written off. This deficiency of the tax laws may be more or less offset, however, by reductions in asset service lives for tax purposes or by acceleration of tax depreciation over the allowable service lives. The evidence in table 3.3 indicates that tax depreciation exceeded consistently measured current-cost depreciation during the period 1962–66, no matter which current-cost concept one chooses. After 1966, tax depreciation continues to exceed the BEA current-cost series and my variant C, but it drops below variant A beginning in 1967 and below variant B beginning in 1973. Thus, unless we believe that firms persistently expected a zero rate of inflation during the late 1960s and early 1970s—the assumption characterizing variant A, and one that seems rather implausible—we must conclude that reductions in tax service lives in 1962 and 1971 have, on the whole, more than compensated for the underdepreciation associated with historical-cost accounting for tax purposes. In any event, tax depreciation allowances in the 1960s and 1970s must certainly be regarded as generous when viewed relative to the situation in the 1940s and 1950s. Moreover, tax write-offs consistently exceeded current-cost replacement requirements since 1961; and although the ratio of tax depreciation to replacement requirements fell sharply in 1974, it still remained well above the levels prevailing before 1961.

Table 3.4 presents seven measures of profit-type income in manufacturing for 1947–74, each one derived using a depreciation series in table 3.3. In all cases, profit-type income is the return to capital net of capital consumption and interest, but before income taxes. The only ingredient that varies from one measure to another is the estimate of capital consumption. A profit-type income series corresponding to my current-cost replacement is not shown because, as I argued above,

Table 3.4 Alternative Estimates of Profit-type Income, Total Manufacturing, 1947–74 (in Billions of Dollars)

		BEA		Coen			
					Current-Cost Depreciation		
Year	Tax Depreciation	Historical-Cost Depreciation	Current-Cost Depreciation	Historical-Cost Depreciation	A	B	C
1947	13.129	13.265	12.275	13.038	6.734	11.080	12.138
1948	16.244	16.437	15.180	15.886	13.568	20.050	14.871
1949	15.353	15.608	14.383	14.862	13.616	15.095	13.856
1950	19.786	19.996	18.721	19.293	15.349	15.698	18.159
1951	23.569	23.967	22.228	23.363	16.939	20.019	21.820
1952	20.845	21.493	19.754	20.746	17.559	23.133	19.261
1953	21.007	22.143	20.414	21.296	19.027	20.852	19.878
1954	18.396	19.946	18.325	19.018	17.486	18.400	17.692
1955	24.137	26.094	24.382	25.086	22.474	22.738	23.749
1956	22.525	24.593	22.414	23.629	16.166	17.557	21.809
1957	21.880	24.230	21.770	23.039	16.430	22.799	20.923
1958	17.425	19.876	17.532	18.459	16.162	21.058	16.540
1959	24.231	26.378	24.087	25.128	22.381	22.811	23.331
1960	22.164	24.480	22.327	23.437	21.194	22.207	21.775
1961	21.031	23.463	21.481	22.496	20.577	21.229	21.042
1962	23.822	27.738	25.869	26.930	24.295	24.783	25.568
1963	26.646	30.933	29.166	30.224	27.454	28.793	28.908
1964	29.516	34.256	32.545	33.615	30.151	31.673	32.287
1965	35.711	40.989	39.251	40.355	36.800	39.028	39.006

Table 3.4 (continued)

		BEA		Coen			
					Current-Cost Depreciation		
Year	Tax Depreciation	Historical-Cost Depreciation	Current-Cost Depreciation	Historical-Cost Depreciation	A	B	C
1966	38.705	44.384	42.454	43.588	39.050	41.339	42.087
1967	34.574	40.799	38.580	39.600	33.186	36.301	37.812
1968	37.277	44.257	41.835	42.731	35.900	40.744	40.618
1969	32.473	39.951	36.923	38.434	27.177	32.213	35.787
1970	22.501	30.141	26.438	28.462	15.324	24.884	25.126
1971	27.637	35.629	31.370	33.892	17.952	28.866	29.821
1972	34.961	43.519	39.058	42.145	31.909	45.177	37.988
1973	35.278	43.717	38.716	42.550	26.358	32.869	37.894
1974	22.788	31.361	24.736	29.987	4.193	17.014	23.617

Note: Profit-type income is gross product originating minus employee compensation, net interest, indirect business taxes, and depreciation.

current-cost replacement is not an appropriate measure of capital consumption for purposes of income measurement.

The two profits series based on historical-cost depreciation are relatively similar, reflecting the similarity of the depreciation estimates. They both remain very close to tax-based profits until 1954, but liberalizations of tax write-offs thereafter lead to growing excesses of consistently measured profits over tax-based profits. By 1974, taxable profits are understating consistently measured profits by 24–27%.

Profits based on the BEA's current-cost depreciation and my variant C display a very different pattern. They fall roughly in line with taxable profits until 1962 and exceed taxable profits for the rest of the period. The excesses are not as great as for the BEA's historical-cost series, but they are sizable, even in 1974.

Profits based on my variant A approximate taxable profits only during the period 1958–67. Aside from a few other isolated years, this series is well below taxable profits as well as the other estimates. Profits are generally acknowledged to be highly unstable, and it is interesting to note how the inflation-adjusted depreciation modifies their instability in this case. The post–World War II recessions or retardations before 1967 were usually periods of deflation or decelerating inflation, either of which tends to moderate the growth of current-cost depreciation in case A and therefore attenuates the decline in profits. This is clearly evident in table 3.4. Taxable profits declined by 5.5% in the 1949 recession, 12.4% in the 1954 recession, and 20.4% in the 1958 recession, but the inflation-adjusted measure rose by 0.4% in 1949 and declined by only 8.1% and 1.6% in 1954 and 1958. When recession is accompanied by inflation or accelerating inflation as in recent years, however, the inflation adjustment leads to more marked deterioration in profits. The most notable example of this is, of course, 1974.

Profits based on my variant B resemble most closely those associated with variant C. When the inflation rate changes sharply, however, the two series part company, as in 1948, 1952, 1956–58, and 1972–74. Since we assume in case B that firms adjust their price expectations in line with their most recent experience, depreciation rises less rapidly in recent years and profits decline less dramatically than in case A. Nonetheless, both case A and case B profits fall substantially below taxable profits in 1974, unlike case C profits or the BEA series.

The BEA's estimates of depreciated stocks of fixed capital are shown in the first two columns of table 3.5, and my estimates of book value of fixed capital appear in the last two columns. It should be recalled that my measure of book value is independent of the price-expectations hypothesis adopted; hence, the current-cost series shown in the last column of table 3.5 is appropriate to cases A, B, and C. Although the four variants are at different levels, their average annual growth rates

Table 3.5 **Alternative Estimates of Book Value of Equipment and Structures, Total Manufacturing, 1947–74 (in Billions of Dollars at End of Year)**

	BEA		Coen	
Year	Historical-Cost Valuation	Current-Cost Valuation	Historical-Cost Valuation	Current-Cost Valuation
1947	27.5	40.2	25.2	33.4
1948	32.0	45.7	29.4	37.9
1949	34.7	47.8	31.4	39.3
1950	37.0	52.6	33.2	42.4
1951	41.3	58.9	37.0	49.2
1952	45.3	62.2	40.4	52.6
1953	49.1	64.5	43.4	55.0
1954	52.6	67.3	46.2	56.6
1955	56.0	73.3	48.9	59.1
1956	61.7	82.1	53.7	66.9
1957	67.6	87.7	58.6	73.5
1958	70.7	88.9	60.3	73.6
1959	72.8	89.5	61.3	73.6
1960	75.6	90.7	63.2	74.2
1961	77.8	91.5	64.6	74.5
1962	80.2	93.1	66.5	76.0
1963	83.2	95.6	68.9	78.3
1964	87.6	100.1	72.8	82.5
1965	94.7	108.6	79.4	89.4
1966	104.5	121.1	88.6	99.5
1967	114.6	133.6	97.6	110.7
1968	122.9	146.5	104.4	119.8
1969	131.8	162.5	112.1	132.8
1970	139.6	176.1	118.3	144.8
1971	145.2	185.1	122.3	155.7
1972	151.7	195.6	127.5	162.2
1973	162.2	216.0	136.9	177.2
1974	176.0	245.2	149.5	199.8

over the entire period are very similar—7.1, 6.9, 6.8, and 6.8%, respectively. However, while each historical-cost variant grows at about the same rate over the subperiods 1947–65 and 1965–74, the current-cost variants grow only about three-fifths as fast in the first subperiod as in the second. The current-cost variants grow especially slowly relative to the historical-cost variants over the period of generally stable prices from 1957 to 1963. It is apparent from these comparisons that differences in service lives and basic depreciation patterns produce only minor variations in the estimates of growth of value of capital. What does produce large variations in the estimates is the valuation basis.

Combining the estimates of profit-type income and value of fixed capital, we can finally arrive at estimates of the rate of return on capital in manufacturing. To calculate the rate of return, we add net interest to profit-type income (table 3.4) and divide the result by the value of total capital—fixed capital (table 3.5) plus inventories. The value of capital is centered at the middle of the year by taking the average of beginning- and end-of-year figures. Omitted from the total capital estimates are land and any residential structures that might be owned by manufacturing firms. The rate of return is gross of income taxes.

Table 3.6 presents rate of return estimates for six variants of profit-type income and value of fixed assets. Table 3.7 shows the same series in index form with 1951 = 100, 1951 being the year in which four of the six series reach their peaks. Because the rate of return estimate for variant B in 1948 is abnormally disturbed by the extraordinary decline in the rate of change of structures prices, 1948 is omitted from table 3.7.

We might first note that the two historical-cost series are generally similar in both level and movement over time. The only notable differences in their fluctuations occur during the business expansions of the mid-1950s and mid-1960 when my historical-cost measure rises more briskly than the BEA's.

The current-cost measures of the rate of return are consistently below the historical-cost measures. Among the current-cost measures, the BEA series and my variant C differ only slightly in level and display nearly identical fluctuations. Relative to the historical-cost measures, they both indicate a more substantial increase in the rate of return from the late fifties to the mid-sixties and a more marked decline in the rate of return in 1974. On the whole, however, the cyclical patterns of these two current-cost series are not radically different from those found in the historical-cost series.

Variants A and B of my current-cost measures tell quite a different story. They both reach their peaks in 1965 rather than 1951, and they show greater resilience in the recessions of 1949, 1954, and 1958 than do the other measures. On the other hand, the combination of recession and high inflation in 1974 produces a more dramatic decline in these variants, with variant A dipping to only 16% of its 1951 level. These results reveal that an inflation adjustment that does not assume perfect foresight tends to moderate movements in the rate of return when prices rise or fall in parallel with general business activity; by the same token, such an inflation adjustment tends to accentuate movements in the rate of return when prices move in a direction contrary to that of general business activity.

Table 3.6 **Alternative Estimates of Gross Rate of Return, Total Manufacturing, 1948–74 (Percentage)**

	BEA		Coen			
				Current-Cost Valuation		
Year	Historical-Cost Valuation	Current-Cost Valuation	Historical-Cost Valuation	A	B	C
1948	28.8	21.6	29.1	21.6	31.9	23.6
1949	25.7	19.4	25.7	20.6	22.8	21.0
1950	30.8	23.6	31.4	21.9	22.4	25.9
1951	32.1	24.3	33.1	20.8	24.6	26.8
1952	25.7	19.6	26.3	19.3	25.4	21.2
1953	24.7	19.3	25.2	19.8	21.7	20.7
1954	21.4	16.9	21.8	17.8	18.7	18.0
1955	26.7	21.4	27.6	22.2	22.4	23.4
1956	23.1	17.9	23.8	14.6	15.9	19.7
1957	21.0	16.1	21.6	13.6	18.9	17.3
1958	16.8	12.8	17.0	13.2	17.2	13.5
1959	21.7	17.4	22.7	17.4	18.5	18.9
1960	19.4	15.8	20.5	16.9	17.7	17.4
1961	18.2	15.1	19.4	16.3	16.8	16.7
1962	20.8	17.7	22.5	18.8	19.2	19.8
1963	22.3	19.3	24.2	20.5	21.5	21.6
1964	23.7	20.8	25.8	21.7	22.7	23.2
1965	26.7	23.6	29.1	24.8	26.3	26.3
1966	26.5	23.3	28.7	24.2	25.6	26.0
1967	22.5	19.6	24.0	19.0	20.7	21.5
1968	22.8	19.6	24.1	19.0	21.4	21.3
1969	19.8	16.5	21.0	14.1	16.4	18.1
1970	15.4	12.1	16.0	8.9	12.9	13.1
1971	16.9	13.1	17.8	9.4	13.7	14.1
1972	19.5	15.2	20.9	14.3	19.4	16.7
1973	18.5	14.1	19.9	11.6	13.9	15.6
1974	12.4	8.5	13.1	3.3	7.3	9.3

Note: Gross rate of return equals profit income plus net interest divided by the average of book values of assets (equipment, structures, and inventories) at the beginning and end of the year.

No matter which series one considers, it is evident that the rate of return on capital has fallen to very low levels in recent years. Does this experience indicate in part a secular decline in the rate of return? I think not. Aside from the historical-cost measures, which are in principle unsatisfactory, in the mid-1960s the estimated rates of return all reach levels that are high by historical standards. If the economy can once again attain high real growth with moderate inflation, the rate of return, appropriately measured, will probably recover to more normal post–World War II levels.

Table 3.7 Alternative Estimates of Gross Rate of Return, Total Manufacturing, 1949–74 (Indexes, 1951 = 100)

	BEA		Coen			
				Current-Cost Valuation		
Year	Historical-Cost Valuation	Current-Cost Valuation	Historical-Cost Valuation	A	B	C
1949	80	80	78	99	93	78
1950	96	97	95	105	91	97
1951	100	100	100	100	100	100
1952	80	81	79	93	103	79
1953	77	79	76	95	88	77
1954	67	70	66	86	76	67
1955	83	88	83	107	91	87
1956	72	74	72	70	65	74
1957	65	66	65	65	77	65
1958	52	53	51	63	70	50
1959	68	72	69	84	75	71
1960	60	65	62	81	72	65
1961	57	62	59	78	68	62
1962	65	73	68	90	78	74
1963	69	79	73	99	87	81
1964	74	86	78	104	92	87
1965	83	97	88	119	107	98
1966	83	96	87	116	104	97
1967	70	81	73	91	84	80
1968	71	81	73	91	87	79
1969	62	68	63	68	67	68
1970	48	50	48	43	52	49
1971	53	54	54	45	56	53
1972	61	63	63	69	79	62
1973	58	58	60	56	57	58
1974	39	35	40	16	30	35

3.5 Concluding Remarks

The statistical results of the previous section indicate that different procedures for estimating depreciation can lead to substantially different assessments of tax depreciation policy and economic performance. Although the choice of asset service lives and depreciation patterns are of some importance, they seem on the whole to be less critical than the formulation of a current-cost concept of depreciation. We have seen that the Commerce Department's concept is appropriate provided, among other things, that firms can either (*a*) perfectly predict the rate of inflation or (*b*) imperfectly predict the rate of inflation but realize appreciation of their depreciation reserves at a rate equal to the actual rate of inflation. Of course, considerable uncertainly surrounds the choice of a price expectations hypothesis and the selection of a valuation procedure for depreciation reserves. I have not attempted to resolve these issues but only tried to highlight their importance and investigate the empirical implications of alternative approaches. With regard to price expectations, I suspect that my case A (the expected inflation rate is always zero) is as unrealistic as the assumption of perfect foresight; case B, or a more complicated form of adaptive expectations, is probably closer to the truth.

Another troublesome set of assumptions which I have explicitly adopted and which the Commerce Department implicitly adopts is that the expected real rate of return on capital is constant and that the expected nominal rate of return equals the real rate plus the expected rate of inflation. The effect of these assumptions is to introduce constancy in the ratios of product prices to capital goods prices; that is, capital goods prices rise or fall at the same rate as product prices. But this is not generally the case in reality; and while there is obviously something wrong with one or both of these assumptions, there are no obvious, workable alternatives to them. It seems that attempts at greater realism in these areas are likely to make an already complex problem a hopelessly complex one.

Notes

1. The revised accounts are presented and discussed in U.S. Department of Commerce (1976*b*). The new approach to measuring capital consumption is described in detail in Young (1975).

2. The service lives tested generally ranged from eight to twenty-two years in increments of two years for equipment and twenty to fifty years in increments of five years for structures. Five alternative loss-of-efficiency patterns were tested: (1) geometric decay at a rate equal to twice the reciprocal of the service life; (2) geometric decay as in (1), but truncated at the end of the service life; (3) a sum-of-years digits pattern; (4) a "one-horse-shay" pattern; and (5) a straight-line pattern. The lives and patterns reported in table 3.1 differ in many instances from those reported in Coen (1975). The current results are derived from somewhat revised data, particularly with regard to tax depreciation parameters (a 1971 Treasury survey of depreciation practices provided more up-to-date information on the parameters); also, they are based both on goodness of fit over the sample period 1949–66 and on accuracy in postsample predictions for 1967–71, whereas the earlier results were based solely on the former.

3. The weights used in computing these averages are proportional to capital expenditures in 1966.

4. In the empirical implementation of equations (20) and (21), it is assumed that r, which represents firms' marginal after-tax rate of discount or desired after-tax marginal rate of return on investments, is constant at a value of 10%

per year. Thus, changes in market rates of interest are assumed not to influence firms' valuations of their fixed assets.

5. Associated with this measure of real replacement is a measure of real capital stock, namely,

$$K_{t\tau} = (I_\tau / c_\tau) - \sum_{j=\tau+1}^{t} R_{j\tau}.$$

Summing $K_{t\tau}$ over all vintages yields a measure of the productive capacity of assets on hand at the end of period t. This is the appropriate measure of capital for analyzing production and real investment decisions.

References

Coen, R. M. 1974. Revised estimates of service lives and capacity depreciation patterns of manufacturing equipment and structures. Prepared for the Office of Tax Analysis, U.S. Treasury Department.

———. 1975. Investment behavior, the measurement of depreciation, and tax policy. *American Economic Review*, March, pp. 59–74.

Gorman, J. A. 1972. Nonfinancial corporations: New measures of output and input. *Survey of Current Business* 52 (March): 21–27, 33.

Hicks, J. R. 1946. *Value and capital*. 2d ed. Oxford: Clarendon Press.

U.S. Department of Commerce. Bureau of Economic Analysis. 1976*a*. *Fixed nonresidential business and residential capital in the United States, 1925–75*. National Technical Information Service, PB 253 725, June.

———. 1976*b*. The national income and product accounts of the United States: Revised estimates, 1929–74. *Survey of Current Business* 56 (January), parts 1 and 2.

U.S. Department of Commerce. Office of Business Economics. 1971. *Fixed nonresidential business capital in the United States, 1925–1970*. National Technical Information Service, COM-71-01111, November.

Young, A. H. 1975. New estimates of capital consumption allowances in the benchmark revision of GNP. *Survey of Current Business* 55 (October): 14–16, 33.

Comment Solomon Fabricant

Professor Coen seeks to measure capital and rates of return by considering how capital consumption enters into the determination of gross

Solomon Fabricant has been associated with New York University and the National Bureau of Economic Research.

capital formation. His approach is ingenious and theoretically appealing. I hope that further work along this line will lead to improvement in the underlying theory and in the data required to apply the theory, and thus eventually to measures deserving of serious consideration. His present measures, however, are not ready to be substituted for those of the Bureau of Economic Analysis (or existing modifications of the BEA's measures), uneasy though we may be with the latter.

Coen starts by noting that businessmen buy the plant and equipment they need with two objectives in mind. One is to replace the assets used up through depreciation, obsolescence, and other forms of capital consumption. The second is to meet the increase in capacity required by increased production. He knows past output and past plant and equipment expenditures, of course. Using these, and a function embodying a neoclassical theory of investment, he estimates the net investment or increase in the capital stock required by the changes in output. The difference between this net investment and the gross investment actually made must be the capital consumption recognized by the businessmen. He then asks, in effect, which among a set of forty possible mortality distributions—combinations of eight asset service lives and five depreciation patterns—would on the average yield a capital consumption allowance series closest to the derived capital consumption series. The calculations are done in real terms, for twenty-one separate manufacturing industries, over the period 1949–66, separately for equipment and for structures.

The procedure and the investment theory underlying it are set forth in Coen's paper in the *American Economic Review* (March 1975), to which the reader must turn if he is to understand the approach. It is sufficient here to recall that Coen assumes, first, a Cobb-Douglas production function. This is readily transposed into an investment function in which desired capital depends on output and the ratio of output price to the price (rental value) of capital's services. He assumes, second, that competition is sufficient to make the marginal product of capital's services equal to their price. And, third, he assumes that the rental price depends on the mortality distribution and the discount rate or rate of interest required to finance net investment (in what is a generalization of the Jorgenson function), with the discount rate assumed to be 10% for all years and industries. Inserting each of the various mortality distributions into his function, in accordance with this procedure, yields a standard error of estimate for each distribution. The best-fitting mortality distribution is the one indicated by the investment behavior of businessmen.

Coen states explicitly that the better mortality distributions are very close to one another, by his test; it cannot be claimed that the one chosen—the best or closest—is more than "marginally superior" to the others. He goes on to suggest, therefore, that "a more discerning test" would use postsample predictions. Disturbing changes in the ranking of the mortality distributions result when, in this paper, he applies his more discerning test to the data for 1967–71. In fact, half of the "best" distributions relating to equipment are no longer those in the *AER* paper, and this is true of two-thirds of those for construction. Also, the differences are often not of the sort suggested in the *AER* paper, namely that a short service life plus a slow depreciation of capacity is roughly equivalent to a long service life plus a fast capacity depreciation. In other words, the more discerning test raises some serious questions about the stability of the results produced by the theory and procedures Coen utilizes.

Coen goes on to make an important distinction between loss of value and loss of efficiency (or productive capacity) as an asset ages. (Coen mentions only aging, but he must mean also the obsolescence that occurs with the passage of time, as well as the wear and tear.) Loss of value reflects not only loss of efficiency but also decline in remaining life, and is a better measure of *economic* depreciation. A corresponding distinction is made between productive capacity and economic value of the capital stock.

It is worth taking a moment to make the distinction clear. Assume no change in the price of an asset over time, and consider a one-horse shay suffering no loss of efficiency by aging, except when the shay finally collapses. Yet there is economic depreciation as it ages; its economic value declines, although its efficiency and gross rental price do not. We may suppose, further, that the businessman owning and operating the shay would think of his net rate of return on the *economic* value of the shay as constant over its life. This implies that his net income is the constant gross rental of the shay minus a *rising* depreciation allowance. Only then will the declining net income, divided by the declining economic value of the shay, be constant. It may be noticed that if at the same time there is a decline in efficiency with age, economic depreciation inclusive of this decline in efficiency may rise less rapidly than in the one-horse-shay case. It may, in fact, remain more or less constant (and reasonably well approximated by a straight-line formula), or it may even decline.

Coen next considers the effect of increases in the prices of capital goods and their significance for calculating the current value of the capital stock and the rate of return. Rather than retrace his steps in arriving at his results, let me indicate what these results look like. The "current-cost depreciation" in the third year of a three-year-old asset is the sum of the historical-cost depreciation in the third year revalued to the current price level, *plus* the amount needed to adjust the first and second years' revalued depreciation to the third, current year's price level. Eventually, as Coen notes, the sum of depreciation charges so calculated will equal the dollar amount needed to replace the asset when it is retired. I suspect here a tendency by Coen to think of the depreciation reserve as a fund held in dollars or fixed-income securities, and of the need to include in the third year's depreciation the loss in purchasing power of the fund (expressed in terms of the price of the particular asset, not of the general price level). In any case, as Coen's table 3.3 shows, current-cost economic depreciation, so derived, is much greater in most years than the BEA's current cost, although in terms of historical cost the two series differ by a much more modest (and stable) amount.

I must admit I have strong doubts that Coen's estimates make sense. I agree with his third assumption, that the economic value of a capital good is (or tends to be) equal to the present value of the expected stream of net money returns it will produce. This is, indeed, the basis of the presumption in the Hulten-Wykoff paper that secondhand values of capital goods provide useful information on economic capital and capital consumption. But I cannot swallow, let alone digest, his other assumptions. As Coen is frank enough to admit, his present assumptions are necessarily somewhat arbitrary. Perhaps they will become more palatable as he proceeds in his research program.

To conclude: Coen's basic idea is intelligent and is consistent with the view that depreciation, profits, investment, and other variables are interrelated. But I have some questions—those already mentioned and some others: about the distinction between maintenance and capital expenditures; the treatment of subsoil assets (Soladay's worry), which is not a negligible item in one or two of the manufacturing groups; the measurement of depreciation as a function of volume of output; and the implications, for the effective application of Coen's procedures and the stability of his results, of Millard Hastay's and other papers in the Universities–National Bureau Committee's conference on the *Regularization of Investment*, published some twenty years ago.

As I have already implied, I look forward to the results of Coen's efforts to extend and improve his interesting analysis.

4 New Books on the Measurement of Capital

Stanley Engerman and Sherwin Rosen

In this chapter we review two recent books: R. J. Gordon, *The Measurement of Durable Goods Prices* (forthcoming), and J. W. Kendrick, *The Formation and Stocks of Total Capital* (1976). The central problems discussed in both books concern conceptually better and more accurate measurement of the input and output of capital stock and the related issue of defining investment. Gordon's chief interest is the technical problem of measuring improvements in the productive capacity of capital goods and the problem of obtaining quality-adjusted investment goods price deflators to provide better measures of real investment and capital stock. His estimates show substantially larger growth of real capital than those generally available. Kendrick's book is wider in scope and presents estimates of a broad view of investment including measures of intangible as well as tangible human capital, which are then used to explain increased output and economic growth in the economy in a way familiar to readers of his earlier works on productivity trends. Kendrick's work represents the most complete test to date of a hypothesis, attributable to T. W. Schultz, that an inclusive measure of the growth of capital stock should be able to account for the entire growth of output. His estimates of total factor productivity growth based on this concept of capital are lower than previous estimates and lend some support to the hypothesis. But unmeasured factors still affect productivity growth. More controversial and uncertain owing to biases in both directions, is Kendrick's empirical result that the rate of return (both gross and net) on human capital exceeded the rate of return on nonhuman capital investment throughout most of the 1929–69 period.

Stanley Engerman is associated with the University of Rochester. Sherwin Rosen is associated with the University of Chicago and the National Bureau of Economic Research.

The authors wish to thank Jeffrey Williamson for comments on an earlier draft and Chitra Ramaswami for research help while we were preparing this paper.

Our comments will be within the rules and conventions of the approaches taken by the authors; thus we shall not ascend to the ethereal heights of the various Cambridge controversies about the theory and measurement of capital.

Both topics have long histories in the theoretical and empirical literature on growth accounting. The proper adjustments for quality change in capital goods have been a major source of controversy for the past two decades of discussion on the sources of economic growth, although the classic article by Denison (1957) precedes this debate by a few years. The position taken by Gordon figured extensively in the debate between Jorgenson-Griliches and Denison,[1] and he both clarifies some of the theoretical issues and produces many detailed measurements and imputations of quality change across a broad spectrum of goods, commodity-by-commodity. The broader definitions of capital proposed by Kendrick have even a longer history. The measurement of tangible human capital, as identified by Kiker (1968), goes back to the pioneer national income accountant William Petty, whose estimates were first published in 1691. Discussion of the conception and estimation of various intangible human components has persisted ever since, and it is probably T. W. Schultz's work in the late 1950s that focused attention on the measurement of the stock of education. While many have appealed to the various components of human and nonhuman intangibles as plausible explanations for "the residual," Kendrick's book represents the most detailed empirical calculations and discussion to date of measuring the amounts and effects of these intangible investments.

Kendrick's central conception of capital rests on the value of resources that society has devoted out of past production to provide for future outputs. First, he broadens the Department of Commerce concept of capital to include stocks of consumer durables and government capital, as well as business tangible physical capital. Second, he calculates several components of tangible and intangible human capital, as well as the intangible value of knowledge specifically created by research and development. The components of human capital include rearing costs, education and training, health, migration, and search, which are usually treated in the official accounts as parts of consumption or as current business expenses. Moreover, some component elements involve imputations for opportunity costs and are ignored in official accounts, while expenditures on research and development either are treated as parts of government expenditure or written off as business expenses. Thus Kendrick's work includes two major types of calculations. First, he reallocates certain items of GNP from consumption to investment. These reallocations more than double the investment-income ratios in the official accounts. Second, he makes imputations for various consumption and intangible investment items. These imputations increase measured investment, but they also increase measured GNP and have a lesser effect on investment-income ratios than the reallocations (see table 4.1).

Table 4.1 **Breakdown of Expenditure Categories, Kendrick's Adjustments and Official GNP, 1929 and 1948**

	1929	Reclassified		1948	Reclassified	
Category	Official GNP (1)	Official GNP (2)	Adjusted GNP (3)	Official GNP (1)	Official GNP (2)	Adjusted GNP (3)
Consumption	77.22	54.10	64.84	173.56	125.00	146.04
Investment	16.23	45.25	54.92	46.01	111.87	139.89
Tangible nonhuman	16.23	29.19	29.47	46.01	75.73	76.63
Tangible human		9.77	9.77		18.28	18.28
Intangible nonhuman and human		6.29	15.69		17.86	44.98
Government	8.50	2.60	6.43	31.55	14.25	35.30
Net exports	1.15	1.15	1.15	6.44	6.44	6.44
Total	103.10	103.10	127.34	257.56	257.56	327.67

Sources:
(1) U.S. Department of Commerce, *The National Income and Product Accounts of the United States, 1929–1965* (Washington, D.C., 1966), table 1.1.
(2) Kendrick (1976, tables 2-1 and 2-1a).
(3) Kendrick (1976, table 2-1).

In essence Kendrick's methods embody in their respective categories specific items that previously have been considered to generate productivity change and account for the residual. It should be noted, however, that his procedures for human capital are somewhat different from those used by Denison,[2] though their measures of physical capital basically are the same. Indeed, Kendrick's treatment of labor inputs differs from his own earlier treatment (Kendrick 1961, 1974; see table 4.2). Both Kendrick and Denison rely on the OBE concepts and measures for physical capital, which apparently capture only a small part, if any, of quality improvements. For human inputs Kendrick follows most of the literature by differentiating the scale of labor input in the form of "raw bodies" from "improved bodies" owing to additional education and training, better health, and so on. His measure of the education component of human capital is based upon costs of schooling, while Denison and most others have used cross-sectional income-education profiles to compute standardized labor input indexes. His treatment of raw bodies imputes investment values to cohorts of persons under fourteen years of age, based upon consumption values and other resources devoted to them. Increased consumption by children in a cohort implicitly

Table 4.2 Selected Measures of "Labor Input," 1948 to 1966 Relative to 1929

Measure	1948[a]	1966[b]
1. Population	120.0	160.6
2. Labor force	129.3	164.3
3. Kendrick		
Persons engaged	126.9	158.8
Man-hours	109.2	129.4
Labor input	119.6	151.1
4. Denison		
Employment-total	126.9	163.3
Employment-NRB	122.9	143.3
Hours-NRB	106.2	115.2
Education NRB	112.1	125.1
Total labor input-NRB	130.2	159.2
5. Kendrick		
Gross human tangible	145.8	246.3
Gross education and training	184.3	366.5
Total gross human capital stock	164.5	308.2
Net human tangible	129.9	240.0
Net education and training	172.2	337.5
Total net human capital stock	152.3	293.3
Total net human capital stock employed in private domestic business economy	168.1	287.1
Total net human capital stock utilized in private domestic economy	147.5	242.4

Sources: Rows 1 and 2: U.S. Department of Commerce, *Historical Statistics of the*
Row 3: Kendrick (1974), pp. 236, 237.
Row 3: Kendrick (1174), pp. 236, 237.
Row 4: Denison (1974), pp. 11, 32 (NRB is Nonresidential Business).
Row 5: Kendrick (1976), Appendix B (Constant Price Estimates).

[a]1929 = 100 for each row.

[b]The lower age cutoff for the labor force (row 2) changed from 1929 to the later years, but the extent of understatement is minor.

allows for quality change in the production of a labor force: the average raw body in the labor force in 1966 is considered to be about 50% larger than the average body in 1929.[3] Those "quality" changes in human investment output that are due to increased measured inputs in their production are incorporated in human capital formation. However, the embodiment of technical change in the physical capital index is imperfect owing to the nature of official investment goods price deflators. The same is true for intangible business capital and its deflator (based on salaries and foregone earnings of research personnel). Note that no allowance for "quality" change in addition to increased costs is imputed. For example, education is considered more productive only when it uses more costly inputs, and no additional output of the educational sector due to increased efficiency in the transmission of new knowledge is allowed.

The major conclusions following from Kendrick's adjustments are that society's provisions for the future have been considerably greater than indicated by the conventional investment-income ratios, and that, in the 1929–69 period, the share of output devoted to investment was increasing because of the growth of intangible investment in humans. Nevertheless, it is still true that the growth of output has exceeded the growth in even this broadly defined capital stock, so that the residual, while lowered, remains. Moreover, cyclical variations in total investment and in the augmented investment-income ratio are less than for the conventionally measured, since the short-run fluctuations in human capital investment are considerably less than in nonhuman goods.

The measurement of physical capital stock forms the basic issue in Gordon's book, which attempts to improve upon conventional physical investment goods price deflators and obtain better measures of real nonhuman investment. More generally, Gordon raises a question of major importance in all national income accounting: What is the definition of a commodity? Is the appropriate definitional unit some generic or specific physical good, or should it be some underlying set of performance characteristics among the class that yields utility or future services? To use Gordon's example, is the desired good a computer measured at cost, or is it the potential number of calculations performed? Is the relevant unit a car or, as is familiar from many studies, a combination of comfort, speed, braking time, and so forth? A similar example given by Griliches and quoted by Gordon is the appropriate definition of output in the birth control sector, where it has been found that the same contraceptive results can be achieved with smaller doses of pills, an improvement in productivity not adequately measured by cost-related indexes and a point that is easily generalized to have broader implications for Kendrick's measurement of the stock of health capital. Gordon's main point is that the transactional units of account—dollars worth of computers, cars, pills, and so on—are not appropriate for growth accounting because they embody arbitrary and changing packages of productive characteristics and that a more appropriate definition should be based on some invariant set of *performance characteristics*. Moreover, Gordon implements these methods by using several modern variants of familiar standardized comparisons of new and old equipment. First, implicit prices of the invariant characteristics of capital goods are imputed from market price data on the transactional units and the performance attributes embodied in them. Then the imputations are used to compute quality-adjusted price indexes that finally are used to deflate capital value expenditures and obtain the desired quality-adjusted real investment indexes.

In this Gordon is carrying on a running battle with several government statistical agencies, but it is often unclear whether the replies to his kind of critique are based on principle or practicality. Thus at times it seems there is acceptance of the usefulness of the concept of quality-adjusted output; but there are also reservations about the practicalities of making adjustments that seem so complex as to be of little use in preparing national income statistics, and there is skepticism about the results to date, which often vary dramatically from study to study. Further, it is important to distinguish issues relating to measurement procedures from questions of the specific magnitude and direction of bias.[4] It does seem that under clearly specified conditions some quality changes are picked up by the conventional deflators. Thus, in cases where two related capital goods of different productive capacity are available in the market at the same time, relative costs are used to provide a quality-corrected linking. This procedure, however, apparently is performed in only a small number of cases, and there remain conceptual problems about the best time for such a linking. For example, if relative costs of production of new goods systematically decline, as is familiar from "learning curve" phenomena, the later the date when the linking is made, the smaller is the measured allowance for quality change. A second case in which quality changes are incorporated by conventional methods is when the improvement is embodied in a specific component that can be separately costed, such as seat belts. Gordon argues, however, that these varieties represent only a minor part of the total, and that conventional procedures therefore omit the bulk of quality improvements in capital goods. By extension, the same is true of consumption goods accounting as well. Given Gordon's analysis of the quality of consumer durable goods, it seems that Kendrick's imputed consumption from this stock is understated. More generally, any attempts to quality-adjust consumer nondurables and services no doubt would have a similar effect. Since the proper adjustment of consumption goods for quality change is not central to Gordon's work, we have not read his adjustments of the investment goods deflators as having any implications for possible differential biases in consumer and investment price indexes.

Gordon's major empirical result is that the rate of growth of the conventional investment price deflator has been too large by several percentage points: there has been a greater rate of quality change over time than is measured by the official accountants (see table 4.3). Consequently, measured growth in capital formation in the areas discussed—producer and consumer durables, autos, and construction—has been severely understated, and their real price increases have been overstated.

It should be noted that neither study provides estimates of broader definitions of GNP, such as the concept of Net Economic Welfare (NEW). Thus there are no direct imputations for the value of housewives' time, leisure, urban amenities and disamenities, changed working conditions, and other consumption aspects of work.[5] In part this reflects

Table 4.3 **Annual Percentage Rates of Change of Gordon's New Alternative Price Index and of Real Investment in Producers Durable Equipment Relative to Official NIA Measures, 1947–70**

	1947–57	1957–70	1947–70
Average deflator for all products			
Official NIA deflator	3.5	1.7	2.4
New alternative index	−0.2	−1.2	−0.7
New minus official	−3.7	−2.9	−3.1
Real investment in producers durable equipment			
Official NIA series	2.9	4.6	3.9
New alternative series	6.7	7.7	7.2
New minus official	3.8	3.1	3.3

Source: Robert J. Gordon, *The Measurement of Durable Goods Prices* (forthcoming).

an issue of principle: Kendrick justifies some omissions on the grounds that he is interested mainly in the production relationships in the economy. This point of view would be most appropriate if these unpriced commodities were "pure" consumption goods completely separable from the measured components. But this assumption about technology and the nature of inputs is too narrow, since such strong separability cannot be maintained. For example, Denison has noted that increased leisure affects worker productivity. But so do providing tickets to ball games, better personnel management, more frequent tea or coffee breaks, and air conditioning. Of course, some of these appear in the accounts as part of other components (air conditioning would be an investment), but corresponding consumption values generally are ignored. Indeed, a neglected major aspect of the entire genre of growth-accounting studies has been the analysis of changing quality of working conditions and the increased value of what is best labeled on-the-job consumption.[6]

Analytically the treatment would be similar to Gordon's measurement of quality change of physical capital, but using different aspects of work activities as the invariant characteristics. Strictly speaking, estimated potential income should be based upon the maximum pecuniary income each member of the population can earn (presumably evaluated at the base period average job quality), not on their actual job selections, which represent transactions in consumption aspects of work and therefore exclude increasingly important values of nonpecuniary income. While some of these issues lie beyond the scope of Kendrick's study, there remain others, concerning the value of housewives' time, and particularly time spent in child-rearing, that do not. Within the spirit of the imputations of foregone earnings for students, an allowance should be made for changing labor force participation of mothers as well as time lost during pregnancy (and maternal death rates), surely among the more important investments made in the course of childbearing.[7] Indeed, could not some of the male-female differential in earnings be regarded as a long-term cost of childbearing? More generally, as market goods are substituted for nonmarket goods (the contemporary analogy to Pigou's example would be the wife who used to provide meals at home but who now works for a fast-food chain and brings home payment in kind), there is a spurious increase in measured output, although since measured input is also increased (spuriously) the net effect on measured productivity change is not transparent.

Gordon's substantive contribution to the growth productivity accounting literature involves the measurement of quality changes for a large number of commodities and industrial units. His conceptual framework is similar to that underlying the construction of hedonic price indexes, where market prices of commodities within each generic class of goods are related to their underlying product attributes by regression or similar methods.[8] The fundamental idea is to distinguish shifts in the observed price-attributes relationship from movements along it, the former being associated with pure price changes for all quality components and the latter associated with pure quality changes within the existing price structure. In the hedonic approach, the coefficients of the estimated price-characteristics regression function are interpreted as implicit prices of the various components of quality, from which quality-adjusted price and quantity indexes are computed by familiar methods.

As outsiders to the ongoing debate on the measurement of capital, it seems clear to us that Gordon appropriately has identified the conceptual issue as the proper definition of a commodity. Do we want a $2'' \times 6''$ radio or do we want x hours of playing time in the future? It is most meaningful to define the radios in terms of playing time, not by the arbitrary and varying packages used to provide it. As a formal matter, Gordon's method of quality adjustment makes most sense when quality change is "quantity augmenting" (the so-called repackaging case). In that case the services of capital enter the production function as the product of the quantity of capital and an elementary function of its quality, the latter represented by a vector of measurable characteristics—a measure of "efficiency units," as it were. (The obvious analogy to Kendrick's differentiation of human capital into "raw bodies" and improved bodies will not pass unnoticed.) This case represents a variety of perfect substitution between quantity and quality attributes. Then the transactional unit of account truly is arbitrary, and the estimated implicit prices of product attributes adequately serve as measures of marginal rates of substitution required for the construction of index numbers. On these terms Gordon's quality adjustments raise issues neither more nor less complex than are familiar from discussions of standard index number problems.

Gordon argues persuasively that the assumption of quantity augmentation and the methods implied by it are better than the official methods, to a first approximation. Yet one may wonder if the approximation is close to true when the efficiency units assumption cannot be maintained. No satisfactory capital aggregate has been shown to exist in such cases and the quantity-augmentation assumption is likely to break down in the presence of indivisibilities and multiple attributes that are not linearly combinable. While both black-and-white and color television sets provide entertainment services, in what sense is it meaningful to say that the latter represents x more units than the former? And granted that there exists between the two a marginal rate of substitution for each consumer unit, revealed preferences for one kind or the other show that most people live off the margin, that there are marginal rents, so that observed price-attribute differences measure the proper marginal rates of substitution for only a small fraction (those truly on the margin of indifference) of the population. This point is readily generalized to cases where a whole spectrum of goods of varying qualities and attributes exist side by side in the market (see Rosen 1974 for a detailed discussion of these points). For example, those who buy smaller, less expensive automobiles evidently do not value the additional attributes provided by larger and more expensive models as much as they value their additional cost. But Gordon's estimation of linear price-attributes surfaces automatically assigns the same implicit prices to everyone independent of their location in the sample space. Problems associated with differences in tastes are thereby simply ignored. Precisely analogous issues arise for capital goods used outright in market production, since machines of alternative specifications embody design characteristics tailored for specific purposes. For example, two motors of one-half horsepower are not obviously equivalent to one or some other number of one-horsepower motors. These are far from standard index number problems. Of course, this issue would be unimportant if price changes on all product varieties within each class of goods were sufficiently uniform that their relative prices were left intact. Then pure price changes virtually are defined by uniform shifts in the price-attributes function, and time dummy shift variables measure these changes quite adequately. However, Gordon's empirical results show that actual price movements are considerably more complex than that.

Related questions exist in cases where alternative varieties of a commodity embody multiple attributes. Gordon's principal example relates to new computers, costing the same as older models, but with twice as much computational speed. His argument that they should be counted as twice as much capital instead of the same amount, as the official methods would do it, is well taken. Yet newer vintages of computers also embody greater core capacity, time-sharing and interactive capabilities, and so on. If it is a package of "computational services" that is to be priced out for productivity analysis, it seems more appropriate to compare the new models with the older ones plus the allied services (e.g., research assistants) that are also embodied ("capitalized," as it were) in the latest vintages but not in the older models. There is no great issue of principle here, but the point is that care must be exercised to guarantee that similar overall packages of total services are being compared. However, there are many practical difficulties of implementing this procedure, since the adjustments required to obtain comparable bundles must be made good for good and case by case. One could conceivably extend this kind of argument to the limit and link the displacement of horse-drawn vehicles by bicycles, trucks, autos, motorcycles, trains, and airplanes by using the production of "transportation services" as the general organizational principle; though not even such a strong advocate as Gordon has attempted to go that far.[9]

In addition, in empirically implementing Gordon's methods there are some genuinely difficult data problems that revolve around the definition of goods. Economic theory is disconcertingly fuzzy about some of its primitive constructs, and the definition of a good is one of them. While Gordon hardly can be faulted for gaps in economic theory, his analytic framework elevates them to a more prominent position than is necessary for many problems in economics. Once we have said that goods of varying qualities within the same generic class should be compared in terms of performance characteristics, there remains the hard work of obtaining adequate measures of these attributes. What performance indicators do we want, and how are multiple indicators of the various dimensions of services to be treated statistically? The fact is that most quality adjustments based on regression methods have had to make do with readily available data, which relate in unknown and imperfect ways to the ideal. Thus, for example, weight is used as a characteristic for hedonic studies of automobile prices. Surely weight is not a utility-bearing characteristic, and one might expect its implicit price to be sensitive to fuel prices. Though Gordon advances some interesting modifications of previous work here, it remains to be seen whether such things as weight, horsepower, and length can adequately proxy true performance characteristics and whether the relationship between measured and desired characteristics remains stable over time.

Gordon presents a large number of adjustments and assumptions for specific items. New hedonic price estimates are presented for some goods, and earlier results of other investigators are used for other goods. For many goods the data are not adequate for thoroughgoing hedonic studies, and so comparisons of closely similar models several years apart (e.g., 1949 Buicks compared with 1970 Chevrolets) are used, on the grounds that these models represent comparable observations on implicit prices for both years, from which pure price shifts can be inferred. Also, for the preponderance of specific items, quality adjustments have been made by linking various vintages of models in Sears Roebuck catalogs, which give detailed information on price and specifications. It should be noted that these latter cases represent observations on durable equipment primarily used in the household sector, which often seem to be extrapolated to much larger scale industrial equipment. We do not feel qualified to discuss these details and so we note only that some of the specific adjustments already have been questioned by several government accountants and are likely to be debated for some time to come. Clearly, whatever principle is finally agreed upon, enormous work remains to fill in the details. Returning this to the respective agencies, we wish only to make a general remark on the implications of these adjustments for growth accounting.

There are two substantial differences of interpretation of measured productivity growth implied by cost-based versus quality-adjusted capital stock measures. First is the specific time period in which productivity change is measured. Second is the classification of technical change as embodied or disembodied.

1. Both methods do allow for measured productivity change, and it is simply not true that quality-adjusted measures define away technical advance, as some have claimed. However, the timing is different. Using quality-adjusted investment data raises GNP in the year the higher-quality goods are produced, increasing the measured residual at the time when the greater future productive capability is introduced into the economy. On the other hand, the conventional method shows a residual in those years in which the actual greater flow of services attributable to those capital goods occurs. Measured input in years subsequent to that in which the quality improvement is introduced is lower in the conventional method than if quality-adjusted indexes are used, but measured output in the year of production is higher in the quality-adjusted method than is shown by the conventional accounts. In actual practice, the problems are more complex, depending on accounting conventions, the precise nature of quality changes, and whether they occur in consumer or producer goods. But it seems that this contrast is the typical one for business investment. This difference in timing obviously is important to students of economic growth, since it yields substantially different interpretations of economic movements and the level of po-

tential output. For these reasons, and since they are based more securely on neoclassical production theory, quality-adjusted methods in principle appear to provide a more reasonable and meaningful set of estimates.

2. Related to this is the question of the extent to which productivity change is to be classified as embodied or disembodied. As shown by Jorgenson (1966), without detailed examination of technical advance for individual capital goods there can be no logically identifiable decomposition of embodied and disembodied technical change. What Gordon attempts to provide here is such a detailed, independent examination and analysis of the actual productive capabilities and characteristics of the capital goods. This is what makes identification of the embodied component possible and what makes such distinctions meaningful both empirically and theoretically. Much of the earlier debate on the correct measurement of capital concentrated too much on whether allowances for the changing nature of capital goods should be made before or after the residual was computed, an issue evidently not worth the heat it generated. In principle, quality-adjusted measures permit proper attribution of increased productive potential where they belong—to individual inputs. Curiously, adherents to the OBE concepts have never questioned similar adjustments in the case of increasing labor quality and have even computed standardized labor input measures based on education. We find this asymmetry puzzling. These distinctions are important for analyzing the sources of growth and for appropriate public policy, since they may point more clearly to some of the specific and ultimate causes of productivity growth.

Although Kendrick's measures of investment in business physical capital follow the official procedures, he is sympathetic to the quality-adjusted approach exemplified by Gordon's work. However, the most interesting, imaginative, and novel aspect of Kendrick's work relates to his treatment of investment in human capital and in intangible nonhuman capital. He gives detailed annual estimates of investment and capital stock for tangible and intangible nonhuman and human investment by sector. As stated above, he uses the conventional non-quality-adjusted measures of tangible nonhuman investment. Intangible nonhuman investment measurement is based upon research and development expenditures. Presumably the returns from these investments accrue from the production of new and better capital and consumer goods. To the extent that costs for research equal benefits it could be argued that this accounting adds a new sector whose output is quality change. In that case, Kendrick's accumulated nonhuman capital could be similar to that provided by quality-adjusted measures, albeit with substantial differences in timing as well as in the nature and form of embodiment. The complexities of interpretation depend also on the extent to which changes due to R&D can be introduced only by embodiment in new capital goods, and on the nature of the price deflators applied to these goods. In this sense the accounting treatment of intangible nonhuman capital need not differ from that of tangible capital, since the output of the former sector is quality change. Clearly, the introduction of a sector producing quality change is a welcome addition to the study of growth accounting. However, it does not at all preclude incorporating the quality changes thereby produced into the measurement of capital inputs.

Tangible human capital is measured by the accumulated costs of rearing children to age fourteen, while intangible human investments are classified as those used to educate individuals, to provide them with training and health, and to improve labor allocation via job search and mobility. Kendrick's demarcation between tangible and intangible human capital is less than distinct. Though we can appreciate the quantity-quality issue confronted, this separation has the effect of splitting expenditures on the under-fourteen group into two categories: tangible (rearing) and intangible (education, health, etc.) and raises some more general issues of substitution possibilities between formal schooling and similar activities performed in the home. Kendrick does not base his estimates of rearing costs on a subsistence concept. Rather, increased consumption expenditures upon children in successive cohorts are used to impute larger stocks, thus implicitly letting increased cost of children generate measures of secularly improved bodies in the labor force. Intangible human investments also are valued at their costs of production, including foregone earnings of both students and the functionally unemployed. Again, increased real expenditures are used to impute increased productive capacity. Those quality improvements in child-rearing techniques, health care, and education not reflected in explicitly higher costs are ignored.

Kendrick's method for estimating the human capital stock is different from that used for nonhuman capital, and this asymmetry is the source of several potential biases in comparing relative productivities of each type of capital and in making inferences about rates of return. The estimates for nonhuman capital are based upon the usual perpetual inventory method, with goods counted as part of gross capital until retirement and depreciated over their life-span. The estimates of human capital are based upon attributing rearing costs, education, and other intangibles to survivors. The treatment of rearing costs has the unusual property that the secular decline in mortality before age fourteen increases the residual. Measured growth in human capital stock is biased downward on this account, because all costs of raising children until age fourteen are attributed to the relevant cohort and no deductions are made for the number who die before age fourteen. Variations in survival rates in a cohort after age fourteen are accounted for, however, in an altered stock of intangible human capital. Further, there are no imputations of the personal consumption value of changed life expectation, based on the appropriate willingness-to-pay concept, which would show a rising trend (the rate of return to human capital investment is too low on this account), nor is sufficient allowance made for the considerable short-run fluctuations in human capital owing to wars.[10]

Kendrick's estimates are original, useful, and important, and within the rules of the game they have a certain justification. We could ask many specific questions: Why should one-half of health care expenditures be regarded as pure consumption? Why not three-fourths or five-ninths? And, more important, why should this ratio be constant over time? Counting all expenditures on rearing costs and education as investment and none as consumption probably overstates the human capital stock. Rearing costs undoubtedly include a large component that increases consumption value to parents rather than adding to productive capacities of children. Kendrick's estimates imply that if hamburgers are purchased for dogs it is consumption, but more hamburgers consumed by children constitute investment. Further, the extent to which wage incomes are lowered owing to costs of on-the-job training remains empirically uncertain, but recent work suggests that the magnitudes exceed the components imputed by Kendrick, tending to reduce his measures of human capital stock and bias the rate of return upward. Some allowances for informal on-the-job investment come in by the back door, since Kendrick does not depreciate intangible human capital before age twenty-eight on these grounds. But surely this assumed equality of depreciation and on-the-job investment leads to understatements of gross investment. No doubt there are other specifics that might be questioned, but this does not detract from the importance of Kendrick's pioneering work.

In essence Kendrick's treatment of child-rearing costs in a free society raises issues similar to those that have been often suggested for a slave society, where the production of a labor force is treated as an investment. There always is some awkwardness in treating children as both consumer and investment goods, since it is not clear whether to regard their consumption as utility to children, to their parents, or to both. Also, the use of per capita estimates to measure welfare over time is complicated because it is sensitive to the mix of expenditures chosen by parents between more goods (or leisure) and more children: the former raises measured per capita welfare and the latter reduces it; yet revealed preferences yield an unambiguous result. A similar issue is involved in Kendrick's breakdown between consumption and investment, as noted above. Note, however, that the formal similarity to the accounting in a slave society does break down, since slaves are treated as intermediate investment goods whose own consumption never enters into output because they are not considered members of the relevant population.

Kendrick's discussion of a tangible human capital sector producing live fourteen-year-old bodies for the economy is in the best tradition of the often-discussed slave-breeding firm.[11] Yet Kendrick's procedure of accumulating the annual costs of production without interest amortization differs from the proper accounting for such a firm.[12] It also provides some asymmetry with the treatment accorded physical capital. Productive humans have a longer gestation period, or period of production (fourteen years in Kendrick's case, to be exact), than do most forms of physical capital. Thus there is a longer period of deferral between the initial investment expenditures and future flows of income than in the case of physical capital. Since "time is money," the slave-breeding firm would not sell at undiscounted accumulated rearing cost but would charge the going rate of its funds tied up in goods-in-process.[13] This problem need not be asymmetrical between human and nonhuman capital, since it involves handling the time needed to produce an asset. In the case of a firm producing durable goods and selling them to users, investment in durables (as opposed to inventory-in-process) is picked up at the time of sale and is measured at the cost of production, which includes an allowance for interest during the period of production. Kendrick's unamortized estimates of the value of human capital therefore understate the relative amount of resources devoted to childbearing investments, understating human caiptal, and thus introduce an upward bias in the rate of return. Since the accumulated value of an annuity of $1 per year for fourteen years at 10% is equal to about twice the undiscounted value, such a consideration is not trivial. And, given the importance of rearing costs in total human capital investment, Kendrick's conclusion as to the relative under- and overinvestment in different forms of capital seems unwarranted.

Kendrick presents three alternative concepts of the stock of human capital: the capital embodied in the total population; the capital embodied in the employed population; and a measure based on man-hours of employment. He does not estimate the rate of return by comparing net labor income with the stock of total population capital but uses the employed population instead. However, this procedure implies a very specific imputation for the value of production in the nonmarket sector: The rate of return on human capital not employed in production in the market is assumed to be identical with that found in the nonmarket sector, an assumption that must be true only at the margin and not on average. Further, one may question his use of employed human capital to estimate relative rates of return, since its treatment is not symmetrical with that of nonhuman capital, which is assumed always to be fully employed. It also misstates expected returns to investment in human capital if employment variations are anticipated. Thus he has adjusted human capital for utilization, but no utilization adjustment is made for the rest of the capital stock, again tending to increase the estimated relative rate of return to human capital. Obviously, the social return to human capital was smaller in the 1930s than estimated by Kendrick, and, while it might be argued that this need not have been true had economic policy been appropriate, the same point can be made for the return to physical capital. Kendrick's method might be justified on the grounds of providing a better measure of productivity of factors actually in use, where output per employed worker provides a partial adjustment. Yet it seems that the comparison of rates of return would be more useful either if nonhuman capital was similarly adjusted or if the denominator for human capital stock was based upon some concept of a standard, normal labor force. Further since the concept he calls "utilization" adjusts for hours worked, the basis for a similar reasonable adjustment for nonhuman capital utilization is suggested.

In his estimates of the returns to human capital Kendrick reduces labor incomes by a provision for maintenance to obtain a net figure, justified as providing symmetry with the treatment of physical capital. Yet the orders of magnitude of these adjustments differ markedly for the two forms of capital, and, in linking maintenance of tangible human capital to a rising consumption standard, it seems that elements of increased consumption are deducted. While in the case of slaves, adjustments for "pure" maintenance might be based on some subsistence concept for those already generating incomes and the expenditures on those not yet employed are regarded as investments, we find Kendrick's discussion unclear on just whose maintenance has been deducted and how the cost of the goods-in-process were treated. The estimated rate of return to the employed stock of human capital evidently should adjust for the maintenance only of those employed, whereas the broader adjustments made by Kendrick appear to include the entire population. This treatment would introduce a downward bias in computed rates of return while also making them sensitive to labor fore participation rates.

We have not touched on many of the other interesting issues contained in both books. Gordon provides new information on the relationships between transactions and list prices and their cyclical changes over time. Kendrick provides much detail on changes in the sectoral composition of investment and their determinants, as well as information on the cyclical variability of various types of investment. Thus both books will be major sources for empirical and policy studies for a long time. Here we have discussed only the broader themes related to the measurement of capital.

Notes

1. See the original articles, replies, and final comments in *Survey of Current Business*, vol. 52 (1972).
2. For Denison's most recent estimates, see Denison (1974).
3. Thus the value of net human tangible capital stock employed in the United States private domestic business to persons engaged rose from $3,032 in 1948 to $3,839 in 1966 (in 1958 dollars). The ratio of net human capital stock employed in the United States private domestic business economy to the estimated number of persons engaged rose from $2,561 in 1929 to $3,032 in 1948. For total net human capital the increases are from $10,319 in 1948 to $15,440 in 1966, and $7,546 in 1929 to $10,319 in 1948.
4. For an extensive discussion of these points and a critique of some of Gordon's earlier work on these problems, see Triplett (1975, pp. 19–82).
5. See, e.g., the work of Nordhaus and Tobin, *Is Growth Obsolete*?, in the NBER Fiftieth Anniversary Colloquium, *Economic Growth* (New York, 1972).
6. See the points raised by Robin C. O. Matthews in his discussion of the work cited note 5.
7. See the discussion of this in Machlup (1962, pp. 52–56). Machlup's book, in addition to discussing many aspects of the conceptual treatment of knowledge, includes calculations of the output of knowledge production in 1958 based upon various adjustments and reclassifications of the national income accounts. His estimate of the final product is $109.2 billion (but no breakdown is provided between consumption and investment). Kendrick's investment in intangibles (which includes health expenditures) is $97.5 billion.
8. See the articles in Griliches (1971).
9. See, however, Fogel (1964) and Fishlow (1965) for discussions of the substitution of railroads for other transport modes.
10. See Usher (1973) and the discussion by Willis.
11. For estimates of the returns to slave females, including the value of their offspring, see Conrad and Meyer (1958). On this see also Fogel and Engerman (1974).
12. Note that Kendrick does not discuss the question whether the appropriate social rate of discount should be zero for his calculations.
13. See also the discussion in Dublin and Lotka (1946, chap. 4).

References

Conrad, Alfred H., and Meyer, John R. 1958. The economics of slavery in the ante-bellum South. *Journal of Political Economy* 66:95–130.

Denison, Edward F. 1957. Theoretical aspects of quality change, capital consumption, and net capital formation. In *Problems of Capital*

Formation, pp. 215–61. National Bureau of Economic Research, Conference on Research in Income and Wealth. Princeton: Princeton University Press.

———. 1974. *Accounting for United States Economic Growth, 1929–1969*. Washington, D.C.: Brookings Institution.

Dublin, Louis I., and Lotka, Alfred J. 1946. *The money value of a man*. New York: Ronald Press.

Fishlow, Albert. 1965. *American railroads and the transformation of the ante-bellum economy*. Cambridge: Harvard University Press.

Fogel, Robert William. 1964. *Railroads and American economic growth*. Baltimore: Johns Hopkins University Press.

Fogel, Robert William, and Engerman, Stanley L. 1974. *Time on the cross*. Boston: Little, Brown.

Gordon, R. J. Forthcoming. *The measurement of durable goods prices*, New York: National Bureau of Economic Research.

Griliches, Zvi, ed. 1971. *Price indexes and quality change*. Cambridge: Harvard University Press.

Jorgenson, Dale W. 1966. The embodiment hypothesis. *Journal of Political Economy* 74:1–17.

Kendrick, John W. 1961. *Productivity trends in the United States*. Princeton: Princeton University Press.

———. 1974. *Postwar productivity trends in the United States, 1948–1969*. General Series no. 98. New York: National Bureau of Economic Research.

———. 1976. *The formation and stocks of total capital*. General Series no. 100. New York: National Bureau of Economic Research.

Kiker, B. F. 1968. *Human capital: In retrospect*. Columbia: University of South Carolina Press.

Machlup, Fritz. 1962. *The production and distribution of knowledge in the United States*. Princeton: Princeton University Press.

Rosen, Sherwin. 1974. Hedonic prices and implicit markets: Product differentiation in pure competition. *Journal of Political Economy* 82:34–55.

Triplett, Jack E. 1975. The measurement of inflation: A survey of research on the accuracy of price indexes. In *The analysis of inflation*, ed. Paul H. Earl, pp. 19–82. Lexington, Mass.: Lexington Books.

Usher, Dan. 1973. An imputation to the measure of economic growth for changes in life expectancy. In *The measurement of economic and social performance*, ed. Milton Moss, pp. 193–226. Studies in Income and Wealth, vol. 38. New York: National Bureau of Economic Research.

Comment John W. Kendrick

Engerman and Rosen have written a thoughtful and balanced review of my new book. They have certainly read and pondered it with care. I am gratified that, despite the deficiencies they have noted—and others will doubtless be found—they consider it a useful pioneering effort that will be a source for empirical and policy studies for some time to come. I hope, further, that the basic approach and conceptual framework will be adopted by others—perhaps eventually by government statistical agencies, at least in part—and the concepts and estimates refined and improved.

The reviewers note that one of the analytical uses to which I put the new estimates was to test the Schultz hypothesis, referred to in the preface, that economic growth can be wholly explained in terms of the accumulation of total capital, broadly defined. At the same time I was also testing the more constrained hypothesis developed in the mid-1950s by Fabricant and me that the growth of the intangible capital stocks resulting from investments designed to improve the quality and efficiency of the tangible factors would account for a significant portion of the increase in total tangible factor productivity. We were, of course, measuring the tangible factor stocks and inputs without adjustment for quality change. The new estimates do support our hypothesis, although I was surprised that less than half of the residual appears to be explained by the growth of real intangible stocks and inputs. I would not expect all of it to be so explained, given the existence of non-investment growth forces, such as increasing returns to scale, changes in economic (allocative) efficiency, and changes in intensity of use of resources. But I also suspect that my estimates of the growth of real total stocks may be understated.

I did not, of course, adjust the tangible investments and capital stocks for quality changes (except to the extent that they were associated with changes in unit real costs), since, as the reviewers recognize, the estimates of real intangible investments and stocks, human and nonhuman, provide an alternative approach to estimating the effect on output of changes in quality and efficiency. If Gordon is right, however, that the construction and producers' equipment price deflators have a significant upward bias, above the quality improvement factor, then my nonhuman tangible investment and stock estimates have a downward bias. The same is probably true of the intangible investment and stock estimates, since the deflators are based largely on input prices. Correction for these biases would result in a larger rate of growth of the real total capital estimates and thus a narrowing of the residual. This factor and several

John W. Kendrick is professor of economics at the George Washington University.

others were discussed in the volume as reasons for believing that the growth of real total capital stocks and inputs accounted for a larger share of the growth of real product than we calculated, although I am convinced that a final residual would, and should, remain.

With respect to a general comment by the reviewers that growth studies tend to neglect imputations, I should mention that in another NBER study I have been involved in developing estimates of imputed values of most nonmarket outputs. In the total capital study, I did develop a number of imputations required for consistency—for examample, the rental values of nonbusiness durable goods and the opportunity cost of students. Since I did not then have completed estimates of the imputed value of unpaid household work, however, I did not include housewives and other unpaid household workers in the employed human capital stock to be related to the income and product estimates.

Engerman and Rosen raise a number of specific questions on concept and methodology that I shall try to address briefly. First, I believe they are right in arguing that rearing costs should include an implicit interest charge, just as the cost of nonhuman capital goods includes an allowance for interest during the period of production. The rearing cost estimates might also have included the value of parents' time devoted to rearing, if such estimates had been available. These adjustments would affect the levels of the tangible human stock estimates, but would have little effect on the movements of the real stocks.

Following the logic of viewing the rearing of children as an alternative to consumption or saving and investment in other forms by the parents, I should probably also have imputed a rental value to the rearing stocks to add to personal consumption outlays. The same should be done for household pets, of course. This would eliminate the paradox noted by the reviewers that under my current procedure, hamburgers purchased for children are counted as an investment while hamburgers for dogs are consumption! If both are investment, the rental values of the resulting stocks represent the consumption utilities to parents and owners.

The reviewers note that I increase both the real basic consumption per child in estimating rearing costs, and that of employed adults in estimating real maintenance costs (for computation of rates of return), in line with the upward trend of real personal consumption expenditures per capita. This has the theoretical justification that customary or conventional subsistence standards are influenced by attained levels. But I must confess that this procedure gave me more reasonable results in estimating rates of return on human investment. Use of the alternative assumption of unchanging minimal subsistence levels resulted in an upward trend in rates of return on human capital.

I would take issue with Engerman and Rosen on one of their points—the criticism of my asymmetrical treatment of human and nonhuman capital in adjusting the former for rates of employment and utilization but not the latter. In a private enterprise system, labor is a cost only when employed, while capital carries a charge, explicit or implicit, regardless of rates of utilization. In productivity analysis, falling rates of utilization tend to reduce productivity, particularly of the capital factor, but also of the labor factor, since there are also "overhead" types of labor. Certainly in calculating private rates of return one should use the employed human capital stock rather than the total as a denominator, since the labor compensation component of national income relates only to employed labor. In the case of capital, it seems to me that declining (rising) rates of utilization should be reflected in declining (rising) rates of return, particularly since nonhuman capital has no alternative use. In the case of human capital, there are alternative uses—nonmarket economic activity and leisure. If a value were imputed to the nonmarket human activities, then it would make sense to relate total compensation of the human factor to its total capital value. But the calculated rates of return in that case would merely reflect the compensation rates used in the imputations for the nonemployed portion of the adult population.

The reviewers inquire about the reasoning behind several of the estimating conventions. Why, for example, do I count all educational outlays as investment? The short answer is that I consider the element of current consumption to be entirely minor compared with the longer-run benefits of increased earning capacity and enjoyment in the future. Why do I assume that half of medical and health outlays are investment? In perusing the literature and talking with experts such as Fuchs and Mushkin, I was persuaded that a substantial portion of such outlays represents consumption in that it does not result in long-term benefits. But another substantial portion does represent investment, in that it increases longevity, reduces time lost owing to illness, and increases vitality. But the experts are not able to allocate the totals. So I decided on half-and-half as the least objectionable and most convenient assumption. More research on this is needed; in the meantime, those who feel strongly that some other allocation is better can easily adjust the estimates.

One final point: the reason we calculate depreciation on educational capital only after several years of work experience is not because of offsets in the form of on-the-job training (for which separate estimates are prepared), but rather because it represents a crude attempt to take some account of learning-by-doing. This is undoubtedly a significant investment aspect of work experience. But innovative as we may have been in developing concepts and measures for various types of investment and capital not hitherto counted, we did not venture to estimate the value of the knowledge and know-how generated by work experience—or the consumption values of productive activity for which the reviewers would also like to have imputations.

If my book sparks additional efforts to refine the concepts and improve the estimates of total investment and capital, I shall feel rewarded. Even though total capital formation does not appear to be the entire proximate cause of economic growth, it is big enough to merit much more work.

5 Capital Gains and Income: Real Changes in the Value of Capital in the United States, 1946–77

Robert Eisner

Personal income may be defined as the algebraic sum of (1) the market value of rights exercised in consumption and (2) the change in the value of the store of property rights between the beginning and the end of the period in question.

Henry Simons

Income is the money value of the net accretion to one's economic power between two points of time.

R. M. Haig

Income No. 1 is thus the maximum amount which can be spent during a period if there is to be an expectation of maintaining intact the capital value of prospective receipts. . . .

Income No. 1 *ex post* equals the value of the individual's consumption *plus* the increment in the money value of his prospect which has accrued during the week; it equals Consumption *plus* Capital accumulation. . . .

We are thus forced back on the central criterion, that a person's income is what he can consume during the week and still expect to be as well off at the end of the week as he was at the beginning.

J. R. Hicks

5.1 Sources and Nature of Capital Gains

The late Howard Hughes and the late J. Paul Getty, the Rockefeller family, and the rich the world over did not gain their wealth by the flow of saving out of conventionally measured income. Rather, they

Robert Eisner is William R. Kenan Professor of Economics at Northwestern University.

This paper was prepared with the critical financial support of National Science Foundation grants 72063, for the Measurement of Economic and Social Performance, and SOC77-17555, for the Distributional and Behavioral Implications of discovered or acquired title to resources that grew enormously in value, or they bought and sold, exchanged and held real assets, securities, and businesses that appreciated.

The wealth of nations has waxed and waned with the acquisition and development of land and its resources and with changes in world demand and supply of the products and services in international commerce. Oil-producing countries have become rich with the discovery of petroleum and increases in its price. Cuba's wealth has declined and grown as much with changes in the price of sugar as with investment by citizens or foreigners. Fortunes of all of the world's raw-material-producing nations have depended mightily on their terms of trade.

Within the United States, in the South and in the West, in particular areas within all regions, in suburbia and farmlands, we have had great increases in wealth, enjoyed by individuals and communities alike, far beyond officially recorded saving. It is clear that the distributions of economic power, of consumption, and of properly measured income have been vastly affected by appreciations in the value of property commonly referred to as capital gains.

National income and product accounts of the United States and elsewhere presume to measure the total of consumption and investment—that is, the current production of goods and services received by households and the accumulation of stocks of goods by producers. Aside from the role of the rest of the world and of government, this total is widely rationalized as income in the sense—to paraphrase Hicks—of what can be consumed during the period of measurement while still leaving society as well off at the end of the period as it was at the beginning. For, at least with perfect elasticity of substitution between capital goods and consumer goods over the relevant range, our measure of net income would then be the amount by which the production and consumption of consumer goods and services could be increased while reducing gross investment to the amount of depreciation or net investment to zero.

Total Income Measurement. Since its presentation at the Toronto Conference in 1976 it has been updated from 1975 to 1977, and many of the statistical series have been revised on the basis of newly available data. A number of consolidated tables have been added, particularly on Martin J. Bailey's suggestion in his comment on the earlier version, to present totals without the double counting implicit in unadjusted summing of individual sectors.

John C. Musgrave, of the Bureau of Economic Analysis of the United States Department of Commerce, and first Helen Tice, then Elizabeth Fogler of the Flow of Funds section of the Federal Reserve Board, have been invaluable guides to data and sources of unpublished tabulations. Those who have labored mightily on the mass of data collection and processing, both on and off the computer, include Marsha Courchane and René Moreno, Jeffrey Silber, Augustine Fosu, John Graham, Roy Webb, and Paul Burik. David Reishus, David Nebhut, and Emily Simons have been of key assistance in the final revisions and updating. As always, Molly Fabian has with good cheer and great skill navigated laborious typing and revisions of tables and manuscript.

The essential difficulty in relating conventional data of consumption and investment to income in the Haig-Simon and Hicksian senses is that investment as currently measured may be poorly related to capital accumulation. Gross investment in conventional accounts is taken as the original cost or supply price of acquisitions by business of capital goods and additional inventories. There are a number of reasons why this measure does not correspond to capital accumulation in the economy.

First, of course, capital goods—that is, goods contributing to future production—are acquired in both government and household sectors. Not only do these contribute to production in those sectors but—particularly with government—because of externalities or transfers at less than cost, they may contribute to future production in the business sector as well. The values of future services or output of a store, warehouse, or factory may be increased by government construction of a highway. These outputs and their values may also be increased by more free or improved public education of labor.

Second, the business sector itself may increase the value of expected future services and output by investing in research and development, training, and other forms of intangible capital not usually counted as part of investment.

Third, because of conditions of monopoly or monopsony, or monopolistic or monopsonistic competition, along with considerations of risk, firms may not acquire capital to the point where the present value of expected future returns from the last unit acquired equals its supply price. The value of capital acquisitions to firms may be more at the time of acquisition than their supply price.

Fourth, after acquisition the value of capital assets may change because of changes in expected prices of the goods and services to be produced or of associated factors of production whose services are to be purchased.

Fifth, after capital goods are acquired, their values may change because of changes in market rates of interest or rates of discount to be applied to expected future returns.

The first three of the considerations above may be met with a comprehensive treatment of capital investment. Such treatments are to be found in recent work by John Kendrick (1976) and in work I have in process (see Eisner 1978 for a preliminary report).

Even with inclusion of all forms of capital in our measurement, capital gains and losses owing to changes in expected prices and interest rates will still need accounting. As far as price changes go, one cannot assume they represent nothing "real." Net income should include consumption plus the money value of real capital accumulation. This means that only the money value of capital gains in excess of those necessary to keep the real value of capital intact should be included in income. There is no reason, however, to expect all prices to move in proportion or hence to expect that, for any individual, firm, or sector, capital gains so defined net of general inflation should be zero. In an open economy, as my introductory remarks have suggested, changes in international relative prices may cause capital gains and losses in individual countries.

Capital gains or losses from changes in the rate of interest or rate of discount of expected future returns may not at first glance seem to fall into the category of our usage of income. Suppose, for example, we are dealing with a perpetual annuity. A fall in the rate of discount would increase the present value of this annuity but would not enable us to consume any more currently without reducing the amount permanently available in the future.

This difficulty disappears, however, when we recognize that the individual's utility function, or the social welfare function implicit in evaluation of society's income, may not call for consumption in perpetuity. "Keeping wealth intact" must involve some at least implicit intertemporal valuations. A fall in the rate of interest may well make it possible for individuals or societies to consume more now while still being indifferent between the new vector of incomes or consumptions available in the future, after the fall in the rate of interest and increased current consumption, and the vector that had been available on the basis of the previous rate of interest, value of capital, and consumption. As individuals or as societies we may have wealth that is the present value of an expected future stream of income that does not correspond to our preferred and planned future consumption. A lowering in the rate of interest may increase the value of that wealth and enable us as a consequence to plan a path of consumption that dominates the previous path.

This is perhaps clearest in the case of an individual contemplating retirement who finds that a change in the rate of discount for his expected future incomes raises his wealth more than it does his desired or planned estate. He is then able to consume more now and still have at least as good a planned consumption path (and planned estate) as before. It may be argued that he will require a larger planned estate if his ultimate motivation is to provide a fixed consumption path for his heirs. But this again would require an assumption, not necessarily warranted, that a future consumption path he preferred for his heirs correspond to the anticipated income stream.

Similarly, a nation may anticipate from its resources a stream of future income that does not correspond to its preferred consumption path. A fall in the rate of interest, which may relate to investment in or from the rest of the world and reflect the differing rates of discount across nations, may raise the capital value of this nation's resources. By selling off some of its increased capital value internationally, the nation as a whole may then consume more now and still be at least as well off as before with regard to future consumption. Here again, therefore, we have a change in the rate of discount that, with no alteration in expected future incomes, involves a capital gain usefully viewed as a component of current income.

Capital gains may also accrue, both for the individual and for the nation, with changes in expected future incomes resulting from the discovery of new resources or new techniques of production. A major source of wealth in the United States has of course been the development of new land, not conventionally included in investment. Along with the land have come literally hundreds of billions of dollars of resources in coal, petroleum, and other minerals. Inventions and innovations, from the cotton gin to the steamboat, the railroad, the telephone, the automobile, and the jet plane have made much of this land and its resources more accessible and more valuable. Such increased values of assets may indeed stem from externalities of investment elsewhere, but they are none the less real and should be taken into account in our measures of capital accumulation and hence of income.

Much of the issue in the relation between capital gains and income is sometimes viewed as a matter of the timing of income (see McElroy 1976). If new resources are discovered, should we count the present capital gain as part of current income, or should we note the increase in income only in the future as revenues are received from the additionally discovered or developed resources? It is sometimes argued that inclusion of capital gains (and subtraction of losses) in measuring current income will make current income all the more unstable and less relevant as a measure of permanent income and welfare. To the extent that our concern is for permanent income, this point is telling. But then we should have to completely revise our conventional accounts, which deal generally with current, measured incomes, regardless of their variance over time. We do not smooth out our national income or gross national product to reflect major fluctuations in corporate and noncorporate profits or in wage income owing to movement in and out of employment and the labor force. It appears best for many purposes to include capital gains in a comprehensive measure of current income and add a comprehensive measure of permanent income that would treat all volatile accretions of economic power equally.

We shall generally make no distinction between realized and unrealized capital gains. Economic power grows as capital gains accrue. Economic power diminishes as capital losses occur. Individuals usually have the option of realizing capital gains, although with some transaction costs and tax penalties. If they choose not to realize their gains, then presumably they feel themselves better off without realization. The gains remain available as a base for further accumulation or even for current consumption without "realization," either by permitting reduction of other saving or accumulation or by offering additional opportunities to borrow with the appreciated capital as collateral.

In principle, transaction costs and tax costs of potential realizations should be recognized in measuring accrued capital gains to individuals and firms, but these frequently are minor. With regard to taxes in the United States, half of realized capital gains have been excluded from taxable personal income. The new tax law of November 1978 raises the exclusion to 60%. (There are further, now expanded exclusions for gains realized on the sale of homes.) But taxable realized capital gains are only the appreciation of those assets actually sold. Thus, for example, if one wishes to realize the gain on $100,000 of assets that have grown in value by 10%, to $110,000, one may sell off $10,000 of the appreciated assets. The capital gains tax applies then only to the gain on the $10,000 of assets that have been sold, or $909. Of this, half would have been excluded from taxable income, so that even at the maximum income tax rate of 70% the total tax would be less than $320 on realization of a gain of $10,000, or little more than 3%. With the new 60% exclusion, the tax is reduced to less than $255, or about 2.5% of the capital gain.

It is of course also true that many individuals and firms may enjoy their capital gains without ever planning to realize them for tax purposes. In the United States one can still avoid capital gains taxation in gifts or bequests. As indicated above, one can accept accrued capital gains as part of saving and thus reduce other saving and increase consumption without "realizing" the capital gains. And one can borrow against assets for consumption or other purposes. Taking into account the lack of taxation in gifts and bequests and the time at which accrued capital gains are eventually realized, Martin Bailey (1969) estimated the effective rate of taxation of capital gains at 8 or 9%.

For nations as well, realization may in essence take place with accrual. Increased wealth affects consumption and international investment flows, whether appreciated assets are actually sold or are used as a base for borrowing or other investment.

Establishing the value of capital for purposes of measuring capital gains and losses involves a number of fundamental problems. In principle, with certainty, perfect knowledge, and perfect markets, and without externalities, the value of capital to individuals, firms, and the economy will equal the present discounted value of its future returns. In fact, we never know future returns, although we can make various efforts to infer expectations of those returns, either our own expectations or those held by firms or investors. Where there have been market transactions we may accept the values established in the markets for the capital directly involved in the transactions.

Only a small portion of capital assets are actually sold in any short period, however. How are we to infer the value of those assets that are not sold? An initially appealing approach would have us group assets as far as possible into homogeneous categories and infer the value of stocks not traded from prices established in the relatively minor flow of actual transactions.

The extent of the difficulties in this approach may be recognized even in the relatively well-suited case of listed securities on organized exchanges. Can we, for example, correctly infer the end-of-year market value of stocks listed on the New York Stock Exchange from the closing prices on 31 December? Could all the shares of General Motors have been sold on that day or even during any other day or reasonably bounded set of days at the prices paid for those shares actually sold?

One evidence that many firms and investors do not view prices of current transactions as reliable measures of the value per share is both the recurrence and the fear of takeovers of companies by tender offers. A stock may be selling at about $11 per share in terms of current transaction flows when an offer may be made to buy enough shares of a company to gain control of it at a price of $21 per share. Cases of this sort are too common to allow confidence that flow transactions prices, particularly with their wide gyrations over relatively short periods of time, are reliable measures of capital value.

Indeed, these considerations do raise further questions with regard to our decision to take "accrued" capital gains at face value. If the amount of accruals is estimated from marginal transactions, are there *potential* realizations for the entire stocks of capital anywhere near equal to those suggested by these marginal prices?

I raise these questions to bring the issues into the open. Nevertheless, in much of our empirical work we do utilize market valuations established on the basis of marginal or flow transactions. Indeed, we and others proceed in essentially similar fashion by using supply prices for the current flow of real goods in estimating market values of corresponding stocks of existing real capital. Such valuations involve essentially application of the "replacement cost" measure that has been adopted by the Bureau of Economic Analysis in estimates of residential and nonresidential capital stocks. These estimates will form an essential part of our analysis. We hence implicitly accept such a valuation for want of a better, available substitute.

Use of replacement cost accounting in the gross valuation of capital stocks leaves a major issue in specifying the depreciation or capital consumption allowances necessary to arrive at net values of capital. The replacement cost is of course at best the value of a new asset. What is the value of existing assets of various ages? Capital gains must equal changes in the value of capital minus net investment. But to calculate net investment we must know not only current gross investment but also the depreciation of existing capital.

For given successive values of net capital stock, the higher the estimate of depreciation and hence the lower the estimate of net investment, the higher will be the estimate of capital gains. Since depreciation and capital gains are properly the two components of total revaluations of existing assets, if the revaluations are known, the estimate of the one depends critically upon the estimate of the other.

Where net capital value is estimated as a cumulative sum of past net investment, the more rapid the rate of depreciation, real or assumed, the lower the value of reported net capital stocks. Also, given the general growth in the rate of gross capital expenditures, the more rapid the rate of depreciation the higher will be annual depreciation charges and the lower will be net investment. Finally, if revaluations are then calculated as the difference between net stock at the end of a period and the sum of the net stock at the end of the previous period plus the intervening net investment, the more rapid the assumed rate of depreciation the lower will be the calculated revaluation. In the limiting steady-state case where all new investment is fully depreciated in the period it is made, there is no net capital carried over for revaluation.

We take depreciation to be the change in value of an asset with the passage of time, given anticipated future returns and given rates of discount. If the value of an asset is a function of calendar time, t, a vector of expected returns, Y, and a vector of discount rates, R, depreciation may be viewed as the partial derivative of that value with respect to time, that is, $V = V(t,Y,R)$, and depreciation equals $\partial V/\partial t$. Capital gains then involve those changes in V occasioned by changes in Y and in R.

Ideally, where we can specify both expected future returns from capital and rates of discount, we can calculate the true economic depreciation to be applied each year to the updated value of the asset. Estimates of economic depreciation along these lines have been attempted by Mendelowitz (1971) for corporate capital and by Graham and Webb (1979) for human capital. We shall incorporate and endeavor to expand upon some of these latter estimates.

For the main, however, we shall again have recourse to accounting conventions and accept the Bureau of Economic Analysis estimates of straight-line depreciation as incorporated in their latest revisions of capital stock series (utilizing 85% of Bulletin F lives and their replacement cost bases). I have argued on a number of occasions that the straight-line depreciation applied by Denison (1967, 1974) is a better measure of economic depreciation than the double-rate, declining-balance depreciation employed by Kendrick (1976), Jorgenson (1974), and others (see Eisner 1973, 1975; Christensen and Jorgenson 1973). Evidence in the work of Coen (1975) and the findings of Mendelowitz (1971), Ramm (1971), and Graham and Webb (1979) reinforce that view.

We have thus far been passing over the component of revaluation of capital assets associated with general price inflation. As I indicated earlier, to avoid money illusion we must surely include in income only that portion of capital gains above what is necessary to maintain real capital or real future consumption intact. On the assumption that the elasticity of price expectations is unity, we may then apply current changes in a general price deflator to calculate the value of capital necessary to keep its purchasing power intact. The "net revaluations," which we will take as the capital gains to be included in income and in net capital accumulation, are therefore the change in the value of capital minus both net investment and that portion of the change in value of capital necessary to keep pace with any general increase in the price level.

Thus, while for gross revaluations we have

$$GR_t = K_t - K_{t-1} - IN_t, \tag{1}$$

for net revaluations, as in McElroy (1971),

$$NR_t = K_t - \left(\frac{P_{t,end}}{P_{t-1,end}}\right) K_{t-1} - \left(\frac{P_{t,end}}{P_t}\right) IN_t, \tag{2}$$

where

NR_t = Net revaluations of the year t
K_t = Net value of capital at the end of the year t
K_{t-1} = Net value of capital at the end of the year $t-1$
$P_{t,end}$ = General price deflator at the end of the year t
$P_{t-1,end}$ = General price deflator at the end of year $t-1$
P_t = Average value of general price deflator in the year t, and
IN_t = Net investment in the year t.[1]

After some consideration, we selected as our general price deflator the implicit deflator for gross national product. In terms of a measure that would indicate the appreciation necessary to keep real value intact, it seemed most appropriate to think in terms of the broadest possible set of goods and services for which capital might be exchanged. In one sense this might be restricted to gross domestic product, as in the work of Shoven and Bulow (1975, 1976). But capital can be used in exchange for not only gross domestic product but that component of gross national product attributed to "rest of the world." In any event, the differences between deflators for gross national product and gross domestic product are trivial.

Net capital accumulation, NCA, will equal the total of net revaluations and net investment, or

$$(3) \qquad NCA_t = NR_t + IN_t.$$

We shall be interested in the extent to which consideration of net revaluations alters the picture of net capital accumulation that we have usually had from considering net investment alone. Differences, as I have suggested, may emerge at the national level as well as in particular sectors.

At the national level, aside from net foreign claims, financial assets and liabilities should essentially cancel out, except for the changes in tangible assets to which they relate. Even this may not be entirely so, as debtors and creditors may attach different subjective rates of discount to expected future payments. At the sectoral level, however, and certainly for individual firms and households, changes in the real value of financial assets and liabilities may bulk large.

Among financial assets and liabilities, equities and bonded debt may change real value because of both changes in nominal market values and changes in the value of money. Other financial items, such as bank deposits and currency, will change value only with the price level.

Tangible wealth may be categorized as human and nonhuman. In the nonhuman category we may include what is generally termed reproducible capital; that is, residential and nonresidential structures and producer and consumer durables, along with inventories. In the category of nonreproducible, tangible capital we have land and natural resources.

Unlike Kendrick, who relates tangible human capital to rearing costs, we also count as tangible his "intangible" human capital stemming from education, training, and other human investment that adds to the productive power of the basic human body. Ideally, we might view all output as the services of capital, human and nonhuman, and take the value of human capital as the sum of its discounted future earnings. Since people are neither bred nor educated for earnings alone, however, we cannot expect with any confidence that the supply price of human capital will equal its present value.

We would like to estimate net revaluations of each category of capital held by the sectors of our "Total Incomes System of Accounts" (Eisner 1975, 1978). These involve: enterprises, further subdivided into business corporate enterprises, business noncorporate enterprises, nonprofit enterprises, and government enterprises; households; and government. In many instances the availability or nonavailability of data has forced us either to classify crudely or to combine sectors. This is most particularly true for households and nonprofit enterprises, which are frequently difficult to disentangle in the accounts, and government enterprises and government, where again data currently available do not permit an easy, reliable separation.

We have had problems with depreciation, alleviated somewhat by the recent BEA replacement-cost, straight-line estimates for structures and equipment. Not all capital has been similarly depreciated, however. Kendrick's human capital stocks, in particular, rely upon double-rate, declining-balance depreciation. We should have liked to employ "economic depreciation," relating to the partial derivative of the value of capital stock with respect to time, as indicated above. In practice we have resorted to straight-line depreciation as the best simple approximation.

5.2 Net Revaluations in the United States since World War II

The record of capital gains and losses, or net revaluations in our terminology, is a striking one in the United States economy since World War II. (For views of part of the record see Bhatia 1970; McElroy 1971.)

The mass of tables we have to present are derived in the main from underlying data pieced together from: (1) the Bureau of Economic Analysis (including some as yet unpublished figures) for stocks, investment flows, and depreciation of business plant and equipment and residential capital, business inventories, and government expenditures for equipment and structures;[2] (2) the Flow of Funds section of the Federal Reserve Board and special tabulations from Helen Tice and then Elizabeth Fogler for financial flows and assets and liabilities by sector, supplemented by estimates of the value of land; (3) investment flows of human capital from Kendrick's *Formation and Stocks of Total Capital.*

We utilized the following additional sources for several special tables: (4) estimated land values by sectors, including government, for the years 1952 to 1968, from table II-1 (p. 344) of Appendix 2, by Grace Milgram, in Goldsmith (1973); (5) estimates of values of national tangible assets, by categories, for 1952 to 1968, in current and constant dollars, from *Historical Statistics of the United States, Colonial Times to 1970*;[3] (6) a paper by John Graham and Roy Webb[4] on the present value of male human capital in 1969, based on Census Public Use Sample data on earnings by age-education cohort, developed into a time series by Graham by applying gross and spendable earnings and population data for the years 1947–75.

The business and residential capital stock data from the Bureau of Economic Analysis are now conveniently in current and 1972 "replacement cost" dollars. Depreciation is consistently taken on a straight-line basis on the assumption of 85% of Bulletin F lives. Financial assets and liabilities in the Flow of Funds accounts or in the special Fogler tabulations were at estimated market value for corporate equities, household equity in unincorporated businesses, direct foreign investment, and life insurance reserves and pension funds. For government and corporate securities and for mortgages, we have converted par values to market by applying New York Stock Exchange bond price indexes or measures of market and par value of government and of corporate securities and of all listed securities, respectively.

Household consumer durables estimates, and government capital stocks, along with other unpublished tables or tables before publication, have been obtained from the Bureau of Economic Analysis through the good offices of John Musgrave. In a number of these instances, as well as with regard to human capital, we have developed our own net investment flows and net stocks by applying perpetual inventory methods with straight-line depreciation. The framework for much of our sectoral analysis regarding nonhuman capital has been the Flow of Funds accounts, supplemented by new estimates on land, and Bureau of Economic Analysis stocks and flows of reproducible capital.

5.2.1 Nonhuman Net Worth, by Sector and in Aggregate

Our first set of basic tables, 5.1 through 5.16, offers figures for net worth, net investment, and gross and net revaluations of nonhuman capital for households, business, government, and the total economy, in current and in 1972 dollars.[5] The household sector here includes personal trusts and nonprofit institutions. Business is taken to comprise noncorporate, corporate nonfinancial, and private financial subsectors. The monetary authority and federally sponsored credit agencies are combined with government. Detailed, item-by-item estimates of net revaluations are offered in tables 5.47 to 5.56.

It should be noted that "noncorporate" includes all of agriculture, both corporate and noncorporate, except for nonresidential fixed capital on corporate farms, which is counted in the corporate sector. The Flow of Funds section estimates 7% of agriculture to be corporate.

The household sector includes household equity in corporate and noncorporate enterprise, the first taken at estimated market value of household-owned corporate stock and the second as the net worth of the noncorporate sector. The private financial sector includes the value of its holdings of nonfinancial corporate shares. In aggregating to develop totals for business and the entire economy, these items are therefore netted out of the household and private financial sectors.

Net worth has of course grown enormously since World War II, and in all sectors gross revaluations have accounted for the bulk of that growth. In households, for example, net worth grew from $677 billion to $5,597 billion from 1945 to 1977, an increase of some $4,920 billion.[6] Of this only $1,938 billion was accounted for by net investment and $2,983 billion, or 61% of the increase, by gross revaluations.

The increase in prices over the thirty-two-year period as a whole, however, more than offset these gross revaluations. Net revaluations in the household sector totaled—$231 billion, an average loss of more than $7 billion per year (table 5.1). In 1972 dollars, total household net revaluations were — $183 billion, yielding a mean annual loss of $5.7 billion (table 5.2).

The mean figures hide a great deal of variance over the years and, as we shall see below, variation by categories of assets and liabilities. The standard deviation of aggregate net revaluations for households is a staggering $129.0 billion in current dollars and $134.1 billion in 1972 dollars (table 5.21). It is also apparent that while net revaluations were positive in eighteen of the thirty-two years, several sharply negative swings kept the mean less than zero. Thus, the inflation immediately following World War II contributed to very considerable real capital losses in the first few postwar years. The years 1969 and 1970 also saw substantial losses and then the stagflation years of 1973 and 1974 contributed a total of $748 billion in negative net revaluations. Indeed, without this episode, and with other net revaluations unchanged, the mean would have run some $16 billion annually over the entire period, more than one-quarter the amount of net investment.

The business sector, summarized in tables 5.3 and 5.4, shows gross revaluations positive in each of the thirty-two years from 1946 to 1975. Net revaluations were positive in twenty-four of the thirty-two years. The constant-dollar total of gross revaluations was almost eleven times that of net investment. The total of net revaluations was 3.4 times the amount of net investment; business sector mean net investment was $6.6 billion in 1972 dollars and mean net revaluations were $22.8 billion per year.

Consideration of the subcategories of business (in tables 5.5 through 5.10) shows that both gross and net revaluations were distinctly higher for the nonfinancial sectors. Dividing the thirty-two years into six five-year subperiods and a final two years, we note that both noncorporate and corporate nonfinancial mean net revaluations were positive in every one of the seven subperiods. The private financial sector, however, suffered total net revaluations of —$102 billion, a mean loss of some $3 billion per year. These were due largely to declines in the market value of bonds and mortgages, occasioned by rising interest rates, owing partly to inflation, and further declines in their real value owing directly to inflation. Along with a mean loss of $4 billion in 1972 dollars on holdings of equity in nonfinancial corporations, these asset declines somewhat outweighed declines in the real value of liabilities (tables

5.10 and 5.54). We may have here a clue to the dominant concern with inflation among the financial community. Their negative net revaluations counterbalanced more than half of net investment.

The big gainer by our calculations—perhaps no surprise to traditional, objecting conservatives—has been government. Net revaluations were positive for our government sector, even with the inclusion of federally sponsored credit agencies and the monetary authority, in no less than twenty-nine of the thirty-two years. The string of net capital gains has been unbroken since 1961. Over the entire thirty-two-year period, mean net revaluations averaged $21 billion per year (table 5.11).

The net worth of the government sector was $17.6 billion at the end of 1945. It grew to $1,070 billion at the end of 1977, despite negative net investment of $149 billion[7] over the intervening years, as gross revaluations were a positive $1,201 billion. Even after the inflation allowance, we come up with a total of positive net revaluations of $675 billion. In 1972 dollars the total was $844 billion and the mean was $26 billion (table 5.12). We can note in tables 5.55 and 5.56 the particular contributing factors but may observe now more generally that the government sector gained from huge declines in the real value of its debt, both because of the direct effect of inflation and because of the increases in interest rates that lowered its nominal market value.

In table 5.13 we report sums of the individual sector magnitudes. Capital gains turn out not to have been a transient factor for which bad years canceled out the good. Net revaluations for the total of our domestic sectors were positive in twenty-three of the thirty-two years; their means were positive in five of the seven subperiods and only very slightly negative in the others. Over the entire thirty-two-year stretch, gross revaluations amounted to $6,357 billion, some three times the total of $2,124 billion of net investment. But even after allowance for inflation, the total of sector net revaluations came to $1,134 billion, a mean of $35 billion per year, or $39 billion in 1972 dollars, as shown in table 5.14.

Tables 5.15 and 5.16 offer economy totals of net worth, net investment, and gross and net revaluations, eliminating the double-counting stemming from household and private financial ownership of noncorporate and corporate nonfinancial business. Tables 5.17 and 5.18 offer matching sector detail for net investment, while tables 5.19 and 5.20 do so for net revaluations. Total gross revaluations are reduced to $4,706 billion but are still some 2.39 times the now $1,967 billion total of net investment. Total net revaluations of non-human capital amounted to $917 billion, a mean of $28.7 billion per year, or $27.2 billion in 1972 dollars. Accumulation or growth in the form of capital gains after allowance for inflation is thus almost half the amount of net investment.

If real increases in net worth are to be taken as net saving, we understate saving seriously when we exclude net revaluations.

While total net revaluations are positive, the differences among sectors and over time are substantial. We have already noted that two of the sectors—households and private financial—are on balance losers over the thirty-two-year period. Standard deviations of annual net revaluations are high in all the sectors. The correlations between the household time series and those of the sectors other than noncorporate are negative, as is that of private financial with government, as shown in table 5.21. These negative correlations reflect the fact that the financial assets of one sector are frequently the liabilities of another. Inclusion with households of such large holders of financial assets as personal trusts and nonprofit institutions serves to accentuate negative correlations of that sector with others.

There are substantial positive correlations among the sectors—corporate, noncorporate, and government—experiencing capital gains. These reflect common movements in values of tangible assets as well as of bonded liabilities.

5.2.2 Tangible Nonhuman Capital

Estimates of net revaluations of tangible, nonhuman capital are striking. Their sums are distinctly positive over our thirty-two-year period for fixed nonresidential and residential capital and for land. They are negative only for consumer durables.

Mean net revaluations of fixed nonresidential business capital were $4.2 billion per year for corporations, $0.8 billion per year for noncorporate enterprises, and $0.3 billion for nonprofit institutions, as may be seen in tables 5.23, 5.24, and 5.25. Thus mean capital gains on fixed nonresidential business capital for all three sectors combined (table 5.26) amounted to $5.4 billion per year, adding more than 30% to the net investment mean of $17.5 billion.

Net revaluations of nonresidential capital were positive for the total of all sectors in twenty-two out of thirty-two years and in six out of the seven subperiods. Seven of the ten negative annual net revaluations came in succession in the years 1958 through 1964. Net revaluations have been positive in each of the years since then.

Gross revaluations over the thirty-two-year period substantially exceeded net investment: $703 billion to $416 billion for corporations, $182 billion to $98 billion in the noncorporate sector, $73 billion to $47 billion for nonprofit institutions, and $958 billion to $561 billion for all business sectors combined. The corresponding net revaluations were $135 billion for corporations, $27 billion for noncorporate enterprises, $9 billion for nonprofit institutions, and $172 billion in total.

Net revaluations for fixed residential capital (excluding land) are about the same. As can be seen in tables 5.27, 5.28, and 5.29, gross revaluations exceeded net investment both for owner-occupied and tenant-occupied residential capital. Capital gains net of inflation totaled \$182 billion for all fixed residential capital, just over one-third of net investment of \$543 billion. Total net revaluations of fixed residential capital were negative in nineteen out of the thirty-two years but were positive in all but three of the years since 1966 and totaled \$152 billion in the years 1976 and 1977. The years 1975 to 1977 indeed fully accounted for the positive balance over the entire postwar period.

Net revaluations on business inventories averaged out to be just about zero, as shown in table 5.30.

Major capital gains are to be found in privately owned land. Net revaluations totaled \$531 billion, averaging more than \$16 billion per year, and were positive in all years except 1946 and 1947, 1969 to 1971, and 1975, as is shown in table 5.31. It may well be argued, of course, that much of the increased value of land stems from land development or investment in land. Our assumption that investment in land is zero hence classifies all increases in land value as revaluations or capital gains. That assumption, however, is consistent with the definition of investment in the BEA income and product accounts.

A somewhat different set of revaluations by sector, derived from estimates of land values put together by Grace Milgram, is found in table 5.32. While the yearly figures for privately held land differ significantly from those in Table 5.31, based upon Federal Reserve Flow of Funds data, the general picture is similar. From Milgram's estimated land values, net revaluations in land were positive in each of her five sectors for all the years from 1953 through 1968 for which her data were available. By her estimates, the value of land rose from \$201 billion at the end of 1952 to \$726 billion at the end of 1968, a total gross revaluation of \$525 billion. Net revaluations in land over this period amounted to \$358 billion, of which \$135 billion was for nonfarm households, \$16 billion was in nonprofit institutions, \$65 billion in unincorporated business plus agriculture, \$64 billion in nonfarm corporations, and \$78 billion in the government sector. Mean net revaluations over the period 1953 to 1968 were \$8.4 billion in nonfarm households, \$1.0 billion in nonprofit institutions, \$4.0 billion each in the noncorporate and corporate sectors, and \$4.9 billion in government, for a total of \$22.4 billion per year in all sectors combined.

5.2.3 Net Revaluations, Saving, and Capital Accumulation

It is informative to consider capital gains and losses in relation to traditional measures of saving and investment. Beginning with households (again including personal trusts and nonprofit institutions), negative mean net revaluations of $7.2 billion over the years 1946 to 1977 offset 23% of mean personal saving of $31.3 billion (table 5.33). The huge negative revaluations of 1973 and 1974, totaling $747 billion, almost completely wiped out the $785 billion of personal saving in all the years from 1946 to 1974. The losses related primarily to the combination of a stock market decline and inflation. While the mean ratio of personal saving to disposable income of 6.2% contrasted with a mean ratio of net revaluations to disposable income of —0.2% over the entire 1946 to 1977 period, there were substantial fluctuations, particularly in the latter. The mean net revaluations ratios were some 50% *more* than the mean personal saving ratios for the subperiods from 1951 to 1955 and from 1961 to 1965.

Another view of net revaluations may be found with conversion of all the saving data to 1972 dollars, using the implicit price deflator for fixed investment. As is shown in table 5.34, mean net revaluations in these 1972 dollars were —$5.7 billion, offsetting almost one-sixth of mean personal saving of $35.8 billion.

The role of net revaluations in a comprehensive measure of capital accumulation comes forth clearly in table 5.35, and corresponding figure 5.1, where we examine tangible assets in particular. Tangible net investment—the acquisition of residential and nonresidential capital, nonprofit investment in plant and equipment, household investment in durable goods, and government fixed investment, all net of depreciation, plus investment in business inventories and investment in land—totaled $1,990 billion from 1946 to 1977, as against only $1,372 billion for the BEA's net private domestic investment. In addition, net revaluations of tangible capital amounted to $931 billion. Thus, tangible net accumulation of nonhuman capital came to $2,920 billion. The means per year were $43 billion for net private domestic investment, $62 billion for tangible net investment of all sectors, $29 billion for net revaluations and $91 billion for net capital accumulation.

Some confirmation of these results for tangible capital may be found by estimating gross revaluations and net revaluations from the data on national tangible assets, provided in both current prices and constant (1958) prices for the years 1952 to 1968 in the Census Bureau's *Historical Statistics of the United States, Colonial Times to 1970*. Calculations from these data indicate total net revaluations of $264 billion over the sixteen years, with a mean annual figure of $16.5 billion, as is shown in table 5.37. Net revaluations were somewhat negative, however, for reproducible assets alone, running to an annual average of —$5.5 billion, with a positive contribution of some $22 billion coming from land. The negative net revaluations on reproducible assets stemmed from sub-

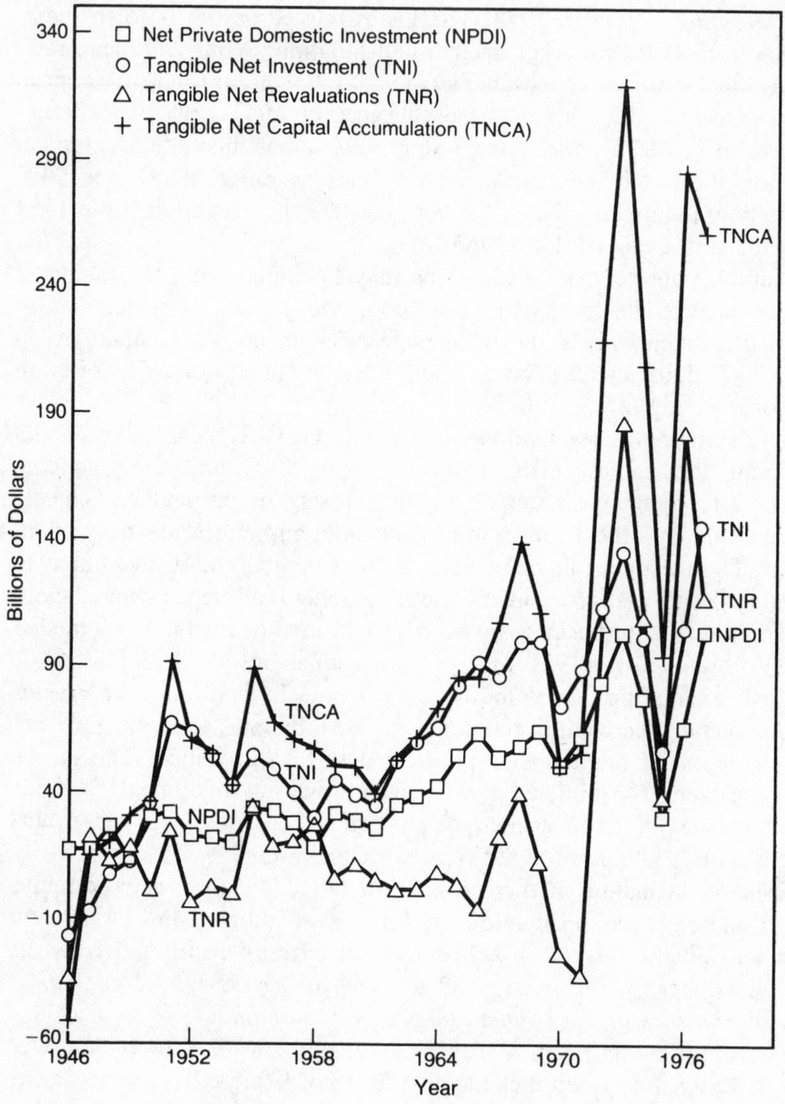

Fig. 5.1 Comparative movements of conventional investment and tangible capital formation, 1946–77. From table 5.35.

stantially negative figures on inventories and consumer and producer durables. Net revaluations for structures were, as in our own data, positive.

5.2.4 Human Capital

An analysis of capital revaluations and capital accumulation is incomplete unless consideration is given to human capital. By various measures, indeed, the amounts of human capital and human capital accumulation considerably exceed the magnitudes for nonhuman capital.

Information on earnings over the life cycle permits estimates of human capital as the present value of future labor earnings. Utilizing census public-use sample data with earnings by age-education cohort, Graham and Webb (1979) have applied a variety of discount rates to estimate the value of male human capital in 1969.

For illustrative purposes, at least, we have taken their estimates with a 7.5% discount rate, using both gross earnings and spendable earnings as a basis for development of time series for net stock. These have been accomplished by Graham by adjusting the 1969 estimates back to 1947 and forward to 1975 in accordance with reported changes in gross earnings and in spendable earnings as well as in population. Using the smaller spendable earnings series, estimates of the value of male human capital show it growing from $1,928 billion at the end of 1947 to $9,133 billion at the end of 1975 (table 5.38). "Gross" accumulation of human capital by this measure thus amounted to $7,205 billion over the twenty-eight-year period, with an annual mean of $257 billion. Applying our usual formulations to abstract from increases in the net stock of capital necessary to keep pace with inflation, we come up with net capital accumulation amounting to $2,249 billion from 1948 to 1975, a mean of $80 billion per year.

After this exercise in present value estimates of male human capital, we utilized the Kendrick series on human capital formation to produce replacement cost estimates of net stocks of human capital in both constant and current dollars. We used Kendrick's flows rather than his stock estimates because we considered his declining-balance depreciation assumptions inappropriate.

Although Kendrick had different assumed lives for various components of human capital, his estimates revealed an implicit average life of human capital of somewhat over fifty years. We took Kendrick's aggregate flows of human capital in constant dollars and applied straight-line depreciation with a fifty-year life throughout to derive net capital stocks in constant dollars, shown (converted to base 1969) in table 5.40. We used the implicit price deflators for gross investment in human capital calculated from Kendrick's aggregate flows in current and constant dollars to reflate the constant-dollar net capital stock series to current replacement-cost dollars. The constant-dollar depreciation was similarly reflated so that net investment and gross revaluation could be distinguished in our usual manner.

We then find, as shown in table 5.39, that net investment in human capital totaled $1,732 billion from 1946 through 1969, with gross revaluations of $1,200 billion accounting for the rest of the increase in the value of human capital. Net revaluations, however, were much less, amounting to $145 billion. Total net capital accumulation, the sum of net investment and net revaluations, was $1,877 from 1946 through 1969, implying a mean annual net capital accumulation of $78 billion,[8] of which $72 billion was net investment and $6 billion was net revaluations. In constant 1969 dollars the picture was similar, but with figures generally higher. Thus mean net investment was $95 billion, mean net revaluations were $8 billion and mean net capital accumulation was $103 billion (table 5.40).

The various components of accumulation of nonhuman and human capital may usefully be juxtaposed. We may view all of human capital as owned by households and compare and combine household investment revaluations and total capital accumulation of nonhuman capital and the corresponding series for human capital. Over the period 1946 to 1969 for which our human capital calculations can also be made from the underlying Kendrick data, we find, as is revealed in table 5.41, that the $1,732 billion net investment in human capital was more than 1.75 times the $971 billion of household net investment in nonhuman capital. The mean annual figure of $72 billion for net investment in human capital contrasted with $40 billion for nonhuman capital.

Net revaluations of nonhuman capital over this period were greater, however. Their total of $272 billion (with a mean annual figure of $11 billion) considerably exceeds the total human capital net revaluations of $145 billion noted above. The estimate of net nonhuman capital accumulation, of $1,242 billion (mean of $52 billion), is markedly less than the $1,877 billion for human capital. Net accumulation of both nonhuman and human capital amounted to $3,119 billion, with a mean of $130 billion.

Put in constant (1969) dollars again, the relative excess of net accumulation of human capital over that of nonhuman capital is even greater. Human capital formation of $2,465 billion was about 1.65 times the nonhuman accumulation of $1,492 billion. In the current dollar series, human capital accumulation was only 1.51 times nonhuman capital accumulation, the difference being considerably accounted for by the relatively larger effect of negative constant-dollar net revaluations of nonhuman capital just after World War II.

Finally, we may usefully compare, in table 5.43 and corresponding figure 5.2, total net formation of nonhuman and human capital with

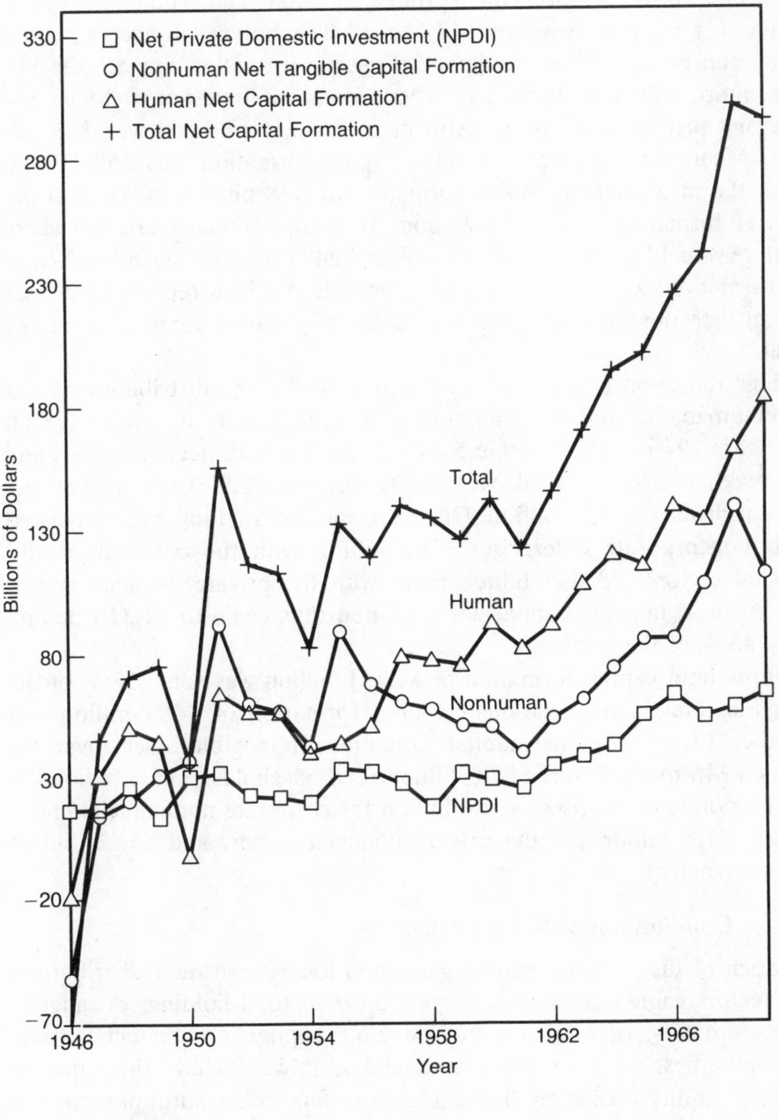

Fig. 5.2 Conventional investment and nonhuman, human, and total capital formation, 1946–69. From table 5.43.

the BEA series of net private domestic investment. Net investment according to the narrow BEA concept, excluding government and household investment (except owner-occupied homes) and also excluding net revaluations, was $801 billion from 1946 through 1969. Our total net tangible formation of nonhuman capital, by contrast, was $1,427 billion. We have of course, included investment by households and government and net revaluations on reproducible assets and land.

To this we may wish to add the $1,877 billion of net formation of human capital. Thus, nonfinancial capital formation was $3,304 billion, more than four times net private domestic investment. Mean annual net private domestic investment from 1946 to 1969 was $33 billion. Mean net tangible nonhuman capital formation was $59 billion. With the mean human capital formation of $78 billion, mean total net capital formation was $138 billion. If these estimates are anywhere near reasonable, one cannot but reflect that, whatever the role of capital formation, what the Bureau of Economic Analysis reports by way of net private domestic investment is a literally minor component of the total.

This reflection is sustained by examination of the distribution of net (nonhuman) capital accumulation of tangible assets by sector for all the years 1946 to 1977 (table 5.44). Including both net investment and net revaluations,[9] the total, we may recall, was $2,920 billion, and the annual mean was $91 billion. Of this, some $498 billion was associated with noncorporate enterprise, $767 billion with the corporate nonfinancial sector, and $45 billion more with the private financial sector. All business tangible capital accumulation thus came to $1,310 billion, only 45% of the total.

Household capital formation of $1,121 billion was some 38% of the tangible total, and government capital formation of $489 billion was another 17%. Mean net capital formation of tangible assets over the years 1946 to 1977 was $35.0 billion for households, $15.6 billion for noncorporate enterprises, $24.0 billion for corporate nonfinancial enterprises, $1.4 billion for the private financial sector, and $15.3 billion for government.

5.2.5 Composition of Net Revaluations

Much of the story on capital gains and losses is in their distribution. All sectors gained, in varying degree, on their total holdings of tangible assets—that is, of land and reproducible capital. On financial assets and liabilities, what we call nontangibles, if we exclude the value of business equity owned by households and financial institutions, net revaluations for the entire economy come close to zero. The mean negative figure of —$0.4 billion is presumably a net loss on dealings with the rest of the world. As is seen, however, in tables 5.45 and 5.46, in current and 1972 dollars respectively, the near-zero total reflects losses of more than $700 billion by households, matched by gains of roughly this amount in the noncorporate, corporate financial, and government sectors.

First, with regard to households (tables 5.47 and 5.48), while the net revaluations on owner-occupied housing in 1972 dollars, for example, came to a modest mean of $3.5 billion, the associated gain in net revaluations on household mortgage debt was $10.3 billion. We have already observed that all sectors were substantial gainers on land; for households, the mean gain in 1972 dollars was $6.8 billion. Households were losers in consumer durables, however, at an average rate of $7.9 billion per year.

Households lost most heavily, as may be imagined with long-run inflation, in their holdings of money, at an average rate of $19.2 billion in 1972 dollars on the total of currency and demand and time deposits. They also lost heavily, to the amount of $5.1 billion per year, on United States government securities and about $2.7 billion on state and local obligations and corporate and foreign bonds. Households were major losers indirectly, if not directly, in life insurance and pension funds, which showed mean net revaluations of —$10.8 billion from 1946 to 1977.

Despite massive fluctuations in value, corporate equities yielded a mean annual gain to households of $4.5 billion in 1972 dollars. Equity in noncorporate business shows a very substantial positive net revaluation, totaling $377 billion and averaging $11.8 billion per year.

It may be reasonable to infer with regard to the household sector that gains came primarily to homeowners (who generally had mortgage debts), to corporate stockholders, and to independent proprietors. It is probable that the majority of relatively lower-income households tended to be net losers, with investments primarily in life insurance and pension funds, savings accounts, and government saving bonds. Egalitarian considerations might suggest these points as an argument for eliminating government restrictions on payment of interest by banks and saving institutions. They might also suggest the advisability of offerings of indexed government bonds that would permit both individuals and their pension funds to protect themselves against losses in the real value of securities because of inflation.

It might also be noted that reduction of taxes on capital gains increases the disparity of tax treatment and widens the dispersion in the total of ordinary after-tax income and net revaluations. Those with savings accounts and corporate and federal government bonds have interest income that is fully taxed and have suffered real nondeductible capital losses. By contrast there were relatively lightly taxed capital gains on land, homes, and mortgage debt, and on corporate equity.

In the noncorporate sector, detailed in tables 5.49 and 5.50, mean total net revaluations were +$11.8 billion in 1972 dollars. The substantial mean annual net revaluation of $8.9 billion in 1972 dollars in land may well reflect capital gains on farms, which are here all lumped with noncorporate enterprises. Somewhat lesser gains on residential structures and nonresidential plant and equipment totaled $36 billion, coming to an annual average of $1.1 billion. The noncorporate sector turned up a loser, however, to the amount of $1 billion per year, on currency and demand deposits.

The corporate nonfinancial sector was a net gainer, in total, of $405 billion over the thirty-two-year period, for an average positive net revaluation of $12.6 billion in 1972 dollars. It actually gained in tangible assets a total of $208 billion—$134 billion in residential structures and nonresidential plant and equipment, $61 billion in land, and $13.5 billion on inventories. The corporate nonfinancial sector was a major loser, however, in financial assets, to a total of $405 billion in 1972 dollars, of which $68 billion could be attributed to currency and deposits, $27 billion to United States government securities, $14 billion to commercial paper, and a quite substantial $206 billion to consumer and trade credit.

The corporate nonfinancial sector's gains on the liability side totaled $601 billion, for an annual average of $18.8 billion in 1972 dollars. These stem considerably from "corporate and foreign bonds" where the total gain was $184 billion, from mortgage debt with a total gain of $94 billion, from "other loans" with a total of $126 billion, and from net trade debt with a total of $156 billion. All this is shown in sum and year by year in table 5.52.

The mean annual negative net revaluations of —$5.7 billion in 1972 dollars in the private financial sector is the result, as is spelled out in table 5.54, of $1,517 billion of negative net revaluations in financial assets almost balanced by $1,327 billion of negative net revaluations in liabilities. By our reckoning, in the years from 1946 to 1977 the private financial sector lost $22 billion on assets in the form of deposits and currency, $54 billion on interbank claims, $131 billion on corporate shares, $243 billion on United States government securities, $92 billion on state and local obligations, $181 billion on corporate and foreign bonds, $402 billion on mortgages, $318 billion on "other loans," $23 billion on security credit, $4 billion on trade credit, and $46 billion on miscellaneous assets. On the other side, negative net revaluations among liabilities caused gains of $761 billion on deposits and currency, $306 billion on life insurance and pension reserves, $13 billion on interbank claims, $37 billion on investment company shares, $23 billion on corporate and foreign bonds, $14 billion on security debt, $3 billion on taxes payable, and $117 billion on miscellaneous liabilities. Our measure of gains in tangible assets for the private financial sector was small, amounting to only $1 billion on residential and nonresidential capital and $5 billion on land.

The government sector, we may recall, was a substantial gainer, with total net revaluations amounting to +$844 billion in 1972 dollars for 1946 to 1977. As is shown in table 5.56, there were gains of $927 billion from negative net revaluations of government liabilities. These amounted to $148 billion for state and local obligations, $592 billion for United States government securities, $12 billion for trade debt, and $40 billion for life insurance and pension funds. Recalling that federally sponsored credit agencies and the Federal Reserve are included in the government sector, we also note $75 billion of gains on currency, demand deposit, and time deposit liabilities, and $45 billion more on vault cash and member bank reserves. Finally, $14 billion was gained on miscellaneous liabilities. The government sector lost $57 billion in 1972 dollars on its financial assets in currency and deposits, $50 billion on gold, SDRs and foreign exchange, some $113 billion on holdings of United States government securities, $4 billion on state and local obligations, $50 billion on mortgages, $64 billion on other loans, $25 billion on taxes receivable, $5 billion on trade credit, and $8 billion on miscellaneous assets. In tangible assets, the government sector gained some $144 billion on structures, plant, and equipment, and $173 billion on land. It lost $22 billion on inventories.

5.3 Summary and Conclusions

We have distinguished revaluations of capital, net of general price-level changes, for inclusion in measures of income and capital accumulation. We have then proceeded to estimate net revaluations in the United States economy from 1946 through 1977 and to present the results in varying detail, along with a number of series for net worth or net capital stocks, net investment, gross revaluations, and related data from our conventional accounts.

We have prepared estimates on major sectors of the economy, and for human and nonhuman capital, the latter broken down in some detail for both tangible assets, including land, and for financial assets and liabilities.

Net revaluations or capital gains turn out on balance, despite considerable fluctuations, particularly in certain financial assets and liabilities, to be substantially positive. Capital gains, at least by our measure in this thirty-two-year period, and even after allowance for general inflation effects, have not been completely offset by capital losses.

On tangible assets alone, mean net revaluations over the years from 1946 to 1977 were +$29.1 billion (or +$28.0 billion in 1972 dollars). Tangible net investment aside from revaluations showed a mean figure of \$62.2 billion. These magnitudes relate to all tangible nonhuman capital, in government and households as well as in business, and include net revaluations of land. An interesting rough comparison is to be found in the mean figure of \$42.9 billion for net private domestic investment in the conventional income and product accounts. Our mean tangible net capital accumulation by contrast is \$91.3 billion. Total tangible capital accumulation from 1946 through 1977 by our measure was \$2,920 billion. Total net private domestic investment reported by the Bureau of Economic Analysis was \$1,372 billion.

Measured net revaluations by our methods were relatively less in the case of human capital, but total mean net capital accumulation was large. For the period 1946 to 1969, for which we were able to make reasonably comparable estimates, mean net private domestic investment was \$33 billion, mean net tangible capital formation of nonhuman capital was \$59 billion, and mean formation of human capital was \$78 billion.

Measured in 1969 dollars and including all household assets, tangible and financial, we find that mean household nonhuman capital accumulation came to \$62 billion, of which \$11 billion was attributed to net revaluations. Mean human capital formation was estimated at \$103 billion, of which \$8 billion was attributed to net revaluations.

The sectoral breakdown indicates major gains by government, substantial positive net revaluations for nonfinancial business, both corporate and noncorporate, and some losses on balance in the financial sector. Households (including personal trusts and nonprofit institutions) also ended up net losers, but variations over time were great and the aggregates subsumed wide differences by category of assets and liabilities. In general, holders of land, owners of homes (especially because of their gains on mortgage debt liabilities), owners of unincorporated business, and, until recently, owners of corporate equity, tended to do well. Those households, probably constituting the majority, who were not relatively well situated in terms of these kinds of investments, tended to be losers because of the substantial negative net revaluations on currency, demand and time deposits, and life insurance and pension funds.

The collection and processing of these data has turned into a mammoth job for the dedicated but small crew of research associates working with me. Updating and taking advantage of more and improved data since the original version of this paper was presented to the 1976 Toronto conference has in itself become a formidable undertaking. As more government resources and those of other researchers are applied to update and improve upon basic relevant data, our own estimates may well be further corrected and sharpened. Our reported gains and losses on financial assets and liabilities depend upon a compounding of data from the Flow of Funds section of the Federal Reserve Board and our own security price indexes and are calculated at highly aggregative levels. The estimates of land values are also highly aggregative and likely to be susceptible of substantial improvement.

As for our estimates of net revaluations of tangible assets, it must be recognized that they depend critically on "replacement cost" calculations rather than market valuations, on the one hand, and on the relation between movements of the implicit price deflators for capital goods and of the general price deflator on the other. Thus, positive net revaluations in tangible assets arise essentially where their prices increase more rapidly than does our GNP implicit price deflator.

That this last has proved true should not be a great surprise. We should generally have been aware of major gains in land prices, the result of direct development and positive externalities from other investment as well as increasing scarcity. And capital goods prices, at least by conventional measures, have tended to rise more than those of other goods.

For human capital, which accounts for such a major portion of total accumulation, our estimated net revaluations appear less, but here the factors remain buried, at least for the moment, in the composition of the implicit price deflators for human capital investment that we have derived from Kendrick's flows.

The magnitude of net revaluations over the thirty-two-year period we have examined, $869 billion in 1972 dollars in nonhuman capital, suggests that we ignore them at some peril in measures of income, saving, and capital accumulation. At the household level, the distribution of personal income will reflect quite imperfectly the distribution or accrual of economic power and the means of economic well-being. Measures of saving and of tangible capital accumulation, so relevant in the perennial choices of individuals and society between the present and the future, should take into account capital gains (and losses) along with all kinds of investment, in human as well as nonhuman capital, in government and household sectors as well as in business. Reform of accounting procedures to eliminate the distorting effects of inflation should include revaluations of existing assets and liabilities corresponding to alterations in the values of flows that reflect changes in relative prices and in the general price level.

Consumption and saving must depend upon all income. The value of current production must relate to the current value of all capital. While much can certainly be done to improve upon the series presented here, one may hope to test their usefulness and relevance even in their current form by introducing them as arguments in the functions for consumption, investment, production, and economic growth that are properly of ultimate concern.

Table 5.1 Net Worth, Net Investment, Gross and Net Revaluations of Nonhuman Capital, Households (Billions of Dollars, 1946–77)

(1) Year	(2) Net Worth	(3) Net Investment	(4) Gross Revaluations	(5) Net Revaluations
1946	726.036	20.276	29.078	− 85.315
1947	783.465	21.083	36.346	− 30.317
1948	818.491	25.158	9.868	− 11.348
1949	854.087	21.405	14.190	28.037
1950	942.501	27.744	60.670	− .373
1951	1,026.869	34.004	50.364	21.144
1952	1,075.934	29.359	19.706	2.548
1953	1,100.852	30.827	− 5.909	− 14.957
1954	1,212.230	29.556	81.822	63.078
1955	1,321.428	32.556	76.641	44.081
1956	1,409.199	36.148	51.623	.093
1957	1,434.300	35.110	−10.009	− 41.611
1958	1,614.727	34.184	146.243	121.181
1959	1,707.997	37.500	55.770	19.325
1960	1,752.304	35.074	9.233	− 8.662
1961	1,908.422	36.160	119.958	94.589
1962	1,903.909	40.922	−45.435	− 81.163
1963	2,050.992	46.232	100.851	73.719
1964	2,182.221	56.498	74.731	39.963
1965	2,352.671	63.115	107.335	49.389
1966	2,400.394	70.185	−22.462	−106.684
1967	2,699.490	71.393	227.703	142.918
1968	3,040.586	75.646	265.450	135.487
1969	3,086.610	60.405	−14.381	−183.417
1970	3,211.841	90.986	34.244	−125.636
1971	3,478.359	94.618	171.901	19.884
1972	3,845.887	107.452	260.076	109.739
1973	3,971.277	125.818	− .428	−308.700
1974	4,102.147	120.920	9.950	−439.649
1975	4,591.715	139.081	350.487	84.803
1976	5,193.564	138.122	463.727	219.359
1977	5,597.180	150.160	253.456	− 62.497
Sums				
1946–50		115.666	150.153	− 99.315
1951–55		156.302	222.625	115.894
1956–60		178.016	252.861	90.326
1961–65		242.927	357.440	176.497
1966–70		368.615	490.554	−137.331
1971–75		587.889	791.986	−533.923
1976–77		288.282	717.183	156.862

Table 5.1 (continued)

Year (1)	Net Worth (2)	Net Investment (3)	Gross Revaluations (4)	Net Revaluations (5)
Means				
1946–50	824.916	23.133	30.031	− 19.863
1951–55	1,147.463	31.260	44.525	23.179
1956–60	1,583.706	35.603	50.572	18.065
1961–65	2,079.643	48.585	71.488	35.299
1966–70	2,887.784	73.723	98.111	− 27.466
1971–75	3,997.877	117.578	158.397	−106.785
1976–77	5,395.372	144.141	358.592	78.431
Sums, 1946–77		1,937.697	2,982.802	−230.990
Means, 1946–77	2,293.678	60.553	93.213	− 7.218

Table 5.2 **Net Worth, Net Investment, Gross and Net Revaluations of Nonhuman Capital, Households (Billions of 1972 Dollars, 1946–77)**

(1) Year	(2) Net Worth	(3) Net Investment	(4) Gross Revaluations	(5) Net Revaluations
1946	1,757.956	49.094	70.407	−206.573
1947	1,602.178	43.115	74.328	− 61.998
1948	1,527.036	46.937	18.411	− 21.171
1949	1,558.552	39.060	25.895	51.163
1950	1,668.143	49.104	107.381	− .660
1951	1,688.929	55.928	82.836	34.776
1952	1,732.583	47.277	31.732	4.103
1953	1,750.162	49.010	− 9.394	− 23.779
1954	1,912.035	46.618	129.057	99.492
1955	2,039.240	50.241	118.273	68.026
1956	2,063.249	52.925	75.583	.137
1957	2,022.991	49.520	−14.117	− 58.690
1958	2,280.688	48.282	206.558	171.159
1959	2,385.470	52.374	77.890	26.991
1960	2,437.141	48.782	12.842	− 12.047
1961	2,665.394	50.503	167.539	132.107
1962	2,644.318	56.836	−63.104	−112.727
1963	2,844.649	64.122	139.876	102.246
1964	2,997.556	77.607	102.653	54.894
1965	3,187.902	85.522	145.441	66.923

Table 5.2 (continued)

(1) Year	(2) Worth Net	(3) Net Investment	(4) Gross Revaluations	(5) Net Revaluations
1966	3,150.124	92.106	−29.478	−140.006
1967	3,430.102	90.715	289.330	181.599
1968	3,703.516	92.139	323.325	165.027
1969	3,551.911	69.511	−16.549	−211.067
1970	3,525.621	99.875	37.590	−137.909
1971	3,627.069	98.663	179.250	20.734
1972	3,845.887	107.452	260.076	109.739
1973	3,746.488	118.696	− .404	−291.226
1974	3,485.257	102.736	8.454	−373.534
1975	3,468.063	105.046	264.718	64.050
1976	3,714.996	98.800	331.707	156.909
1977	3,724.005	99.907	168.634	− 41.581
Sums				
1946–50		227.310	296.422	−239.240
1951–55		249.073	352.505	182.618
1956–60		251.884	358.757	127.550
1961–65		334.590	492.405	243.444
1966–70		444.346	604.219	−142.356
1971–75		532.593	712.094	−470.236
1976–77		198.707	500.341	115.328
Means				
1946–50	1,622.773	45.462	59.284	− 47.848
1951–55	1,824.590	49.815	70.501	36.524
1956–60	2,237.908	50.377	71.751	25.510
1961–65	2,867.964	66.918	98.481	48.689
1966–70	3,472.255	88.869	120.844	− 28.471
1971–75	3,634.553	106.519	142.419	− 94.047
1976–77	3,719.500	99.354	250.171	57.664
Sums, 1946–77		2,238.504	3,316.741	−182.892
Means, 1946–77	2,679.350	69.953	103.648	− 5.715

Table 5.3 **Net Worth, Net Investment, Gross and Net Revaluations of Nonhuman Capital, and Business (Billions of Dollars, 1946–77)**

(1) Year	(2) Net Worth	(3) Net Investment	(4) Gross Revaluations	(5) Net Revaluations
1946	399.223	3.409	42.545	−16.585
1947	449.353	9.002	41.127	4.585
1948	478.359	12.975	16.032	3.867
1949	491.321	7.704	5.258	13.330
1950	539.014	8.756	38.937	4.148
1951	575.114	10.318	25.783	9.149
1952	593.587	11.477	6.996	− 2.555
1953	609.328	8.039	7.701	2.756
1954	627.749	4.174	14.248	3.969
1955	651.983	5.284	18.948	2.240
1956	694.615	8.258	34.375	9.141
1957	740.446	7.137	38.695	23.203
1958	758.126	1.584	16.096	3.319
1959	766.535	3.029	5.380	−11.587
1960	798.530	1.420	30.574	22.587
1961	801.853	2.200	1.124	−10.311
1962	842.767	12.420	28.494	13.524
1963	851.018	3.343	4.909	− 6.960
1964	879.528	8.884	19.626	5.335
1965	908.483	7.852	21.103	− 2.015
1966	975.663	15.400	51.781	19.444
1967	1,006.183	3.249	27.270	− 6.651
1968	1,056.394	1.137	49.073	1.272
1969	1,109.912	3.269	50.249	− 7.979
1970	1,196.494	7.030	80.007	23.176
1971	1,240.342	−14.956	58.348	2.780
1972	1,331.282	− 8.486	99.426	46.878
1973	1,593.686	5.661	256.743	151.621
1974	1,979.900	−22.573	408.787	232.315
1975	2,139.149	−12.217	171.466	45.814
1976	2,429.262	.320	289.793	177.578
1977	2,641.827	.483	212.083	66.391
Sums				
1946–50		41.846	143.899	9.345
1951–55		39.292	73.676	15.559
1956–60		21.428	125.120	46.663
1961–65		34.699	75.256	− .427
1966–70		30.085	258.380	29.262
1971–75		−52.571	994.770	479.408
1976–77		.803	501.876	243.969

Table 5.3 (continued)

(1) Year	(2) Net Worth	(3) Net Investment	(4) Gross Revaluations	(5) Net Revaluations
Means				
1946–50	471.454	8.369	28.780	1.869
1951–55	611.552	7.858	14.735	3.112
1956–60	751.650	4.286	25.024	9.333
1961–65	856.730	6.940	15.051	– .085
1966–70	1,069.020	6.017	51.676	5.852
1971–75	1,656.872	–10.514	198.954	95.882
1976–77	2,535.545	.401	250.938	121.985
Sums, 1946–77		115.582	2,172.977	823.779
Means, 1946–77	1,004.921	3.612	67.906	25.743

Note: Excludes private financial corporate shares.

Table 5.4 **Net Worth, Net Investment, Gross and Net Revaluations of Nonhuman Capital, Business (Billions of 1972 Dollars, 1946–77)**

(1) Year	(2) Net Worth	(3) Net Investment	(4) Gross Revaluations	(5) Net Revaluations
1946	966.643	8.254	103.014	–40.157
1947	918.923	18.409	84.105	9.377
1948	892.462	24.207	29.910	7.214
1949	896.572	14.058	9.594	24.325
1950	954.006	15.496	68.913	7.342
1951	945.912	16.970	42.407	15.047
1952	955.857	18.483	11.265	– 4.113
1953	968.725	12.780	12.245	4.381
1954	990.142	6.584	22.473	6.261
1955	1,006.146	8.154	29.242	3.455
1956	1,017.005	12.091	50.329	13.382
1957	1,044.353	10.066	54.575	32.725
1958	1,070.800	2.238	22.735	4.688
1959	1,070.580	4.230	7.515	–16.182
1960	1,110.612	1.975	42.522	31.414
1961	1,119.907	3.073	1.570	–14.402
1962	1,170.510	17.250	39.575	18.783
1963	1,180.331	4.636	6.808	– 9.653
1964	1,208.144	12.204	26.959	7.328
1965	1,231.006	10.640	28.596	– 2.732

Table 5.4 (continued)

(1) Year	(2) Net Worth	(3) Net Investment	(4) Gross Revaluations	(5) Net Revaluations
1966	1,280.400	20.210	67.954	25.518
1967	1,278.505	4.127	34.651	− 8.453
1968	1,286.717	1.385	59.773	1.551
1969	1,277.229	3.762	57.825	− 9.182
1970	1,313.886	7.717	87.823	25.440
1971	1,293.370	−15.596	60.842	2.900
1972	1,331.282	− 8.486	99.426	46.878
1973	1,503.478	5.340	242.212	143.039
1974	1,682.157	−19.178	347.312	197.380
1975	1,615.670	− 9.228	129.506	34.602
1976	1,737.669	.229	207.291	127.023
1977	1,757.703	.321	141.107	44.173
Sums				
1946–50		80.424	295.536	8.101
1951–55		62.971	117.632	25.031
1956–60		30.600	177.676	66.027
1961–65		47.803	103.508	− .676
1966–70		37.201	308.026	34.874
1971–75		−47.148	879.298	424.799
1976–77		.550	348.398	171.196
Means				
1946–50	925.721	16.085	59.107	1.620
1951–55	973.356	12.594	23.526	5.006
1956–60	1,062.670	6.120	35.535	13.205
1961–65	1,181.980	9.561	20.702	− .135
1966–70	1,287.347	7.440	61.605	6.975
1971–75	1,485.191	− 9.430	175.860	84.960
1976–77	1,747.686	.275	174.199	85.598
Sums, 1946–77		212.401	2,230.074	729.352
Means, 1946–77	1,189.897	6.638	69.690	22.792

Note: Excludes private financial corporate shares.

Table 5.5 **Net Worth, Net Investment, Gross and Net Revaluations of Nonhuman Capital, Noncorporate Nonfarm, and Farm (Billions of Dollars, 1946–77)**

(1) Year	(2) Net Worth	(3) Net Investment	(4) Gross Revaluations	(5) Net Revaluations
1946	222.778	1.506	25.990	− 6.659
1947	249.365	1.864	24.722	4.470
1948	259.020	5.130	4.526	− 2.220
1949	260.263	.914	.329	4.686
1950	288.730	3.723	24.744	6.357
1951	309.720	2.609	18.381	9.495
1952	312.101	1.066	1.316	− 3.766
1953	314.473	1.352	1.019	− 1.567
1954	319.447	− .929	5.904	.623
1955	330.296	− .617	11.465	3.006
1956	351.296	.795	20.205	7.489
1957	367.471	1.102	15.074	7.260
1958	391.299	1.852	21.976	15.624
1959	396.840	− 1.209	6.750	− 1.980
1960	405.868	1.044	7.984	3.848
1961	412.567	1.876	4.823	− .996
1962	424.809	1.399	10.843	3.185
1963	436.516	2.194	9.513	3.527
1964	449.443	.855	12.072	4.776
1965	471.256	2.143	19.670	7.882
1966	502.726	2.377	29.093	12.408
1967	529.265	.116	26.423	8.977
1968	567.233	2.965	35.003	9.803
1969	597.675	− 6.159	36.601	5.559
1970	623.406	8.309	17.422	−13.297
1971	647.572	− 3.457	27.622	− 1.413
1972	710.752	− 7.899	71.079	43.723
1973	846.559	− 3.152	138.959	83.095
1974	951.168	−11.688	116.297	22.539
1975	1,007.519	− 8.097	64.449	4.156
1976	1,152.627	− 9.595	154.703	102.098
1977	1,260.618	−16.645	124.636	56.015
Sums				
1946–50		13.137	80.315	6.634
1951–55		3.481	38.085	7.791
1956–60		3.584	71.988	32.241
1961–65		8.467	56.921	18.373
1966–70		7.608	144.542	23.450
1971–75		−34.293	418.406	152.100
1976–77		−26.240	279.339	158.113

Table 5.5 (continued)

(1) Year	(2) Net Worth	(3) Net Investment	(4) Gross Revaluations	(5) Net Revaluations
Means				
1946–50	256.031	2.627	16.063	1.327
1951–55	317.207	.696	7.617	1.558
1956–60	382.555	.717	14.398	6.448
1961–65	438.918	1.693	11.384	3.675
1966–70	564.061	1.522	28.908	4.690
1971–75	832.714	− 6.859	83.681	30.420
1976–77	1,206.623	−13.120	139.669	79.056
Sums, 1946–77		−24.256	1,089.597	398.703
Means, 1946–77	511.584	− .758	34.050	12.459

Table 5.6 **Net Worth, Net Investment, Gross and Net Revaluations of Nonhuman Capital, Noncorporate Nonfarm, and Farm (Billions of 1972 Dollars, 1946–77)**

(1) Year	(2) Net Worth	(3) Net Investment	(4) Gross Revaluations	(5) Net Revaluations
1946	539.415	3.646	62.942	−16.124
1947	509.948	3.812	50.557	9.142
1948	483.246	9.571	8.443	− 4.142
1949	474.932	1.668	.600	8.551
1950	511.026	6.589	43.794	11.252
1951	509.408	4.291	30.232	15.617
1952	502.579	1.717	2.119	− 6.064
1953	499.957	2.149	1.620	− 2.491
1954	503.860	− 1.465	9.312	.983
1955	509.716	− .952	17.694	4.638
1956	514.342	1.164	29.583	10.964
1957	518.295	1.554	21.260	10.239
1958	552.682	2.616	31.039	22.067
1959	554.246	− 1.689	9.428	− 2.765
1960	564.490	1.452	11.104	5.352
1961	576.211	2.620	6.736	− 1.392
1962	590.013	1.943	15.060	4.424
1963	605.432	3.043	13.194	4.891
1964	617.367	1.174	16.582	6.560
1965	638.558	2.904	26.654	10.680

Table 5.6 (continued)

(1) Year	(2) Net Worth	(3) Net Investment	(4) Gross Revaluations	(5) Net Revaluations
1966	659.746	3.119	38.180	16.284
1967	672.510	.147	33.574	11.406
1968	690.905	3.611	42.634	11.940
1969	687.773	− 7.087	42.119	6.397
1970	684.310	9.121	19.124	−14.596
1971	675.257	− 3.605	28.803	− 1.473
1972	710.752	− 7.899	71.079	43.723
1973	798.641	− 2.974	131.094	78.391
1974	808.129	− 9.930	98.808	19.150
1975	760.966	− 6.116	48.677	3.139
1976	824.483	− 6.863	110.660	73.032
1977	838.735	−11.075	82.925	37.269
Sums				
1946–50		25.287	166.336	8.679
1951–55		5.740	60.976	12.683
1956–60		5.098	102.414	45.859
1961–65		11.684	78.225	25.163
1966–70		8.912	175.632	31.431
1971–75		−30.523	378.461	142.930
1976–77		−17.938	193.585	110.300
Means				
1946–50	503.713	5.057	33.267	1.736
1951–55	505.104	1.148	12.195	2.537
1956–60	540.811	1.020	20.483	9.172
1961–65	605.516	2.337	15.645	5.033
1966–70	679.049	1.782	35.126	6.286
1971–75	750.749	− 6.105	75.692	28.586
1976–77	831.609	− 8.969	96.792	55.150
Sums, 1946–77		8.259	1,155.629	377.046
Means, 1946–77	612.123	.258	36.113	11.783

Table 5.7 **Net Worth, Net Investment, Gross and Net Revaluations of Nonhuman Capital, Nonfinancial Corporations (Billions of Dollars, 1946–77)**

(1) Year	(2) Net Worth	(3) Net Investment	(4) Gross Revaluations	(5) Net Revaluations
1946	152.851	.800	18.561	− 3.742
1947	188.899	6.529	21.519	7.392
1948	198.877	7.109	10.869	5.967
1949	207.429	7.961	.591	3.967
1950	228.523	3.988	17.106	2.406
1951	252.323	9.229	14.572	7.479
1952	265.036	7.743	4.969	.747
1953	277.032	6.021	5.975	3.755
1954	285.763	4.785	3.946	− .750
1955	309.867	6.523	17.580	9.920
1956	342.225	7.107	25.251	13.195
1957	367.854	5.199	20.430	12.783
1958	379.715	2.506	9.355	2.991
1959	399.962	5.849	14.398	5.857
1960	405.281	.545	4.774	.607
1961	415.237	4.409	5.548	− .285
1962	429.007	8.174	5.596	− 2.172
1963	439.725	6.283	4.435	− 1.645
1964	457.783	10.817	7.241	− .201
1965	488.676	12.321	18.572	6.428
1966	530.737	11.982	30.080	12.627
1967	579.587	16.206	32.644	13.889
1968	617.916	6.933	31.395	3.712
1969	695.913	10.452	67.545	33.245
1970	726.727	.449	30.365	− 5.166
1971	747.797	3.934	17.136	−16.883
1972	806.619	6.887	51.936	19.983
1973	941.156	− 1.351	135.887	72.394
1974	1,139.764	−25.054	223.662	120.099
1975	1,244.263	7.679	96.820	24.008
1976	1,313.476	13.472	55.741	− 9.868
1977	1,439.537	− 3.411	129.472	50.808
Sums				
1946–50		26.387	68.645	15.989
1951–55		34.301	47.043	21.150
1956–60		21.206	74.208	35.433
1961–65		42.004	41.391	2.126
1966–70		46.022	192.029	58.307
1971–75		− 7.905	525.441	219.600
1976–77		10.061	185.213	40.940

Table 5.7 (continued)

(1) Year	(2) Net Worth	(3) Net Investment	(4) Gross Revaluations	(5) Net Revaluations
Means				
1946–50	193.716	5.277	13.729	3.198
1951–55	278.004	6.860	9.409	4.230
1956–60	379.007	4.241	14.842	7.087
1961–65	446.086	8.401	8.278	.425
1966–70	630.176	9.204	38.406	11.661
1971–75	975.920	− 1.581	105.088	43.920
1976–77	1,376.506	5.031	92.607	20.470
Sums, 1946–77		172.076	1,133.971	393.545
Means, 1946–77	539.611	5.377	35.437	12.298

Table 5.8 **Net Worth, Net Investment, Gross and Net Revaluations of Nonhuman Capital, Nonfinancial Corporations (Billions of 1972 Dollars, 1946–77)**

(1) Year	(2) Net Worth	(3) Net Investment	(4) Gross Revaluations	(5) Net Revaluations
1946	370.100	1.937	44.942	− 9.061
1947	369.937	13.352	44.005	15.116
1948	371.040	13.263	20.279	11.133
1949	378.520	14.527	1.078	7.239
1950	404.465	7.058	30.276	4.258
1951	415.006	15.179	23.967	12.300
1952	426.789	12.469	8.002	1.203
1953	440.433	9.572	9.500	5.969
1954	450.731	7.547	6.224	− 1.183
1955	478.189	10.066	27.130	15.309
1956	501.061	10.406	36.971	19.319
1957	518.835	7.333	28.815	18.030
1958	536.321	3.540	13.214	4.224
1959	558.606	8.169	20.109	8.180
1960	563.673	.758	6.639	.844
1961	579.941	6.158	7.748	− .398
1962	595.843	11.353	7.772	− 3.016
1963	609.882	8.714	6.151	− 2.281
1964	628.823	14.859	9.947	− .276
1965	662.162	16.695	25.165	8.710

Table 5.8 (continued)

(1) Year	(2) Net Worth	(3) Net Investment	(4) Gross Revaluations	(5) Net Revaluations
1966	696.506	15.724	39.475	16.571
1967	736.451	20.592	41.479	17.647
1968	752.638	8.445	38.241	4.522
1969	800.820	12.028	77.728	38.256
1970	797.725	.493	33.332	− 5.671
1971	779.767	4.102	17.868	−17.605
1972	806.619	6.887	51.936	19.983
1973	887.883	− 1.275	128.196	68.297
1974	968.363	−21.286	190.027	102.038
1975	939.775	5.800	73.127	18.133
1976	939.539	9.637	39.872	− 7.059
1977	957.776	− 2.269	86.143	33.805
Sums				
1946–50		50.138	140.579	28.684
1951–55		54.834	74.823	33.598
1956–60		30.205	105.748	50.597
1961–65		57.779	56.782	2.739
1966–70		57.282	230.253	71.326
1971–75		− 5.772	461.154	190.845
1976–77		7.367	126.015	26.746
Means				
1946–50	378.812	10.028	28.116	5.737
1951–55	442.229	10.967	14.965	6.720
1956–60	535.699	6.041	21.150	10.119
1961–65	615.330	11.556	11.356	.548
1966–70	756.828	11.456	46.051	14.265
1971–75	876.482	− 1.154	92.231	38.169
1976–77	948.657	3.684	63.007	13.373
Sums, 1946–77		251.832	1,195.354	404.534
Means, 1946–77	622.632	7.870	37.355	12.642

Table 5.9 **Net Worth, Net Investment, Gross and Net Revaluations of Nonhuman Capital, Private Financial (Billions of Dollars, 1946–77)**

(1) Year	(2) Net Worth	(3) Net Investment	(4) Gross Revaluations	(5) Net Revaluations
1946	28.519	1.294	− 2.011	− 6.988
1947	24.363	.958	− 5.114	− 7.738
1948	26.024	1.024	.637	− .023
1949	31.698	1.336	4.338	4.781
1950	31.178	2.393	− 2.913	− 5.241
1951	23.335	− .673	− 7.170	− 8.121
1952	28.327	4.281	.711	.277
1953	30.777	1.743	.707	.464
1954	40.292	5.117	4.398	3.840
1955	35.990	5.795	−10.097	− 11.241
1956	27.071	2.163	−11.081	− 12.508
1957	30.692	.430	3.191	2.586
1958	23.520	8.063	−15.235	− 15.845
1959	12.421	4.669	−15.768	− 16.339
1960	33.688	3.450	17.816	17.676
1961	35.508	11.067	− 9.247	− 9.825
1962	47.019	− .544	12.055	11.402
1963	45.500	7.521	− 9.039	− 9.762
1964	55.945	10.132	.313	− .541
1965	47.467	8.661	−17.139	− 18.719
1966	36.792	− 3.283	− 7.392	− 9.017
1967	19.873	14.877	−31.797	− 33.385
1968	16.683	14.135	−17.325	− 18.603
1969	−42.307	− 5.093	−53.897	− 54.672
1970	− 2.409	7.678	32.220	34.182
1971	40.943	29.762	13.590	13.060
1972	59.160	41.805	−23.589	− 26.277
1973	8.779	−32.277	−18.103	− 21.411
1974	36.319	−41.288	68.828	70.145
1975	84.525	38.008	10.197	6.650
1976	200.959	37.085	79.349	73.972
1977	166.486	7.553	−42.025	− 54.303
Sums				
1946–50		7.005	− 5.063	− 15.209
1951–55		16.263	−11.451	− 14.781
1956–60		18.775	−21.077	− 24.430
1961–65		36.837	−23.057	− 27.446
1966–70		28.314	−78.190	− 81.494
1971–75		36.010	50.924	42.167
1976–77		44.638	37.324	19.669

Table 5.9 (continued)

(1) Year	(2) Net Worth	(3) Net Investment	(4) Gross Revaluations	(5) Net Revaluations
Means				
1946–50	28.357	1.401	– 1.013	– 3.042
1951–55	31.744	3.253	– 2.290	– 2.956
1956–60	25.479	3.755	– 4.215	– 4.886
1961–65	46.288	7.367	– 4.611	– 5.489
1966–70	5.727	5.663	–15.638	– 16.299
1971–75	45.945	7.202	10.185	8.433
1976–77	183.723	22.319	18.662	9.834
Sums, 1946–77		187.842	–50.592	–101.525
Means, 1946–77	40.161	5.870	– 1.581	– 3.173

Table 5.10 **Net Worth, Net Investment, Gross and Net Revaluations of Nonhuman Capital, Private Financial (Billions of 1972 Dollars, 1946–77)**

(1) Year	(2) Net Worth	(3) Net Investment	(4) Gross Revaluations	(5) Net Revaluations
1946	69.053	3.133	– 4.870	– 16.920
1947	49.823	1.959	– 10.457	– 15.824
1948	48.553	1.910	1.188	– .044
1949	57.844	2.438	7.916	8.725
1950	55.182	4.235	– 5.157	– 9.276
1951	38.380	– 1.107	– 11.792	– 13.357
1952	45.615	6.894	1.144	.446
1953	48.930	2.771	1.125	.738
1954	63.553	8.071	6.937	6.057
1955	55.540	8.943	– 15.582	– 17.348
1956	39.636	3.167	– 16.225	– 18.314
1957	43.289	.606	4.500	3.647
1958	33.221	11.388	– 21.518	– 22.379
1959	17.348	6.521	– 22.022	– 22.820
1960	46.854	4.798	24.779	24.584
1961	49.592	15.457	– 12.914	– 13.722
1962	65.304	– .756	16.743	15.835
1963	63.107	10.431	– 12.537	– 13.540
1964	76.848	13.918	.430	– .743
1965	64.319	11.736	– 23.223	– 25.365

Table 5.10 (continued)

(1) Year	(2) Net Worth	(3) Net Investment	(4) Gross Revaluations	(5) Net Revaluations
1966	48.284	– 4.308	– 9.701	– 11.833
1967	25.252	18.903	– 40.402	– 42.421
1968	20.321	17.217	– 21.102	– 22.658
1969	–48.684	– 5.861	– 62.022	– 62.913
1970	– 2.644	8.428	35.367	37.521
1971	42.694	31.034	14.171	13.619
1972	59.160	41.805	– 23.589	– 26.277
1973	8.282	–30.450	– 17.078	– 20.199
1974	30.857	–35.079	58.477	59.597
1975	63.840	28.707	7.702	5.022
1976	143.747	26.527	56.759	52.913
1977	110.769	5.025	– 27.961	– 36.130
Sums				
1946–50		13.676	– 11.379	– 33.339
1951–55		25.572	– 18.169	– 23.463
1956–60		26.481	– 30.485	– 35.282
1961–65		50.786	– 31.503	– 37.534
1966–70		34.379	– 97.859	–102.304
1971–75		36.017	39.683	31.761
1976–77		31.552	28.798	16.783
Means				
1946–50	56.091	2.735	– 2.276	– 6.668
1951–55	50.403	5.114	– 3.634	– 4.693
1956–60	36.070	5.296	– 6.097	– 7.056
1961–65	63.834	10.157	– 6.301	– 7.507
1966–70	8.506	6.876	– 19.572	– 20.461
1971–75	40.967	7.203	7.937	6.352
1976–77	127.258	15.776	14.399	8.391
Sums, 1946–77		218.464	–120.913	–183.378
Means, 1946–77	47.933	6.827	– 3.779	– 5.731

Table 5.11 **Net Worth, Net Investment, Gross and Net Revaluations of Nonhuman Capital, Government (Billions of Dollars, 1946–77)**

(1) Year	(2) Net Worth	(3) Net Investment	(4) Gross Revaluations	(5) Net Revaluations
1946	11.852	− 36.074	30.328	30.363
1947	26.876	− 22.308	37.332	37.244
1948	17.638	− 22.546	13.308	12.639
1949	−7.440	− 17.572	−7.506	− 7.284
1950	7.718	− 2.180	17.338	17.957
1951	58.045	30.022	20.305	19.817
1952	88.940	27.436	3.459	2.179
1953	107.545	15.387	3.218	2.405
1954	117.460	6.000	3.915	2.059
1955	166.662	11.411	37.791	34.528
1956	206.375	10.850	28.864	22.240
1957	214.232	4.461	3.396	− 1.227
1958	230.311	− 5.975	22.054	18.421
1959	252.173	.757	21.106	15.953
1960	247.673	2.865	−7.365	−10.000
1961	265.806	− 4.770	22.903	19.403
1962	273.643	2.076	5.761	.817
1963	296.904	8.126	15.135	11.223
1964	314.552	2.999	14.649	9.664
1965	350.672	5.993	30.127	21.816
1966	379.762	6.298	22.792	10.304
1967	416.703	− .670	37.611	24.449
1968	468.615	8.985	42.927	22.929
1969	560.194	12.040	79.539	53.410
1970	594.108	− 6.721	40.635	12.215
1971	619.461	− 25.368	50.721	23.528
1972	687.073	− 7.345	74.957	48.783
1973	857.624	1.894	168.657	114.447
1974	967.447	− 4.606	114.429	19.044
1975	979.272	− 72.058	83.882	24.633
1976	985.542	− 46.008	52.278	2.082
1977	1,069.895	− 32.316	116.669	58.537
Sums				
1946–50		−100.680	90.800	90.920
1951–55		90.256	68.688	60.987
1956–60		12.958	68.054	45.387
1961–65		14.424	88.575	62.924
1966–70		19.932	223.504	123.307
1971–75		−107.483	492.647	230.434
1976–77		− 78.324	168.947	60.619

Table 5.11 (continued)

(1) Year	(2) Net Worth	(3) Net Investment	(4) Gross Revaluations	(5) Net Revaluations
Means				
1946–50	11.329	– 20.136	18.160	18.184
1951–55	107.730	18.051	13.738	12.197
1956–60	230.153	2.592	13.611	9.077
1961–65	300.315	2.885	17.715	12.585
1966–70	483.876	3.986	44.701	24.661
1971–75	822.176	– 21.497	98.529	46.087
1976–77	1,027.718	– 39.162	84.473	30.310
Sums, 1946–77		–148.917	1,201.213	674.578
Means, 1946–77	369.792	– 4.654	37.538	21.081

Table 5.12 **Net Worth, Net Investment, Gross and Net Revaluations of Nonhuman Capital, Government (Billions of 1972 Dollars, 1946–77)**

(1) Year	(2) Net Worth	(3) Net Investment	(4) Gross Revaluations	(5) Net Revaluations
1946	28.697	– 87.346	73.432	73.519
1947	54.961	– 45.620	76.344	76.163
1948	32.906	– 42.063	24.828	23.580
1949	–13.576	– 32.066	–13.696	–13.292
1950	13.660	– 3.858	30.686	31.783
1951	95.468	49.378	33.396	32.593
1952	143.220	44.180	5.570	3.509
1953	170.978	24.463	5.116	3.823
1954	185.268	9.464	6.175	3.248
1955	257.194	17.610	58.319	53.283
1956	302.160	15.886	42.260	32.562
1957	302.161	6.292	4.789	– 1.730
1958	325.298	– 8.439	31.149	26.019
1959	352.197	1.057	29.477	22.280
1960	344.469	3.985	–10.243	–13.908
1961	371.237	– 6.662	31.987	27.100
1962	380.060	2.883	8.002	1.135
1963	411.795	11.270	20.991	15.566
1964	432.077	4.120	20.123	13.275
1965	475.166	8.121	40.823	29.561

Table 5.12 (continued)

(1) Year	(2) Net Worth	(3) Net Investment	(4) Gross Revaluations	(5) Net Revaluations
1966	498.375	8.265	29.910	13.522
1967	529.483	− .851	47.791	31.066
1968	570.786	10.944	52.286	27.928
1969	644.642	13.855	91.529	61.461
1970	652.149	− 7.378	44.605	13.408
1971	645.945	− 26.453	52.890	24.534
1972	687.073	− 7.345	74.957	48.783
1973	809.079	1.787	159.111	107.969
1974	821.960	− 3.913	97.221	16.180
1975	739.631	− 54.424	63.355	18.605
1976	704.966	− 32.910	37.395	1.489
1977	711.839	− 21.501	77.624	38.947
Sums				
1946–50		−210.953	191.594	191.754
1951–55		145.095	108.577	96.457
1956–60		18.780	97.433	65.223
1961–65		19.732	121.925	86.637
1966–70		24.835	266.121	147.386
1971–75		− 90.349	447.534	216.070
1976–77		− 54.411	115.019	40.436
Means				
1946–50	23.330	− 42.191	38.319	38.351
1951–55	170.426	29.019	21.715	19.291
1956–60	325.257	3.756	19.487	13.045
1961–65	414.067	3.946	24.385	17.327
1966–70	579.087	4.967	53.224	29.477
1971–75	740.738	− 18.070	89.507	43.214
1976–77	708.403	− 27.205	57.509	20.218
Sums, 1946–77		−147.271	1,348.202	843.963
Means, 1946–77	396.291	− 4.602	42.131	26.374

Table 5.13 **Net Worth, Net Investment, Gross and Net Revaluations of Nonhuman Capital, Sum of Sectors (Billions of Dollars, 1946–77)**

(1) Year	(2) Net Worth	(3) Net Investment	(4) Gross Revaluations	(5) Net Revaluations
1946	1,142.036	−12.198	101.951	− 72.341
1947	1,264.968	8.126	114.805	11.051
1948	1,320.050	15.875	39.208	5.015
1949	1,346.037	14.044	11.942	34.187
1950	1,498.650	35.668	116.945	21.106
1951	1,670.292	75.191	96.452	49.814
1952	1,770.338	69.885	30.161	1.985
1953	1,830.679	55.330	5.010	− 9.900
1954	1,975.192	44.529	99.985	68.850
1955	2,164.243	55.668	133.380	80.294
1956	2,336.166	57.063	114.862	30.509
1957	2,414.549	46.302	32.082	− 20.209
1958	2,639.572	40.630	184.393	142.372
1959	2,769.393	47.566	82.256	22.816
1960	2,844.814	42.978	32.442	3.469
1961	3,037.540	48.742	143.985	102.886
1962	3,078.387	52.027	−11.180	− 67.931
1963	3,269.637	70.356	120.895	77.062
1964	3,459.944	81.301	109.006	53.661
1965	3,710.742	92.233	158.565	66.796
1966	3,850.411	87.559	52.111	− 80.362
1967	4,244.918	101.922	292.584	156.848
1968	4,711.033	108.664	357.450	153.328
1969	4,898.085	71.645	115.407	−145.875
1970	5,153.673	100.701	154.886	− 97.702
1971	5,534.132	99.489	280.970	38.176
1972	6,109.491	140.900	434.459	195.951
1973	6,625.395	90.932	424.972	− 60.175
1974	7,196.845	38.284	533.166	−207.822
1975	7,907.294	104.613	605.835	144.250
1976	8,846.168	133.076	805.798	387.643
1977	9,533.716	105.341	582.208	48.560
Sums				
1946–50		61.515	384.851	− .982
1951–55		300.603	364.988	191.043
1956–60		234.539	446.035	178.957
1961–65		344.659	521.271	232.474
1966–70		470.491	972.438	− 13.763
1971–75		474.218	2,279.402	110.380
1976–77		238.417	1,388.006	436.203

Table 5.13 (continued)

(1) Year	(2) Net Worth	(3) Net Investment	(4) Gross Revaluations	(5) Net Revaluations
Means				
1946–50	1,314.348	12.303	76.970	− .196
1951–55	1,882.149	60.121	72.998	38.209
1956–60	2,600.899	46.908	89.207	35.791
1961–65	3,311.250	68.932	104.254	46.495
1966–70	4,571.624	94.098	194.488	− 2.753
1971–75	6,674.631	94.844	455.880	22.076
1976–77	9,189.942	119.209	694.003	218.102
Sums, 1946–77		2,124.442	6,356.991	1,134.312
Means, 1946–77	3,754.825	66.389	198.656	35.447

Table 5.14 **Net Worth, Net Investment, Gross and Net Revaluations of Nonhuman Capital, Sum of Sectors (Billions of 1972 Dollars, 1946–77)**

(1) Year	(2) Net Worth	(3) Net Investment	(4) Gross Revaluations	(5) Net Revaluations
1946	2,765.221	− 29.536	246.853	−175.159
1947	2,586.847	16.618	234.777	22.599
1948	2,462.781	29.618	73.149	9.356
1949	2,456.272	25.627	21.793	62.386
1950	2,652.476	63.128	206.980	37.357
1951	2,747.191	123.669	158.639	81.929
1952	2,850.786	112.537	48.567	3.197
1953	2,910.460	87.965	7.967	− 15.740
1954	3,115.447	70.235	157.705	108.597
1955	3,339.879	85.908	205.834	123.908
1956	3,420.448	83.548	168.172	44.668
1957	3,405.571	65.305	45.247	− 28.504
1958	3,728.210	57.387	260.442	201.090
1959	3,867.867	66.432	114.882	31.866
1960	3,956.627	59.775	45.121	4.825
1961	4,242.375	68.076	201.096	143.695
1962	4,275.538	72.259	−15.527	− 94.349
1963	4,534.865	97.580	167.675	106.882
1964	4,752.671	111.678	149.735	73.710
1965	5,028.107	124.978	214.860	90.509

Table 5.14 (continued)

(1) Year	(2) Net Worth	(3) Net Investment	(4) Gross Revaluations	(5) Net Revaluations
1966	5,053.035	114.906	68.386	−105.462
1967	5,393.798	129.506	371.772	199.297
1968	5,738.166	132.356	435.384	186.759
1969	5,636.462	82.446	132.805	−167.866
1970	5,657.161	110.539	170.018	−107.247
1971	5,770.732	103.741	292.982	39.809
1972	6,109.491	140.900	434.459	195.951
1973	6,250.373	85.784	400.919	− 56.768
1974	6,114.566	32.528	452.987	−176.569
1975	5,972.275	79.013	457.579	108.949
1976	6,327.731	95.191	576.393	277.284
1977	6,343.124	70.087	387.365	32.310
Sums				
1946–50		105.455	783.552	− 43.461
1951–55		480.314	578.712	301.891
1956–60		332.447	633.864	253.945
1961–65		474.571	717.839	320.447
1966–70		569.753	1,178.365	5.481
1971–75		441.966	2,038.926	111.372
1976–77		165.278	963.758	309.594
Means				
1946–50	2,584.719	21.091	156.710	− 8.692
1951–55	2,992.753	96.063	115.742	60.378
1956–60	3,675.745	66.489	126.773	50.789
1961–65	4,566.711	94.914	143.568	64.089
1966–70	5,495.724	113.951	235.673	1.096
1971–75	6,043.487	88.393	407.785	22.274
1976–77	6,335.428	82.639	481.879	154.797
Sums, 1946–77		2,569.784	6,895.016	1,259.269
Means, 1946–77	4,358.330	80.306	215.469	39.352

Table 5.15 **Net Worth, Net Investment, Gross and Net Revaluations of Nonhuman Capital, Total, Excluding Households' Corporate and Noncorporate Equity and Private Financial Corporate Shares (Billions of Dollars, 1946–77)**

(1) Year	(2) Net Worth	(3) Net Investment	(4) Gross Revaluations	(5) Net Revaluations
1946	810.948	– 15.029	85.271	–36.885
1947	909.083	4.802	93.333	19.701
1948	955.335	9.481	36.771	12.203
1949	968.264	9.929	2.999	19.097
1950	1,066.845	29.921	68.660	– .475
1951	1,194.022	69.911	57.267	23.930
1952	1,275.942	65.568	16.351	– 3.979
1953	1,340.851	51.929	12.980	2.173
1954	1,402.998	39.846	22.301	– .560
1955	1,523.510	48.914	71.596	33.766
1956	1,653.837	52.481	77.848	18.223
1957	1,754.166	44.072	56.257	19.144
1958	1,838.601	26.400	58.035	27.538
1959	1,927.928	41.883	47.445	5.955
1960	1,997.250	38.853	30.468	10.271
1961	2,062.785	31.396	34.140	5.311
1962	2,158.229	56.128	39.316	.593
1963	2,248.585	57.985	32.372	1.568
1964	2,362.250	67.672	45.993	7.822
1965	2,505.117	76.920	65.947	3.105
1966	2,677.675	90.192	82.367	– 7.558
1967	2,872.525	78.081	116.768	22.223
1968	3.139.288	89.286	177.476	38.974
1969	3,412.529	85.523	187.718	12.541
1970	3,650.485	84.555	153.400	–22.950
1971	3,856.936	62.854	143.598	–28.215
1972	4,235.730	104.034	274.760	108.402
1973	4,908.407	143.404	529.273	189.551
1974	5,668.526	107.599	652.520	99.154
1975	6,136.225	66.958	400.739	37.678
1976	6,746.863	105.861	504.777	180.215
1977	7,413.245	139.320	527.063	118.286
Sums				
1946–50		39.104	287.034	13.641
1951–55		276.168	180.495	55.330
1956–60		203.689	270.053	81.131
1961–65		290.101	217.768	18.399
1966–70		427.637	717.729	43.230
1971–75		484.849	2,000.890	406.570
1976–77		245.181	1,031.840	298.501

Table 5.15 (continued)

(1) Year	(2) Net Worth	(3) Net Investment	(4) Gross Revaluations	(5) Net Revaluations
Means				
1946–50	942.095	7.821	57.407	2.728
1951–55	1,347.465	55.234	36.099	11.066
1956–60	1,834.356	40.738	54.011	16.226
1961–65	2,267.393	58.020	43.554	3.680
1966–70	3,150.500	85.527	143.546	8.646
1971–75	4,961.165	96.970	400.178	81.314
1976–77	7,080.054	122.591	515.920	149.251
Sums, 1946–77		1,966.729	4,705.809	916.802
Means, 1946–77	2,708.593	61.460	147.057	28.650

Table 5.16 **Net Worth, Net Investment, Gross and Net Revaluations of Nonhuman Capital, Total, Excluding Households' Corporate and Noncorporate Equity and Private Financial Shares (Billions of 1972 Dollars, 1946–77)**

(1) Year	(2) Net Worth	(3) Net Investment	(4) Gross Revaluations	(5) Net Revaluations
1946	1,963.554	– 36.390	206.465	–89.306
1947	1,859.067	9.820	190.866	40.288
1948	1,782.343	17.689	68.603	22.767
1949	1,766.906	18.118	5.474	34.850
1950	1,888.220	52.957	121.521	– .840
1951	1,963.852	114.985	94.190	39.356
1952	2,054.656	105.585	26.329	– 6.406
1953	2,131.719	82.559	20.638	3.454
1954	2,212.932	62.849	35.175	– .882
1955	2,351.094	75.485	110.487	52.106
1956	2,421.431	76.839	113.978	26.681
1957	2,474.142	62.160	79.345	27.002
1958	2,596.895	37.288	81.971	38.896
1959	2,692.636	58.495	66.263	8.318
1960	2,777.817	54.038	42.376	14.284
1961	2,880.985	43.850	47.681	7.417
1962	2,997.540	77.955	54.606	.822
1963	3,118.704	80.422	44.897	2.177
1964	3,244.850	92.958	63.179	10.745
1965	3,394.469	104.229	89.360	4.206

Table 5.16 (continued)

(1) Year	(2) Net Worth	(3) Net Investment	(4) Gross Revaluations	(5) Net Revaluations
1966	3,514.011	118.362	108.092	– 9.920
1967	3,649.969	99.212	148.372	28.237
1968	3,823.739	108.753	216.171	47.474
1969	3,926.962	98.415	216.016	14.431
1970	4,007.119	92.815	168.387	–25.192
1971	4,021.832	65.540	149.737	–29.420
1972	4,235.730	104.034	274.760	108.402
1973	4,630.573	135.287	499.316	178.823
1974	4,816.079	91.419	554.392	84.243
1975	4,634.609	50.573	302.673	28.457
1976	4,826.082	75.723	361.071	128.908
1977	4,932.298	92.695	350.675	78.701
Sums				
1946–50		62.194	592.929	7.759
1951–55		441.463	286.819	87.628
1956–60		288.820	383.933	115.181
1961–65		399.414	299.723	25.367
1966–70		517.557	857.038	55.030
1971–75		446.853	1,780.878	370.505
1976–77		168.418	711.746	207.609
Means				
1946–50	1,852.018	12.439	118.586	1.552
1951–55	2,142.851	88.293	57.364	17.526
1956–60	2,592.584	57.764	76.787	23.036
1961–65	3,127.310	79.883	59.945	5.073
1966–70	3,784.360	103.511	171.408	11.006
1971–75	4,467.765	89.371	356.176	74.101
1976–77	4,879.190	84.209	355.873	103.805
Sums, 1946–77		2,324.719	4,913.066	869.079
Means, 1946–77	3,112.275	72.647	153.533	27.159

Table 5.17 **Net Investment, Nonhuman Capital, by Sector and Total Economy (Billions of Dollars, 1946–77)**

(1) Year	(2) Households, Excluding Corporate and Noncorporate Equity	(3) Non-corporate	(4) Corporate Non-financial	(5) Private Financial, Excluding Corporate Shares	(6) Govern-ment	(7) Total Economy
1946	17.636	1.506	.800	1.103	− 36.074	−15.029
1947	18.108	1.864	6.529	.609	− 22.308	4.802
1948	19.052	5.130	7.109	.736	− 22.546	9.481
1949	19.797	.914	7.961	− 1.171	− 17.572	9.929
1950	23.345	3.723	3.988	1.045	− 2.180	29.921
1951	29.571	2.609	9.229	− 1.520	30.022	69.911
1952	26.655	1.066	7.743	2.668	27.436	65.568
1953	28.503	1.352	6.021	.666	15.387	51.929
1954	29.672	− .929	4.785	.318	6.000	39.846
1955	32.219	− .617	6.523	− .622	11.411	48.914
1956	33.373	.795	7.107	.356	10.850	52.481
1957	32.474	1.102	5.199	.836	4.461	44.072
1958	30.791	1.852	2.506	− 2.774	− 5.975	26.400
1959	38.097	− 1.209	5.849	− 1.611	.757	41.883
1960	34.568	1.044	.545	− .169	2.865	38.853
1961	33.966	1.876	4.409	− 4.085	− 4.770	31.396
1962	41.632	1.399	8.174	2.847	2.076	56.128
1963	46.516	2.194	6.283	− 5.134	8.126	57.985
1964	55.789	.855	10.817	− 2.788	2.999	67.672
1965	63.075	2.143	12.321	− 6.612	5.993	76.920
1966	68.494	2.377	11.982	1.041	6.298	90.192
1967	75.502	.116	16.206	−13.073	− .670	78.081
1968	79.164	2.965	6.933	− 8.761	8.985	89.286
1969	70.214	− 6.159	10.452	− 1.024	12.040	85.523
1970	84.246	8.309	.449	− 1.728	− 6.721	84.555
1971	103.178	− 3.457	3.934	−15.433	− 25.368	62.854
1972	119.865	− 7.899	6.887	− 7.474	− 7.345	104.034
1973	135.849	− 3.152	− 1.351	10.164	1.894	143.404
1974	134.778	−11.688	−25.054	14.169	− 4.606	107.599
1975	151.233	− 8.097	7.679	−11.799	− 72.058	66.958
1976	151.549	− 9.595	13.472	− 3.557	− 46.008	105.861
1977	171.153	−16.645	− 3.411	20.539	− 32.316	139.320
Sums						
1946–50	97.938	13.137	26.387	2.322	−100.680	39.104
1951–55	146.620	3.481	34.301	1.510	90.256	276.168
1956–60	169.303	3.584	21.206	− 3.362	12.958	203.689
1961–65	240.978	8.467	42.004	−15.772	14.424	290.101
1966–70	377.620	7.608	46.022	−23.545	19.932	427.637

Table 5.17 (continued)

(1) Year	(2) Households, Excluding Corporate and Noncorporate Equity	(3) Non-corporate	(4) Corporate Non-financial	(5) Private Financial, Excluding Corporate Shares	(6) Govern-ment	(7) Total Economy
1971–75	644.903	−34.293	− 7.905	−10.373	−107.483	484.849
1976–77	322.702	−26.240	10.061	16.982	− 78.324	245.181
Means						
1946–50	19.588	2.627	5.277	.464	− 20.136	7.821
1951–55	29.324	.696	6.860	.302	18.051	55.234
1956–60	33.861	.717	4.241	− .672	2.592	40.738
1961–65	48.196	1.693	8.401	− 3.154	2.885	58.020
1966–70	75.524	1.522	9.204	− 4.709	3.986	85.527
1971–75	128.981	− 6.859	− 1.581	− 2.075	− 21.497	96.970
1976–77	161.351	−13.120	5.030	8.491	− 39.162	122.591
Sums, 1946–77	2,000.064	−24.256	172.076	−32.238	−148.917	1,966.729
Means, 1946–77	62.502	− .758	5.377	− 1.007	− 4.654	61.460

Table 5.18 **Net Investment, Nonhuman Capital, by Sector and Total Economy (Billions of 1972 Dollars, 1946–77)**

(1) Year	(2) Households, Excluding Corporate and Noncorporate Equity	(3) Non-corporate	(4) Corporate Non-financial	(5) Private Financial, Excluding Corporate Shares	(6) Govern-ment	(7) Total Economy
1946	42.702	3.646	1.937	2.671	− 87.346	−36.390
1947	37.031	3.812	13.352	1.245	− 45.620	9.820
1948	35.545	9.571	13.263	1.373	− 42.063	17.689
1949	36.126	1.668	14.527	− 2.137	− 32.066	18.118
1950	41.319	6.589	7.058	1.849	− 3.858	52.957
1951	48.637	4.291	15.179	− 2.500	49.378	114.985
1952	42.922	1.717	12.469	4.297	44.180	105.585
1953	45.316	2.149	9.572	1.059	24.463	82.559
1954	46.801	− 1.465	7.547	.502	9.464	62.849
1955	49.721	.952	10.066	− .960	17.610	75.485
1956	48.862	1.164	10.406	.521	15.886	76.839
1957	45.802	1.554	7.333	1.179	6.292	62.160
1958	43.489	2.616	3.540	− 3.918	− 8.439	37.288

Table 5.18 (continued)

(1) Year	(2) Households, Excluding Corporate and Noncorporate Equity	(3) Non-corporate	(4) Corporate Non-financial	(5) Private Financial, Excluding Corporate Shares	(6) Govern-ment	(7) Total Economy
1959	53.208	− 1.689	8.169	− 2.250	1.057	58.495
1960	48.078	1.452	.758	− .235	3.985	54.038
1961	47.439	2.620	6.158	− 5.705	− 6.662	43.850
1962	57.822	1.943	11.353	3.954	2.883	77.955
1963	64.516	3.043	8.714	− 7.121	11.270	80.422
1964	76.634	1.174	14.859	− 3.829	4.120	92.958
1965	85.468	2.904	16.695	− 8.959	8.121	104.229
1966	89.887	3.119	15.724	1.367	8.265	118.362
1967	95.936	.147	20.592	−16.612	− .851	99.212
1968	96.424	3.611	8.445	−10.671	10.944	108.753
1969	80.798	− 7.087	12.028	− 1.179	13.855	98.415
1970	92.476	9.121	.493	− 1.897	− 7.378	92.815
1971	107.589	− 3.605	4.102	−16.093	− 26.453	65.540
1972	119.865	− 7.899	6.887	− 7.474	− 7.345	104.034
1973	128.160	− 2.974	− 1.275	9.589	1.787	135.287
1974	114.510	− 9.930	−21.286	12.038	− 3.913	91.419
1975	114.225	− 6.116	5.800	− 8.912	− 54.424	50.573
1976	108.404	− 6.863	9.637	− 2.545	− 32.910	75.723
1977	113.875	−11.075	− 2.269	13.665	− 21.501	92.695
Sums						
1946–50	192.723	25.286	50.137	5.001	−210.953	62.194
1951–55	233.397	5.740	54.833	2.398	145.095	441.463
1956–60	239.439	5.097	30.206	− 4.703	18.781	288.820
1961–65	331.879	11.684	57.779	−21.660	19.732	399.414
1966–70	455.521	8.911	57.282	−28.992	24.835	517.557
1971–75	584.349	−30.524	− 5.772	−10.852	− 90.348	446.853
1976–77	222.279	−17.938	7.368	11.120	− 54.411	168.418
Means						
1946–50	38.545	5.057	10.027	1.000	− 42.191	12.439
1951–55	46.679	1.148	10.967	.480	29.019	88.293
1956–60	47.888	1.019	6.041	− .941	3.756	57.764
1961–65	66.376	2.337	11.556	− 4.332	3.946	79.883
1966–70	91.104	1.782	11.456	− 5.798	4.967	103.511
1971–75	116.870	− 6.105	− 1.154	− 2.170	− 18.070	89.371
1976–77	111.140	− 8.969	3.684	5.560	− 27.206	84.209
Sums, 1946–77	2,259.587	8.256	251.833	−47.688	−147.269	2,324.719
Means, 1946–77	70.612	.258	7.870	− 1.490	− 4.602	72.647

Table 5.19 **Net Revaluations, Nonhuman Capital, by Sector and Total Economy (Billions of Dollars, 1946–77)**

(1) Year	(2) Households, Excluding Corporate and Noncorporate Equity	(3) Non-corporate	(4) Corporate Non-financial	(5) Private Financial, Excluding Shares Corporate	(6) Govern-ment	(7) Total Economy
1946	− 50.663	− 6.659	− 3.742	− 6.184	30.363	−36.885
1947	− 22.128	4.470	7.392	− 7.277	37.244	19.701
1948	− 4.303	− 2.220	5.967	.120	12.639	12.203
1949	13.051	4.686	3.967	4.677	− 7.284	19.097
1950	− 22.580	6.357	2.406	− 4.615	17.957	− .475
1951	− 5.036	9.495	7.479	− 7.825	19.817	23.930
1952	− 3.603	− 3.766	.747	.464	2.179	− 3.979
1953	− 2.988	− 1.567	3.755	.568	2.405	2.173
1954	− 6.588	.623	− .750	4.096	2.059	− .560
1955	− 3.002	3.006	9.920	−10.686	34.528	33.766
1956	− 13.158	7.489	13.195	−11.543	22.240	18.223
1957	− 2.832	7.260	12.783	3.160	− 1.227	19.144
1958	5.798	15.624	2.991	−15.296	18.421	27.538
1959	1.589	− 1.980	5.857	−15.464	15.953	5.955
1960	− 2.316	3.848	.607	18.132	−10.000	10.271
1961	− 3.781	− .996	− .285	− 9.030	19.403	5.311
1962	− 13.748	3.185	− 2.172	12.511	.817	.593
1963	− 2.695	3.527	− 1.645	− 8.842	11.223	1.568
1964	− 7.177	4.776	− .201	.760	9.664	7.822
1965	− 16.696	7.882	6.428	−16.325	21.816	3.105
1966	− 37.306	12.408	12.627	− 5.591	10.304	− 7.558
1967	4.425	8.977	13.889	−29.517	24.449	22.223
1968	14.773	9.803	3.712	−12.243	22.929	38.974
1969	− 32.890	5.559	33.245	−46.783	53.410	12.541
1970	− 58.341	−13.297	− 5.166	41.639	12.215	−22.950
1971	− 54.523	− 1.413	−16.883	21.076	23.528	−28.215
1972	12.741	43.723	19.983	−16.828	48.783	108.402
1973	− 76.517	83.095	72.394	− 3.868	114.447	189.551
1974	−152.205	22.539	120.099	89.677	19.044	99.154
1975	− 32.769	4.156	24.008	17.650	24.633	37.678
1976	.555	182.098	− 9.868	85.348	2.082	180.215
1977	− 6.642	56.015	50.808	−40.432	58.537	118.286
Sums						
1946–50	− 86.623	6.634	15.990	−13.279	90.919	13.641
1951–55	− 21.217	7.791	21.151	−13.383	60.988	55.330
1956–60	− 10.919	32.241	35.433	−21.011	45.387	81.131
1961–65	− 44.097	18.374	2.125	−20.926	62.923	18.399
1966–70	−109.339	23.450	58.307	−52.495	123.307	43.230

Table 5.19 (continued)

(1) Year	(2) Households, Excluding Corporate and Noncorporate Equity	(3) Non-corporate	(4) Corporate Non-financial	(5) Private Financial, Excluding Shares Corporate	(6) Govern-ment	(7) Total Economy
1971–75	−303.273	152.100	219.601	107.707	230.435	406.570
1976–77	− 6.087	158.113	40.940	44.916	60.619	298.501
Means						
1946–50	− 17.325	1.327	3.198	− 2.656	18.184	2.728
1951–55	− 4.243	1.558	4.230	− 2.677	12.198	11.066
1956–60	− 2.184	6.448	7.087	− 4.202	9.077	16.226
1961–65	− 8.819	3.675	.425	− 4.185	12.585	3.680
1966–70	− 21.868	4.690	11.661	−10.499	24.661	8.646
1971–75	− 60.655	30.420	43.920	21.541	46.087	81.314
1976–77	− 3.044	79.057	20.470	22.458	30.310	149.251
Sums, 1946–77	−581.555	398.703	393.547	31.529	674.578	916.802
Means, 1946–77	− 18.174	12.459	12.298	.985	21.081	28.650

Table 5.20 **Net Revaluations, Nonhuman Capital, by Sector and Total Economy (Billions of 1972 Dollars, 1946–77)**

(1) Year	(2) Households, Excluding Corporate and Noncorporate Equity	(3) Non-corporate	(4) Corporate Non-Financial	(5) Private Financial, Excluding Corporate Shares	(6) Govern-ment	(7) Total Economy
1946	−122.668	−16.124	− 9.061	−14.972	73.519	−89.306
1947	− 45.252	9.142	15.116	−14.881	76.163	40.288
1948	− 8.027	− 4.142	11.133	.223	23.580	22.767
1949	23.817	8.551	7.239	8.535	−13.292	34.850
1950	− 39.965	11.252	4.258	− 8.168	31.783	− .840
1951	− 8.284	15.617	12.300	−12.870	32.593	39.356
1952	− 5.802	− 6.064	1.203	.748	3.509	− 6.406
1953	− 4.750	− 2.491	5.969	.903	3.823	3.454
1954	− 10.391	.983	− 1.183	6.461	3.248	− .882
1955	− 4.632	4.638	15.309	−16.492	53.283	52.106
1956	− 19.263	10.964	19.319	−16.901	32.562	26.681
1957	− 3.993	10.239	18.030	4.456	− 1.730	27.002
1958	8.189	22.067	4.224	−21.603	26.019	38.896

Table 5.20 (continued)

(1) Year	(2) Households, Excluding Corporate and Noncorporate Equity	(3) Non-corporate	(4) Corporate Non-Financial	(5) Private Financial, Excluding Corporate Shares	(6) Govern-ment	(7) Total Economy
1959	2.220	– 2.765	8.180	–21.597	22.280	8.318
1960	– 3.222	5.352	.844	25.218	–13.908	14.284
1961	– 5.281	– 1.392	– .398	–12.612	27.100	7.417
1962	– 19.096	4.424	– 3.016	17.375	1.135	.822
1963	– 3.736	4.891	– 2.281	–12.263	15.566	2.177
1964	– 9.858	6.560	– .276	1.044	13.275	10.745
1965	– 22.623	10.680	8.710	–22.122	29.561	4.206
1966	– 48.960	16.284	16.571	– 7.337	13.522	– 9.920
1967	5.624	11.406	17.647	–37.506	31.066	28.237
1968	17.995	11.940	4.522	–14.911	27.928	47.474
1969	– 37.848	6.397	38.256	–53.835	61.461	14.431
1970	– 64.040	–14.596	– 5.671	45.707	13.408	–25.192
1971	– 56.854	– 1.473	–17.605	21.978	24.534	–29.420
1972	12.741	43.723	19.983	–16.828	48.783	108.402
1973	– 72.185	78.391	68.297	– 3.649	107.969	178.823
1974	–129.317	19.150	102.038	76.192	16.180	84.243
1975	– 24.750	3.139	18.133	13.330	18.605	28.457
1976	.396	73.032	– 7.059	61.050	1.489	128.908
1977	– 4.419	37.269	33.805	–26.901	38.947	78.701
Sums						
1946–50	–192.095	8.679	28.685	–29.263	191.753	7.759
1951–55	– 33.859	12.683	33.598	–21.250	96.456	87.628
1956–60	– 16.069	45.857	50.597	–30.427	65.223	115.181
1961–65	– 60.594	25.163	2.739	–28.578	86.637	25.367
1966–70	–127.229	31.431	71.325	–67.882	147.385	55.030
1971–75	–270.365	142.930	190.846	91.023	216.071	370.505
1976–77	– 4.023	110.301	26.746	34.149	40.436	207.609
Means						
1946–50	– 38.419	1.736	5.737	– 5.853	38.351	1.552
1951–55	– 6.772	2.537	6.720	– 4.250	19.291	17.526
1956–60	– 3.214	9.171	10.119	– 6.085	13.045	23.036
1961–65	– 12.119	5.033	.548	– 5.716	17.327	5.073
1966–70	– 25.446	6.286	14.265	–13.576	29.477	11.006
1971–75	– 54.073	28.586	38.169	18.205	43.214	74.101
1976–77	– 2.012	55.151	13.373	17.074	20.218	103.805
Sums, 1946–77	–704.234	377.044	404.536	–52.228	843.961	869.079
Means, 1946–77	– 22.007	11.783	12.642	– 1.632	26.374	27.159

Table 5.21 **Net Revaluations, 1946–77, Standard Deviations by Sector and Simple Correlation Matrix (Billions of Current and 1972 Dollars)**

(1) Households	(2) Households, Excluding Corporate and Noncorporate Equity	(3) Noncorporate	(4) Corporate Nonfinancial	(5) Private Financial	(6) Private Financial Excluding Corporate Shares	(7) Government	(8) Total Economy [2+3+4+6+7]
A. STANDARD DEVIATIONS							
Billions of Current Dollars							
129.0	32.8	24.9	26.0	26.7	28.3	23.4	53.4
Billions of 1972 Dollars							
134.1	35.8	20.7	22.8	25.5	26.5	26.5	49.1
B. CORRELATION MATRIX							
1972 Dollars/Current Dollars							
Households	—	−.038	−.742	−.126	—	−.375	−.143
Households, excluding							
corporate and							
noncorporate equity	1.000	−.086	−.683	—	−.506	−.313	−.164
Noncorporate	.065	1.000	.382		.246	.488	.945
Corporate nonfinancial	−.421	.425	1.000		.180	.524	.571
Private financial	—						
Private financial,							
excluding				1.000	—	−.490	.132
corporate shares	−.338	.116	.108	—	1.000	−.349	.267
Government	−.410	.309	.365	−.553	−.465	1.000	.546
Total economy	.158	.896	.591	−.043	.142	.289	1.000

Table 5.22 **Net Stocks, Net Investment, Gross and Net Revaluations of Fixed Nonresidential Capital, Nonfinancial Corporate (Billions of Dollars, 1946–77)**

(1) Year	(2) Net Capital Stock	(3) Net Investment	(4) Gross Revaluations	(5) Net Revaluations
1946	85.4	5.9	9.0	−3.2
1947	106.0	9.7	10.9	2.8
1948	120.6	8.4	6.2	3.3
1949	128.0	4.9	2.5	4.5
1950	141.7	5.3	8.4	− .8
1951	157.3	6.8	8.7	4.3
1952	167.3	6.0	4.0	1.4
1953	177.0	6.9	2.8	1.4
1954	185.4	5.5	2.9	− .1
1955	202.8	6.8	10.6	5.6
1956	226.2	9.2	14.2	6.2
1957	243.8	9.3	8.3	3.2
1958	251.2	3.1	4.3	.1
1959	258.8	4.3	3.3	−2.3
1960	265.9	6.0	1.1	−1.6
1961	271.2	4.5	.8	−3.0
1962	279.8	7.0	1.6	−3.5
1963	289.1	6.9	2.4	−1.6
1964	303.8	10.4	4.3	− .6
1965	328.9	17.2	7.9	− .2
1966	363.2	21.6	12.7	.7
1967	397.1	18.6	15.3	2.3
1968	438.0	19.6	21.4	2.1
1969	489.2	22.4	28.8	4.0
1970	537.3	17.1	31.1	5.7
1971	580.1	14.9	27.8	2.4
1972	629.4	19.0	30.4	5.3
1973	721.8	27.5	64.8	14.1
1974	852.9	26.2	104.9	23.0
1975	953.5	11.1	89.5	34.9
1976	1,032.5	12.5	66.6	16.3
1977	1,126.9	23.1	71.3	8.7
Sums				
1946–50		34.2	37.1	6.6
1951–55		32.0	29.1	12.6
1956–60		31.9	31.2	5.5
1961–65		46.0	17.1	−9.0
1966–70		99.1	109.3	14.9
1971–75		98.7	317.4	79.6
1976–77		35.5	137.9	24.9

Table 5.22 (continued)

(1) Year	(2) Net Capital Stock	(3) Net Investment	(4) Gross Revaluations	(5) Net Revaluations
Means				
1946–50	116.4	6.8	7.4	1.3
1951–55	177.9	6.4	5.8	2.5
1956–60	249.2	6.4	6.2	1.1
1961–65	294.6	9.2	3.4	−1.8
1966–70	445.0	19.8	21.9	3.0
1971–75	747.5	19.7	63.5	15.9
1976–77	1,079.7	17.8	68.9	12.5
Sums, 1946–77		377.5	679.0	135.2
Means, 1946–77	384.7	11.8	21.2	4.2

Table 5.23 **Net Stocks, Net Investment, Gross and Net Revaluations of Fixed Nonresidential Capital, All Corporate (Billions of Dollars, 1946–77)**

(1) Year	(2) Net Capital Stock	(3) Net Investment	(4) Gross Revaluations	(5) Net Revaluations
1946	86.7	6.0	9.2	−3.2
1947	107.7	9.8	11.2	2.9
1948	122.3	8.4	6.1	3.2
1949	129.8	5.0	2.5	4.6
1950	143.8	5.5	8.5	− .8
1951	159.5	6.9	8.9	4.4
1952	169.8	6.2	4.0	1.3
1953	179.6	7.0	2.8	1.4
1954	188.2	5.7	2.9	− .2
1955	206.1	7.2	10.7	5.6
1956	230.0	9.5	14.4	6.3
1957	247.9	9.6	8.3	3.1
1958	255.6	3.3	4.3	.0
1959	263.7	4.8	3.3	−2.5
1960	271.0	6.2	1.1	−1.7
1961	276.6	4.8	.8	−3.1
1962	285.3	7.1	1.6	−3.6
1963	295.3	7.5	2.5	−1.6
1964	311.0	11.3	4.4	− .6
1965	337.6	18.4	8.2	− .2

Table 5.23 (continued)

(1) Year	(2) Net Capital Stock	(3) Net Investment	(4) Gross Revaluations	(5) Net Revaluations
1966	373.7	23.1	13.0	.8
1967	409.7	20.2	15.7	2.4
1968	453.7	21.8	22.2	2.2
1969	508.6	24.9	30.0	4.3
1970	560.6	19.8	32.3	5.8
1971	607.5	17.9	28.9	2.3
1972	661.5	22.0	32.0	5.7
1973	760.5	30.6	68.4	15.0
1974	899.2	29.1	109.6	23.2
1975	1,005.1	14.0	92.0	34.3
1976	1,089.4	15.7	68.6	15.5
1977	1,190.4	26.6	74.4	8.3
Sums				
1946–50		34.7	37.6	6.8
1951–55		33.0	29.4	12.6
1956–60		33.4	31.4	5.3
1961–65		49.0	17.6	−9.0
1966–70		109.7	113.3	15.5
1971–75		113.7	330.8	80.4
1976–77		42.3	143.0	23.7
Means				
1946–50	118.1	6.9	7.5	1.4
1951–55	180.6	6.6	5.9	2.5
1956–60	253.6	6.7	6.3	1.1
1961–65	301.2	9.8	3.5	−1.8
1966–70	461.3	21.9	22.7	3.1
1971–75	786.8	22.7	66.2	16.1
1976–77	1,139.9	21.2	71.5	11.9
Sums, 1946–77		415.8	703.1	135.3
Means, 1946–77	399.6	13.0	22.0	4.2

Table 5.24 **Net Stocks, Net Investment, Gross and Net Revaluations of Fixed Nonresidential Capital, Noncorporate (Billions of Dollars, 1946–77)**

(1) Year	(2) Net Capital Stock	(3) Net Investment	(4) Gross Revaluations	(5) Net Revaluations
1946	24.6	2.1	2.7	− .8
1947	31.8	3.7	3.5	1.1
1948	37.4	3.7	1.9	1.0
1949	40.7	2.7	.6	1.2
1950	46.3	3.1	2.5	− .5
1951	51.8	2.5	2.9	1.5
1952	54.3	1.5	1.0	.2
1953	56.5	1.8	.3	− .1
1954	58.1	1.1	.5	− .5
1955	62.9	1.9	2.9	1.3
1956	68.5	1.8	3.9	1.4
1957	72.3	1.8	2.0	.5
1958	74.1	1.0	.8	− .4
1959	76.6	1.9	.6	−1.1
1960	78.6	1.7	.3	− .5
1961	80.6	1.4	.5	− .6
1962	83.3	1.8	1.0	− .6
1963	86.9	2.4	1.3	.1
1964	91.4	3.0	1.4	− .0
1965	98.4	4.5	2.6	.1
1966	107.6	5.2	4.0	.4
1967	116.2	4.1	4.6	.8
1968	128.0	4.5	7.2	1.6
1969	142.7	5.1	9.7	2.5
1970	156.4	4.2	9.4	2.0
1971	166.5	1.9	8.2	.8
1972	179.0	3.3	9.3	2.1
1973	203.9	5.5	19.4	5.0
1974	235.8	4.9	27.0	3.9
1975	258.5	4.2	18.5	3.3
1976	277.5	4.3	14.6	.9
1977	299.9	5.4	17.1	.3
Sums				
1946–50		15.3	11.1	2.0
1951–55		8.9	7.6	2.4
1956–60		8.1	7.7	− .1
1961–65		13.0	6.7	−1.0
1966–70		23.1	34.9	7.3
1971–75		19.9	82.2	15.2
1976–77		9.7	31.7	1.2

Table 5.24 (continued)

(1) Year	(2) Net Capital Stock	(3) Net Investment	(4) Gross Revaluations	(5) Net Revaluations
Means				
1946–50	36.2	3.1	2.2	.4
1951–55	56.7	1.8	1.5	.5
1956–60	74.0	1.6	1.5	− .0
1961–65	88.1	2.6	1.3	− .2
1966–70	130.2	4.6	7.0	1.5
1971–75	208.8	4.0	16.4	3.0
1976–77	288.7	4.9	15.9	.6
Sums, 1946–77		98.1	182.0	27.0
Means, 1946–77	110.9	3.1	5.7	.8

Table 5.25 **Net Stocks, Net Investment, Gross and Net Revaluations of Fixed Nonresidential Capital, Nonprofit Institutions (Billions of Dollars, 1946–77)**

(1) Year	(2) Net Capital Stock	(3) Net Investment	(4) Gross Revaluations	(5) Net Revaluations
1946	7.0	.1	1.2	.2
1947	8.3	.1	1.2	.6
1948	9.0	.4	.3	.1
1949	9.4	.6	− .1	.0
1950	10.9	.8	.7	− .0
1951	12.6	.8	.8	.5
1952	13.5	.7	.2	− .0
1953	14.1	.8	− .1	− .3
1954	15.1	1.0	− .1	− .3
1955	16.9	1.0	.8	.4
1956	19.2	1.2	1.1	.4
1957	20.6	1.3	.1	− .3
1958	21.8	1.5	− .3	− .7
1959	23.2	1.5	− .1	− .6
1960	24.8	1.6	.0	− .2
1961	26.7	1.8	.2	− .2
1962	29.3	2.1	.5	− .0
1963	31.8	2.0	.5	.1
1964	34.6	2.1	.7	.1
1965	38.4	2.5	1.3	.4

Table 5.25 (continued)

(1) Year	(2) Net Capital Stock	(3) Net Investment	(4) Gross Revaluations	(5) Net Revaluations
1966	42.9	2.5	1.9	.5
1967	47.1	2.3	1.9	.4
1968	53.1	2.3	3.7	1.4
1969	60.8	2.5	5.3	2.3
1970	67.8	2.3	4.6	1.5
1971	74.1	2.4	4.0	.8
1972	82.0	2.5	5.4	2.1
1973	95.0	2.0	10.9	4.4
1974	109.1	1.5	12.6	1.9
1975	115.0	.9	5.0	−2.0
1976	119.6	1.1	3.6	−2.5
1977	126.1	.9	5.7	−1.5
Sums				
1946–50		2.0	3.2	.8
1951–55		4.4	1.6	.3
1956–60		7.2	.7	−1.5
1961–65		10.5	3.1	.3
1966–70		11.9	17.5	6.1
1971–75		9.4	37.8	7.2
1976–77		1.9	9.2	−4.0
Means				
1946–50	8.9	.4	.6	.2
1951–55	14.4	.9	.3	.1
1956–60	21.9	1.4	.1	− .3
1961–65	32.2	2.1	.6	.1
1966–70	54.3	2.4	3.5	1.2
1971–75	95.0	1.9	7.6	1.4
1976–77	122.8	1.0	4.6	−2.0
Sums, 1946–77		47.1	73.2	9.3
Means, 1946–77	43.1	1.5	2.3	.3

Table 5.26 **Net Stocks, Net Investment, Gross and Net Revaluations of Fixed Nonresidential Capital, All Business and Nonprofit (Billions of Dollars, 1946–77)**

(1) Year	(2) Net Capital Stock	(3) Net Investment	(4) Gross Revaluations	(5) Net Revaluations
1946	118.3	8.1	13.1	−3.7
1947	147.8	13.6	15.9	4.6
1948	168.7	12.6	8.3	4.3
1949	179.9	8.3	2.9	5.8
1950	201.0	9.4	11.7	−1.3
1951	223.9	10.3	12.6	6.4
1952	237.5	8.4	5.3	1.5
1953	250.1	9.6	3.0	1.0
1954	261.4	7.9	3.3	− .9
1955	286.0	10.2	14.4	7.3
1956	317.8	12.4	19.4	8.1
1957	340.9	12.7	10.4	3.3
1958	351.5	5.8	4.8	−1.1
1959	363.4	8.1	3.8	−4.1
1960	374.4	9.5	1.4	−2.4
1961	383.9	8.0	1.5	−3.9
1962	397.9	10.9	3.1	−4.1
1963	414.0	11.9	4.3	−1.4
1964	437.1	16.5	6.6	− .5
1965	474.5	25.3	12.1	.3
1966	524.2	30.8	18.9	1.7
1967	573.0	26.6	22.3	3.5
1968	634.7	28.6	33.1	5.2
1969	712.1	32.4	44.9	9.1
1970	784.8	26.3	46.4	9.4
1971	848.1	22.3	41.0	3.9
1972	922.5	27.8	46.6	9.9
1973	1,059.5	38.2	98.7	24.5
1974	1,244.1	35.5	149.1	29.0
1975	1,378.6	19.2	115.4	35.6
1976	1,486.4	21.1	86.8	13.9
1977	1,616.4	32.9	97.1	7.0
Sums				
1946–50		52.0	51.9	9.6
1951–55		46.3	38.7	15.3
1956–60		48.6	39.8	3.7
1961–65		72.5	27.5	−9.7
1966–70		144.7	165.6	28.9
1971–75		142.9	450.9	102.8
1976–77		53.9	183.9	20.9

Table 5.26 (continued)

(1) Year	(2) Net Capital Stock	(3) Net Investment	(4) Gross Revaluations	(5) Net Revaluations
Means				
1946–50	163.2	10.4	10.4	1.9
1951–55	251.8	9.3	7.7	3.1
1956–60	349.6	9.7	8.0	.7
1961–65	421.5	14.5	5.5	−1.9
1966–70	645.8	28.9	33.1	5.8
1971–75	1,090.6	28.6	90.2	20.6
1976–77	1,551.4	27.0	91.9	10.5
Sums, 1946–77		561.0	958.3	171.6
Means, 1946–77	553.6	17.5	29.9	5.4

Table 5.27 **Net Stocks, Net Investment, Gross and Net Revaluations of Fixed Residential Capital (Billions of Dollars, 1946–77)**

(1) Year	(2) Net Capital Stock	(3) Net Investment	(4) Gross Revaluations	(5) Net Revaluations
1946	160.7	3.7	20.2	− 2.9
1947	189.7	6.3	22.7	7.9
1948	208.2	9.2	9.3	4.1
1949	220.9	8.5	4.2	7.7
1950	245.9	14.0	11.1	− 5.0
1951	269.5	11.3	12.2	4.6
1952	284.8	11.2	4.1	− .4
1953	297.6	11.5	1.3	− 1.1
1954	314.0	12.3	4.2	− .9
1955	337.3	15.4	7.8	− .7
1956	355.9	13.4	5.3	− 7.9
1957	374.8	12.2	6.7	− 1.3
1958	399.8	12.9	12.1	5.6
1959	426.0	17.1	9.1	− .0
1960	443.0	13.8	3.2	− 1.3
1961	457.5	13.9	.6	− 5.9
1962	473.9	15.8	.6	− 8.0
1963	494.6	17.2	3.5	− 3.3
1964	515.5	17.0	3.8	− 4.6
1965	533.2	16.6	1.1	−12.6

Table 5.27 (continued)

(1) Year	(2) Net Capital Stock	(3) Net Investment	(4) Gross Revaluations	(5) Net Revaluations
1966	550.2	14.2	2.8	−16.3
1967	594.3	13.7	30.4	11.0
1968	675.9	17.8	63.8	35.2
1969	740.7	19.4	45.3	7.6
1970	777.3	17.2	19.4	−18.8
1971	825.4	28.2	19.9	−17.0
1972	917.6	37.2	55.0	19.1
1973	1,056.6	36.2	102.8	29.0
1974	1,184.7	20.2	107.9	−11.0
1975	1,293.6	15.0	94.0	18.1
1976	1,449.4	27.3	128.5	60.0
1977	1,672.9	43.3	180.2	92.0
Sums				
1946–50		41.8	67.4	11.8
1951–55		61.6	29.7	1.5
1956–60		69.3	36.4	− 5.0
1961–65		80.6	9.7	−34.3
1966–70		82.3	161.7	18.7
1971–75		136.8	379.6	38.1
1976–77		70.6	308.7	151.9
Means				
1946–50	205.1	8.4	13.5	2.4
1951–55	300.6	12.3	5.9	.3
1956–60	399.9	13.9	7.3	− 1.0
1961–65	494.9	16.1	1.9	− 6.9
1966–70	667.7	16.5	32.3	3.7
1971–75	1,055.6	27.4	75.9	7.6
1976–77	1,561.2	35.3	154.4	76.0
Sums, 1946–77		543.0	993.1	182.5
Means, 1946–77	585.7	17.0	31.0	5.7

Table 5.28 **Net Stocks, Net Investment, Gross and Net Revaluations of Fixed Residential Capital, Owner-Occupied (Billions of Dollars, 1946–77)**

(1) Year	(2) Net Capital Stock	(3) Net Investment	(4) Gross Revaluations	(5) Net Revaluations
1946	90.7	4.1	11.4	− 1.4
1947	110.6	7.1	12.8	4.3
1948	125.9	9.7	5.6	2.6
1949	136.8	8.3	2.6	4.7
1950	156.8	12.9	7.1	− 3.1
1951	175.9	11.0	8.0	3.1
1952	189.4	10.4	3.1	.1
1953	201.3	10.8	1.1	− .5
1954	216.2	11.9	3.0	− .5
1955	236.7	14.8	5.6	− .3
1956	253.5	13.0	3.9	− 5.4
1957	270.0	11.3	5.1	− .6
1958	290.6	11.1	9.5	4.8
1959	312.4	14.2	7.5	.9
1960	327.1	11.6	3.1	− .2
1961	339.0	10.6	1.3	− 3.5
1962	351.5	11.2	1.3	− 5.1
1963	367.2	12.6	3.2	− 1.9
1964	383.4	12.8	3.3	− 2.9
1965	397.5	12.9	1.2	− 9.0
1966	411.3	11.3	2.5	−11.7
1967	445.8	11.3	23.1	8.6
1968	507.7	13.4	48.5	27.1
1969	555.2	12.7	34.8	6.5
1970	581.8	11.4	15.2	−13.4
1971	619.0	21.4	15.8	−11.9
1972	690.0	28.9	42.2	15.2
1973	795.7	27.1	78.6	23.1
1974	895.9	17.8	82.4	− 7.3
1975	983.0	15.8	71.2	13.7
1976	1,108.9	27.7	98.2	45.9
1977	1,288.4	40.7	138.8	71.1
Sums				
1946–50		42.1	39.6	7.2
1951–55		59.0	20.9	1.9
1956–60		61.2	29.2	− .6
1961–65		60.2	10.3	−22.4
1966–70		60.0	124.2	17.1
1971–75		111.0	290.2	32.8
1976–77		68.4	237.0	117.0

Table 5.28 (continued)

(1) Year	(2) Net Capital Stock	(3) Net Investment	(4) Gross Revaluations	(5) Net Revaluations
Means				
1946–50	124.2	8.4	7.9	1.4
1951–55	203.9	11.8	4.2	.4
1956–60	290.7	12.2	5.8	− .1
1961–65	367.7	12.0	2.1	− 4.5
1966–70	500.4	12.0	24.8	3.4
1971–75	796.7	22.2	58.0	6.6
1976–77	1,198.6	34.2	118.5	58.5
Sums, 1946–77		462.0	751.3	153.0
Means, 1946–77	431.7	14.4	23.5	4.8

Table 5.29 **Net Stocks, Net Investment, Gross and Net Revaluations of Fixed Residential Capital, Tenant-Occupied (Billions of Dollars, 1946–77)**

(1) Year	(2) Net Capital Stock	(3) Net Investment	(4) Gross Revaluations	(5) Net Revaluations
1946	70.0	−.4	8.7	− 1.5
1947	79.1	−.8	9.9	3.5
1948	82.3	−.5	3.7	1.5
1949	84.1	.2	1.6	2.9
1950	89.1	1.0	4.0	− 2.0
1951	93.6	.3	4.2	1.5
1952	95.4	.8	1.0	− .5
1953	96.3	.7	.2	− .6
1954	97.8	.4	1.1	− .5
1955	100.6	.6	2.2	− .4
1956	102.4	.4	1.4	− 2.5
1957	104.8	.9	1.5	− .7
1958	109.2	1.8	2.6	.8
1959	113.6	2.9	1.5	− .9
1960	115.9	2.2	.1	− 1.1
1961	118.5	3.3	−.7	− 2.4
1962	122.4	4.6	−.7	− 2.9
1963	127.4	4.7	.3	− 1.4
1964	132.1	4.2	.5	− 1.6
1965	135.7	3.7	−.1	− 3.6

Table 5.29 (continued)

(1) Year	(2) Net Capital Stock	(3) Net Investment	(4) Gross Revaluations	(5) Net Revaluations
1966	138.9	2.9	.3	− 4.6
1967	148.5	2.3	7.3	2.4
1968	168.2	4.4	15.3	8.1
1969	185.5	6.8	10.5	1.1
1970	195.5	5.8	4.2	− 5.4
1971	206.4	6.8	4.1	− 5.2
1972	227.6	8.3	12.9	3.9
1973	260.9	9.1	24.2	5.9
1974	288.8	2.4	25.5	− 3.7
1975	310.7	−.8	22.7	4.4
1976	340.5	−.4	30.3	14.0
1977	384.6	2.6	41.4	20.9
Sums				
1946–50		−.4	27.8	4.5
1951–55		2.7	8.8	− .5
1956–60		8.1	7.2	− 4.5
1961–65		20.4	−.6	−12.0
1966–70		22.3	37.5	1.6
1971–75		25.8	89.4	5.3
1976–77		2.1	71.7	35.0
Means				
1946–50	80.9	−.1	5.6	.9
1951–55	96.7	.5	1.8	− .1
1956–60	109.2	1.6	1.4	− .9
1961–65	127.2	4.1	−.1	− 2.4
1966–70	167.3	4.5	7.5	.3
1971–75	258.9	5.2	17.9	1.1
1976–77	362.6	1.1	35.9	17.5
Sums, 1946–77		81.0	241.9	29.5
Means, 1946–77	153.9	2.5	7.6	.9

Table 5.30 Business Inventories: Stocks, Investment, Gross and Net Revaluations, 1946–77

(1) Year	(2) Stocks	(3) Investment	(4) Gross Revaluations	(5) Net Revaluations
1946	73.7	7.6	−1.2	−13.0
1947	86.9	− 0.1	13.3	6.7
1948	90.6	4.0	− .3	− 2.7
1949	81.0	− 3.0	−6.6	− 5.1
1950	98.8	8.0	9.8	3.8
1951	112.1	10.7	2.6	− .5
1952	109.4	3.2	−5.9	− 7.7
1953	110.1	1.1	− .4	− 1.3
1954	107.2	− 1.6	−1.3	− 3.1
1955	112.1	5.6	− .7	− 3.6
1956	121.8	4.4	5.3	.9
1957	126.7	1.2	3.7	1.0
1958	128.9	− 1.4	3.6	1.5
1959	132.3	5.1	−1.7	− 4.6
1960	136.2	3.5	.4	− 1.0
1961	138.4	2.3	− .1	− 2.1
1962	145.2	6.4	.4	− 2.3
1963	151.5	6.2	.1	− 2.0
1964	157.6	5.8	.3	− 2.3
1965	172.7	9.3	5.8	1.5
1966	189.1	14.0	2.4	− 3.9
1967	202.2	10.2	2.9	− 3.9
1968	215.3	7.6	5.5	− 4.3
1969	236.2	9.7	11.2	− 1.0
1970	244.2	4.0	4.0	− 8.2
1971	261.9	6.4	11.2	− .3
1972	288.6	9.9	16.8	5.5
1973	353.6	19.3	45.7	22.2
1974	422.3	10.8	57.9	17.9
1975	428.3	−14.7	16.1	− 5.7
1976	459.7	−15.3	46.7	24.6
1977	498.6	25.1	13.8	− 2.9
Sums				
1946–50		16.4	15.1	−10.3
1951–55		19.0	−5.7	−16.3
1956–60		12.7	11.4	− 2.2
1961–65		30.1	6.4	− 7.1
1966–70		45.6	25.9	−21.2
1971–75		31.7	147.8	39.5
1976–77		9.8	60.5	21.7

Table 5.30 (continued)

(1) Year	(2) Stocks	(3) Investment	(4) Gross Revaluations	(5) Net Revaluations
Means				
1946–50	86.2	3.3	3.0	− 2.1
1951–55	110.2	3.8	−1.1	− 3.3
1956–60	129.2	2.5	2.3	− .4
1961–65	153.1	6.0	1.3	− 1.4
1966–70	217.4	9.1	5.2	− 4.2
1971–75	350.1	6.3	29.6	7.9
1976–77	479.1	4.7	30.3	10.9
Sums, 1946–77		165.2	284.4	4.0
Means, 1946–77	193.5	5.2	8.9	.1

Table 5.31 **Values, Gross and Net Revaluations of Privately Held Land (Billions of Dollars, 1946–77)**

(1) Year	(2) Value (End of Year)	(3) Gross Revaluations	(4) Net Revaluations
1946	140.1	10.5	−11.0
1947	149.6	9.4	− 3.3
1948	155.3	5.7	1.7
1949	160.6	5.3	7.9
1950	178.9	18.3	7.1
1951	193.2	14.3	8.8
1952	203.1	9.8	6.6
1953	208.5	5.5	3.8
1954	221.3	12.8	9.3
1955	241.5	20.2	14.4
1956	268.2	26.7	17.4
1957	288.9	20.6	14.7
1958	315.9	27.1	22.1
1959	340.8	24.9	17.8
1960	358.6	17.8	14.3
1961	375.0	16.4	11.3
1962	399.7	24.7	17.7
1963	415.9	16.2	10.6
1964	438.2	22.3	15.3
1965	466.7	28.5	17.0

Table 5.31 (continued)

(1) Year	(2) Value (End of Year)	(3) Gross Revaluations	(4) Net Revaluations
1966	500.7	34.0	17.6
1967	531.6	30.9	13.5
1968	564.0	32.4	7.1
1969	588.5	24.5	− 6.6
1970	610.2	21.8	− 8.3
1971	623.9	13.7	−14.8
1972	703.3	79.4	52.9
1973	827.5	124.2	68.8
1974	969.9	142.3	50.0
1975	1,030.1	60.2	− 1.5
1976	1,193.5	163.5	109.5
1977	1,304.1	110.6	39.0
Sums			
1946–50		49.3	2.4
1951–55		62.6	42.9
1956–60		117.1	86.3
1961–65		108.1	72.0
1966–70		143.5	23.3
1971–75		419.8	155.4
1976–77		274.1	148.5
Means			
1946–50	156.9	9.9	.5
1951–55	213.5	12.5	8.6
1956–60	314.5	23.4	17.3
1961–65	419.1	21.6	14.4
1966–70	559.0	28.7	4.7
1971–75	830.9	84.0	31.1
1976–77	1,248.8	137.0	74.2
Sums, 1946–77		1,174.5	530.7
Means, 1946–77	467.7	36.7	16.6

Table 5.32 Values and Net Revaluations of Land by Sector (Billions of Dollars, 1952–68, from Milgram Data)

(1) Year	(2) Households, Excluding Nonprofit Institutions	(3) Non-profit Institutions	(4) Non-corporate Plus Farm	(5) Corporate Nonfarm	(6) Government	(7) Total
			A. Values (End of Year)			
1952	58.7	6.3	80.0	21.8	34.5	201.3
1953	64.9	7.3	81.0	26.1	39.0	218.3
1954	72.7	7.9	84.0	27.5	41.7	233.8
1955	84.9	9.1	89.6	33.2	48.1	264.9
1956	97.3	10.3	97.8	38.4	54.0	297.8
1957	108.9	11.2	104.3	43.8	60.9	329.1
1958	121.9	12.5	112.8	48.5	66.6	362.3
1959	140.0	13.9	117.1	54.9	73.0	398.9
1960	148.6	14.9	119.8	58.1	79.0	420.4
1961	161.9	16.4	126.6	64.0	86.9	455.8
1962	172.9	17.8	134.3	69.6	94.0	488.6
1963	184.8	19.4	142.1	76.1	101.9	524.3
1964	198.0	21.1	151.1	82.7	110.1	563.0
1965	212.7	22.9	161.8	88.7	117.4	603.5
1966	224.5	24.8	172.8	96.5	127.4	646.0
1967	237.7	26.9	183.3	103.3	135.8	687.0
1968	250.9	28.6	192.7	110.0	144.2	726.4
			B. Net Revaluations			
1953	5.7	.9	.3	4.1	4.2	15.3
1954	6.7	.5	1.6	1.0	2.0	11.8
1955	10.3	1.0	3.4	5.0	5.3	24.9
1956	9.1	.8	4.8	3.9	4.0	22.7
1957	9.4	.7	4.3	4.5	5.7	24.7
1958	11.1	1.1	6.7	3.9	4.6	27.5
1959	15.4	1.1	1.8	5.3	4.9	28.5
1960	7.1	.9	1.5	2.6	5.2	17.3
1961	11.2	1.3	5.1	5.1	6.8	29.4
1962	8.0	1.1	5.4	4.4	5.5	24.4
1963	9.5	1.4	5.9	5.5	6.6	28.8
1964	10.1	1.4	6.6	5.3	6.5	29.9
1965	9.5	1.2	6.7	3.8	4.4	25.8
1966	4.3	1.1	5.3	4.7	5.9	21.2
1967	5.4	1.2	4.5	3.5	4.0	18.6
1968	1.9	.4	.7	1.8	2.0	6.8

Table 5.32 (continued)

(1) Year	(2) Households, Excluding Nonprofit Institutions	(3) Non-profit Insti-tutions	(4) Non-corporate Plus Farm	(5) Corporate Nonfarm	(6) Govern-ment	(7) Total
		B. Net Revaluations				
Sums						
1953–55	22.7	2.4	5.4	10.1	11.6	52.1
1956–60	52.2	4.6	19.0	20.4	24.6	120.8
1961–65	48.3	6.4	29.7	24.2	29.8	138.3
1966–68	11.6	2.8	10.5	9.9	11.8	46.5
Means						
1953–55	7.6	.8	1.8	3.4	3.9	17.4
1956–60	10.4	.9	3.8	4.1	4.9	24.2
1961–65	9.7	1.3	5.9	4.8	6.0	27.7
1966–68	3.9	.9	3.5	3.3	3.9	15.5
Sum, 1953–68	134.8	16.1	64.6	64.5	77.6	357.7
Mean, 1953–68	8.4	1.0	4.0	4.0	4.9	22.4

Table 5.33 **Personal Income and Saving and Household Net Revaluations of Nonhuman Capital, 1946–77**

(1) Year	(2) Personal Income (PI)	(3) Disposable Personal Income (DPI)	(4) Personal Saving (PS)	(5) Net Revaluations (NR)	(6) Disposable Personal Income Plus Net Revaluations	(7) Personal Saving Plus Net Revaluations (PS+NR)	(8) PS ÷ DPI	(9) NR ÷ DPI	(10) (PS+NR) ÷ DPI
			Billions of Dollars					*Percentage*	
1946	177.3	158.6	13.4	− 85.3	73.3	− 71.9	8.5	−53.8	−45.3
1947	189.8	168.4	4.9	− 30.3	138.1	− 25.4	2.9	−18.0	−15.1
1948	208.5	187.4	10.6	− 11.3	176.1	− .8	5.7	− 6.1	− .4
1949	205.6	187.1	6.7	28.0	215.2	34.8	3.6	15.0	18.6
1950	226.1	205.5	10.8	− .4	205.1	10.5	5.3	− .2	5.1
1951	253.7	224.8	14.8	21.1	245.9	35.9	6.6	9.4	16.0
1952	270.4	236.4	16.0	2.5	238.9	18.6	6.8	1.1	7.9
1953	286.1	250.7	17.0	− 15.0	235.7	2.0	6.8	− 6.0	.8
1954	288.2	255.7	15.6	63.1	318.8	78.6	6.1	24.7	30.3
1955	308.8	273.4	14.9	44.1	317.5	59.0	5.4	16.1	21.6
1956	330.9	291.3	19.7	.1	291.3	19.8	6.8	.0	6.8
1957	349.3	306.9	20.6	− 41.6	265.3	− 21.0	6.7	−13.6	− 6.9
1958	359.3	317.1	21.7	121.2	438.3	142.9	6.8	38.2	45.1
1959	382.1	336.1	18.8	19.3	355.4	38.1	5.6	5.7	11.3
1960	399.7	349.4	17.1	− 8.7	340.7	8.4	4.9	− 2.5	2.4
1961	415.0	362.9	20.2	94.6	457.5	114.8	5.6	26.1	31.6
1962	440.7	383.9	20.4	− 81.2	302.7	− 60.8	5.3	−21.1	−15.8
1963	463.1	402.8	18.8	73.7	476.5	92.5	4.7	18.3	23.0
1964	495.7	437.0	26.1	40.0	477.0	66.1	6.0	9.1	15.1
1965	537.0	472.2	30.3	49.4	521.5	79.7	6.4	10.5	16.9
1966	584.9	510.4	33.0	−106.7	403.7	− 73.7	6.5	−20.9	−14.4
1967	626.6	544.5	40.9	142.9	687.5	183.8	7.5	26.2	33.8
1968	685.2	588.1	38.1	135.5	723.6	173.6	6.5	23.0	29.5
1969	745.8	630.4	35.1	−183.4	447.0	−148.3	5.6	−29.1	−23.5
1970	801.3	685.9	50.6	−125.6	560.3	− 75.1	7.4	−18.3	−10.3

Table 5.33 (continued)

(1) Year	(2) Personal Income (PI)	(3) Disposable Personal Income (DPI)	(4) Personal Saving (PS)	(5) Net Revaluations (NR)	(6) Disposable Personal Income Plus Net Revaluations	(7) Personal Saving Plus Net Revaluations (PS+NR)	(8) PS ÷ DPI	(9) NR ÷ DPI	(10) (PS+NR) ÷ DPI
			Billions of Dollars					*Percentage*	
1971	859.1	742.8	57.3	19.9	762.7	77.2	7.7	2.7	10.4
1972	942.5	801.3	49.4	109.7	911.0	159.1	6.2	13.7	19.9
1973	1,052.4	901.7	70.3	−308.7	593.0	−238.4	7.8	−34.2	−26.4
1974	1,154.9	984.6	71.7	−439.6	545.0	−368.0	7.3	−44.7	−37.4
1975	1,255.5	1,086.7	83.6	84.8	1,171.5	168.5	7.7	7.3	15.5
1976	1,380.9	1,184.4	66.0	219.4	1,403.7	285.4	5.6	18.5	24.1
1977	1,529.0	1,303.0	66.9	− 62.5	1,240.5	4.4	5.1	− 4.8	.3
Sums									
1946–50	1,007.3	907.1	46.6	− 99.3	807.8	− 52.8			
1951–55	1,407.2	1,240.9	78.2	115.9	1,356.8	194.1			
1956–60	1,821.3	1,600.8	97.8	90.3	1,691.1	188.1			
1961–65	2,351.4	2,058.7	115.8	176.5	2,235.2	292.3			
1966–70	3,443.8	2,959.4	197.6	−137.3	2,822.1	60.3			
1971–75	5,264.5	4,517.1	332.3	−533.9	3,983.1	−201.6			
1976–77	2,909.8	2,487.4	133.0	156.9	2,644.2	289.8			
Means									
1946–50	201.5	181.4	9.3	− 19.9	161.6	− 10.6	5.2	−12.6	− 7.4
1951–55	281.4	248.2	15.6	23.2	271.4	38.8	6.3	9.1	15.4
1956–60	364.3	320.2	19.6	18.1	338.2	37.6	6.2	5.6	11.7
1961–65	470.3	411.7	23.2	35.3	447.0	58.5	5.6	8.6	14.2
1966–70	688.8	591.9	39.5	− 27.5	564.4	12.1	6.7	− 3.8	2.9
1971–75	1,052.9	903.4	66.5	−106.8	796.6	− 40.3	7.3	−10.9	− 3.6
1976–77	1,454.9	1,243.7	66.5	78.4	1,322.1	144.9	5.4	6.9	12.2
Sums, 1946–77	18,205.4	15,771.4	1,001.3	−231.0	15,540.4	770.3			
Means, 1946–77	568.9	492.9	31.3	− 7.2	485.6	24.1	6.2	− .2	6.0

Table 5.34 **Personal Income and Saving and Household Net Revaluations of Nonhuman Capital (1972 Dollars, 1946–77)**

(1) Year	(2) Disposable Personal Income (DPI)	(3) Personal Saving (PS)	(4) Net Revaluations (NR)	(5) Disposable Personal Income Plus Net Revaluations	(6) Personal Saving Plus Net Revaluations (PS+NR)	(7) PS ÷ DPI	(8) NR ÷ DPI	(9) (PS+NR) ÷ DPI
			Billions of Dollars				*Percentage*	
1946	332.4	32.6	−206.6	125.8	−174.0	9.8	−62.1	−52.4
1947	318.8	10.1	− 62.0	256.8	− 51.9	3.2	−19.4	−16.3
1948	335.5	19.8	− 21.2	314.3	− 1.4	5.9	− 6.3	− .4
1949	336.1	12.3	51.2	387.3	63.5	3.7	15.2	18.9
1950	361.9	19.2	− .7	361.2	18.5	5.3	− .2	5.1
1951	371.6	24.3	34.8	406.4	59.1	6.5	9.4	15.9
1952	382.1	25.8	4.1	386.2	29.9	6.8	1.1	7.8
1953	397.5	27.0	− 23.8	373.7	3.2	6.8	− 6.0	.8
1954	402.1	24.5	99.5	501.6	124.0	6.1	24.7	30.8
1955	425.9	23.0	68.0	493.9	91.0	5.4	16.0	21.4
1956	444.9	28.8	.1	445.0	28.9	6.5	.0	6.5
1957	453.9	29.0	− 58.7	395.2	− 29.7	6.4	−12.9	− 6.5
1958	459.0	30.6	171.2	630.2	201.8	6.7	37.3	44.0
1959	477.4	26.3	27.0	504.4	53.3	5.5	5.7	11.2
1960	487.3	23.7	− 12.0	475.3	11.7	4.9	− 2.5	2.4
1961	500.6	28.2	132.1	632.7	160.3	5.6	26.4	32.0
1962	521.6	28.3	−112.7	408.9	− 84.4	5.4	−21.6	−16.2
1963	539.2	26.1	102.2	641.4	128.3	4.8	19.0	23.8
1964	577.3	35.9	54.9	632.2	90.8	6.2	9.5	15.7
1965	612.4	41.0	66.9	679.3	107.9	6.7	10.9	17.6
1966	643.6	43.3	−140.0	503.6	− 96.7	6.7	−21.8	−15.0
1967	669.8	51.9	181.6	851.4	233.5	7.8	27.1	34.9
1968	695.2	46.4	165.0	860.2	211.4	6.7	23.7	30.4
1969	712.3	40.4	−211.1	501.2	−170.7	5.7	−29.6	−24.0
1970	741.6	55.5	−137.9	603.7	− 82.4	7.5	−18.6	−11.1

Table 5.34 (continued)

(1) Year	(2) Disposable Personal Income (DPI)	(3) Personal Saving (PS)	(4) Net Revaluations (NR)	(5) Disposable Personal Income Plus Net Revaluations	(6) Personal Saving Plus Net Revaluations (PS+NR)	(7) PS ÷ DPI	(8) NR ÷ DPI	(9) (PS+NR) ÷ DPI
			Billions of Dollars				*Percentage*	
1971	769.0	59.8	20.7	789.7	80.5	7.8	2.7	10.5
1972	801.3	49.4	109.7	911.0	159.1	6.2	13.7	19.9
1973	856.0	66.3	−291.2	564.8	−224.9	7.8	−34.0	−26.3
1974	842.0	60.9	−373.5	468.5	−312.7	7.2	−44.4	−37.1
1975	859.7	63.2	64.1	923.8	127.2	7.3	7.5	14.8
1976	890.1	47.2	156.9	1,047.0	204.1	5.3	17.6	22.9
1977	926.3	44.5	− 41.6	884.7	2.9	4.8	− 4.5	.3
Sums								
1946–50	1,684.7	93.9	−239.2	1,445.5	−145.3			
1951–55	1,979.2	124.6	182.6	2,161.8	307.3			
1956–60	2,322.5	138.4	127.5	2,450.0	266.0			
1961–65	2,751.1	159.5	243.4	2,994.5	402.9			
1966–70	3,462.5	237.5	−142.4	3,320.1	95.2			
1971–75	4,128.0	299.6	−470.2	3,657.8	−170.7			
1976–77	1,816.4	91.8	115.3	1,931.7	207.0			
Means								
1946–50	336.9	18.8	− 47.8	289.1	− 29.1	5.6	−14.6	− 9.0
1951–55	395.8	24.9	36.5	432.4	61.5	6.3	9.0	15.4
1956–60	464.5	27.7	25.5	490.0	53.2	6.0	5.5	11.5
1961–65	550.2	31.9	48.7	598.9	80.6	5.8	8.8	14.6
1966–70	692.5	47.5	− 28.5	664.0	19.0	6.9	− 3.8	3.0
1971–75	825.6	59.9	− 94.0	731.6	− 34.1	7.3	−10.9	− 3.7
1976–77	908.2	45.9	57.7	965.9	103.5	5.1	6.6	11.6
Sums, 1946–77	18,144.4	1,145.3	−182.9	17,961.5	962.4			
Means, 1946–77	567.0	35.8	− 5.7	561.3	30.1	6.2	− .5	5.7

Table 5.35 **BEA Net Private Domestic Investment, Tangible Net Investment, Net Revaluations and Net Capital Accumulation, Nonhuman Capital (Billions of Dollars, 1946–77)**

(1) Year	(2) Net Private Domestic Investment	(3) Tangible Net Investment	(4) Tangible Net Revaluations	(5) Capital Accumulation Tangible Net
1946	16.8	−17.6	−33.9	−51.5
1947	16.8	− 7.5	22.0	14.4
1948	25.6	7.1	13.1	20.2
1949	13.3	12.1	18.6	30.7
1950	30.0	35.1	1.5	36.6
1951	31.6	66.6	24.7	91.3
1952	22.5	63.3	− 3.6	59.7
1953	21.7	53.6	2.5	56.1
1954	19.6	42.0	− .1	41.9
1955	33.1	54.3	34.2	88.4
1956	32.2	48.7	18.8	67.6
1957	27.2	39.7	20.5	60.2
1958	17.8	29.6	27.6	57.1
1959	31.4	44.2	6.1	50.3
1960	28.7	38.3	11.5	49.8
1961	25.3	34.1	5.3	39.4
1962	34.5	51.7	1.4	53.1
1963	38.0	59.4	1.8	61.2
1964	42.1	65.0	8.4	73.4
1965	54.5	81.4	3.4	84.8
1966	62.7	91.0	− 5.9	85.2
1967	53.8	85.0	22.3	107.3
1968	57.7	98.8	39.4	138.2
1969	63.7	99.0	12.4	111.4
1970	50.0	73.8	−24.0	49.9
1971	61.2	87.8	−32.4	55.4
1972	82.9	112.5	106.3	218.8
1973	102.3	134.0	185.9	319.9
1974	76.9	100.2	108.8	209.0
1975	30.0	56.2	37.6	93.8
1976	65.2	103.9	182.0	285.9
1977	102.6	146.3	114.3	260.6
Sums				
1946–50	102.5	29.2	21.3	50.5
1951–55	128.5	279.7	57.8	337.5
1956–60	137.3	200.5	84.5	285.1
1961–65	194.4	291.5	20.4	311.9
1966–70	287.9	447.6	44.3	491.9
1971–75	353.3	490.7	406.2	896.9
1976–77	167.8	250.2	296.3	546.5

Table 5.35 (continued)

(1) Year	(2) Net Private Domestic Investment	(3) Tangible Net Investment	(4) Tangible Net Revaluations	(5) Capital Accumulation Tangible Net
Means				
1946–50	20.5	5.8	4.3	10.1
1951–55	25.7	55.9	11.6	67.5
1956–60	27.5	40.1	16.9	57.0
1961–65	38.9	58.3	4.1	62.4
1966–70	57.6	89.5	8.9	98.4
1971–75	70.7	98.1	81.2	179.4
1976–77	83.9	125.1	148.2	273.3
Sums, 1946–77	1,371.7	1,989.6	930.6	2,920.2
Means, 1946–77	42.9	62.2	29.1	91.3

Table 5.36 **National Tangible Assets in Current Prices: Gross Revaluations (Billions of Dollars, 1953–68)**

		Reproducible Assets													Land[c]		
			Structures						Equipment[a]		Inventories[b]						
				Nonfarm													
											Private		Public		Private		Public
Year (1)	Total Tangible Assets (2)	Total Structures (3)	Total Nonfarm Structures[a] (4)	Public Nonresidential (5)	Institutional (6)	Other Private Nonresidential (7)	Residential (8)	Farm Structures (9)	Producer Durables (10)	Consumer Durables (11)	Farm (12)	Nonfarm (13)	(14)	Farm (15)	Nonfarm (16)	(17)
1953	17.0	1.5	.6	1.1	.1	.5	−.8	−.4	1.3	−1.2	−.3	1.1	−.2	−2.1	13.1	4.5
1954	21.5	6.3	3.4	1.3	.0	.4	1.8	.0	2.2	−1.4	1.4	.4	.1	2.4	10.1	2.7
1955	63.0	33.1	26.4	7.4	.8	5.4	11.8	1.0	7.0	−1.2	−1.3	2.1	.0	3.0	20.5	6.4
1956	83.8	51.8	32.9	11.1	1.2	7.4	11.9	1.3	10.7	3.6	.6	3.4	.5	5.5	20.6	5.9
1957	60.2	29.2	14.3	5.7	.4	3.3	4.7	.4	7.7	4.4	.6	1.7	.4	4.5	19.6	6.9
1958	50.0	16.8	9.4	2.5	−.1	.2	6.2	.5	4.3	2.1	.3	.2	.2	7.3	20.2	5.7
1959	55.7	19.9	12.1	2.1	−.2	.7	8.9	.6	2.3	4.8	.0	.7	.1	4.6	24.8	6.4
1960	30.6	10.9	6.4	2.4	.1	−.5	3.8	.8	.0	−3.8	10.1	.1	−.0	.4	13.3	6.0
1961	39.2	3.6	12.3	5.6	.4	1.6	4.8	.5	−.2	−.3	−10.5	−.0	.0	5.8	21.9	7.9
1962	19.1	20.4	20.4	8.3	.6	2.8	8.7	−.4	−.3	.3	.1	−.0	−.0	5.2	−13.6	7.1
1963	93.9	24.5	23.7	7.7	.8	1.9	12.7	.5	.5	−.6	−.1	1.2	−.1	7.4	54.1	7.9
1964	66.6	27.7	25.1	8.6	1.0	2.8	12.3	.6	2.0	−.0	.1	.8	.1	7.9	22.8	8.2
1965	77.8	37.8	33.3	12.9	1.2	5.4	12.2	1.5	3.9	−1.4	.4	2.8	.2	9.8	22.9	7.3
1966	99.8	58.3	50.1	16.7	1.6	8.2	21.7	2.2	7.6	−1.6	1.0	3.0	.5	7.5	24.0	10.0
1967	125.9	85.6	37.0	21.4	2.1	9.5	31.8	1.9	9.3	3.3	.0	7.2	.0	8.3	23.6	8.4
1968	106.3	67.0	87.0	13.1	2.9	14.3	24.7	1.5	9.7	5.6	.7	−2.2	.4	7.8	23.1	8.4
Sums																
1953–55	101.4	40.8	30.4	9.8	.9	6.3	12.8	.6	10.5	−3.7	−.1	3.5	−.0	3.3	43.7	13.6
1956–60	280.2	128.5	75.0	23.8	1.4	11.1	35.5	3.6	25.1	11.1	11.6	6.2	1.2	22.3	98.5	30.9
1961–65	296.5	113.9	115.0	43.1	3.9	14.6	50.7	2.6	5.8	−2.1	−10.1	4.7	.2	36.1	108.1	38.4
1966–68	332.0	210.9	174.2	51.3	6.6	32.1	78.1	5.5	26.6	7.4	1.7	7.9	.9	23.6	70.7	26.8

Table 5.36 (continued)

Year (1)	Total Tangible Assets (2)	Reproducible Assets: Structures: Total Structures (3)	Total Nonfarm Structures[a] (4)	Nonfarm: Public Nonresidential (5)	Nonfarm: Institutional (6)	Nonfarm: Other Private Nonresidential (7)	Nonfarm: Residential (8)	Farm Structures (9)	Equipment[a]: Producer Durables (10)	Equipment[a]: Consumer Durables (11)	Inventories[b]: Private: Farm (12)	Inventories[b]: Private: Nonfarm (13)	Inventories[b]: Public (14)	Land[c]: Private: Farm (15)	Land[c]: Private: Nonfarm (16)	Land[c]: Public (17)
Means																
1953–55	33.8	13.6	10.1	3.3	.3	2.1	4.3	.2	3.5	− 1.2	− .0	1.2	−.0	1.1	14.6	4.5
1956–60	56.0	25.7	15.0	4.8	.3	2.2	7.1	.7	5.0	2.2	2.3	1.2	.2	4.5	19.7	6.2
1961–65	59.3	22.8	23.0	8.6	.8	2.9	10.1	.5	1.2	− .4	− 2.0	.9	.0	7.2	21.6	7.7
1966–68	110.7	70.3	58.1	17.1	2.2	10.7	26.0	1.8	8.9	2.5	.6	2.6	.3	7.9	23.6	8.9
Sums, 1953–68	1,010.2	494.2	394.6	127.9	12.8	64.1	177.1	12.3	68.1	12.7	3.1	22.3	2.3	85.3	321.0	109.7
Means, 1953–68	63.1	30.9	24.7	8.0	.8	4.0	11.1	.8	4.3	.8	.2	1.4	.1	5.3	20.1	6.9

Source: Calculated from series F349–364, "National Tangible Assets in Current Prices," and F365–376, "National Reproducible Assets in Constant (1958) Prices," both excluding Alaska and Hawaii, of *U.S. Department of Commerce, Bureau of the Census, Historical Statistics of the United States, Colonial Times to 1970*, Part 1 (Washington, D.C.: GPO, 1975).

[a]Constant-dollar net stock "estimates derived by 'perpetual inventory' method that is intended to reflect reproduction cost of different types of assets. Estimates are obtained by: (*a*) reducing each year's gross capital expenditures in current prices to 1958 price level by means of appropriate construction cost or wholesale price indexes; (*b*) depreciating gross capital expenditures in accordance with an assumed length of life for different types of assets, thus obtaining net capital expenditures for each year in 1958 prices; (*c*) cumulating net capital expenditures for as many years backwards as corresponds to the assumed length of life of the type of asset involved".

Current-dollar net stock "estimates obtained by multiplying the *constant dollar* figures shown in series F365–376 by the appropriate price index for current year." We then calculate net investment in constant dollars as the first difference of constant-dollar net capital stocks reported in series F365–376. Reflation to current-dollar net investment is accomplished by applying implicit deflators calculated by dividing the current dollar stocks of series F349–364 by the constant dollar stocks of series F365–376.

[b]Current-dollar stock estimates are based on book values. Constant-dollar stock estimates reflect book values reduced by means of wholesale price indexes.

[c]Estimates are based on census or similar data. For other private land, estimates are derived by application of rough ratios of land to structure values for different types of real estate. Excludes subsoil assets." We assume zero investment and depreciation in land.

Table 5.37 National Tangible Assets, in Current Prices: Net Revaluations (Billions of Dollars, 1953–68)

		Reproducible Assets												Land[c]		
			Structures						Equipment[a]		Inventories[b]					
				Nonfarm							Private		Public	Private		Public
Year (1)	Total Tangible Assets (2)	Total Structures (3)	Total Nonfarm Structures[a] (4)	Public Nonresidential (5)	Institutional (6)	Other Private Nonresidential (7)	Residential (8)	Farm Structures (9)	Producer Durables (10)	Consumer Durables (11)	Farm (12)	Nonfarm (13)	(14)	Farm (15)	Nonfarm (16)	(17)
1953	7.5	−6.3	−4.3	−.1	−.0	−.4	−3.1	−.7	.2	−1.9	−.5	.4	−.3	−2.7	12.3	4.2
1954	1.5	−10.1	−6.9	−1.3	−.2	−1.6	−3.1	−.5	−.3	−3.0	1.1	−1.0	−.1	1.3	8.2	2.0
1955	29.6	5.8	9.3	3.0	.3	2.0	3.7	.2	2.8	−3.9	−1.8	−.2	−.4	1.2	17.3	5.3
1956	30.9	8.9	5.8	4.2	.4	2.0	−1.0	.1	4.0	−.7	−.1	−.1	−.1	2.8	15.2	4.0
1957	26.9	2.4	−2.7	1.3	−.1	−.0	−3.2	−.4	3.4	1.7	.1	−.4	.1	2.8	16.0	5.7
1958	22.2	−5.4	−4.7	−1.2	−.5	−2.6	−.3	−.1	.8	−.1	−.1	−1.5	−.1	5.9	17.1	4.6
1959	17.9	−10.0	−7.0	−3.0	−.8	−3.1	−.1	−.2	−2.5	1.8	−.5	−1.5	−.3	2.6	20.3	4.9
1960	11.9	−3.7	−2.9	−.1	−.2	−2.3	−.6	.4	−2.3	−5.2	9.9	−1.0	−.2	−.6	−10.9	5.2
1961	12.3	−17.5	−1.2	1.9	−.0	−.9	−1.5	−.1	−3.5	−2.4	−11.0	−1.6	−.3	4.5	18.5	6.8
1962	−17.5	−7.9	2.1	3.2	−.0	−.7	.1	−1.2	−4.7	−2.5	−.4	−2.0	−.3	3.4	−18.4	5.5
1963	65.0	1.9	9.0	3.5	.4	−.8	5.8	−.1	−3.0	−2.7	−.5	−.5	−.4	5.9	50.6	6.6
1964	29.7	−.6	6.6	3.3	.4	−.6	3.7	−.1	−2.3	−2.8	−.3	−1.3	−.2	6.0	17.8	6.5
1965	16.2	−9.3	2.4	4.0	.1	−.2	−2.0	.4	−3.2	−6.0	−.3	−.6	−.2	6.7	14.4	4.4
1966	10.9	−9.6	5.8	3.7	.1	.1	1.6	.6	−2.9	−8.3	−.0	−2.1	.0	2.9	11.7	5.9
1967	31.7	13.5	−9.9	7.4	.5	.8	10.8	.3	−2.0	−3.7	−.9	1.8	−.4	3.6	10.7	4.0
1968	−32.4	−39.6	19.2	−7.7	.5	1.6	−6.1	−.8	−7.2	−4.8	−.6	−10.2	−.3	.9	4.3	2.0
Sums																
1953–55	38.6	−10.6	−2.0	1.6	.1	−.1	−2.5	−1.0	2.6	−8.9	−1.1	−.7	−.8	−.1	37.8	11.6
1956–60	109.9	−7.7	−11.4	1.1	−1.1	−6.0	−5.0	−.3	3.4	−2.4	9.3	−4.4	−.6	13.6	79.5	24.6
1961–65	105.7	−33.4	19.0	16.0	.9	−3.2	6.2	−1.1	−16.7	−16.4	−12.4	−5.9	−1.3	26.5	82.8	29.8
1966–68	10.2	−35.7	15.1	3.3	1.0	2.5	6.2	.1	−12.0	−16.8	−1.5	−10.4	−.7	7.4	26.7	11.8

Table 5.37 (continued)

Year (1)	Total Tangible Assets (2)	Reproducible Assets: Structures: Total Structures (3)	Total Nonfarm Structures[a] (4)	Nonfarm: Public Nonresidential (5)	Nonfarm: Institutional (6)	Nonfarm: Other Private Nonresidential (7)	Nonfarm: Residential (8)	Farm Structures (9)	Equipment[a]: Producer Durables (10)	Equipment[a]: Consumer Durables (11)	Inventories[b]: Private: Farm (12)	Inventories[b]: Private: Nonfarm (13)	Inventories[b]: Public (14)	Land[c]: Private: Farm (15)	Land[c]: Private: Nonfarm (16)	Land[c]: Public (17)
Means																
1953–55	12.9	− 3.5	− .7	.5	.0	− .0	− .8	− .3	.9	− 3.0	− .4	− .2	− .3	−.0	12.6	3.9
1956–60	22.0	− 1.5	− 2.3	.2	− .2	−1.2	−1.0	− .1	.7	− .5	1.9	− .9	− .1	2.7	15.9	4.9
1961–65	21.1	− 6.7	3.8	3.2	.2	− .6	1.2	− .2	− 3.3	− 3.3	− 2.5	− 1.2	− .3	5.3	16.6	6.0
1966–68	3.4	−11.9	5.0	1.1	.3	.8	2.1	.0	− 4.0	− 5.6	− .5	− 3.5	− .2	2.5	8.9	3.9
Sums, 1953–68	264.4	−87.5	20.7	22.0	.9	−6.7	6.0	−2.3	−22.7	−44.5	− 5.7	−21.4	−3.4	47.4	226.8	77.6
Means, 1953–68	16.5	− 5.5	1.3	1.4	.1	− .4	.3	− .1	− 1.4	− 2.8	− .4	− 1.3	− .2	3.0	14.2	4.9

Source: Calculated from series F349–364, "National Tangible Assets in Current Prices," and F365–376, "National Reproducible Assets in Constant (1958) Prices," both excluding Alaska and Hawaii, of *U.S. Department of Commerce, Bureau of the Census, Historical Statistics of the United States, Colonial Times to 1970*, Part 1 (Washington, D.C.: GPO, 1975).

[a]Constant-dollar net stock "estimates derived by 'perpetual inventory' method which is intended to reflect reproduction cost of different types of assets. Estimates are obtained by: (*a*) reducing each year's gross capital expenditures in current prices to 1958 price level by means of appropriate construction cost or wholesale price indexes; (*b*) depreciating gross capital expenditures in accordance with an assumed length of life for different types of assets, thus obtaining net capital expenditures for each year in 1958 prices; (*c*) cumulating net capital expenditures for as many years backwards as corresponds to the assumed length of life of the type of asset involved".

Current-dollar net stock "estimates obtained by multiplying the *constant dollar* figures shown in series F365–376 by the appropriate price index for current year." We then calculate net investment in constant dollars as the first difference of constant-dollar net capital stocks reported in series F365–376. Reflation to current-dollar net investment is accomplished by applying implicit deflators calculated by dividing the current dollar stocks of series F349–364 by the constant dollar stocks of series F365–376.

[b]Current-dollar stock estimates are based on book values. Constant-dollar stock estimates reflect book values reduced by means of wholesale price indexes.

[c]Estimates are based on census or similar data. For other private land, estimates are derived by application of rough ratios of land to structure values for different types of real estate. Excludes subsoil assets." We assume zero investment and depreciation in land.

Table 5.38 **Male Human Capital, from Present Values of Prospective Earnings, 1969, Population and Gross and Spendable Earnings Series (Billions of Dollars, 1947–75)**

	Net Stock		"Gross" Capital Accumulation		Net Capital Accumulation	
(1) Year	(2) From Gross Earnings	(3) From Spendable Earnings	(4) From Gross Earnings	(5) From Spendable Earnings	(6) From Gross Earnings	(7) From Spendable Earnings
1947	2,059	1,928				
1948	2,251	2,130	192	202	136	150
1949	2,346	2,220	95	90	133	126
1950	2,521	2,360	175	140	11	− 15
1951	2,791	2,572	270	212	193	140
1952	2,974	2,712	183	140	137	98
1953	3,176	2,871	202	159	173	133
1954	3,269	2,946	93	75	44	31
1955	3,498	3,123	229	177	142	99
1956	3,708	3,297	210	174	75	54
1957	3,911	3,451	203	154	121	81
1958	4,067	3,578	156	127	89	68
1959	4,355	3,797	288	219	198	140
1960	4,526	3,912	177	115	125	75
1961	4,708	4,058	182	146	117	90
1962	4,968	4,255	260	197	173	122
1963	5,184	4,401	216	146	146	86
1964	5,422	4,686	238	285	151	212
1965	5,709	4,953	287	267	145	144
1966	5,998	5,143	289	190	87	15
1967	6,242	5,322	244	179	36	1
1968	6,661	5,631	419	309	123	56
1969	7,148	5,960	487	329	120	19
1970	7,524	6,297	376	337	11	33
1971	8,096	6,834	572	537	221	243
1972	8,731	7,421	635	587	291	296
1973	9,390	7,863	659	442	− 29	−143
1974	10,037	8,346	647	483	−400	−394
1975	10,732	9,133	695	787	96	289
Sums						
1947–50			462	432	280	261
1951–55			977	763	689	501
1956–60			1,034	789	608	418
1961–65			1,183	1,041	732	654
1966–70			1,815	1,344	377	124
1971–75			3,208	2,836	179	291

Table 5.38 (continued)

(1) Year	Net Stock (2) From Gross Earnings	(3) From Spendable Earnings	"Gross" Capital Accumulation (4) From Gross Earnings	(5) From Spendable Earnings	Net Capital Accumulation (6) From Gross Earnings	(7) From Spendable Earnings
Means						
1947–50	2,294	2,160	154	144	93	87
1951–55	3,142	2,845	195	153	138	100
1956–60	4,113	3,607	207	158	122	84
1961–65	5,198	4,471	237	208	146	131
1966–70	6,715	5,671	363	269	75	25
1971–75	9,397	7,919	642	567	36	58
Sums, 1947–75			8,679	7,205	2,865	2,249
Means, 1947–75	5,241	4,524	310	257	102	80

Source: Prepared by John Graham, adjusting the 7.5% discount 1969 present values in his paper with Roy Webb, "Present Value Estimates of Human Capital Stocks," to changing earnings and population indicated in BLS data.

Table 5.39 **Human Capital: Net Stocks, Gross and Net Investment, Gross and Net Revaluations, and Net Capital Accumulation (Billions of Dollars, 1946–69)**

(1) Year	(2) Net Capital Stock (NCS)	(3) Gross Investment (GI)	(4) Deprecia-tion (D)	(5) Net Investment (NI)	(6) Gross Revaluations (GR)	(7) Net Revaluations (NR)	(8) Net Capital Accumulation (NCA=NI+NR)
1946	507.4	47.9	27.7	20.2	38.1	−38.4	−18.2
1947	585.0	55.1	31.4	23.7	54.0	7.0	30.6
1948	651.1	60.9	34.4	26.5	39.6	23.8	50.3
1949	684.5	61.2	35.7	25.6	7.8	18.9	44.5
1950	732.0	66.8	37.5	29.3	18.1	−31.1	− 1.8
1951	818.8	76.5	41.1	35.4	51.4	28.7	64.0
1952	889.2	83.1	43.9	39.2	31.2	17.3	56.5
1953	952.9	88.6	46.1	42.5	21.2	13.7	56.2
1954	1,009.6	89.6	48.2	41.3	15.4	− 1.0	40.4
1955	1,080.8	99.2	50.8	48.4	22.8	− 4.6	43.8
1956	1,174.4	108.4	54.2	54.2	39.5	− 3.2	51.0
1957	1,280.2	117.3	58.1	59.1	46.7	20.1	79.3
1958	1,380.4	122.6	61.7	60.9	39.3	16.6	77.5
1959	1,487.1	134.2	65.2	69.0	37.7	6.2	75.2
1960	1,594.9	141.5	68.8	72.7	35.1	19.4	92.1
1961	1,700.6	148.5	72.4	76.1	29.6	6.1	82.3
1962	1,824.5	160.8	76.5	84.3	39.6	7.3	91.6
1963	1,958.7	171.9	80.8	91.1	43.1	16.7	107.8
1964	2,112.4	187.5	85.7	101.8	51.9	18.2	120.1
1965	2,284.7	205.4	91.1	114.3	58.0	1.2	115.5

Table 5.39 (continued)

(1) Year	(2) Net Capital Stock (NCS)	(3) Gross Investment (GI)	(4) Deprecia-tion (D)	(5) Net Investment (NI)	(6) Gross Revaluations (GR)	(7) Net Revaluations (NR)	(8) Net Capital Accumulation (NCA=NI+NR)
1966	2,506.8	230.4	97.7	132.8	89.3	6.5	139.3
1967	2,730.2	245.2	104.1	141.0	82.4	− 7.5	133.5
1968	3,026.0	274.7	113.4	161.3	134.4	1.0	162.3
1969	3,380.9	305.6	124.6	181.0	173.9	2.3	183.3
Sums							
1946–50		291.9	166.6	125.3	157.6	−19.9	105.4
1951–55		436.9	230.1	206.8	142.0	54.1	260.8
1956–60		623.9	308.1	315.8	198.3	59.2	375.0
1961–65		874.1	406.5	467.6	222.2	49.7	517.3
1966–69		1,055.9	439.7	616.1	480.1	2.2	618.4
Means							
1946–50	632.0	58.4	33.3	25.1	31.5	− 4.0	21.1
1951–55	950.2	87.4	46.0	41.4	28.4	10.8	52.2
1956–60	1,383.4	124.8	61.6	63.2	39.7	11.8	75.0
1961–65	1,976.2	174.8	81.3	93.5	44.4	9.9	103.5
1966–69	2,911.0	264.0	109.9	154.0	96.0	.6	154.6
Sums, 1946–69		3,282.7	1,551.1	1,731.6	1,200.2	145.3	1,876.9
Means, 1946–69	1,514.7	136.8	64.6	72.2	50.0	6.1	78.2

Source: Underlying data and assumptions from John W. Kendrick, *The Formation and Stocks of Total Capital*; depreciation, net investment and net capital stock recalculated with straight-line depreciation.

Table 5.40 **Human Capital: Net Stocks, Gross and Net Investment, Gross and Net Revaluations, and Net Capital Accumulation (Billions of 1969 Dollars, 1946–69)**

(1) Year	(2) Net Capital Stock (NCS)	(3) Gross Investment (GI)	(4) Deprecia-tion (D)	(5) Net Investment (NI)	(6) Gross Revaluations (GR)	(7) Net Revaluations (NR)	(8) Net Capital Accumulation (NCA=NI+NR)
1946	1,151.9	108.7	62.8	45.9	86.5	−87.1	−41.2
1947	1,200.4	113.0	62.4	50.6	110.7	14.3	64.9
1948	1,251.4	117.0	66.1	51.0	76.2	45.7	96.6
1949	1,300.0	116.3	67.7	48.6	14.8	35.8	84.4
1950	1,354.3	123.6	69.4	54.2	33.5	−57.1	−2.9
1951	1,415.4	132.2	71.1	61.1	88.9	49.6	110.7
1952	1,480.7	138.3	73.0	65.3	51.9	28.8	94.1
1953	1,549.8	144.2	75.1	69.1	34.5	22.2	91.4
1954	1,615.9	143.3	77.2	61.1	24.6	−1.6	64.6
1955	1,691.7	155.2	79.5	75.7	35.6	−7.3	68.5
1956	1,773.5	163.7	81.9	81.8	59.6	−4.8	77.0
1957	1,859.4	170.3	84.4	85.9	67.8	29.2	115.1
1958	1,945.1	172.7	86.9	85.8	55.4	23.4	109.2
1959	2,039.7	184.0	89.5	94.6	51.8	8.5	103.1
1960	2,137.1	189.6	92.2	97.4	47.0	26.0	123.3
1961	2,237.2	195.4	95.3	100.1	39.0	8.1	108.2
1962	2,345.7	206.8	98.4	108.4	50.9	9.4	117.8
1963	2,460.0	215.9	101.5	114.4	54.2	21.0	135.4
1964	2,584.6	229.4	104.8	124.6	63.5	22.3	146.9
1965	2,720.7	244.5	108.5	136.1	69.1	1.5	137.5

Table 5.40 (continued)

(1) Year	(2) Net Capital Stock (NCS)	(3) Gross Investment (GI)	(4) Deprecia-tion (D)	(5) Net Investment (NI)	(6) Gross Revaluations (GR)	(7) Net Revaluations (NR)	(8) Net Capital Accumulation (NCA=NI+NR)
1966	2,872.8	264.1	111.9	152.2	102.3	7.4	159.6
1967	3,029.4	272.1	115.6	156.5	91.4	− 8.4	148.1
1968	3,199.9	290.5	119.9	170.6	142.2	1.1	171.6
1969	3,380.9	305.6	124.6	181.0	173.9	2.3	183.3
Sums							
1946–50		578.7	328.4	250.3	321.7	−48.4	201.8
1951–55		713.3	375.8	337.4	235.6	91.8	429.3
1956–60		880.3	434.9	445.4	281.6	82.4	527.8
1961–65		1,092.0	508.4	583.6	276.6	62.3	645.9
1966–69		1,132.2	471.9	660.2	509.8	2.4	662.7
Means							
1946–50		115.7	65.7	50.1	64.3	− 9.7	40.4
1951–55		142.7	75.2	67.5	47.1	8.4	85.8
1956–60		176.1	87.0	89.1	56.3	16.5	105.6
1961–65		219.4	101.7	116.7	55.3	12.5	129.2
1966–69		283.0	118.0	165.1	127.5	.6	165.7
Sums, 1946–69		4,396.4	2,119.5	2,276.9	1,625.4	190.5	2,467.4
Means, 1946–69		183.2	88.3	94.9	67.7	7.9	102.8

Source: From table 5.39, using implicit price deflators calculated from Kendrick's current and constant-dollar figures for gross investment in human capital.

Table 5.41 **Net Revaluations and Net Capital Accumulation, Human and Nonhuman Capital, Households (Billion of Dollars, 1946–69)**

	Nonhuman Capital			Human Capital			Total Capital		
(1) Year	(2) Net Investment (NI)	(3) Net Revaluations (NR)	(4) Net Capital Accumulation (NCA)	(5) Net Investment (NI)	(6) Net Revaluations (NR)	(7) Net Capital Accumulation (NCA)	(8) Net Investment (NI)	(9) Net Revaluations (NR)	(10) Net Capital Accumulation (NCA)
1946	20.3	— 85.3	— 65.0	20.2	—38.4	— 18.2	40.5	—123.7	— 83.2
1947	21.1	— 30.3	— 9.2	23.7	7.0	30.7	44.8	— 23.3	21.5
1948	25.2	— 11.3	13.8	26.5	23.8	50.3	51.7	12.5	64.1
1949	21.4	28.0	49.4	25.6	18.9	44.5	47.0	46.9	93.9
1950	27.7	— .4	27.4	29.3	—31.1	— 1.8	57.0	— 31.5	25.6
1951	34.0	21.1	55.1	35.4	28.7	64.1	69.4	49.8	119.2
1952	29.4	2.5	31.9	39.2	17.3	56.5	68.6	19.8	88.4
1953	30.8	— 15.0	15.9	42.5	13.7	56.2	73.3	— 1.3	72.1
1954	29.6	63.1	92.6	41.3	— 1.0	40.3	70.9	62.1	132.9
1955	32.6	44.1	76.6	48.4	— 4.6	43.8	81.0	39.5	120.4
1956	36.1	.1	36.2	54.2	— 3.2	51.0	90.3	— 3.1	87.2
1957	35.1	— 41.6	— 6.5	59.1	20.1	79.2	94.2	— 21.5	72.7
1958	34.2	121.2	155.4	60.9	16.6	77.5	95.1	137.8	232.9
1959	37.5	19.3	56.8	69.0	6.2	75.2	106.5	25.5	132.0
1960	35.1	— 8.7	26.4	72.7	19.4	92.1	107.8	10.7	118.5
1961	36.2	94.6	130.7	76.1	6.1	82.2	112.3	100.7	212.9
1962	40.9	— 81.2	— 40.2	84.3	7.3	91.6	125.2	— 73.9	51.4
1963	46.2	73.7	120.0	91.1	16.7	107.8	137.3	90.4	227.8
1964	56.5	40.0	96.5	101.8	18.2	120.0	158.3	58.2	216.5
1965	63.1	49.4	112.5	114.3	1.2	115.5	177.4	50.6	228.0

Table 5.41 (continued)

	Nonhuman Capital			Human Capital			Total Capital		
(1) Year	(2) Net Investment (NI)	(3) Net Revaluations (NR)	(4) Net Capital Accumulation (NCA)	(5) Net Investment (NI)	(6) Net Revaluations (NR)	(7) Net Capital Accumulation (NCA)	(8) Net Investment (NI)	(9) Net Revaluations (NR)	(10) Net Capital Accumulation (NCA)
1966	70.2	−106.7	− 36.5	132.8	6.5	139.3	203.0	−100.2	102.8
1967	71.4	142.9	214.3	141.0	− 7.5	133.5	212.4	135.4	347.8
1968	75.6	135.5	211.1	161.3	1.0	162.3	236.9	136.5	373.4
1969	60.4	−183.4	−123.0	181.0	2.3	183.3	241.4	−181.1	60.3
Sums									
1946–50	115.7	− 99.3	16.3	125.3	−19.8	105.5	241.0	−119.1	121.8
1951–55	156.3	115.9	272.2	206.8	54.1	260.9	363.1	170.0	533.1
1956–60	178.0	90.3	268.3	315.9	59.1	375.0	493.9	149.4	643.3
1961–65	242.9	176.5	419.4	467.6	49.5	517.1	710.5	226.0	936.5
1966–69	277.6	− 11.7	265.9	616.1	2.3	618.4	893.7	− 9.4	884.3
Means									
1946–50	23.1	− 19.9	3.3	25.1	− 4.0	21.1	48.2	− 23.8	24.4
1951–55	31.3	23.2	54.4	41.4	10.8	52.2	72.6	34.0	106.6
1956–60	35.6	18.1	53.7	63.2	11.8	75.0	98.8	29.9	128.7
1961–65	48.6	35.3	83.9	93.5	9.9	103.4	142.1	45.2	187.3
1966–69	69.4	− 2.9	66.5	154.0	.6	154.6	223.4	− 2.3	221.1
Sums, 1946–60	970.5	271.7	1,242.2	1,731.7	145.2	1,876.9	2,702.2	416.9	3,119.1
Means, 1946–69	40.4	11.3	51.8	72.2	6.1	78.2	112.6	17.4	130.0

Table 5.42 **Net Revaluations and Net Capital, Accumulation, Human and Nonhuman Capital, Households (Billions of 1969 Dollars, 1946–69)**

	Nonhuman Capital			Human Capital			Total Capital		
(1) Year	(2) Net Invest-ment (NI)	(3) Net Revalua-tions (NR)	(4) Net Capital Accumu-lation (NCA)	(5) Net Invest-ment (NI)	(6) Net Revalua-tions (NR)	(7) Net Capital Accumu-lation (NCA)	(8) Net Invest-ment (NI)	(9) Net Revalua-tions (NR)	(10) Net Capital Accumu-lation (NCA)
1946	42.7	−179.6	−136.9	45.9	−87.3	−41.4	88.6	−266.9	−178.3
1947	37.4	− 53.8	16.4	48.7	14.4	63.0	86.1	− 39.5	46.6
1948	40.8	− 18.4	22.4	51.0	45.8	96.7	91.7	27.4	119.1
1949	33.9	44.4	78.4	48.6	35.9	84.4	82.5	88.3	162.8
1950	42.7	− .6	42.1	54.3	−57.6	− 3.3	96.9	− 58.2	38.8
1951	48.6	30.2	78.8	61.2	49.7	110.9	109.8	79.9	189.7
1952	41.1	3.6	44.6	65.2	28.8	94.0	106.3	32.3	138.6
1953	42.6	− 20.7	21.9	69.1	22.3	91.4	111.7	1.6	113.3
1954	40.5	86.4	126.9	66.1	− 1.6	64.5	106.6	84.8	191.4
1955	43.6	59.1	102.7	75.7	− 7.2	68.5	119.4	51.9	171.3
1956	46.0	.1	46.1	81.9	− 4.8	77.0	127.9	− 4.7	123.1
1957	43.0	− 51.0	− 8.0	85.8	29.2	114.9	128.8	− 21.8	107.0
1958	41.9	148.7	190.6	85.8	23.4	109.2	127.7	172.1	299.8
1959	45.5	23.5	69.0	94.7	8.5	103.2	140.2	32.0	172.1
1960	42.4	− 10.5	31.9	97.5	26.0	123.5	139.9	15.5	155.4
1961	43.9	114.8	158.7	100.1	8.0	108.2	144.0	122.8	266.8
1962	49.4	− 97.9	− 48.5	108.4	9.4	117.7	157.7	− 88.5	69.2
1963	55.7	88.8	144.5	114.4	21.0	135.4	170.1	109.8	279.9
1964	67.4	47.7	115.1	124.6	22.3	146.9	192.0	70.0	262.0
1965	74.3	58.2	132.5	136.1	1.4	137.5	210.4	59.6	270.0

Table 5.42 (continued)

(1) Year	Nonhuman Capital (2) Net Investment (NI)	(3) Net Revaluations (NR)	(4) Net Capital Accumulation (NCA)	Human Capital (5) Net Investment (NI)	(6) Net Revaluations (NR)	(7) Net Capital Accumulation (NCA)	Total Capital (8) Net Investment (NI)	(9) Net Revaluations (NR)	(10) Net Capital Accumulation (NCA)
1966	80.0	−121.6	− 41.6	152.1	7.4	159.6	232.1	−114.2	117.9
1967	78.8	157.7	236.5	156.5	− 8.3	148.2	235.3	149.4	384.7
1968	80.0	143.4	223.4	170.5	1.1	171.6	250.6	144.4	395.0
1969	60.4	−183.4	−123.0	181.0	2.3	183.3	241.4	−181.1	60.3
Sums									
1946–50	197.5	−208.0	− 10.5	248.4	−48.9	199.5	445.9	−256.9	189.0
1951–55	216.3	158.6	375.0	337.4	91.9	429.3	553.7	250.5	804.3
1956–60	218.9	110.8	329.7	445.5	82.2	527.8	664.4	193.0	857.4
1961–65	290.7	211.6	502.3	583.6	62.1	645.7	874.3	273.7	1,148.0
1966–69	299.3	− 3.9	295.3	660.1	2.5	662.6	959.4	− 1.5	957.9
Means									
1946–50	39.5	− 41.6	− 2.1	49.7	− 9.8	39.9	89.2	− 51.4	37.8
1951–55	43.3	31.7	75.0	67.5	18.4	85.9	110.7	50.1	160.9
1956–60	43.8	22.2	65.9	89.1	16.4	105.6	132.9	38.6	171.5
1961–65	58.1	42.3	100.5	116.7	12.4	129.1	174.9	54.7	229.6
1966–69	74.8	− 1.0	73.8	165.0	.6	165.6	239.9	− .4	239.5
Sums, 1946–60	1,222.7	269.0	1,491.8	2,275.0	189.9	2,464.9	3,497.8	458.9	3,956.6
Means, 1946–69	50.9	11.2	62.2	94.8	7.9	102.7	145.7	19.1	164.9

Table 5.43 BEA Net Private Domestic Investment and Total Net Capital Formation, Nonhuman and Human (Billions of Dollars, 1946–69)

		Net Capital Formation		
(1) Year	(2) Net Private Domestic Investment	(3) Nonhuman (Tangible)	(4) Human	(5) Total
1946	16.8	−51.5	−18.2	−69.7
1947	16.8	14.4	30.7	45.1
1948	25.6	20.2	50.3	70.5
1949	13.3	30.7	44.5	75.2
1950	30.0	36.6	− 1.8	34.8
1951	31.6	91.3	64.1	155.4
1952	22.5	59.7	56.5	116.2
1953	21.7	56.1	56.2	112.3
1954	19.6	41.9	40.3	82.2
1955	33.1	88.4	43.8	132.2
1956	32.2	67.6	51.0	118.6
1957	27.2	60.2	79.2	139.4
1958	17.8	57.1	77.5	134.6
1959	31.4	50.3	75.2	125.5
1960	28.7	49.8	92.1	141.9
1961	25.3	39.4	82.2	121.6
1962	34.5	53.1	91.6	144.7
1963	38.0	61.2	107.8	169.0
1964	42.1	73.4	120.0	193.4
1965	54.5	84.8	115.5	200.3
1966	62.7	85.2	139.3	224.5
1967	53.8	107.3	133.5	240.8
1968	57.7	138.2	162.3	300.5
1969	63.7	111.4	183.3	294.7
Sums				
1946–50	102.5	50.5	105.5	156.0
1951–55	128.5	337.5	260.9	598.4
1956–60	137.3	285.1	375.0	660.1
1961–65	194.4	311.9	517.1	829.0
1966–69	237.9	442.1	618.4	1,060.5
Means				
1946–50	20.5	10.1	21.1	31.2
1951–55	25.7	67.5	52.2	119.7
1956–60	27.5	57.0	75.0	132.0
1961–65	38.9	62.4	103.4	165.8
1966–69	59.5	110.5	154.6	265.1
Sums, 1946–69	800.6	1,427.0	1,876.9	3,303.9
Means, 1946–69	33.4	59.5	78.2	137.7

Table 5.44 Net Capital Accumulation of Tangible Assets by Sector (Billions of Dollars, 1946–77)

(1) Year	(2) Households	(3) Non-corporate	(4) Corporate Non-financial	(5) Private Financial	(6) Govern-ment	(7) Totals
1946	−4.2	−3.8	7.1	.1	− 50.7	−51.5
1947	18.0	6.7	16.2	.3	− 26.7	14.4
1948	21.4	5.1	15.9	−.0	− 22.1	20.2
1949	26.8	6.7	8.1	.1	− 10.9	30.7
1950	21.2	12.3	10.6	.1	− 7.8	36.6
1951	25.0	13.5	20.8	.2	31.8	91.3
1952	18.7	−1.4	9.5	.2	32.7	59.7
1953	18.9	.1	10.6	.0	26.5	56.1
1954	18.6	2.5	4.4	.3	16.0	41.9
1955	29.8	5.6	20.1	.5	32.5	88.4
1956	19.7	7.8	25.0	.5	14.6	67.6
1957	22.7	10.5	15.7	.3	11.0	60.2
1958	25.4	17.2	3.1	.2	11.2	57.1
1959	30.0	1.1	10.0	.5	8.7	50.3
1960	19.4	9.5	10.4	.2	10.2	49.8
1961	14.8	2.0	6.8	.4	15.4	39.4
1962	18.2	9.7	11.4	.3	13.6	53.1
1963	25.6	10.3	9.7	.7	14.9	61.2
1964	26.0	11.5	17.5	1.1	17.3	73.4
1965	24.4	15.4	27.8	1.6	15.8	84.8
1966	15.5	17.9	35.6	1.8	14.4	85.2
1967	43.4	11.1	31.1	2.1	19.7	107.3
1968	72.4	14.3	22.9	2.6	25.9	138.2
1969	37.6	6.0	35.2	3.2	29.4	111.4
1970	7.3	−5.6	22.5	3.2	22.5	49.9
1971	15.4	7.0	13.2	3.0	16.8	55.4
1972	84.5	50.0	41.8	4.0	38.5	218.8
1973	85.1	83.8	76.6	4.7	69.6	319.9
1974	21.5	12.7	107.0	3.7	64.1	209.0
1975	47.9	2.7	24.9	2.3	15.9	93.8
1976	120.6	110.1	45.0	2.9	7.3	285.9
1977	149.3	45.7	50.6	4.0	11.0	260.6
Sums						
1946–50	83.3	27.0	57.9	.5	−118.2	50.5
1951–55	111.0	20.3	65.4	1.3	139.5	337.5
1956–60	117.1	46.1	64.2	1.8	55.8	285.1
1961–65	109.1	48.8	73.2	4.0	76.9	311.9
1966–70	176.2	43.7	147.3	12.9	111.8	491.9
1971–75	254.5	156.2	263.6	17.7	204.9	896.9
1976–77	269.9	155.8	95.6	6.9	18.3	546.5

Table 5.44 (continued)

(1) Year	(2) Households	(3) Non-corporate	(4) Corporate Non-financial	(5) Private Financial	(6) Government	(7) Totals
Means						
1946–50	16.7	5.4	11.6	.1	– 23.6	10.1
1951–55	22.2	4.1	13.1	.3	27.9	67.5
1956–60	23.4	9.2	12.8	.4	11.2	57.0
1961–65	21.8	9.8	14.6	.8	15.4	62.4
1966–70	35.2	8.7	29.5	2.6	22.4	98.4
1971–75	50.9	31.2	52.7	3.5	41.0	179.4
1976–77	135.0	77.9	47.8	3.5	9.2	273.3
Sums, 1946–77	1,121.0	497.9	767.2	45.2	488.9	2,920.2
Means, 1946–77	35.0	15.6	24.0	1.4	15.3	91.3

Table 5.45 **Net Revaluations of Reproducible Assets, Land, and Nontangible Nonhuman Capital by Sector (Billions of Dollars, Sums and Means, 1946–77)**

(1) Sector	(2) Reproducible Assets	(3) Land	(4) All Tangibles	(5) Nontangibles	(6) Total Net Worth
			Sums		
Households, excluding corporate and noncorporate equity	–52.1	189.9	137.8	–719.4	–581.6
Noncorporate	27.5	288.3	315.8	82.9	398.7
Corporate nonfinancial	161.0	48.2	209.2	184.3	393.5
Private financial, excluding corporate shares	.5	4.3	4.8	26.7	31.5
Government	110.0	153.1	263.1	411.5	674.6
Total economy	247.0	683.7	930.7	– 13.9	916.8
			Means		
Households, excluding corporate and noncorporate equity	– 1.6	5.9	4.3	– 22.5	– 18.2
Noncorporate	.9	9.0	9.9	2.6	12.5
Corporate nonfinancial	5.0	1.5	6.5	5.8	12.3
Private financial, excluding corporate shares	.02	.14	.2	.8	1.0
Government	3.4	4.8	8.2	12.9	21.1
Total economy	7.7	21.4	29.1	– .4	28.7

Table 5.46 **Net Revaluations of Reproducible Assets, Land and Nontangible Nonhuman Capital by Sector (Billions of 1972 Dollars, Sums and Means, 1946–77)**

(1) Sector	(2) Reproducible Assets	(3) Land	(4) All Tangibles	(5) Nontangibles	(6) Total Net Worth
			Sums		
Households, excluding corporate and noncorporate equity	−125.9	216.0	90.1	−794.4	−704.2
Noncorporate	11.9	248.3	296.2	80.8	377.0
Corporate nonfinancial	147.6	60.9	208.5	196.1	404.5
Private financial, excluding corporate shares	1.0	5.1	6.1	− 58.3	− 52.2
Government	121.4	172.7	294.1	549.8	844.0
Total economy	156.0	739.0	895.0	− 26.0	869.0
			Means		
Households, excluding corporate and noncorporate equity	− 3.9	6.8	2.8	− 24.8	− 22.0
Noncorporate	.4	8.9	9.3	2.5	11.8
Corporate nonfinancial	4.6	1.9	6.5	6.1	12.6
Private financial, excluding corporate shares	.03	.2	.2	− 1.8	− 1.6
Government	3.8	5.4	9.2	17.2	26.4
Total economy	4.9	23.1	28.0	− .8	27.2

Table 5.47 **Households, Net Revaluations in Detail, Nonhuman Capital (Billions of Dollars, 1946–77)**

(1) Year	(2) Total Tangible Assets	(3) Total Reproducible Assets	(4) Owner-Occupied Housing	(5) Nonprofit Fixed Capital	(6) Consumer Durables	(7) Land	(8) Total Financial Assets	(9) Dem. Dep., Currency, and Time Dep.	(10) U.S. Gov't Securities	(11) State and Local Obligations	(12) Corporate and Foreign Bonds	(13) Commercial Paper
1946	−10.586	−9.425	−1.240	.180	−8.365	−1.161	−80.849	−18.497	−12.511	−1.202	−1.547	0
1947	1.856	.963	3.960	.706	−3.703	.893	−36.692	−10.606	−8.335	−.828	−.941	0
1948	1.746	1.104	2.439	.174	−1.510	.643	−14.189	−3.190	−1.454	−.135	−.146	0
1949	7.504	5.444	4.367	.150	.927	2.059	22.313	1.981	2.760	.349	.287	0
1950	−4.808	−6.911	−2.781	−.126	−4.004	2.103	−1.078	−8.514	−6.064	−.774	−.403	−.001
1951	4.269	2.831	2.923	.572	−.665	1.438	12.748	−3.862	−4.555	−.622	−.418	−.000
1952	.528	−2.146	.112	−.016	−2.241	2.674	.559	−2.284	−1.278	−.229	.105	−.000
1953	−1.453	−4.200	−.420	−.264	−3.516	2.747	−14.203	−1.222	.072	−.002	−.104	−.000
1954	−2.441	−5.566	−.408	−.311	−4.848	3.125	64.752	−2.634	−.461	−.093	.170	−.001
1955	3.128	−3.284	−.279	.391	−3.396	6.411	34.824	−4.430	−4.158	−1.104	−.256	−.003
1956	−2.839	−8.731	−5.117	.296	−3.910	5.893	−8.614	−6.832	−5.539	−1.692	−.290	−.004
1957	3.458	−1.647	−.564	−.357	−.726	5.105	−45.767	−4.157	1.427	.379	−.913	−.003
1958	9.507	1.787	4.516	−.640	−2.089	7.720	103.876	−3.502	−4.593	−1.650	−.177	−.002
1959	7.373	−3.949	.873	−.624	−4.198	11.322	1.580	−4.831	−4.443	−1.695	−.680	−.001
1960	−.800	−3.940	−.120	−.268	−3.552	3.140	−3.116	−2.378	4.576	1.511	.045	−.000
1961	−2.805	−8.454	−3.329	−.285	−4.840	5.649	91.751	−3.551	−2.384	−1.062	.052	−.000
1962	−3.991	−10.571	−4.822	−.129	−5.620	6.581	−78.118	−4.951	.742	.397	.091	−.001
1963	−1.207	−7.393	−1.785	.050	−5.658	6.186	68.731	−4.157	−2.347	−.886	−.112	−.001
1964	−4.055	−9.687	−2.806	.071	−6.952	5.633	40.506	−5.410	−.661	−.325	.027	−.001
1965	−10.150	−16.651	−8.606	.215	−8.260	6.502	44.659	−9.314	−4.707	−1.991	−.442	−.001
1966	−18.041	−18.538	−11.231	.338	−7.646	.497	−105.921	−13.505	−2.979	−1.308	−1.277	−.044
1967	12.362	4.146	8.303	.514	−4.671	8.215	107.280	−14.599	−6.719	−2.524	−1.256	−.050
1968	34.968	21.127	26.117	1.756	−6.745	13.841	76.278	−21.814	−6.254	−2.080	−1.403	−.017
1969	1.009	−1.368	6.311	2.351	−10.029	2.376	−236.415	−26.772	−14.745	−6.498	−4.466	−.116
1970	−22.649	−21.502	−12.914	1.296	−9.884	−1.147	−109.869	−26.470	1.966	.402	−1.093	−.121

Table 5.47 (continued)

(1) Year	(2) Total Tangible Assets	(3) Total Repro-ducible Assets	(4) Owner-Occupied Housing	(5) Nonprofit Fixed Capital	(6) Consumer Durables	(7) Land	(8) Total Financial Assets	(9) Dem. Dep., Currency, and Time Dep.	(10) U.S. Gov't Securities	(11) State and Local Obligations	(12) Corporate and Foreign Bonds	(13) Com-mercial Paper
1971	-29.859	-21.731	-11.439	.628	-10.920	-8.128	41.800	-27.091	-1.719	-1.396	.843	-.044
1972	22.845	4.725	14.758	2.322	-12.355	18.120	63.827	-28.365	-3.563	-2.077	-1.444	-.044
1973	21.057	7.846	22.435	4.639	-19.228	13.211	-405.712	-59.077	-15.015	-6.882	-6.420	-.219
1974	-19.307	-26.328	-7.075	1.786	-21.038	7.021	-486.993	-91.324	3.598	1.506	-11.364	-.938
1975	10.951	7.106	13.319	-1.855	-4.358	3.845	44.953	-57.131	-6.288	-2.978	.230	-.640
1976	62.041	32.802	44.703	-1.885	-9.917	29.240	158.411	-52.398	-1.061	-.505	5.303	-.392
1977	68.166	50.013	69.229	-.769	-18.447	18.153	-213.612	-67.303	-14.959	-7.743	-6.466	-.540
Sums												
1946–50	-4.288	-8.825	6.745	1.085	-16.655	4.537	-110.495	-38.824	-25.605	-2.589	-2.750	-.001
1951–55	4.031	-12.365	1.928	.373	-14.666	16.396	98.681	-14.431	-10.380	-2.050	-.503	-.005
1956–60	16.700	-16.480	-.412	-1.594	-14.475	33.180	47.959	-21.701	-8.572	-3.147	-2.016	-.011
1961–65	-22.207	-52.756	-21.347	-.079	-31.330	30.550	167.528	-27.382	-9.357	-3.867	-.383	-.003
1966–70	7.648	-16.134	16.585	6.255	-38.975	23.782	-268.647	-103.158	-28.732	-12.007	-9.495	-.348
1971–75	5.688	-28.382	31.998	7.519	-67.899	34.069	-742.130	-262.988	-22.888	-11.827	-18.156	-1.884
1976–77	130.207	82.815	113.932	-2.754	-28.364	47.392	-55.201	-119.701	-16.020	-8.248	-1.163	-.932
Means												
1946–50	-.858	-1.765	1.349	.217	-3.331	.907	-22.099	-7.765	-5.121	-.518	-.550	-.000
1951–55	.806	-2.473	.386	.075	-2.933	3.279	19.736	-2.886	-2.076	-.410	-.101	-.001
1956–60	3.340	-3.296	-.082	-.319	-2.895	6.636	9.592	-4.340	-1.714	-.629	-.403	-.002
1961–65	-4.441	-10.551	-4.269	-.016	-6.266	6.110	33.506	-5.476	-1.871	-.773	-.077	-.001
1966–70	1.530	-3.227	3.317	1.251	-7.795	4.756	-53.729	-20.632	-5.746	-2.401	-1.899	-.070
1971–75	1.138	-5.676	6.400	1.504	-13.580	6.814	-148.426	-52.588	-4.598	-2.365	-3.631	-.377
1976–77	65.104	41.408	56.966	-1.377	-14.182	23.696	-27.600	-59.851	-8.010	-4.124	-.581	-.466
Sums, 1946–77	137.778	-52.127	149.430	10.806	-212.364	189.905	-862.304	-588.187	-121.655	-43.735	-34.466	-3.184
Means, 1946–77	4.306	-1.629	4.670	.338	-6.636	5.935	-26.947	-18.381	-3.802	-1.367	-1.077	-.099

Table 5.47 (continued)

(1) Year	(14) Corporate Equity (at Market)	(15) Mortgages	(16) Pension Funds, Life Insurance	(17) Equity in Non-corporate Business	(18) Misc. Assets	(19) Total Assets	(20) Mortgage Debt	(21) Other Loans and Credit	(22) Trade Credit	(23) Misc. Liabil-ities	(24) Total Liabil-ities	(25) Net Worth
1946	− 27.993	− 2.304	− 8.910	− 6.659	− 1.226	− 91.435	− 3.588	− 1.741	− .089	− .702	− 6.120	− 85.315
1947	− 12.659	− 1.746	− 5.323	4.471	− .726	− 34.835	− 2.972	− 1.241	− .055	− .250	− 4.518	− 30.317
1948	− 4.825	− .320	− 1.675	− 2.220	− .224	− 12.443	− .581	− .427	− .018	− .070	− 1.095	− 11.348
1949	10.300	.656	1.147	4.686	.147	29.817	1.396	.330	.013	.041	1.780	28.037
1950	15.850	− 1.486	− 5.382	6.357	− .662	− 5.887	− 3.450	− 1.777	− .059	− .227	− 5.513	− .373
1951	16.685	− 1.187	− 2.487	9.495	− .301	17.017	− 3.145	− .847	− .027	− .108	− 4.127	21.144
1952	9.917	− .246	− 1.486	− 3.766	− .173	1.087	− .847	− .536	− .017	− .060	− 1.460	2.548
1953	−10.402	− .079	− .807	− 1.566	− .092	− 15.655	− .350	− .305	− .010	− .034	− .698	− 14.957
1954	69.043	.011	− 1.709	.623	− .195	62.311	− .003	− .662	− .021	− .081	− .767	63.078
1955	44.077	− 1.250	− .736	3.006	− .322	37.952	− 4.781	− 1.158	− .035	− .156	− 6.129	44.081
1956	5.762	− 2.238	− 4.790	7.489	− .479	− 11.453	− 9.348	− 1.899	− .055	− .245	− 11.546	.093
1957	− 46.039	.179	− 3.614	7.259	− .283	− 42.309	.647	− 1.169	− .034	− .141	− .698	− 41.611
1958	99.759	− 1.602	.248	15.624	− .228	113.383	− 6.693	− .955	− .029	− .120	− 7.797	121.181
1959	19.716	− 1.951	− 2.250	− 1.980	− .304	8.952	− 8.829	− 1.332	− .042	− .170	− 10.373	19.325
1960	− 10.194	1.281	− 1.660	3.848	− .146	− 3.916	5.535	− .687	− .022	− .081	4.746	− 8.662
1961	99.366	− 1.042	1.579	− .996	− .211	88.946	− 4.455	− 1.034	− .031	− .124	− 5.643	94.589
1962	− 70.600	.242	− 6.941	3.185	− .283	− 82.109	.694	− 1.425	− .043	− .172	− .945	− 81.163
1963	72.887	− .914	.958	3.526	− .222	67.525	− 4.803	− 1.208	− .035	− .148	− 6.195	73.719
1964	42.364	− .220	.236	4.776	− .280	36.451	− 1.672	− 1.605	− .045	− .190	− 3.512	39.963
1965	58.203	− 2.064	− 2.425	7.881	− .483	34.509	− 11.688	− 2.804	− .077	− .312	− 14.880	49.389
1966	− 81.786	− 2.254	− 14.465	12.408	− .712	−123.962	− 12.614	− 4.109	− .112	− .443	− 17.278	−106.684
1967	129.516	− 3.247	− 2.011	8.977	− .807	119.642	− 18.285	− 4.345	− .122	− .523	− 23.276	142.918
1968	110.911	− 2.902	− 8.696	9.803	− 1.269	111.246	− 16.751	− 6.438	− .185	− .868	− 24.242	135.487
1969	−156.086	− 7.304	− 24.400	5.558	− 1.587	−235.407	− 42.460	− 8.275	− .242	− 1.012	− 51.990	−183.417
1970	− 53.998	.633	− 16.369	−13.297	− 1.523	−132.518	2.484	− 8.284	− .254	− .829	− 6.882	−125.636

Table 5.47 (continued)

(1) Year	(14) Corporate Equity (at Market)	(15) Mortgages	(16) Pension Funds, Life Insurance	(17) Equity in Non-corporate Business	(18) Misc. Assets	(19) Total Assets	(20) Mortgage Debt	(21) Other Loans and Credit	(22) Trade Credit	(23) Misc. Liabil-ities	(24) Total Liabil-ities	(25) Net Worth
1971	75.820	.691	−2.398	−1.412	−1.495	11.941	1.284	−8.178	−.257	−.791	−7.943	19.884
1972	53.275	−2.105	5.917	43.723	−1.490	86.672	−13.533	−8.370	−.262	−.902	−23.067	109.739
1973	−315.278	−8.128	−74.813	83.094	−2.974	−384.655	−56.068	−17.662	−.536	−1.689	−75.955	−308.700
1974	−309.983	−5.220	−91.369	22.540	−4.443	−506.305	−36.362	−27.328	−.841	−2.124	−66.656	−439.649
1975	113.416	−1.283	−1.797	4.155	−2.731	55.905	−10.811	−16.315	−.547	−1.225	−28.898	84.803
1976	116.706	2.436	−11.257	102.099	−2.519	220.453	17.180	−14.386	−.516	−1.185	1.093	219.359
1977	−111.870	−8.669	−48.813	56.015	−3.264	−145.446	−61.998	−18.661	−.668	−1.621	−82.949	−62.497
Sums												
1946–50	−19.328	−5.200	−20.143	6.635	−2.690	−114.783	−9.195	−4.856	−.209	−1.208	−15.468	−99.315
1951–55	129.320	−2.751	−7.225	7.791	−1.083	102.712	−9.127	−3.507	−.109	−.439	−13.182	115.894
1956–60	69.004	−4.331	−12.067	32.240	−1.441	64.658	−18.688	−6.042	−.182	−.756	−25.668	90.326
1961–65	202.220	−3.998	−6.594	18.373	−1.481	145.322	−21.923	−8.076	−.230	−.946	−31.175	176.497
1966–70	−51.443	−15.074	−65.941	23.450	−5.899	−260.999	−87.627	−31.451	−.915	−3.674	−123.668	−137.331
1971–75	−382.750	−16.045	−164.460	152.100	−13.132	−736.442	−115.490	−77.854	−2.443	−6.732	−202.519	−533.923
1976–77	4.835	−6.233	−60.070	158.113	−5.783	75.007	−44.819	−33.047	−1.184	−2.806	−81.856	156.862
Means												
1946–50	−3.866	−1.040	−4.029	1.327	−.538	−22.957	−1.839	−.971	−.042	−.242	−3.094	−19.863
1951–55	25.864	−.550	−1.445	1.558	−.217	20.542	−1.825	−.701	−.022	−.088	−2.636	23.179
1956–60	13.801	−.866	−2.413	6.448	−.288	12.932	−3.738	−1.208	−.036	−.151	−5.134	18.065
1961–65	40.444	−.800	−1.319	3.675	−.296	29.064	−4.385	−1.615	−.046	−.189	−6.235	35.299
1966–70	−10.289	−3.015	−13.188	4.690	−1.180	−52.200	−17.525	−6.290	−.183	−.735	−24.734	−27.466
1971–75	−76.550	−3.209	−32.892	30.420	−2.626	−147.288	−23.098	−15.571	−.489	−1.346	−40.504	−106.785
1976–77	2.418	−3.116	−30.035	79.057	−2.891	37.504	−22.409	−16.524	−.592	−1.403	−40.928	78.431
Sums, 1946–77	−48.141	−53.632	−336.500	398.703	−31.508	−724.525	−306.868	−164.833	−5.273	−16.561	−493.536	−230.990
Means, 1946–77	−1.504	−1.676	−10.516	12.459	−.985	−22.641	−9.590	−5.151	−.165	−.518	−15.423	−7.218

Table 5.48 **Households, Net Revaluations in Detail, Nonhuman Capital (Billions of 1972 Dollars, 1946–77)**

(1) Year	(2) Total Tangible Assets	(3) Total Repro-ducible Assets	(4) Owner-Occupied Housing	(5) Nonprofit Fixed Capital	(6) Consumer Durables	(7) Land	(8) Total Financial Assets	(9) Dem. Dep., Currency, and Time Dep.	(10) U.S. Gov't Securities	(11) State and Local Obligations	(12) Corporate and Foreign Bonds	(13) Com-mercial Paper
1946	−25.632	− 22.821	− 3.003	.437	− 20.255	−2.811	−195.761	− 44.786	− 30.294	− 2.910	− 3.746	0
1947	3.796	1.970	8.097	1.444	− 7.572	1.826	− 75.034	− 21.688	− 17.046	− 1.693	− 1.924	0
1948	3.258	2.059	4.551	.326	− 2.817	1.199	− 26.473	− 5.951	− 2.713	− .251	− .273	0
1949	13.693	9.935	7.969	.274	1.692	3.757	40.717	3.616	5.036	.638	.524	0
1950	− 8.510	− 12.232	− 4.921	− .223	− 7.087	3.722	− 1.909	− 15.068	− 10.733	− 1.369	− .714	− .002
1951	7.021	4.656	4.808	.941	− 1.094	2.365	20.968	− 6.351	− 7.491	− 1.023	− .687	− .001
1952	.850	− 3.455	.180	− .025	− 3.609	4.305	.901	− 3.677	− 2.058	− .368	.169	− .000
1953	− 2.309	− 6.677	− .668	− .420	− 5.589	4.368	− 22.580	− 1.943	.114	− .004	− .166	− .001
1954	− 3.850	− 8.779	− .643	− .490	− 7.646	4.929	102.132	− 4.154	− .727	− .147	.267	− .002
1955	4.826	− 5.068	− .430	.604	− 5.241	9.894	53.741	− 6.837	− 6.417	− 1.704	− .395	− .004
1956	− 4.156	− 12.784	− 7.492	.433	− 5.725	8.628	− 12.612	− 10.004	− 8.111	− 2.477	− .424	− .006
1957	4.877	− 2.323	− .796	− .504	− 1.024	7.200	− 64.551	− 5.864	2.012	.535	− 1.287	− .005
1958	13.429	2.524	6.379	− .904	− 2.950	10.904	146.717	− 4.946	− 6.487	− 2.331	− .250	− .004
1959	10.297	− 5.516	1.219	− .872	− 5.863	15.813	2.206	− 6.747	− 6.206	− 2.368	− .950	− .002
1960	− 1.112	− 5.479	− .166	− .372	− 4.941	4.367	− 4.334	− 3.308	6.365	2.102	.062	− .000
1961	− 3.918	− 11.807	− 4.649	− .399	− 6.760	7.889	128.144	− 4.960	− 3.329	− 1.483	.073	− .000
1962	− 5.542	− 14.682	− 6.697	− .180	− 7.806	9.140	−108.497	− 6.876	1.031	.552	.126	− .001
1963	− 1.674	− 10.253	− 2.475	.069	− 7.847	8.580	95.328	− 5.765	− 3.256	− 1.229	− .156	− .001
1964	− 5.570	− 13.307	− 3.855	.098	− 9.550	7.737	55.640	− 7.431	− .908	− .447	.037	− .001
1965	−13.753	− 22.563	−11.661	.292	− 11.193	8.810	60.513	− 12.620	− 6.378	− 2.697	− .598	− .001
1966	−23.676	− 24.329	−14.739	.444	− 10.034	.652	−139.004	− 17.723	− 3.909	− 1.716	− 1.676	− .058
1967	15.707	5.268	10.550	.653	− 5.935	10.439	136.315	− 18.550	− 8.538	− 3.207	− 1.596	− .064
1968	42.592	25.733	31.811	2.138	− 8.216	16.859	92.908	− 26.570	− 7.618	− 2.534	− 1.709	− .021
1969	1.161	− 1.574	7.262	2.705	− 11.541	2.734	−272.054	− 30.808	− 16.968	− 7.477	− 5.140	− .133
1970	−24.861	− 23.602	−14.176	1.423	− 10.849	−1.259	−120.603	− 29.055	2.158	.442	− 1.200	− .132

Table 5.48 (continued)

(1) Year	(2) Total Tangible Assets	(3) Total Repro-ducible Assets	(4) Owner-Occupied Housing	(5) Nonprofit Fixed Capital	(6) Consumer Durables	(7) Land	(8) Total Financial Assets	(9) Dem. Dep., Currency, and Time Dep.	(10) U.S. Gov't Securities	(11) State and Local Obligations	(12) Corporate and Foreign Bonds	(13) Com-mercial Paper
1971	−31.136	−22.660	−11.928	.655	−11.387	−8.476	43.587	−28.249	−1.792	−1.456	.879	−.045
1972	22.845	4.725	14.758	2.322	−12.355	18.120	63.827	−28.365	−3.563	−2.077	−1.444	−.044
1973	19.865	7.402	21.165	4.376	−18.139	12.463	−382.747	−55.733	−14.165	−6.493	−6.057	−.206
1974	−16.403	−22.368	−6.011	1.517	−17.875	5.965	−413.762	−77.591	3.057	1.279	−9.655	−.797
1975	8.271	5.367	10.060	−1.401	−3.291	2.904	33.953	−43.151	−4.749	−2.249	.174	−.483
1976	44.379	23.463	31.976	−1.420	−7.093	20.915	113.313	−37.481	−.759	−.361	3.793	−.280
1977	45.353	33.275	46.060	−.512	−12.273	12.078	−142.124	−44.779	−9.953	−5.151	−4.302	−.359
Sums												
1946–50	−13.395	−21.088	12.693	2.258	−36.040	7.693	−258.459	−83.878	−55.750	−5.586	−6.132	−.002
1951–55	6.538	−19.324	3.246	.610	−23.180	25.862	155.162	−22.963	−16.580	−3.246	−.811	−.008
1956–60	23.334	−23.578	−.856	−2.219	−20.502	46.912	67.427	−30.868	−12.426	−4.539	−2.850	−.016
1961–65	−30.456	−72.612	−29.337	−.120	−43.155	42.156	231.127	−37.653	−12.840	−5.304	−.517	−.004
1966–70	10.922	−18.503	20.708	7.364	−46.575	29.425	−302.437	−122.705	−34.875	−14.493	−11.320	−.408
1971–75	3.443	−27.535	28.044	7.469	−63.047	30.977	−655.143	−233.088	−21.213	−10.995	−16.104	−1.576
1976–77	89.732	56.738	78.037	−1.931	−19.366	32.993	−28.811	−82.260	−10.712	−5.513	−.509	−.640
Means												
1946–50	−2.679	−4.218	2.539	.452	−7.208	1.539	−51.692	−16.776	−11.150	−1.117	−1.226	−.000
1951–55	1.308	−3.865	.649	.122	−4.636	5.172	31.032	−4.593	−3.316	−.649	−.162	−.002
1956–60	4.667	−4.716	−.171	−.444	−4.100	9.382	13.485	−6.174	−2.485	−.908	−.570	−.003
1961–65	−6.091	−14.522	−5.867	−.024	−8.631	8.431	46.225	−7.531	−2.568	−1.061	−.103	−.001
1966–70	2.184	−3.701	4.142	1.473	−9.315	5.885	−60.487	−24.541	−6.975	−2.899	−2.264	−.082
1971–75	.689	−5.507	5.609	1.494	−12.609	6.195	−131.029	−46.618	−4.243	−2.199	−3.221	−.315
1976–77	44.866	28.369	39.018	−.966	−9.683	16.496	−14.405	−41.130	−5.356	−2.756	−.254	−.320
Sums, 1946–77	90.118	125.902	112.536	13.429	−251.865	216.018	−791.133	−613.415	−164.396	−49.676	−38.243	−2.653
Means, 1946–77	2.816	−3.934	3.517	.420	−7.871	6.751	−24.723	−19.169	−5.137	−1.552	−1.195	−.083

Table 5.48 (continued)

(1) Year	(14) Corporate Equity (at Market)	(15) Mortgages	(16) Pension Funds, Life Insurance	(17) Equity in Non-corporate Business	(18) Misc. Assets	(19) Total Assets	(20) Mortgage Debt	(21) Other Loans and Credit	(22) Trade Credit	(23) Misc. Liabil-ities	(24) Total Liabil-ities	(25) Net Worth
1946	-67.781	-5.578	-21.574	-16.124	-2.969	-221.392	-8.689	-4.214	-.216	-1.700	-14.819	-206.573
1947	-25.888	-3.570	-10.886	9.144	-1.484	-71.238	-6.077	-2.538	-.113	-.511	-9.240	-61.998
1948	-9.002	-.597	-3.125	-4.142	-.417	-23.215	-1.083	-.796	-.033	-.131	-2.044	-21.171
1949	18.795	1.196	2.093	8.551	.268	54.410	2.547	.602	.023	.076	3.247	51.163
1950	28.053	-2.630	-9.526	11.252	-1.171	-10.419	-6.106	-3.146	-.105	-.402	-9.758	-.660
1951	27.443	-1.953	-4.091	15.617	-.495	27.988	-5.173	-1.394	-.044	-.177	-6.788	34.776
1952	15.969	-.397	-2.393	-6.065	-.279	1.751	-1.364	-.863	-.028	-.097	-2.352	4.103
1953	-16.538	-.125	-1.283	-2.490	-.146	-24.889	-.557	-.485	-.015	-.054	-1.110	-23.779
1954	108.900	.018	-2.696	.982	-.308	98.282	-.005	-1.044	-.032	-.128	-1.210	99.492
1955	68.020	-1.930	-1.136	4.639	-.496	58.568	-7.378	-1.786	-.054	-.241	-9.459	68.026
1956	8.436	-3.276	-7.014	10.964	-.702	-16.769	-13.686	-2.780	-.080	-.359	-16.905	.137
1957	-64.936	.252	-5.098	10.238	-.399	-59.674	.912	-1.649	-.048	-.199	-.984	-58.690
1958	140.903	-2.263	.351	22.068	-.322	160.146	-9.454	-1.349	-.042	-.169	-11.013	171.159
1959	27.536	-2.725	-3.143	-2.765	-.425	12.503	-12.331	-1.860	-.059	-.237	-14.487	26.991
1960	-14.177	1.782	-2.308	5.353	-.203	-5.446	7.699	-.956	-.030	-.112	6.601	-12.047
1961	138.780	-1.455	2.205	-1.391	-.295	124.226	-6.221	-1.443	-.043	-.173	-7.881	132.107
1962	-98.055	.336	-9.641	4.424	-.393	-114.040	.964	-1.980	-.059	-.238	-1.313	-112.727
1963	101.091	-1.268	1.328	4.891	-.309	93.654	-6.662	-1.676	-.048	-.205	-8.592	102.246
1964	58.192	-.303	.324	6.561	-.385	50.070	-2.296	-2.204	-.062	-.262	-4.824	54.894
1965	78.866	-2.797	-3.286	10.679	-.655	46.760	-15.838	-3.799	-.104	-.422	-20.163	66.923
1966	-107.330	-2.958	-18.982	16.283	-.934	-162.680	-16.554	-5.392	-.147	-.581	-22.674	-140.006
1967	164.569	-4.125	-2.556	11.407	-1.026	152.023	-23.234	-5.521	-.156	-.665	-29.576	181.599
1968	135.092	-3.535	-10.592	11.941	-1.546	135.500	-20.403	-7.842	-.225	-1.058	-29.527	165.027
1969	-179.616	-8.406	-28.078	6.396	-1.826	-270.894	-48.861	-9.523	-.279	-1.164	-59.827	-211.067
1970	-59.273	.695	-17.969	-14.596	-1.672	-145.464	2.727	-9.093	-.279	-.910	-7.555	-137.909

Table 5.48 (continued)

(1) Year	(14) Corporate Equity (at Market)	(15) Mortgages	(16) Pension Funds, Life Insurance	(17) Equity in Non-corporate Business	(18) Misc. Assets	(19) Total Assets	(20) Mortgage Debt	(21) Other Loans and Credit	(22) Trade Credit	(23) Misc. Liabil-ities	(24) Total Liabil-ities	(25) Net Worth
1971	79.061	.720	− 2.500	− 1.472	− 1.559	12.451	1.338	− 8.528	− .268	− .825	− 8.283	20.734
1972	53.275	− 2.105	5.917	43.723	− 1.490	86.672	− 13.533	− 8.370	− .262	− .902	− 23.067	109.739
1973	−297.432	− 7.668	− 70.579	78.391	− 2.806	−362.882	− 52.894	− 16.662	− .505	− 1.594	− 71.656	−291.226
1974	−263.367	− 4.435	− 77.628	19.150	− 3.775	−430.165	− 30.894	− 23.218	− .714	− 1.805	− 56.632	−373.534
1975	85.661	− .969	− 1.357	3.138	− 2.063	42.224	− 8.165	− 12.323	− .413	− .925	− 21.826	64.050
1976	83.481	1.743	− 8.052	73.032	− 1.802	157.692	12.289	− 10.290	− .369	− .848	.782	156.909
1977	− 74.431	− 5.768	− 32.477	37.269	− 2.172	− 96.771	− 41.250	− 12.416	− .445	− 1.079	− 55.189	− 41.581
Sums												
1946–50	− 55.822	−11.179	− 43.018	8.681	− 5.773	−271.854	− 19.408	− 10.093	− .444	− 2.668	− 32.614	−239.240
1951–55	203.795	− 4.386	− 11.599	12.683	− 1.724	161.700	− 14.477	− 5.571	− .173	− .696	− 20.918	182.618
1956–60	97.762	− 6.231	− 17.213	45.858	− 2.051	90.761	− 26.860	− 8.594	− .259	− 1.076	− 36.789	127.550
1961–65	278.874	− 5.486	− 9.070	25.163	− 2.037	200.671	− 30.053	− 11.102	− .317	− 1.301	− 42.773	243.444
1966–70	− 46.558	−18.329	− 78.177	31.431	− 7.004	−291.515	−106.326	− 37.371	−1.085	− 4.377	−149.159	−142.356
1971–75	−342.801	−14.456	−146.148	142.930	−11.691	−651.700	−104.148	− 69.101	−2.164	− 6.051	−181.464	−470.236
1976–77	9.049	− 4.025	− 40.529	110.301	− 3.973	60.921	− 28.961	− 22.706	− .814	− 1.926	− 54.407	115.328
Means												
1946–50	− 11.164	− 2.236	− 8.604	1.736	− 1.155	− 54.371	− 3.882	− 2.019	− .089	− .534	− 6.523	− 47.848
1951–55	40.759	− .877	− 2.320	2.537	− .345	32.340	− 2.895	− 1.114	− .035	− .139	− 4.184	36.524
1956–60	19.552	− 1.246	− 3.443	9.172	− .410	18.152	− 5.372	− 1.719	− .052	− .215	− 7.358	25.510
1961–65	55.775	− 1.097	− 1.814	5.033	− .407	40.134	− 6.011	− 2.220	− .063	− .260	− 8.555	48.689
1966–70	− 9.312	− 3.666	− 15.635	6.286	− 1.401	− 58.303	− 21.265	− 7.474	− .217	− .875	− 29.832	− 28.471
1971–75	− 68.560	− 2.891	− 29.230	28.586	− 2.338	−130.340	− 20.830	− 13.820	− .433	− 1.210	− 36.293	− 94.047
1976–77	4.525	− 2.013	− 20.265	55.150	− 1.987	30.461	− 14.480	− 11.353	− .407	− .963	− 27.203	57.664
Sums, 1946–77	144.299	−64.092	−345.752	377.047	−34.254	−701.016	−330.233	−164.540	−5.256	−18.096	−518.124	−182.892
Means, 1946–77	4.509	− 2.003	− 10.805	11.783	− 1.070	− 21.907	− 10.320	− 5.142	− .164	− .565	− 16.191	− 5.715

Table 5.49 Noncorporate Nonfarm, and Farm, Net Revaluations in Detail, Nonhuman Capital (Billions of Dollars, 1946–77)

(1) Year	(2) Total Tangible Assets	(3) Total Repro-ducible Assets	(4) Residential Structures	(5) Nonresidential Plant and Equipment	(6) Inven-tories	(7) Land	(8) Total Financial Assets	(9) Demand Deposits and Currency
1946	− 5.856	1.836	− 1.389	− .796	4.020	−7.691	− 3.045	− 2.535
1947	4.628	8.496	3.061	1.081	4.354	−3.868	− 1.853	− 1.526
1948	− 2.029	− 2.219	1.331	1.008	− 4.558	.190	− .582	− .475
1949	4.908	1.249	3.032	1.199	− 2.982	3.659	.371	.293
1950	6.221	.346	− 2.091	− .467	2.904	5.875	− 1.600	− 1.222
1951	8.963	3.083	1.350	1.485	.247	5.880	− .718	− .542
1952	− 3.782	− 5.318	− .141	.159	− 5.337	1.536	− .396	− .289
1953	− 1.526	− 1.483	− .393	− .120	− .970	− .042	− .202	− .144
1954	.843	− 3.284	− .569	− .474	− 2.242	4.127	− .419	− .296
1955	2.200	− 3.211	− .419	1.307	− 4.099	5.412	− .680	− .476
1956	5.927	− .824	− 2.632	1.424	.384	6.750	− 1.015	− .699
1957	7.663	1.395	− .633	.472	1.557	6.267	− .603	− .411
1958	14.479	3.473	1.129	− .433	2.778	11.006	− .500	− .343
1959	− 3.472	− 5.317	− .854	−1.073	− 3.391	1.846	− .656	− .443
1960	5.023	− 2.393	− 1.512	− .460	− .421	7.415	− .299	− .195
1961	− 1.813	− 4.437	− 2.205	− .609	− 1.623	2.624	− .412	− .261
1962	3.367	− 3.784	− 2.821	− .556	− .407	7.151	− .544	− .340
1963	2.566	− 3.838	− 1.513	.069	− 2.395	6.404	− .422	− .257
1964	4.377	− 4.185	− 1.880	− .038	− 2.266	8.561	− .516	− .306
1965	5.328	− 2.229	− 3.883	.101	1.554	7.557	− .836	− .483
1966	9.540	− 6.460	− 4.119	.439	− 2.780	16.000	− 1.163	− .654
1967	4.492	.799	2.594	.769	− 2.564	3.693	− 1.181	− .645
1968	5.622	7.005	7.218	1.575	− 1.788	−1.382	− 1.668	− .889
1969	− 5.131	2.983	.576	2.485	− .078	−8.114	− 2.017	− 1.038
1970	−14.003	− 7.445	− 5.368	2.048	− 4.126	−6.558	− 1.959	− .968

Table 5.49 (continued)

(1) Year	(2) Total Tangible Assets	(3) Total Repro-ducible Assets	(4) Residential Structures	(5) Nonresidential Plant and Equipment	(6) Inven-tories	(7) Land	(8) Total Financial Assets	(9) Demand Deposits and Currency
1971	− 2.144	− 1.992	− 4.918	.809	2.118	− .152	− 1.877	− .891
1972	39.213	11.569	3.819	2.105	5.644	27.644	− 1.808	− .820
1973	66.134	17.382	− 1.988	5.037	14.333	48.752	− 3.556	− 1.538
1974	9.980	−17.184	−12.832	3.946	− 8.298	27.164	− 5.306	− 2.176
1975	.166	3.054	5.949	3.308	− 6.203	−2.888	− 3.204	− 1.239
1976	105.548	22.275	26.813	.950	− 5.487	83.273	− 2.815	− 1.026
1977	38.367	18.207	18.841	.294	− .928	20.160	− 3.467	− 1.179
Sums								
1946–50	7.873	9.708	3.945	2.023	3.740	−1.835	− 6.710	− 5.465
1951–55	6.699	−10.214	− .171	2.358	−12.401	16.913	− 2.416	− 1.746
1956–60	29.619	− 3.666	− 4.502	− .070	.906	33.285	− 3.074	− 2.090
1961–65	13.825	−18.472	−12.302	−1.032	− 5.137	32.297	− 2.730	− 1.648
1966–70	.521	− 3.118	.903	7.316	−11.336	3.639	− 7.988	− 4.194
1971–75	113.349	12.829	− 9.970	15.205	7.594	100.520	−15.751	− 6.665
1976–77	143.915	40.482	45.654	1.244	− 6.415	103.433	− 6.283	− 2.205
Means								
1946–50	1.575	1.942	.789	.405	.748	− .367	− 1.342	− 1.093
1951–55	1.340	− 2.043	− .034	.472	− 2.480	3.383	− .483	− .349
1956–60	5.924	− .733	− .900	− .014	.181	6.657	− .615	− .418
1961–65	2.765	− 3.694	− 2.460	− .206	− 1.027	6.459	− .546	− .330
1966–70	.104	− .624	.181	1.463	− 2.267	.728	− 1.598	− .839
1971–75	22.670	2.566	− 1.994	3.041	1.519	20.104	− 3.150	− 1.333
1976–77	71.958	20.241	22.627	.622	− 3.208	51.717	− 3.141	− 1.103
Sums, 1946–77	315.800	27.549	23.555	27.044	−23.050	288.252	−44.951	−24.014
Means, 1946–77	9.869	.861	.736	.845	− .720	9.008	− 1.405	− .750

Table 5.49 (continued)

(1) Year	(10) Consumer Credit	(11) Misc. Assets	(12) Total Assets	(13) Mortgages	(14) Other Loans	(15) Net Trade Debt	(16) Total Liabil-ities	(17) Net Worth
1946	− .244	− .265	− 8.901	− 1.613	− .836	.209	− 2.242	− 6.659
1947	− .163	− .164	2.775	− 1.191	− .582	.078	− 1.695	4.470
1948	− .055	− .053	− 2.611	− .217	− .188	.013	− .391	− 2.220
1949	.041	.037	5.279	.461	.125	.008	.593	4.686
1950	− .209	− .169	4.621	− 1.095	− .588	− .054	− 1.736	6.357
1951	− .099	− .077	8.245	− .938	− .284	− .028	− 1.250	9.495
1952	− .060	− .047	− 4.178	− .223	− .174	− .015	− .412	− 3.766
1953	− .032	− .026	− 1.728	− .067	− .087	− .007	− .161	− 1.567
1954	− .067	− .056	.424	.008	− .178	− .029	− .199	.623
1955	− .108	− .096	1.520	− 1.088	− .308	− .090	− 1.486	3.006
1956	− .167	− .149	4.912	− 1.921	− .500	− .156	− 2.577	7.489
1957	− .102	− .090	7.059	.203	− .309	− .094	− .200	7.260
1958	− .083	− .074	13.979	− 1.300	− .262	− .083	− 1.645	15.624
1959	− .113	− .101	− 4.128	− 1.667	− .369	− .113	− 2.148	− 1.980
1960	− .055	− .049	4.723	1.119	− .187	− .056	.875	3.848
1961	− .079	− .072	− 2.225	− .885	− .274	− .070	− 1.229	− .996
1962	− .107	− .097	2.824	.100	− .378	− .083	− .361	3.185
1963	− .088	− .077	2.143	− 1.004	− .323	− .056	− 1.383	3.527
1964	− .111	− .099	3.860	− .437	− .425	− .054	− .915	4.776
1965	− .187	− .166	4.492	− 2.571	− .743	− .076	− 3.390	7.882
1966	− .267	− .241	8.377	− 2.823	− 1.135	− .074	− 4.031	12.408
1967	− .274	− .262	3.311	− 4.390	− 1.251	− .024	− 5.665	8.977
1968	− .388	− .391	3.954	− 4.022	− 1.825	− .002	− 5.849	9.803
1969	− .471	− .508	− 7.148	−10.160	− 2.327	− .219	− 12.706	5.559
1970	− .461	− .529	−15.962	− .108	− 2.326	− .231	− 2.865	−13.297

Table 5.49 (continued)

(1) Year	(10) Consumer Credit	(11) Misc. Assets	(12) Total Assets	(13) Mortgages	(14) Other Loans	(15) Net Trade Debt	(16) Total Liabil- ities	(17) Net Worth
1971	−.445	−.541	−4.021	−.339	−2.258	−.011	−2.609	−1.413
1972	−.426	−.561	37.405	−4.068	−2.250	−.000	−6.318	43.723
1973	−.848	−1.170	62.579	−15.777	−4.698	−.042	−20.516	83.095
1974	−1.290	−1.840	4.674	−10.418	−7.309	−.138	−17.866	22.539
1975	−.787	−1.178	−3.038	−2.545	−4.428	−.221	−7.194	4.156
1976	−.699	−1.090	102.733	4.861	−3.923	−.303	.634	102.098
1977	−.876	−1.412	34.900	−15.692	−4.985	−.438	−21.115	56.015
Sums								
1946–50	−.630	−.615	1.163	−3.655	−2.070	.254	−5.471	6.634
1951–55	−.367	−.303	4.283	−2.308	−1.031	−.169	−3.509	7.791
1956–60	−.520	−.463	26.545	−3.567	−1.627	−.501	−5.696	32.241
1961–65	−.572	−.511	11.094	−4.797	−2.143	−.339	−7.278	18.373
1966–70	−1.862	−1.932	−7.467	−21.502	−8.865	−.550	−30.917	23.450
1971–75	−3.796	−5.290	97.598	−33.146	−20.943	−.413	−54.502	152.100
1976–77	−1.575	−2.503	137.633	−10.831	−8.908	−.741	−20.480	158.113
Means								
1946–50	−.126	−.123	.233	−.731	−.414	.051	−1.094	1.327
1951–55	−.073	−.061	.857	−.462	−.206	−.034	−.702	1.558
1956–60	−.104	−.093	5.309	−.713	−.325	−.100	−1.139	6.448
1961–65	−.114	−.102	2.219	−.959	−.429	−.068	−1.456	3.675
1966–70	−.372	−.386	−1.493	−4.300	−1.773	−.110	−6.183	4.690
1971–75	−.759	−1.058	19.520	−6.629	−4.189	−.083	−10.900	30.420
1976–77	−.787	−1.251	68.816	−5.416	−4.454	−.371	−10.240	79.056
Sums, 1946–77	−9.320	−11.617	270.849	−79.807	−45.587	−2.460	−127.854	398.703
Means, 1946–77	−.291	−.363	8.464	−2.494	−1.425	−.077	−3.995	12.459

Table 5.50 Noncorporate Nonfarm, and Farm, Net Revaluations in Detail, Nonhuman Capital (Billions of 1972 Dollars, 1946–77)

(1) Year	(2) Total Tangible Assets	(3) Total Repro-ducible Assets	(4) Residential Structures	(5) Nonresidential Plant and Equipment	(6) Inven-tories	(7) Land	(8) Total Financial Assets	(9) Demand Deposits and Currency
1946	−14.179	4.444	− 3.363	−1.927	9.735	−18.623	− 7.374	− 6.139
1947	9.464	17.374	6.261	2.210	8.904	− 7.910	− 3.789	− 3.120
1948	− 3.785	− 4.140	2.483	1.880	− 8.503	.355	− 1.087	− .886
1949	8.957	2.279	5.533	2.187	− 5.441	6.678	.677	.534
1950	11.011	.613	− 3.700	− .827	5.141	10.398	− 2.832	− 2.163
1951	14.742	5.070	2.221	2.443	.406	9.672	− 1.181	− .892
1952	− 6.090	− 8.564	− .227	.257	− 8.594	2.474	− .638	− .465
1953	− 2.426	− 2.358	− .625	− .191	− 1.542	− .068	− .321	− .229
1954	1.330	− 5.180	− .897	− .747	− 3.536	6.510	− .661	− .466
1955	3.395	− 4.956	− .646	2.017	− 6.326	8.351	− 1.050	− .734
1956	8.677	− 1.206	− 3.853	2.085	.562	9.884	− 1.486	− 1.023
1957	10.808	1.968	− .893	.666	2.196	8.840	− .851	− .580
1958	20.450	4.905	1.594	− .612	3.923	15.545	− .706	− .484
1959	− 4.849	− 7.427	− 1.193	−1.498	− 4.736	2.578	− .917	− .618
1960	6.985	− 3.328	− 2.102	− .640	− .586	10.313	− .416	− .271
1961	− 2.532	− 6.197	− 3.080	− .850	− 2.267	3.664	− .575	− .365
1962	4.677	− 5.255	− 3.918	− .772	− .566	9.932	− .755	− .473
1963	3.558	− 5.323	− 2.098	.096	− 3.322	8.882	− .586	− .357
1964	6.012	− 5.748	− 2.583	− .052	− 3.113	11.760	− .709	− .420
1965	7.220	− 3.020	− 5.262	.137	2.105	10.240	− 1.133	− .655
1966	12.519	− 8.478	− 5.405	.576	− 3.649	20.997	− 1.526	− .858
1967	5.708	1.015	3.296	.978	− 3.258	4.692	− 1.500	− .819
1968	6.848	8.532	8.792	1.918	− 2.178	− 1.684	− 2.032	− 1.082
1969	− 5.904	3.433	.663	2.859	− .090	− 9.337	− 2.321	− 1.195
1970	−15.371	− 8.173	− 5.892	2.248	− 4.529	− 7.199	− 2.150	− 1.063

Table 5.50 (continued)

(1) Year	(2) Total Tangible Assets	(3) Total Repro- ducible Assets	(4) Residential Structures	(5) Nonresidential Plant and Equipment	(6) Inven- tories	(7) Land	(8) Total Financial Assets	(9) Demand Deposits and Currency
1971	− 2.236	− 2.077	− 5.129	.843	2.209	− .159	− 1.957	− .929
1972	39.213	11.569	3.819	2.105	5.644	27.644	− 1.808	− .820
1973	62.391	16.398	− 1.875	4.752	13.521	45.993	− 3.354	− 1.451
1974	8.479	−14.600	−10.902	3.353	− 7.051	23.079	− 4.508	− 1.849
1975	.125	2.307	4.493	2.499	− 4.685	− 2.181	− 2.420	− .936
1976	75.499	15.934	19.180	.679	− 3.925	59.566	− 2.014	− .734
1977	25.527	12.114	12.536	.196	− .618	13.413	− 2.307	− .785
Sums								
1946–50	11.469	20.571	7.213	3.522	9.835	− 9.102	−14.405	−11.774
1951–55	10.951	−15.988	− .174	3.778	−19.592	26.939	− 3.851	− 2.786
1956–60	42.072	− 5.087	− 6.448	.001	1.359	47.160	− 4.376	− 2.977
1961–65	18.935	−25.543	−16.940	−1.441	− 7.161	44.478	− 3.758	− 2.269
1966–70	3.800	− 3.670	1.454	8.579	−13.703	7.471	− 9.530	− 5.017
1971–75	107.972	13.597	− 9.594	13.552	9.639	94.375	−14.048	− 5.986
1976–77	101.026	28.047	31.715	.875	− 4.543	72.979	− 4.321	− 1.519
Means								
1946–50	2.294	4.114	1.443	.704	1.967	− 1.820	− 2.881	− 2.355
1951–55	2.190	− 3.198	− .035	.756	− 3.918	5.388	− .770	− .557
1956–60	8.414	− 1.017	− 1.290	.000	.272	9.432	− .875	− .595
1961–65	3.787	− 5.109	− 3.388	− .288	− 1.432	8.896	− .752	− .454
1966–70	.760	− .734	.291	1.716	− 2.741	1.494	− 1.906	− 1.003
1971–75	21.594	2.719	− 1.919	2.710	1.928	18.875	− 2.810	− 1.197
1976–77	50.513	14.024	15.858	.437	− 2.271	36.490	− 2.160	− .759
Sums, 1946–77	296.226	11.926	7.226	28.865	−24.166	284.300	−54.289	−32.328
Means, 1946–77	9.257	.373	.226	.902	− .755	8.884	− 1.697	− 1.010

Table 5.50 (continued)

(1) Year	(10) Consumer Credit	(11) Misc. Assets	(12) Total Assets	(13) Mortgages	(14) Other Loans	(15) Net Trade Debt	(16) Total Liabil-ities	(17) Net Worth
1946	− .592	− .643	−21.552	− 3.906	− 2.028	.506	− 5.428	−16.124
1947	− .334	− .336	5.675	− 2.436	− 1.189	.159	− 3.467	9.142
1948	− .102	− .099	− 4.872	− .404	− .350	.024	− .730	− 4.142
1949	.075	.068	9.633	.841	.228	.015	1.083	8.551
1950	− .370	− .300	8.179	− 1.937	− 1.041	− .095	− 3.073	11.252
1951	− .162	− .127	13.561	− 1.543	− .467	− .045	− 2.056	15.617
1952	− .097	− .076	− 6.728	− .359	− .281	− .024	− .664	− 6.064
1953	− .051	− .041	− 2.747	− .106	− .139	− .012	− .256	− 2.491
1954	− .106	− .089	.669	.012	− .280	− .046	− .314	.983
1955	− .167	− .148	2.345	− 1.679	− .475	− .139	− 2.293	4.638
1956	− .245	− .217	7.192	− 2.813	− .732	− .228	− 3.773	10.964
1957	− .144	− .127	9.957	.286	− .436	− .133	− .282	10.239
1958	− .117	− .105	19.744	− 1.836	− .370	− .117	− 2.324	22.067
1959	− .157	− .141	− 5.765	− 2.329	− .515	− .157	− 3.001	− 2.765
1960	− .077	− .069	6.570	1.556	− .260	− .079	1.217	5.352
1961	− .110	− .101	− 3.108	− 1.235	− .383	− .098	− 1.716	− 1.392
1962	− .148	− .134	3.922	.138	− .525	− .115	− .502	4.424
1963	− .122	− .107	2.973	− 1.393	− .448	− .078	− 1.919	4.891
1964	− .153	− .136	5.303	− .600	− .583	− .074	− 1.257	6.560
1965	− .253	− .225	6.087	− 3.484	− 1.006	− .103	− 4.593	10.680
1966	− .351	− .317	10.993	− 3.705	− 1.489	− .096	− 5.291	16.284
1967	− .349	− .333	4.208	− 5.578	− 1.590	− .031	− 7.199	11.406
1968	− .473	− .477	4.816	− 4.898	− 2.223	− .002	− 7.124	11.940
1969	− .541	− .585	− 8.225	−11.691	− 2.678	− .252	− 14.622	6.397
1970	− .506	− .581	−17.521	− .118	− 2.553	− .254	− 2.925	−14.596

Table 5.50 (continued)

(1) Year	(10) Consumer Credit	(11) Misc. Assets	(12) Total Assets	(13) Mortgages	(14) Other Loans	(15) Net Trade Debt	(16) Total Liabil-ities	(17) Net Worth
1971	− .464	− .564	− 4.193	− .353	− 2.355	− .012	− 2.720	− 1.473
1972	− .426	− .561	37.405	− 4.068	− 2.250	− .000	− 6.318	43.723
1973	− .800	− 1.104	59.036	−14.884	− 4.432	− .039	− 19.355	78.391
1974	− 1.096	− 1.563	3.971	− 8.852	− 6.210	− .118	− 15.179	19.150
1975	− .594	− .890	− 2.295	− 1.922	− 3.345	− .167	− 5.434	3.139
1976	− .500	− .780	73.486	3.477	− 2.806	− .217	.454	73.032
1977	− .583	− .940	23.220	−10.441	− 3.316	− .291	− 14.048	37.269
Sums								
1946–50	− 1.322	− 1.309	− 2.936	− 7.842	− 4.381	.608	− 11.615	8.679
1951–55	− .584	− .482	7.100	− 3.676	− 1.642	− .266	− 5.583	12.683
1956–60	− .740	− .659	37.696	− 5.136	− 2.313	− .713	− 8.162	45.859
1961–65	− .786	− .703	15.176	− 6.573	− 2.946	− .467	− 9.987	25.163
1966–70	− 2.220	− 2.292	− 5.729	−25.991	−10.534	− .636	− 37.161	31.431
1971–75	− 3.380	− 4.682	93.924	−30.078	−18.591	− .336	− 49.005	142.930
1976–77	− 1.083	− 1.720	96.706	− 6.964	− 6.123	− .508	− 13.595	110.300
Means								
1946–50	− .264	− .262	− .587	− 1.568	− .876	.122	− 2.323	1.736
1951–55	− .117	− .096	1.420	− .735	− .328	− .053	− 1.117	2.537
1956–60	− .148	− .132	7.539	− 1.027	− .463	− .143	− 1.632	9.172
1961–65	− .157	− .141	3.035	− 1.315	− .589	− .093	− 1.997	5.033
1966–70	− .444	− .458	− 1.146	− 5.198	− 2.107	− .127	− 7.432	6.286
1971–75	− .676	− .936	18.785	− 6.016	− 3.718	− .067	− 9.801	28.586
1976–77	− .541	− .860	48.353	− 3.482	− 3.061	− .254	− 6.797	55.150
Sums, 1946–77	−10.115	−11.846	241.937	−86.260	−46.530	−2.319	−135.109	377.046
Means, 1946–77	− .316	− .370	7.561	− 2.696	− 1.454	− .072	− 4.222	11.783

Table 5.51 **Nonfinancial Corporations, Net Revaluations in Detail, Nonhuman Capital (Billions of Dollars, 1946–77)**

(1) Year	(2) Total Tangible Assets	(3) Total Repro-ducible Assets	(4) Structures, Plant and Equipment	(5) Inven-tories	(6) Land	(7) Total Financial Assets	(8) Currency, Demand and Time Dep.	(9) U.S. Gov't Securities	(10) State and Local Obligations	(11) Com-mercial Paper	(12) Security R.P.S.
1946	−4.727	− 2.556	−3.256	.700	−2.170	− 11.969	− 3.353	− 3.209	− .062	− .005	0
1947	5.314	5.586	2.967	2.619	− .271	− 6.949	− 1.932	− 1.583	− .040	− .009	0
1948	5.476	4.581	3.405	1.176	.895	− 1.990	− .604	− .257	− .006	− .004	0
1949	4.826	2.621	4.695	−2.073	2.205	1.775	.387	.598	.020	.005	0
1950	.458	1.358	− .846	2.204	− .900	− 6.948	− 1.726	− 1.360	− .046	− .025	0
1951	5.485	4.031	4.406	− .375	1.455	− 3.894	− .785	− 1.211	− .047	− .011	0
1952	1.408	− .982	1.395	−2.376	2.390	− 1.908	− .447	− .326	− .015	− .009	0
1953	2.836	1.757	1.411	.346	1.080	− .806	− .227	.007	− .001	− .006	0
1954	.901	− 1.091	− .109	− .981	1.992	− 1.854	− .477	− .128	− .007	− .016	0
1955	8.222	5.779	5.564	.215	2.443	− 4.237	− .791	− 1.227	− .025	− .028	0
1956	10.814	6.179	6.060	.118	4.635	− 6.177	− 1.159	− 1.287	− .116	− .045	0
1957	5.712	2.472	3.204	− .733	3.240	− 2.507	− .667	.374	.023	− .028	0
1958	2.172	− 1.108	.182	−1.290	3.281	− 3.703	− .537	− 1.142	− .143	− .021	0
1959	.865	− 3.634	−2.354	−1.279	4.499	− 5.181	− .702	− 1.655	− .208	− .022	0
1960	1.149	− 2.475	−1.605	− .870	3.625	.231	− .321	1.665	.190	− .014	0
1961	− .582	− 3.470	−3.162	− .308	2.888	− 2.959	− .486	− .433	− .077	− .041	0
1962	−1.653	− 5.492	−3.634	−1.859	3.840	− 3.141	− .696	.241	.015	− .062	0
1963	−3.058	− .983	−1.599	.616	−2.075	− 3.221	− .591	− .285	− .129	− .060	0
1964	.260	− .709	− .639	− .070	.969	− 3.631	− .737	− .011	− .020	− .092	− .003
1965	1.955	− .746	− .538	− .207	2.701	− 6.834	− 1.197	− .432	− .267	− .170	− .012
1966	− .378	− 1.186	.268	−1.454	.807	− 9.068	− 1.645	− .119	− .058	− .234	− .026
1967	2.706	1.425	2.611	−1.186	1.281	− 9.863	− 1.669	− .206	− .212	− .312	− .026
1968	−4.892	.598	3.237	−2.639	−5.490	− 14.643	− 2.400	− .362	− .249	− .604	− .042
1969	2.657	3.841	4.322	− .481	−1.183	− 19.260	− 2.699	− 1.056	− .256	− .930	− .123
1970	.365	1.276	5.103	−3.827	− .910	− 18.025	− 2.448	− .300	.115	− .993	− .090

Table 5.51 (continued)

(1) Year	(2) Total Tangible Assets	(3) Total Repro-ducible Assets	(4) Structures, Plant and Equipment	(5) Inven-tories	(6) Land	(7) Total Financial Assets	(8) Currency, Demand and Time Dep.	(9) U.S. Gov't Securities	(10) State and Local Obligations	(11) Com-mercial Paper	(12) Security R.P.S.
1971	−7.165	− .633	1.704	−2.337	−6.532	− 18.165	− 2.424	− .639	− .208	− .686	− .029
1972	12.956	6.373	6.099	.274	6.583	− 17.716	− 2.506	− .103	− .265	− .787	− .082
1973	32.933	26.525	15.007	11.518	6.408	− 36.621	− 4.979	− .322	− .467	− 1.784	− .320
1974	66.659	51.439	22.446	28.992	15.221	− 55.158	− 7.198	− .075	.118	− 2.835	− .432
1975	25.241	27.384	34.754	−7.370	−2.143	− 34.593	− 4.301	− .679	− .194	− 1.783	− .231
1976	20.014	23.078	19.498	3.580	−3.064	− 30.300	− 3.831	− .106	− .034	− 1.669	− .307
1977	10.318	9.799	12.001	−2.202	.519	− 40.633	− 4.777	− 1.937	− .354	− 2.167	− .631
Sums											
1946–50	11.348	11.590	6.964	4.626	− .242	− 26.082	− 7.228	− 5.812	− .135	− .039	0
1951–55	18.852	9.494	12.666	−3.172	9.358	− 12.700	− 2.728	− 2.886	− .094	− .070	0
1956–60	20.712	1.433	5.487	−4.054	19.279	− 17.337	− 3.385	− 2.044	− .255	− .130	0
1961–65	−3.076	−11.400	−9.573	−1.828	8.324	− 19.786	− 3.708	− .921	− .478	− .425	− .015
1966–70	.459	5.954	15.541	−9.587	−5.495	− 70.859	−10.861	− 2.044	− .660	− 3.074	− .308
1971–75	130.624	111.087	80.010	31.077	19.538	−162.252	−21.409	− 1.817	−1.017	− 8.075	−1.095
1976–77	30.332	32.877	31.499	1.378	−2.545	− 70.934	− 8.607	− 2.045	− .387	− 3.836	− .939
Means											
1946–50	2.270	2.318	1.393	.925	− .048	− 5.216	− 1.446	− 1.162	− .027	− .008	0
1951–55	3.770	1.899	2.533	− .634	1.872	− 2.540	− .546	− .577	− .019	− .014	0
1956–60	4.142	.287	1.097	− .811	3.856	− 3.467	− .677	− .409	− .051	− .026	0
1961–65	− .615	− 2.280	−1.915	− .366	1.665	− 3.957	− .742	− .184	− .096	− .085	− .003
1966–70	.092	1.191	3.108	−1.917	−1.099	− 14.172	− 2.172	− .409	− .132	− .615	− .062
1971–75	26.125	22.217	16.002	6.215	3.908	− 32.450	− 4.282	− .363	− .203	− 1.615	− .219
1976–77	15.166	16.439	15.749	.689	−1.273	− 35.467	− 4.304	− 1.022	− .194	− 1.918	− .469
Sums, 1946–77	209.250	161.033	142.593	18.440	48.217	−379.949	−57.928	−17.569	−3.027	−15.648	−2.356
Means, 1946–77	5.539	5.032	4.456	.576	1.507	− 11.873	− 1.810	− .549	− .095	− .489	− .074

Table 5.51 (continued)

(1) Year	(13) Consumer and Trade Credit	(14) Misc. Assets	(15) Total Assets	(16) Corporate and Foreign Bonds	(17) Mortgage Debt	(18) Other Loans	(19) Profit Taxes Payable	(20) Net Trade Debt	(21) Misc. Liabil-ities	(22) Total Liabil-ities	(23) Net Worth
1946	−4.038	−1.303	−16.696	−4.197	−1.666	−2.180	−1.638	−2.856	−.417	−12.954	−3.742
1947	−2.600	−.784	−1.634	−3.134	−1.329	−1.465	−.906	−1.962	−.231	−9.026	7.392
1948	−.862	−.257	3.486	−.740	−.250	−.480	−.306	−.635	−.071	−2.482	5.967
1949	.578	.187	6.601	1.138	.537	.300	.194	.418	.047	2.634	3.967
1950	−2.891	−.900	−6.490	−2.964	−1.248	−1.331	−1.023	−2.103	−.226	−8.895	2.406
1951	−1.420	−.419	1.592	−2.498	−1.034	−.661	−.569	−1.019	−.106	−5.887	7.479
1952	−.850	−.261	−.501	.359	−.232	−.419	−.320	−.574	−.063	−1.247	.747
1953	−.434	−.145	2.030	−.956	−.071	−.214	−.157	−.292	−.034	−1.725	3.755
1954	−.909	−.317	−.953	1.208	.006	−.434	−.298	−.611	−.075	−.203	−.750
1955	−1.621	−.546	3.984	−2.299	−1.192	−.728	−.477	−1.111	−.129	−5.936	9.920
1956	−2.673	−.898	4.637	−2.361	−2.161	−1.235	−.733	−1.866	−.203	−8.558	13.195
1957	−1.624	−.586	3.205	−7.334	.187	−.787	−.384	−1.137	−.123	−9.579	12.783
1958	−1.343	−.517	−1.531	−1.032	−1.571	−.630	−.249	−.936	−.102	−4.521	2.991
1959	−1.870	−.724	−4.316	−5.517	−2.033	−.859	−.323	−1.299	−.141	−10.173	5.857
1960	−.925	−.363	1.381	.790	1.296	−.440	−.158	−.646	−.070	.773	.607
1961	−1.366	−.555	−3.540	−.226	−1.107	−.662	−.207	−.950	−.103	−3.255	−.285
1962	−1.861	−.777	−4.793	−.120	.111	−.896	−.286	−1.291	−.139	−2.622	−2.172
1963	−1.509	−.647	−6.279	−1.283	−1.202	−.734	−.237	−1.068	−.110	−4.634	−1.645
1964	−1.932	−.836	−3.370	−.035	−.363	−.954	−.297	−1.385	−.137	−3.170	−.201
1965	−3.328	−1.427	−4.879	−3.687	−2.769	−1.712	−.500	−2.413	−.225	−11.307	6.428
1966	−4.937	−2.049	−9.446	−11.669	−3.082	−2.657	−.716	−3.635	−.315	−22.073	12.627
1967	−5.270	−2.168	−7.157	−8.627	−4.590	−2.956	−.608	−3.932	−.332	−21.046	13.889
1968	−7.814	−3.171	−19.535	−7.153	−4.382	−4.481	−.811	−5.928	−.492	−23.247	3.712
1969	−10.222	−3.974	−16.603	−23.547	−10.792	−6.032	−.925	−7.928	−.623	−49.848	33.245
1970	−10.287	−4.022	−17.660	3.042	.101	−6.253	−.680	−8.063	−.641	−12.494	−5.166

Table 5.51 (continued)

(1) Year	(13) Consumer and Trade Credit	(14) Misc. Assets	(15) Total Assets	(16) Corporate and Foreign Bonds	(17) Mortgage Debt	(18) Other Loans	(19) Profit Taxes Payable	(20) Net Trade Debt	(21) Misc. Liabilities	(22) Total Liabilities	(23) Net Worth
1971	−9.947	−4.031	−25.330	6.687	−.121	−5.986	−.576	−7.817	−.634	−8.447	−16.883
1972	−9.907	−4.066	−4.760	−5.607	−4.321	−5.918	−.565	−7.717	−.613	−24.743	19.983
1973	−20.274	−8.474	−3.688	−27.841	−16.936	−13.097	−1.141	−15.656	−1.410	−76.082	72.394
1974	−31.376	−13.360	11.502	−45.935	−11.314	−22.790	−1.793	−24.217	−2.548	−108.597	120.099
1975	−18.887	−8.517	−9.352	1.051	−3.209	−13.969	−.951	−14.598	−1.683	−33.360	24.008
1976	−16.455	−7.896	−10.286	20.756	5.312	−11.403	−.874	−12.693	−1.515	−.418	−9.868
1977	−20.700	−10.067	−30.316	−30.242	−17.738	−14.340	−1.101	−15.836	−1.868	−81.124	50.808
Sums											
1946–50	−9.812	−3.056	−14.734	−9.897	−3.955	−5.157	−3.679	−7.137	−.898	−30.723	15.989
1951–55	−5.235	−1.688	6.152	−4.185	−2.523	−2.455	−1.821	−3.606	−.407	−14.998	21.150
1956–60	−8.434	−3.089	3.375	−15.455	−4.282	−3.951	−1.847	−5.883	−.640	−32.058	35.433
1961–65	−9.996	−4.242	−22.862	−5.351	−5.330	−4.960	−1.527	−7.107	−.713	−24.988	2.126
1966–70	−38.529	−15.383	−70.400	−47.955	−22.744	−22.379	−3.739	−29.486	−2.403	−128.707	58.307
1971–75	−90.391	−38.449	−31.628	−71.645	−35.902	−61.761	−5.028	−70.005	−6.887	−251.228	219.600
1976–77	−37.156	−17.963	−40.602	−9.486	−12.426	−25.743	−1.975	−28.529	−3.383	−81.542	40.940
Means											
1946–50	−1.962	−.611	−2.947	−1.979	−.791	−1.031	−.736	−1.427	−.180	−6.145	3.198
1951–55	−1.047	−.338	1.230	−.837	−.505	−.491	−.364	−.721	−.081	−3.000	4.230
1956–60	−1.687	−.618	.675	−3.091	−.856	−.790	−.369	−1.177	−.128	−6.412	7.087
1961–65	−1.999	−.848	−4.572	−1.070	−1.066	−.992	−.305	−1.421	−.143	−4.998	.425
1966–70	−7.706	−3.077	−14.080	−9.591	−4.549	−4.476	−.748	−5.897	−.481	−25.741	11.661
1971–75	−18.078	−7.690	−6.326	−14.329	−7.180	−12.352	−1.006	−14.001	−1.377	−50.246	43.920
1976–77	−18.578	−8.982	−20.301	−4.743	−6.213	−12.871	−.988	−14.265	−1.691	−40.771	20.470
Sums, 1946–77	−199.552	−83.870	−170.699	−163.974	−87.163	−126.406	−19.617	−151.754	−15.331	−564.244	393.545
Means, 1946–77	−6.236	−2.621	−5.334	−5.124	−2.724	−3.950	−.613	−4.742	−.479	−17.633	12.298

Table 5.52 **Nonfinancial Corporations, Net Revaluations in Detail, Nonhuman Capital (Billions of 1972 Dollars, 1946–77)**

(1) Year	(2) Total Tangible Assets	(3) Total Repro-ducible Assets	(4) Structures, Plant and Equipment	(5) Inven-tories	(6) Land	(7) Total Financial Assets	(8) Currency, Demand, and Time Deposits	(9) U.S. Gov't Securities	(10) State and Local Obligations	(11) Com-mercial Paper	(12) Security R.P.S
1946	−11.445	− 6.190	− 7.884	1.694	−5.255	− 28.982	− 8.118	− 7.770	− .150	− .012	0
1947	10.867	11.422	6.067	5.356	− .555	− 14.210	− 3.952	− 3.238	− .083	− .018	0
1948	10.217	8.547	6.353	2.194	1.670	− 3.714	− 1.127	− .480	− .011	− .008	0
1949	8.806	4.783	8.567	− 3.783	4.023	3.239	.706	1.090	.036	.009	0
1950	.811	2.404	− 1.498	3.901	−1.592	− 12.298	− 3.055	− 2.408	− .082	− .045	0
1951	9.022	6.629	7.247	− .618	2.393	− 6.404	− 1.291	− 1.992	− .078	− .019	0
1952	2.267	− 1.581	2.246	− 3.827	3.848	− 3.073	− .720	− .525	− .024	− .014	0
1953	4.509	2.793	2.243	.550	1.716	− 1.282	− .361	.011	− .001	− .010	0
1954	1.421	− 1.720	− .173	− 1.548	3.142	− 2.924	− .753	− .202	− .011	− .025	0
1955	12.688	8.918	8.586	.332	3.769	− 6.539	− 1.221	− 1.894	− .038	− .043	0
1956	15.832	9.046	8.873	.173	6.786	− 9.044	− 1.696	− 1.884	− .170	− .066	0
1957	8.056	3.486	4.519	− 1.033	4.570	− 3.536	− .940	.528	.032	− .040	0
1958	3.068	− 1.565	.257	− 1.823	4.634	− 5.231	− .759	− 1.613	− .202	− .029	0
1959	1.208	− 5.075	− 3.288	− 1.787	6.283	− 7.236	− .980	− 2.311	− .291	− .030	0
1960	1.598	− 3.443	− 2.233	− 1.210	5.041	.322	− .447	2.316	.264	− .019	0
1961	− .812	− 4.846	− 4.417	− .430	4.034	− 4.132	− .679	− .605	− .107	− .057	0
1962	− 2.295	− 7.628	− 5.047	− 2.582	5.333	− 4.362	− .967	.334	.021	− .087	0
1963	− 4.241	− 1.364	− 2.218	.854	−2.877	− 4.468	− .820	− .396	− .179	− .083	0
1964	.358	− .974	− .878	− .096	1.332	− 4.987	− 1.012	− .015	− .028	− .127	− .004
1965	2.649	− 1.010	− .729	− .281	3.660	− 9.260	− 1.622	− .586	− .362	− .230	− .016
1966	− .497	− 1.556	.352	− 1.908	1.059	− 11.900	− 2.159	− .157	− .075	− .307	− .034
1967	3.438	1.811	3.318	− 1.507	1.628	− 12.533	− 2.121	− .262	− .270	− .397	− .033
1968	− 5.959	.728	3.943	− 3.215	−6.687	− 17.835	− 2.923	− .441	− .304	− .736	− .052
1969	3.058	4.420	4.973	− .553	−1.362	− 22.164	− 3.106	− 1.215	− .294	− 1.071	− .142
1970	.401	1.400	5.602	− 4.201	− .999	− 19.786	− 2.687	− .329	.126	− 1.090	− .099

Table 5.52 (continued)

(1) Year	(2) Total Tangible Assets	(3) Total Repro-ducible Assets	(4) Structures, Plant and Equipment	(5) Inven-tories	(6) Land	(7) Total Financial Assets	(8) Currency, Demand, and Time Deposits	(9) U.S. Gov't Securities	(10) State and Local Obligations	(11) Com-mercial Paper	(12) Security R.P.S
1971	− 7.472	− .660	1.776	− 2.437	−6.811	− 18.941	− 2.528	− .666	− .217	− .924	− .030
1972	12.956	6.373	6.099	.274	6.583	− 17.716	− 2.506	− .103	− .265	− .787	− .082
1973	31.069	25.023	14.157	10.866	6.046	− 34.548	− 4.698	− .303	− .441	− 1.683	− .302
1974	56.635	43.703	19.071	24.632	12.932	− 46.863	− 6.116	− .063	.100	− 2.408	− .367
1975	19.064	20.682	26.249	− 5.567	−1.618	− 26.127	− 3.248	− .513	− .146	− 1.347	− .175
1976	14.316	16.508	13.947	2.561	−2.191	− 21.674	− 2.740	− .077	− .024	− 1.194	− .220
1977	6.865	6.520	7.984	− 1.465	.345	− 27.035	− 3.178	− 1.289	− .235	− 1.442	− .420
Sums											
1946–50	19.257	20.966	11.605	9.362	−1.710	− 55.964	−15.546	−12.805	− .289	− .074	0
1951–55	29.907	15.039	20.149	− 5.110	14.868	− 20.223	− 4.346	− 4.602	− .152	− .110	0
1956–60	29.763	2.449	8.128	− 5.680	27.314	− 24.725	− 4.822	− 2.965	− .367	− .185	0
1961–65	− 4.342	−15.823	−13.289	− 2.534	11.481	− 27.210	− 5.101	− 1.267	− .656	− .583	− .020
1966–70	.443	6.803	18.187	−11.384	−6.361	− 84.217	−12.996	− 2.404	− .817	− 3.600	− .360
1971–75	112.253	95.121	67.353	27.769	17.131	−144.196	−19.096	− 1.649	− .970	− 7.149	− .956
1976–77	21.181	23.028	21.932	1.096	−1.846	− 48.709	− 5.918	− 1.366	− .259	− 2.636	− .640
Means											
1946–50	3.851	4.193	2.321	1.872	− .342	− 11.193	− 3.109	− 2.561	− .058	− .015	0
1951–55	5.981	3.008	4.030	− 1.022	2.974	− 4.045	− .869	− .920	− .030	− .022	0
1956–60	5.953	.490	1.626	− 1.136	5.463	− 4.945	− .964	− .593	− .073	− .037	0
1961–65	− .868	− 3.165	− 2.658	− .507	2.296	− 5.442	− 1.020	− .253	− .131	− .117	− .004
1966–70	.089	1.361	3.637	− 2.277	−1.272	− 16.843	− 2.599	− .481	− .163	− .720	− .072
1971–75	22.451	19.024	13.471	5.554	3.426	− 28.839	− 3.819	− .330	− .194	− 1.430	− .191
1976–77	10.591	11.514	10.966	.548	− .923	− 24.354	− 2.959	− .683	− .130	− 1.318	− .320
Sums, 1946–77	208.461	147.584	134.064	13.520	60.877	−405.244	−67.826	−27.058	−3.510	−14.337	−1.976
Means, 1946–77	6.514	4.612	4.190	.422	1.902	− 12.664	− 2.120	− .846	− .110	− .448	− .062

Table 5.52 (continued)

(1) Year	(13) Consumer and Trade Credit	(14) Misc. Assets	(15) Total Assets	(16) Corporate and Foreign Bonds	(17) Mortgage Debt	(18) Other Loans	(19) Profit Taxes Payable	(20) Net Trade Debt	(21) Misc. Liabil-ities	(22) Total Liabil-ities	(23) Net Worth
1946	− 9.776	− 3.155	− 40.427	− 10.162	− 4.033	− 5.279	− 3.965	− 6.916	− 1.010	− 31.365	− 9.061
1947	− 5.316	− 1.602	− 3.342	− 6.408	− 2.717	− 2.997	− 1.852	− 4.011	− .472	− 18.458	15.116
1948	− 1.609	− .479	6.503	− 1.382	− .466	− .895	− .571	− 1.184	− .132	− 4.630	11.133
1949	1.055	.342	12.045	2.077	.979	.547	.353	.763	.087	4.806	7.239
1950	− 5.116	− 1.592	− 11.487	− 5.246	− 2.208	− 2.356	− 1.811	− 3.722	− .401	− 15.744	4.258
1951	− 2.336	− .688	2.618	− 4.108	− 1.701	− 1.086	− .935	− 1.677	− .175	− 9.682	12.300
1952	− 1.368	− .421	− .806	.579	− .373	− .674	− .515	− .924	− .102	− 2.009	1.203
1953	− .690	− .230	3.227	− 1.520	− .112	− .341	− .250	− .464	− .054	− 2.742	5.969
1954	− 1.434	− .500	− 1.503	1.905	.009	− .684	− .470	− .963	− .118	− .320	− 1.183
1955	− 2.501	− .843	6.148	− 3.547	− 1.840	− 1.124	− .737	− 1.714	− .198	− 9.160	15.309
1956	− 3.913	− 1.315	6.788	− 3.456	− 3.164	− 1.808	− 1.073	− 2.732	− .297	− 12.530	19.319
1957	− 2.290	− .826	4.520	− 10.344	.263	− 1.110	− .542	− 1.604	− .174	− 13.510	18.030
1958	− 1.897	− .731	− 2.162	− 1.458	− 2.219	− .890	− .352	− 1.321	− .145	− 6.386	4.224
1959	− 2.611	− 1.012	− 6.028	− 7.706	− 2.839	− 1.200	− .451	− 1.814	− .198	− 14.208	8.180
1960	− 1.287	− .505	1.920	1.098	1.803	− .611	− .219	− .898	− .097	1.076	.844
1961	− 1.908	− .776	− 4.944	− .316	− 1.546	− .925	− .289	− 1.326	− .144	− 4.546	− .398
1962	− 2.584	− 1.079	− 6.658	− .167	.154	− 1.245	− .398	− 1.794	− .193	− 3.641	− 3.016
1963	− 2.093	− .897	− 8.709	− 1.779	− 1.668	− 1.019	− .329	− 1.482	− .152	− 6.428	− 2.281
1964	− 2.654	− 1.148	− 4.630	− .048	− .498	− 1.310	− .408	− 1.902	− .188	− 4.354	− .276
1965	− 4.510	− 1.934	− 6.611	− 4.996	− 3.753	− 2.320	− .678	− 3.270	− .304	− 15.321	8.710
1966	− 6.479	− 2.689	− 12.396	− 15.314	− 4.044	− 3.487	− .939	− 4.770	− .413	− 28.967	16.571
1967	− 6.696	− 2.754	− 9.094	− 10.962	− 5.832	− 3.756	− .772	− 4.996	− .422	− 26.742	17.647
1968	− 9.517	− 3.863	− 23.794	− 8.713	− 5.337	− 5.458	− .987	− 7.220	− .600	− 28.316	4.522
1969	− 11.762	− 4.573	− 19.105	− 27.097	−12.419	− 6.941	− 1.065	− 9.123	− .717	− 57.362	38.256
1970	− 11.292	− 4.415	− 19.385	3.339	.111	− 6.864	− .747	− 8.851	− .703	− 13.714	− 5.671

Table 5.52 (continued)

(1) Year	(13) Consumer and Trade Credit	(14) Misc. Assets	(15) Total Assets	(16) Corporate and Foreign Bonds	(17) Mortgage Debt	(18) Other Loans	(19) Profit Taxes Payable	(20) Net Trade Debt	(21) Misc. Liabil-ities	(22) Total Liabil-ities	(23) Net Worth
1971	− 10.372	− 4.204	− 26.413	6.973	− .127	− 6.242	− .601	− 8.151	− .661	− 8.808	−17.605
1972	− 9.907	− 4.066	− 4.760	− 5.607	− 4.321	− 5.918	− .565	− 7.717	− .613	− 24.743	19.983
1973	− 19.127	− 7.995	− 3.479	− 26.265	−15.978	− 12.356	− 1.077	− 14.770	− 1.330	− 71.775	68.297
1974	− 26.657	−11.351	9.772	− 39.027	− 9.612	− 19.363	− 1.524	− 20.575	− 2.164	− 92.266	102.038
1975	− 14.265	− 6.433	− 7.063	.793	− 2.424	− 10.551	− .719	− 11.026	− 1.271	− 25.196	18.133
1976	− 11.771	− 5.648	− 7.358	14.847	3.800	− 8.157	− .625	− 9.080	− 1.084	− .299	− 7.059
1977	− 13.773	− 6.698	− 20.170	− 20.121	−11.801	− 9.541	− .732	− 10.536	− 1.243	− 53.975	33.805
Sums											
1946–50	− 20.762	− 6.487	− 36.707	− 21.121	− 8.445	− 10.980	− 7.846	− 15.070	− 1.929	− 65.391	28.684
1951–55	− 8.331	− 2.682	9.684	− 6.692	− 4.018	− 3.909	− 2.907	− 5.742	− .647	− 23.914	33.598
1956–60	− 11.997	− 4.389	5.038	− 21.866	− 6.156	− 5.620	− 2.638	− 8.369	− .910	− 45.559	50.597
1961–65	− 13.749	− 5.833	− 31.552	− 7.306	− 7.310	− 6.819	− 2.101	− 9.773	− .981	− 34.290	2.739
1966–70	− 45.746	−18.293	− 83.775	− 58.746	−27.521	− 26.506	− 4.510	− 34.961	− 2.856	−155.101	71.326
1971–75	− 80.329	−34.048	− 31.943	− 63.133	−32.462	− 54.430	− 4.485	− 62.239	− 6.039	−222.788	190.845
1976–77	− 25.543	−12.346	− 27.528	− 5.274	− 8.002	− 17.697	− 1.358	− 19.616	− 2.326	− 54.273	26.746
Means											
1946–50	− 4.152	− 1.297	− 7.341	− 4.224	− 1.689	− 2.196	− 1.569	− 3.014	− .386	− 13.078	5.737
1951–55	− 1.666	− .536	1.937	− 1.338	− .804	− .782	− .581	− 1.148	− .129	− 4.783	6.720
1956–60	− 2.399	− .878	1.008	− 4.373	− 1.231	− 1.124	− .528	− 1.674	− .182	− 9.112	10.119
1961–65	− 2.750	− 1.167	− 6.310	− 1.461	− 1.462	− 1.364	− .420	− 1.955	− .196	− 6.858	.548
1966–70	− 9.149	− 3.659	− 16.755	− 11.749	− 5.504	− 5.301	− .902	− 6.992	− .571	− 31.020	14.265
1971–75	− 16.066	− 6.810	− 6.389	− 12.627	− 6.492	− 10.886	− .897	− 12.448	− 1.208	− 44.558	38.169
1976–77	− 12.772	− 6.173	− 13.764	− 2.637	− 4.001	− 8.849	− .679	− 9.808	− 1.163	− 27.137	13.373
Sums, 1946–77	−206.457	−84.079	−196.782	−184.138	−93.914	−125.962	−25.845	−155.770	−15.688	−601.317	404.534
Means, 1946–77	− 6.452	− 2.627	− 6.149	− 5.754	− 2.935	− 3.936	− .808	− 4.868	− .490	− 18.791	12.642

Table 5.53 Private Financial, Net Revaluations in Detail, Nonhuman Capital (Billions of Dollars, 1946–77)

(1) Year	(2) Total Tangible Assets	(3) Total Repro-ducible Assets	(4) Resident Structures	(5) Non-residential Plant and Equipment	(6) Land	(7) Total Financial Assets	(8) Currency, Demand, and Time Deposits	(9) Interbank Claims	(10) Corporate Shares	(11) Gov't Securities
1946	−.011	.016	−.006	.022	−.027	−42.805	−.753	−3.003	−.804	−24.210
1947	.169	.186	.011	.176	−.017	−27.750	−.457	−1.737	−.461	−14.723
1948	−.106	−.081	.007	−.087	−.025	−6.024	−.142	−.551	−.143	−2.559
1949	.087	.096	.071	.025	−.009	8.710	.091	.363	.104	4.343
1950	−.071	−.081	−.064	−.017	.010	−23.440	−.418	−1.370	−.626	−9.404
1951	.102	.074	.007	.068	.028	−16.683	−.196	−.623	−.296	−6.720
1952	.032	−.016	.001	−.017	.048	−4.686	−.117	−.367	−.187	−1.900
1953	−.029	−.026	−.001	−.025	−.004	−2.271	−.062	−.190	−.104	.098
1954	−.049	−.105	−.067	−.038	.057	−1.697	−.132	−.376	−.256	−.697
1955	.128	.041	.002	.039	.087	−19.126	−.222	−.579	−.555	−6.186
1956	.240	.119	.066	.053	.121	−28.311	−.336	−.860	−.965	−7.301
1957	−.042	−.113	−.072	−.041	.071	−8.008	−.199	−.505	−.574	1.945
1958	.058	−.020	.080	−.101	.078	−21.101	−.169	−.387	−.549	−7.233
1959	.065	−.097	.008	−.104	.161	−26.749	−.227	−.490	−.875	−4.702
1960	−.009	−.095	−.054	−.040	.086	−12.446	−.106	−.223	−.456	5.774
1961	.093	−.033	.020	−.053	.126	−13.859	−.163	−.306	−.795	−3.606
1962	.056	−.079	−.044	−.035	.135	−3.265	−.231	−.411	−1.109	1.045
1963	.114	.043	.045	−.002	.071	−15.697	−.185	−.313	−.920	−2.768
1964	.140	−.042	−.030	−.012	.182	−9.034	−.226	−.380	−1.301	−.789
1965	.320	.040	−.044	.084	.280	−36.733	−.365	−.623	−2.394	−5.536
1966	.302	.049	.015	.035	.252	−46.386	−.494	−.890	−3.426	−2.777
1967	.392	.083	.041	.042	.308	−59.680	−.501	−.969	−3.868	−7.949
1968	.330	.169	.008	.161	.161	−62.742	−.725	−1.444	−6.360	−6.935
1969	.608	.251	−.013	.264	.357	−125.636	−.834	−1.812	−7.889	−11.611
1970	.388	.057	−.060	.118	.331	−24.932	−.792	−1.825	−7.457	−1.571

Table 5.53 (continued)

(1) Year	(2) Total Tangible Assets	(3) Total Reproducible Assets	(4) Resident Structures	(5) Nonresidential Plant and Equipment	(6) Land	(7) Total Financial Assets	(8) Currency, Demand, and Time Deposits	(9) Interbank Claims	(10) Corporate Shares	(11) Gov't Securities
1971	.119	.092	.136	−.044	.027	−31.950	−.830	−1.912	−8.016	−4.566
1972	.785	.275	−.100	.376	.510	−67.464	−.903	−1.940	−9.449	−6.482
1973	1.545	1.084	.125	.960	.461	−197.166	−1.803	−4.250	−17.543	−16.136
1974	.807	.190	.009	.181	.617	−175.888	−2.880	−7.316	−19.532	5.503
1975	−.722	−.364	.247	−.611	−.358	−85.077	−1.979	−4.136	−11.000	−8.841
1976	−1.032	−1.033	−.251	−.783	.002	−14.871	−1.725	−3.520	−11.376	−1.445
1977	.006	−.175	.250	−.425	.180	−213.529	−2.113	−4.309	−13.871	−25.303
Sums										
1946–50	.069	.137	.018	.119	−.068	−91.309	−1.679	−6.298	−1.931	−46.553
1951–55	.184	−.031	−.059	.027	.216	−44.462	−.729	−2.134	−1.398	−15.405
1956–60	.312	−.206	.028	−.234	.518	−71.723	−1.037	−2.466	−3.420	−11.517
1961–65	.723	−.070	−.052	−.018	.793	−78.587	−1.169	−2.033	−6.519	−11.655
1966–70	2.020	.610	−.010	.620	1.410	−319.375	−3.346	−6.940	−29.000	−30.843
1971–75	2.534	1.278	.415	.862	1.257	−557.545	−8.394	−19.735	−65.541	−30.522
1976–77	−1.026	−1.208	−.000	−1.207	.182	−228.400	−3.838	−7.829	−25.246	−26.748
Means										
1946–50	.014	.027	.004	.024	−.014	−18.262	−.336	−1.260	−.386	−9.311
1951–55	.037	−.006	−.012	.005	.043	−8.892	−.146	−.427	−.280	−3.081
1956–60	.062	−.041	.006	−.047	.104	−14.345	−.207	−.493	−.684	−2.303
1961–65	.145	−.014	−.010	−.004	.159	−15.717	−.234	−.407	−1.304	−2.331
1966–70	.404	.122	−.002	.124	.282	−63.875	−.669	−1.388	−5.800	−6.169
1971–75	.507	.256	.083	.172	.251	−111.509	−1.679	−3.947	−13.108	−6.104
1976–77	−.513	−.604	−.000	−.604	.091	−114.200	−1.919	−3.915	−12.623	−13.374
Sums, 1946–77	4.817	.509	.340	.169	4.308	−1,391.401	−20.193	−47.434	−133.054	−173.242
Means, 1946–77	.151	.016	.011	.005	.135	−43.481	−.631	−1.482	−4.158	−5.414

Table 5.53 (continued)

(1) Year	(12) State and Local Obligations	(13) Corporate and Foreign Bonds	(14) Mortgages	(15) Other Loans	(16) Security Credit	(17) Trade Credit	(18) Misc. Financial Assets	(19) Total Assets	(20) Currency, Demand, and Time Deposits	(21) Insurance and Pension Reserves
1946	-1.174	-3.146	-4.151	-3.917	-.989	-.070	-.587	-42.816	-25.248	-7.702
1947	-.859	-2.574	-3.521	-2.747	-.293	-.048	-.329	-27.580	-13.645	-4.533
1948	-.148	-.680	-.891	-.920	-.073	-.016	-.101	-6.129	-4.154	-1.417
1949	.415	.982	1.653	.631	.052	.011	.065	8.797	2.632	.966
1950	-.944	-2.833	-4.094	-3.099	-.292	-.051	-.308	-23.511	-11.542	-4.519
1951	-.867	-2.434	-3.730	-1.512	-.134	-.024	-.147	-16.580	-5.251	-2.090
1952	-.306	.330	-.994	-.959	-.076	-.015	-.093	-4.654	-3.100	-1.251
1953	.001	-1.012	-.386	-.513	-.045	-.008	-.051	-2.300	-1.642	-.683
1954	-.125	1.211	-.005	-1.072	-.111	-.017	-.117	-1.746	-3.521	-1.453
1955	-1.353	-2.356	-5.533	-1.896	-.214	-.029	-.203	-18.997	-5.900	-.323
1956	-1.889	-2.429	-10.626	-3.209	-.320	-.047	-.328	-28.071	-8.989	-4.158
1957	.412	-7.543	.881	-2.004	-.176	-.030	-.215	-8.050	-5.412	-3.232
1958	-2.157	-1.025	-7.584	-1.635	-.148	-.026	-.188	-21.043	-4.548	.560
1959	-1.940	-5.855	-9.869	-2.284	-.207	-.038	-.261	-26.685	-6.217	-1.827
1960	1.925	.675	6.294	-1.186	-.099	-.019	-.133	12.438	-3.018	-1.453
1961	-1.369	-.299	-5.123	-1.789	-.156	-.028	-.224	-13.766	-4.543	1.881
1962	.186	-.244	.548	-2.464	-.225	-.039	-.321	-3.209	-6.369	-6.533
1963	-1.412	-1.569	-5.945	-2.088	-.197	-.032	-.268	-15.583	-5.335	1.286
1964	-.477	-.269	-2.169	-2.775	-.251	-.040	-.358	-8.894	-6.903	.648
1965	-3.164	-4.308	-14.320	-4.935	-.397	-.067	-.624	-36.412	-11.766	-1.744
1966	-1.780	-12.884	-15.155	-7.419	-.548	-.098	-.917	-46.084	-16.878	-13.499
1967	-5.318	-8.895	-22.478	-7.933	-.647	-.106	-1.014	-59.288	-18.083	-1.007
1968	-5.205	-6.976	-20.541	-11.777	-1.072	-.158	-1.549	-62.412	-26.841	-7.265
1969	-10.007	-23.317	-51.251	-15.493	-1.226	-.203	-1.993	-125.028	-32.491	-22.619
1970	-1.515	4.658	2.711	-15.752	-1.026	-.211	-2.152	-24.543	-31.868	-14.694

Table 5.53 (continued)

(1) Year	(12) State and Local Obligations	(13) Corporate and Foreign Bonds	(14) Mortgages	(15) Other Loans	(16) Security Credit	(17) Trade Credit	(18) Misc. Financial Assets	(19) Total Assets	(20) Currency, Demand, and Time Deposits	(21) Insurance and Pension Reserves
1971	−5.188	6.997	.450	−15.439	−1.014	−.210	−2.222	−31.831	−32.698	−.706
1972	−5.890	−5.564	−17.744	−15.888	−1.192	−.225	−2.188	−66.680	−34.420	7.596
1973	−16.525	−27.277	−71.605	−34.648	−2.197	−.487	−4.694	−195.621	−71.649	−71.491
1974	5.029	−44.131	−44.475	−56.539	−2.484	−.753	−8.308	−175.080	−110.627	−86.386
1975	−6.407	1.254	−12.000	−34.124	−1.385	−.468	−5.811	−85.799	−68.772	1.262
1976	−1.091	19.521	21.340	−29.079	−1.515	−.412	−5.568	−15.902	−62.197	−8.517
1977	−16.952	−30.449	−73.460	−36.911	−2.196	−.497	−7.469	−213.524	−79.262	−45.331
Sums										
1946–50	−2.710	−8.253	−10.803	−10.053	−1.595	−.173	−1.261	−91.240	−51.957	−17.205
1951–55	−2.651	−4.262	−10.647	−5.952	−.580	−.094	−.610	−44.277	−19.414	−5.800
1956–60	−3.650	−16.177	−20.905	−10.318	−.949	−.160	−1.126	−71.411	−28.184	−10.110
1961–65	−6.237	−6.687	−27.008	−14.051	−1.227	−.207	−1.794	−77.864	−34.915	−4.461
1966–70	−23.825	−47.413	−106.715	−58.374	−4.519	−.776	−7.624	−317.355	−126.160	−59.083
1971–75	−28.980	−68.722	−145.373	−156.637	−8.274	−2.143	−23.224	−555.011	−318.166	−149.725
1976–77	−18.043	−10.929	−52.120	−65.990	−3.710	−.910	−13.037	−229.426	−141.459	−53.848
Means										
1946–50	−.542	−1.651	−2.161	−2.011	−.319	−.035	−.252	−18.248	−10.391	−3.441
1951–55	−.530	−.852	−2.129	−1.190	−.116	−.019	−.122	−8.855	−3.883	−1.160
1956–60	−.730	−3.235	−4.181	−2.064	−.190	−.032	−.225	−14.282	−5.637	−2.022
1961–65	−1.247	−1.337	−5.402	−2.810	−.245	−.041	−.359	−15.573	−6.983	−.892
1966–70	−4.765	−9.483	−21.343	−11.675	−.904	−.155	−1.525	−63.471	−25.232	−11.817
1971–75	−5.796	−13.744	−29.075	−31.327	−1.655	−.429	−4.645	−111.002	−63.633	−29.945
1976–77	−9.021	−5.464	−26.060	−32.995	−1.855	−.455	−6.518	−114.713	−70.729	−26.924
Sums, 1946–77	−86.096	−162.443	−373.571	−321.374	−20.855	−4.463	−48.676	−1,386.585	−720.255	−300.233
Means, 1946–77	−2.690	−5.076	−11.674	−10.043	−.652	−.139	−1.521	−43.331	−22.508	−9.382

Table 5.53 (continued)

(1) Year	(22) Interbank Claims	(23) Investment Company Shares	(24) Corporate and Foreign Bonds	(25) Mortgages	(26) Other Loans	(27) Security Debt	(28) Taxes Payable	(29) Misc. Liabil-ities	(30) Total Liabil-ities	(31) Net Worth
1946	− .123	− .213	− .050	− .007	− .150	− .530	− .075	− 1.731	− 35.828	− 6.988
1947	− .058	− .123	− .060	− .017	− .129	− .180	− .037	− 1.062	− 19.843	− 7.738
1948	− .017	− .038	− .030	− .004	− .048	− .044	− .010	− .343	− 6.106	− .023
1949	.011	.032	.030	.010	.042	.037	.009	.245	4.016	4.781
1950	− .090	− .227	− .143	− .026	− .261	− .198	− .057	− 1.206	− 18.270	− 5.241
1951	− .048	− .104	− .131	− .023	− .131	− .089	− .029	− .564	− 8.459	− 8.121
1952	− .023	− .062	.018	− .009	− .084	− .048	− .022	− .349	− 4.931	.277
1953	− .011	− .034	− .115	− .003	− .046	− .027	− .014	− .191	− 2.765	.464
1954	− .020	− .085	.099	− .001	− .095	− .066	− .030	− .415	− 5.586	3.840
1955	− .042	− .185	− .190	− .050	− .191	− .122	− .038	− .716	− 7.756	− 11.241
1956	− .079	− .325	− .236	− .082	− .327	− .171	− .052	− 1.144	− 15.563	− 12.508
1957	− .045	− .198	− .739	.013	− .187	− .093	− .034	− .709	− 10.636	2.586
1958	− .032	− .196	− .060	− .074	− .142	− .080	− .029	− .599	− 5.198	− 15.845
1969	− .047	− .321	− .679	− .086	− .202	− .109	− .035	− .823	− 10.345	− 16.339
1960	− .026	− .169	− .055	.070	− .113	− .052	− .018	− .405	− 5.239	17.676
1961	− .040	− .295	.025	− .058	− .178	− .085	− .025	− .622	− 3.941	− 9.825
1962	− .062	− .410	.047	− .011	− .267	− .124	− .031	− .851	− 14.610	11.402
1963	− .048	− .331	− .231	− .077	− .258	− .106	− .024	− .696	− 5.821	− 9.762
1964	− .059	− .457	− .162	.007	− .361	− .135	− .028	− .902	− 8.353	− .541
1965	− .092	− .844	− .659	− .105	− .660	− .224	− .046	− 1.553	− 17.693	− 18.719
1966	− .124	− 1.238	− 1.564	− .013	− 1.026	− .322	− .062	− 2.340	− 37.067	− 9.017
1967	− .148	− 1.416	− .941	− .225	− 1.021	− .399	− .056	− 2.607	− 25.903	− 33.385
1968	− .262	− 2.311	− .683	− .184	− 1.482	− .687	− .077	− 4.019	− 43.810	− 18.603
1969	− .403	− 2.789	− 2.657	− .421	− 2.405	− .806	− .099	− 5.665	− 70.356	− 54.672
1970	− .488	− 2.460	.275	− .087	− 2.638	− .698	− .112	− 5.955	− 58.725	34.182

Table 5.53 (continued)

(1) Year	(22) Interbank Claims	(23) Investment Company Shares	(24) Corporate and Foreign Bonds	(25) Mortgages	(26) Other Loans	(27) Security Debt	(28) Taxes Payable	(29) Misc. Liabil-ities	(30) Total Liabil-ities	(31) Net Worth
1971	− .576	− 2.419	.610	− .214	− 2.363	− .686	− .115	− 5.724	− 44.892	13.060
1972	− .683	− 2.482	− 1.092	− .340	− 2.395	− .744	− .104	− 5.740	− 40.403	− 26.277
1973	− 1.804	− 4.156	− 4.387	− .678	− 5.997	− 1.387	− .202	− 12.458	− 174.210	− 21.411
1974	− 3.490	− 4.495	− 6.726	− .205	−10.767	− 1.610	− .306	− 20.612	− 245.225	70.145
1975	− 2.101	− 2.432	.450	− .324	− 6.463	− .904	− .175	− 12.989	− 92.448	6.650
1976	− 1.710	− 2.335	2.850	.218	− 5.243	− 1.029	− .158	− 11.754	− 89.875	73.972
1977	− 2.169	− 2.691	− 5.069	−1.118	− 6.824	− 1.478	− .231	− 15.048	− 159.221	− 54.303
Sums										
1946–50	− .276	− .569	− .253	− .044	− .547	− .915	− .169	− 4.097	− 76.031	− 15.209
1951–55	− .142	− .470	− .319	− .085	− .547	− .352	− .133	− 2.234	− 29.496	− 14.781
1956–60	− .227	− 1.209	− 1.769	− .159	− .971	− .505	− .167	− 3.680	− 46.981	− 24.430
1961–65	− .301	− 2.337	− .981	− .245	− 1.724	− .674	− .154	− 4.625	− 50.418	− 27.446
1966–70	− 1.426	−10.214	− 5.570	− .931	− 8.573	− 2.911	− .407	− 20.586	− 235.861	− 81.494
1971–75	− 8.655	−15.984	−11.145	−1.761	−27.985	− 5.331	− .902	− 57.523	− 597.178	42.167
1976–77	− 3.878	− 5.026	− 2.220	− .899	−12.067	− 2.507	− .389	− 26.801	− 249.095	19.669
Means										
1946–50	− .055	− .114	− .051	− .009	− .109	− .183	− .034	− .819	− 15.206	− 3.042
1951–55	− .028	− .094	− .064	− .017	− .109	− .070	− .027	− .447	− 5.899	− 2.956
1956–60	− .045	− .242	− .354	− .032	− .194	− .101	− .033	− .736	− 9.396	− 4.886
1961–65	− .060	− .467	− .196	− .049	− .345	− .135	− .031	− .925	− 10.084	− 5.489
1966–70	− .285	− 2.043	− 1.114	− .186	− 1.715	− .582	− .081	− 4.117	− 47.172	− 16.299
1971–75	− 1.731	− 3.197	− 2.229	− .352	− 5.597	− 1.066	− .180	− 11.505	− 119.436	8.433
1976–77	− 1.939	− 2.513	− 1.110	− .450	− 6.034	− 1.253	− .194	− 13.401	− 124.548	9.834
Sums, 1946–77	−14.907	−35.809	−22.256	−4.123	−52.414	−13.194	−2.321	−119.547	−1,285.060	−101.525
Means, 1946–77	− .466	− 1.119	− .696	− .129	− 1.638	− .412	− .073	− 3.736	− 40.158	− 3.173

Table 5.54 Private Financial, Net Revaluations in Detail, Nonhuman Capital (Billions of 1972 Dollars, 1946–77)

(1) Year	(2) Total Tangible Assets	(3) Total Repro-ducible Assets	(4) Residential Structures	(5) Nonres-idential Plant and Equipment	(6) Land	(7) Total Financial Assets	(8) Currency, Demand, and Time Deposits	(9) Interbank Claims	(10) Corporate Shares	(11) U.S. Gov't Securities
1946	−.026	.039	−.014	.053	−.065	−103.645	−1.824	−7.272	−1.948	−58.621
1947	.346	.381	.022	.359	−.035	−56.748	−.935	−3.552	−.943	−30.109
1948	−.197	−.151	.013	−.163	−.047	−11.238	−.264	−1.028	−.267	−4.773
1949	.158	.174	.129	.046	−.016	15.894	.166	.662	.190	7.926
1950	−.125	−.143	−.113	−.029	.018	−41.487	−.740	−2.424	−1.108	−16.644
1951	.168	.122	.011	.111	.046	−27.439	−.323	−1.024	−.487	−11.053
1952	.051	−.026	.001	−.027	.077	−7.545	−.189	−.591	−.302	−3.059
1953	−.047	−.041	−.001	−.040	−.006	−3.611	−.098	−.302	−.165	.156
1954	−.077	−.166	−.106	−.060	.089	−2.677	−.209	−.593	−.404	−1.100
1955	.198	.064	.003	.061	.134	−29.515	−.342	−.893	−.856	−9.546
1956	.351	.174	.097	.077	.178	−41.451	−.491	−1.260	−1.413	−10.690
1957	−.059	−.159	−.101	−.058	.100	−11.295	−.281	−.712	−.809	2.744
1958	.082	−.029	.114	−.142	.111	−29.803	−.238	−.546	−.776	−10.216
1959	.090	−.135	.010	−.146	.225	−37.359	−.317	−.685	−1.223	−6.567
1960	−.012	−.132	−.076	−.056	.120	17.310	−.148	−.310	−.634	8.031
1961	.130	−.046	.028	−.074	.176	−19.356	−.228	−.428	−1.110	−5.037
1962	.078	−.109	−.061	−.048	.187	−4.534	−.321	−.570	−1.540	1.451
1963	.158	.060	.063	−.003	.098	−21.771	−.257	−.434	−1.277	−3.839
1964	.192	−.058	−.041	−.017	.250	−12.409	−.310	−.522	−1.787	−1.084
1965	.434	.055	−.060	.114	.379	−49.773	−.494	−.845	−3.243	−7.501
1966	.396	.065	.019	.045	.331	−60.874	−.648	−1.168	−4.496	−3.644
1967	.497	.106	.052	.054	.392	−75.832	−.637	−1.232	−4.915	−10.100
1968	.402	.205	.009	.196	.196	−76.421	−.883	−1.759	−7.747	−8.448
1969	.700	.289	−.015	.304	.411	−144.576	−.960	−2.085	−9.078	−13.361
1970	.426	.063	−.066	.129	.363	−27.367	−.869	−2.003	−8.186	−1.725

Table 5.54 (continued)

(1) Year	(2) Total Tangible Assets	(3) Total Repro-ducible Assets	(4) Residential Structures	(5) Nonres-idential Plant and Equipment	(6) Land	(7) Total Financial Assets	(8) Currency, Demand, and Time Deposits	(9) Interbank Claims	(10) Corporate Shares	(11) U.S. Gov't Securities
1971	.124	.096	.141	–.046	.028	– 33.316	– .865	– 1.994	– 8.359	– 4.761
1972	.785	.275	–.100	.376	.510	– 67.464	– .903	– 1.940	– 9.449	– 6.482
1973	1.457	1.023	.117	.905	.435	– 186.005	– 1.701	– 4.010	– 16.550	– 15.222
1974	.686	.161	.007	.154	.524	– 149.437	– 2.447	– 6.216	– 16.595	4.675
1975	–.545	–.275	.187	–.461	–.271	– 64.257	– 1.495	– 3.260	– 8.308	– 6.677
1976	–.738	–.739	–.179	–.560	.001	– 10.637	– 1.234	– 2.518	– 8.137	– 1.034
1977	.004	–.116	.166	–.283	.120	– 142.069	– 1.406	– 2.867	– 9.229	– 16.835
Sums										
1946–50	.156	.301	.036	.266	–.145	– 197.224	– 3.597	–13.614	– 4.076	–102.221
1951–55	.294	–.047	–.092	.045	.341	– 70.786	– 1.161	– 3.403	– 2.213	– 24.602
1956–60	.453	–.281	.044	–.325	.733	– 102.599	– 1.476	– 3.513	– 4.855	– 16.698
1961–65	.992	–.098	–.071	–.028	1.090	– 107.844	– 1.609	– 2.798	– 8.957	– 16.010
1966–70	2.422	.728	–.001	.729	1.694	– 385.070	– 3.997	– 8.246	– 34.422	– 37.278
1971–75	2.507	1.280	.352	.928	1.226	– 500.481	– 7.410	–17.419	– 59.262	– 28.467
1976–77	–.734	–.855	–.013	–.842	.121	– 152.706	– 2.640	– 5.385	– 17.366	– 17.869
Means										
1946–50	.031	.060	.007	.053	–.029	– 39.445	– .719	– 2.723	– .815	– 20.444
1951–55	.059	–.009	–.018	.009	.068	– 14.157	– .232	– .681	– .443	– 4.920
1956–60	.091	–.056	.009	–.065	.147	– 20.520	– .295	– .703	– .971	– 3.340
1961–65	.198	–.020	–.014	–.006	.218	– 21.569	– .322	– .560	– 1.791	– 3.202
1966–70	.484	.146	–.000	.146	.339	– 77.014	– .799	– 1.649	– 6.884	– 7.456
1971–75	.501	.256	.070	.186	.245	– 100.096	– 1.482	– 3.484	– 11.852	– 5.693
1976–77	–.367	–.428	–.006	–.421	.061	– 76.353	– 1.320	– 2.692	– 8.683	– 8.934
Sums, 1946–77	6.089	1.028	.256	.772	5.061	–1,516.708	–21.890	–54.380	–131.150	–243.146
Means, 1946–77	.190	.032	.008	.024	.158	– 47.397	– .684	– 1.699	– 4.098	– 7.598

Table 5.54 (continued)

(1) Year	(12) State and Local Obligations	(13) Corporate and Foreign Bonds	(14) Mortgages	(15) Other Loans	(16) Security Credit	(17) Trade Credit	(18) Misc. Financial Assets	(19) Total Assets	(20) Currency, Demand, and Time Deposits	(21) Insurance and Pension Reserves
1946	− 2.842	− 7.618	− 10.051	− 9.485	− 2.396	− .169	− 1.421	− 103.671	− 61.132	− 18.648
1947	− 1.756	− 5.265	− 7.200	− 5.618	− .599	− .098	− .673	− 56.402	− 27.903	− 9.270
1948	− .276	− 1.269	− 1.289	− 1.716	− .136	− .029	− .189	− 11.435	− 7.751	− 2.644
1949	.757	1.791	3.017	1.151	.095	.021	.118	16.053	4.804	1.763
1950	− 1.671	− 5.015	− 7.245	− 5.485	− .517	− .091	− .546	− 41.612	− 20.429	− 7.999
1951	− 1.427	− 4.003	− 6.134	− 2.487	− .220	− .039	− .241	− 27.270	− 8.636	− 3.437
1952	− .493	.531	− 1.601	− 1.544	− .123	− .024	− .150	− 7.494	− 4.991	− 2.015
1953	.001	− 1.609	− .613	− .815	− .071	− .013	− .081	− 3.657	− 2.611	− 1.086
1954	− .197	1.909	− .008	− 1.691	− .174	− .027	− .184	− 2.753	− 5.553	− 2.292
1955	− 2.089	− 3.636	− 8.538	− 2.925	− .330	− .045	− .313	− 29.317	− 9.106	− .499
1956	− 2.765	− 3.557	− 15.558	− 4.698	− .469	− .069	− .481	− 41.100	− 13.161	− 6.088
1957	.580	− 10.638	1.242	− 2.826	− .248	− .042	− .303	− 11.354	− 7.633	− 4.559
1958	− 3.047	− 1.448	− 10.712	− 2.309	− .209	− .037	− .266	− 29.721	− 6.423	.791
1959	− 2.710	− 8.178	− 13.784	− 3.189	− .290	− .052	− .364	− 37.269	− 8.683	− 2.551
1960	2.677	.939	8.754	− 1.650	− .137	− .026	− .186	17.298	− 4.198	− 2.021
1961	− 1.913	− .417	− 7.155	− 2.499	− .218	− .039	− .313	− 19.226	− 6.346	2.627
1962	.258	− .338	.762	− 3.422	− .313	− .054	− .446	− 4.457	− 8.845	− 9.073
1963	− 1.958	− 2.176	− 8.245	− 2.896	− .274	− .044	− .372	− 21.613	− 7.399	1.784
1964	− .655	− .369	− 2.979	− 3.811	− .345	− .055	− .491	− 12.217	− 9.482	.890
1965	− 4.288	− 5.837	− 19.404	− 6.687	− .537	− .091	− .846	− 49.339	− 15.943	− 2.363
1966	− 2.336	− 16.908	− 19.888	− 9.736	− .719	− .128	− 1.203	− 60.478	− 22.150	− 17.715
1967	− 6.758	− 11.302	− 28.562	− 10.080	− .822	− .135	− 1.288	− 75.334	− 22.978	− 1.280
1968	− 6.340	− 8.497	− 25.020	− 14.345	− 1.305	− .192	− 1.886	− 76.020	− 32.693	− 8.848
1969	−11.516	− 26.832	− 58.977	− 17.828	− 1.411	− .234	− 2.293	− 143.876	− 37.389	− 26.029
1970	− 1.663	5.113	2.975	− 17.291	− 1.126	− .232	− 2.362	− 26.941	− 34.981	− 16.129

Table 5.54 (continued)

(1) Year	(12) State and Local Obligations	(13) Corporate and Foreign Bonds	(14) Mortgages	(15) Other Loans	(16) Security Credit	(17) Trade Credit	(18) Misc. Financial Assets	(19) Total Assets	(20) Currency, Demand, and Time Deposits	(21) Insurance and Pension Reserves
1971	− 5.409	7.296	.469	− 16.099	− 1.058	− .219	− 2.317	− 33.192	− 34.096	− .736
1972	− 5.890	− 5.564	− 17.744	− 15.888	− 1.192	− .225	− 2.188	− 66.680	− 34.420	7.596
1973	−15.589	− 25.733	− 67.552	− 32.686	− 2.073	− .460	− 4.429	− 184.548	− 67.593	− 67.444
1974	4.273	− 37.495	− 37.787	− 48.036	− 2.111	− .640	− 7.059	− 148.751	− 93.991	− 73.395
1975	− 4.839	.947	− 9.063	− 25.773	− 1.046	− .353	− 4.389	− 64.803	− 51.943	.953
1976	− .780	13.963	15.265	− 20.800	− 1.084	− .295	− 3.983	− 11.375	− 44.490	− 6.093
1977	−11.279	− 20.259	− 48.875	− 24.558	− 1.461	− .331	− 4.969	− 142.065	− 52.736	− 30.160
Sums										
1946–50	− 5.789	− 17.375	− 22.768	− 21.153	− 3.553	− .366	− 2.711	− 197.067	−112.412	− 36.798
1951–55	− 4.204	− 6.808	− 16.894	− 9.463	− .919	− .149	− .969	− 70.491	− 30.897	− 9.328
1956–60	− 5.264	− 22.882	− 30.058	− 14.673	− 1.352	− .228	− 1.600	− 102.146	− 40.098	− 14.428
1961–65	− 8.556	− 9.137	− 37.022	− 19.316	− 1.688	− .284	− 2.467	− 106.852	− 48.015	− 6.135
1966–70	−28.612	− 58.426	−129.471	− 69.280	− 5.384	− .921	− 9.033	− 382.648	−150.190	− 70.001
1971–75	−27.455	− 60.549	−131.676	−138.483	− 7.480	−1.897	−20.382	− 497.974	−282.043	−133.027
1976–77	−12.059	− 6.296	− 33.611	− 45.358	− 2.544	− .626	− 8.952	− 153.440	− 97.226	− 36.253
Means										
1946–50	− 1.158	− 3.475	− 4.554	− 4.231	− .711	− .073	− .542	− 39.413	− 22.482	− 7.360
1951–55	− .841	− 1.362	− 3.379	− 1.893	− .184	− .030	− .194	− 14.098	− 6.179	− 1.866
1956–60	− 1.053	− 4.576	− 6.012	− 2.935	− .270	− .046	− .320	− 20.429	− 8.020	− 2.886
1961–65	− 1.711	− 1.827	− 7.404	− 3.863	− .338	− .057	− .493	− 21.370	− 9.603	− 1.227
1966–70	− 5.722	− 11.685	− 25.894	− 13.856	− 1.077	− .184	− 1.807	− 76.530	− 30.038	− 14.000
1971–75	− 5.491	− 12.110	− 26.335	− 27.697	− 1.496	− .379	− 4.076	− 99.595	− 56.409	− 26.605
1976–77	− 6.030	− 3.148	− 16.805	− 22.679	− 1.272	− .313	− 4.476	− 76.720	− 48.613	− 18.126
Sums, 1946–77	−91.939	−181.472	−401.500	−317.727	−22.920	−4.471	−46.114	−1,510.619	−760.880	−305.970
Means, 1946–77	− 2.873	− 5.671	− 12.547	− 9.929	− .716	− .140	− 1.441	− 47.207	− 23.777	− 9.562

Table 5.54 (continued)

(1) Year	(22) Interbank Claims	(23) Investment Company Shares	(24) Corporate and Foreign Bonds	(25) Mortgages	(26) Other Loans	(27) Security Debt	(28) Taxes Payable	(29) Misc. Liabil-ities	(30) Total Liabil-ities	(31) Net Worth
1946	−.297	−.516	−.122	−.018	−.363	−1.283	−.181	−4.190	−86.751	−16.920
1947	−.119	−.251	−.122	−.035	−.265	−.367	−.075	−2.172	−40.578	−15.824
1948	−.032	−.072	−.056	−.008	−.089	−.082	−.018	−.640	−11.391	−.044
1949	.020	.059	.056	.019	.077	.067	.017	.448	7.328	8.725
1950	−.159	−.402	−.253	−.045	−.463	−.351	−.101	−2.135	−32.336	−9.276
1951	−.079	−.171	−.216	−.037	−.216	−.146	−.047	−.928	−13.913	−13.357
1952	−.036	−.100	.029	−.014	−.136	−.078	−.035	−.562	−7.940	.446
1953	−.017	−.053	−.183	−.004	−.073	−.043	−.023	−.303	−4.396	.738
1954	−.031	−.134	.157	−.002	−.149	−.104	−.047	−.654	−8.810	6.057
1955	−.064	−.285	−.293	−.077	−.294	−.188	−.059	−1.105	−11.969	−17.348
1956	−.115	−.476	−.346	−.119	−.479	−.250	−.077	−1.675	−22.786	−18.314
1957	−.063	−.280	−1.042	.018	−.264	−.132	−.048	−1.000	−15.001	3.647
1958	−.045	−.276	−.084	−.105	−.201	−.112	−.041	−.847	−7.342	−22.379
1959	−.065	−.449	−.949	−.120	−.282	−.152	−.049	−1.149	−14.449	−22.820
1960	−.036	−.234	−.077	.097	−.157	−.073	−.024	−.563	−7.286	24.584
1961	−.056	−.411	.035	−.082	−.249	−.118	−.035	−.868	−5.504	−13.722
1962	−.086	−.569	.065	−.015	−.371	−.173	−.043	−1.182	−20.292	15.835
1963	−.067	−.460	−.321	−.107	−.358	−.147	−.033	−.966	−8.074	−13.540
1964	−.081	−.628	−.222	.010	−.496	−.186	−.038	−1.240	−11.474	−.743
1965	−.125	−1.143	−.893	−.143	−.894	−.304	−.063	−2.105	−23.975	−25.365
1966	−.163	−1.625	−2.053	−.017	−1.347	−.423	−.082	−3.071	−48.645	−11.833
1967	−.188	−1.799	−1.195	−.286	−1.297	−.507	−.072	−3.312	−32.914	−42.421
1968	−.319	−2.815	−.832	−.224	−1.805	−.837	−.094	−4.895	−53.361	−22.658
1969	−.464	−3.210	−3.058	−.484	−2.768	−.928	−.114	−6.519	−80.962	−62.913
1970	−.535	−2.700	.301	−.096	−2.896	−.766	−.123	−6.537	−64.462	37.521

Table 5.54 (continued)

(1) Year	(22) Interbank Claims	(23) Investment Company Shares	(24) Corporate and Foreign Bonds	(25) Mortgages	(26) Other Loans	(27) Security Debt	(28) Taxes Payable	(29) Misc. Liabil-ities	(30) Total Liabil-ities	(31) Net Worth
1971	−.601	−2.523	.636	−.223	−2.464	−.715	−.120	−5.968	−46.811	13.619
1972	−.683	−2.482	−1.092	−.340	−2.395	−.744	−.104	−5.740	−40.403	−26.277
1973	−1.702	−3.921	−4.139	−.640	−5.658	−1.309	−.191	−11.753	−164.349	−20.199
1974	−2.966	−3.819	−5.715	−.174	−9.148	−1.368	−.260	−17.513	−208.348	59.597
1975	−1.587	−1.837	.340	−.245	−4.882	−.683	−.132	−9.810	−69.825	5.022
1976	−1.223	−1.670	2.038	.156	−3.751	−.736	−.113	−8.407	−64.288	52.913
1977	−1.443	−1.791	−3.373	−.744	−4.540	−.983	−.154	−10.012	−105.935	−36.130
Sums										
1946–50	−.586	−1.182	−.498	−.087	−1.103	−2.015	−.358	−8.690	−163.729	−33.339
1951–55	−.227	−.744	−.506	−.135	−.868	−.559	−.211	−3.552	−47.028	−23.463
1956–60	−.324	−1.715	−2.497	−.229	−1.382	−.719	−.238	−5.234	−66.864	−35.282
1961–65	−.415	−3.212	−1.337	−.337	−2.368	−.927	−.212	−6.361	−69.318	−37.534
1966–70	−1.670	−12.148	−6.836	−1.108	−10.113	−3.459	−.484	−24.334	−280.344	−102.304
1971–75	−7.539	−14.581	−9.969	−1.621	−24.546	−4.818	−.807	−50.784	−529.735	31.761
1976–77	−2.666	−3.461	−1.335	−.588	−8.291	−1.719	−.266	−18.419	−170.223	16.783
Means										
1946–50	−.117	−.236	−.100	−.017	−.221	−.403	−.072	−1.738	−32.746	−6.668
1951–55	−.045	−.149	−.101	−.027	−.174	−.112	−.042	−.710	−9.406	−4.693
1956–60	−.065	−.343	−.499	−.046	−.276	−.144	−.048	−1.047	−13.373	−7.056
1961–65	−.083	−.642	−.267	−.067	−.474	−.185	−.042	−1.272	−13.864	−7.507
1966–70	−.334	−2.430	−1.367	−.222	−2.023	−.692	−.097	−4.867	−56.069	−20.461
1971–75	−1.508	−2.916	−1.994	−.324	−4.909	−.964	−.161	−10.157	−105.947	6.352
1976–77	−1.333	−1.730	−.667	−.294	−4.145	−.860	−.133	−9.210	−85.112	8.391
Sums, 1946–77	−13.427	−37.043	−22.977	−4.103	−48.671	−14.217	−2.577	−117.375	−1,327.241	−183.378
Means, 1946–77	−.420	−1.158	−.718	−.128	−1.521	−.444	−.081	−3.668	−41.476	−5.731

Table 5.55 Government, Net Revaluations in Detail, Nonhuman Capital, (Billions of Dollars, 1946–77)

(1) Year	(2) Total Tangible Assets	(3) Total Repro-ducible Assets	(4) Residential Structures	(5) Nonres-idential Plant and Equipment	(6) Inven-tories	(7) Land	(8) Total Financial Assets	(9) Demand Deposits, Currency, and Time Deposits	(10) Gold, SDRs, & Foreign Exchange
1946	−12.695	−10.837	−.109	−3.988	−6.741	−1.858	−16.876	−3.445	−4.206
1947	9.990	10.299	.060	12.634	−2.394	−.309	−9.350	−.894	−2.452
1948	8.007	7.703	−.486	9.756	−1.567	.304	−2.423	−.276	−.782
1949	1.259	−.079	.105	.908	−1.092	1.339	2.354	.205	.517
1950	−.303	−1.744	−.101	−1.250	−.393	1.442	−7.991	−.910	−2.133
1951	5.920	5.900	.007	8.389	−2.496	.020	−4.765	−.409	−.926
1952	−1.775	−4.411	.003	−.305	−4.109	2.636	−2.188	−.261	−.497
1953	2.699	−1.516	−.013	−3.445	1.942	4.215	−.731	−.134	−.245
1954	.651	−1.393	−.013	−6.981	5.600	2.044	−1.708	−.272	−.486
1955	20.511	15.216	−.007	12.528	2.695	5.295	−5.022	−.431	−.768
1956	4.684	.633	−.150	2.099	−1.315	4.050	−7.253	−.604	−1.147
1957	3.746	−1.955	−.016	.569	−2.508	5.700	−1.141	−.339	−.681
1958	1.346	−3.304	.146	−2.931	−.519	4.650	−4.980	−.270	−.516
1959	1.283	−3.629	.049	−2.490	−1.188	4.912	−5.393	−.378	−.644
1960	6.115	.875	.003	1.936	−1.063	5.240	2.176	−.195	−.292
1961	10.445	3.675	−.089	4.951	−1.187	6.771	−3.303	−.306	−.380
1962	3.669	−1.821	−.143	.690	−2.368	5.490	−1.341	−.429	−.484
1963	3.359	−3.221	−.073	−2.027	−1.121	6.579	−3.347	−.366	−.354
1964	7.646	1.147	−.107	−.065	1.320	6.499	−2.494	−.490	−.414
1965	5.989	1.569	−.304	.603	1.271	4.419	−7.595	−.821	−.626
1966	2.718	−3.135	−.388	−1.425	−1.322	5.853	−8.023	−1.149	−.828
1967	2.335	−1.645	.294	−.773	−1.166	3.980	−11.919	−1.274	−.831
1968	3.369	1.417	.912	2.692	−2.187	1.952	−13.588	−1.873	−1.193
1969	13.284	12.395	.227	10.539	1.629	.889	−24.937	−2.113	−1.476
1970	11.930	11.063	−.418	15.610	−4.130	.868	−9.152	−2.126	−1.380

Table 5.55 (continued)

(1) Year	(2) Total Tangible Assets	(3) Total Repro-ducible Assets	(4) Residential Structures	(5) Nonres-idential Plant and Equipment	(6) Inven-tories	(7) Land	(8) Total Financial Assets	(9) Demand Deposits, Currency, and Time Deposits	(10) Gold, SDRs, & Foreign Exchange
1971	6.652	7.903	−.369	9.804	− 1.533	−1.251	− 11.774	− 2.423	− 1.199
1972	30.541	15.586	.583	11.785	3.218	14.955	− 14.647	− 2.661	− 1.118
1973	64.212	57.703	.851	41.722	15.130	6.509	− 41.298	− 5.495	− 2.193
1974	50.640	37.850	−.247	29.997	8.099	12.790	− 29.047	− 8.138	− 3.105
1975	1.921	− 6.889	.456	− 6.053	− 1.291	8.810	− 24.934	− 4.707	− 1.869
1976	− 4.571	−22.868	1.509	−23.468	− .909	18.297	− 10.422	− 4.035	− 1.682
1977	− 2.520	−12.495	2.294	−12.982	− 1.807	9.975	− 50.424	− 4.993	− 2.080
Sums									
1946–50	6.259	5.341	−.530	18.059	−12.188	.918	− 34.287	− 5.320	− 9.055
1951–55	28.006	13.796	−.023	10.186	3.632	14.209	− 14.413	− 1.507	− 2.921
1956–60	17.173	− 7.380	.031	− .817	− 6.594	24.553	− 16.591	− 1.786	− 3.280
1961–65	31.107	1.350	−.716	4.152	− 2.086	29.757	− 18.081	− 2.411	− 2.257
1966–70	33.636	20.095	.627	26.643	− 7.175	13.541	− 67.618	− 8.536	− 5.707
1971–75	153.966	112.153	1.274	87.255	23.623	41.813	−121.699	−23.424	− 9.485
1976–77	− 7.091	−35.363	3.803	−36.450	− 2.716	28.271	− 60.846	− 9.028	− 3.762
Means									
1946–50	1.252	1.068	−.106	3.612	− 2.438	.184	− 6.857	− 1.064	− 1.811
1951–55	5.601	2.759	−.005	2.037	.726	2.842	− 2.883	− .301	− .584
1956–60	3.435	− 1.476	.006	− .163	− 1.319	4.911	− 3.318	− .357	− .656
1961–65	6.221	.270	−.143	.830	− .417	5.951	− 3.616	− .482	− .451
1966–70	6.727	4.019	.125	5.329	− 1.435	2.708	− 13.524	− 1.707	− 1.141
1971–75	30.793	22.431	.255	17.451	4.725	8.363	− 24.340	− 4.685	− 1.897
1976–77	− 3.546	−17.681	1.902	−18.225	− 1.358	14.136	− 30.423	− 4.514	− 1.881
Sums, 1946–77	263.056	109.992	4.467	109.028	− 3.503	153.064	−333.535	−52.012	−36.468
Means, 1946–77	8.221	3.437	.140	3.407	− .109	4.783	− 10.423	− 1.625	− 1.140

Table 5.55 (continued)

(1) Year	(11) U.S. Gov't Securities	(12) State and Local Obligations	(13) Mortgages	(14) Other Loans	(15) Taxes Receivable	(16) Trade Credit	(17) Misc. Assets	(18) Total Assets	(19) State and Local Obligations
1946	−5.531	−.314	−.420	−1.058	−1.570	−.084	−.247	−29.571	−2.752
1947	−3.601	−.181	−.242	−.946	−.900	−.005	−.130	.640	−1.908
1948	−.599	−.030	−.040	−.350	−.305	0	−.040	5.584	−.319
1949	1.003	.072	.094	.247	.193	0	.024	3.614	.855
1950	−2.307	−.160	−.238	−1.099	−1.027	−.018	−.100	−8.294	−1.924
1951	−1.932	−.137	−.223	−.499	−.576	−.020	−.044	1.155	−1.673
1952	−.649	−.040	−.071	−.290	−.325	−.033	−.024	−3.963	−.590
1953	.019	.001	−.026	−.156	−.159	−.018	−.012	1.969	−.001
1954	−.244	−.016	.003	−.324	−.302	−.039	−.028	−1.057	−.241
1955	−2.241	−.150	−.328	−.518	−.471	−.063	−.051	15.489	−2.677
1956	−2.994	−.193	−.648	−.781	−.705	−.089	−.092	−2.569	−3.878
1957	.800	.047	−.015	−.463	−.371	−.051	−.066	2.605	.860
1958	−2.789	−.189	−.500	−.379	−.242	−.034	−.061	−3.634	−4.139
1959	−2.398	−.146	−.868	−.522	−.313	−.038	−.085	−4.111	−3.990
1960	2.515	.165	.457	−.256	−.155	−.018	−.044	8.291	3.791
1961	−1.463	−.088	−.387	−.378	−.204	−.025	−.070	7.142	−2.596
1962	.372	.038	.103	−.535	−.275	−.035	−.097	2.327	.636
1963	−1.503	−.057	−.269	−.461	−.230	−.032	−.077	.011	−2.484
1964	−.466	−.010	−.083	−.606	−.291	−.044	−.091	5.152	−.833
1965	−3.450	−.115	−.840	−1.044	−.480	−.077	−.143	−1.606	−5.537
1966	−2.266	−.057	−1.207	−1.537	−.655	−.130	−.192	−5.305	−3.202
1967	−5.284	−.147	−1.877	−1.621	−.519	−.182	−.185	−9.584	−8.201
1968	−4.856	−.126	−1.978	−2.356	−.665	−.291	−.250	−10.219	−7.661
1969	−11.069	−.277	−5.483	−3.086	−.749	−.379	−.305	−11.652	−17.038
1970	−.270	−.011	−.911	−3.191	−.567	−.354	−.342	2.778	−1.008

Table 5.55 (continued)

(1) Year	(11) U.S. Gov't Securities	(12) State and Local Obligations	(13) Mortgages	(14) Other Loans	(15) Taxes Receivable	(16) Trade Credit	(17) Misc. Assets	(18) Total Assets	(19) State and Local Obligations
1971	− 3.439	− .036	− .498	− 3.046	− .509	− .269	− .355	− 5.121	− 6.815
1972	− 4.488	− .038	− 2.438	− 2.876	− .511	− .188	− .329	15.894	− 8.187
1973	−15.323	− .267	− 9.879	− 5.978	− 1.034	− .329	− .799	22.914	− 23.682
1974	4.226	.041	− 8.674	− 9.871	− 1.644	− .529	−1.353	21.593	6.804
1975	− 6.179	− .234	− 3.611	− 6.246	− .899	− .370	− .818	−23.013	− 9.528
1976	− 1.041	− .037	3.828	− 5.492	− .885	− .350	− .726	−14.993	− 1.619
1977	−18.578	− .802	−14.495	− 6.935	− 1.250	− .394	− .898	−52.944	− 25.128
Sums									
1946–50	−11.036	− .614	− .845	− 3.206	− 3.609	− .107	− .494	−28.028	− 6.047
1951–55	− 5.048	− .342	− .645	− 1.786	− 1.832	− .173	− .159	13.593	− 5.182
1956–60	− 4.867	− .316	− 1.574	− 2.402	− 1.787	− .231	− .348	.582	− 7.357
1961–65	− 6.510	− .232	− 1.476	− 3.024	− 1.481	− .213	− .478	13.026	− 10.814
1966–70	−23.745	− .618	−11.456	−11.791	− 3.155	−1.337	−1.274	−33.982	− 37.110
1971–75	−25.204	− .533	−25.100	−28.016	− 4.597	−1.686	−3.654	32.267	− 41.409
1976–77	−19.618	− .839	−10.667	−12.427	− 2.135	− .744	−1.626	−67.937	− 26.747
Means									
1946–50	− 2.207	− .123	− .169	− .641	− .722	− .021	− .099	− 5.606	− 1.209
1951–55	− 1.010	− .068	− .129	− .357	− .366	− .035	− .032	2.719	− 1.036
1956–60	− .973	− .063	− .315	− .480	− .357	− .046	− .070	.116	− 1.471
1961–65	− 1.302	− .046	− .295	− .605	− .296	− .043	− .096	2.605	− 2.163
1966–70	− 4.749	− .124	− 2.291	− 2.358	− .631	− .267	− .255	− 6.796	− 7.422
1971–75	− 5.041	− .107	− 5.020	− 5.603	− .919	− .337	− .731	6.453	− 8.282
1976–77	− 9.809	− .419	− 5.333	− 6.214	− 1.067	− .372	− .813	−33.969	− 13.374
Sums, 1946–77	−96.027	−3.493	−51.764	−62.653	−18.595	−4.490	−8.033	−70.479	−134.667
Means, 1946–77	− 3.001	− .109	− 1.618	− 1.958	− .581	− .140	− .251	− 2.202	− 4.208

Table 5.55 (continued)

(1) Year	(20) U.S. Gov't Securities	(21) Mortgages	(22) Trade Debt	(23) Pension Funds, Life Insurance	(24) Currency, Demand Deposits, Time Deposits	(25) Vault Cash, Member Bank Reserves	(26) Misc. Liabil-ities	(27) Total Liabil-ities	(28) Net Worth
1946	− 46.437	0	− .398	− 1.208	− 5.122	− 2.996	− 1.022	− 59.935	30.363
1947	− 28.818	0	− .108	− .790	− 2.702	− 1.732	− .546	− 36.604	37.244
1948	− 4.950	0	− .025	− .258	− .791	− .549	− .163	− 7.055	12.639
1949	8.894	0	.019	.181	.490	.361	.098	10.898	− 7.284
1950	− 19.579	0	− .137	− .863	− 1.981	− 1.358	− .409	− 26.252	17.957
1951	− 14.824	0	− .086	− .398	− .868	− .634	− .179	− 18.662	19.817
1952	− 4.304	0	− .087	− .235	− .483	− .372	− .091	− 6.142	2.179
1953	.203	0	− .034	− .124	− .247	− .187	− .046	− .436	2.405
1954	− 1.583	0	− .068	− .257	− .502	− .371	− .095	− 3.116	2.059
1955	− 14.327	0	− .107	− .413	− .794	− .570	− .150	− 19.039	34.528
1956	− 17.918	0	− .165	− .632	− 1.156	− .846	− .214	− 24.809	22.240
1957	4.749	− .006	− .103	− .382	− .668	− .496	− .122	3.832	− 1.227
1958	− 16.475	− .047	− .086	− .312	− .520	− .379	− .096	− 22.055	18.421
1959	− 14.173	− .074	− .116	− .424	− .682	− .480	− .125	− 20.064	15.953
1960	15.348	.012	− .056	− .206	− .320	− .218	− .059	18.291	−10.000
1961	− 8.404	− .048	− .084	− .302	− .445	− .298	− .085	− 12.261	19.403
1962	2.498	− .001	− .116	− .409	− .588	− .399	− .112	1.510	.817
1963	− 7.405	− .041	− .092	− .329	− .474	− .303	− .083	− 11.212	11.223
1964	− 2.082	− .008	− .111	− .412	− .602	− .366	− .100	− 4.513	9.664
1965	− 15.183	− .090	− .187	− .681	− .992	− .598	− .155	− 23.423	21.816
1966	− 8.596	− .083	− .285	− .966	− 1.410	− .854	− .212	− 15.609	10.304
1967	− 21.750	− .111	− .327	− 1.004	− 1.490	− .913	− .236	− 34.033	24.449
1968	− 19.681	− .083	− .483	− 1.432	− 2.130	− 1.331	− .347	− 33.148	22.929
1969	− 40.862	− .206	− .580	− 1.740	− 2.604	− 1.609	− .424	− 65.062	53.410
1970	− 1.636	.043	− .540	− 1.718	− 2.575	− 1.547	− .455	− 9.437	12.215

Table 5.55 (continued)

(1) Year	(20) U.S. Gov't Securities	(21) Mortgages	(22) Trade Debt	(23) Pension Funds, Life Insurance	(24) Currency, Demand Deposits, Time Deposits	(25) Vault Cash, Member Bank Reserves	(26) Misc. Liabil-ities	(27) Total Liabil-ities	(28) Net Worth
1871	− 15.162	.033	− .495	− 1.692	− 2.522	− 1.546	− .450	− 28.649	23.528
1972	− 18.167	− .025	− .461	− 1.679	− 2.489	− 1.479	− .403	− 32.889	48.783
1973	− 54.768	− .152	− .907	− 3.323	− 4.950	− 2.848	− .902	− 91.533	114.447
1974	15.636	− .070	− 1.469	− 4.983	− 7.630	− 4.197	− 1.543	2.549	19.044
1975	− 25.744	− .006	− 1.015	− 3.059	− 4.924	− 2.414	− .956	− 47.645	24.633
1976	− 4.284	.041	− 1.053	− 2.738	− 4.598	− 1.983	− .840	− 17.075	2.082
1977	− 72.202	− .090	− 1.466	− 3.476	− 5.730	− 2.341	− 1.047	−111.482	58.537
Sums									
1946–50	− 90.890	0	− .650	− 2.938	−10.107	− 6.274	− 2.042	−118.948	90.920
1951–55	− 34.836	0	− .362	− 1.425	− 2.895	− 2.134	− .561	− 47.395	60.987
1956–60	− 28.469	− .115	− .525	− 1.957	− 3.347	− 2.421	− .615	− 44.805	45.387
1961–65	− 30.575	− .187	− .589	− 2.133	− 3.100	− 1.963	− .535	− 49.898	62.924
1966–70	− 92.525	− .440	− 2.215	− 6.860	−10.210	− 6.254	− 1.674	−157.289	123.307
1971–75	− 98.206	− .219	− 4.346	−14.735	−22.515	−12.484	− 4.253	−198.167	230.434
1976–77	− 76.487	− .048	− 2.519	− 6.215	−10.328	− 4.324	− 1.887	−128.556	60.619
Means									
1946–50	− 18.178	0	− .130	− .588	− 2.021	− 1.255	− .408	− 23.790	18.184
1951–55	− 6.967	0	− .072	− .285	− .579	− .427	− .112	− 9.479	12.197
1956–60	− 5.694	− .023	− .105	− .391	− .669	− .484	− .123	− 8.961	9.077
1961–65	− 6.115	− .037	− .118	− .427	− .620	− .393	− .107	− 9.980	12.585
1966–70	− 18.505	− .088	− .443	− 1.372	− 2.042	− 1.251	− .335	− 31.458	24.661
1971–75	− 19.641	− .044	− .869	− 2.947	− 4.503	− 2.497	− .851	− 39.633	46.087
1976–77	− 38.243	− .024	− 1.260	− 3.107	− 5.164	− 2.162	− .944	− 64.278	30.310
Sums, 1946–77	−451.988	−1.010	−11.208	−36.262	−62.501	−35.854	−11.568	−745.057	674.578
Means, 1946–77	− 14.125	− .032	− .350	− 1.133	− 1.953	− 1.120	− .361	− 23.283	21.081

Table 5.56 Government, Net Revaluations in Detail, Nonhuman Capital, (Billions of 1972 Dollars, 1946–77)

(1) Year	(2) Total Tangible Assets	(3) Total Repro-ducible Assets	(4) Residential Structures	(5) Nonres-idential Plant and Equipment	(6) Inven-tories	(7) Land	(8) Total Financial Assets	(9) Demand Deposits, Currency, and Time Deposits	(10) Gold, SDRs, & Foreign Exchange
1946	−30.738	−26.240	−.263	−9.656	−16.321	−4.498	−40.863	−8.342	−10.185
1947	20.430	21.062	.122	25.836	−4.896	−.632	−19.121	−1.829	−5.014
1948	14.938	14.371	−.906	18.201	−2.924	.568	−4.521	−.515	−1.459
1949	2.298	−.145	.193	1.656	−1.993	2.443	4.296	.374	.944
1950	−.536	−3.088	−.179	−2.213	−.696	2.552	−14.144	−1.610	−3.775
1951	9.736	9.704	.012	13.797	−4.106	.033	−7.837	−.673	−1.522
1952	−2.858	−7.103	.004	−.491	−6.616	4.245	−3.523	−.420	−.800
1953	4.291	−2.410	−.021	−5.477	3.087	6.701	−1.161	−.213	−.390
1954	1.027	−2.197	−.020	−11.011	8.833	3.224	−2.694	−.428	−.766
1955	31.652	23.482	−.010	19.333	4.159	8.171	−7.750	−.666	−1.185
1956	6.858	.927	−.220	3.073	−1.926	5.930	−10.619	−.884	−1.679
1957	5.283	−2.757	−.023	.803	−3.537	8.040	−1.609	−.478	−.961
1958	1.901	−4.667	.206	−4.140	−.734	6.568	−7.034	−.381	−.729
1959	1.792	−5.069	.068	−3.478	−1.660	6.861	−7.533	−.528	−.900
1960	8.505	1.217	.004	2.692	−1.478	7.288	3.027	−.272	−.406
1961	14.589	5.133	−.124	6.915	−1.658	9.456	−4.613	−.427	−.530
1962	5.095	−2.529	−.199	.959	−3.289	7.624	−1.863	−.595	−.672
1963	4.658	−4.467	−.101	−2.811	−1.554	9.125	−4.642	−.507	−.491
1964	10.502	1.576	−.148	−.090	1.813	8.927	−3.426	−.673	−.568
1965	8.115	2.127	−.412	.817	1.722	5.988	−10.291	−1.112	−.848
1966	3.567	−4.114	−.509	−1.870	−1.735	7.681	−10.529	−1.509	−1.087
1967	2.967	−2.090	.374	−.983	−1.481	5.057	−15.145	−1.619	−1.056
1968	4.103	1.726	1.110	3.279	−2.664	2.378	−16.550	−2.281	−1.453
1969	15.287	14.264	.261	12.128	1.875	1.023	−28.696	−2.431	−1.699
1970	13.096	12.143	−.459	17.135	−4.534	.952	−10.046	−2.334	−1.514

Table 5.56 (continued)

(1) Year	(2) Total Tangible Assets	(3) Total Repro-ducible Assets	(4) Residential Structures	(5) Nonres-idential Plant and Equipment	(6) Inven-tories	(7) Land	(8) Total Financial Assets	(9) Demand Deposits, Currency, and Time Deposits	(10) Gold, SDRs, & Foreign Exchange
1971	6.937	8.241	− .384	10.224	− 1.598	−1.304	− 12.277	− 2.527	− 1.250
1972	30.541	15.586	.583	11.785	3.218	14.955	− 14.647	− 2.661	− 1.118
1973	60.577	54.437	.803	39.361	14.274	6.140	− 38.960	− 5.184	− 2.069
1974	43.024	32.158	− .210	25.486	6.881	10.867	− 24.679	− 6.914	− 2.638
1975	1.451	− 5.203	.344	− 4.572	− .975	6.654	− 18.832	− 3.555	− 1.412
1976	− 3.270	−16.357	1.080	−16.787	− .650	13.088	− 7.455	− 2.886	− 1.203
1977	− 1.677	− 8.313	1.526	− 8.637	− 1.202	6.637	− 33.549	− 3.322	− 1.384
Sums									
1946–50	6.393	5.960	−1.033	33.824	−26.831	.432	− 74.353	−11.922	−19.488
1951–55	43.848	21.475	− .035	16.152	5.358	22.373	− 22.965	− 2.400	− 4.664
1956–60	24.338	−10.349	.036	− 1.049	− 9.335	34.687	− 23.768	− 2.542	− 4.674
1961–65	42.960	1.839	− .984	5.789	− 2.967	41.121	− 24.836	− 3.315	− 3.109
1966–70	39.020	21.929	.778	29.690	− 8.538	17.091	− 80.966	−10.174	− 6.808
1971–75	142.531	105.218	1.136	82.283	21.800	37.312	−109.395	−20.841	− 8.488
1976–77	− 4.946	−24.671	2.606	−25.424	− 1.852	19.724	− 41.004	− 6.208	− 2.587
Means									
1946–50	1.279	1.192	− .207	6.765	− 5.366	.086	− 14.871	− 2.384	− 3.898
1951–55	8.770	4.295	− .007	3.230	1.072	4.475	− 4.593	− .480	− .933
1956–60	4.868	− 2.070	.007	− .210	− 1.867	6.937	− 4.754	− .508	− .935
1961–65	8.592	.368	− .197	1.158	− .593	8.224	− 4.967	− .663	− .622
1966–70	7.804	4.386	.156	5.938	− 1.708	3.418	− 16.193	− 2.035	− 1.362
1971–75	28.506	21.044	.227	16.457	4.360	7.462	− 21.879	− 4.168	− 1.698
1976–77	− 2.473	−12.335	1.303	−12.712	− .926	9.862	− 20.502	− 3.104	− 1.293
Sums, 1946–77	294.142	121.402	2.504	141.264	−22.366	172.740	−377.286	−57.403	−49.818
Means, 1946–77	9.192	3.794	.078	4.415	− .699	5.398	− 11.790	− 1.794	− 1.557

Table 5.56 (continued)

(1) Year	(11) U.S. Gov't Securities	(12) State and Local Obligations	(13) Mortgages	(14) Other Loans	(15) Taxes Receivable	(16) Trade Credit	(17) Misc. Assets	(18) Total Assets	(19) State and Local Obligations
1946	−13.392	−.761	−1.016	−2.563	−3.801	−.204	−.599	−71.601	−6.663
1947	−7.365	−.370	−.495	−1.934	−1.840	−.009	−.265	1.309	−3.901
1948	−1.118	−.057	−.075	−.652	−.569	0	−.076	10.418	−.595
1949	1.829	.131	.172	.450	.353	0	.044	6.594	1.561
1950	−4.083	−.283	−.421	−1.945	−1.818	−.032	−.177	−14.680	−3.406
1951	−3.178	−.225	−.368	−.821	−.947	−.033	−.072	1.899	−2.752
1952	−1.045	−.064	−.114	−.467	−.523	−.053	−.038	−6.382	−.950
1953	.030	.001	−.041	−.248	−.252	−.029	−.020	3.130	−.002
1954	−.385	−.025	.004	−.511	−.476	−.062	−.044	−1.667	−.380
1955	−3.458	−.232	−.506	−.799	−.728	−.097	−.079	23.903	−4.130
1956	−4.384	−.282	−.948	−1.144	−1.032	−.130	−.135	−3.761	−5.678
1957	1.128	.066	−.022	−.653	−.524	−.073	−.093	3.674	1.213
1958	−3.939	−.267	−.706	−.536	−.342	−.047	−.086	−5.133	−5.846
1959	−3.349	−.204	−1.212	−.729	−.438	−.054	−.118	−5.741	−5.573
1960	3.497	.230	.636	−.356	−.216	−.025	−.061	11.532	5.273
1961	−2.044	−.124	−.541	−.528	−.285	−.036	−.098	9.976	−3.626
1962	.517	.053	.143	−.744	−.382	−.049	−.134	3.232	.883
1963	−2.084	−.079	−.373	−.639	−.319	−.045	−.106	.016	−3.445
1964	−.640	−.014	−.113	−.832	−.400	−.060	−.125	7.076	−1.144
1965	−4.675	−.156	−1.138	−1.415	−.651	−.104	−.193	−2.177	−7.503
1966	−2.974	−.075	−1.584	−2.017	−.860	−.171	−.252	−6.962	−4.203
1967	−6.714	−.186	−2.385	−2.059	−.660	−.232	−.235	−12.178	−10.421
1968	−5.914	−.153	−2.409	−2.870	−.810	−.354	−.305	−12.446	−9.331
1969	−12.738	−.319	−6.309	−3.551	−.862	−.436	−.351	−13.409	−19.606
1970	−.297	−.012	−1.000	−3.503	−.622	−.389	−.376	3.050	−1.107

Table 5.56 (continued)

(1) Year	(11) U.S. Gov't Securities	(12) State and Local Obligations	(13) Mortgages	(14) Other Loans	(15) Taxes Receivable	(16) Trade Credit	(17) Misc. Assets	(18) Total Assets	(19) State and Local Obligations
1971	− 3.586	− .037	− .519	− 3.176	− .530	− .281	− .370	− 5.340	− 7.107
1972	− 4.488	− .038	− 2.438	− 2.876	− .511	− .188	− .329	15.894	− 8.187
1973	− 14.456	− .252	− 9.320	− 5.639	− .976	− .311	− .754	21.617	− 22.342
1974	3.590	.035	− 7.369	− 8.386	− 1.397	− .450	−1.150	18.346	5.780
1975	− 4.667	− .177	− 2.728	− 4.718	− .679	− .280	− .618	−17.381	− 7.196
1976	− .744	− .026	2.738	− 3.929	− .633	− .251	− .521	−10.725	− 1.158
1977	− 12.360	− .533	− 9.644	− 4.614	− .831	− .262	− .598	−35.226	− 16.719
Sums									
1946–50	− 24.129	−1.340	− 1.835	− 6.645	− 7.676	− .245	−1.073	−67.960	− 13.004
1951–55	− 8.037	− .544	− 1.024	− 2.845	− 2.925	− .273	− .253	20.883	− 8.214
1956–60	− 7.047	− .458	− 2.253	− 3.418	− 2.552	− .329	− .494	.570	− 10.612
1961–65	− 8.926	− .319	− 2.022	− 4.157	− 2.037	− .293	− .657	18.123	− 14.835
1966–70	− 28.637	− .745	−13.688	−14.001	− 3.813	−1.582	−1.518	−41.946	− 44.667
1971–75	− 23.607	− .469	−22.374	−24.795	− 4.093	−1.508	−3.220	33.135	− 39.051
1976–77	− 13.105	− .560	− 6.906	− 8.543	− 1.464	− .513	−1.119	−45.950	− 17.877
Means									
1946–50	− 4.826	− .268	− .367	− 1.329	− 1.535	− .049	− .215	−13.592	− 2.601
1951–55	− 1.607	− .109	− .205	− .569	− .585	− .055	− .051	4.177	− 1.643
1956–60	− 1.409	− .092	− .451	− .684	− .510	− .066	− .099	.114	− 2.122
1961–65	− 1.785	− .064	− .404	− .831	− .407	− .059	− .131	3.625	− 2.967
1966–70	− 5.727	− .149	− 2.738	− 2.800	− .763	− .316	− .304	− 8.389	− 8.933
1971–75	− 4.721	− .094	− 4.475	− 4.959	− .819	− .302	− .644	6.627	− 7.810
1976–77	− 6.552	− .280	− 3.453	− 4.271	− .732	− .256	− .559	−22.975	− 8.938
Sums, 1946–77	−113.487	−4.435	−50.103	−64.403	−24.561	−4.743	−8.334	−83.144	−148.261
Means, 1946–77	− 3.546	− .139	− 1.566	− 2.013	− .768	− .148	− .260	− 2.598	− 4.633

Table 5.56 (continued)

(1) Year	(20) U.S. Gov't Securities	(21) Mortgages	(22) Trade Debt	(23) Pension Funds, Life Insurance	(24) Currency, Demand Deposits, Time Deposits	(25) Vault Cash, Member Bank Reserves	(26) Misc. Liabil-ities	(27) Total Liabil-ities	(28) Net Worth
1946	−112.438	0	− .964	− 2.926	−12.403	− 7.253	− 2.474	−145.121	73.519
1947	− 58.933	0	− .221	− 1.616	− 5.526	− 3.541	− 1.116	− 74.854	76.163
1948	− 9.235	0	− .047	− .481	− 1.476	− 1.024	− .304	− 13.162	23.580
1949	16.230	0	.034	.331	.894	.659	.179	19.886	−13.292
1950	− 34.653	0	− .242	− 1.527	− 3.506	− 2.404	− .725	− 46.463	31.783
1951	− 24.381	0	− .142	− .654	− 1.428	− 1.042	− .294	− 30.694	32.593
1952	− 6.931	0	− .108	− .378	− .779	− .599	− .146	− 9.891	3.509
1953	.322	0	− .054	− .197	− .392	− .298	− .073	− .693	3.823
1954	− 2.497	0	− .107	− .405	− .792	− .585	− .150	− 4.915	3.248
1955	− 22.110	0	− .165	− .637	− 1.226	− .880	− .232	− 29.381	53.283
1956	− 26.234	0	− .241	− .926	− 1.692	− 1.239	− .313	− 36.323	32.562
1957	6.698	− .008	− .145	− .539	− .943	− .700	− .172	5.404	− 1.730
1958	− 23.270	− .067	− .122	− .441	− .735	− .536	− .135	− 31.152	26.019
1959	− 19.794	− .103	− .162	− .592	− .952	− .671	− .175	− 28.022	22.280
1960	21.346	.017	− .078	− .287	− .446	− .304	− .082	25.440	−13.908
1961	− 11.737	− .067	− .117	− .422	− .621	− .416	− .119	− 17.124	27.100
1962	3.470	− .001	− .161	− .568	− .817	− .553	− .156	2.098	1.135
1963	− 10.271	− .056	− .128	− .456	− .657	− .421	− .116	− 15.550	15.566
1964	− 2.860	− .011	− .152	− .566	− .826	− .502	− .137	− 6.199	13.275
1965	− 20.573	− .122	− .253	− .923	− 1.344	− .810	− .210	− 31.738	29.561
1966	− 11.281	− .109	− .374	− 1.268	− 1.850	− 1.121	− .279	− 20.485	13.522
1967	− 27.637	− .141	− .415	− 1.276	− 1.894	− 1.160	− .300	− 43.244	31.066
1968	− 23.972	− .101	− .588	− 1.744	− 2.595	− 1.621	− .422	− 40.375	27.928
1969	− 47.022	− .237	− .667	− 2.003	− 2.997	− 1.851	− .488	− 74.870	61.461
1970	− 1.796	.047	− .593	− 1.885	− 2.827	− 1.698	− .500	− 10.359	13.408

Table 5.56 (continued)

(1) Year	(20) U.S. Gov't Securities	(21) Mortgages	(22) Trade Debt	(23) Pension Funds, Life Insurance	(24) Currency, Demand Deposits, Time Deposits	(25) Vault Cash, Member Bank Reserves	(26) Misc. Liabilities	(27) Total Liabilities	(28) Net Worth
1971	− 15.811	.035	− .516	− 1.764	− 2.630	− 1.612	− .470	− 29.874	24.534
1972	− 18.167	− .025	− .461	− 1.679	− 2.489	− 1.479	− .403	− 32.889	48.783
1973	− 51.668	− .144	− .856	− 3.135	− 4.670	− 2.687	− .851	− 86.351	107.969
1974	13.285	− .059	− 1.248	− 4.233	− 6.483	− 3.566	− 1.311	2.166	16.180
1975	− 19.444	− .004	− .766	− 2.310	− 3.719	− 1.823	− .722	− 35.986	18.605
1976	− 3.065	.030	− .753	− 1.959	− 3.289	− 1.419	− .601	− 12.214	1.489
1977	− 48.039	− .060	− .975	− 2.313	− 3.812	− 1.558	− .697	− 74.173	38.947
Sums									
1946–50	−199.029	0	− 1.441	− 6.220	−22.017	−13.564	− 4.440	−259.714	191.754
1951–55	− 55.597	0	− .576	− 2.270	− 4.616	− 3.404	− .895	− 75.573	96.457
1956–60	− 41.254	− .161	− .747	− 2.784	− 4.768	− 3.450	− .877	− 64.653	65.223
1961–65	− 41.970	− .257	− .811	− 2.935	− 4.266	− 2.702	− .737	− 68.514	86.637
1966–70	−111.708	− .541	− 2.638	− 8.176	−12.162	− 7.452	− 1.988	−189.332	147.386
1971–75	− 91.805	− .198	− 3.847	−13.121	−19.990	−11.167	− 3.755	−182.935	216.070
1976–77	− 51.104	− .030	− 1.729	− 4.272	− 7.102	− 2.976	− 1.298	− 86.386	40.436
Means									
1946–50	− 39.806	0	− .288	− 1.244	− 4.403	− 2.713	− .888	− 51.943	38.351
1951–55	− 11.119	0	− .115	− .454	− .923	− .681	− .179	− 15.115	19.291
1956–60	− 8.251	− .032	− .149	− .557	− .954	− .690	− .175	− 12.931	13.045
1961–65	− 8.394	− .051	− .162	− .587	− .853	− .540	− .147	− 13.703	17.327
1966–70	− 22.342	− .108	− .528	− 1.635	− 2.432	− 1.490	− .398	− 37.866	29.477
1971–75	− 18.361	− .040	− .769	− 2.624	− 3.998	− 2.233	− .751	− 36.587	43.214
1976–77	− 25.552	− .015	− .864	− 2.136	− 3.551	− 1.488	− .649	− 43.193	20.218
Sums, 1946–77	−592.467	−1.187	−11.789	−39.778	−74.920	−44.715	−13.990	−927.107	843.963
Means, 1946–77	− 18.515	− .037	− .368	− 1.243	− 2.341	− 1.397	− .437	− 28.972	26.374

Table 5.57 GNP Implicit Price Deflators, 1945-IV to 1978-I

(1) Year	(2) First Quarter	(3) Second Quarter	(4) Third Quarter	(5) Fourth Quarter
1945	0	0	0	39.980
1946	41.540	43.100	44.800	46.630
1947	48.470	49.000	49.860	51.420
1948	52.290	52.900	53.790	53.530
1949	52.980	52.490	52.430	52.440
1950	52.280	52.720	54.300	55.160
1951	56.890	57.180	57.200	57.800
1952	57.690	57.640	58.000	58.650
1953	58.730	58.880	59.080	58.810
1954	59.540	59.740	59.610	59.900
1955	60.440	60.760	61.180	61.500
1956	62.030	62.540	63.250	63.770
1957	64.510	64.770	65.370	65.440
1958	65.690	65.830	66.210	66.410
1959	66.980	67.450	67.700	67.950
1960	68.420	68.550	68.810	68.940
1961	68.850	69.180	69.480	69.590
1962	70.170	70.410	70.600	71.030
1963	71.320	71.370	71.580	72.070
1964	72.280	72.530	72.930	73.080
1965	73.680	74.060	74.560	74.920
1966	75.680	76.570	77.020	77.730
1967	78.190	78.480	79.240	80.150
1968	81.180	82.120	82.880	84.040
1969	84.950	86.050	87.400	88.480
1970	89.810	90.910	91.740	92.990
1971	94.400	95.730	96.530	97.380
1972	98.760	99.450	100.290	101.440
1973	103.040	104.840	106.730	109.010
1974	111.580	114.280	117.700	121.450
1975	123.740	125.040	127.210	129.330
1976	131.470	133.060	134.560	136.350
1977	138.130	140.520	142.190	144.230
1978	146.710	0	0	0

Table 5.58 **Implicit Price Deflators for Fixed Investment, 1946–77, and for Human Capital, 1946–69**

(1) Year	(2) Fixed Investment Deflator (1972 = 100)	(3) Fixed Investment Deflator (1969 = 100)	(4) Human Capital Deflator (1969 = 100)
1946	41.3	47.5	44.0
1947	48.9	56.3	48.7
1948	53.6	61.7	52.0
1949	54.8	63.1	52.7
1950	56.5	65.0	54.0
1951	60.8	70.0	57.8
1952	62.1	71.5	60.1
1953	62.9	72.4	61.5
1954	63.4	73.0	62.5
1955	64.8	74.6	63.9
1956	68.3	78.6	66.2
1957	70.9	81.6	68.9
1958	70.8	81.5	71.0
1959	71.6	82.4	72.9
1960	71.9	82.7	74.6
1961	71.6	82.4	76.0
1962	72.0	82.9	77.8
1963	72.1	83.0	79.6
1964	72.8	83.8	81.7
1965	73.8	84.9	84.0
1966	76.2	87.7	87.3
1967	78.7	90.6	90.1
1968	82.1	94.5	94.6
1969	86.9	100.0	100.0
1970	91.1	104.8	
1971	95.9	110.4	
1972	100.0	115.1	
1973	106.0	122.0	
1974	117.7	135.4	
1975	132.4	152.4	
1976	139.8	160.9	
1977	150.3	173.0	

Table 5.59 **Bond Price Indexes Used in Par-to-Market Conversions, 1945–77**

(1) Year	(2) U.S. and State and Local Gov't Securities	(3) Corporate and Foreign Bonds	(4) All Listed Bonds
1945	105.310	99.090	103.640
1946	104.300	98.140	102.640
1947	101.230	95.240	99.620
1948	101.800	95.780	100.180
1949	104.090	97.940	102.430
1950	102.550	96.490	100.930
1951	99.000	93.150	97.430
1952	98.740	96.200	97.810
1953	99.670	95.210	98.320
1954	100.670	99.480	100.070
1955	97.270	97.760	97.080
1956	93.240	97.400	91.590
1957	97.350	88.090	94.850
1958	92.220	89.050	91.280
1959	88.830	83.770	87.480
1960	95.900	86.410	93.210
1961	94.090	88.130	92.260
1962	96.950	90.220	94.970
1963	95.620	90.450	94.200
1964	96.560	92.310	95.430
1965	93.730	91.320	93.070
1966	94.260	84.410	91.500
1967	90.630	82.070	87.940
1968	89.290	82.250	86.690
1969	82.050	72.120	77.800
1970	86.810	80.780	83.600
1971	87.860	89.930	89.110
1972	87.800	91.480	90.400
1973	82.820	85.710	85.160
1974	96.380	76.350	87.680
1975	98.160	84.130	91.890
1976	102.560	97.030	100.390
1977	98.430	93.130	96.520

Appendix: Sources and Methods

Marsha Courchane

Most of the summary tables dealing with nonhuman capital, including all of tables 5.1 to 5.31 and 5.44 to 5.46 and parts of others, are drawn from, or based upon data underlying, tables 5.47 to 5.56. The latter present net revaluations in detail for each of our five major sectors—households, noncorporate, nonfinancial corporate, private financial, and government, in current and in 1972 dollars. Sources and methods are therefore first reported for tables 5.47 to 5.56, which are then used as references for the earlier tables.

Net revaluations are calculated, as shown in the text (eq. 2), from data on end-of-year stocks, K, net investment, I, and GNP implicit price deflators. Net investment in financial assets and liabilities was generally taken as the first difference of their stocks (in current dollars, and before the application of bond price indexes, BPI, to convert from par to market value when applicable). For reproducible tangible assets, net investment was calculated as: (*a*) gross investment minus depreciation charges, or (*b*) the first difference of constant-dollar net stocks converted to current dollars by their own implicit stock deflator. Investment in land was assumed to be zero.

Current-dollar figures are generally presented in odd-numbered tables, and 1972 dollar results are shown in even-numbered tables. Unless otherwise indicated, the implicit price deflator for fixed investment is used to convert from current to 1972 dollars.

Table 5.47, Households, Current Dollars

Total tangible assets = total reproducible assets + land

Total reproducible assets = residential structures + nonprofit plant and equipment + consumer durables

Owner-occupied housing

K—Owner-occupied nonfarm—Musgrave [5.5.a][1]

I—Owner-occupied nonfarm—Musgrave [5.6.a]

Gross investment minus depreciation [5.5.a]

Nonprofit fixed capital

Residential structures

K—Musgrave [5.7, current dollars]

I—First differences of constant dollar net stocks, Musgrave [5.7, 1972 dollars], converted to current dollars by multiplying by the implicit price deflator for residential structures, SCB [11.a, table 7.1]

Nonresidential plant and equipment

K—Musgrave [5.1.a, current dollars]

*Number in brackets refer to "Sources" listed at the end of this appendix.

Parts of this appendix are drawn from the description of sources and methods prepared jointly by Marsha Courchane and René Moreno, Jr., for the original version of the paper.

I—Musgrave [5.1.a, historical cost, gross investment] minus [5.1.a, current-dollar depreciation]

Consumer durables
K—Musgrave [8]
I—Gross investment minus depreciation [8]

Land
K—FED [7]

Currency, demand deposits, and time deposits
K—FED [7]

U.S. government securities
K—FED [7] times BPI for U.S. and state and local governments

State and local obligations
K—FED [7] times BPI for U.S. and state and local governments

Corporate and foreign bonds
K—FED [7] times BPI for corporate and foreign bonds

Commercial paper
K—FED [7], open market paper plus money market fund shares

Corporate equities
K—FED [7]
I—FED [7], flow item, net purchase of corporate shares

Mortgages
K—FED [7] times BPI for all listed bonds

Life insurance and pension funds
K—FED [7]
I—FED [7], flow item

Noncorporate equities
K—Net worth, noncorporate sector
I—Net investment, noncorporate sector

Miscellaneous assets
K—FED [7], miscellaneous assets plus security credit

Mortgage debt
K—FED [7], home and other mortgages, times BPI for all listed bonds

Other loans and credit
K—FED [7], installment consumer credit, other consumer credit, bank loans n.e.c., and other loans

Trade credit
K—FED [7]

Miscellaneous liabilities
K—FED [7], security credit and deferred and unpaid life insurance premiums

Table 5.48, Households, 1972 Dollars
Table 5.47 converted to 1972 dollars using implicit price deflators for fixed investment, SCB [11.a, table 7.1]

Table 5.49, Noncorporate Nonfarm, and Farm, Current Dollars

Residential structures and nonresidential plant and equipment

Residential structures

K—SCB [11.b] Noncorporate, table 6, minus Musgrave [5.5.a] and Musgrave [5.7], current dollars

I—First difference of constant-dollar net stocks, SCB [11.b.], noncorporate, converted to current dollars with residential structures implicit price deflators, SCB [11.a., table 7.1] minus (net investment, owner-occupied nonfarm residential [5.6.a, 5.5.a.] and net investment, nonprofit residential capital [5.7] as computed in table 31).

Nonresidential plant and equipment

K—Musgrave [5.1.b], current-dollar net stocks, minus Musgrave [5.1.a], current-dollar net stocks.

I—Musgrave [5.1.b], historical dollars, gross investments minus [5.1.b], current dollars, depreciation; minus Musgrave [5.1.a], historical dollars, gross investments minus [5.1.a] current dollars, depreciation.

Fixed nonresidential corporate farm capital is included in the nonfinancial corporate sector. Flow of Funds data, utilized for the items below, however, include all of farm business with noncorporate.

Inventories

K—FED [7]

I—FED [7]

Land

K—FED [7]

Currency and demand deposits

K—FED [7]

Consumer credit

K—FED [7]

Miscellaneous assets

K—FED [7]

Mortgage debt

K—FED [7] times BPI for all listed bonds.

Other loans

K—FED [7], bank loans n.e.c., and other loans

Trade debt

K—FED [7]

Table 5.50, Noncorporate Nonfarm, and Farm, 1972 Dollars

Table 5.49 converted to 1972 dollars using implicit price deflators for fixed investment, SCB [11.a, table 7.1]

Table 5.51, Nonfinancial Corporations, Current Dollars

Residential structures + nonresidential plant and equipment

Residential structures

K—SCB [11.b, tables 6, 8]

I—First differences of constant-dollar net stocks multiplied by residential investment deflator from SCB [11.a., table 7.1]

Nonresidential plant and equipment

K—Musgrave [5.1.c]

I—Musgrave [5.1.c] historical costs gross investment minus current dollar depreciation

Inventories

K—FED [7]

I—FED [7]

Land

K—FED [8A]

Currency, demand deposits, and time deposits

K—FED [7]

U.S. government securities

K—FED [7] times BPI for U.S. and state and local governments.

State and local obligations

K—FED [7] times BPI for U.S. and state and local governments

Commercial paper

K—FED [7]

Security R.P.s

K—FED [7]

Consumer and trade credit

K—FED [7]

Miscellaneous assets

K—FED [7]

Corporate and foreign bonds

K—FED [7] (including tax-exempt bonds) times BPI for corporate and foreign bonds

Mortgage debt

K—FED [7] times BPI for all listed bonds

Other loans

K—FED [7] (includes bank loans n.e.c., open market paper, acceptances, finance company loans, and U.S. government loans)

Profit taxes payable

K—FED [7]

Net trade debt

K—FED [7]

Miscellaneous liabilities

K—FED [7]

Table 5.52, Nonfinancial Corporations, 1972 Dollars
Table 5.51 converted to 1972 dollars using implicit price deflators for fixed investment, SCB [11.a, table 7.1]

Table 5.53, Private Financial, Current Dollars
Residential structures + nonresidential plant and equipment
Residential:
K—SCB [11.b, table 6] (total corporate minus nonfinancial)
I—First differences of constant dollar net stocks of residential structures multiplied by residential investment deflator from SCB [11.a, table 7.1]
Nonresidential:
K—Musgrave [5.1.d minus 5.1.c]
I—Musgrave [(5.1.d)–(5.1.c), historical cost, gross investment] minus [(5.1.d.)–(5.1.c), current-dollar depreciation].
Land
K—FED [8A]
Currency, demand deposits, and time deposits
K—FED [7]
Interbank claims
K—FED [7]
Corporate shares
K—FED [7]
U.S. government securities
K—FED [7] (includes U.S. Treasury securities and federal agency securities) times BPI for U.S. and state and local governments
State and local obligations
K—FED [7] times BPI for U.S. and state and local governments
Corporate and foreign bonds
K—FED [7] times BPI for corporate and foreign bonds
Mortgages
K—FED [7] times BPI for all listed bonds
Other loans and credit
K—FED [7] (sum of bank loans n.e.c., other loans, private short-term paper, and consumer credit)
Security credit
K—FED [7]
Trade credit
K—FED [7]
Miscellaneous assets
K—FED [7]
Currency, demand deposits, and time deposits
K—FED [7]

Life insurance and pension funds
K—FED [7]
Investment company shares
K—FED [7]
Corporate and foreign bonds
K—FED [7] times BPI for corporate and foreign bonds
Mortgages
K—FED [7] times BPI for all listed bonds
Other loans and credit
K—FED [7] (sum of bank loans n.e.c., private short term paper, and other loans)
Security debt
K—FED [7]
Taxes payable
K—FED [7]
Miscellaneous liabilities
K—FED [7]

Table 5.54, Private Financial, 1972 Dollars
Table 5.53 converted to 1972 dollars using implicit price deflator for fixed investment, SCB [11.a, table 7.1]

Table 5.55, Government, Current Dollars
The government sector includes U.S. government, state and local governments, federally sponsored credit agencies, monetary authorities and mortgage pools. Capital stocks of government may be held by some or all of these components.
Residential structures + nonresidential plant and equipment
Residential structures:
K—Musgrave [5.2.c current dollars]
I—Musgrave [5.11.a, historical-dollar gross investment] minus Musgrave [5.11.b, current-dollar depreciation]
Nonresidential plant and equipment
K—Musgrave [5.2.a], current dollars, plus [5.2.b], current dollars
I—Musgrave [5.3 plus 5.4], historical cost, gross investment minus [5.8 plus 5.9], current cost, depreciation
Inventories
K—Musgrave [5.2.d], current dollars
I—First differences of constant dollar net stocks, Musgrave [5.2.d, 1972 dollars] converted to current dollars by the average of the implicit price deflators.
Land
K—Milgram [4, p.344] for 1952–68; for 1945–51 and 1969–75, data for K were extrapolated, using total private land stocks, from

FED [7].

$$GL_t = PL,F_t \; \frac{GL,M_{1952}}{PL,F_{1952}} \quad \text{for } t = 1945 \text{ to } 1951$$

$$GL_t = PL,F_t \; \frac{GL,M_{1968}}{PL,F_{1968}} \quad \text{for } t = 1969 \text{ to } 1975,$$

where GL = government land; M = Milgram
PL = private land; F = FED

Currency and demand deposits
K—FED [7]
Vault cash and member bank reserves
K—FED [7]
Gold, special drawing rights, and official foreign exchange
K—FED [7]
U.S. government securities
K—FED [7] times BPI for U.S. and state and local governments
State and local obligations
K—FED [7] times BPI for U.S. and state and local governments
Mortgages
K—FED [7], home and other mortgages, times BPI for all listed bonds
Other loans
K—FED [7], other loans, loans to S and L associations, farmers and co-ops, acceptances, and bank loans, n.e.c.
Taxes payable
K—FED [7]
Trade credit
K—FED [7]
Miscellaneous assets
K—FED [7], federal agencies open market paper and RPs, and all miscellaneous assets
State and local obligations
K—FED [7] times BPI for U.S. and state and local governments
U.S. government securities
K—FED [7], other loans and credit market instruments times BPI for U.S. and state and local governments
Mortgages
K—FED [7] times BPI for all listed bonds
Trade debt
K—FED [7]
Life insurance and pension funds
K—FED [7], sum of U.S. government life insurance and retirement funds

Currency and demand deposits
  K—FED [7], Monetary Authorities
Vault cash and member bank reserves
  K—FED [7], Monetary Authorities
Miscellaneous liabilities
  K—FED [7]

Table 5.56, Government, 1972 Dollars
Table 5.55 converted to 1972 dollars using implicit price deflators for fixed investment, SCB [11.a, table 7.1]

Table 5.57, GNP Implicit Price Deflators
Quarterly GNP deflators from SCB [11.a, table 7.1] and revised benchmarks

Table 5.58, Implicit Price Deflators for Fixed Investment
Fixed investment deflators (1972 = 100), SCB [11.a, table 7.1].
Fixed investment deflators (1969 = 100), by dividing the fixed investment deflators (1972 = 100), by the deflator (1972 = 100) for 1969 and multiplying by 100.

Table 5.59, Bond Price Indexes
All indexes are market value as a percentage of par value.
All listed bonds (New York Stock Exchange) are from
  NYSE *Fact Book* [6.a], for 1951 to 1977
  and from NYSE *Yearbook* [6.b], for 1945 to 1950
U.S. and state and local government securities
  1951–77 listed bonds by major group—U.S. government and New York City NYSE *Fact Book* [6.a]
  1945–50 extrapolated from 1951 using:

$$\text{BPI, Government}_{t-1} = \text{BPI, Government}_t \ \frac{\text{BPI, All}_{t-1}}{\text{BPI, All}_t}$$

U.S. companies
  1951–77 listed bonds by major group–total U.S. companies NYSE *Fact Book* [6.a]
  1945–50 extrapolated from 1951 using:

$$\text{BPI U.S. Co.}_{t-1} = \text{BPI U.S. Co.}_t \ \frac{\text{BPI, All}_{t-1}}{\text{BPI, All}_t}$$

Table 5.1, Households, Current Dollars
Net worth
  Total assets minus total liabilities for categories shown in table 5.47.

Net investment

Acquisitions of assets net of depreciation charges where applicable plus reduction of liabilities, summed for all assets and liabilities appearing in table 5.47.

Gross revaluations

Sum of gross revaluations of assets minus sum of gross revaluations of liabilities as indicated in equation (1) of the text for all assets and liabilities listed in table 5.47.

Net revaluations

Sum of net revaluations of assets minus sum of net revaluations of liabilities as indicated in equation (2) of the text for all assets and liabilities listed in table 5.47.

Table 5.2, Households, 1972 Dollars
Table 5.1 converted to 1972 dollars using the implicit price deflator for fixed investment, SCB [11.a, table 7].

Table 5.3, Business = table 5.5 + table 5.7 + table 5.9 excluding private financial corporate shares, current dollars

Table 5.4, Business = table 5.6 + table 5.8 + table 5.10 excluding private financial corporate shares, 1972 dollars
Table 5.3 converted to 1972 dollars using the implicit price deflators for fixed investment, SCB [11.a, table 7.1]

Table 5.5, Noncorporate Nonfarm and Farm, Current Dollars
Based upon data underlying table 5.49, otherwise similar to table 5.1.

Table 5.6, Noncorporate Nonfarm, and Farm, 1972 Dollars
Table 5.5 converted to 1972 dollars using the implicit price deflators for fixed investment, SCB [11.a, table 7.1]

Table 5.7, Nonfinancial Corporations, Current Dollars
Based upon data underlying table 5.53, otherwise similar to table 5.1.

Table 5.8, Nonfinancial Corporations, 1972 Dollars
Table 5.7 converted to 1972 dollars using the implicit price deflators for fixed investment, SCB [11.a, table 7.1]

Table 5.9, Private Financial, Current Dollars
Based upon data underlying table 5.53, otherwise similar to table 5.1.

Table 5.10, Private Financial, 1972 Dollars
Table 5.9 converted to 1972 dollars using the implicit price deflators for fixed investment, SCB [11.a, table 7.1]

Table 5.11, Government, Including Federally Sponsored Credit Agencies and Monetary Authorities, Current Dollars
Based upon data underlying table 5.55, otherwise similar to table 5.1.

Table 5.12, Government, Including Federally Sponsored Credit Agencies and Monetary Authorities, 1972 Dollars
Table 5.11 converted to 1972 dollars using the implicit price deflators for fixed investment, SCB [11.a, table 7].

Table 5.13, Sum of Sectors = tables 5.1 + 5 + 7 + 9 + 11, Current Dollars

Table 5.14, Sum of Sectors = tables 5.2 + 6 + 8 + 10 + 12, 1972 Dollars
Table 5.13 converted to 1972 dollars using the implicit price deflators for fixed investment, SCB [11.a, table 7.1].

Table 5.15, Total, Current Dollars
Table 5.13 excluding households' corporate and noncorporate equity and private financial corporate shares.

Table 5.16, Total, 1972 Dollars
Total 5.14 excluding households' corporate and noncorporate equity and private financial corporate shares.

Table 5.17, Investment by Sector and Total, Current Dollars
Net investment in current dollars excluding households' corporate and noncorporate equity and private financial corporate shares.

Table 5.18, Investment by Sector and Total, 1972 Dollars
Table 5.17 converted to 1972 dollars using the implicit price deflators for fixed investment, SCB [11.a, table 7.1].

Table 5.19, Net Revaluations by Sector, Current Dollars

(a) Households from table 5.47, col. 25–col. 14–col. 17.
(b) Noncorporate from table 5.49, col. 17.
(c) Nonfinancial corporations from table 5.51, col. 5.23.
(d) Private financial from table 5.53, col. 33–col. 10.
(e) Government, including federally sponsored credit agencies and monetary authorities, from table 5.55, col. 28.

Table 5.20, Net Revaluations by Sector, 1972 Dollars
Table 5.19 converted to 1972 dollars, using the implicit deflator for fixed investment, SCB [11.a, table 7.1]

Table 5.21, Net Revaluations: Standard Deviations and Simple Correlation Matrix
Based on figures from: tables 5.47 and 5.48, col. 25; tables 5.53 and 5.54, col. 32; and tables 5.19 and 5.20.

Table 5.22, Nonfinancial Corporate

K—table 5.51, nonresidential plant and equipment
I—table 5.51, nonresidential plant and equipment

Table 5.23, All Corporate
K—tables 5.51 and 53, nonresidential plant and equipment
I—tables 5.51 and 53, nonresidential plant and equipment

Table 5.24, Noncorporate
K—table 5.49, nonresidential plant and equipment
I—table 5.49, nonresidential plant and equipment

Table 5.25, Nonprofit Institutions
K—table 5.47, nonprofit plant and equipment
I—table 5.47, nonprofit plant and equipment

Table 5.26 (= table 5.23 + table 5.24 + table 5.25)

Table 5.27 (= table 5.28 + table 5.29)

Table 5.28, Owner-Occupied Residential Capital
K—Musgrave [5.5.a plus 5.5.b], net stocks, current dollars
I—Musgrave [5.6.a plus 5.6.b], historical cost, gross investment minus [5.5.a plus 5.5.b], current-dollar depreciation

Table 5.29, Tenant-Occupied Residential Capital
K—SCB [11.b, table 6]
I—First differences of constant-dollar net stocks, SCB [11.b, table 8] converted to current dollars using the implicit price deflators for residential investment, SCB [11.a, table 7.1]

Table 5.30, Business Inventories
K—SCB [11.c, table 5.9]
I—First differences of constant-dollar net stocks, SCB [11.c, table 5.10], converted to current dollars using an implicit price deflator,

$$P_t = \frac{K_t \text{ current dollars}}{K_t \text{ constant dollars}},$$

where K_t current is from SCB [11.c, table 5.9]

Table 5.31, Privately Held Land
K—Fogler [8A] summing land values for all nongovernment sectors
I—equals zero throughout

Table 5.32, Land by Sector
K—Values for all sectors from Milgram [4, p. 344]
I—equals zero throughout

Table 5.33, Personal Income and Savings, Current Dollars
Personal income, disposable personal income, and personal saving from SCB [11.c, table 2]
Net revaluations from table 5.1, col. 5

Table 5.34, Personal Income and Saving, 1972 Dollars
Disposable personal income from SCB [11.a, table 2.1]. Personal saving, from table 5.33, was converted to 1972 dollars using the implicit price deflator for personal consumption expenditures [SCB, 11.a, table 7.1], and the deflator for fixed investment was used for net revaluations.

Table 5.35, Investment and Capital Accumulations, Current Dollars
Net private domestic investment from SCB [11.a, table 5.2].
Tangible net investment from summing net investments on tangible assets from tables 5.47, 49, 51, 53, and 55.
Tangible net revaluations from summing net revaluations on tangible assets from tables 5.47, 49, 51, 53, and 55.
Tangible net capital accumulation = tangible net investment + net revaluations

Table 5.36 and 5.37, Tangible Assets
Sources and methods indicated in footnotes to tables 5.36 and 5.37.

Table 5.38
Net capital stock:
From gross earnings—using the 1969 figure from Graham-Webb [2], K_{69} = \$7,148 billion, then:

$$K_t = K_{69} \ \frac{Pop_t}{Pop_t} \ \frac{GE_t}{GE_{69}} .$$

where Pop_t = male population size in year t, from Historical Statistics [10, table A24].
and GE_t = average annual gross earnings in year t, from Economic Report [12, table B-29, p. 205].

From spendable earnings—using the 1969 figure from Graham-Webb [2], K_{69} = \$5,960 billion, and spendable earnings rather than gross earnings from Economic Report [12, table B-29, p. 205], otherwise similar to method for gross earnings.

"Gross" capital accumulation (GCA):
From gross earnings—$GCA_t = K_t - K_{t-1}$, where K_t is net stock from gross earnings in year t (col. 2).
From spendable earnings—$GCA_t = K_t - K_{t-1}$, where K_t is net stock from spendable earnings in year t (col. 3)

Net capital accumulation (NCA):

From gross earnings: $NCA_t = K_t - K_{t-1} \ \frac{P_{t,end}}{P_{t-1,end}}$,

where K_t is net stock from gross earnings in year t (col. 2) and $P_{t,end}$ is as defined in note 1 to the text.
From spendable earnings: where K_t is net stock in year t calculated from spendable earnings (col. 3), otherwise similar to NCA for gross earnings.

Table 5.39

To obtain net stocks of human capital, we assumed a fifty-year service life and used gross investment figures from 1894 to 1969 to apply a perpetual inventory method with straight-line depreciation. The underlying data are from Kendrick [3, table B-5]—total gross investment (human tangibles and nontangibles) in 1958 dollars (I_t) and Kendrick [3, table B-17]—total gross stocks in 1958 dollars (G_t), for the years 1929 to 1969. For 1894 to 1919, gross investment was obtained from the assumed identity $G_t - G_{t-1} \equiv I_t - I_{t-50}$. Hence,

$$I_{t-50} \equiv G_{t-1} + I_t - G_t, \text{ for } t = 1944 \text{ to } 1969.$$

For the years 1920 to 1928, the following interpolation was used:

$$I_t = I_{1919} \frac{I_{1929}}{I_{1919}} {}^{.1(t-1919)} \quad 1919 < t < 1929.$$

For 1929 to 1969, Kendrick [3, table 11] was used. Applying the perpetual inventory method with straight-line depreciation, we obtain net stocks and depreciation for the years 1946 to 1969. Net investment is then the difference between gross investment and depreciation for each year. These are then converted to current dollars using an implicit human capital total gross investment deflator, calculated from Kendrick's current- and constant-dollar figures for gross investment in human capital. Gross and net revaluations then follow as per equations (1) and (2) in the text. Net capital accumulation = net investment + net revaluations.

Table 5.40

Table 5.39 converted to 1969 dollars using implicit price deflators calculated from Kendrick's [3] current- and constant-dollar figures for gross investment in human capital.

Table 5.41

Net capital accumulation = net investment + net revaluations
Nonhuman capital
  Net investment from table 5.1, col. 3
  Net revaluations from table 5.1, col. 5
Human capital
  Net investment from table 5.40, col. 5
  Net revaluations from table 5.39, col. 7
Total capital = nonhuman capital + human capital

Table 5.42

Table 5.41 converted to 1969 dollars using the implicit price deflator for fixed investment on nonhuman capital, and for gross investment in human capital, as used for table 5.40 on human capital. For these deflators, see table 5.58.

Table 5.43, from table 5.35 and table 5.39

Table 5.44, Net Capital Accumulation of Tangible Assets, Current Dollars
Net capital accumulation = net investment + net revaluations.
Net investment for households, noncorporate, nonfinancial corporations, private financial, and government sectors equals the acquisition of assets net of depreciation charges when applicable, plus the reduction in liabilities summed for all assets and liabilities appearing in tables 5.47, 49, 51, 53, and 55, respectively. Net revaluations for these respective sectors relates to net worth and equals the difference between net revaluations on total assets and on total liabilities as shown in the separate sector tables.

Table 5.45, Reproducible Assets, Current Dollars
Figures for household, noncorporate, nonfinancial corporations, private financial, and government sectors, respectively, from tables 5.47, 49, 51, 53, and 55.

Table 5.46, Reproducible Assets, 1972 Dollars
Figures for household, noncorporate, nonfinancial corporations, private financial, and government sectors, respectively, from tables 5.48, 50, 52, 54, and 56.

Sources

[1] Federal Reserve System. Board of Governors. 1978. *Flow of Funds accounts*, August 1973, September 1974.

[2] Graham, John, and Webb, Roy. 1976. "Present-value estimates of human capital stocks." Published in *Review of Income and Wealth*, 1979, as "Stocks and depreciation of human capital: New evidence from a present value perspective."

[3] Kendrick, John W. 1976. *The formation and stocks of total capital*. New York: Columbia University Press for NBER.

[4] Milgram, Grace. 1973. Estimates of the value of land in the United States held by various sectors of the economy, annually, 1952–1968. In *Institutional investors and corporate stock*, Raymond W. Goldsmith. ed. New York: NBER.

[5.1–5.11] Musgrave, John. 1978. Unpublished data from the Bureau of Economic Analysis, U.S. Department of Commerce, all furnished in summer 1978. Descriptions follow.

[5.1] Fixed nonresidential capital, current cost, structures and equipment, and Fixed nonresidential business capital, by major type, historical cost.

[5.1.a] Nonprofit business

[5.1.b] Noncorporate business

[5.1.c] Nonfinancial corporate business

[5.1.d] All corporate business

[5.2] Reproducible tangible capital, government (including military), current and constant (1972 = 100) cost valuation.

[5.2.a] Nonresidential—equipment

[5.2.b] Nonresidential—structures

[5.2.c] Residential

[5.2.d] Inventories

[5.3] Fixed nonresidential capital, federal government (including military), investment data, historical cost valuation. Equipment and structures.

[5.4] Fixed nonresidential capital, state and local government, investment data, historical cost valuation. Equipment and structures.

[5.5] Residential capital, business, current cost valuation.

[5.5.a] Owner-occupied nonfarm

[5.5.b] Owner-occupied farm

[5.6] Residential capital, business, by tenure group, investment data, historical cost.

[5.6.a] Owner-occupied nonfarm

[5.6.b] Owner-occupied farm

[5.7] Nonprofit residential capital, current and constant (1972 = 100) cost valuation.

[5.8] Reproducible tangible capital, federal government (including military), straight-line depreciation current cost. Equipment and structures.

[5.9] Reproducible tangible capital, state and local government, straight-line depreciation, current cost. Equipment and structures.

[5.10] Residential capital, by legal form of organization, investment data, historical cost valuation. Government (total).

[5.11] Residential capital, government, current cost valuation, straight-line depreciation.

[6] New York Stock Exchange

[6.a.] *Fact Book*, 1951–78.

[6.b.] *Yearbook*, 1945–50.

[7] Board of Governors of the Federal Reserve System. 1978. Sector balance sheets with tangible assets at replacement cost, year end levels, 1945–1978, and sector/flow reconciliation statements, year end flows. Unpublished printouts developed from a project worked on first by Helen Tice and later by Elizabeth Fogler [FED].

[8] Musgrave, John. 1978. Consumer durables: Stocks and depreciation, total. Unpublished.

[8A] Board of Governors of the Federal Reserve System. 1978. Land, net stocks (unpublished tables), November 1978.

[9] U.S. Department of Commerce. Bureau of Economic Analysis. 1976. *Fixed nonresidential and residential capital in the United States, 1925–1975*. June [FNRCUS].

[10] U.S. Department of Commerce. Bureau of Economic Analysis. 1975. *Historical statistics of the United States, colonial times to 1970, Bicentennial edition.* Washington, D.C.

[11] U.S. Department of Commerce. Bureau of Economic Analysis. 1976. *Survey of Current Business* [SCB].

[11.a] January 1976, part 2.

[11.b] April 1976.

[12] U.S. Government Printing Office. 1976. *Economic report of the President*, January 1976. Washington, D.C.

Notes

1. When quarterly investment data are available we may use

$$\frac{P_t, \text{end}}{4} \sum_{i=1}^{4} \frac{IN_{t,i}}{P_{t,i}} \text{ instead of } \frac{P_t, \text{end}}{P_t} \quad IN_t,$$

where $IN_{t,i}$ is net investment of the ith quarter, at annual rates, and $P_{t,i}$ is the general price deflator of the ith quarter. We have taken as the general price deflator at the end of the year t,

$$P_{t,}\text{end} = (P_{t+1,1} + P_{t,4})/2,$$

where $P_{t+1,1}$ is the first-quarter deflator of the year $t+1$ and $P_{t,4}$ is the fourth-quarter deflator of the year t. With quarterly price deflators available but investment only annual, we have used annual investment, IN_t, instead of $IN_{t,i}$, so that the final term in (2) was generally taken as

$$\frac{P_t, \text{end}}{4} \sum_{i=1}^{4} \frac{IN_t}{P_{t,i}}.$$

2. The article by John Musgrave in the *Survey of Current Business* (April 1976) is a major published source, supplemented by revised figures for the most recent years.

3. U.S. Department of Commerce (1975), Series F349-364, F365-376.

4. To be published in *The Review of Income and Wealth*, 1979.

5. Current-dollar estimates are generally to be found in odd-numbered tables, estimates in 1972 dollars in even-numbered tables.

6. Calculated from table 5.1. Net worth at the end of 1945 equals net worth at the end of 1946 minus net investment and gross revaluations of 1946.

7. Reflecting in large part depreciation and disposal of military equipment after World War II and the large federal government deficits of 1975 to 1977.

8. The Kendrick-derived net capital accumulation of $1,864 billion from 1948 to 1969 compares remarkably with the present value total net accumulation of $1,925 billion over the same period taken from table 5.38. The latter deals only with male earnings, however. Other conceptual or definitional problems aside, it would apparently take a higher rate of discount than 7.5% to equate the present value of all human capital with its supply price.

9. Summaries of net revaluations of reproducible assets, land and total tangibles by sector are shown in tables 5.45 and 5.46.

References

Bailey, Martin J. 1969. Capital gains and income taxation. In *The Taxation of income from capital*, ed. Arnold C. Harberger and Martin J. Bailey, pp. 11–49. Washington, D.C.: Brookings Institution.

Bhatia, Kul B. 1970. Accrued capital gains, personal income and saving in the United States, 1948–64. *Review of Income and Wealth* 16 (December): 363–78.

Christensen, Laurits R., and Jorgensen, Dale W. 1973. Measuring economic performance in the private sector. In *The measurement of economic and social performance*. ed. Milton Moss, pp. 233–338. Studies in Income and Wealth, vol. 38. New York: National Bureau of Economic Research.

Coen, Robert M. 1975. Investment behavior, the measurement of depreciation, and tax policy. *American Economic Review* 65 no. 1 (March): 59–74.

Denison, Edward F. 1967. *Why growth rates differ: Postwar experience in nine Western countries*. Washington, D.C.: Brookings Institution.

———. 1973. *Accounting for United States economic growth 1929–1969*. Washington, D.C.: Brookings Institution.

Eisner, Robert. 1973. Comment. In *The measurement of economic and social performance*, Moss, Milton ed. pp. 343–49. Studies in Income and Wealth, vol. 38. New York: National Bureau of Economic Research.

———. 1975. TISA: Total incomes system of accounts. Paper presented to the Fourteenth General Conference of the International Association for Research in Income and Wealth, Aulanko, Finland.

———. 1978. Total incomes in the United States, 1959 and 1969. *Review of Income and Wealth* 24, no. 1 (March): 41–70.

Goldsmith, Raymond W., ed. 1973. *Institutional investors and corporate—A background study*. New York: National Bureau of Economic Research.

Graham, John, and Webb, Roy. 1979. Stocks and depreciation of human capital: New evidence from a present value perspective. *Review of Income and Wealth* 25, no. 2 (June): 209–24.

Haig, Robert M. 1959. The concept of income: Economic and legal aspects. In *Readings in the economics of taxation*, ed. Richard A. Musgrave and Carl S. Shoup, pp. 54–76. Homewood, Ill.: Irwin (originally published 1921).

Hicks, John R. 1946. *Value and capital*. Oxford: Clarendon Press.

Jorgenson, Dale W. 1974. The economic theory of replacement and depreciation. In *Econometrics and economic theory*, ed. W. Sellekaerts, pp. 189–221. London: Macmillan.

Kendrick, John W. 1976. *The formation and stocks of total capital*. New York: National Bureau of Economic Research.

McElroy, Michael B. 1971. Capital gains and the concept and measurement of purchasing power. In *1970 Proceedings of the American Statistical Association, Business and Economics Statistics Section*, pp. 132–39. Washington, D.C.: ASA.

———. 1976. Capital gains and social income. *Economic Inquiry* 14, no. 2 (June): 221–40.

Mendelowitz, Allan I. 1971. The measurement of economic depreciation. In *1970 Proceedings of the American Statistical Association, Business and Economics Statistics Section,* pp. 140–48. Washington, D.C.: ASA.

Musgrave, John C. 1976. Fixed nonresidential business and residential capital in the United States, 1925–75. *Survey of Current Business* 54, no. 4 (April): 42–52.

Ramm, Wolfhard. 1971. Measuring the services of household durables: The case of automobiles. In *1970 Proceedings of the American Statistical Association, Business Economics Statistics Section*, pp. 149–58. Washington, D.C.: ASA.

Seltzer, Lawrence H. 1951. *The nature and tax treatment of capital gains and losses*. New York: National Bureau of Economic Research.

Shoven, John B., and Bulow, Jeremy I. 1975. Inflation accounting and nonfinancial corporate profits: Physical assets. *Brookings Papers on Economic Activity* 3:557–611.

———. 1976. Inflation accounting and nonfinancial corporate profits: Financial assets and liabilities. *Brookings Papers on Economic Activity* 1:15–66.

Simons, Henry. 1938. *Personal income taxation*. Chicago.

U.S. Department of Commerce. Bureau of the Census. 1975. *Historical Statistics of the United States, Colonial Times to 1970, Part I.* Washington, D.C.: GPO.

Comment   Martin J. Bailey

The Eisner paper provides a significant addition to the stock of well-constructed data on income and wealth; future scholars will use it fruitfully. Moreover, the proposal to include capital gains in national income is well taken; I liked it when I first proposed it, and I like it now, except for those capital gains that are due to changes in the real rate of interest. Therefore my comments involve comparatively minor points.

The reason it is important to measure the capital gains component of income is that tax laws and traditional accounting practices have led to the reporting of true economic income as capital gains. Depreciation practices, charging off of research and development and similar expenses against current income, and related practices now lead to the systematic understatement of income in the national accounts. Whether

Martin J. Bailey is associated with the University of Maryland, College Park, Maryland.

these practices merely "defer" the reporting of income or lead to the conversion of ordinary income into reported capital gains, the appropriate corrective is to add accrued capital gains to income, including accruals to market values of assets in excess of their book values.

However, additions to wealth that result from a fall in the real interest rate are not income. Permanent income does include accruals to wealth due to all other causes, because such accruals could be consumed without impairing the ability to go on consuming at the same level forever. In contrast, consuming additions to wealth that result from a fall in the interest rate *would* impair the ability to go on consuming at the same level. A change in wealth due to changes in the interest rate reflects a price change, not a tangible change in goods available. If one thinks that permanent income is the appropriate variable for the consumption function, these arguments settle the matter. If, instead, one thinks wealth is the appropriate variable, or that there is a wealth effect in consumption, one might find it expedient to include this type of capital gain in income, as an alternative to putting in wealth as an explicit variable. This questionable thought is the only exception I can think of to my point here. In any event, Eisner includes this type of capital gain mainly in his financial estimates, not in the tangible assets.

In listing the reasons that we mismeasure capital accumulation, Eisner might mention as a sixth reason that gross errors in our price indexes of capital goods, uncovered by Robert Gordon's work, also contribute to mismeasurement.

It was disappointing that Eisner insisted on strict use of straight-line depreciation. Coen's earlier work on this issue, among other work, suggests that different depreciation patterns are appropriate for different types of assets; various authors have found that declining balance is accurate for machinery. Although I feel diffident about asking Eisner to do more work on his data, it would be little more than a clerical task to show alternative estimates using the main candidates for depreciation.

As Eisner correctly states, there is an element of double counting in his financial estimates owing to his inclusion of capital gains within corporations without an offsetting item for increased net worth; the increased net worth he includes in household sector capital gains, as he properly should. Purely financial capital gains should net out to zero, except for real capital losses on currency issued by the Treasury. Although Eisner did not prepare his totals to produce this complete netting out, he presents the data with which the interested user can do it himself—a redeeming virtue that applies to many other possible criticisms of his procedures.

Net revaluations of tangible assets would look quite different if they could be estimated with secondhand prices rather than replacement cost—they would have swings comparable to those in the stock market. Regrettably, it is impractical to try to construct estimates of revaluations on this basis.

In conclusion, we should appreciate the important contribution this work contains; it is valuable and useful.

Comment J. W. S. Walton

I welcome this paper, which I regard as an important contribution to the application of macroeconomics. It is well established that the command over resources of an individual or household is affected by capital gains or losses on assets held, and the paper seeks to quantify these influences, for example, on the real income of households, in relation to the similar influences on the real income of other groups of economic entities. This seems quite compatible with preserving the identity in the conventional accounts between product and the sum of factor incomes contributing to that product. In the conventional accounting framework, consumption out of capital gains is regarded as dissaving. For the total economy, real income will vary in relation to real product only according to shifts in international transfers or in the terms of trade; but an excess of aggregate domestic use of resources over either aggregate income or aggregate product is still possible when there is an expectation of a substantial future increase in the future provision of resources domestically. [I have only to look at the number of Arabs walking around the streets of London to appreciate that consumption can be generated by an increase in either the real income or the real wealth represented by a given product.]

At a disaggregated level within the domestic economy, command over resources is further affected by the effects of changes in the buying power of the income streams arising from financial claims, particularly as the result of inflation.

The United Nations Statistical Office has produced an accounting framework, in the shape of guidelines for the compilation of national and sector balance sheets. In these a reconciliation account connects conventional incomes with the changes between opening and closing net assets. The framework, incidentally, shows separately the "net worth" of corporations, defined as their total wealth—total assets less liabilities to third parties—from which is deducted the market value of the equity interest of the proprietors, and this net worth is regarded as part of the independent wealth of the corporate sector; no double counting is there-

J. W. S. Walton is associated with the Central Statistical Office, London.

fore necessary. The system of valuation is broadly by market values or replacement cost rather than according to economic value, so that "goodwill" is not provided for. It is in terms of current prices and costs, so that the system leaves quite open the question to what extent the gross revaluation surplus should be regarded as spendable income or as necessary to provide for the maintenance of opening wealth.

Professor Eisner's solution to this problem is to use as a numeraire the nationally available "basket" of goods and services—the GNP deflator. I worry about the implications of using this system of estimation—or any other using a general price index—upon the concept of business "income," taking this in the sense of the amount of trading surplus that is available for distribution (or, if not distributed, for internally financed capital expansion) after maintaining the "wealth" of the business. This gets to the heart of the current debate about systems of inflation accounting, in particular how to estimate what is needed to *maintain* the opening "wealth" of a business. Accountants have, of course, always regarded income as the growth of net assets, and the debate on how to allow for the effect of inflation on net assets reflects two rather different views of the object served by business accounts, which have been called the "equity" and the "entity" concepts.

According to the "equity" concept, in going from gross to net revaluations one would deduct from gross revaluations the amount needed to maintain the purchasing power to the shareholder of his opening stake—this is very similar to Professor Eisner's procedure. According to the "entity" concept, the shareholders' interest is regarded as stemming from the viability of the business as a going concern, so that one would initially regard the gross revaluation as a provision needed for maintenance of what has been called the "substance of the business." It is fairly readily agreed that the "substance of the business" will include physical assets (though the debate continues about whether to include monetary items, in particular monetary working capital), so that gross revaluations on fixed assets and inventories—when estimated by use of replacement cost or of the concept of "deprival" value formulated by the United Kingdom Sandilands Committee—are primarily regarded as representing funds required within the business. On this basis, *net* revaluations on fixed assets and inventories, in the sense of being regarded as part of the distributable surplus, will be zero or very small. However, such a systems of valuation ignores "goodwill," in the sense of the excess of the economic value (the present value of the future income stream) of a collection of assets over their current replacement cost, and evidently this excess—if it could have a value placed upon it—would rank for inclusion in net revaluations, even according to the "entity" concept. Similarly, economic value, if applied to monetary assets and liabilities, will in principle generate gross revaluation surpluses or deficits, against which assessments would be required of the amounts needed for maintenance of the "substance of the business."

In considering the relationship between the aggregated conventional accounts and the more comprehensive accounts in their disaggregated form, it is instructive to look at the gross revaluations arising on inventories—the difference between their value at the time materials are purchased and their value at the time they are taken into the productive process. The initial position is that these revaluation surpluses are needed within the business, for example, to maintain a given relationship between the volume of materials held as stock and the volume of output. But this relationship of course varies, and, in addition, businessmen would say that "good buying" (or bad buying)—for instance, a lengthening of the pipeline of materials in successful anticipation of a rise in its price, where the gain exceeds the additional financing cost—is part of income. In Professor Eisner's framework such an element of the gross revaluations on inventories would remain in the net revaluations and could likewise be treated as part of income. It is of course quite possible in theory for a single business to be persistently successful in entrepreneurial activity of this kind—at the expense of someone else. In just the same way, pure speculative activity can generate gains, whether they are called income or capital gains, that provide command over resources to the successful speculator.

6 Measurement of Income and Product in the Oil and Gas Mining Industries

John J. Soladay

6.1 Introduction

We are currently in a period of national concern over the depletion of our stock of natural resources. Unfortunately, however, the "energy crisis" is being debated with little or no reliable evidence available on the value and depreciation of that stock. In view of these problems, this study examines two of the most important minerals, oil and gas, that, at market value, account for approximately half of all natural resource extraction in the United States. It attempts to contribute toward an understanding of the real trade-offs implied by alternative rates of resource utilization by providing economically meaningful measures of both the value and the depreciation of the stock of developed oil and gas resources. Depletion, correctly measured, is treated as capital consumption, with a corresponding negative effect on measured income. I hope the data provided will be a useful input to informed policy decisions concerning these resources.

In this study I define and apply new measures of output, income, capital accumulation, and capital consumption in the oil and gas mining industries. The current Bureau of Economic Analysis (BEA) estimates of income and product in these industries are closely aligned with accounting measures of depreciation and investment that have, at best, a tenuous relationship with economically meaningful measures and pro-

John J. Soladay is an economist with Exxon Corporation. This paper was written while he was an assistant professor of economics at Pennsylvania State University.

This study represents the reestimation of the empirical relationships in the author's doctoral dissertation. The dissertation was completed at the Economics Department of Northwestern University under the direction of Professor Robert Eisner. I gratefully acknowledge his invaluable supervision and advice.

vide little information on the value of additions to, and consumption of, national wealth in natural resources. For example, at present, additions to national wealth in petroleum are not directly counted as investment. The BEA measures investment as expenditures involved in searching for and developing these minerals. For example, suppose our economy comprised only one firm, producing one product—crude oil. This firm spends $1 million exploring and developing crude oil and acquires additional crude oil stocks having a present value of $2 million. The BEA measure of investment would be $1 million, whereas the revised measure in this study would be $2 million. The costs of acquisition are used as a measure of investment in BEA accounts. In this study I count the present value of the additional resources as investment. The costs of acquisition are not an appropriate measure of the value of resource additions to wealth because acquisition capital gains (the difference between the value and the acquisition cost of an asset) may be considerable and should be included in a measure of this industry's income and product. As one consequence of the BEA's procedure, reported profits understate industry net revenue.

Current BEA depreciation estimates are also calculated using the acquisition cost base. Regardless of the depreciation formulas used, however, the data to which they are applied are inappropriate. In addition, the accounting formulas bear little resemblance to the utilization or consumption of the resource stock. The major part of BEA depreciation data for this industry is taken directly from tax returns, which report depreciation based on allowable depreciation schedules determined by tax law.[1] These data are unlikely to reflect economic depreciation because firms have an incentive to report tax depreciation charges so as to maximize the present value of expected after-tax returns. Furthermore, the BEA depreciates investment expenditures that are charged to current account by firms for tax purposes at an even rate over a twenty-year period. The rationale for this schedule is nothing more than an estimated average service life of twenty years for drilling equipment. Since the net revenue generated by equipment can change radically over its service life, however, this procedure is clearly not appropriate; it is very unlikely that depreciation would be identical over the period of utilization.

In contrast to the BEA's methods, this study measures investment by estimating directly the value of additions to the developed resource stock. My depreciation estimates are based upon the change in the value of resource capital in the production process rather than the tax depreciation schedules currently used.

The procedure followed in this study is essentially as follows:

1. The BEA measure of investment in this industry is replaced by estimates of the value of additions to the stock of oil and gas reserves.

2. The BEA depreciation measure is replaced by estimating the change in the value of the existing stock of developed oil and gas reserves (net of new additions).

3. In computing the present value of additional oil and gas reserves, it is assumed that the time path of output from any given pool of reserves is technologically given. Separate paths are estimated for each of these minerals. The greater part of the empirical work for this essay consisted in estimating the shape of these paths.

4. The production time path estimates are applied to each barrel of oil in order to attribute a time path of revenue to that oil and thereby calculate the present value.

5. Revised national income accounts are devised for the oil and gas mining industries in order to account properly for investment and disinvestment in these industries. The value of newly discovered and developed resources is included in capital formation, income, and output. Depletion, correctly measured, is treated as capital consumption with a corresponding negative effect on measured income.

6.2 Measurement of Income and Product in the Oil Industry: Theory

6.2.1 Current Accounting Procedures of the National Income Division of the Bureau of Economic Analysis

The major source of BEA national income data is the Internal Revenue Service (IRS) summary data for tax returns. The BEA adjusts reported taxable income in deriving data on business and national income appearing in the national income accounts. These adjustments are especially important in crude oil and natural gas mining because of the tax privileges granted these industries. For example, the depletion allowance permitted all oil and gas firms to deduct 22% of gross revenue from net revenue in reporting taxable income until 1975.[2] This allowance was constrained to be no more than 50% of predepletion allowance net revenue. Although the depletion allowance was deducted from gross income in arriving at taxable income, it was again added to taxable income in arriving at business and national income (U.S. Department of Commerce, OBE 1954, p. 92). The BEA's rationale for not recognizing the depletion of natural resources as an expense or charge against income is that their initial discovery or acquisition is not included in fixed capital or inventories and these are not included in income (Hagen and Budd 1958, p. 264).

Capital outlays for oil and gas well drilling and exploration, which are charged to current expense in the individual firm accounts, are included in the new construction component of gross private domestic investment in the national income accounts. An estimate of the depreciation on such items is included in capital consumption. The difference between such capital outlays and their corresponding capital consumption is entered into income in the national income accounts (*Survey of Current Business* [August 1965], p. 13). These capital outlays are depreciated by the BEA on a straight-line basis over twenty years, that is, at 5% of the initial outlay per year.

The BEA's treatment of investment and depreciation in the oil and gas mining industries is consistent with its treatment of these measures in other industries. Since capital outlays charged to current expense on firm accounts are depreciated in the national income accounts, the acquisition costs on new oil and gas resources are counted as investment. The depletion allowance was not counted as an additional expense, since this would entail double counting depreciation of oil and gas assets. Although firms were permitted such double counting on tax returns, it was corrected in the national income accounts. Furthermore, the depletion allowance in no sense reflected depreciation. Permitting firms to charge 22% of total revenue as an expense for depletion was incorrect, since the costs of acquiring these resources are already depreciated. The BEA's procedure of including the depletion allowance in national income is preferable not because the initial discovery is not included in fixed capital,[3] but because the expenditures associated with natural resource acquisition are already depreciated.

The BEA classifies companies into industries according to their major activity. Since many crude oil and natural gas firms are vertically integrated, with their major activity in manufacturing, they are classified accordingly. The result has been a consistent underreporting of mining gross product. This problem has been discussed by Lerner (1958). The BEA has adjusted for this bias by constructing a series on the gross product in mining which adjusts for the establishment-company industrial reporting bias, Gottsegen (1967).

6.2.2 The Revised Measures of Income and Product

This section presents the structure of my revised gross product statements. In summary of the previous section, my definition of net product is the sum of employee compensation, indirect business taxes, and profits. My profit series includes royalty payments, net interest, monopoly rents, and acquisition capital gains or losses. I do not attempt to measure windfall capital gains;[4] however, I think it useful to present the definitions and calculations in a manner exhibiting their explicit inclusion. My revised statements of the productive contribution of this industry are meant to reflect the effect of additions to national wealth in developed oil and gas resources as well as the depreciation of the existing stock of developed resources. The following equations will aid in the presentation of definitions:

Let

$R^{j,i}_t$ = the expectation in period j, of the net revenue in period t, from a mineral asset acquired in period i;

$V^{j,i}_t$ = the expectation, in period j, of the present value, at the beginning of period t, of mineral assets acquired in period i;

D^i_t = the depreciation, in period t, of mineral assets acquired in period i;

D_t = the depreciation in period t of all existing mineral assets;

C^i_t = the capital gains in period t, from mineral assets acquired in period i;

r_t = the discount rate in period t.

Assume $r_t = r_{t+j}$ for all j.

Then we may define $V^{t,t}_t$, D^i_t, and C^i_{t+1} as

(1) $$V^{t,t}_t = \sum_{\tau=0}^{\infty} = \frac{R^{t,t}_{t+\tau}}{(1+r)^\tau};$$

(2) $$D^i_t = V^{t,i}_t - V^{t,i}_{t+1};$$

(3) $$D_t = \sum_{i=0}^{t} D^i_t = \sum_{i=0}^{t} (V^{t,i}_t - V^{t,i}_{t+1});$$

(4) $$C^i_{t+1} = V^{t+1,i}_{t+1} - V^{t,i}_{t+1}.$$

The object is to create a time series on depreciation (D_t) and present value ($V^{t,t}_t$) of oil and gas resources. Equations (1) and (3) are used to accomplish this task. These equations are connected to other variables by the following agebraic relationships. Let

V^i_t = the present value at the beginning of period t of the mineral asset acquired in period i;

E^i_t = the revenue in period t generated by a mineral asset acquired in period i;

E_t = the revenue in period t generated by crude oil production from all vintages;

Q^i_t = production in year t from new oil acquired in year i;

Q^P_t = predicted output in year t from all vintages;

Q^R_t = reported aggregate production in year t;

D^i_t = the depreciation in year t from a mineral asset acquired in period i;

D_t = aggregate oil depreciation in year t;

$r =$ the discount rate;
$w_i =$ the production time path coefficient representing the ratio of current production from new oil reported i years previously to the quantity of new oil reported i years ago;
$b_t =$ average revenue per barrel of predicted oil production in year t;
$N_t =$ the quantity of new oil reported in year t.

Our calculations as based on two main assumptions. The first is that the discovery of one barrel of reserves in year t will result in extra output of oil of w_i in the year $t + i$, where the series of w_i represents technical coefficients and where $\sum_{i=0}^{\infty} w^i \leq 1$ because production from reported reserves cannot exceed the amount of the reserves available. If follows immediately that

$$Q_t = w_o N_t + w_1 N_{t-1} + \ldots + w_n N_{t-n}. \tag{5}$$

This equation is used to estimate the w_i from time series cross-sectional data on output ($Q^R{}_t$) and new oil (N_t). Identical procedures are followed for gas.

The present value of new oil additions is calculated as the stream of new revenues originating from production. A new oil addition reported in year t is evaluated in year t as

$$V^t{}_t = \sum_{\tau=0}^{T} \frac{E^t{}_{t+\tau}}{(1+r)^\tau}.$$

Similarly, we can express the present value of new oil reported in year i and evaluated n years later in year t as

$$V^i{}_t = \sum_{\tau=0}^{T-n} \frac{E^i{}_{t+\tau}}{(1+r)^\tau},$$

where i also denotes vintage.

We calculate the amount of net revenue in year t attributable to oil initially reported in year i as:

$$E^i{}_t = \frac{E_t}{Q^P{}_t} \times Q^i{}_t,$$

where $\frac{E_t}{Q^P{}_t}$ represents average revenue per unit of predicted output

and
$$Q^P{}_t = \sum_{i=0}^{15} w_i N_{t-i};$$

$$Q^i{}_t = w_i N_{t-i}.$$

Observations on net revenue include the years 1948 to 1974. Since the estimated service life of new oil is sixteen years (twenty-six years for natural gas) and we are attempting to calculate the present value of new oil from 1948 to 1974, it was necessary to project average revenue for the years 1975 to 1989 (1999 for natural gas). The observed relationship between current and lagged ratios of revenue to predicted output is assumed to generate forecasts of future revenue.

We assume average revenue per barrel of oil expected in 1975 is a weighted average of past ratios; that is,

$$b_{75} = c_o + \sum_{i=1}^{n} d_i \, b_{t-i}$$

$$b^*_{75} = b_{75}$$

and that expectations are met, so that 1976 average revenue is

$$b^*_{1976} = c_o + d_1 \, b^*_{75} + \sum_{i=2}^{n} d_i \, b_{t-i}.$$

Iteration is continued until 1985 (1999 for natural gas).

6.3 Description of the Data

6.3.1 Introduction

This section represents an attempt to analyze a number of problems arising from the data used in this study. Certain problems are solved in my estimates; others remain. My task was to acquire data permitting me to estimate a relationship between expenditures on acquisitions of developed crude oil and the eventual revenue generated by these additions. To some extent, the data sources defined my method of approaching the problem of acquiring estimates of present value and depreciation. Since sufficient data are not available to allow a direct estimate of the relationship between acquisition costs and net revenue, I proceed stepwise. I first estimate a relationship between additions to the mineral stock and production. Yearly net revenue is then attributed to these current and past additions to the developed oil stock, thus enabling me to derive estimates of the net revenue stream resulting from additions to the stock of developed oil. I then discount this stream and acquire estimates of present value and depreciation. Differences between the value of new oil and the cost of acquiring it provide information on acquisition capital gains (or losses).

In section 6.3.2 I examine the natural of crude oil reserves data and consider some of the consequences for my estimates of using these data. Section 6.3.3 treats the BEA acquisition cost data, and section 6.3.4

examines the net revenue data used in this study. Section 6.3.5 considers some of the problems raised by the joint-product nature of oil and gas acquisition and production.

6.3.2 The Nature of Crude Oil Reserves Data

The American Petroleum Institute (API) publishes annual estimates of proved crude oil reserves. Reserves are defined by the API as volumes of crude oil that geological and engineering information indicates are recoverable "beyond reasonable doubt, under existing economic and operating conditions" (Lovejoy and Homan 1965, pp. 17–19).

The API breaks down the new oil added each year into three categories: new pools discovered during the year, extensions of old pools, and revisions of previous estimates. Estimates in these categories may be described as follows.

New pools or discoveries. These are previously undeveloped and possibly unknown oil pools that are brought to the producing stage during the year.

Extensions of existing reservoirs. New reserves sometimes result from the drilling of additional development wells after the year of initial discovery.

Revisions. Revised estimates frequently arise from additional information concerning the performance of a reservoir or from new processes that increase recovery. The reserves figures published by the API are not used as an indication of the recoverable oil at any time but correspond more closely to oil that can eventually be produced under current operating conditions—that is, a working inventory.

The typical relationship between the eventual recovery from a pool and the amount of oil initially reported by the API as oil contained in a new pool discovery is not known. Extensions and revisions are credited by the API to additions to reserves of the year in which the extensions and revisions are noted, not to reserves of the year of initial discovery. If we could attribute all extensions and revisions during 1946 to 1974 to new pools discovered over the period (excluding the large Alaskan reserve, reported in 1970 and not producing in 1974), the data indicate that, on average, 7.06 times the amount of oil initially reported in new pools is eventually reported as producible.

The relationship between reserves eventually reported as producible from a pool and those initially reported has interesting implications for our accounting of capital acquisitions. We note that 50% of the additional reserves attributed to previously reported new oil are due to revisions. As mentioned above, these reserves are not all directly associated with additional development in existing pools. The revisions (if unexpected) represent increases in the evaluation of existing oil assets that can be considered windfall capital gains. Firms must generally expect the eventual recovery from new pools to exceed the conservative estimates of the API. Ideally, then, we should count the expected future revenues and expenditures (associated with the extensions category) in the year in which these expectations were formed. Unfortunately, data are not available that would permit us to attribute extensions and revisions back to the initial year in which the pools were reported, and even if these data were available, there would be no way of testing whether these quantities of additional oil were expected at the initial acquisition date of the new pool.

Because of data restrictions, I am forced to treat the quantity of new oil (new pools + extensions + revisions) reported by the API as resulting solely from current investment; and any capital gains on acquisition (difference between cost and value of new oil) are attributed not to date of the initial expectation but to the current period. Unexpected additional reserves that are reported in the current period and may be considered windfall capital gains will be included in the value of new oil and will show up in the income accounts as acquisition capital gains rather than as windfall gains.

6.3.3 An Analysis of Acquisition Cost Data

My acquisition cost data on new oil and gas basically comprise the weighted sums of two entries in the National Income Accounts. The first, "Petroleum and Natural Gas Well Drilling and Exploration," includes: (1) all capital outlays for new oil and gas that are expensed on firm account (for tax purposes), and (2) those acquisition costs that are depreciated on firm account and result in the construction of fixed structures on new oil and gas property. The second entry is "Mining and Oil Field Machinery." Costs included under this item represent durable equipment other than that in fixed structures. Some of these reported costs represent purchases of equipment for mining other than oil and gas. Fortunately, such costs are relatively small. To correct for them, I have multiplied the data for mining and oil field machinery by the ratio of the BEA Gross Product in Oil and Gas to the BEA Gross Product in Mining in the corresponding year. This item was added to Petroleum and Natural Gas Well Drilling and Exploration to obtain acquisition costs for oil and gas. Some of the implications of treating investment outlays as acquisition costs of currently reported new oil and gas are treated in Soladay (1974, pp. 24–25).

6.3.4 Net Revenue Data

Net revenue data for the years 1948 to 1974 for oil and gas mining were derived mainly from the BEA gross product statements. Data on net interest, capital consumption allowances, and profits are available for the two industries combined. After-tax profits are not reported. We approximated joint after-tax profits by multiplying yearly reported profits by one minus the ratio of yearly corporate profits tax liability to corporate profits (both of which are reported in the national income accounts as totals for crude petroleum and natural gas).

Royalty payments are also considered a component of net revenue and were derived from industry survey data (Joint Association Survey). These payments are usually a fixed percentage of gross sales paid to landowners whose property is used for oil or gas extraction. They are treated as payments to the real estate industry by the BEA (Ruggles 1949, p. 53). Although they represent a flow of funds from oil mining firms and, as such, cannot be considered as revenue available to the firms, these payments are generated by the oil industry and may be considered payments for the oil contained in the landowner's property rather than for his real estate. Thus, royalty payments represent part of the surplus generated by the mining activity and are considered here as part of net revenue originating in mining regardless of whether the firm owns the land in which the natural resources are contained. Because they are payments from mining operators to resource owners, royalty payments are included in the gross product and net revenue generated in mining.

Net interest is treated as a cost of current production by the BEA. Since net interest represents a net payment for the use of borrowed capital, it constitutes a claim on net revenue, originating in the oil industry, that is transferred to bondholders. As part of income distributed to owners of the firm's capital, net interest should be treated not as a current cost but again as a component of net income generated in mining.

Since I also estimate depreciation, the original net revenue data include BEA capital consumption allowances. In reporting profits in my revised gross product statements, capital consumption allowances are reported separately.

6.3.5 Conceptual and Data Problems related to the Joint-Product Nature of Crude Petroleum and Natural Gas

The BEA data on acquisition expenditures and gross product are reported only for the combination of the crude oil and natural gas mining activities. Because no data are available for either mineral separately, we are faced with a number of difficulties in attempting to acquire separate estimates of the present value and depreciation of oil and of gas. Because of the joint-product nature of oil and gas, a problem arises when we attempt to acquire separate cost and revenue estimates for these minerals. I believe that the additional information gained from the individual estimates reflects a great deal more than these arbitrary allocations, however, and hence it seems worthwhile to me. A more complete discussion of the joint-product nature of these resources is provided in Soladay (1974, pp. 26–27).

Acquisition costs. Fortunately, no aggregative bias is introduced into my results by the somewhat arbitrary apportionment of the acquisition-cost data. With total acquisition costs given, the segregation I perform merely allocates capital gains among minerals. Acquisition capital gains for the combination do not change. I attribute the BEA acquisition costs to oil and gas by using weighted ratios of new reserves. For example, the ratio for oil was calculated as the product of the current oil price and new oil reserves divided by the sum of the product of the current oil price and new reserves and the product of the current gas price and new gas reserves. This ratio was multiplied by acquisition costs for oil and gas in order to determine oil acquisition costs. Acquisition costs for gas were calculated in a similar manner.

Net revenue data. Revenue was allocated between minerals in the same fashion as acquisition costs. In this case the product of the current price and production for each mineral was divided by the sum of the price and output products for both minerals. This ratio, when multiplied by joint revenue, yielded the revenue attributable to each mineral separately.

6.4 The Empirical Evidence

6.4.1 Introduction

This section presents my estimates of the value of new oil, the capital gains associated with the acquisition of that oil, and the depreciation and value of the entire oil stock for the period 1948 to 1974. To reiterate, my approach to the problems of acquiring economically meaningful magnitudes for the variables mentioned above is to estimate first the relationship between additions to the oil stock and production. This relationship, which is referred to as the production time path, indicates current and future output from new oil assets acquired during the estimation period. Knowledge of the production time path permits us to attribute yearly net revenue to these current and past additions to the developed oil stock, thus enabling us to acquire estimates of present value and depreciation.

Section 6.4.2 presents my estimates of the production time path for oil; in section 6.4.3 the production time path for natural gas is presented; in section 6.4.4 I explore the problem of allocating net revenue among the production from current and past additions to the developed oil and gas stock. Finally, section 6.4.5 presents my numerical solutions.

6.4.2 The Production Time Path Estimates for Oil

Data on crude oil reserves and production were acquired for the years 1948 to 1974 for the eighteen states that accounted for approximately 98% of United States production and reserves during the period.[5] The source of data on reserves and production was the American Gas Institute and the American Petroleum Institute (1975).

All the state data on production, reserves, and new oil are expressed as ratios to the reserves at the end of 1960 in each state. This procedure permits us to adjust for size differences among states. Current oil output (Q_t) can be expressed as the sum of contributions to current output of current and past additions to the resource stock (N_t):

$$Q_t = w_o N_t + w_1 N_{t-1} + w_2 N_{t-2} + \ldots + w_n N_{t-n}. \tag{6}$$

This section presents the results of a number of attempts to estimate the parameters of the production time path. The rational lag estimator is used to derive these estimates, which utilize several groupings of data on eighteen states for the years 1948 to 1974. The different groupings of state data were used in hope of ascertaining the degree to which estimation results were sensitive to the types of regressions run on the same basic data.

Several estimating equations were used in an attempt to acquire information on the production profile. A direct estimate of the beginning of the production profile provided information on the initial buildup in production. A modified Koyck equation was also used that allowed for the production buildup. I also made use of the instrumental variables technique in an attempt to remove difficulties associated with using a lagged dependent variable. Results were not much different from OLS.[6]

The rational lag estimator was used in more general form in equation (7) (see table 6.1). This equation permitted the buildup in production during the first few years but did not constrain remaining production to lie on a geometrically declining path, as did the Koyck equations. I found that this estimating equation performed better than others used in deriving the production time path weights. The coefficients on more than two lagged values of new oil or production tended to become insignificantly different from zero. Of course, the significance test on individual coefficients whose variables are to some degree multicollinear is an insufficient test of the significance of individual coefficients, but in

Table 6.1 Output as a Function of Current and Lagged New Oil and Lagged Output

(Eq. 7) $q_t = \sum_{i=0}^{4} b_{5i}n_{t-i} + \sum_{i=1}^{2} c_{5i}q_{t-i} + u_t$

Variable or Statistic	Regression Coefficients and Standard Errors: Overall	State Cross-sectional	State Time-Series
n_t	.0570	.0579	.0550
	(.0066)	(.0068)	(.0067)
n_{t-1}	.0260	.0281	.0255
	(.0072)	(.0074)	(.0072)
n_{t-2}	.0046	.0093	.0046
	(.0069)	(.0072)	(.0070)
q_{t-1}	.0686	.9649	.9517
	(.0485)	(.0485)	(.0485)
q_{t-2}	−.0960	−.1084	−.0950
	(.0450)	(.0449)	(.0456)
Σn	.0876	.0953	.0851
	(.0101)	(.0112)	(.0108)
Σq	.8726	.8565	.8567
	(.0164)	(.0182)	(.0197)
r.d.f.[a]	426	403	409
DW	2.0178	2.0223	2.0196
R^2	.9151	.9128	.8663
F	918.490	1117.25	691.903
SE	.0110392	.0107873	.0109356
α	.6876	.6641	.5939
	(.1435)	(.1429)	(.1292)

[a]Residual variance degrees of freedom. Of the original sample of twenty-seven years for eighteen states, or 486 observations for each variable, two years of observations were lost in generating the lagged values of new oil and an additional year was lost in calculating the new oil variable as current output plus the difference between reserves at the end of this year and the end of last year (see definition of page 00). With twenty-four remaining years of observations (432) we lost one degree of freedom for each mean calculated and one for each variable on the right-hand side. Since there is only one mean in the overall, we have 426 degrees of freedom, the eighteen means in the state time series (one for each state) give us 409 degrees of freedom and finally the twenty-two means (one for each year) in the cross section give us 403 degrees of freedom.

many instances the sums of coefficients changed very little, yielding no or generally insignificant changes in recovery rates or in the shape of derived production time paths. Additional coefficients also approached zero or became negative.

Turning to the new oil coefficients of equation (7) we note that their sums were 0.0876 in the overall, 0.0851 in the time series, and 0.0953 in the cross section. The time-series and cross-sectional sums of new oil coefficients are not statistically different, since the difference between coefficient sums is less than the standard error of the difference.[7] There is, however, a possibility that these sums of coefficients are biased downward because of an error-in-variables problem. Approximately 75% of United States oil is produced in states that regulate production by prorating market demand; five of the eighteen states in our sample were regulated by this system. Each of these states limits production to forecasts of quantities demanded. These forecasted quantities (net of predicted unregulated production) are then allocated among regulated wells by permitting regulated wells to produce state-determined percentages of an assigned maximum allowable production level. These maximums are not directly related to capacity or reported revenues.[8] The divergence between observable new oil and other units of production capacity (among market-demand states and between market-demand states and the remaining states with other types of production restrictions) contributes to a problem of errors in variables.

Turning to the sum of lagged production coefficients, we note no appreciable difference between the estimates, the overall, time-series, and cross-section sums of coefficients being 0.8726, 0.8567 and 0.8567 respectively. To test for autocorrelation, the error term u_t was regressed on u_{t-1}. The coefficient of u_{t-1} was not significantly different from zero, indicating no serial correlation. This test was used instead of the Durbin h test because the Durbin h was not calculable.[9]

My estimate of the recovery rate was 0.6876 in the overall, 0.5939 in the time series, and 0.6641 in the cross section. The differences among the overall, time-series, and cross-sectional recovery rates are not statistically significant.

The production time path derived from the cross-section regression of equation (7) reported in the Appendix was selected for use in my estimates of the value of new oil and depreciation. The criteria used were the higher R^2 and lower standard error of estimate of the equation. In addition, the cross-sectional results appeared less affected by the errors-in-variables problem present in the time series results.

My estimate of the amount of oil recovered per barrel reported apparently contradicts the description of new oil data as reported by the API. Results indicate that 66% of reported new oil is produced, while the API indicates that 100% is producible.

To determine how well my production time path estimate performed when applied to aggregate United States data on new oil, I constructed a predicted output series to be used in comparisons with United States reported output over the period 1948 to 1974. The predicted output series was constructed by applying the structural coefficients of equation (7)[10] for the overall regression to data on United States new oil over the period 1933 to 1974.[11] Note that the data used to construct the predicted series differ from the state data sample for the period 1948 to 1974 used in the estimation of equation (7).[12]

Since the predicted output series summed to 69% of reported output over the sample period, the estimate of the recovery rate is biased downward. As a rough check on the recovery rate estimate, I note, for illustrative purposes only, that if we blow up the production time path weights so that they sum to unity (by dividing each of the weights by their sum), the sum of predicted output over the entire period would amount to 103.7% of reported output. It appears that difficulties associated with errors in variables for new oil data outweigh the distributed lag bias associated with using lagged dependent variables. Since the amount of net revenue attributed to oil production is allocated evenly over predicted output, the fact that the recovery rate is less than unity does not necessarily produce any bias in our results. To the extent that predicted output is lower than actual output, average revenue per barrel will be higher than actual average revenue.

6.4.3 The Production Time Path Estimates for Natural Gas

Reserves, production, and new gas data are compiled by the American Gas Association (AGA). The concepts used by the AGA in defining natural gas reserves are quite similar to those used by the API concerning crude oil reserves.

Data on natural gas reserves and production were acquired for seventeen states over the period 1948 to 1974.[13] These states accounted for approximately 98% of United States gas production and reserves over the period. The state data on reserves were compiled by the AGA. The same econometric techniques that were used for oil were also applied to natural gas. To adjust for size differences among the states in our sample, all variables are divided by the 1960 value of state reserves.

In an attempt to determine the production time path for new gas, we estimated the modified Koyck equation (8). The number of new gas lags used was extended to four, since the sum of new gas coefficients continued to increase up to that point. The sum of new gas coefficients was 0.0428, 0.0584, and 0.0430 in the overall, time-series, and cross-sectional regressions. The lower cross-sectional sum of new gas coefficients may be due to a more severe errors-in-variables problem in the cross section. To the extent that institutional differences between reported and producible new gas are more important across states than are differences between reported and producible new gas over time, the cross-sectional sums of new gas coefficients will be lower.

The lagged production coefficients were 0.9168 in the overall, 0.9319 in the time-series, and 0.9140 in the cross-sectional regressions. The Durbin h statistic indicates autocorrelation in the overall and cross-sectional regressions; no autocorrelation is indicated in the time-series regression. The presence of autocorrelation in the overall and cross-sectional regressions will produce biased estimates of coefficients and therefore make the overall and cross-sectional results less reliable.

Ratios of eventual recovery to the quantity of new gas reported are 0.5144, 0.8576, and 0.5000 in the overall, time-series, and cross-sectional regressions. Apparently, the lower estimates of recovery rates in the overall and cross-sectional regressions originated because both new gas and lagged output coefficients were lower than the time-series coefficients; for example, 0.0430 and 0.9140 in the cross-sectional as opposed to 0.0584 and 0.9319 in the time-series. Since the Durbin-Watson statistic is biased, it is not used to indicate whether positive or negative autocorrelation exists. However, the lower lagged output coefficients in the cross-sectional regressions would be consistent with negative autocorrelation, while the lower cross-sectional new gas coefficients might be considered as due to a more severe errors-in-variables problem. The time-series results appear more reasonable than the cross-sectional or overall results because no autocorrelation is indicated in the time series and the time series standard error of estimate is lower.

In an attempt to determine whether additional lagged values of production would alter my results, I ran additional regressions. No significant difference in recovery rates occurred in any of the regressions. I take this as indicating that the modified Koyck equation discussed above is a reasonable specification of the production time path. The table in the Appendix presents the estimates of the structural coefficients derived from table 6.2. The better performance of the time-series estimating equation leads to its selection in generating the structural coefficients. Since the sum of the first sixteen structural coefficients is only 62% of the sum to infinity, the length of the structural equation is extended to twenty-six periods. The sum of coefficients thereby expanding to 81% of the sum to infinity. During this period the coefficients sum to 0.6977, or 81% of their sum to infinity.

6.4.4 Numerical Solutions

Oil. As described in sections 6.2 and 6.3, industry net revenue and acquisition cost was first allocated among oil and gas by using weighted ratios of production and new reserves. Then the net revenue for each mineral in each time period was distributed evenly over the contributions to current output of current and lagged values of new reserves. To calculate the present value of new oil and new gas I had to project average revenue for the years 1975 to 1989 for oil and from 1975 to 1999 for natural gas. This task was performed by testing a number of equations relating current and lagged ratios of revenue to predicted output for each mineral. I selected one equation for each mineral on

Table 6.2 **Gas Output as a Function of Current and Lagged New Gas and Lagged Output**

(Eq. 8) $q_t = \sum_{i=0}^{4} c_{4i}n_{t-i} + c_{51}q_{t-1}$

Variable or Statistic	Regression Coefficients and Standard Errors		
	Overall	State Time-Series	State Cross-sectional
n_t	.0171	.0188	.0170
	(.0041)	(.0039)	(.0040)
n_{t-1}	.0043	.0042	.0035
	(.0044)	(.0042)	(.0043)
n_{t-2}	.0076	.0125	.0089
	(.0057)	(.0054)	(.0056)
n_{t-3}	−.0056	−.0007	−.0093
	(.0059)	(.0056)	(.0058)
n_{t-4}	.0194	.0236	.0229
	(.0061)	(.0058)	(.0060)
q_{t-1}	.9168	.9319	.9140
	(.0151)	(.0163)	(.0150)
Σn	.0428	.0584	.0430
	(.0076)	(.0083)	(.0072)
r.d.f.	367	351	346
R^2	.9201	.9059	.9206
F	847.008	708.840	853.263
SEE	.00805809	.00750854	.00764782
DW	1.7460	2.0180	1.7270
Dh	2.5685	.1833	2.7578
α	.5144	.8576	.5000
	(.1466)	(.2511)	(.1350)

the basis of minimum standard error of estimate and used it to generate the expected average revenue series for each mineral. These expected net revenue paths were then discounted in order to acquire the present value and depreciation variables described in section 6.2.

A number of discount rates were used in the present value and depreciation calculations. Since the net revenue variables were presented in terms of constant 1972 dollars, the effect of inflation was netted out. It follows that the appropriate rate of interest to use in discounting net revenue should not be the market rate of interest facing petroleum firms, since that rate includes a component for the expected rate of inflation. Nominal interest rates would be appropriate only if current-dollar estimates of net revenue were being discounted.

The nominal Aaa corporate bond rate ranged from 2.82 in 1948 to 8.57 in 1974. These rates present an upper limit on the discount factor because they include an inflation premium.

No attempt will be made in this study to estimate expected rates of inflation. Knowledge of the geometric mean rate of inflation and the various long-term corporate bond rates will be used to present a range of estimates of depreciation and the present value of new oil. The mean rate of inflation over the period 1953 to 1974 was 4.6%.[14] Yohe and Karnosky (1969) of the Saint Louis Federal Reserve Bank estimate long-term real rates of interest from 1960 to 1969 that range from (in three series) 2 to 4%. These estimates offer added information concerning a lower limit on interest rates to be applied. The geometric mean Aaa corporate bond rate was 5.8% from 1955 to 1974. Depreciation and present value were therefore computed using interest rates of 3%, 5%, and 7%.

I calculated depreciation and present value of the stock of oil resources as well as the present value of additions to the stock, using interest rates of 3%, 5%, and 7%. At 3% interest, the mean value of depreciation was $4.3 billion, while the mean value of the stock was $31.1 billion and the mean value of new oil was $5.4 billion. The 1970 entry for the value of new oil, $23.8 billion, reflects the large quantity of new oil reported in Alaska. These Alaskan reserves were assumed not to produce until 1978 and to continue production until 1993. The average revenue predictions are extended over this period. The drop in the depreciation series from $5.0 billion in 1969 to from $4.1 billion in 1970 to $4.2 billion in 1974 is due to the negative depreciation of new oil in Alaska. Since all revenues from Alaskan oil are discounted fewer periods from 1970 to 1977, the present value of these reserves must increase and thereby depreciate negatively. Mean depreciation, value of the oil stock, and value of new oil were $3.6, $26.7, and $4.5 billion respectively, calculated at a 7% interest rate.

Table 6.3 gives estimates of (1) the present value of new oil (calculated using 5% interest); (2) the cost of new oil; and (3) the resulting acquisition capital gains. I have also reported the results of my calculations of (4) the value of the capital stock in oil, and (5) depreciation.

An examination of table 6.3 indicates substantial acquisition capital gains averaging $3.0 billion per year or 61% of the value of new oil acquired each year. Mean depreciation ($3.9 billion) was 13% of the mean value of the oil stock over the period. The $19.4 billion value of new oil in 1970 reflects mainly the acquisition of Alaskan reserves, which are assumed, as before, not to produce until 1978.

Gas. The arithmetic manipulations are identical to those used for oil. Numerical solutions for depreciation and present value of the entire gas stock as well as new gas additions for interest rates of 3% and 7% were obtained. Using the 3% rate, we note that mean depreciation was $1.4 billion, or 6.46% of the mean value of the gas stock ($21.5 bil-

Table 6.3 **Value of New Oil, Acquisition Costs, Acquisition Capital Gains, Value of the Oil Stock, and Depreciation over the Period 1948–74 (Millions of 1972 Dollars)**

Year	V'_t	C_t	$V'_t - C_t = ACG_t$	V_t	D_t
1948	5,314	1,377	3,937	19,715	3,420
1949	4,423	1,329	3,094	20,718	3,010
1950	3,596	1,402	2,194	21,304	3,364
1951	6,251	1,884	4,367	24,191	3,644
1952	3,944	1,947	1,997	24,491	3,500
1953	4,814	1,963	2,851	25,805	4,057
1954	4,238	2,396	1,842	25,986	3,857
1955	4,275	2,159	2,116	26,404	4,412
1956	4,419	2,050	2,369	26,411	4,445
1957	3,589	2,255	1,334	25,555	4,343
1958	3,855	1,681	2,174	25,067	4,196
1959	5,473	2,098	3,375	26,344	4,106
1960	3,596	1,758	1,838	25,834	3,906
1961	4,143	1,722	2,421	26,071	3,925
1962	3,477	1,648	1,829	25,623	4,124
1963	3,527	1,602	1,925	25,026	4,236
1964	4,403	1,914	2,489	25,193	3,777
1965	5,168	1,958	3,210	26,584	4,035
1966	5,135	1,995	3,140	27,684	4,229
1967	5,236	1,773	3,463	28,691	4,451
1968	4,422	2,002	2,420	28,662	4,381
1969	3,899	2,467	1,432	28,180	4,623
1970	19,416	2,920	16,496	42,973	3,614
1971	4,453	1,884	2,569	43,812	3,846
1972	3,068	1,543	1,525	43,034	3,407
1973	4,353	1,766	2,587	43,980	3,422
1974	4,146	1,835	2,311	44,704	3,604
Sum	132,633	51,328	81,305	778,042	105,934
Mean	4,912	1,901	3,011	28,816	3,923

Note: Interest rate = 5%; the price deflator used was the implicit price deflator of oil and gas mining gross product (S1C13).

lion). The mean value of new gas was \$1.9 billion. At 7% interest, mean depreciation (\$9.2 billion) was 5.44% of the mean value of the gas stock (\$17 billion). The average value of new gas was \$1.35 billion.[15]

Table 6.4 presents the numerical solutions for (1) the present value of new gas reported in the current period; (2) the acquisition cost of currently acquired new gas; (3) capital gains or losses associated with acquisition; (4) the value of the entire capital stock in natural gas; and (5) depreciation. The interest rate used is 5%.

Table 6.4 **Present Value of New Gas, Acquisition Capital Gains, Value of the Gas Stock, and Depreciation over the Period 1948–74 (Millions of 1972 Dollars)**

Year	V^t_t	C_t	$V^t_t - C_t = ACG_t$	V_t	D_t
1948	1,009	331	678	9,269	352
1949	951	293	658	9,868	294
1950	931	556	375	10,505	356
1951	1,277	500	777	11,426	504
1952	1,167	684	483	12,089	514
1953	1,698	831	867	13,273	722
1954	814	364	450	13,365	681
1955	1,909	918	991	14,593	769
1956	2,201	1,135	1,066	16,025	815
1957	1,814	775	1,039	17,024	698
1958	1,751	912	839	18,077	740
1959	1,949	853	1,096	19,286	918
1960	1,334	948	386	19,702	1,092
1961	1,679	917	762	20,289	1,155
1962	1,932	1,199	733	21,066	1,223
1963	1,826	1,178	648	21,669	1,348
1964	2,054	1,077	977	22,375	1,139
1965	2,189	1,132	1,057	23,425	1,393
1966	2,090	1,213	877	24,122	1,563
1967	2,272	1,155	1,117	24,831	1,693
1968	1,431	1,011	420	24,569	1,684
1969	882	719	163	23,767	1,776
1970	3,919	385	3,534	25,910	1,607
1971	1,046	1,364	−318	25,349	1,839
1972	1,026	1,726	−700	24,536	1,723
1973	734	1,493	−759	23,547	2,016
1974	931	1,359	−428	22,462	1,703
Sum	42,816	25,028	17,788	512,419	30,317
Mean	1,586	927	659	18,978	1,123

Note: Interest rate = 5%.

We note in table 6.4 substantial capital gains in new gas acquisition. While the mean value of new gas was \$1.6 billion, the mean cost of acquiring it was \$0.93 billion, indicating average acquisition capital gains of 0.66, or 41% of the value of new gas on average. The value of the gas stock was rising substantially from \$9.3 billion in 1948 to \$25.9 billion in 1970. From 1971 to 1974 the value of the gas stock declined from \$25.3 billion in 1971 to \$22.5 billion in 1974 because of the smaller additions of new gas reserves over the period 1971–74. The mean value of the gas stock was \$19.0 billion over the entire period.

The average value of the new gas reserves from 1971 to 1974 was \$0.9 billion, compared with the \$1.6 billion mean value of new gas over the entire period. Depreciation also increased fairly steadily over the period, from \$0.3 billion in 1948 to \$1.7 billion in 1974, with a mean value of \$1.1 billion. Over the period, depreciation was approximately 5.9% of the value of of total gas reserves.

6.5 Integration of Results into the National Income Accounts

6.5.1 The BEA and the Revised Accounts

This section presents my estimates of income and production in the crude oil and natural gas mining industries. These estimates are meant to reflect the economic definitions underlying the gross product statement of the oil and gas mining activities. The results provide us with measures of additions to national wealth in oil and gas minerals as well as the depreciation and value of the current stock of developed oil and gas resources.

The concept of income I apply in constructing gross product statements in the crude oil and natural gas mining industries is that income equals consumption plus change in wealth. The value of newly discovered and developed resources is included in capital formation, and in output. The value of new oil and gas, net of investment expenditures responsible for their acquisition however, are, also included as income (acquisition capital gain), to be recorded in the year in which the new acquisitions are made. The diminution over time of the value of existing oil and gas assets is considered depreciation.

Table 6.5 exhibits the present value (measured at the beginning of the period) of currently acquired new oil and gas as well as the cost associated with the acquisition of those minerals. The difference between the value and costs of new oil indicates acquisition capital gains. As noted previously, acquisition capital gains refer not only to gains on physical capital but also to the surplus the firm realizes on all capital expenditures, whether or not they result directly in tangible capital. Column 4 lists the present value, also measured at the beginning of the period of the entire oil and gas stock, and, finally, depreciation is listed in column 5. Over the period 1948 to 1974, the mean value of newly acquired oil and gas (\$6.5 billion) was 2.3 times the mean cost of acquiring those minerals, resulting in average acquisition capital gains of \$3.7 billion. We also note that the average value of the capital stock in developed oil and gas resources was \$47.8 billion. The value of the oil and gas stock increased steadily from a low of \$28.9 billion to \$69.2 billion in 1971, one year after the reporting of oil in Prudhoe Bay, Alaska (assumed to begin production in 1978). Relatively low

Table 6.5 **Present Value of New Oil and Gas, Acquisition Costs, Acquisition Capital Gains, Value of Oil and Gas Reserves and Depreciation over the Period 1948–74 (Millions of 1972 Dollars)**

Year	V^t_t	C_t	ACG_t	V_t	D_t
1948	6,323	1,708	4,615	28,984	3,772
1949	5,374	1,622	3,752	30,586	3,304
1950	4,527	1,958	2,569	31,809	3,720
1951	7,528	2,384	5,144	35,617	4,148
1952	5,111	2,631	2,480	36,580	4,014
1953	6,512	2,794	3,718	39,078	4,779
1954	5,052	2,760	2,292	39,351	4,538
1955	6,184	3,077	3,107	40,997	5,181
1956	6,620	3,185	3,435	42,436	5,260
1957	5,403	3,030	2,373	42,579	5,041
1958	5,606	2,593	3,013	43,144	4,936
1959	7,422	2,951	4,471	45,630	5,024
1960	4,930	2,706	2,224	45,536	4,998
1961	5,822	2,639	3,183	46,360	5,080
1962	5,409	2,847	2,562	46,689	5,347
1963	5,353	2,780	2,573	46,695	5,584
1964	6,457	2,991	3,466	47,568	4,916
1965	7,357	3,090	4,267	50,009	5,428
1966	7,225	3,208	4,017	51,806	5,792
1967	7,508	2,928	4,580	53,522	6,144
1968	5,853	3,013	2,840	53,231	6,065
1969	4,781	3,186	1,595	51.947	6,399
1970	23,335	3,305	20,030	68,883	5,221
1971	5,499	3,248	2,251	69,161	5,685
1972	4,094	3,269	825	67,570	5,130
1973	5,087	3,259	1,828	67,527	5,438
1974	5,077	3,194	1,883	67,166	5,307
Sum	175,449	76,356	99,093	1,290,461	136,251
Mean	6,498	2,828	3,670	47,795	5,046

additions to reserves from 1971 to 1974, on average \$4.4 billion, account for the minor decline in the value of the oil and gas stock to \$67.2 billion in 1974. Depreciation increased from \$3.7 billion in 1948 to \$6.4 billion in 1969. The decline in the series to from \$5.2 billion in 1970 to \$5.3 billion in 1974 is due predominantly to the negative depreciation associated with the Alaskan oil over this period. Mean depreciation (\$5.0 billion) was 10% of the average value of the stock of developed resources over the period 1948 to 1974.

Table 6.6 presents the BEA gross product series; my revised series is presented in table 6.7. Employee compensation and indirect business taxes are the same in both series. In the revised series, net interest and royalty payments are included in profits. In addition, and far more important quantitatively, acquisition capital gains are included in profits. Furthermore, instead of using the tax formulas for depreciation, depreciation in the revised accounts was calculated in accord with the definitions in section 6.2, as the change in the value of existing assets.

Average employee compensation was $2.3 billion and average indirect business taxes were $0.7 billion. Revised gross product had a mean value of $14.7 billion, while average BEA gross product was only $9.6 billion. On average, over the period 1948 to 1974, the revised series was

Table 6.6 **BEA Gross Product Crude Petroleum and Natural Gas Mining (Millions of 1972 Dollars)**

Year	Gross Product	Employee Compensation	Net Interest	CCA	IBT	Profits
1948	6,335	1,266	22	1,063	310	3,674
1949	5,993	1,252	18	1,119	369	3,235
1950	6,582	1,344	33	1,318	412	3,475
1951	7,432	1,582	34	1,551	462	3,803
1952	7,684	1,752	26	1,654	515	3,737
1953	8,035	1,827	24	1,820	526	3,838
1954	8,098	1,762	24	1,778	485	4,049
1955	8,846	1,889	25	2,157	529	4,246
1956	9,244	2,050	25	2,169	571	4,429
1957	9,208	2,058	25	2,065	560	4,500
1958	8,653	1,924	27	2,159	570	3,973
1959	9,192	2,127	28	2,295	666	4,076
1960	9,094	2,081	29	2,510	713	3,761
1961	9,316	2,125	20	2,548	770	3,853
1962	9,577	2,214	35	2,653	760	3,915
1963	9,950	2,310	49	2,802	788	4,001
1964	10,003	2,377	47	2,820	815	3,944
1965	10,229	2,446	32	2,893	787	4,071
1966	10,707	2,634	33	3,040	880	4,120
1967	11,193	2,626	39	3,036	877	4,615
1968	11,624	2,803	38	3,121	962	4,700
1969	11,958	3,018	77	3,210	1,006	4,647
1970	12,264	3,133	97	3,394	1,065	4,575
1971	12,185	3,280	91	3,400	1,162	4,252
1972	12,308	3,229	115	3,556	1,153	4,255
1973	12,186	3,296	211	3,144	1,166	4,369
1974	12,048	2,889	252	2,275	1,265	5,367
Sum	259,944	61,294	1,476	65,550	20,144	111,480
Mean	9,628	2,270	55	2,428	746	4,129

Table 6.7 **Revised Gross Product Crude Petroleum and Natural Gas Mining (Millions of 1972 Dollars)**

Year	Gross Product	Employee Compensation	CCA	IBT	Profits
1948	11,837	1,266	3,772	310	6,489
1949	10,514	1,252	3,304	369	5,589
1950	9,987	1,344	3,720	412	4,511
1951	13,556	1,582	4,148	462	7,364
1952	11,144	1,752	4,014	515	4,863
1953	12,814	1,827	4,779	526	5,682
1954	11,380	1,762	4,538	485	4,595
1955	13,022	1,889	5,181	529	5,423
1956	13,781	2,050	5,260	571	5,900
1957	12,750	2,058	5,041	560	5,091
1958	12,735	1,924	4,936	570	5,305
1959	14,840	2,127	5,024	666	7,023
1960	12,515	2,081	4,998	713	4,723
1961	13,722	2,125	5,080	770	5,747
1962	13,431	2,214	5,347	760	5,110
1963	13,901	2,310	5,584	788	5,219
1964	14,866	2,377	4,916	815	6,758
1965	15,950	2,446	5,428	787	7,289
1966	16,329	2,634	5,792	880	7,023
1967	17,401	2,626	6,144	877	7,754
1968	16,178	2,803	6,065	962	6,348
1969	15,356	3,018	6,399	1,006	4,933
1970	34,314	3,133	5,221	1,065	24,895
1971	16,584	3,280	5,685	1,162	6,457
1972	15,143	3,229	5,130	1,153	5,631
1973	16,122	3,296	5,438	1,166	6,222
1974	16,228	2,889	5,307	1,265	6,767
Sum	396,400	61,294	136,251	20,144	178,711
Mean	14,681	2,270	5,046	746	6,619

53% higher than the BEA series. The relatively high value of new oil and gas acquired in 1970 ($23.3 billion) is due to the reporting of Alaskan reserves. As evidenced in 1970, our estimates are more sensitive to changes in wealth in natural resources. I believe this property is consistent with what we are attempting to measure when constructing gross product statements. Changes in natural resource wealth enter the BEA national income accounts only as acquisition costs, and future depreciation of those costs ignores often significant differences between the cost and the present value of newly acquired mineral assets. The mean value of acquisition capital gains ($3.6 billion) accounts for 73% of the difference between the two series.

Turning to the depreciation series, we note that mean BEA depreciation was $2.4 billion over the entire period, while mean depreciation in my series was $5.1 billion, an average of 2.12 times the BEA series. One reason for the higher revised series is that my base for depreciation is the value of new oil and gas (mean value 1948 to 1974 of $6.5 billion) rather than acquisition costs (mean = $2.8 billion). The difference between these two bases ($3.7 billion), which represents acquisition capital gains, accounts for a substantial portion of the $2.6 billion average discrepancy between the BEA and revised depreciation series. In addition to the difference in the bases, I calculate depreciation as reductions in present value; the BEA uses accounting rules that I believe are not well related to economic depreciation.

6.5.2 Summary

In this study I have attempted to measure income and product in the crude oil and natural gas mining industries in a manner consistent with generally accepted definitions of income and value. The results are in no sense final but rather are interpreted as preliminary estimates of income and product in the oil and gas industries.

To reiterate, the basis of this project has been the definition of income as consumption plus the increase in wealth. The concept of wealth or value in natural resources relates to the stream of net revenue expected to result from their utilization. Gross capital accumulation or investment in any year hence consists of the present value of the current and future revenue from new oil and gas reported in that year. Purchases of physical plant and equipment are treated as embodied in the new oil and gas and are therefore not depreciated separately. The diminution over time of the value of the originally anticipated revenue stream, at its originally anticipated discount rates and expected prices, represents what I consider depreciation.

The current BEA estimates of income and product are closely aligned with accounting measures of depreciation and investment and have an often tenuous relationship with economically meaningful magnitudes. Currently, investment is measured not as the addition to national wealth in minerals over time but as expenditures involved in the search for, and development of, these minerals. Consequently, current measures of investment are accurate only when there is no divergence between the value of newly acquired oil and gas assets and the acquisition costs currently used as measures of investment. Since acquisition capital gains may be considerable, however, they should not be excluded from the income of this industry. Thus, BEA reported profits will understate the net revenue of the industry when these acquisition capital gains are positive.

Current BEA depreciation estimates are also calculated using the acquisition cost base. Regardless of the depreciation formulas used, the data to which they are applied is inappropriate. In addition, the accounting formulas bear little resemblance to the utilization or changes in the value of the resource stock.

In contrast to the BEA's methods, my estimates of investment were derived by estimating directly the value of additions to the developed resource stock. Depreciation estimates were obtained by ascertaining the change in the present value of the existing stock (net of new additions) of developed oil and gas resources. One shortcoming of my study is that this measure of depreciation is consistent with the concepts of income and value only in the absence of windfall capital gains and losses. (Windfall capital gains are assumed to be zero while acquisition capital gains are captured in the valuation of resources.) The revised estimate of output, investment, and depreciation were based upon my estimates of the utilization and revenue generated by current and past additions to the developed stock of these minerals.

Appendix

Table 6.A.1 Oil and Gas Production Time Path Coefficients

$Q_t = w_o N_t + w_1 N_{t-1} + \ldots + w_t N_{t-t}$

Oil: Structural Coefficient	Oil: State Cross-Sectional	Gas: Structural Coefficient	Gas: State Time-Series
w_0	.0579	w_0	.0188
w_1	.0840	w_1	.0217
w_2	.0840	w_2	.0327
w_3	.0720	w_3	.0298
w_4	.0604	w_4	.0514
w_5	.0504	w_5	.0479
w_6	.0421	w_6	.0446
w_7	.0352	w_7	.0416
w_8	.0294	w_8	.0388
w_9	.0245	w_9	.0361
w_{10}	.0205	w_{10}	.0337
w_{11}	.0171	w_{11}	.0314
w_{12}	.0143	w_{12}	.0292
w_{13}	.0119	w_{13}	.0272
w_{14}	.0100	w_{14}	.0254
w_{15}	.0083	w_{15}	.0237
		w_{16}	.0220
		w_{17}	.0205
		w_{18}	.0191
		w_{19}	.0178
		w_{20}	.0166
		w_{21}	.0155
		w_{22}	.0144
		w_{23}	.0135
		w_{24}	.0125
		w_{25}	.0117
$\sum_{i=o}^{15} w_i$	.6220	$\sum_{i=o}^{25} w_i$	.6977
$\sum_{i=o}^{\infty} w_i$	.6641	$\sum_{i=o}^{\infty} w_i$	.8576
$\frac{\sum_{i=o}^{15} w_i}{\sum_{i=o}^{\infty} w_i}$	.9366	$\frac{\sum_{i=o}^{25} w_i}{\sum_{i=o}^{\infty} w_i}$	.8136

Notes

1. The BEA currently calculates aggregate depreciation on the basis of 85% of the service lives specified in the 1942 edition of Bulletin F issued by the IRS. The difference between the old depreciation (taken directly from tax returns) and the current series is reported as a capital consumption adjustment that is included in income (Young 1975). However, this revision is not currently reported on an industry basis and therefore does not apply to the BEA depreciation data included in this study.

2. The 1975 Tax Reduction Act eliminated percentage depletion for oil, for taxpayers owning production per day in the calendar year in excess of 2,000 barrels per day in 1975; in 1976 it would drop to 1,800; and it was to decline thereafter until 1981, when it would level off at 1,000 barrels per day. The depletion allowance for major intrastate gas producers was abolished as of 1 January 1975, and for major interstate producers this was effective 1 July 1976. The 22% depletion allowance for small independent producers was continued until 1980, after which it will decrease annually to a final level of 15% in 1984.

3. The initial rationale cited in Hagen and Budd (1958, p. 5) was published when capital outlays charged to current expense for tax purposes were not included in new construction in the national income accounts.

4. Although the definitions of value and depreciation are couched in terms of expected values of variables, the present estimation procedure uses ex post measurements of these variables. Since data on the output and cost expectations of firms involved in oil and gas exploration do not exist, to my knowledge, expectations are assumed to be perfect; that is, the values of expected variables are assumed to be identical to the values of observed current variables. Firms involved in oil production have a wealth of information upon which to base expectations. This information, which is not available to me, certainly goes beyond the lagged observed variables used in most expectations models. I believe that the assumption of perfect expectations introduces less error to my results than an attempt to bring in estimates of expectations. Furthermore, it should be noted that the assumption of perfect expectations does not preclude the existence of acquisition capital gains (defined as the difference between the value and cost of new oil and gas), which are attributed here to the presence of monopoly elements or other imperfections in these industries.

5. The states included in the sample were Kansas, Louisiana, New Mexico, Texas, Oklahoma, Arkansas, California, Colorado, Mississippi, Montana, Nebraska, Wyoming, Illinois, Indiana, Ohio, Pennsylvania, Kentucky, and Virginia.

6. Full information on these results and my interpretation of them will be provided upon request.

7. Standard error of the difference equals $(.0108^2 + .0112^2)^{1/2} = .0156$.

8. A fuller discussion is provided in Lovejoy and Homan (1967) and MacDonald (1971).

9. $Dh = r\sqrt{\dfrac{n}{1 - nV(c_{51})}}$; since $nV(c_{51}) > 1$, the test was inapplicable.

10. Since the initial sixteen production time path weights sum to 93.7% of their sum to infinity, the predicted output series was blown up by the ratio $1/0.937 = 1.0677$.

11. Before 1945, new oil included a number of elements that were reclassified after 1945 and not included in post-1945 data on new oil. I made a rough adjustment for this classification change by deflating pre-1945 new oil by the ratio of

new oil as reported under the later classification in 1945 to new oil as reported under the old classification.

12. The data sample on which the structural estimates were based was different. To generate the predicted series aggregate, new oil data for the period 1933 to 1974 were acquired. As noted previously, pre-1946 new oil data were not comparable in definition to post-1946 data, and my adjustment of the early series was only a rough approximation. It may also be plausible to believe that these early quantities of new oil also differed in reporting characteristics concerning the quantities of new oil that were reported as producible.

13. The states included in the sample were Arkansas, California, Colorado, Illinois, Kansas, Kentucky, Louisiana, Michigan, Mississippi, Montana, New Mexico, Ohio, Oklahoma, Pennsylvania, Texas, West Virginia, and Wyoming.

14. The implicit price deflator of GNP was used.

15. Full data are available from the author.

References

American Gas Association, American Petroleum Institute, and Canadian Petroleum Association. 1975. *Reserves of crude oil, natural gas liquids, and natural gas in the United States and Canada and United States productive capacity as of December 31, 1974.* Vol. 29, May 1975. Published jointly.

Eisner, Robert. 1967. A permanent income theory for investment: Some empirical exploration. *American Economic Review* 57 (June): 389.

Gottsegen, J. 1967. Revised estimates of G.N.P. by major industry. *Survey of Current Business* 47(4) (April): 18–24.

Hagen, E., and Budd, E. 1958. The product side: Some theoretical aspects. In *A critique of the United States income and product accounts.* Studies in Income and Wealth, vol. 22. New York: National Bureau of Economic Research.

Johnston, John 1972. *Econometric methods.* 2d ed. New York: McGraw-Hill.

Lerner, J. 1958. Extractive industries. In *A critique of the United States income and product accounts.* Studies in Income and Wealth, vol. 22. New York: National Bureau of Economic Research.

Lovejoy, W., and Homan, P. 1965. *Methods of estimating reserves of crude oil, natural gas and natural gas liquids.* Baltimore: Johns Hopkins University Press.

———. 1967. *Economic aspects of oil conservation regulation.* Baltimore: Johns Hopkins University Press.

MacDonald, S. 1971. *Petroleum conservation in the United States: An economic analysis.* Baltimore: Johns Hopkins University Press.

Ruggles, R. 1949. *Introduction to national income and income analysis.* New York: McGraw-Hill.

Soladay, John. 1974. The measurement of income and product in the oil and gas mining industry. Ph.D. diss., Northwestern University.

U.S. Department of Commerce. Bureau of Economic Analysis. 1965. The national income and product accounts of the United States: Revised estimates, 1929–64. *Survey of Current Business* 45 (August): 6–22.

U.S. Department of Commerce. Office of Business Economics. 1954. *National income, 1954*. Washington, D.C.: Government Printing Office.

Yohe, W., and Karnosky, D. 1969. Interest rates and price level changes, 1952–96. *Review of the Federal Reserve Bank of St. Louis* 51(12) (December): 18–38.

Young, Allan H. 1975. New estimates of capital consumption allowances revision of GNP in the benchmark. *Survey of Current Business* 55 (October): 14–16, 33.

7 The Measurement of Capital Aggregates: A Postreswitching Problem

Murray Brown

7.1 Introduction

The problem of capital measurement is a postreswitching problem in the sense that the literature that centered on reswitching and attendant perversities contributed little to our knowledge of the conditions for capital aggregation. But it did serve to focus attention on the problem itself—to motivate the inquiry by indicating in no uncertain terms that the failure to satisfy certain aggregation conditions (namely, the Gorman conditions) could lead to results qualitatively different from those one would expect from the so-called neoclassical parables (those based on aggregate neoclassical production specifications). There is now a considerable consensus on this point, and so the inquiry must proceed beyond reswitching into more detailed and empirically oriented analyses of capital aggregation. That is the principal concern of the present paper. But before taking this up, it may be useful to give a brief review of the reswitching phenomenon. Its implications, presented after the review, should be examined closely because they motivate further work and also embody a critique of what has been done using aggregate capital measures.

The misspecification that may result from using improper aggregates is not negligible. It affects the empirical foundations of production and distribution analyses (and all the spinoff implications these have for pricing, productivity, etc.). It will not go away if we merely look it in the eye and pass on, and hence it is bound to return in devilishly unpredictable forms to render those analyses unacceptable.

The body of this chapter is a critical examination of conditions that must be satisfied for the empirical specification of capital aggregates at

Murray Brown is associated with the Department of Economics, State University of New York at Buffalo, Amherst campus.

various levels of aggregation. Here one must turn away from the capital-theoretic reswitching literature and look critically at the aggregation conditions associated with functional form and relative prices, inter alia. These include the Leontief-Solow conditions, Fisher's aggregation analysis, the Gorman conditions, the Houthakker-Sato approach, Hicksian composite commodity aggregation, the Brown-Chang conditions, and the statistical case for production aggregation.

On the basis of this review, I feel that two recommendations can be adequately defended. The first is addressed to the development of the output, capital, and labor data used in production analysis. Since the very existence of stable aggregates is questionable, one must at the least suspend judgment on studies using such aggregates. It follows that problems requiring aggregates must be treated in such a way that the aggregates are justified empirically. To do that requires that sufficiently disaggregated data be available upon which aggregation conditions can be tested. Thus, the first recommendation is that these be made available to allow for such tests. For output and labor, the data requisite can be reasonably satisfied; with respect to capital, it may be very costly to develop sufficiently disaggregated data on the numerous physical capital items to allow for acceptably rigorous applications of the aggregation conditions. Of course there are many data, already developed, that can be made available for aggregation analysis; where the confidentiality rule is not violated, they may be found useful to this end.

In view of the problem of the intractability of the data with respect to capital, and in view of certain theoretical problems, the second recommendation concerns the kind of tests one can reasonably hope to apply. I argue at some length below that composite commodity aggregation is the approach that requires our attention at the moment. For the reasons, I am afraid one has to read on.

7.2 A Brief Review of Reswitching and Capital Aggregation

The possibility of reswitching was originally discovered by Sraffa, who published his results in 1960. Apparently, members of Sraffa's seminars at Cambridge University were aware of the phenomenon well before the results appeared in print. In 1956 Joan Robinson published a version of the reswitching phenomenon called the Ruth Cohen Curiosum. After Sraffa's publication, Samuelson (1962) showed the conditions under which aggregate neoclassical analysis (parable) is possible; these conditions assumed reswitching away. This was related to Champernowne's (1953–54) excellent treatment of chain indexation of capital and since this was the first published demonstration of the reswitching difficulties encountered by aggregate neoclassical-type production analysis, we shall begin there.[1]

Consider an economy in which two commodities are produced in fixed proportions: a consumption good, say corn, produced by means of labor and capital, and capital, produced by means of labor and itself. There are many techniques, and each technique is associated with a particular specification of the capital good. For n heterogeneous capital goods (heterogeneous either in the physical sense as in Samuelson's model or in the sense of different lengths of time required in producing particular capital as in Champernowne's model), the technology of the economy can be described by a book of "blueprints" that is simply a set of the following technique matrixes:

$$\underbrace{\alpha = \begin{array}{l} \\ \text{Labor} \\ \text{Capital type } \alpha \end{array} \begin{array}{cc} \text{Corn} & \text{Capital type } \alpha \\ \end{array} \begin{bmatrix} a_{lo} & a_{l1} \\ a_{1o} & a_{11} \end{bmatrix}, \quad \beta = \begin{array}{l} \\ \text{Labor} \\ \text{Capital type } \beta \end{array} \begin{array}{cc} \text{Corn} & \text{Capital type } \beta \end{array} \begin{bmatrix} b_{lo} & b_{l1} \\ b_{1o} & b_{11} \end{bmatrix}, \gamma, \delta, \ldots}_{n \text{ techniques}}$$

Let capital be infinitely durable.[2] In a competitive equilibrium there are zero profits and hence the value of the output must equal the cost of production:

(1) $$P_o Y_o = W_o L_o + r\, K_{1o}(\alpha)\, P_1(\alpha)$$

(2) $$P_1(\alpha)\, Y_1(\alpha) = W_o L_1 + r\, K_{11}(\alpha)\, P_1(\alpha),$$

where P_o = price of consumption goods,
$P_1(\alpha)$ = price of capital (denoted by subscript 1) good type α,
Y_o = output of consumption good,
$Y_1(\alpha)$ = output of capital good (by subscript 1) type α,
r = rate of profit,
W_o = nominal wage rate,
$K_{1j}(\alpha)$ = amount of capital good type α used in producing one unit of good j, $j = o, 1$, and
L_j = amount of labor employed in producing one unit of good j, $j = o,1$.

Dividing (1) and (2) by Y_o and $Y_1(\alpha)$, respectively, the price equations are obtained:

(3) $$P_o = a_{lo} W_o + r\, a_{1o}\, P_1(\alpha)$$

(4) $$P_1(\alpha) = a_{l1} W_o + r\, a_{11}\, P_1(\alpha),$$

where $a_{lj} = L_j / Y_j$ and $a_{1j} = K_{lj}/Y_j$, $j = o,1$.

Therefore, for the particular technique matrix α, solving (3) and (4) for the wage rate and capital price, both normalized by the consumption good price, gives

$$(5) \qquad W_o/P_o = \frac{1 - a_{11}r}{(1 - a_{11}r)\, a_{lo} + a_{1o}a_{l1}r}$$

$$(6) \qquad P_1(\alpha)/P_o = \frac{a_{l1}}{(1 - a_{11}r)\, a_{lo} + a_{1o}a_{l1}r}\,.$$

Note that, if $m \equiv \dfrac{a_{1o}/a_{lo}}{a_{l1}/a_{11}} > 1$, the consumption section is the more capital intensive, whereas if $m < 1$, the capital sector is more capital intensive. One must keep that in mind for what is to follow.

Equation (5) is the well-known wage curve or wage-profit relationship; (6) relates relative prices to the profit rate. Much of the story turns on the properties of these two equations.[3]

Motivated by Joan Robinson, Champernowne (1953) tried to find a unit in which capital goods can be measured such that the conventional production function can be constructed and marginal productivity theory can be preserved. To do this, he proposed the Divisia type of chain index. An example shows how the chain index of capital is found and how the conventional production function emerges. In the model above, assume that the economy's technology consists of three techniques, where each requires a different capital good.

Figure 7.1*a* depicts the $W_o/P_o - r$ relationship, and figures 7.1*b*, 7.1*c*, and 7.1*d* show the price-profit rate relationships for each technique. The intercepts of the wage curves on the ordinate are $1/a_{lo}(\alpha)$ for the α technique, $1/a_{lo}(\beta)$ for the β technique, and $1/a_{lo}(\gamma)$ for the γ technique; on the abscissa, they are $1/a_{11}(\alpha)$, $1/a_{11}(\beta)$, and $1/a_{11}(\gamma)$. The α technique is more capital intensive (higher a_{11} and lower a_{lo} coefficients) than the β technique, which in turn is more capital intensive than the γ technique. Except at the switch points, r_1 and r_2, economy-wide forces will select that single technique that yields the highest real wage rate for a given profit rate. Thus, in this simple example, α is selected from zero to r_1 profit rate, β from r_1 to r_2, and γ for $r > r_2$. Clearly, as r increases, capital intensity falls. And that is the "well-behaved" case that underlies the aggregate neoclassical postulate.

When one compares (5) and (6) across techniques, one must take care. It is meaningful to compare the $W_o/P_o - r$ relations, but it is illegitimate to compare the price-profit equations across techniques in this model. The basic reason is that W_o/P_o for techniques α, β, and γ have the same dimensions, while $P_1(\alpha)/P_o$, $P_1(\beta)/P_o$ and $P_1(\gamma)/P_o$ have different dimensions.[4]

However, the ratios of the capital values in terms of the consumption good *at equal-profit* points are comparable and this is what is required for the chain index of capital. Their capital values in terms of the price of the consumption good at $r = r_1$ where techniques α and β are equally profitable can be obtained by substituting r_1 into their respective equa-

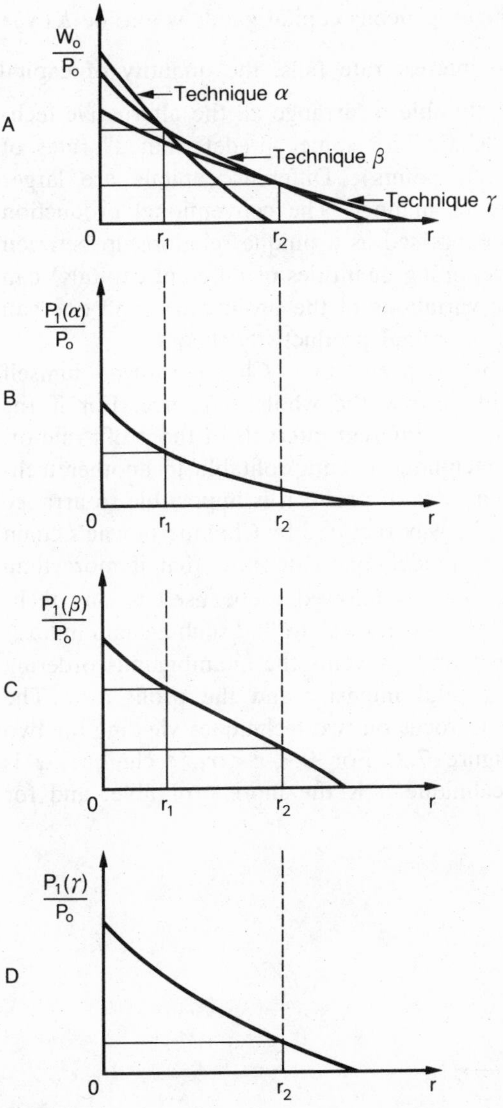

A
$\frac{W_o}{P_o}$
Technique α
Technique β
Technique γ
0
r_1
r_2
r
B
$\frac{P_1(\alpha)}{P_o}$
0
r_1
r_2
r
C
$\frac{P_1(\beta)}{P_o}$
0
r_1
r_2
r
D
$\frac{P_1(\gamma)}{P_o}$
0
r_2
r

Fig. 7.1

tions (6). Pairs of comparable ratios can be found, and, consequently, a chain index of capital can be erected. Let the base of the index be the real value of γ equipment at r_2, which can be derived from (1) and (2); call it $K(\gamma)$. Suppose the ratio of capital costs $\left[\frac{P_1(\beta)}{P_o}\Sigma K_{1j}(\beta) \Big/ \frac{P_1(\gamma)}{P_o}\Sigma K_{1j}(\gamma)\right]$ of the β to the γ technique at r_2 is 3 : 1, and that the ratio of the capital costs of the α to β technique at r_1 is 6 : 5. Then a chain index of these three heterogeneous capital goods would be $K(\gamma)\cdot(1 : 3 : 3\frac{6}{5})$. Thus, as the interest rate falls, the quantity of capital rises. Champernowne is clearly able to arrange all the alternative techniques of production in a "chain" for some "predetermined" rates of profit (chosen at equal-profit points). Different capitals are larger than others in an unambiguous manner. The conventional production function in which output is expressed as a unique relationship between labor and capital (here representing quantities of different capitals) can be traced out by parametric variations of the profit rates, and one can go on to do straightforward marginal productivity theory.

Of course the example is a special one. Champernowne himself showed that reswitching will destroy the whole sequence. For if the same technique is selected at two different intervals of the profit rate or, stated in another way, if a technique is equiprofitable to another technique at more than two given rates of profit, it is impossible to arrange the alternative techniques in the way required by Champernowne's chain index. (In a different type of model, one can show that if more than one [heterogeneous] capital good is allowed to be used in any technique matrix, then in general there is no way to find such a chain index.)

It is easy to see that reswitching prevents the unambiguous ordering of techniques in terms of capital intensity and the profit rate. The simplest way to show that is to focus on two techniques yielding the two wage curves depicted in figure 7.2. For $0 < r < r_1$, technique α is adopted; for $r_1 < r < r_2$, technique β is the more profitable, and for

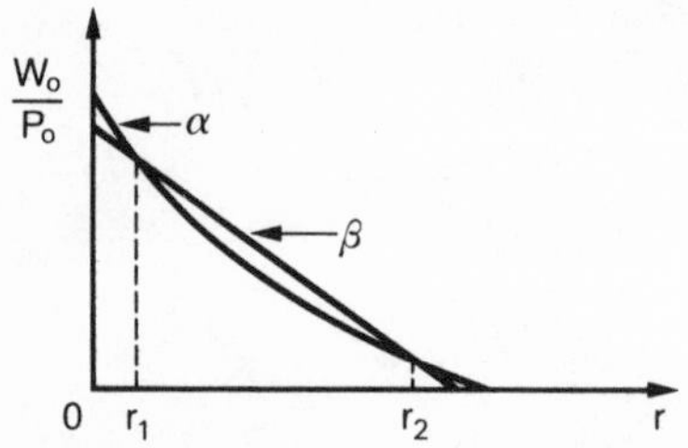

Fig. 7.2

$r > r_2$, technique α comes back or reswitches. Since $1/a_{lo}(\alpha) > 1/a_{lo}(\beta)$ and $1/a_{11}(\alpha) > 1/a_{11}(\beta)$, as the profit rate rises monotonically from $r = 0$ the economy adopts the less capital-intensive technique; but, as r continues to rise, there comes a point where it readopts the less capital-intensive technique. That is one of the reasons Champernowne's index breaks down. Another difficulty—called capital reversal—results when the wage frontier (the envelope of the wage curves) is concave from below. But the reswitching phenomenon is enough to show us that the chain index solution to the capital measurement problem is unacceptable. Note that the reason for the so-called perverse reswitching case is that the coefficient ratio is not unity, or more generally that it is such that it allows two intersections of the wage curves along the frontier.

Samuelson, in his well-known "surrogate production" model (1962), defended aggregate neoclassical production theory. He compared the simple heterogeneous capital model given above (which, as he said, is more realistic) with the neoclassical smooth, malleable-capital model. By a very special assumption that the $W_o/P_o - r$ relation for each technique is linear, the simple neoclassical malleable-capital model, in which output and capital are "jelly," can be a good approximation to the more realistic heterogeneous capital model given above.

Suppose the economy's technology implies the factor-price frontier derived from the wage curves in figure 7.3. Each segment on the frontier is associated with a specific method of production (and therefore a specific capital good). By increasing the number of techniques, a continuous frontier is generated, and hence a continuous switch from one technique to another will be expected as the rate of profit changes. Samuelson then argues that a general good, K, called jelly, can be found such that the factor price trade-off relation generated by the conventional neoclassical production function (with capital jelly as an in-

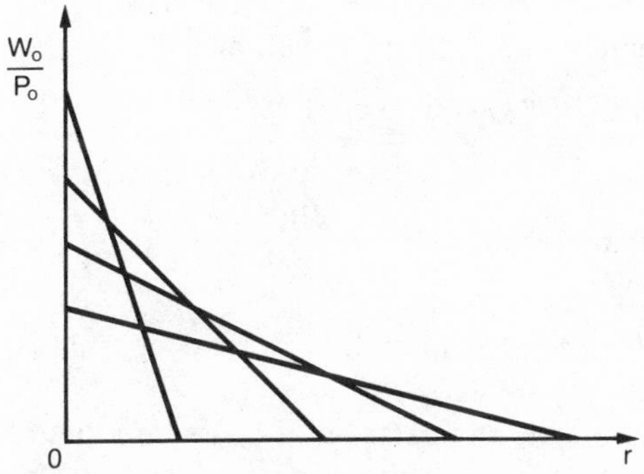

Fig. 7.3 The factor price frontier is the envelope of these wage curves.

put) is a good approximation to the factor-price frontier obtained from the simple heterogeneous capital model. The more realistic model can thus be represented by a neoclassical production function with all the usual aggregate neoclassical properties (i.e., differentiability, positive marginal products, constant returns, etc.). By means of the invisible hand of competition, the marginal product of the capital jelly equals the reward to capital jelly, and the marginal product of labor equals the real wage rate. Duality theory permits one to show the following: $Y \equiv C + PrK = F(L,J) = LF(1,J/L) = Lf(J/L)$; in a perfectly competitive economy, we have

$$W^* = \frac{\partial Y}{\partial L} = f(J/L) - \frac{J}{L} \cdot f'(J/L)$$

$$r = \frac{\partial Y}{\partial J} = f'(J/L),$$

where $W^* = W_o/P_o$; the assumptions of positive marginal products and diminishing or constant returns implies

$$\frac{dW^*}{d(J/L)} = -\frac{J}{L} \cdot f''(J/L) > 0 \tag{7}$$

$$\frac{dr}{d(J/L)} = f''(J/L) < 0. \tag{8}$$

Thus W^* is an increasing function of J/L and r is a decreasing function of J/L. The factor-price relation (trade-off) of the production function can be traced out by parametric variations of J/L. Graphically, this trade-off is given in figures 7.4 *a*, *b*, *c*, and *d*, where figure 7.4*d* clearly mimics figure 7.3. That is, the more realistic heterogeneous capital model can be approximated as closely as we like by increasing the density of techniques, which allows us to employ the neoclassical single-malleable-capital model. Samuelson further shows that the simple Marshallian elasticity of the factor-price frontier is a measure of the distribution of income. By equations (7) and (8), we have

$$\frac{dW^*}{dr} = -\frac{(J/L) \cdot f''(J/L)}{f''(J/L)} = -\frac{J}{L}.$$

Therefore the simple Marshallian elasticity $= -\dfrac{dW^*}{dr}\dfrac{r}{W^*} = \dfrac{J\,r}{LW^*} =$ ratio of relative shares.

Finally, one can show that $C/L = \gamma(r)$ is monotone decreasing, that is, $\gamma' < 0$.

All of Samuelson's aggregation results rest on the assumption of linear factor-price relations. That is, the *m* ratio must equal unity. (The equality of sectoral factor ratios satisfies the Gorman conditions; see below.) This assumption completely excludes reswitching. Being linear,

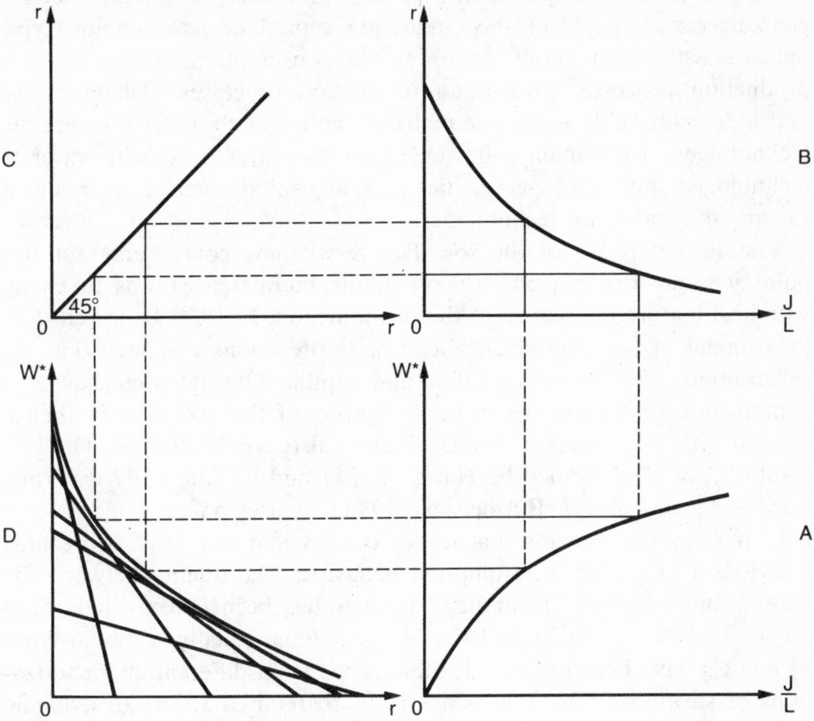

Fig. 7.4

each factor-price curve intersects another at the most only once. The technique will never come back again at different intervals of the rate of profit. The assumption of no reswitching is crucial to the development of a surrogate production function.[5]

Given that assumption, one arrives at the simplest neoclassical (Clarkian) parable, in which there is one homogeneous malleable physical capital (actually, one can measure capital in value terms in this case, but the value capital behaves like a physical quantity), no joint production, and smooth substitutability of labor and the capital aggregate. The marginal productivity relationships determine the functional income distribution and all the other variables in the general equilibrium system upon which the parable is based.

After the Samuelson article appeared, Levhari published a paper that attempted to show that reswitching was not possible in an economy in which the technique matrix is indecomposable. There was a flurry of effective refutations of that theorem, and in November 1966 a symposium in the *Quarterly Journal of Economics* presented them and also forced agreement on a large number of problems. Reswitching and other perversities are potentially present in models containing heterogeneous capital items of the circulating capital or fixed capital type, many consumption goods or only one consumption good, Austrian production processes, Walrasian production processes, decomposable and indecomposable technique matrixes, and smooth as well as discrete technologies. Reswitching, however, is associated only with discrete technologies, but other perversities such as capital reversal are relevant to smooth production technologies.

The second phase of the so-called reswitching controversy (at this point it is no longer a controversy in the literal sense) was taken up with spelling out the nature of the phenomenon. In 1969 I showed that, in a model of the type given above, if the technology is such that the substitution effects between labor and capital outweigh the change in composition or the change in the weighting of the two sectors, then a general type of perversity cannot occur (also see Brown 1973). This result has been confirmed by Hatta (1974) and by Sato (1976*b*) using a more general model. Burmeister (1977) focuses on the concept of a regular economy showing that it is necessary and sufficient to preclude paradoxical aggregate consumption behavior. The duality between the wage frontier and the technology frontier has been investigated (Sato 1974; Burmeister and Kuga 1970; Bruno 1969). Finally, different types of models have been examined; these range from different characterizations of steady-state models (Cass 1976; Zarembka 1976) to dynamic models (Oguchi 1977).

7.3 The Implications

One way to spell out the implications of what has been presented above is to compare the neoclassical parable to the intertemporal general equilibrium model containing many heterogeneous capital goods (Samuelson 1976; also see Nuti 1976). The following is a list of some steady-state properties of the neoclassical parable, some of which have been indicated above but do not hold generally:

a) $-\partial C_{t+1}/\partial C_t = 1 + r_t$,
b) $\partial^2 C_{t+1}/\partial C^2_t \leq 0$,
c) $W_o/P_i = f_i(r) = f(r)$, factor-price frontier trade-off,
d) $r = f'(K/L)$, marginal productivity, $f'' < 0$,
e) $C/L = \gamma(r)$, monotone decreasing, $\gamma'(\ ) < 0$,
f) $C/L = \theta(K/L)$, monotone increasing, $\theta'(\ ) > 0$,
g) K/Y or capital-output ratio declining with profit rate,
g') K/L declining with profit rate,

h) no reswitching possible,
i) no capital reversals,
j) elasticity of (r,w) frontier = wage share/profit share.[6]

Clearly, not all of these hold generally. It has been stressed repeatedly that (*h*) does not hold in general and therefore the neoclassical parable goes by the way. But (*a*), (*b*), and (*c*) do hold up in very general circumstances. Even if joint production is present, one can still accept the wage-profit trade-off that is dual to the consumption-growth rate relation just as it is in the nonjoint production case (Burmeister and Kuga 1970). Continuing, (*e*) does not hold in general, nor do (*f*), (*g*), and (*g*′). The neoclassical parable and its implications are thus generally untenable.[7]

What does this mean for those who want to measure capital at various levels of aggregation? If the conditions for no reswitching and no capital reversal ($m = 1$ covers both, but the conditions, $m \neq 1$ and the wage-profit frontier concave from below, permit capital reversals), then the capital aggregates are unstable. This means they are not invariant to changes in relative prices (Brown 1973). One may construct them as is usually done, but it is unlikely that they do not change with changes in the profit rate as Robinson has noted. Of course, that in turn means that the production function estimated on the basis of those capital aggregates is no longer a physical-technical relationship, for it now contains market variables. One cannot have much confidence in predictions based on such an unstable relationship.

7.4 Separability, Duality, Price, and Quantity Capital Indexes

We begin the discussion of the conditions underlying capital aggregates with those that require restrictions on functional form. For most of the exposition, we need treat only two sectors, in each of which there are three factors of production, two physically heterogeneous kinds of capital (x_{1j} and x_{2j}; $j = 1,2$), and labor (x_{oj}; $j = 1,2$). The original statement of this type of aggregation is attributable to Leontief (1947). The theorem is applicable to a partial equilibrium approach (analyzing the behavior of a single sector while treating the other sectors as exogenous) as well as to a general equilibrium analysis (in which feedback effects are permitted between sectors). In all the models, the capital goods are thought to be produced within the economy. They are akin to intermediate goods, but they are not "netted out" as is often done with inputs of materials. In many applications, the latter are indeed netted out so that these models refer to value-added magnitudes. Of course, as will become clear, the aggregation theorems based on the

Leontief results can encompass all types of goods. Finally, we abstract from depreciation and joint production in the initial exposition, returning to it briefly at a later point.

Suppose we focus on two production functions:

$$(9) \qquad y_j = f^j\,(x_{0j}, x_{1j}, x_{2j}), \quad j = 1{,}2,$$

where y_j are the outputs of the two sectors which we can take to be value-added measures for the moment. The functions f^j can be taken to have strictly positive marginal products (i.e., $f^j_i = (\partial f^j/\partial x_{ij}) > 0$; $i = 0{,}1{,}2$. For the Leontief theorem, the production functions f^j are taken to be strictly quasi-concave over the economic region.[8] They can be characterized by any degree of returns to scale; the freedom allowed by the Leontief theorem in this respect is one of its main advantages.

The Leontief theorem itself simply states that the necessary and sufficient condition to write f^j in equation (9) as

$$(10) \qquad y_j = f^j(x_{0j}, x_j), \quad j = 1{,}2,$$

where $\qquad x_j = g(x_{1j}, x_{2j}),$

is that

$$(11) \qquad \frac{\partial}{\partial x_{0j}}\left[\frac{\partial f^j}{\partial x_{1j}} \Big/ \frac{\partial f^j}{\partial x_{2j}}\right] = 0.$$

(For a simple proof, see Green 1964.) This condition, meaning that the marginal rate of substitution between the capital items is independent of labor, is called weak separability.[9] Note that it allows for aggregation of capital inputs within each sector; in other words, it permits intrasectoral aggregation.

Since weak separability is the basis for many of the aggregation results in this particular area of aggregation theory, it is worthwhile to interpret its meaning here. In the first place, it requires that changes in the labor (or any noncapital input) not affect the substitution possibilities between the capital inputs. Suppose labor input is ten, and the two capital substitution possibilities are, say, three x_1 to one x_2 and two x_1 to three x_2, both combinations yielding one hundred units of output. Now let labor input increase to twenty, which, combined with the same capital ratios, yields two hundred units of output. In this case the Leontief condition holds. (This example is based on Green 1964, pp. 11–12.) As Solow indicates (1955, p. 103), the condition will not often be satisfied, even approximately, in the real world. Some examples such as brick buildings and wooden buildings or aluminum fixtures and steel fixtures turn out to be cases where the capital items are homogeneous except in name. For more complex cases—bulldozers and trucks or sound amplification equipment and desks in a classroom—the technical substitution possibilities will probably depend on the amount of the labor input.

Yet there is a class of situations, according to Solow, in which the weak separability condition may be expected to hold. Suppose the production of y_j can be decomposed into two stages, one in which something called x_j is produced out of x_{1j} and x_{2j}, alone, and the second stage requiring this substance in combination with labor x_{0j} to produce y_j. More specifically, suppose that the "production" of x_j is given by

$$x_j = g^j(x_{1j}, x_{2j}); \tag{12}$$

for example, if x_{1j} and x_{2j} are two kinds of electricity-generating equipment and x_j is electric power, then generating capacity would be an index of the capital inputs. Clearly, the functions g^j in (12) are capital index functions, and it is important to know their properties. One way to do that is to follow Solow's article, where he shows that the g^j functions are linearly homogeneous (given that the F^j functions are linearly homogeneous and that the weak separability condition applies). Green (1964, chap. 4) does the same; but now an additional problem must be considered.

Examine (10) again, and see that the three factors of production are partitioned into two groups, a labor "group" x_{0j} and a capital group x_j. When there are only two groups, the weak separability condition is sufficient to allow for that decomposition and to yield price and quantity indexes for each group.[10] That is, if there are only two groups, it is sufficient (see Green 1964, p. 21) for there to exist a quantity index (12) in each sector and a sectoral capital price index: $p_{x_j} = p_{x_j}(p_{1j}, p_{2j})$. Moreover, it can be shown that, if the production function is homothetic,[11] the expenditure on the capital aggregate in each sector is $p_{x_j} x_j$, which, when added to the expenditure on the labor input, $p_{0j} x_{0j}$, adds up to total expenditure.

But when there are more than two groups, and of course that is probably the case, weak separability is no longer sufficient. Strotz (1959) and Gorman (1959) show that not only must the weak separability condition hold, but, in addition, each quantity index must be a function homogeneous of degree one in its inputs. These conditions, called homogeneous functional separability by Green (1964, p. 25), are necessary and sufficient[12] for each group expenditure to equal the sum of the expenditures on each item in the group; that is,

$$E^{j}{}_{r} = p_{i_r j}\, x_{i_r} j, \quad r = 1,2, \ldots, S,$$

where S is the number of groups into which the factors of production are partitioned.

It is customary to prove the above results by using duality theory. (See Shephard 1953.) Let us partition the inputs of (9) into labor and capital groups for each sector; that is, let x_{0j} and g^j (x_{1j}, x_{2j}) be the two groups.[13] Suppose that the g^j are homogeneous functions (they are quantity index functions) and that corresponding price indexes (homogeneous functions of prices) can be specified: $p_{x_{0j}}$ *and* p_{x_j} (p_{1j}, p_{2j}). Then, following Shephard (1953), the following aggregation conditions must apply:

(*a*) $\sum_{i=0}^{3} p_{x_{ij}} x_{ij} = p_{x_{0j}} x_{0j} + p_j g^j$

(*b*) $F^j(x_{0j}, x_{1j}, x_{2j})$ can be expressed as $F^j[x_{0j}, g^j(x_{1j}, x_{2j})]$, where g^j are homogeneous functions.

(*c*) Minimum cost, C^j, can be expressed as a function, $C^j(y_j, p_{x_{0j}}, p_{x_j})$; that is, as a function of the sectoral output rate and the price indexes.

(*d*) The aggregate cost function, $C^j(y_j, p_{x_{0j}}, p_{x_j})$ may be derived from the aggregate production function, $F^j(x_{0j}, g^j(\cdot))$ as $C^j(y_j, p_{x_{0j}}, p_{x_j}) = \min_{x_{0j}, g^j} (p_{x_{0j}} x_{0j} + p_j g^j)$, where g^j is given above and the prices are taken as parameters from the firm or sector's point of view.

If these conditions apply, then clearly each sector need concern itself with only two factors of production, and one can obtain all the information from the two-factor formulations that one does from the formulation involving all the elementary factors (in our simple exposition, there are only three).

The aggregation problem is solved if the production functions are such that F^j are arbitrary increasing functions of x_{0j} and g^j $(j = 1,2)$, and the g^j are homogeneous of degree one in their respective arguments; in other words, the production functions are homothetic.[14]

Duality between cost and production functions is involved precisely here, yielding information on the implied price indexes. For it is one of the enduring results of duality theory that if the production function in each sector is homothetic, then the sector's cost function factors into a product of $f^j(y_j)$, which is the inverse function of F^j (recall that the F^j are assumed to be monotonically increasing and also assume that $F^j(0) = 0$), and a function

$$\Gamma^j(p_{x_{0j}}, p_{x_{1j}}, p_{x_{2j}})$$

that is homogeneous of degree one in the prices; that is,

$$C^j(y_j, p_{x_{0j}}, p_{x_{1j}}, p_{x_{2j}}) = f^j(y_j) \cdot \Gamma^j(p_{x_{0j}}, p_{x_{1j}}, p_{x_{2j}}).$$

This considerably simplifies the cost function; it is worth repeating that, to do this, homotheticity of the production function and the independence of prices and quantities are required.

Using this well-known result, it is a simple matter to form subindexes for the two groups. Thus, in terms of costs for each group:

$$\min_{x_{0j}} (p_{x_{0j}} x_{0j}) = x_{0j}\Gamma^{0j}(p_{x_{0j}})$$

(13) and

$$\min_{x_{ij}} \left(\sum_{i=1}^{2} p_{x_{ij}} x_{ij} \right) = x_j \Gamma^{1j} (p_{x_{1j}}, p_{x_{2j}}).$$

where, recall, x_j is given by $g^j(x_{1j}, x_{2j})$ for g^j homogeneous of degree one; and Γ^{0j} and Γ^{1j} are homogeneous functions of degree one. Putting the two together, we can write:

$$C^j(y_j, p_{x_{0j}}, P_{x_{1j}}, p_{x_{2j}}) =$$

(14)

$$= \min_{x_{0j}, x_j} [x_{0j}\Gamma^{0j}(p_{0j}) + x_j\Gamma^{1j}(p_{1j}, p_{2j})],$$

where x_{0j} and x_j are restricted by

$$y_j = F^j(x_{0j}, x_j).$$

As Strotz and Gorman have demonstrated, the procedure for obtaining subindexes can be thought of as occurring in two stages: the first minimizes total costs by choosing the optimal proportion of each group of factors, whereas the second stage involves the minimization problems for each of the subgroups in (13) in which group costs are minimized separately given total costs.

The result is that $g^j(\cdot)$ and $\Gamma^{1j}(\cdot)$ are quantity (of capital) and capital price index numbers—they are the aggregates we seek—that simultaneously accomplish four things: the first is that they reflect the optimal inputs obtained from minimizing cost with respect to homothetic production surfaces; second, they are generalized index numbers that satisfy three fundamental Fisherian properties;[15] third, they satisfy the aggregation conditions (*a*)–(*d*), and, finally, they are consistent with the two-stage Gorman-Strotz optimization procedure. This is an extraordinary list of accomplishments, obtained at the cost of two seemingly harmless assumptions.

But there are limitations, and they are not negligible. The basic limitation of the duality theory and the resulting indexes can be seen from a simple example. Consider a firm using only two factors of production, x_0 and x_1, whose production follows the homogeneous of degree one CES form, which is obviously homothetic; that is,

$$y = \gamma(\kappa_0 x_0{}^{-a} + \kappa_1 x_1{}^{-a})^{-\frac{1}{a}} \cdot$$

The first-order conditions can be written in marginal rate of substitution form:

$$\frac{\kappa_1}{\kappa_0}\left(\frac{x_0}{x_1}\right)^{1+a} = \frac{E_1}{E_0}\frac{p_1}{p_0},$$

where $E_i = 1 + 1/e_i$, e_i is the elasticity of supply of the ith factor, and the p_i are the factor prices. The cost function is

$$C = \left(\frac{1}{\gamma}y\right)\left[\kappa_0 p^a{}_0\left[1 + \underline{a}EP^{-\frac{a}{1+a}}\right]^a + \kappa_1 p^a{}_1 \left[1 + \underline{a}^{-1}E^{-1}P^{\frac{a}{1+a}}\right]^a\right]^{\frac{1}{a}},$$

where $\underline{a} = \kappa_0/\kappa_1$, $E = E_0/E_1$, and $P = p_0/p_1$. Clearly, if $\partial E/\partial x_0 = \partial E/\partial x_1 = 0$, the cost function factors into two expressions, one in output that is homogeneous of degree one and the other in the p_i that is also homogeneous of degree one (note that P is homogeneous of degree zero in the p_i).

However, if factor-supply elasticities are related to the quantities of the factors themselves, and hence to the output, then the cost function does not factor into two terms that are homogeneous of degree one. This means, inter alia, that price and quantity of factor input indexes computed as expressions homogeneous of degree one misspecify the actual price and quantity changes, not because of the usual index number problems but because of the distortions introduced by imperfect competition in factor markets. (It can be shown that quantity output and price indexes would suffer a similar fate as a result of the presence of imperfect competition on the output side.) One can expect this to occur in those industries largely controlled by few firms, in time periods over which the factor supply elasticities are likely to change, and between firms in industries largely controlled by a few firms that coexist with smaller firms.

Suppose that industry price and quantity indexes homogeneous of degree one are constructed and that an analyst, using that data, aims to test hypotheses related to the degree of imperfect competition in that industry. That is, the data are constructed on the assumption that the firm or industry is competitive in factor markets,[16] and the analyst uses that data to test the degree to which that firm or industry is competitive. Clearly, the outcome must be biased. Or suppose a productivity analysis were undertaken using price and quantity indexes constructed as above; the productivity measure is clearly affected.

A practical difficulty with the approach based on weak separability and homotheticity is that it requires microdata on physical inputs and outputs to test the aggregation conditions. We do not have measures in physical units of the numerous capital items that enter production processes at even the most disaggregated level of production. But, even were they available, it may be difficult to accept the assumption of competition that underlies the construction of this type of aggregate.

7.5 Fisher's Extensions of Functional Form Conditions: Intersectoral and Intrasectoral Aggregation

Perhaps the most extensive analysis of aggregation conditions focusing on functional form has been done by Frank Fisher (1965; 1968*a*,*b*; 1969). Not only does he consider capital, labor, and output aggregation, but he also includes the difficult problems of fixed and movable factors.

Fisher introduces optimizing conditions for the economy into aggregation analysis. Thus, suppose the production functions are

$$y_j = F^j(x_{0j}, x_{1j}), \tag{15}$$

where capital may differ from firm to firm and for simplicity all firms' outputs are indistinguishable and there is only one kind of labor. Under what condition is it possible to write total output Y as given by the aggregate production function:

$$Y = \sum_j y_j = F(x_0, x_1), \tag{16}$$

where $x_0 = x_0(x_{01}, x_{02}, \ldots, x_{0n})$ and $x_1 = x_1(x_{11}, x_{12}, \ldots, x_{1n})$ are indexes of aggregate labor and capital, respectively. This, then, is solely a question of intersectoral aggregation.

If only restrictions on functional form were considered, the necessary and sufficient conditions for intersectoral aggregation are that every firm's production function be additively separable in capital and labor; that is, each F^j be of the form: $F^j(x_{0j}, x_{1j}) = Q^j(x_{0j}) + \Psi^j(x_{1j})$. That these conditions are extremely restrictive has been noted by Fisher and others.

Here Fisher notes that these conditions are answers to the wrong question. A production function, he states, describes the maximum level of output that can be achieved if the inputs are efficiently employed. Accordingly, one should ask not for the conditions under which total production can be written as (16) under any economic conditions, but rather for the conditions under which it can be written once production has been organized to get the maximum output achievable with the given factors. Thus, efficient production requires that Y be maximized given x_0 and x_1, a circumstance that introduces allocative decisions into the aggregate procedure. If one wishes to analyze production within a market system (or a centrally controlled one), then it does not seem reasonable to ignore the optimizing conditions for aggregation purposes.

Suppose in the simplest case that labor is movable and only labor can be allocated to firms to maximize total output. Letting Y^* be that maximal output, one can evidently write $Y^* = G(x_0, x_{11}, x_{12}, \ldots, x_{1n})$, there being no labor aggregation problem, since the values of x_{0j} are determined in the course of the maximizing procedure. The entire problem is the existence of a capital aggregate. Recalling that the weak separability condition (that MRS between x_{1i} and x_{1j} be independent of x_0 in G) is both necessary and sufficient for the existence of a group capital index, Fisher proceeds to draw the implication of this condition for the form of the original firm production functions in (15). He finds that under the assumption of strictly diminishing returns to labor ($F^j_{0j,0j} < 0$; $j = 1,2, \ldots, n$; where the subscripts denote differentiation), a necessary and sufficient condition for capital aggregation is that every firm's production function satisfy a partial differential equation in the form $F^j_{0j,1j}/F^j_{1j} F^j_{0j,0j} = g(F^j_{0j})$, where g is the same function for all firms. Further, assuming constant returns to scale, capital augmenting technical differences turns out to be the only case under constant returns in which a capital aggregate exists.

This means that each firm's production function be written as $F^j(x_{0j}, x_{1j}) = F^1(x_{0j}, b_j x_{1j})$, where the b_j are positive constants. Such a requirement is highly restrictive, since a different capital good is equivalent in all respects to more of the same capital good. For example, sound amplification equipment in a classroom is considered to be three times the number of desks in the same classroom. One requires a very complicated transformation scheme that somehow allows the varied and myriad capital goods to be accounted for in the same units.

The capital augmentation result and the notion of capital generalized constant returns[17] are important contributions of Fisher's analysis. He utilizes these basics in more complicated models, some of which are discussed below. But the general message that comes out of the work is that the conditions for output, capital, and labor aggregation are unlikely to be satisfied exactly.

Are they likely to be approximated? All we really care about is whether aggregate production functions provide an adequate approximation to reality in terms of the empirical values of the output, labor, and capital variables. Thus, for approximate capital aggregation it would suffice for technical differences among firms to be approximately capital augmenting.

But this is not a useful result. "The reason for being unhappy with capital aggregation, for example, is not merely that one thinks technical differences are not likely all to be exactly capital augmenting but that one thinks there are some differences that are not anything like capital augmenting" (Fisher 1969, p. 570). The interesting question is whether an aggregate production function gives a satisfactory approximation in a bounded region defined by the empirical values of capital and labor. Clearly, one must define what one means by a satisfactory approximation and also decide how badly the conditions are violated.

Fisher arrives at a generally negative conclusion: it appears that the only way to accept such approximations would be to admit certain well-defined irregularities in production functions, irregularities that are not exhibited by the aggregate production function in practice. Such an escape from the stringent conditions for aggregation will be available, if at all, only in rather special cases.

In view of this, Fisher asks why production functions with parameters estimated from factor payments turn out to fit input and output data so well. Since the matter is too complicated to treat analytically, he suggests experimenting with constructed data in which the aggregation conditions are known not to be satisfied. Aggregate production functions are then estimated on these data (in the latest study, the CES is used; see Fisher, Solow, and Kearl 1974). It turns out that the aggregate Cobb-Douglas predicts wages well whenever labor's share is roughly constant; with the CES, generalizations are more difficult to obtain. In spite of the special nature of the constructed data (all micro-units exhibit constant returns to scale), several other suggestive results emerge from this Monte Carlo type of study: composition effects can seriously distort aggregate elasticity of substitution estimates; and the wage equation estimates are more reliable than the production function estimates, though combining the two allows one to track output and factor prices closely. Thus aggregate production functions can work in special cases. And that is precisely their problem. We would require a catalog of unknown proportions to indicate their areas of applicability. Even then, one could not allay the doubt that the results are special in one way or another, and it may be difficult to specify which way it is.

7.6 The Gorman Aggregation Conditions

The Gorman (1953) conditions are developed along lines similar to those followed by Fisher. It is assumed that the optimal conditions for the distribution of given totals of moveable inputs among firms are satisfied. These efficiency conditions (which imply Pareto optimality) require that the marginal rates of substitution (MRS) between the ith and jth factors be the same for all firms:

$$\frac{\partial F^i}{\partial x_{ki}} \Big/ \frac{\partial F^i}{\partial x_{hi}} = \frac{\partial F^j}{\partial x_{kj}} \Big/ \frac{\partial F^j}{\partial x_{hj}}, \qquad i,j = 1, \ldots, n; \quad k = 1, \ldots, n; \quad h = 1, \ldots, m. \tag{17}$$

If all firms use some labor input, the given totals of the factors of production must be well-defined aggregates:

(18) $$x_r = \sum_{s=1}^{n} x_{rs}.$$

These, together with (17) imply a transformation surface: $G(y_1, y_2, \ldots, y_n; x_0, x_1, \ldots, x_m)$.[18]

Given that (17) holds and that isoproduct surfaces are convex, then Gorman shows that intersectoral aggregation of the production functions (equation 9) requires that the expansion paths for all firms be parallel straight lines through their respective origins. There will then exist functions, h^1, and h^2 and F, such that $Y = \sum_{j=1}^{2} h^j(y_j) = F(x_0,x_1,x_2)$, where F is homogeneous of degree one in its inputs. Hence, each F^j will be expressible as a function of F. Also, if the expansion paths are required to be parallel, the optimal ratios of the factors must be the same for all firms. An example may be useful here.

Suppose the F^j were CES, that is,

$$y_j = \left[b_{1j}x_{1j}^{(\sigma_j-1)/\sigma_j} + b_{2j}x_{2j}^{(\sigma_j-1)/\sigma_j} + b_{3j}x_{0j}^{(\sigma_j-1)/\sigma_j} \right]^{\sigma_j/(\sigma_j-1)},$$

then the marginal rates of substitution equilibrium conditions would be

(19) $$\frac{\partial F^j}{\partial x_{1j}} \bigg/ \frac{\partial F^j}{\partial x_{2j}} = \frac{b_{1j}}{b_{2j}} \left[\frac{x_{2j}}{x_{1j}} \right]^{1/\sigma_j} = \frac{p_1(r+\delta_1)}{p_2(r+\delta_2)}$$

(20) $$\frac{\partial F^j}{\partial x_{1j}} \bigg/ \frac{\partial F_j}{\partial x_{0j}} = \frac{b_{1j}}{b_{3j}} \left[\frac{x_{0j}}{x_{1j}} \right]^{1/\sigma_j} = p_1(r+\delta_1), \quad j = 1,2,$$

where the b_{ij} and σ_j are constants, the prices are normalized by the wage rate, and δ_j are constant declining-balance type depreciation coefficients. It is readily seen that the expansion paths are straight lines through their origin; moreover, the two conditions in (19) and the two in (20) imply parallel expansion paths if $b_{11}/b_{21} = b_{12}/b_{22}$, $b_{11}/b_{31} = b_{12}/b_{32}$, $\sigma_1 = \sigma_2$. Thus, under these conditions, intersectoral aggregation is possible. Note that, in the example above, satisfaction of the conditions entails that the production function F^1 has the form AF^2 with A an arbitrary positive constant. The two capital goods can be regarded as identical except for a choice of units. This ensures the feasibility of aggregation, but the requirement is so stringent that it is not likely to be satisfied in practice.

7.7 Economywide and Sectoral Weights in Divisia Input Price Indexes: The Gorman Conditions Again

The Gorman conditions turn up in unexpected places,[19] and one of those is in the weights on the Divisia indexes of capital inputs in a sectoral context. I shall show here that the practice of using economy-wide deflators to obtain real capital measures within a sector requires that the Gorman conditions be satisfied for all sectors in the economy. That is a patent impossibility, and hence that procedure involves a misspecification of unknown proportions.

Consider the value of capital used in the jth sector:

(21) $$v_j = \sum_{i=1}^{2} q_i x_{ij}, \quad j = 1,2.$$

Take its total differential[20] and express it in relative terms:

(22) $$\hat{v}_j = \sum_i w_{ij}\hat{q}_i + \sum_i w_{ij}\hat{x}_{ij}, \quad j = 1,2,$$

where the "hatted" variables represent relative changes, that is $\hat{v}_j = dv_j/v_j$, and so on, and $w_{ij} = q_i x_{ij}/v_j$, which is simply the costs of the ith capital item in the jth sector as a proportion of the sector's total capital costs.

The two components of $\hat{v}_j$ in equation (22) are called Wicksell effects, the first being the price Wicksell effect (PWE) while the second is the real Wicksell effect (RWE).

Suppose the two capital items in the jth sector (say, shearing machines and lathes) are to be treated as an aggregate. For several reasons (see Usher 1973, chap. 7), one must start with the value magnitudes (21) and (22) and derive the real aggregate from them. Referring to (22), it is thus necessary to eliminate the PWE. This is usually done by deflating the value of the capital aggregate (i.e., v_j) by a Divisia or chain index. In relative change terms, a commonly used index is

(23) $$\hat{q}^* = \sum_{h=1}^{2} w_{h.}\hat{q}_h,$$

where $$w_{h.} = \frac{\sum_{j=1}^{2} q_h x_{hj}}{\sum_{j=1}^{2} v_j}.$$[21]

The $w_{h.}$ are (possibly) changing Divisia weights; that is, $w_{h.}$ represents the economywide costs of the hth capital item as a proportion of total costs of all capital items. Note that $\hat{q}^*$ is an economywide measure that corresponds to an economywide Divisia or chain index. If the Bureau of Labor Statistics (BLS) wholesale price index (WPI) (or some variant of it) is used, an economywide input index is implied.[22] However, note that relative changes in the BLS WPI and $\hat{q}^*$ differ unless all depreciation rates are zero or the same.

Now, "deflate" (22) by (23)—that is, deduct $\hat{q}^*$ from $\hat{v}_j$; this yields $\hat{x}^*_j$, say: $\hat{x}^*_j = \sum_i (w_{ij} - w_{i.})\hat{p}_i + \sum_i w_{ij}\hat{x}_{ij}$. Recall that the deflation procedure, to be successful, must make the PWE vanish, leaving only $\sum_i w_{ij}\hat{x}_{ij}$. This implies that $\sum_i (w_{ij} - w_{i.})\hat{p}_i = 0$. Since $\hat{p}_i > 0$,[23] a necessary and sufficient condition for the PWE to vanish by this deflation procedure can be shown to be $x_{11}/x_{21} = x_{12}/x_{22}$. In turn, this can be shown to be identical to the Gorman conditions (parallel, straight-line expansion paths) if the production functions are homogeneous of degree one.

How does one interpret this result? Someone analyzing production in a single sector that uses two types of capital to produce it deflates the total cost of these two capital inputs by a price index of the two items that contains weights representing the proportions of costs of each item in the total costs of all capital produced. In doing that, the analyst has assumed (whether knowingly or not) that the Gorman conditions are satisfied. Clearly, they cannot be satisfied in realistic situations, and hence the PWE is not eliminated. A price effect remains in the "real capital aggregate," and every function specifying that aggregate must be unstable. (Clearly, one can isolate the direction of the resulting bias by an analysis of the sectoral and economywide weights.) Though the result above is subject to several qualifications,[24] one arrives at the discomforting conclusion that using an economywide index to deflate capital costs within a sector to derive a real measure of capital almost inevitably fails to purge the price Wicksell effect completely, and thus the resulting data fluctuate with prices. Since data estimation procedures are often used to derive data on which production functions are estimated, misspecifications are bound to be present.

7.8 Houthakker-Sato Aggregation

In a paper having a succès d'estime,[25] Houthakker (1955–56) found a way around the difficulties encountered by Solow-Fisher and Hicks by postulating that factor proportions are distributed in a certain way among the firms over which the aggregation is to take place. The introduction of the distribution function is novel, though there is an analogue from consumption theory on the distribution of income among consumers (see Katzner 1970, pp. 139 ff.). In subsequent work, the Houthakker idea was taken up by Levhari (1968) and Sato (1975), the latter developing it very fully.

In Houthakker's paper, each firm is assumed to operate under two-factor (labor and capital) fixed coefficients production conditions:

$$y_j = \alpha_j k_j = \beta_{0j} x_{0j}, \tag{24}$$

where k_j is the jth firm's capital-labor ratio. Efficiency conditions require that the firm is above its shutdown point if its quasi rent is nonnegative; that is, $y_j - p_0 x_{0j} = y_j(1 - p_0/\beta_j) \geq 0$ or $\beta_j \geq p_0$, where the labor input is taken to be homogeneous among firms so that all firms face the same wage rate. The distribution of capacity output of the firms is determined by the α_j and k_j and one can define a capacity distribution function as

$$\phi(\beta) = \sum_{a} \alpha k(\alpha,\beta). \tag{25}$$

The right-hand side is clearly the total productive capacity of firms with the labor efficiency level of β. To find the total productive capacity over all firms, one must integrate over β; thus

$$Y(p_0) = \int_{p_0}^{\beta_0} \phi(\beta) d\beta, \tag{26}$$

and total employment is

$$L(p_0) = \int_{p_0}^{\beta_0} \frac{\phi(\beta)}{\beta} d\beta, \tag{27}$$

where β_0 is the supremum of β (clearly, the β are taken to be bounded from above). Suppose the density function follows a Pareto distribution:

$$\phi(\beta) = C\beta^{-1/(1-a)}. \tag{28}$$

Inserting this into $Y(p_0)$ and $L(p_0)$ and eliminating p_0 from the two equations, one obtains the aggregate production function:

$$Y = J^{1-a} L^{a}, \quad 0 < a < 1, \tag{29}$$

where the aggregate capital, J, can clearly be found from

$$J = \int_{0}^{\beta_0} \phi(\beta) d\beta. \tag{30}$$

Thus, in the Houthakker model, if all firms operate according to Leontief production functions and if the β_j are distributed according to Pareto, the aggregate production function is Cobb-Douglas. Clearly, the weak separability property (in any of its variants) is unnecessary here.

Sato's procedure is only slightly different, but it yields far more general results. He begins with the micro production functions and the productive capacity function associated with the labor coefficient. He then derives necessary and sufficient conditions for the existence of an aggregate production function with capital and labor aggregates. That is, the following equalities must hold:

$$\text{(31)} \quad \begin{aligned} &i)\ L(p_0) = \int_{p_0}^{\beta_0} \frac{\phi(\beta)}{\beta}\, d\beta = \frac{1}{\beta_0} H \left(\frac{p_0}{\beta_0}\right) J \\ &ii)\ Y(p_0) = \int_{p_0}^{\beta_0} \phi(\beta)\, d\beta = G\left[H\left(\frac{p_0}{\beta_0}\right)\right] J, \end{aligned}$$

where J is given by (30) and the H and G functions satisfy the middle equalities of equations (31.i) and (31.ii), respectively.

Using this procedure, a host of results can be obtained. The micro production functions can now be allowed to have elasticities of substitution exceeding zero, and the distribution functions need no longer be of the Pareto form. Levhari (1968) had already derived an aggregate CES function using the Houthakker procedure, specifying zero elasticity of substitution micro production functions. Sato is able to treat this and the original Houthakker result as special cases of his more general approach.

The aggregate production function derived in this manner is a short-run relationship, since it describes the employment-output relation given the efficiency distribution. If the efficiency distribution shifts, the short-run aggregate production function also shifts, but the resulting factor proportions may not lie along the ex ante production function.[26] Generally, one considers the elasticity of substitution of the ex post or clay production process to be less than that of the ex ante production function. Sato shows (1975, pp. 134 ff.) that, if the efficiency distribution is stable in form, the resulting estimates should reveal the ex ante production function. Thus, the burden of the analysis that generates the desired aggregates shifts from the underlying production functions themselves to the stability of the distribution function.

Is the distribution function inherently unstable when the variables vary? (Sato's estimates, 1975, p. 205, are not uniformly acceptable.) Do firms entering the industry have the same distribution of productive capacities as those leaving? (See Sato 1975, p. 30.) Clearly, the presence of nonneutral technical change implies a change in the slope of the Pareto curve, since capacity will be added at the low end of the scale of input ratios (see Sato 1975, p. 140). At the very least, the estimation problems associated with the distribution function are just as formidable as those of the production function itself. Moreover, recall that one must estimate the distribution function in addition to the production function, thus compounding the difficulties.

There is one further estimation problem with the Houthakker-Sato approach that requires some discussion. The distribution of productive capacities does not appear to be independent of the macro production function. The disturbances on each of the econometric forms are probably correlated (certainly shocks in the distribution function affect aggregate output); thus there is a simultaneous equation estimating problem that differs from that treated in the literature on error specification in production models (see, e.g., Zellner, Kmenta, and Dreze 1966). This problem does not appear to be recognized, much less resolved. One may wish to classify the simultaneity problem as another practical difficulty (see Sato 1975, pp. 201–2).

Glancing back at (24) and (29), one notices that the original Houthakker problem was the intersectoral aggregation of two-factor production functions. When more than two factors are considered, one has to invoke the familiar separability conditions (Sato 1975, pp. 65 ff.) in order to do intrasectoral aggregation. The addition of the distribution function is useful only in intersectoral aggregation; nothing is added to the traditional analysis of indexes of capital goods and prices. Hence, the national income statistician interested in the theoretical foundations of those indexes would not turn to the Houthakker approach.

The question of whether the Houthakker-Sato procedure is more or less restrictive than either those based on the weak separability property or the composite commodity condition is a difficult one to handle. The introduction of the distribution function complicates any comparison, since one has little basis for knowing if its specification and estimation is more or less restrictive than the requirements of the alternative aggregation procedures. That in one respect it allows for a (possibly) more limited range of possibilities (e.g., micro elasticities of substitution greater than unity are ruled out [Sato 1975, p. 61]) than weak separability, and so on, is clear. That it is an essentially short-run analysis puts it on the same footing as composite commodity aggregation but makes it less desirable than the Gorman theorem. That it is difficult to test empirically gives it the same grades on this account as the weak separability approach. That it allows for more general micro production processes than the Gorman theorem (except for the elasticity of substitution restriction above) is a significant point in its favor. That it requires fairly restrictive assumptions on stability of the distribution function detracts from the previous point.[27] And that intrasectoral aggregation requires some sort of restrictive weak separability or composite property as well as the somewhat restrictive stability conditions of the distribution function—that also is clear. Thus, much is clear yet, nevertheless, a comparison cannot yield an unambiguous answer on which procedure is preferable. It remains to say that the Houthakker-Sato approach must be subjected to further work to resolve some of the outstanding problems indicated above.

7.9 Commodity Aggregation Approach

Up to this point I have focused on the conditions for aggregation that arise out of the form of the production function (weak separability, homotheticity, etc.). The Hicks (1946) commodity aggregation approach that I now consider sidesteps those considerations of functional form. Hicks writes: "a collection of physical things can always be treated as if they were divisible into units of a single commodity so long as their relative prices can be assumed to remain unchanged, in the particular problem at hand" (1946, p. 33). Thus, let q_{ij} be the capital user costs; that is, $q_{ij} = p_{ij}(r_{ij} + \delta_{ij})$, $(i = 1,2)$ in its simplest form, where p_{ij} is the price of the ith capital good in the jth sector, r_{ij} is the net own interest rate, and δ_{ij} is the depreciation rate on the ith capital good. If the system is in equilibrium and depreciation is independent of the output rate, then the variables defining user costs are independent of the sector with which the capital is associated and the net own interest rates for all capitals are the same; therefore,

$$q_i = p_i(r + \delta_i). \tag{32}$$

For our purposes, we can use (32) to illustrate the present aggregation procedure.

Now, define the value of capital in the jth sector as

$$v_j \equiv \sum_i^2 q_i x_{ij} = q_1 \sum_i^2 \frac{q_i}{q_1} x_{ij}, \quad j = 1,2, \tag{33}$$

where the last equality would hold just as well were we to replace q_1 by q_2. Hicks proves that if $\left[\frac{q_1}{q_i}\right] d \left[\frac{q_i}{q_1}\right] = 0$, one can decompose v_j into two components, a "price" component, q_1, and a quantity component, $\sum_i^2 \frac{q_i}{q_1} x_{ij}$. With a slight modification, these components serve as price and quantity indexes of aggregate capital in the jth sector. Clearly, any number proportional to q_1, say $q^* = \alpha q_1$, would serve as the capital price index. Thus, the factor reversal test for price-quantity indexes is satisfied. Moreover, one can obtain "real" sectoral aggregate capital by deflating v_j by q^* and economywide "real" aggregate capital by deflating Σv_j by q^*. Finally, note that both the quantity and price indexes are homogeneous of degree one.

There are several reasons why prices of goods within a group may move in proportion to each other. Suppose certain prices are administered (fixed) over a relevant time period under conditions of monopoly (Fisher 1969, p. 572). Conversely, goods that are within a competitive industry or group would tend to move together in the long run. They may move together because of governmental price or incomes policy. Or, if the economy were in a balanced, steady-state growth or if it were stationary, prices would be constant and of course proportional to each other. Finally, if the labor shares in all firms are equal, then relative prices are constant (see below).

This is a very simple aggregating device, yet its exact form requires the stringent proportionality condition. However, approximations do not wreak havoc with the composite commodity conditions as they do with the functional form procedure. Clearly, commodity aggregation is unlikely to hold in general, but it may hold approximately for certain subgroupings (see Diewert 1974) and for some groups for certain periods and cycles but not for others. I shall elaborate upon this in a forthcoming study. Note that it has been used for theoretical purposes to justify partial and comparative static equilibrium analyses (see Arrow and Hahn 1971, pp. 7, 253).

It may also be the case that some prices are proportional to each other over certain time periods and not over others. For example, the trend and eight-year cycle could be the same for two prices, but they may differ over shorter-run cycles. Does this mean that the prices fail to satisfy the commodity aggregation theorem? Not at all, for a long-term grouping of the corresponding quantities is possible, whereas that grouping would make no sense in the short run.

Following this line of thought, one can consider the possibility that there is a systematic lead-lag relationships between the two prices but that, aside from that, they are proportional to each other. Does the lead or lag prevent the application of the commodity aggregation theorem? Again, the answer depends on the use to which the grouping is to be put.

There are many problems with this approach, the main one being that the q_j are not prices—rather, they are per unit capital rental values. Thus they are conglomerates of several factors that may change in various ways. Another problem is that published prices generally refer to total output, whereas a value-added price is the more appropriate concept. I shall elaborate on these and other matters relating to commodity aggregation in a forthcoming paper.

7.10 The Brown-Chang General Equilibrium Approach

The principal shortcoming of the preceding aggregation approaches is that they are done in a compartmentalized manner. That is, the restrictions on functional form required by the Gorman theorem are discussed in abstraction from their effect on prices; and the composite commodity theorem is derived without reference to economywide forces affecting prices of the items in the composite.

The Brown-Chang analysis remedies that deficiency in the literature by treating prices as endogenous within a simple general equilibrium model. Recall that the Gorman conditions focus on factor proportions while the composite commodity theorem emphasizes relative factor prices. But both factor proportions and factor prices are endogenous in a general equilibrium context, and hence any restriction on, or requirement of, one set of variables must affect the other.

Refer back to the little two-sector production function model (eq. 9), taking each to be homogeneous of degree one. Now add a zero profit condition for each sector:

$$p_j y_j / x_{0j} = 1 + q_1 x_{1j}/x_{0j} + q_2 x_{2j}/x_{0j}, \quad j = 1,2. \tag{34}$$

All prices are measured in terms of the nominal wage. For simplicity, assume for the moment that machines last forever (or one could also assume that depreciation rates are the same for both equipments) and thus the gross rental rates become: $q_i = p_i r$, where r is the only exogenous variable in the system. Parenthetically, we remark that one can "close" the system completely by specifying a relationship between net own rates of productivity and the rate of time preference (see Solow 1963) or by postulating that the fiscal monetary authorities control r to obtain a distributional objective (see Sraffa 1960). We require one other set of conditions—the marginal productivity equilibrium conditions must hold for each sector, that is,

$$\text{(35)} \qquad \begin{aligned} f^j_0 &= \frac{\partial f^j}{\partial x_{0j}} = 1/p_0, \quad j = 1,2 \\ f^j_i &= \frac{\partial f^j}{\partial x_{ij}} = p_i r/p_j, \quad i,j = 1,2. \end{aligned}$$

These, together with (34) place us firmly within the world of perfect competition.

Brown and Chang now set out to find the conditions for the aggregation of the capital aggregates in a composite commodity sense; that is, under what conditions can one specify a $q^1{}_j$ and q such that

$$\text{(36)} \qquad \begin{aligned} &i)\; x_j = \sum_{i=1}^{2} \frac{q_i}{q^1{}_j}\, x_{ij}, \quad j = 1,2 \\ &\text{and} \\ &ii)\; \mathrm{x} = \sum_{h=1}^{2} \frac{q^1{}_h}{q}\, x_h ? \end{aligned}$$

Clearly, this requires

$$\frac{d(q_1/q_2)}{dr} = \frac{d(p_1/p_2)}{dr} = 0.$$

Thus, solving (34) for the p_j in terms of r, taking the ratio of the two expressions and then differentiating with respect to r, one finds

$$\text{(37)} \qquad \frac{d(p_1/p_2)}{dr} = \frac{1}{p^2_2 r\Delta}\left(P_1\frac{y_1}{x_{01}} - p_2\frac{y_2}{x_{02}}\right),$$

where $$\Delta \equiv \left(\frac{y_1}{x_{01}} - \frac{x_{11}}{x_{01}}r\right)\left(\frac{y_2}{x_{02}} - \frac{x_{22}}{x_{02}}r\right) - \frac{x_{12}}{x_{02}}\frac{x_{21}}{x_{01}}r^2.$$

The term in parentheses in (37) represents the difference in the wage shares in the two sectors.

Thus we arrive at the principal Brown-Chang result: commodity aggregation is assured, (36) holds, if the labor shares in the two sectors are equal. As an example, suppose the production functions are CES; aggregation of the two capital goods is possible—both intersectorally and intrasectorally—if

$$a_1\left(\frac{y_1}{x_{01}}\right)^{\frac{1}{\sigma_1}-1} = \frac{x_{01}}{p_1y_1} = a_2\left(\frac{y_2}{x_{02}}\right)^{\frac{1}{\sigma_2}-1} = \frac{x_{02}}{p_2y_2},$$

where a_i and σ_i $(i = 1,2)$ are constants. This condition requires that the production functions be restricted in a particular way, but the restriction appears to be weaker than the Gorman conditions, since factor ratios do not all have to be the same at all rates of interest.

In the general equilibrium model of production presented above, the equal-labor share condition guarantees the constancy of relative commodity prices (provided depreciation rates are equal), thereby permitting intrasectoral as well as complete aggregation of the capital items in the system. The condition can be applied to models with joint products and can be generalized to models with many primary factors; it can be applied to the capital goods as a group, to all sectors in the economy including the consumption good sector, and to a subgroup of capital goods sectors—the decomposable case—that does not require inputs from sectors outside the group. The decomposable case is particularly useful, since no matter how many groups of capital goods are in the economy, as long as there is a particular group whose production does not require capital inputs from sectors outside the group, the commodity aggregation condition applies, provided labor shares in that group are equal. In the decomposable case, however, the equal-labor share condition alone is not sufficient to guarantee aggregation of a proper subgroup of capital goods. If capital goods are divided into more than two groups, it is possible to derive more detailed conditions for aggregation. But these conditions are expected to be more stringent and therefore less likely to hold.

Intuitively, the equal-labor share condition amounts to equal capital/labor cost ratios in each industry—a variant of Marx's case of equal organic composition of capital. When the depreciation rates are the same for each capital good, this condition is equivalent to the equal factor intensity condition in value terms; that is, the *aggregate value* of capital/labor ratios are the same in every industry.

When there is an increase in the rate of interest, the increase in rental costs of capital in each industry depends upon (with identical rates of depreciation for each capital good) the *aggregate* value of capital employed in that industry. This explains why it is the capital intensity in value terms, not in physical terms, that is crucial in determining the effect on prices resulting from a change in the rate of interest. When every industry has the same capital intensity in value terms, an increase in the rate of interest will increase the cost of every commodity in the same proportion, thereby maintaining constant relative prices.

If the depreciation rates of different capital goods are different, the commodity price ratios and rental rates will not remain fixed as a result of a change in the rate of interest, even though the wage shares are equal in all sectors. However, Sato (1976*a*) has shown that if production is taken net of depreciation, the equal-labor share condition still applies.

The logic of the Brown-Chang and the Gorman aggregation conditions of a many-sector, many-capital, equal-depreciation rate model can now be examined. Suppose that there are n capital goods sectors and m consumption goods sectors. When the equal-labor share condition together with equal rates of depreciation for each capital good is satisfied, the relative commodity prices and the relative rental rates of capital are always constant. We can then apply the Hicksian aggregation theorem to perform intrasectoral aggregation over all capital inputs. When we appropriately choose the same units of measurement for the aggregated capital inputs in each sector, the system is reduced to one with n capital goods sectors and m consumption goods sectors, each with two factors of production, aggregated capital and labor. Now the equal-labor share condition in this two-factor model amounts to equal capital intensities in value terms as well as in physical terms. At this point the Gorman conditions are satisfied and intersectoral aggregation is possible. If all wage shares are equal in the capital good sectors, all these capital goods may be aggregated into a single capital good sector. A similar argument applies to the aggregation of the consumption goods sectors. The resulting system becomes the familiar two-sector, one-capital-good model.

Further aggregation of the two-sector model into a one-sector aggregative model can be achieved if the wage shares are equal in the two sectors. This implies the satisfaction of the Gorman conditions, and the production functions in the two sectors clearly differ only by an efficiency unit.

The commodity aggregation approach depends on the constancy of relative prices. In this case aggregation is completely independent of demand conditions. Clearly, this is not the only case allowing aggregation. For example, based on demand or utility functions, one can carry out aggregation of several outputs and production functions into an economywide production function (see Sato 1975).

In the general equilibrium model, it is not possible for the conditions of the Gorman theorem to be satisfied without simultaneously satisfying the condition for commodity aggregation (see Zarembka 1976). If the production functions happen to have a form such that the expansion paths for both firms are parallel straight lines through their respective origins, then (as noted above) the optimal factor ratios must be the same. Since all firms face the same factor prices, labor shares clearly must be the same in both sectors, and thus the commodity aggregation condition is satisfied in this model.

This leads to the unexpected result that the satisfaction of the Gorman conditions allows only intersectoral aggregation (see above), but if those conditions are satisfied in a general equilibrium type model, then the conditions for commodity aggregation are also satisfied, which means that intersectoral, intrasectoral, and full aggregation are permitted. In other words, if the very stringent Gorman conditions restricting the form of the production function are met (allowing only intersectoral aggregation), then the capital goods prices are proportional to each other (and to a capital price index), so that one need not stop with intersectoral aggregation but can proceed to aggregate all the capital items in each capital good sector and all the capital items among the many capital goods sectors.

The converse of this proposition clearly does not hold. For, even if all labor shares were to be equal, all optimal factor ratios do not have to be the same, so that if conditions for commodity aggregation hold, the Gorman conditions do not have to hold. It is possible for sectoral labor shares to be equal without all factor ratios being equal. Thus the conditions for commodity aggregation are somewhat weaker than that required by the theorem that focuses on the form of the production functions.

The equal-labor share condition is weaker than the Gorman condition in another respect. The latter requires that all capital items be used in each sector for intersectoral aggregation to hold, while the equal-labor share condition allows for the absence of capital items, since we have assumed only that labor is indispensable in each line of production. Certainly, in many sectors there are many corners, that is, numerous capital items not actually employed in production, and hence the Brown-Chang condition is weaker than the Gorman condition.

How do the Brown-Chang results relate to the other principal restriction on functional form procedure developed by Fisher? Fisher's discussion of the case of two-factor (fixed capital, movable labor) constant returns to scale contains a result similar to that found by Brown and Chang. There, a necessary and sufficient condition for the existence of an aggregate capital stock (obtained from all vintages) is that the average product of labor shall be the same for all vintages. Also, in his discussion of aggregation of fixed and movable capital items in the constant returns to scale case, Fisher (1968*b*, p. 422) shows that a necessary condition for total capital aggregation is that the average product of every kind of labor be the same in every firm whenever all movable factors (labor and movable capital) are optimally allocated. In the two cases cited above, he assumes that only one homogeneous output is produced, which must be the same for all firms. Therefore, with identical output prices in Fisher's models, equal average product of labor in every sector is equivalent to the equal-labor share condition. The Brown-Chang model assumes that all factors are movable, thus assuming away the problem of aggregating fixed factors.

Perhaps the most relevant way to compare the Brown-Chang model and Fisher's is to examine his aggregation of movable factors. Fisher discusses extensively full aggregation as well as subaggregation. In particular, he finds that what is required for subaggregation is that given the relative wages (relative prices) of the labor inputs (outputs) to be included in the aggregate, every firm employs those inputs (produces those outputs) in the same proportion. This is very close to parallel expansion paths. Note, however, that some fixed factors are assumed to exist and are left out of the aggregate in the case above. When there are no fixed factors, the condition that every firm employ all movable factors in the same proportion naturally implies the equal-labor share condition for the Brown-Chang model. The converse, of course, is not true, which implies that the equal-labor share condition may be more general than Fisher's result in this context. It is important to note that in Fisher's analyses, he uses conditions of technical efficiency (maximize the last output, given the amounts of the other outputs and the amounts of the inputs) while assuming the existence of some fixed factors that cannot be moved around over different uses so as to equalize marginal products. In the Brown-Chang analysis, it is assumed that all factors are movable so as to satisfy the equilibrium conditions. Clearly, the use of the equilibrium conditions makes aggregation easier. Finally, in the Brown-Chang model capital outputs are produced to be used as capital inputs. This is closely related to the capital aggregation problems associated with the recent reswitching debate.

What are the shortcomings of the Brown-Chang results? Certainly the general equilibrium model is not as general as one would like (such as that proposed by Arrow and Hahn 1971, chap. 5), but that is not a fundamental problem, since one would conjecture that many of the results would hold in a more general model. The real problem is the same as that encountered by the aggregation theory described above, which is based on duality theory, and that is the necessity for assuming competition in factor markets. The equal-labor share condition, though less restrictive than the Gorman conditions in certain respects, is still a stringent one. This is coupled with the fact that it cannot be applied in an economy where competition is suspected of being imperfect.

7.11 Structural versus Nominalistic Aggregation and a Paradox in Aggregation Analyses

We can now introduce an important distinction in aggregation theory. Consistent aggregates can be specified for essentially two reasons. The first is associated with the restrictions on functional form based in one way or another on the weak separability property of the underlying production functions. These give rise to proportional factor inputs. We know that, if this property is present, then whatever the behavior of the myriad aspects of the economy, consistent aggregation is preserved. That is, prices can change in a proportional or nonproportional manner because of supply shifts, say, and the aggregates would be unaffected. This says that if the physical-technical properties of production that manifest this property remain unchanged, the aggregates are preserved whether or not monopoly forces are present, whether relative supplies of factors change, whether disequilibrium effects are present, whether the economy is a steady-state growth path, whether an incomes policy is enforced, and so on. In short, knowing that the aggregates are conditional upon the properties of the production function is enormously economical. (Only nonneutral technical change would offset the aggregates.) We call this "structural" aggregation.

Going to commodity aggregation, we cannot infer this. Prices could be proportional to each other for a variety of reasons, and the resulting aggregates are subject to change owing to changes in any one of them. Thus, observing constancy of relative prices and basing the aggregation procedure on them would be questionable. If one is able to derive aggregates in this way at all, they are less likely to be stable than those derived from a knowledge of the properties of the production functions. Obviously, the resulting aggregates are real groupings in name only—hence we call this nominalistic.

It is one of the paradoxes of aggregation analysis that it may not be possible to derive the structural type of aggregates until and unless one can first obtain the nominalistic type. The reasoning is as follows. In order to test for weak separability (inter alia) underlying the structural aggregates, one must have data on the myriad physical capital items used in a given production unit. These data do not exist, nor are they likely to become available. Data on expenditures exist for many categories, but to obtain the physical data on the items within those categories, price indexes must be used to deflate them. But the very existence of price indexes that allow for consistent aggregation is the point in question; for one does not know that the production functions are homogeneous of degree one in the elementary inputs in each group index, since that is the object of the test. Mention could also be made of the current impossibility of estimating production functions with thousands of inputs even were the physical data available.

But one can test for nominalistic factor aggregation, and though that does not yield inferences directly with respect to the production function, one could use the resulting aggregates in estimating the aggregated production function over the sample for which the nominalistic aggregates hold. Aside from engineering approaches, that seems to be the only feasible way of going about it, thus giving rise to the paradox.

7.12 The Statistical Case (?) for Aggregative Analysis

The argument for specifying aggregative relationships directly rather than focusing on micro aspects of economic and technological behavior finds expression in the econometric literature. It is necessary to examine it to determine if and when it can be applied to the production and capital aggregation problems under discussion here. The intent is to make precise an aspect of the crude notion that macro relationships are preferable because of offsetting errors among the micro components. This is a purely statistical approach, and if it could be implemented it would afford a means of bypassing the difficulties of satisfying the aggregation conditions noted above.

In Theil's original work along this line, he found that the micro equations are the more appropriate ones to estimate under the assumptions of perfect (micro) model specification and nonstochastic regressors. This was developed further by Grunfeld and Griliches (1960), who indicate that there are circumstances in which an aggregate variable may be forecast with more precision than an aggregate of forecasts from the micro equations. Such a result arises from the possibility that micro equations are less well specified than the macro equation. The problem with the Grunfeld-Griliches analysis is that it is very difficult to be precise about when and the extent to which the micro equations are less well specified than the macro equation. In fact, one is reduced to articulating special cases and examples of the alleged specification bias rather than a general analysis. But, as we shall see, that is not the main objection to the whole procedure.

Rejecting the Grunfeld-Griliches approach, Orcutt, Watts, and Edwards (see Edwards and Orcutt 1969 for references) focus on the difficulty of obtaining suitable micro data. In general they find that it is better to forecast on the basis of an aggregate of micro forecasts rather than doing a macro forecast. In any event, the focus of the literature has switched to the measurement errors attached to micro and macro data. If micro data is subject to more measurement error than aggregate data, there is the trade-off of the loss from the specification bias resulting from aggregation and the potential gain from the reduction in the inaccuracy of the measured aggregate data.

Aigner and Goldfeld (1974) consider the problems of estimation and prediction when the data on independent variables contain less measurement error than the micro data. Greene (1975), correcting an error in their model, does the same. The last reference I make to this literature is Welsch and Kuh (1976), who employ a general random coefficient model to determine how the variances of the coefficients behave as the number of micro units increase.

To give an idea of one line of development, let us follow Greene's analysis of the very simple offsetting errors case. Suppose there are only two micro equations,

$$\begin{aligned} Y_1 &= \beta_1 X_1 + u_1 \\ Y_2 &= \beta_2 X_2 + u_2, \end{aligned} \tag{38}$$

where the measured values of the micro variables are

$$\begin{aligned} y_1 &= Y_1 + w \\ y_2 &= Y_2 - w \end{aligned} \tag{39}$$

and

$$\begin{aligned} x_1 &= X_1 + v \\ x_2 &= X_2 - v. \end{aligned} \tag{40}$$

The macro variables, $(Y_1 + Y_2) = (y_1 + y_2)$ and $(X_1 + X_2) = (x_1 + x_2)$, are clearly assumed to be measured without error.[28]
After combination,

$$
(41) \qquad \begin{aligned} &i)\ y_1 = \beta_1 x_1 + \epsilon_1 \\ &ii)\ y_2 = \beta_2 x_2 + \epsilon_2, \end{aligned}
$$

where $\epsilon_1 = u_1 + \beta_1 v - w$ and $\epsilon_2 = u_2 - \beta_2 v + w$. The macro equation is simply the addition of these, which is,

$$
(42) \qquad (y_1 + y_2) = \beta(x_1 + x_2) + \epsilon,
$$

where $\epsilon = u_1 + u_2 + (\beta_1 - \beta)\, x_1 + (\beta_2 - \beta)\, x_2 + (\beta_1 - \beta_2)\, v$. All variables are taken to be independent and normally distributed with zero means; that is, $(X_1, X_2) \sim N(0, \Sigma_x)$, $(u_1, u_2) \sim N(0, \Sigma_u)$, $w \sim N(0, \sigma^2_w)$ and $v \sim N(0, \sigma^2_v)$, where

$$
\Sigma_x = \begin{bmatrix} \sigma^2_{x_1} & \sigma_{x_1 x_2} \\ \sigma_{x_1 x_2} & \sigma^2_{x_2} \end{bmatrix}; \quad \Sigma_u = \begin{bmatrix} \sigma^2_{u_1} & \sigma_{u_1 u_2} \\ \sigma_{u_1 u_2} & \sigma^2_{u_2} \end{bmatrix}.
$$

The error terms in (41) involve the βs, and thus the estimation problem is akin to a classic errors-in-variables problem. The limiting values to which the least-squares estimates of β_i tend in probability can be shown to be

$$
\text{plim}\ \hat{\beta}_i = \beta_i \Big/ 1 + \frac{\sigma^2_v}{\sigma^2_{x_i}} .
$$

This gives the familiar result that the micro parameter $\hat{\beta}_i$ is in fact an underestimate of β_i.

Now, going to the macro equation, (42), one finds that

$$
\text{plim}\ (\hat{\beta}) = \gamma\beta_1 + (1 - \gamma)\, \beta_2,
$$

where

$$
\gamma = (\sigma^2_{x_1} + \sigma_{x_1 x_2}) / (\sigma^2_{x_1} + \sigma^2_{x_2} + 2\sigma_{x_1 x_2}),
$$

which is also inconsistent. Hence, in deciding whether to use the micro or the macro equations when measurement errors offset each other in the micro variables, the choice devolves upon two sets of inconsistent estimators. A preliminary conclusion can be reached here without further analysis; and that suggests that if β_1 and β_2 are close together and if the measurement error is large, one would be advised to estimate the macro equation (42) and use $\hat{\beta}$ as an estimate of each β_i rather than estimate each β_i separately from (41). This result is made more precise by specifying the mean square errors of the estimators and comparing them. However, this large sample result is not an interesting one, since an instrumental variable estimator, using $(x_1 + x_2) = (X_1 + X_2)$, can be shown to dominate both micro and macro least-square estimators (Greene 1975).

Even in the small sample case, there is an opportunity for the macro estimator to outperform the micro in spite of the presence of "aggregation bias." Here aggregation bias is represented by $\beta_1 \neq \beta_2$. It is found that, though there are exceptions, in most cases in which there is aggregation bias, the micro estimator is superior. However, when observation errors are introduced, there is an inevitable trade-off between aggregation bias and measurement errors of the micro data. It is found that as the error variance increases relative to the "true" variables, the advantage of the micro estimator declines, which is not an unexpected result.

There are many different results in this literature. Some studies support prediction in certain circumstances from disaggregated data (e.g., Edwards and Orcutt 1969). Using different models, Grunfeld and Griliches (1960) and perhaps Aigner and Goldfeld (1974) and Greene (1975) find superiority in certain circumstances in macro analysis. In the Welsch and Kuh (1976) analysis, it is difficult to say which is superior.[29] A summing-up results in the characterization of the glass as half-full or half-empty and hence is not very informative.

There are two immediate problems with this analysis. The first is that the model itself is extremely simple: linear specifications, variances of the exogenous variables identical, and no measurement error on the macro variables. The last assumption is quite restrictive, for there is no reason to believe that, in general, the macro variables are free of measurement error if the micro data from which they are computed are not. If and when this type of analysis proceeds to examine macro measurement error, there will be three elements to the trade-off that will have to be considered: micro and macro measurement error and aggregation bias. Whether the resulting analysis will be more than impressionistic remains to be seen.

The second problem with this statistical approach is a fundamental one within the context of aggregation of production and capital. It devolves upon the notion of aggregation bias, which here simply means $\beta_1 \neq \beta_2$. But, in the reswitching literature, not only may the form of the macro relationship differ from the micro equations, but the macro equation probably will contain different variables. The difference between the macro equation and the micro equation is not only that the former is in some sense an aggregate of the micro relationships, but that the two types of specifications may differ. Moreover, it is very, very hard (if not impossible) to know even the approximate specification of the macro relationship without knowing the properties of the micro equations. Therefore one is forced to treat the micro relationships directly; for, in spite of the alleged measurement error, there is simply no way of proceeding. The statistical approach provides us with interesting and suggestive, though tentative, results; but it is at present irrelevant to the problem of aggregation of production and capital.

7.13 Conclusions

The review of aggregation theory leads to two general conclusions: the first is that if one ignores the potential aggregation bias, qualitatively incorrect predictions result, which indicates the importance of the problem for the areas of production, income distribution, productivity, and pricing; the second is that at present there is only one basis, flawed though it is, for testing capital aggregates, and that is the commodity aggregation approach. None of the procedures that focus on functional form is feasible because, aside from the stringency of the conditions they require, they need an inordinate amount of micro physical data that simply are not available. Thus, the only feasible procedure is commodity aggregation, for the requisite data appear to be available and the conditions do not rule out imperfect competition. The principal shortcoming is that it allows for the specification only of nominalistic aggregates. But if they exist, then at least one could test for more enduring aggregates based on restrictions on functional form. That seems to be the appropriate course of action, given our review of the theoretical and statistical bases for aggregation.

Notes

1. This review does not pretend to be a definitive statement of the problem. In fact, no such thing exists, though reviews from one or another point of view are available; see Harcourt (1972), Blaugh (1974), Samuelson (1976), and Burmeister (1976).

2. Bruno, Burmeister, and Sheshinski (1966) show that there is no essential difference between the circulating-capital and the fixed-capital models as far as the important capital-theoretic issues are concerned.

3. Before doing any analysis with this model, it is necessary to ensure that the technique is feasible, which means that P_1/P_o must be positive. See Hicks (1965, pp. 97–98). If $r < 1/a_{11}$, one can show by differentiating (6) that $P_1(\alpha)/P_o$ will be an increasing or decreasing function of the rate of profit, depending on whether the capital good sector is more or less capital intensive than the consumption good sector. The curves in figures 7.1*a–d* are drawn with the assumption that the consumption sector is more capital intensive than the capital sector. Note that, if $m = 1$, relative prices are independent of the profit rate. But this is unimportant for Champernowne's chain index.

4. See Brown (1969). W_o/P_o has the dimension:

$$\dim \frac{\$\text{ labor}}{\$\text{ corn}} = \frac{\text{Labor}}{\text{Corn}},$$

which is invariant to changes in technique. However,

$$\dim\left[\frac{P_1(\alpha)}{P_o}\right] = \frac{\$/\text{capital type } \alpha}{\$/\text{corn}} = \left[\frac{\text{capital } \alpha}{\text{corn}}\right]^{-1},$$

which does not have the same dimension as $P_1(\beta)/P_o$ and $P_1(\gamma)/P_o$.

5. The condition that the factor-price relation should be linear in Samuelson's surrogate production is stronger than that required for the construction of Champernowne's chain index. To find a chain index, only one intersection between any pair of techniques is required. Straight-line factor-price relations are not necessary in Champernowne's construction. However, if these ratios are identical for all techniques, there is only one intersection between any pair of techniques (Hicks 1965, p. 154). It is in this sense that the condition for constructing a chain index is somewhat weaker than that for the surrogate production function. Yet, if the simple Marshallian elasticity at each point on the frontier is to be used to measure the distribution of income, it is necessary and sufficient that the factor-price curves should be linear.

6. Initial and terminal capital stocks and all other consumptions are understood to be held constant in (*a*) and (*b*). If there are many capital goods with no joint production, the wage rate in terms of every good's price forms a factor-price or wage-profit frontier in (*c*); this is a generalization of the model used above to illustrate the chain index and the surrogate production function. If the rate of growth, g, is positive, then the monotone relations in (*e*) and (*f*) are taken to hold only for $r > g$ and for K/L less than the golden rule capital-labor ratio associated with $r = g$. If there are many capital goods (the general model), then in (*g*) and (*g*′), $\Sigma P_i K_i / P_i Y_i$ is to be expressed in terms of some numeraire.

7. It may be useful to indicate what reswitching does not imply. It does not imply that marginal analysis is silly; one can use smoothly differentiable production functions or specify a production possibility set that is closed and convex (this is more general in one sense but it rules out increasing returns), and there is a considerable intersection of implications that results from the two specifications; the choice should be empirically determined. It does not imply that there are inherent contradictions in capitalistic production; one has to refer to an entirely different literature to try to show that. Finally, it does not imply that general equilibrium theory is silly because in that theory one can specify as many heterogeneous capital items as one wishes, treating each as a separate good with its own market, etc.; no aggregates need be involved.

8. For any two distinct points in input space, x_{ij} and x'_{ij}, strict quasi-concavity is defined by $f^j[(1-\alpha)x_{0j} + \alpha x'_{0j}, (1-\alpha)x_{1j} + \alpha x'_{1j}, (1-\alpha)x_{2j} + \alpha x'_{2j}] >$ $\min\,[f^j(x_{0j}, x_{1j}, x_{2j}), f^j(x'_{0j}, x'_{1j}, x'_{2j})]$, where $0 < \alpha < 1$.

9. There are essentially two concepts of separability that are important here. The first is weak separability, already defined. The other is strong separability: consider a function F of n variables; it is called strongly separable with respect to a partition $\{N_1, \ldots, N_S\}$ if the marginal rate of substitution between two inputs i and j from different subsets of inputs N_S and N_t, respectively, does not depend upon inputs outside of N_S and N_t; that is, let $y = f[\phi^1(x^{(1)}) + \phi^2(x^{(2)}) + \ldots + \phi^S(x^{(s)})]$, where ϕ^i $(i = 1, \ldots, S)$ are functions of the subsectors $x^{(i)}$ and f is a monotone-increasing function of the ϕ_i; then

$$\frac{\partial\left[\dfrac{\partial\phi^i}{\partial x_t^{(i)}} \Big/ \dfrac{\partial\phi^j}{\partial x_s^{(i)}}\right]}{\partial x_k} = 0,\ i\epsilon N_S,\ j\epsilon N_T;\ kN_S \text{U} N_T (S \neq T).$$

If the function is weakly separable, it can be written as $y = f[\phi^1(x^{(1)}), \phi^2(x^{(2)}), \ldots, \phi^S(x^{(s)})]$. For proofs of these propositions, see Goldman and Uzawa (1964).

10. Weak separability is not both necessary and sufficient to accomplish this, since indexes can be formed if the weights on the inputs within a group index behave in a certain way (see below). The behavior of the weights can be independent of the form of the production function.

11. A function of $x_1, x_2, \ldots, x_n$ factors of production is homothetic if it can be written as $\phi^j(\sigma^j(x_1, x_2, \ldots, x_n))$, where σ^j are homogeneous of degree one and ϕ^j are continuous monotonically increasing functions of σ^j. Actually, less restrictive ϕ^j functions (namely, upper semicontinuous functions; see Shephard 1970, pp. 92 ff.) produce similar results.

12. These conditions are necessary and sufficient if one focuses on the form of the production function alone (Green 1964, p. 28). They are merely necessary if one allows for the commodity aggregation condition to hold (see below) or if something is going on "behind the scene" (see Brown and Chang 1976).

13. This can be generalized in several directions when n-factors ($n > 3$) are considered. First, the number of partitions can obviously be extended; second, the number of items in each group can be variable provided no item is allowed to be in more than one group; third, one can allow for several groups and many individual factors (in the text, we have one grouping of capital items and another "group" consisting of the labor input); finally, the F^j and g_j need not be continuous; they can be finite, nondecreasing, nonnegative upper semicontinuous functions (Shephard 1970, pp. 20 ff.). The last extension allows for discontinuities, provided the functions are continuous only from the right.

14. Note that weak separability does not require the g^j function to be homogeneous.

15. They are: (*i*) if all prices and quantities are fixed between time point t_1 and t_0, then $g^j{}_{t_1} = \Gamma^{1i}{}_{r_1 t_0} = 1$; (*ii*) if all prices (quantities) at t_1 are proportional to those at t_0, then $g^j{}_{t_1 t_0} = \Gamma^{1j}{}_{t_1 t_0} = \alpha$, where α is the factor of proportionality; and (*iii*) $g^j{}_{t_1 t_0} \Gamma^{1j}{}_{t_1 t_0} = \sum_{i=1}^{2} p^1{}_{ij} x^1{}_{ij} \Big/ \sum_{i=1}^{2} p^0{}_{ij} x^0{}_{ij}$.

16. This assumption is tenuous at best in light of the commonly held view that capital markets are notoriously imperfect.

17. Fisher (1969, p. 560) finds that capital aggregation is possible under somewhat less restrictive conditions than under capital augmenting technical differences. This involves the case in which each firm's production function becomes one of constant returns after a transformation of the capital inputs; that is, $F^j(x_{0j}, x_{1j}) = F^j[H^j(x_{1j}), x_{0j}]$, where the f^j are homogeneous of degree one and the H^j are monotonic. Despite the fact that this is more general than capital augmentation, it is itself very restrictive.

18. It is known that if all firm's production functions are quasi-concave and homogeneous of degree $\lambda (0 < \lambda \leq 1)$, then G is convex.

19. For example, the Hicksian condition, $m = 1$, which rules out reswitching (1965), and Zarembka's conditions for aggregation (1975) are simply the Gorman conditions in two of their guises.

20. To be precise, one must take the differential in terms of the exogenous variable. Here we can treat the interest rate as exogenous (see discussion of the Brown-Chang conditions below).

21. Actually, the Bureau of Labor Statistics wholesale price index follows the Lespeyres formula, but in a modified form. When new weights are introduced, the chain-link device is employed, at the linkage points, implies a Divisia index.

22. To see what is involved, note that the WPI weights represent the total net selling value of commodities produced, processed, or imported into the United States and flowing into primary markets; see BLS (1971, pp. 103–4). The weights in the WPI correspond to the $w_{.h}$ and hence are economywide weights.

23. We assume that the system satisfied the Hawkins-Simon conditions (see Brown and Chang 1976).

24. The equal or zero depreciation assumption is one. Another is the assumption that production functions are homogeneous of degree one.

25. See for example, Solow (1967, pp. 46–48).

26. The ex ante production function describes the factor substitution possibilities before capital is installed; that is, it is the putty part of the putty-clay appelation representing the whole range of blueprints for the production process available to the firm in its planning stage.

27. Using a different approach, Sonnenschein (1973) has shown that (*a*) for a given aggregate expenditure and for prices and aggregate demands—all of which satisfy the aggregate budget constraint—and (*b*) any set of rates of change of aggregate demands with respect to prices and total expenditure (these must satisfy the homogeneity constraint), then there is a finite collection of utility maximizing consumers with equal total expenditures. An aggregate demand system is the result, but it is peculiar to the point (prices, aggregate demands, etc.) that is initially taken as given. Thus the implied aggregate demand systems (the functions themselves) are conditional upon prices, etc. This difficulty is similar to that affecting the Houthakker-Sato distribution function.

28. The case where the macro variables contain some measurement error has yet to be worked out in an acceptable manner.

29. In analyzing the affect of aggregation on the reduction in the variance of parameter estimates, Welsch and Kuh use a model that is similar to Green's except for one important characteristic. The former model allows for random coefficients; that is, $E(\beta_i) = \beta$. This is seemingly more general than Green's model, but in fact Welsch and Kuh have assumed away one of the most interesting aspects of the analysis; namely, aggregation bias. For they do not allow the β_i to vary in a nonstochastic manner among the micro units. However, they advise that the relative efficiency of aggregation could be severely reduced by differences in micro behavior (1976, p. 362).

References

Aigner, D. J., and Goldfeld, S. M. 1974. Estimation and prediction from aggregate data when aggregates are measured more accurately than their components. *Econometrica* 47:113–34.

Arrow, K. J., and Hahn, F. H. 1971. *General competitive analysis*. San Francisco: Holden-Day.

Blaugh, M. 1974. *The Cambridge revolutions: Success or failure: A critical analysis of Cambridge theories of value and distribution*. London: Institute of Economic Affairs.

Brown, M. 1969. Substitution-composition effects, capital intensity, uniqueness and growth. *Economic Journal* 79:334–47.

——— 1973. Toward an econometric accommodation of the capital perversity phenomenon. *Econometrica* 41:937–54.

Brown, M., and Chang, W. W. 1976. Capital aggregation in a general equilibrium model of production. *Econometrica* 44 (November): 1179–1200.

Brown, M.; Sato K.; and Zarembka, P. 1976. *Essays in modern capital theory*. Amsterdam: North-Holland.

Bruno, M. 1969. Fundamental duality relations in the pure theory of capital and growth. *Review of Economic Studies* 36:39–53.

Bruno, M.; Burmeister, E.; and Sheshinski, E. 1966. The nature and implications of the reswitching of techniques. *Quarterly Journal of Economics* 80:526–53.

Burmeister, E. 1977. On the social significance of the reswitching controversy. *Revue d'Economie Politique*. In press.

Burmeister, E., and Kuga, K. 1970. The factor-price frontier in a neoclassical multi-sector model. *International Economic Review* 11:162–74.

Cass, D. 1976. The Hamiltonian representation of static competitive or efficient allocation. In *Essays in modern capital theory,* ed. M. Brown, K. Sato, and P. Zarembka. Amsterdam: North-Holland.

Champernowne, D. G. 1953. The production function and the theory of capital: A comment. *Review of Economic Studies* 21:112–35.

Diewert, W. E. 1974. A note on aggregation and elasticities of substitution. *Canadian Journal of Economics* 12:12–20.

Edwards, B., and Orcutt, G. H. 1969. Should aggregation prior to estimation be the rule. *Review of Economics and Statistics* 51:409–20.

Fisher, F. 1965. Embodied technical change and the existence of an aggregate capital stock. *Review of Economic Studies* 32:263–88.

———. 1968*a*. Embodied technology and the existence of labour and output aggregates. *Review of Economic Studies* 35:391–412.

———. 1968*b*. Embodied technology and the aggregation of fixed and movable capital goods. *Review of Economic Studies* 35:417–28.

———. The existence of aggregate production functions. *Econometrica* 37:553–77.

Fisher, F. M.; Solow, R. M.; and Kearl, J. R. 1974. Aggregate production functions: Some CES experiments. Working paper, Department of Economics, M.I.T. Cambridge, Mass.

Goldman, S. M., and Uzawa, H. 1964. A note on separability in demand analysis. *Econometrica* 32:387–98.

Gorman, W. M. 1953. Community preference fields. *Econometrica* 21:63–80.

———. 1959. Separable utility and aggregation. *Econometrica* 27:469–81.

Green, H. A. J. 1964. *Aggregation in economic analysis: An introductory survey*. Princeton: Princeton University Press.

Greene, W. H. 1975. Estimation and prediction from aggregate data when aggregates are measured more accurately than their components: Some further results. Discussion Paper 7513, Social Systems Research Institute, University of Wisconsin, Madison, Wisc.

Grunfeld, Y., and Griliches, Z. 1960. Is aggregation necessarily bad. *Review of Economics and Statistics* 42:1–13.

Harcourt, G. C. 1972. *Some Cambridge controversies in the theory of capital*. Cambridge: Cambridge University Press.

Hatta, T. 1974. The paradox in capital theory and complementarity of inputs. Department of Economics, Ohio State University.

Hicks, J. 1946. *Value and capital*. London: Oxford University Press.

———. 1965. *Capital and growth*. New York: Oxford University Press.

Houthakker, H. S. 1955–56. The Pareto distribution and the Cobb-Douglas production function in activity analysis. *Review of Economic Studies* 23:27–31.

Katzner, D. W. 1970. *Static demand theory*. New York: Macmillan.

Leontief, W. W. 1947. Introduction to a theory of the internal structure of functional relationships. *Econometrica* 15:361–73.

Levhari, D. 1968. A note on Houthakker's aggregate production function in a multifirm industry. *Econometrica* 36:151–54.

Nuti, D. M. 1976. On the rates of return on investment. In *Essays in modern capital theory*, ed. M. Brown, K. Sato, and P. Zarembka. Amsterdam: North-Holland.

Oguchi, N. 1977. *Dynamic growth models and capital perversities*. Ph.D. Diss., Department of Economics, SUNYAB.

Robinson, J. 1956. *The accumulation of capital*. London: Macmillan.

Samuelson, P. A. 1962. Parable and realism in capital theory: The surrogate production function. *Review of Economic Studies* 29:193–206.

———. 1976. Interest rate determinations and oversimplifying parables: A summing up. In *Essays in modern capital theory*, ed. M. Brown, K. Sato, and P. Zarembka. Amsterdam: North-Holland.

Sato, K. 1974. The neoclassical postulate and the technology frontier in capital theory. *Quarterly Journal of Economics* 88:353–84.

———. 1975. *Production functions and aggregation*. Amsterdam: North-Holland.

———. 1976*a*. A note on capital and output aggregation in a general equilibrium model of production. Department of Economics, SUNYAB.

———. 1976*b*. Perversity in a multisector neoclassical production system. Discussion Paper number 380. Department of Economics, SUNYAB.

Shephard, R. 1953. *Cost and production functions*. Princeton: Princeton University Press.

———. 1970. *Theory of cost and production functions*. Princeton: Princeton University Press.

Solow, R. M. 1955. The production function and the theory of capital. *Review of Economic Studies* 23:101–8.

———. 1963. *Capital theory and the rate of return*. Amsterdam: North-Holland.

———. 1967. Some recent developments in the theory of production. In *The theory and empirical analysis of production*, ed. M. Brown. Studies in Income and Wealth, no. 31. New York: National Bureau of Economic Research.

Sonnenschein, H. 1973. The utility hypothesis and market demand theory. *Western Economic Journal* 11:404–10.

Sraffa, P. 1960. *Production of commodities by means of commodities: A prelude to a critique of economic theory*, Cambridge: Cambridge University Press.

Strotz, R. 1959. The utility tree: A correction and further appraisal. *Econometrica* 27:482–88.

U.S. Department of Labor. Bureau of Labor Statistics. 1971. *BLS handbook of methods*. Bulletin 1711. Washington, D.C.

Usher, D. 1973. The measurement of economic growth. Discussion Paper no. 131, Institute for Economic Research, Queen's University, Kingston, Ontario.

Welsch, R. E., and Kuh, E. 1976. The variances of regression coefficient estimates using aggregate data. *Econometrica* 44:353–64.

Zarembka, P. 1975. Capital heterogeneity, aggregation, and the two-sector model. *Quarterly Journal of Economics* 79:103–14.

———. 1976. Characterizations of technology in capital theory. In *Essays in modern capital theory*, ed. M. Brown, K. Sato, and P. Zarembka. Amsterdam: North-Holland.

Zellner, A.; Kmenta, J.; and Dreze, J. 1966. Specification and estimation of Cobb-Douglas production function models. *Econometrica* 34:784–95.

Comment Edwin Burmeister

Murray Brown's paper provides a comprehensive survey of the theoretical and practical problems associated with capital aggregation. It should be required reading for every econometrician before he is allowed access to his computer! The paper is long, and I shall have space only to briefly summarize some of the results, along with a few comments of my own.

Brown begins with a review of the neoclassical parable and the so-called reswitching controversy that reached its peak with the November 1966 *Quarterly Journal of Economics* Symposium, "Paradoxes in Capital Theory" (1966). The primary issue can be easily explained. Suppose there exist two alternative Leontief-Sraffa production techniques, *a* and *b*, both using a homogeneous labor input and *n* types of heterogeneous capital inputs. Suppose also that there is a single consumption good. In a steady-state equilibrium the technique employed will maximize the real wage W/P_c or minimize P_c/W, the price of final output in terms of the single primary factor, labor. Thus in figure C7.1*a* and *b*, technique *a* will be used for $0 \leqq r < r_1$ and $r_2 < r \leqq r^*$, while technique *b* will be used for $r_1 < r < r_2$. Both techniques are viable and may coexist at the *switch points* r_1 and r_2.

The crucial observation is that all physical quantities, for example, the stocks of capital goods and the output of the final consumption good, depend only on the technique employed. Thus, suppose we define any indexes of "capital" for techniques *a* and *b*, say K^a and K^b, that depend only upon the technique employed. Clearly the existence of reswitching makes it obvious that the techniques cannot be ordered in terms of such indexes and the steady-state profit rate because, when there is reswitching, at least one technique in employed for two disjoint intervals of the profit rate.

That physical quantities depend only on the technique employed is illustrated in figure C7.1*b* where equilibrium consumption is plotted for alternative steady-state profit rates. Note that $C = C^a$ when technique *a* is employed ($0 \leqq r < r_1$ and $r_2 < r \leqq r^*$), while $C = C^b$ when technique *b* is employed ($r_1 < r < r_2$). If the technology consists of smooth neoclassical production functions, figure C7.1*b* is replaced by figure C7.2. Although reswitching is precluded in these circumstances,[1] *paradoxical consumption behavior* may still exist; that is, steady-state consumption

Edwin Burmeister is Commonwealth Professor of Economics at the University of Virginia.

Research support from the Center for Advanced Studies at the University of Virginia and the National Science Foundation is acknowledged with thanks. I am also grateful to John Whitaker for helpful comments.

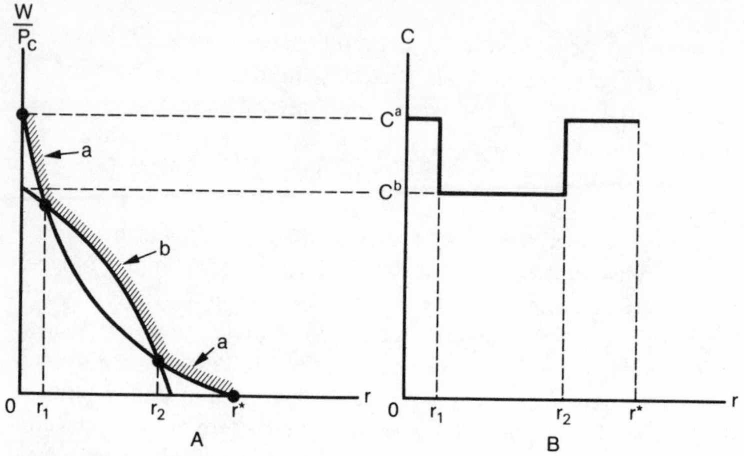

Fig. C7.1

may rise with the profit rate, as illustrated in figure C7.2. Thus there cannot exist a well-behaved neoclassical production function (across steady states),

$$C = F(K,L),$$

where C is consumption, L is the fixed labor supply, and K is some index of capital that always falls with an increase in the steady-state profit rate. Brown refers to my own result that such an aggregate production function can be defined if, and only if,

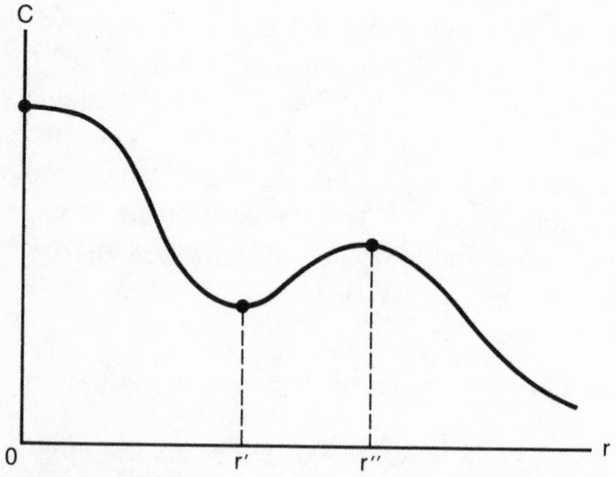

Fig. C7.2

$$\sum_{i=1}^{n} p_i \frac{dk_i}{dr} < 0 \text{ for all feasible } r,$$

where p_i is the price of the ith capital good in terms of any numeraire and k_i is the capital-labor ratio for capital of type i, $i = 1, \ldots, n$.[2]

I agree fully with Brown's stated conclusion that "the neoclassical parable and its implications are generally untenable" (p. 15). Freak cases such as Samuelson's surrogate production function example are of little comfort.

In section 7.4 Brown reviews capital aggregation theorems that work because the form of the production function is restricted. The original Leontief (1947) theorem concerns

$$Q = F(L, K_1, K_2);$$

if

$$\frac{\partial}{\partial L}\left[\frac{\partial F}{\partial K_1} \bigg/ \frac{\partial F}{\partial K_2}\right] = 0,$$

then there exists an aggregate production function

$$Q = F(L, K),$$

where "aggregate capital" is given by some function

$$K = G(K_1, K_2).$$

Brown then discusses additional problems that arise when there are more than two groups of inputs, and he summarizes the results due to Strotz (1959) and Gorman (1959), as well as the application of the duality between cost and production functions stemming from Shephard's work (1953). He concludes with two objections to this approach.

1. Price and quantity indexes are constructed *assuming* perfect competition in factor markets, and in many instances this assumption is obviously false.

2. The basic micro data required for the construction of capital indexes, even when they conceptually exist, generally are unobserved. I should like to add a third problem.

3. Suppose K_1 and K_2 are two physically different types of capital goods. Using the production function for industry 1, F^1, we construct an index for "capital" in that industry, say $G^1(K_{11}, K_{21})$. But, using a different production function for industry 2, having the same physical inputs, in general we have a different index $G^2(K_{12}, K_{22})$. Thus even if we consider *all* points for which the quantities of the physical inputs are the same in both industries and $K_{11} = K_{12}$, $K_{21} = K_{22}$, in general $G^1 \neq \lambda G^2$ for any scalar $\lambda > 0$. This means that an aggregate production function for the whole economy need not exist, even when sectoral capital aggregation is possible.

The problem of intersectoral aggregation—the basis for my last objection—has been studied in a series of papers by Frank Fisher (1965, 1968*a*, *b*, 1969). We now have *n* industry production functions

$$Q_j = F^j(L_j, K_j), \quad j = 1, \ldots, n,$$

and ask when we can find an aggregate production function

$$Q = \sum_{j=1}^{n} Q_j = F(L, K),$$

where

$$L = L(L_1, \ldots, L_n),$$
$$K = K(K_1, \ldots, K_n).$$

Essentially the Fisher sufficient condition is that, when labor is optimally allocated, every production function must differ only by the degree of capital augmentation or, as Brown states, "For example, sound amplification equipment in a classroom is considered to be three times the number of desks in the same classroom." I agree with the negative feelings expressed by both Fisher and Brown for progress along this line.

The Gorman (1953) aggregation conditions require that all firms have homothetic production functions with parallel expansion paths through the origin, in which case we may express

$$Q_j = F^j(L_j, K_{1j}, \ldots, K_{nj}), \quad j = 1, \ldots, n,$$

in the aggregate form

$$Q = \sum_{j=1}^{n} h^j(Q_j) = F(L, K_1, \ldots, K_n),$$

where

$$L = \sum_{j=1}^{n} L_j$$

and

$$K_i = \sum_{j=1}^{n} K_{ij}, \quad i = 1, \ldots, n.$$

If in addition the production functions $F^j(\cdot)$ exhibit constant returns to scale, then by renumbering the isoquants the production functions may be made identical; that is, outputs are identical except for the units in which they are measured. Brown proceeds to show how such unrealistic conditions are often assumed implicitly when one uses a price index for capital goods as a deflator to measure "real capital" in an industry.

The Houthakker (1955–56) approach discussed in section 7.8, although ingenious, seems to me of little relevance for the primary issue at hand. Its usefulness is limited to the intersectoral aggregation of production functions with two factor inputs, and even then there are formidable estimation difficulties stated by Brown.

All the aggregation procedures discussed so far rely on functional form restrictions. Alternatively, the Hicks (1946) composite commodity theorem allows aggregation of heterogeneous commodities if their relative prices remain constant for the problem under consideration. The relevant question is then which hypothetical alternatives are to be investigated.

The Hicks theorem is the basis for the Brown and Chang (1976) general equilibrium aggregation results. This model requires the following assumptions:

1. There is no joint production.
2. The rate of profit r is exogenous; for example, r may be determined exogenously by the rate of time preference or by fiscal and monetary policy (section 7.10).
3. There is no technological change.
4. Steady-state equilibrium always prevails so that we may express capital net rentals rates as

$$q_i = p_i r$$

rather than the more general form

$$q_i = p_i r - \dot{p}_i$$

that allows for capital gains and losses.

5. There is perfect competition in factor markets (section 7.10).

I fear that any one of these five reasons is sufficient to reject the model as empirically unrealistic; but suppose we accept it. For such a model Marxians know that relative prices are constant if, and only if, there is "equal organic composition of capital" and the "cost of labor/value of capital" ratio is the same function of r for every industry:

$$\frac{WL_j}{\sum_{i=1}^{n} P_i K_{ij}} = \psi(r), \quad j = 1, \ldots, n.$$

This condition, of course, leads to a labor theory of value in which relative prices reflect the ratio of *total* embodied labor; that is,

$$\frac{p_i(r)}{p_j(r)} = \frac{l_i}{l_j} = constant \quad \text{for all } r,$$

where the vector of total embodied labor is given by

$$l = (l_1, \ldots, l_n) = \frac{P}{W}(r = 0) = p(0)$$
$$= [p_1(0), \ldots, p_n(0)].$$

It is also a theorem that such a labor theory of value is valid *if, and only if*, prices are a markup on unit labor costs:

$$\frac{P_i}{W}(r) \equiv p_i(r) = \alpha(r) a_{Li}(r),$$

where

$$a_{Li}(r) = \frac{L_i}{Q_i}, \quad i = 1, \ldots, n,$$

and where $\alpha(r)$ is the same markup function for all industries. As Brown and Chang state the result,

$$\text{labor's relative share} = \frac{WL_i}{P_i Q_i} = \frac{a_{Li}}{P_i}$$
$$= \text{the same function of } r \text{ alone}$$
$$= \frac{1}{\alpha(r)}, \quad i = 1, \ldots, n.$$

I am afraid few econometricians would be willing to assume such stringent conditions. The Marxian case of equal organic composition is precisely that freak situation in which capital theoretic problems due to heterogeneity do not arise![3]

Moreover, the condition that labor's relative share be the same function of r for every industry surely imposes *some* restrictions on the production functions. For example, it is certainly sufficient that

$$Q_j = F^j(L_j, K_{1j}, \ldots, K_{nj}) =$$
$$L_j^{\beta}[\phi^j(K_{1j}, \ldots, K_{nj})]^{1-\beta}, \quad j = 1, \ldots, n,$$

where $0 < \beta = \textit{constant} < 1$ and $\phi^j(\cdot)$ is concave and homogeneous of degree one. In this case, of course,

$$\text{labor's relative share} = \frac{1}{\alpha(r)} = \beta, \quad j = 1, \ldots, n.$$

In general, when β may vary with r, one wonders what *necessary* functional form restrictions are implied by the Brown-Chang-Marx condition and how these restrictions relate to those of Solow, Gorman, Fisher, and others.

In section 7.11 Brown makes the important distinction between nominalistic and structural aggregation. He points out the paradox that nominalistic aggregation based upon the observed constancy of relative prices is usually a prerequisite for determining whether the underlying functional forms themselves allow aggregation. There is an "uncertainty principle" at work.

To estimate functional forms directly, we would require unavailable microeconomic data. Thus, as a practical necessity, nominalistic aggregation is required to estimate a set of production functions and to ask whether they satisfy any known sufficient conditions allowing additional aggregation. But, even if we discover that the answer is yes, we can never be certain that this affirmative conclusion is true in general because the conditions that permitted nominalistic aggregation in the first place may not remain valid over time. Moreover, the Hicks composite commodity approach yields an aggregate function that is related in a very complex way to the underlying micro functions; there might be an identification problem whereby certain specific restrictions on the micro functions cannot be tested using the aggregate function.

I do not think we should be too apologetic about this result. After all, economists are confronted with an impossible task when they are asked to estimate production functions without all the microeconomic input data! It *is* progress to recognize logical impossibilities, even when they are distressing.

It is difficult to find an optimistic note on which to close. My conclusion is that, given the current state of the art, the real-world facts contradict every set of conditions that would allow for theoretically rigorous capital aggregation. So where do we go from here? Three avenues of research remain relatively unexplored:

1. Further analysis of the Fisher type of Monte Carlo experiments may at least help us to understand more precisely the reasons why an aggregate production function sometimes "works," at least for tracking wages and, to a lesser degree, output. Although research in this direction is probably tedious, presumably some approximation theorems can be proved that would indicate error bounds on aggregate production function predictions for certain specified microeconomic structures.

2. Statistical cases can be made for aggregation in some instances, as Brown discusses in section 7.12, and perhaps further research in this direction will yield fruitful results.

3. Derivation of production functions from underlying engineering data remains an unexplored area, although it is unclear whether such derivations will yield results that permit aggregation of heterogeneous inputs.

I am not very optimistic about success along any of these roads; one must ponder what to do if we are dissatisfied with the theoretical foundations of current econometric work. I have one revolutionary suggestion: Perhaps for the purpose of answering many macroeconomic questions—particularly about inflation and unemployment—we should disregard the concept of a production function at the microeconomic level. The economist who succeeds in finding a suitable replacement will be a prime candidate for a future Nobel prize.

Finally, I turn to an additional difficulty that precludes aggregation of many multisector models into a *dynamic* one-sector Solow-Swan model. First, consider a dynamic multisector model in which prices are predicted with perfect short-run foresight; that is, $E(\dot{p}_i/p_i) = \dot{p}_i/p_i$ for all commodities. The work by Hahn (1966), Samuelson (1967, 1972*a*), Kuga (1977), myself,[4] and others shows that the rest point or steady-state equilibrium for such a model is not stable, but rather it is a saddle point in the space of capital-labor ratios and relative prices. Thus *any* aggregation procedure that gives rise to a dynamically stable evolution for an index of the capital-labor ratio incorrectly reflects the inherent instability of the underlying microeconomic model.[5]

Second, suppose we follow the Burmeister and Graham (1974, 1975) adaptive type of price expectations mechanism. Then stability is possible, but so far we know of only very stringent sufficient stability conditions; for example, the inverse of the input coefficient matrix must have a negative diagonal and positive off-diagonal elements at all feasible factor price ratios.[6] In addition to the restrictions imposed by aggregation, we now must *assume* that some such stability conditions hold, for the microeconomic data required to test for stability conditions are unavailable.

This is an especially unhappy state of affairs because it is completely unrealistic to assume that our observed data always are generated by steady-state equilibria. We must look at dynamic microeconomic structure; if aggregation to a stable one-sector model is possible, it is probably necessary that unstable microeconomic components of an aggregate index would cancel out to yield dynamic stability of the index.

I conjecture that something close to the converse also is true. That is, if a multisector model admits aggregation to a stable one-sector model without assuming that the economy is always in steady-state equilibrium, then most likely the underlying microeconomic model is stable.

In closing I note that, if this conjecture is correct, then there is a serious conceptual difficulty. The problem is not merely aggregation, but the fact that we do not yet have any satisfactory theoretical justifications for supposing stability of disaggregated dynamic models with heterogeneous capital goods.

Notes

1. See Burmeister and Dobell (1970, theorem 5, p. 279).

2. See Burmeister (1977). Also see Burmeister and Dobell (1970, pp. 282–94), Burmeister and Turnovsky (1972), Burmeister (1974), Brock and Burmeister

(1976), and Burmeister (1976, 1979). The work of Burmeister and Hammond (1977) proves that points for which the expression

$$\sum_{i=1}^{n} p_i \frac{dk_i}{dr}$$

is positive are dynamically unstable rest points if the economy follows a max-min rule.

3. These results about "equal organic composition of capital" are stated and proved in Burmeister (1979). The so-called transformation problem between Marxian values and competitive prices arises because "equal organic composition of capital" is a freak case; see, for example, Samuelson (1972*b*, *c*).

4. See Burmeister and Dobell (1970, pp. 297–306), Burmeister and Graham (1974, 1975), Brock and Burmeister (1976), and Burmeister et al. (1973).

5. Preliminary computer simulations suggest that divergence away from steady-state equilibrium may be quite rapid; see Burmeister et al. (1973).

6. Stability of a heterogeneous capital good model with technological change is another formidable problem, except in the special case when there is labor-augmenting technical progress at the *same rate* in every sector.

References

Brock, William A., and Burmeister, Edwin. 1976. Regular economies and conditions for uniqueness of steady states in optimal multi-sector economic models. *International Economic Review* 17 (February): 105–20.

Brown, M., and Chang, W. W. 1976. Capital aggregation in a general equilibrium model of production. *Econometrica* 44: (November): 1179–1200.

Burmeister, E. 1974. Synthesizing the neo-Austrian and alternative approaches to capital theory: A survey. *Journal of Economic Literature* 12 (June): 413–56.

———. 1976. Real Wicksell effects and regular economies. In *Essays in modern capital theory*, ed. M. Brown, K. Sato, and P. Zarembka, pp. 145–64. Amsterdam: North-Holland.

———. 1977. On the social significance of the reswitching controversy. *Revue d'Economie Politique*. March–April.

———. 1979. Critical observations on the labor theory of value and Sraffa's standard commodity. Discussion paper, University of Virginia.

Burmeister, E.; Caton, C.; Dobell, A. R.; and Ross, S. A. 1973. The saddlepoint property and the structure of dynamic heterogeneous capital good models. *Econometrica* 41:79–96.

Burmeister, E., and Dobell, A. R. 1970. *Mathematical theories of economic growth*. New York: Macmillan.

Burmeister, E., and Graham, D. A. 1974. Multi-sector economic models with continuous adaptive expectations. *Review of Economic Studies* 41:323–36.

———. 1975. Price expectations and global stability in economic systems. *Automatica* 11:487–97.

Burmeister, E., and Hammond, P. J. 1977. Maximin paths of heterogeneous capital accumulation and the instability of paradoxical steady states. *Econometrica* 45:853–71.

Burmeister, E., and Turnovsky, Stephen J. 1972. Capital deepening response in an economy with heterogeneous capital goods. *American Economic Review* 62 (December): 842–53.

Fisher, F. 1965. Embodied technical change and the existence of an aggregate capital stock. *Review of Economic Studies* 32:263–88.

Fisher, F. 1968*a*. Embodied technology and the existence of labour and output aggregates. *Review of Economic Studies* 35:391–412.

———. 1968*b*. Embodied technology and the aggregation of fixed and movable capital goods. *Review of Economic Studies* 35:417–28.

——— 1969. The existence of aggregate production functions. *Econometrica* 37:553–77.

Gorman, W. M. 1953. Community preference fields. *Econometrica* 21:63–80.

———. 1959. Separable utility and aggregation. *Econometrica* 27:469–81.

Hahn, F. H. 1966. Equilibrium dynamics with heterogeneous capital goods. *Quarterly Journal of Economics* 80:633–46.

Hicks, J. 1946. *Value and capital.* London: Oxford University Press.

Houthakker, H. S. 1955–56. The Pareto distribution and the Cobb-Douglas production function in activity analysis. *Review of Economic Studies* 23:27–31.

Kuga, K. 1977. General saddlepoint property of the steady state of a growth model with heterogeneous capital goods. *International Economic Review* 18 (February): 29–59.

Leontief, W. W. 1947. Introduction to a theory of the internal structure of functional relationships. *Econometrica* 15:361–73.

Paradoxes in capital theory: A symposium. 1966. *Quarterly Journal of Economics* 80, no. 4 (November): 503–83.

Samuelson, P. A. 1967. Indeterminacy of development in a heterogeneous-capital model with constant saving propensity. In *Essays on the theory of optimal economic growth*, pp. 219–31. Cambridge, Mass.: MIT Press.

———. 1972*a*. The general saddlepoint property of optimal-control motions. *Journal of Economic Theory* 5:102–20.

———. 1972*b*. The "transformation" from Marxian "values" to competitive "prices": A process of rejection and replacement. In *The collected scientific papers of Paul A. Samuelson*, ed. Robert C. Merton, vol. 3. Cambridge: M.I.T. Press.

———. 1972*c*. Understanding the Marxian notion of exploitation: A summary of the so-called transformation problem between Marxian values and competitive prices. In *The collected scientific papers of Paul A. Samuelson*, ed. Robert C. Merton, vol. 3. Cambridge: M.I.T. Press.

Shephard, R. 1953. *Cost and production functions*. Princeton: Princeton University Press.

Strotz, R. 1959. The utility tree: A correction and further appraisal. *Econometrica* 27:482–88.

8 Aggregation Problems in the Measurement of Capital

W. E. Diewert

8.1 Introduction and Overview

In his Introduction to this volume, Dan Usher has provided us with a rather comprehensive discussion on the purposes of capital measurement as well as the problems of defining capital in the context of a specific purpose.

With Usher's introduction in mind, the scope of the present paper can readily be defined: I will concentrate on the problems of defining and measuring capital in the context of estimating production functions and measuring total factor productivity, with particular emphasis on the associated index number problems.

However, before discussing the special problems involved in aggregating capital, I will first discuss the general problem of aggregating over goods in section 8.2 and the general problem of aggregating over sectors in section 8.3. The material presented in these sections is for the most part not new, although much of it is fairly recent and not widely known. Usher's new definition of real capital is discussed in section 8.2.6 along with some other definitions.

In section 8.4 I discuss some of the aggregation problems that are specifically associated with capital. In particular, the problem of defining capital as an instantaneous stock or a service flow is discussed along with the concomitant problems of measuring depreciation.

In section 8.5 I present some new material on the measurement of total factor productivity and technical progress. In this section, capital

W. E. Diewert is associated with the Department of Economics at the University of British Columbia, Vancouver.

The author is indebted to E. R. Berndt, C. Blackorby, P. Chinloy, M. Denny, L. J. Lau, D. Usher, and F. Wykoff for helpful comments.

does not play a more important role than any other factor of production, so that one could question its inclusion in a paper that is supposed to be restricted to capital aggregation problems. However, past discussions of technical change have emphasized the possibility that technical change may be embodied in new capital goods (see Jorgenson 1966), and thus I decided to include section 8.5.

One of the most difficult problems in the measurement of capital is the problem of new goods. This is of course not specific to capital, and so in section 8.6 I present some suggestions for solving the new goods problem in general.

In section 8.7 I briefly consider a problem that occurs when measuring capital as well as other inputs and outputs: the problem of aggregating over time; that is, How should "monthly" estimates of a capital good be constructed? or, given monthly estimates, How should we construct an annual estimate of the capital component?

In section 8.8 I conclude by making some concrete recommendations to national income accountants based on the material in the previous sections. Some mathematical proofs are contained in the Appendix.

8.2 Methods for Justifying Aggregation over Goods

8.2.1 Price Proportionality: Hicks's Aggregation Theorem

Hicks (1946, pp. 312–13) showed (in the context of twice-differentiable utility functions) that if the prices of a group of goods change in the same proportion, that group of goods behaves just as if it were a single commodity. This aggregation theorem and the homogeneous weak separability method (which will be discussed in the following section) are the two most general methods we have for justifying aggregation over goods. Alternative statements and proofs of Hicks's aggregation theorem in the consumer context can be found in Wold (1953, pp. 109–10), Gorman (1953, pp. 76–77), and Diewert (1978*a*).

Versions of Hicks's aggregation theorem also exist in the producer context, particularly in the context of measuring real value added (see Khang 1971; Bruno 1978; Diewert 1978*a*). Below, I sketch yet another version of Hicks's aggregation theorem in the producer context, a version that does not make use of any restrictive differentiability assumptions.

Suppose there are $N + M$ goods that a given firm can produce or use as an input and that the set of feasible input-output combinations of goods is a set $S \equiv \{(x,y)\} \equiv \{(x_1,x_2, \ldots ,x_N,y_1,y_2, \ldots ,y_M)\}$, where x_n represents the quantity of good n produced (used as an input if $x_n < 0$) and y_m represents the quantity of good $N + m$ produced by the firm (used as an input if $y_m < 0$). We assume that the firm can buy or sell the first N goods at the positive prices $(w_1, w_2, \ldots, w_N) \equiv w \gg 0_N$[1] and the last M goods at the positive prices $(p_1, p_2, \ldots, p_M) \equiv p \gg 0_M$. We assume that the firm behaves competitively and attempts to solve the following *microeconomic profit-maximization problem*:

$$(1) \qquad \max_{x,y}\{w \cdot x + p \cdot y : (x,y) \in S\} \equiv \Pi(w,p).$$

The solution to the above profit-maximization problem (if one exists)[2] is a function of the prices w,p that the producer is facing and is called the (*micro*) *profit function* Π. It can be shown (see McFadden 1978 or Diewert 1973*a*) that under suitable regularity conditions on the technology S, the profit function completely characterizes the underlying technology. This duality property will prove very useful in subsequent sections of this chapter.

The firm's *gross*[3] or *restricted*[4] or *variable*[5] profit function Π^* is defined as

$$(2) \qquad \Pi^*(w,y) \equiv \max_x\{w \cdot x : (x,y) \in S\}.$$

The usual interpretation of the maximization problem (2) is that the firm is maximizing only with respect to its variable inputs and output x, while the inputs (and or outputs) y remain fixed in the short run. It can also be shown under suitable regularity conditions on S that a knowledge of the variable profit function Π^* is sufficient to completely determine the underlying technology S.[6] Thus, we will use the variable profit function to define an aggregate technology.

Suppose the prices of the first N goods vary in strict proportion; that is,

$$(3) \qquad (w_1, w_2, \ldots, w_N) = (p_0\alpha_1, p_0\alpha_2, \ldots, p_0\alpha_N),$$

where $p_0 > 0$ is a scalar that varies over time while the proportionality constants $(\alpha_1, \alpha_2, \ldots, \alpha_N) \equiv \alpha \gg 0_N$ remain fixed over time.

We can now define a *macro technology set* S_α using the variable profit function Π^* and the vector of constants α as follows:

$$(4) \qquad S_\alpha \equiv \{(y_0, y) : y_0 \leq \Pi^*(\alpha, y), \text{ where } y \text{ is such that there exists an } x \text{ such that } (x,y) \in S\}.$$

We will see that y_0 can be interpreted as an aggregate of the components of x; that is, $y_0 = w \cdot x / p_0$. It is easy to show that the macro technology set S_α inherits many of the properties of the micro technology set S. For example, if S is a convex set[7] (which is a generalization of the Hicksian [1946, p. 81] diminishing marginal rates of transformation regularity conditions on S), then S_α is also a convex set.[8] Moreover, if S exhibits constant returns to scale,[9] then S_α also exhibits constant returns to scale.[10]

Given that the macro technology set S_α has been defined, we may now define the *macro profit maximizations problem*:

(5) $$\max_{y_0,y}\{p_0y_0 + p\cdot y : (y_0,y)\epsilon S\} \equiv \Pi(p_0,p).$$

The following theorem shows that if the price proportionality assumption in (3) is satisfied, then the macro profit maximization problem (5) is completely consistent with the underlying "true" micro profit maximization problem (1).

(6) *Thorem*: If (x^*,y^*) is a solution to the micro profit maximization problem (1) and the price proportionality assumption (3) holds, then (y^*_0,y^*) is a solution to the macro profit maximization (5), where the aggregate y^*_0 is defined by

(7) $$y^*_0 \equiv w\cdot x^*/p_0.$$

Note that, if the vector of constants α is known, the aggregate y^*_0 can be calculated from observable price and quantity data.

The theorem above shows that, if the factors of proportionality $(\alpha_1,\alpha_2,\ldots,\alpha_N) \equiv \alpha$ remain constant over time, then the true micro technology S can be replaced by the macro technology S_α. However, in most practical situations, α will not remain constant over time, though it may be *approximately* constant, in which case the set S_α will be *approximately* constant also, and this approximate constancy may suffice for empirical work. Perhaps a concrete example would make this point clearer.

Suppose the technology of the firm can be represented by a *translog variable profit function*[11] Π^* which is defined by the following equation:

(8) $$\ln \Pi^*(w^r,y^r) \equiv \beta_0 + \sum_{i=1}^{N} \beta_i \ln w^r_i + \tfrac{1}{2} \sum_{i=1}^{N}\sum_{h=1}^{N} \beta_{ih} \ln w^r_i \ln w^r_h + \sum_{i=1}^{N}\sum_{j=1}^{M} \gamma_{ij} \ln w^r_i \ln y^r_j + \sum_{j=1}^{M} \delta_j \ln y^r_j + \tfrac{1}{2} \sum_{j=1}^{M}\sum_{k=1}^{M} \delta_{jk} \ln y^r_j \ln y^r_k,$$

where $w^r \equiv (w^r_1,w^r_2,\ldots,w^r_N) \rangle\rangle 0_N$ is the vector of prices for the first N goods in period r where $r = 1,2,\ldots,T$ ($x^r \equiv (x^r_1,x^r_2,\ldots,x^r_N)$ is the corresponding quantity vector) and $y^r \equiv (y^r_1,y^r_2,\ldots,y^r_M) \rangle\rangle 0_M$ is a vector of purchases and sales of the last M goods in period r ($p^r \equiv (p^r_1,p^r_2,\ldots,p^r_M)$ is the corresponding vector of prices). Because the logarithm of a negative number is not defined, we have temporarily changed our sign convention and made all components of y^r positive whether the corresponding goods are outputs or inputs. Thus if the $N + M$th good during period r is an output, $y^r_m > 0$ and $p^r_m > 0$; however, if the $N + m$ th good during period r is an input, set $y^r{}_m > 0$ equal to the absolute value of the amount of input and set $p^r{}_m < 0$ equal to minus the input price.

The technological parameters β_{ih} in (8) satisfy the symmetry restrictions $\beta_{ih} = \beta_{hi}$ for $1 \leq i < h \leq N$, and the δ_{jk} satisfy the restrictions $\delta_{jk} = \delta_{kj}$ for $1 \leq j < k \leq M$. In order that the translog variable profit function $\Pi^*(w,y)$ be linearly homogeneous in w, the following restrictions on the parameters in (8) must be satisfied:

$$(9) \qquad \sum_{i=1}^{N} \beta_i = 1; \ \sum_{h=1}^{N} \beta_{ih} = 0 \text{ for } i = 1,2, \ldots ,N; \ \sum_{i=1}^{N} \gamma_{ij} = 0 \text{ for } j = 1,2, \ldots ,M.$$

Now let the w^r prices vary approximately proportionately over time; that is,

$$(10) \qquad w^r \equiv (w^r{}_1, w^r{}_2, \ldots , w^r{}_N) = (p^r{}_0 \alpha_1 e^{\epsilon^r{}_1}, p^r{}_0 \alpha_2 e^{\epsilon^r{}_2}, \ldots , p^r{}_0 \alpha_N e^{\epsilon^r{}_N}),$$

where $p^r{}_0$ represents the general level of prices of the first N goods, the α_i represent fixed factors of proportionality, and the $\epsilon^r{}_i$ represent perturbations in these fixed factors of proportionality.

If we deflate $\Pi^*(w^r,y^r) = w^r \cdot x^r$ by $p_0{}^r$ (which converts a nominal value added into a "real" value added), then (10) and (8) yield

$$(11) \qquad \ln w^r \cdot x^r / p^r{}_0 = \beta_0 + \sum_{i=1}^{N} \beta_i \ln \alpha_i + \tfrac{1}{2} \sum_{i=1}^{N} \sum_{h=1}^{N} \beta_{ih} \ln \alpha_i \ln \alpha_h + \sum_{j=1}^{M} \delta_j \ln y^r{}_j + \sum_{i=1}^{N} \sum_{j=1}^{M} \gamma_{ij} \ln \alpha_i \ln y^r{}_j + \tfrac{1}{2} \sum_{j=1}^{M} \sum_{k=1}^{M} \delta_{jk} \ln y^r{}_j \ln y^r{}_k + \epsilon^r,$$

where the Hicks's aggregate approximation error ϵ^r in period r is defined as

$$(12) \qquad \epsilon^r \equiv \sum_{i=1}^{N} \left[\beta_i + \sum_{h=1}^{N} \beta_{ih} \ln \alpha_h + \sum_{j=1}^{N} \gamma_{ij} \ln y^r{}_j \right] \epsilon^r{}_i + \tfrac{1}{2} \sum_{i=1}^{N} \sum_{h=1}^{N} \beta_{ih} \epsilon^r{}_i \epsilon^r{}_h.$$

Note that the left-hand side of (11) is observable (if $p^r{}_0$ is known), while the right-hand side is a conventional translog production function in the quantities y^r if the error term ϵ^r is neglected. Note how shifts in the price proportionality constants $\alpha \equiv (\alpha_1, \alpha_2, \ldots , \alpha_N)$ will systematically shift this translog production function.

If the perturbations ϵ^r_i defined above are such that $E\epsilon^r_i = 0$ and $E\epsilon^r_i\epsilon^t_h = \delta_{rt}\sigma_{ih}$ for $i,h = 1,2,\ldots,N$ and $r,s = 1,2,\ldots,T$, where E denotes the expectation operator and δ_{rt} equals 0 if $r \neq t$ but $\delta_{rt} = 1$ if $r = t$, then it is trivial to show that the error ϵ^r will have a constant bias[12] that will be absorbed into the constant if regression techniques are used in order to estimate the parameters of (11). Thus, with the above stochastic assumptions,[13] the production function that corresponds to the macro technology set S_α could be unbiasedly estimated up to a scaling factor, provided that the underlying technology S could be adequately approximated by the translog variable profit function Π^* defined by (8). This last proviso will be satisfied for moderate variations in prices and quantities, since the translog variable profit function can provide a second-order approximation to an arbitrary twice-differentiable variable profit function that in turn provides a complete description of the underlying technology S under suitable regularity conditions.

Thus it appears that the assumption of approximate price proportionality provides a rather powerful justification for aggregating over commodities.

Note that the aggregation method studied in this section did not restrict the technology in any essential way; rather, the set of prices that producers faced was restricted. In the following section, a method of aggregating over commodities is outlined that depends on the technology's satisfying certain restrictive assumptions.

8.2.2 Homogeneous Weak Separability

The second major method justifying commodity aggregation is due to Leontief (1947) and Shephard (1953, pp. 61–71; 1970, pp. 145–46; see also Solow 1955–56; Green 1964; Arrow 1974; Geary and Morishima 1973), and I will outline this method below. To cover both producer and consumer theory applications of this method of aggregation, we assume cost minimizing (instead of profit maximizing) behavior on the part of producers.

Suppose the microeconomic production (or utility) function f^* where $u = f^*(x,z)$ is output (or utility), $x \geq 0_N$ is a nonnegative N-dimensional vector of commodity inputs to be aggregated, and $z \geq 0_M$ is an M-dimensional vector of "other" commodity inputs. The producer's (or consumer's) total minimum cost function is defined as:

$$(13) \qquad C^*(u; p,w) \equiv \min_{x,z} \{p \cdot x + w \cdot z : f^*(x,z) \geq u\},$$

where $p \equiv (p_1,p_2,\ldots,p_N) \gg 0_N$ is a vector of positive input prices and $w \equiv (w_1,w_2,\ldots,w_M) \gg 0_M$ is a vector of "other" input prices. The Shephard (1953, 1970) duality theorem (see also Samuelson 1953–54; Uzawa 1964; McFadden 1978; Hanoch 1978; and Diewert 1971) states that, under certain regularity conditions, the total cost function C^* completely determines the production function f^*. Thus restrictions on the production function f^* translate into restrictions on the cost function C^* and vice versa. We will make use of this fact below.

To justify the aggregation of the commodities x, Shephard assumed that x was *homogeneously weakly separable*[14] from the "other" commodities z; that is, he assumed that the micro function f^* could be written as

$$f^*(x,z) = \hat{f}[f(x),z], \tag{14}$$

where $\hat{f}$ is a *macro* production (or utility) function (satisfying the same regularity conditions as f^*) and f is an *aggregator* function that is assumed to satisfy the following regularity conditions.

(15) *Conditions on* f:
i) f is defined for $x \rangle\rangle 0_N$ and $f(x) > 0$ (*positivity*);
ii) $f(\lambda x) = \lambda f(x)$ for $\lambda > 0$, $x \rangle\rangle 0_N$ (*linear homogeneity*);
iii) $f(\lambda x^1 + (1-\lambda)x^2) \geq \lambda f(x^1) + (1-\lambda)f(x^2)$ for $0 \leq \lambda \leq 1$, $x^1 \rangle\rangle 0_N$, $x^2 \rangle\rangle 0_N$ (*concavity*).

The macro function $\hat{f}$ has a cost function dual defined by

$$\hat{C}(u; p_0,w) \equiv \min_{y,z}\{p_0 y + w \cdot z\colon \hat{f}(y,z) \geq u\}, \tag{16}$$

where $p_0 > 0$ is the price of the aggregate, y. The aggregator function f also has a total cost function dual defined by

$$\begin{aligned} C(y;p) &\equiv \min_x\{p \cdot x\colon f(x) \geq y\} \\ &= y \min_{x/y}\{p \cdot x/y\colon f(x/y) \geq 1\} \text{ using (15.ii)} \\ &\equiv yc(p). \end{aligned} \tag{17}$$

It turns out that the unit cost function $c(p)$ satisfies the same regularity conditions as f; that is, $c(p)$ is positive, linearly homogeneous, and concave for $p \rangle\rangle 0_N$ (see Samuelson 1953–54; Diewert 1974*b*). Moreover, given a unit-cost function $c(p)$ satisfying the conditions (15), the production function dual may be defined as[15]

$$f(x) \equiv 1/max_p\{c(p)\colon p \cdot x = 1, p \geq 0_N\}. \tag{18}$$

With the above preliminaries disposed of, we can now outline the Shephard-Solow-Arrow results. Suppose $p^* \cdot x^* + w^* \cdot z^* = C^*(u^*; p^*,w^*)$; that is, x^*,z^* is a solution to the micro cost minimization problem (13) when micro prices p^*,w^* (and utility or output u^*) prevail. If the micro function f^* is homogenously weakly separable (i.e., f^* satisfies eq. 14) and *if the functional form for the aggregator function f* *is known* (or the functional form for its unit-cost function $c(p)$ is known), then the aggregate y^* can be defined as

(19) $$y^* \equiv f(x^*) \text{ (or } y^* \equiv p^* \cdot x^* / c(p^*)),$$

and the price of the aggregate may be defined as

(20) $$p^*_0 \equiv p^* \cdot x^* / f(x^*) \text{ (or } p^*_0 \equiv c(p^*)),$$

and $p^*_0 y^* + w^* \cdot z^* = \hat{C}(u^*; p^*_0, w^*)$; that is, y^*, z^* is a solution to the macro cost minimization problem (16) with prices p^*_0, w^* (and utility or output u^*).[16]

There are, of course, at least two problems with this aggregation method: (*a*) the micro function f^* may not be homogeneously weakly separable in practice, and (*b*) the functional form for the aggregator function f is generally unknown. In the remainder of this section, our attention will be directed toward solving the second difficulty.

Let $p^r \gg 0_N$, $w^r \gg 0_M$ for $r = 0, 1, \ldots, T$. If x^r, z^r is a solution to $\min_{x,z}\{p^r \cdot x + w^r \cdot z\colon \hat{f}[f(x), z] \geq u^r\}$ and if $\hat{f}$ is increasing in its first argument, it is easy to see that x^r must be a solution to the following *aggregator maximization problem.*

(21) $$\max_x \{f(x)\colon p^r \cdot x \leq p^r \cdot x^r; x \geq 0_N\} \quad r = 0, 1, \ldots, T.$$

In other words, if an economic agent wishes to minimize the cost of achieving a certain utility or output level when the micro function f^* is weakly separable (i.e., $f^*(x,z) = \hat{f}[f(x), z]$) and the macro function $\hat{f}$ is increasing in its first argument, then the "intermediate input" (or "real value added" or "category subutility") $f(x)$ must be a maximum subject to an expenditure constraint.

Notice that (21) involves only the (unknown) aggregator function f and observable prices and quantities, $\{p^r, x^r\}$ for $r = 0, 1, \ldots, T$. If f is differentiable, then the first-order necessary conditions for a maximum yield the following identity after the Lagrange multiplier is eliminated:

(22) *Lemma*: (Konyus and Byushgens 1926, p. 155; Hotelling 1935, pp. 71–74; Wold 1944, pp. 69–71). Suppose f *is* differentiable and $x^r > 0_N$ is a solution to $\max_x\{f(x)\colon p^r \cdot x \leq p^r \cdot x^r, x \geq 0_N\}$, where $p^r \gg 0_N$. Then

$$\frac{p^r}{p^r \cdot x^r} = \frac{\nabla f(x^r)}{x^r \cdot \nabla f(x^r)},$$

where $\nabla f(x^r)$ is the vector of first-order partial derivatives evaluated at x^r.

Corollary:[17] If f is also homogeneous of degree one (i.e., $f(\lambda x) = \lambda f(x)$ for every $\lambda > 0$), then

(23) $$\frac{p^r}{p^r \cdot x^r} = \frac{\nabla f(x^r)}{f(x^r)}.$$

The above corollary suggests the following *Method I* (due to Arrow 1974) for determining the aggregator function f given the micro data $\{p^r, x^r\}$, $r = 0,1,2, \ldots, T$: simply assume a convenient functional form for f and use the relations (23) to econometrically estimate the unknown parameters. For example, suppose that f is the *homogeneous translog function* (Christensen, Jorgenson, and Lau 1971):

(24) $$\ln f(x^r) \equiv \beta_0 + \sum_{n=1}^{N} \beta_n \ln x^r_n + \tfrac{1}{2} \sum_{j=1}^{N} \sum_{k=1}^{N} \beta_{jk} \ln x^r_j \ln x^r_k, \quad r = 0,1, \ldots, T,$$

where $\sum_{n=1}^{N} \beta_n = 1$, $\beta_{jk} = \beta_{kj}$ and $\sum_{k=1}^{N} \beta_{jk} = 0$ for $j = 1,2, \ldots, N$.

With the above parameter restrictions, f turns out to be linearly homogeneous. Application of (23) yields the following system of equations that is linear in the unknown parameters:

(25) $$\frac{p^r_n}{p^r \cdot x^r} = \frac{\beta_n + \sum_{k=1}^{N} \beta_{nk} \ln x^r_k}{x^r_n}, \quad \begin{array}{l} n = 1,2, \ldots, N \\ r = 0,1,2, \ldots, T, \end{array}$$

where $p^r \equiv (p^r_1, p^r_2, \ldots, p^r_N)$ and $x^r \equiv (x^r_1, x^r_2, \ldots, x^r_N)$. Notice that the parameter β_0 is not identified, but once the other parameters are determined, an estimate for β_0 may be obtained by solving $f(x^0) = 1$ for β_0 (*base period normalization*). For an econometric application of this method in the context of estimating a real value-added production function, see Berndt and Christensen (1973).

Instead of econometrically estimating the parameters of the aggregator function f, we may attempt to estimate the parameters of its unit cost function, $c(p)$. In this context, the following result is useful.

(26) *Lemma*: (Shephard 1953, p. 11; Samuelson 1953–54) If f satisfies (15), $p^r \cdot x^r = \min_x \{p^r \cdot x : f(x) \geq f(x^r)\} = c(p^r) f(x^r)$ for $r = 0,1, \ldots T$, and the unit cost function c is differentiable at p^r, then

$$x^r = \nabla c(p^r) f(x^r), \quad r = 0,1, \ldots, T.$$

(27) *Corollary*:[18] $x^r / p^r \cdot x^r = \nabla c(p^r) / c(p^r)$, $r = 0,1, \ldots, T$.

The above corollary suggests the following *Method II* (also due to Arrow 1974) for determining the dual c to the aggregator function f

given the micro data $\{p^r, x^r\}$, $r = 1,2, \ldots, T$: assume a functional form for $c(p)$ and use the relations (27) to estimate the unknown parameters of $c(p)$. For example, suppose that c is the *translog unit cost function* (Christensen, Jorgenson, and Lau 1971):

$$(28) \qquad \ln c(p^r) \equiv \gamma_0 + \sum_{n=1}^{N} \gamma_n \ln p^r_n + \tfrac{1}{2} \sum_{j=1}^{N} \sum_{k=1}^{N} \gamma_{jk} \ln p^r_j \ln p^r_k, \quad r = 0,1, \ldots, T,$$

where $\sum_{n=1}^{N} \gamma_n = 1$, $\gamma_{jk} = \gamma_{kj}$ and $\sum_{k=1}^{N} \gamma_{jk} = 0$ for $j = 1,2, \ldots, N$.

Application of Shephard's lemma (27) yields the following system of equations that is linear in the unknown parameters:

$$(29) \qquad \frac{x^r_n}{p^r \cdot x^r} = \frac{\gamma_n + \sum_{k=1}^{N} \gamma_{nk} \ln p^r_k}{p^r_n}, \quad n = 1,2, \ldots, N, \; r = 0,1,2, \ldots, T.$$

Notice that the parameter γ_0 is not identified, but once the other parameters are determined an estimate for γ_0 may be obtained by solving the equation $p^0 \cdot x^0 / c(p^0) = 1$ (*base period normalization*), which makes $f(x^0) = 1$.

Note that the translog unit cost function generates an aggregator function via (18) that does not in general[19] coincide with the translog aggregator function defined by (24). Thus, in general, the two translog functional forms correspond to *different* tastes or technologies, although either functional form can approximate the same underlying (differentiable) technology to the second order.

At this point I should mention *Method III* for determining the ratio of the aggregates, $f(x^r)/f(x^0)$. This final method involves assuming a functional form for the aggregator function f that is consistent with an index number formula (which is a function of observable prices and quantities for the two periods under consideration). The method assumes that x^r is a solution to the aggregator maximization problem defined by (21),[20] and it will be studied in greater detail in section 8.2.4. When reading section 8.2.4, recall that it was the assumption of expenditure minimizing behavior (which is consistent with profit maximizing behavior), plus the assumption that the technology was homogeneously weakly separable in the x goods that led us to conclude that x^r was a solution to the aggregator maximization problem $\max_x\{f(x) : p^r \cdot x \leq p^r \cdot x^r\}$, where f is the linearly homogeneous aggregator function.

In the next section, I outline another method for aggregating over goods, a method due to François Divisia (1926).

8.2.3 The Divisia Index and Various Discrete Approximations

The most frequently suggested index to be used in the measurement of total factor productivity is the Divisia (1926, p. 40) index. Let us briefly outline Solow's (1957) derivation of the index.[21]

Suppose a linearly homogeneous, concave, nondecreasing in x production function F exists where $y(t) = F(x(t); t)$, $y(t)$ is output at time t, and $x(t) \equiv (x_1(t), x_2(t), \ldots, x_N(t))$ is a vector of inputs at time t. If the production function exhibits neutral technical change (see Blackorby, Lovell, and Thursby 1976 for a formal definition), then it can be written as $F(x(t); t) = A(t)f(x(t))$, where $A(t)$ is the cumulative multiplicative shift factor for the production function at time t. If we totally differentiate the following equation

$$(30) \qquad y(t) = A(t)f(x(t))$$

with respect to time and divide by $y(t)$, we obtain

$$(31) \qquad \frac{\dot{y}(t)}{y(t)} = \frac{\dot{A}(t)}{A(t)} + A(t) \sum_{i=1}^{N} \frac{\partial f[x(t)]}{\partial x_i} \frac{\dot{x}_i(t)}{y(t)},$$

where a dot over a variable signifies a derivative with respect to time. Let $p(t) \equiv (p_1(t), \ldots, p_N(t))$ be the vector of input prices at time t relative to the price of output, which is set equal to one. Then, if inputs are being paid the value of their marginal products, $A(t)\partial f[x(t)]/\partial x_i = p_i(t)$, and if we define the ith input's share of output as $s_i(t) \equiv p_i(t)x_i(t)/y(t)$, $i = 1,2, \ldots, N$, then (31) may be rewritten as

$$(32) \qquad \frac{\dot{A}(t)}{A(t)} = \frac{\dot{y}(t)}{y(t)} - \sum_{i=1}^{N} s_i(t) \frac{\dot{x}_i(t)}{x_i(t)}.$$

If $\dot{A}(t)/A(t) = 0$, there is no exogenous shift in the production function owing to technical progress, increasing returns to scale, or any other cause; that is, the growth of output is completely accounted for by the growth of inputs.

We can integrate (32) (given continuous data on output, inputs, and prices) to obtain the cumulative index of total factor productivity from time $t = 0$ to time $t = T$:

$$(33) \qquad \frac{A(T)}{A(0)} = \frac{y(T)/y(0)}{e^{\int_0^T \sum_{i=1}^{N} s_i(t)\, \dot{x}_i(t)/x_i(t)\, dt}},$$

where the denominator on the right-hand side of (33) is the Divisia index of input growth between, say, time 0 and T, $X(T)/X(0)$.

Richter (1966) and Jorgenson and Griliches (1967) have generalized equations (32) and (33) by replacing the single output term

$\dot{y}(t)/y(t)$ in (32) with a share-weighted average of the growth rates of many outputs, and the term $y(T)/y(0)$ in (33) with a Divisia index of output growth.

Since the right-hand sides of (32) and (33) are in principle observable, the technical change term $A(t)$ can, in principle, be estimated.[22] But in practice data do not come in nice continuous series; rather they come at discrete intervals. Thus the continuous formulas (32) and (33) must be approximated using discrete data.

Let us now introduce some new notation that is appropriate when data come at discrete intervals. Let the vector of period r inputs be $x^r \equiv (x^r{}_1,x^r{}_2,\ldots,x^r{}_N)$ and period r prices be $p^r \equiv (p^r{}_1,p^r{}_2,\ldots,p^r{}_N)$ for $r = 0,1$.

Denote the denominator of (33) as $X(1)/X(0)$, when $T = 1$. If the input shares are approximately constant, then $\ln X(1)/X(0)$ approximately equals $\sum_{i=1}^{N} s_i \ln x^1{}_i/x^0{}_i$. For any number z close to 1, $\ln z$ can be accurately approximated by $-1 + z$, so that $X(1)/X(0)$ approximately equals $\sum_{i=1}^{N} s_i x^1{}_i/x^0{}_i$. Thus the Divisia index of input growth $X(1)/X(0)$ can be approximated by a share-weighted rate of growth of the quantity relatives $x^1{}_i/x^0{}_i$, $i = 1,2,\ldots,N$. If we choose base-period shares, the resulting index is the Laspeyres quantity index Q_L:

$$(34) \qquad Q_L(p^0,p^1;x^0,x^1) \equiv \sum_{i=1}^{N} \frac{p^0{}_i x^0{}_i}{p^0 \cdot x^0} (x^1{}_i/x^0{}_i) = \frac{p^0 \cdot x^1}{p^0 \cdot x^0},$$

where $p^0 \cdot x^r \equiv \sum_{I=i}^{N} p^0{}_i x^r{}_i$ denotes the inner product between the vectors p^0 and x^r, $r = 0,1$. On the other hand, if we choose current-period prices and base-period quantities to form shares, the resulting index is the Paasche quantity index Q_P:

$$(35) \qquad Q_p(p^0,p^1;x^0,x^1) \equiv \sum_{i=1}^{N} \frac{p^1{}_i x^0{}_i}{p^1 \cdot x^0} (x^1{}_i/x^0{}_i) = \frac{p^1 \cdot x^1}{p^1 \cdot x^0}.$$

A third way of approximating the share-weighted rate of growth of inputs that apepars in (32) would be to take a geometric mean of the index Q_L and Q_P:

$$(36) \qquad Q_2(p^0,p^1;x^0,x^1) \equiv (p^0 \cdot x^1 p^1 \cdot x^1 / p^0 \cdot x^0 p^1 \cdot x^0)^{1/2}.$$

The index Q_2 is Irving Fisher's (1922) ideal quantity index. The price index that corresponds to Q_2 is P_2 defined implicitly by Fisher's weak factor reversal test:

$$(37) \qquad P_2(p^0,p^1;x^0,x^1)\, Q_2(p^0,p^1,x^0,x^1) = p^1 \cdot x^1 / p^0 \cdot x^0;$$

that is, the product of the price index times the quantity index equals the expenditure ratio between the two periods. Fisher called P_2 and Q_2

ideal indexes because they satisfied (37) and also $P_2(p^0,p^1;x^0,x^1) \equiv Q_2(x^0,x^1;p^0,p^1)$; that is, the price and quantity indexes turn out to have the same functional form, except that the role of prices and quantities are reversed for the two indexes.

The integral expression for the Divisia index of inputs found in (33) suggests some further discrete approximations. If the input shares $s_i(t)$ remain constant between 0 and 1, then the log of the Divisia index becomes:

$$\ln e^{\int_0^1 \sum_{i=1}^{N} s_i \dot{x}_i(t)/x_i(t)\,dt} = \sum_{i=1}^{N} s_i \ln x^1_i/x^0_i.$$

Since the shares $s_i(t)$ are not generally the same for periods 0 and 1, Törnqvist (1936) suggested the following discrete approximation Q_0 to the continuous Divisia quantity index:

$$(38)\qquad \ln Q_0(p^0,p^1;x^0,x^1) \equiv \sum_{i=1}^{N} \tfrac{1}{2}\left[\frac{p^0{}_i x^0{}_i}{p^0\cdot x^0} + \frac{p^1{}_i x^1{}_i}{p^1\cdot x^1}\right]\cdot \ln[x^1{}_i/x^0{}_i].$$

Star and Hall (1976) develop an analytic expression for the difference between the discrete approximation Q_0 defined by (38) and the continuous Divisia index. They conclude that the approximation error will be small provided the shares do not fluctuate wildly.

The Törnqvist price index P_0 can be defined by the formula for Q_0 except that prices and quantities are interchanged; more explicitly:

$$(39)\qquad \ln P_0(p^0,p^1;x^0,x^1) \equiv \sum_{i=1}^{N} \left[\tfrac{1}{2}\frac{p^0{}_i x^0{}_i}{p^0\cdot x^0} + \tfrac{1}{2}\frac{p^1{}_i x^1{}_i}{p^1\cdot x^1}\right]\cdot \ln[p^1{}_i/p^0{}_i].$$

Given the price index P_0, an implicit Törnqvist quantity index $\tilde{Q}_0$ may be defined using Fisher's weak factor reversal test:

$$(40)\qquad \tilde{Q}_0(p^0,p^1;x^0,x^1) \equiv [p^1\cdot x^1/p^0\cdot x^0]/P_0(p^0,p^1;x^0,x^1).$$

Kloek (1967) and Theil (1968) showed that the Törnqvist indexes Q_0, P_0, and $\tilde{Q}_0$ had some good approximation properties. Kloek noted that Q_0 was not well defined if some quantities were zero, while P_0 was not well defined if some prices were zero. Thus he advocated using the price index P_0 and the quantity index $\tilde{Q}_0$, since prices are usually nonzero. I will return to this problem of zero prices and quantities in section 8.6.2.

We have now defined five reasonable-looking discrete approximations to the Divisia quantity index. The problem is that the theory of Divisia indexes outlined above does not tell us which discrete index number formula should be used in empirical applications, even though it is known that the Laspeyres and Paasche quantity indexes can differ considerably from the other indexes.[23]

It turns out that the economic theory of exact index numbers[24] enables us to discriminate more sharply among the above index number formulas. I will briefly outline this theory.

8.2.4 Exact and Superlative Index Number Formulas

Suppose the production function (or aggregator function) is $y = f(x_1,x_2,\ldots,x_N) = f(x)$, where y is output (or the aggregate), x is a vector of inputs (or goods to be aggregated), and f is a nondecreasing, linearly homogeneous and concave function. Suppose further that, given a positive vector of input prices $p \equiv (p_1,p_2,\ldots,p_N)$, the producer attempts to minimize the cost of producing a given output level. The solution to the cost minimization problem is the total cost function $C(y;p)$, which decomposes into a unit-cost function $c(p)$ times the output level owing to the linear homogeneity of the aggregator function f;[25] that is,

$$(41) \qquad C(y;p) \equiv \min_x\{p\cdot x:\ f(x) = y\} = c(p)y.$$

It is natural to identify $c(p)$ with the price of output; that is, as being the price of the aggregate good y.

Suppose we are given price and quantity data for two periods, p^0,p^1,x^0,x^1. Define a *price index* simply as a function P of prices and quantities, $P(p^0,p^1;x^0,x^1)$, while a *quantity index* $Q(p^0,p^1;x^0,x^1)$ is another function of prices and quantities for the two periods. We generally assume that the price and quantity indexes satisfy Fisher's weak factor reversal test; that is, P and Q satisfy

$$(42) \qquad P(p^0,p^1;\ x^0,x^1)\ Q(p^0,p^1;x^0,x^1) = p^1\cdot x^1/p^0\cdot x^0.$$

A given functional form for a quantity index Q is defined to be *exact* for a functional form for the aggregator function f if given output levels y^0,y^1, input price vectors $p^0,p^1;x^0$ a solution to the period 0 cost minimization problem (41) and x^1 a solution to the period 1 cost minimization problem (41), then

$$(43) \qquad f(x^1)/f(x^0) = Q(p^0,p^1;\ x^0,x^1)$$

for all $y^0 > 0$, $y^1 > 0$, $p^0 \gg 0_N$, $p^1 \gg 0_N$.[26] Similarly, a given functional form for a price index P is defined to be *exact* for a functional form for the aggregator function f (and its derived unit cost function c) if given output levels y^0,y^1, input price vectors $p^0,p^1;x^r$ a solution to the period r cost minimization problem (41) for $r = 0,1$, then

(44) $$c(p^1)/c(p^0) = P(p^0,p^1; x^0,x^1).$$

Thus the quantity index Q equals the ratio of the "outputs" y^1/y^0, and the price index P equals the ratio of the unit costs (or the ratio of the "prices" of the "outputs") $c(p^1)/c(p^0)$, provided Q and P are exact for some f. Note that for $r = 0,1$,

$$C(y^r; p^r) \equiv \min_x\{p^r \cdot x: f(x) = y^r\} = p^r \cdot x^r = c(p^r)y^r,$$

and, using (43) and (44),

$$\begin{aligned} P(p^0,p^1; x^0,x^1)\, Q(p^0,p^1; x^0,x^1) &= [c(p^1)/c(p^0)]\,[f(x^1)/f(x^0)] \\ &= c(p^1)y^1 \,/\, c(p^0)y^0 \\ &= p^1 \cdot x^1/p^0 \cdot x^0, \end{aligned}$$

so that exact price and quantity indexes satisfy the weak factor reversal test (43).[27]

With the above theoretical considerations disposed of, we can now return to the problem of evaluating the five alternative discrete approximations to the Divisia quantity index. It seems that we could define two other discrete approximations to the Divisia quantity index by defining the Laspeyres and Paasche price indexes analogously to the Laspeyres and Paasche quantity indexes (defined by equations 34 and 35), except that the roles of prices and quantities are reversed and then the implicit Laspeyres and Paasche quantity indexes, $\tilde{Q}_L$ and $\tilde{Q}_P$, may be defined by the weak factor reversal test (42):

(45) $$\begin{aligned} \tilde{Q}_L(p^0,p^1; x^0,x^1) &\equiv [p^1 \cdot x^1/p^0 \cdot x^0]/P_L(p^0,p^1; x^0,x^1) \\ &= p^1 \cdot x^1/p^1 \cdot x^0 \\ &\equiv Q_P(p^0,p^1; x^0,x^1), \\ \tilde{Q}_P(p^0,p^1; x^0,x^1) &\equiv [p^1 \cdot x^1/p^0 \cdot x^0]/P_P(p^0,p^1; x^0x^1) \\ &= p^0 \cdot x^1/p^0 \cdot x^0 \\ &\equiv Q_L(p^0,p^1; x^0,x^1). \end{aligned}$$

Thus the quantity index that corresponds to the Laspeyres price index is the Paasche quantity index, and the Paasche price index corresponds to the Laspeyres quantity index.

Konyus and Byushgens (1926) have shown that:[28] (*a*) the Laspeyres and Paasche quantity indexes are exact for a fixed coefficients (or Leontief) aggregator function of the form $f_L(x_1,x_2, \ldots ,x_N \equiv \min\{x_i/a_i: i = 1,2, \ldots ,N\}$, where the $a_i > 0$ are fixed coefficients, and (*b*) Fisher's ideal quantity index Q_2 defined by (36) is exact for a *homogeneous quadratic aggregator function* of the form $f_2(x_1,x_2, \ldots ,x_N) \equiv$

$\left(\sum_{i=1}^{N}\sum_{j=1}^{N} a_{ij}x_ix_j\right)^{1/2}$, where $a_{ij} = a_{ji}$ and the matrix of coefficients $[a_{ij}]$ is such that f_2 is concave and nondecreasing over the relevant range of quantities. Thus, under the assumption of cost-minimizing behavior and if the aggregator function is the homogeneous quadratic defined above, then we have

$$y^1/y^0 = \left(\sum_{i=1}^{N}\sum_{j=1}^{N} a_{ij}x^1{}_ix^1{}_j\right)^{1/2} \Big/ \left(\sum_{i=1}^{N}\sum_{j=1}^{N} a_{ij}x^0{}_ix^0{}_j\right)^{1/2}$$
$$\equiv Q_2(p^0,p^1;x^0,x^1).$$

Thus we can calculate the "output" ratio y^1/y^0 by calculating Q_2, *which can be evaluated without knowing what the a_{ij} coefficients are.*

On the other hand, Diewert (1976) has shown that the Törnqvist quantity index Q_0 defined by (38) is exact for the *homogeneous translog aggregator function* f, defined by

$$\ln f_0(x_1,x_2,\ldots,x_N) \equiv \beta_0 + \sum_{i=1}^{N} \beta_i \ln x_i + \tfrac{1}{2} \sum_{i=1}^{N}\sum_{j=1}^{N} \beta_{ij} \ln x_i \ln x_j,$$

where the parameters β_i and $\beta_{ij} = \beta_{ji}$ are such that $f_0(x)$ is concave, nondecreasing, and linearly homogeneous over the relevant range of xs. In order that f_0 be linearly homogeneous, it is necessary and sufficient that the following restrictions be satisfied:

$$(46) \qquad \sum_{i=1}^{N} \beta_i = 1; \ \sum_{j=1}^{N} \beta_{ij} = 0 \text{ for } i = 1,2,\ldots,N;$$
$$\sum_{i=1}^{N} \beta_{ij} = 0 \text{ for } j = 1,2,\ldots,N.$$

Thus the homogeneous translog aggregator function has exactly the same number of independent parameters as the homogeneous quadratic aggregator function defined earlier, namely $N(N+1)/2$ independent parameters. Moreover, it turns out that both aggregator functions are capable of providing a second-order differential[29] approximation to an arbitrary twice continuously differentiable, linearly homogeneous function.

It was also shown in Diewert (1976) that the implicit Törnqvist quantity index $\tilde{Q}_0$ defined by equation (40) above is exact for the aggregator function $\tilde{f}_0$ that has as its dual the translog unit cost function $c_0(p)$ defined by

$$\ln c_0(p_1,p_2,\ldots,p_N) = \beta^*{}_0 + \sum_{i=1}^{N} \beta^*{}_i \ln p_i$$
$$+ \tfrac{1}{2} \sum_{i=1}^{N}\sum_{j=1}^{N} \beta^*{}_{ij} \ln p_i \ln p_j,$$

where $$\sum_{i=1}^{N} \beta^*_{i} = 1, \beta^*_{ij} = \beta^*_{ji}, \text{ and}$$

$$\sum_{i=1}^{N} \beta^*_{ij} = 0 \text{ for } j = 1,2, \ldots, N.$$

(The restrictions $\sum_{j=1}^{N} \beta^*_{ij} = 0$ for $i = 1,2, \ldots, N$ follow from the symmetry restrictions $\beta^*_{ij} = \beta^*_{ji}$.) The translog unit cost function can provide a second-order differential approximation to an arbitrary twice continuously differentiable unit cost function, which in turn is capable of completely describing the corresponding linearly homogeneous aggregator function.

The fixed coefficients aggregator function has a linear unit cost function (equal to $\sum_{i=1}^{N} a_i p_i$) which can provide only a first-order approximation to an arbitrary twice-differentiable unit-cost function. Thus the Törnqvist price index P_0 should be preferred to the Laspeyres and Paasche price indexes P_L and P_P, respectively.

Thus the economic theory of exact index numbers has enabled us to discriminate somewhat between the five discrete approximations to the Divisia quantity index that we have considered: the indexes Q_2, Q_0, and $\tilde{Q}_0$ are to be preferred to Q_L and Q_P, since the former are exact for functional forms for the underlying aggregator function (or its dual unit cost function) that are more flexible than the very restrictive fixed coefficients aggregator function.

That the indexes Q_2, Q_0, and $\tilde{Q}_0$ are approximately equivalent can be demonstrated in another way (which does not depend on the assumption that the producer attempted to minimize the cost of producing the aggregate during the two periods). Diewert (1978*b*) showed that when prices in the two periods are equal (i.e., $p^0 = p^1 = p$) and quantities are also equal (i.e., $x^0 = x^1 = x$), then

$$\begin{aligned}(47) \qquad & Q_2(p,p; x,x) = Q_0(p,p; x,x) = \tilde{Q}_0(p,p; x,x)\\ & \nabla Q_2(p,p; x, x) = \nabla Q_0(p,p; x,x) = \\ & \nabla \tilde{Q}_0(p,p; x,x) \text{ and}\\ & \nabla^2 Q_2(p,p; x,x) = \nabla^2 Q_0(p,p; x,x) = \\ & \nabla^2 \tilde{Q}_0(p,p; x,x);\end{aligned}$$

that is, the three "better" quantity indexes differentially approximate each other to the second order at any point where the two price vectors are equal and the two quantity vectors are equal.[30] Thus for small changes in prices and quantities between the two periods, the three indexes should give the same answer to the second order.[31] The equalities in (47) can be derived simply by evaluating and differentiating the appropriate index number formula—no assumptions about minimizing behavior are required.

Diewert (1976) defined a price index (quantity index) to be *superlative* if it is exact for a unit cost function c (aggregator function f) capable of providing a second-order differential approximation to an arbitrary twice-differentiable linearly homogeneous function. Since a linearly homogeneous translog function can provide a second-order approximation to an arbitrary twice-differentiable linearly homogeneous function (see Lau 1974), it can be seen that P_0 defined by (39) is a superlative price index and Q_0 defined by (38) is a superlative quantity index. In general, "superlative" indexes are exact for "flexible" functional forms for the underlying aggregator function.

It is easy to show that the three "better" quantity indexes are superlative indexes. Are there any other superlative indexes? The answer is yes, as the following examples show.

For $r \neq 0$, define the quadratic mean of order r price index P_r as

$$(48) \qquad P_r(p^0,p^1;x^0,x^1) \equiv \left[\frac{\sum_{k=1}^{N} (p^1{}_k x^1{}_k / p^1 \cdot x^1)(p^0{}_k / p^1{}_k)^{r/2}}{\sum_{i=1}^{N} (p^0{}_i x^0{}_i / p^0 \cdot x^0)(p^1{}_i / p^0{}_i)^{r/2}} \right]^{1/r}.$$

It can be shown (Diewert 1976) that P_r is exact for the quadratic mean of order r unit cost function,

$$c_r(p) \equiv \left(\sum_{i=1}^{N} \sum_{j=1}^{N} b_{ij} p_i^{r/2} p_j^{r/2} \right)^{1/r}.$$

Since c_r can approximate an arbitrary unit cost function to the second order, P_r is a superlative price index.

For $r \neq 0$, define the quadratic mean of order r quantity index Q_r as

$$(49) \qquad Q_r(p^0,p^1;x^0,x^1) \equiv \left[\frac{\sum_{i=1}^{N} (p^0{}_i x^0{}_i / p^0 \cdot x^0)(x^1{}_i / x^0{}_i)^{r/2}}{\sum_{j=1}^{N} (p^1{}_j x^1{}_j / p^1 \cdot x^1)(x^0{}_j / x^1{}_j)^{r/2}} \right]^{1/r}.$$

It can similarly be shown that Q_r is exact for the quadratic mean of order r aggregator function,[32]

$$f_r(x) \equiv \left(\sum_{i=1}^{N} \sum_{j=1}^{N} a_{ij} x_i^{r/2} x_j^{r/2} \right)^{1/r}, \text{ and}$$

that Q_r is a superlative quantity index.

The reason for our notation P_2 and Q_2 for the Fisher ideal price and quantity indexes should now be evident: they are special cases of (48) and (49) when $r = 2$.

We can now also explain our reason for choosing the notation P_0 and Q_0 for the Törnqvist price and quantity indexes: it can be shown that $f_r(x)$ tends to $f_0(x)$, the homogeneous translog functional form, as r tends to zero under certain conditions, which we explain below. Thus Q_0 is in some sense a limiting case of Q_r.

It is no loss of generality to choose units of measurement for "output" y so that $\Sigma_i\Sigma_j a_{ij} = 1$. Let us further redefine the a_{ij} as $a_{ii} = \beta_i + 2\beta_{ii}r^{-1}$, and $a_{ij} \equiv 2\beta_{ij}r^{-1}$ for $i \neq j$, where $\Sigma_i\beta_i = 1$, $\beta_{ij} = \beta_{ji}$ *and* $\Sigma_i\beta_{ij} = 0$ for $j = 1,2,\ldots,N$. Then the equation that defines the quadratic mean of order r becomes

$$y = \left[\sum_{i=1}^{N} \beta_i x^r{}_i + 2r^{-1} \sum_{i=1}^{N} \sum_{j=1}^{N} \beta_{ij} x^{r/2}{}_i x^{r/2}{}_j\right]^{1/r}.$$

Now raise each side of this equation to the power r, subtract 1 from each side of the resulting equation, divide both sides by r, and upon making use of the restrictions on the β_i and β_{ij}, we may write the result as

$$\frac{y^r - 1}{r} = \Sigma_i\beta_i \frac{(x^r{}_i - 1)}{r} + \tfrac{1}{2}\Sigma_i\Sigma_j\beta_{ij} \frac{(x^{r/2}{}_i - 1)}{r/2} \frac{(x^{r/2}{}_j - 1)}{r/2}.$$

If we take limits of both sides of this equation as r tends to zero, we obtain (since, using L'Hospital's rule, $\lim \lambda \to 0 (x^\lambda - 1)/\lambda = \ln x$)

$$\ln y = \Sigma_i\beta_i \ln x_i + \tfrac{1}{2}\Sigma_i\Sigma_j\beta_{ij} \ln x_i \ln x_j,$$

which is the homogeneous translog functional form since, the β_i and β_{ij} satisfy the restrictions (46). The above proof that f_0 is a limiting case of f_r owes much to suggestions made by L. J. Lau.

The following theorems indicate that it does not matter which superlative index is used in empirical work with time series data: they will all give virtually the same answer.

(50) *Theorem* (Diewert 1978*b*): For any $r \neq 0$, $P_r(p^0,p^1; x^0,x^1) = P_0(p^0,p^1; x^0,x^1)$ and the first- and second-order partial derivatives of the two functions coincide provided $p^0 = p^1 \rangle\rangle 0_N$ (all price components are positive) and $x^0 = x^1 > 0_N$ (at least one quantity component is positive).

(51) *Theorem* (Diewert 1978*b*): For any $r \neq 0$, the quantity index Q_r differentially approximates Q_0 to the second order at any point where the prices and quantities for the two periods are equal; that is, $Q_r(p^0,p^1; x^0,x^1) = Q_0(p^0,p^1; x^0,x^1)$, and the first- and second-order partial

derivatives of the two functions coincide provided $p^0 = p^1 > 0_N$ and $x^0 = x^1 \rangle\rangle 0_N$.

Thus, if changes in prices and quantities are small, all the superlatives indexes P_r and Q_r will give virtually the same answer, even if economic agents are not engaging in optimizing behavior.[33] Some empirical evidence on the degree of closeness of the various indexes to each other is available in Fisher (1922), Ruggles (1967), and Diewert (1978*b*).

Theorems (50) and (51) suggest that using the *chain principle* (i.e., the base is changed to the previous period $t-1$ rather than maintaining a fixed base when calculating the change in the aggregate going from period $t-1$ to period t) in calculating aggregates will minimize the differences between the various index number formulas, since the changes in prices and quantities will generally be small between adjacent periods.[34] Furthermore, as we saw in the previous section, the Paasche, Laspeyres, and any superlative index number can be regarded as discrete approximations to the continuous-line integral Divisia index, which has some useful optimality properties from the viewpoint of economic theory (see Malmquist 1953; Wold 1953; Richter 1966; and Hulten 1973 on these optimality properties). These discrete approximations will be closer to the Divisia index if the chain principle is used.

8.2.5 Two-Stage Aggregation

To reduce the number of commodities, macroeconomic models generally employ index numbers of prices and quantities. However, very often an index number that is used in an economic model has been constructed in two or more stages, and thus the question arises: Does the two-stage procedure give the same answer as the single-stage procedure? It is true that the usually employed Paasche and Laspeyres indexes have this property of consistency in aggregation, but these index numbers are consistent only with very restrictive functional forms for the underlying aggregator function, as we have seen in section 8.2.4.

Diewert (1978*b*) shows that superlative indexes have an approximate consistency-in-aggregation property. This result was obtained by utilizing some results due to the Finnish economist Vartia (1974, 1976), who proposed a discrete approximation to the continuous Divisia price or quantity index that has the following two remarkable properties: (*a*) the price index and the corresponding quantity index (which is defined by the same formula except that prices and quantities are interchanged) satisfy Fisher's (1922) factor-reversal test (i.e., the product of the price and quantity indexes equal the expenditure ratio for the two periods under consideration) and (*b*) the price or quantity index has the property of *consistency in aggregation*.

Vartia defines an index number formula to be consistent in aggregation if the value of the index calculated in two stages necessarily coincides with the value of the index as calculated in an ordinary way, that is, in a single stage.

As we saw in section 8.2.4, the economic theory of index numbers is concerned with rationalizing functional forms for index numbers with functional forms for the underlying aggregator function. Diewert (1978*b*) shows that the Vartia I price and quantity indexes are consistent only with a Cobb-Douglas aggregator function. This is perhaps not surprising, since thus far the only way the two-stage method of calculating index numbers has been justified from the viewpoint of the economic theory of index numbers has been to assume that the underlying aggregator function is weakly separable in the same partition that corresponds to the two stages.[35] Thus, to justify the two-stage method of constructing index numbers for any partition of variables, one so far has had to assume that the aggregator function is weakly separable in any partition of its variables; but then the results of Leontief (1947) and Gorman (1968*b*) imply that the aggregator function is strongly separable in the coordinatewise partition of its variables. If we also assume that aggregator function is linearly homogeneous, then, using Bergson's (1936) results, it can be seen that the aggregator function must be a mean of order r (Hardy, Littlewood, and Polya 1934); that is, a CES function. However, it turns out that the Vartia price and quantity indexes are exact only for a mean of order 0 (or Cobb-Douglas) aggregator function.

In spite of the rather negative result that the Vartia I price and quantity indexes are exact only for a Cobb-Douglas aggregator function, Diewert (1978*b*) shows that for small changes in prices and quantities these indexes have some rather good approximation properties. I outline these results due to Vartia and Diewert below.

Define the Vartia (1974, 1976)[36] price index $P_V(p^0,p^1; x^0,x^1)$ as

$$(52) \qquad \ln P_V(p^0,p^1; x^0,x^1) \equiv \sum_{i=1}^{N} L(p^1_i x^1_i, p^0_i x^0_i)/L(p^1 \cdot x^1, p^0 \cdot x^0) \ln(p^1_i/p^0_i),$$

where the logarithmic mean function L introduced by Vartia (1974) and Sato (1976*a*) is defined by $L(a,b) \equiv (a-b)/(\ln a - \ln b)$ for $a \neq b$ and $L(a,a) \equiv a$.

The Vartia quantity index $Q_V(p^0,p^1; x^0,x^1)$ is defined by

$$(53) \qquad \ln Q_V(p^0,p^1; x^0,x^1) \equiv \sum_{i=1}^{N} L(p^1_i x^1_i, p^0_i x^0_i)/L(p^1 \cdot x^1, p^0 \cdot x^0) \ln(x^1_i/x^0_i) = \ln P_V(x^0,x^1; p^0,p^1);$$

that is, the price and quantity indexes have the same functional form except that the role of prices and quantities are interchanged. Vartia shows that P_V and Q_V satisfy the factor-reversal test and have the property of consistency in aggregation.

Since the price index P_0 defined in section 8.2.3 resembles somewhat the Vartia price index P_V defined by (52), the following theorems may not be too surprising.

(54) *Theorem* (Diewert 1978*b*): The Vartia price index differentially approximates the superlative price index P_0 to the second order at any point where the prices and quantities for the two periods are equal; that is, $P_V(p^0,p^1;x^0,x^1) = P_0(p^0,p^1;x^0,x^1)$, and the first- and second-order partial derivatives of the two functions coincide provided that $p^0 = p^1 \gg 0_N$ and $x^0 = x^1 \gg 0_N$.

(55) *Theorem* (Diewert 1978*b*): The Vartia quantity index differentially approximates the superlative quantity index Q_0 to the second order at any point where the prices and quantities for the two periods are equal.

Thus $P_V(p^0,p^1;x^0,x^1)$ will be close to $P_0(p^0,p^1;x^0,x^1)$ provided p^0 is close to p^1 and x^0 is close to x^1. If we call an index that can approximate a superlative index differentially to the second order at any point where $p^0 = p^1$ and $x^0 = x^1$ a *pseudosuperlative* index, it can be seen that the Vartia price and quantity indexes are pseudosuperlative.

Recall theorems (50) and (51). Theorems (54) and (50) imply that the Vartia price index P_V approximates all the superlative indexes P_0 and P_r, while theorems (55) and (51) imply that the Vartia quantity index Q_V approximates all the superlative indexes Q_0 and Q_r to the second order.

For many years it was thought that the indexes P_0 and Q_0 had the property of consistency in aggregation. However, although P_0 and Q_0 are not consistent in aggregation, the results above show why they are approximately consistent in aggregation: each P_0 subindex can be approximated to the second order by a Vartia index of the same size, while the "macro" P_0 index can be approximated to the second order by a "macro" Vartia index. Thus the macro index of the subindexes is approximated to the second order by a Vartia macro index of Vartia subindexes which is identically equal to a Vartia index of the original micro components, which in turn approximates to the second order a P_0 index in the micro components. Therefore, for time-series data where indexes are constructed by chaining observations in successive periods, we would expect P_0 and Q_0 to be approximately consistent in aggregation.

The same conclusion holds for the quadratic mean of order r price indexes P_r and quantity indexes Q_r: they will be approximately consistent in aggregation, since each P_r approximates P_V and each Q_r approximates Q_V.

Some empirical evidence is available that tends to support the theoretical results above. Parkan (1975) compared the price indexes P_0, P_2, and $\tilde{P}_0$ (defined implicitly by the weak factor reversal test, using Q_0 as the quantity index) and the quantity indexes Q_0, Q_2, and $\tilde{Q}_0$ using some Canadian postwar consumption data on thirteen goods. He also calculated the nonparametric price and quantity indexes defined by Diewert (1973*b*, p. 424). Parkan then computed all four price indexes and all four quantity indexes in two stages, calculating four subaggregates in each case, then aggregating these subaggregates using the same index number formula. It was found that the resulting total of eight price indexes generally coincided to three significant figures, and the eight quantity indexes similarly closely approximated each other. Similar empirical results are reported in Diewert (1978*b*). The theoretical results cited above provide an explanation for this rather convenient empirical phenomenon.

To summarize, the arguments above show that constructing aggregate price and quantity indexes by aggregating in two (or more) stages will give approximately the same answer that a one-stage index would, provided that either a superlative index or the Vartia index is used.[37]

8.2.6 The Measurement of Real Input, Real Output, and Real Value Added

In this section we will study the various definitions of real output, input, and value added that economists have proposed, including the definition of real capital that Usher proposed in the introduction to this volume. We shall also indicate how various index number formulas can be used to closely approximate the various notions of real input and output.

First it is necessary to recall the definition of the firm's *variable profit function* from section 8.2.1:

$$(56)\qquad \Pi(x,p) \equiv \max_y\{p \cdot y: (x,y) \in S\},$$

where S is the firm's technologically feasible set, $(x,y) \equiv (x_1,x_2, \ldots ,x_N, y_1,y_2, \ldots ,y_M)$ is a vector that indicates the firm's production or input demand for each of the $N + M$ goods, and $p \equiv (p_1,p_2, \ldots ,p_M) \gg 0_M$ is a vector of positive prices. In this section we will assume that the x goods are all inputs and that $x \gg 0_N$. On the other hand, negative components of y will continue to indicate that the corresponding good is used as an input. With these sign conventions, it can be shown (see Diewert 1973*a*; Gorman 1968*a*; or Lau 1976) that if S is a nonempty, closed, convex set with certain boundedness and free disposal properties, then $\Pi(x,p)$ will be a nonnegative, nondecreasing, and concave function in x for any fixed p; that is, $\Pi(x,p)$ regarded as a function of x will have the usual regularity properties that a neoclassical production function possesses.

Thus a *real input index X* can sensibly be defined as

$$X(x^0,x^1;p^*) \equiv \Pi(x^1,p^*)/\Pi(x^0,p^*), \tag{57}$$

where $x^0 \equiv (x^0{}_1,\ldots,x^0{}_N)$ is period 0 input, $x^1 \equiv (x^1{}_1,\ldots,x^1{}_N)$ is period 1 input, and $p^* \rangle\rangle\, 0_M$ is a reference price vector. Sato (1976*b*, p. 438) calls X defined by (57) a *true index of real value added*, and he notes that the definition does not require any assumption of optimizing behavior on the part of the producer with respect to inputs (although profit-maximizing behavior with respect to outputs and intermediate inputs in the y goods is of course required). Sato also notes that a separability assumption on the technology is required in order to make X defined by (57) independent of p^*; that is, we require that $\Pi(p,x) = r(p)f(x)$ for some functions r and f, which implies that the x inputs are separable from y.

We now study the problem of approximating (57) by observable data; that is, by means of an index number formula. However, it is first necessary to present some general material taken from Diewert (1976) that will be used repeatedly in this section.

Let z be an N-dimensional vector and define the quadratic function $f(z)$ as

$$\begin{aligned} f(z) &\equiv a_0 + a^Tz + \tfrac{1}{2}z^TAz \\ &= a_0 + \sum_{i=1}^{N} a_iz_i + \sum_{i=1}^{N}\sum_{j=1}^{N} a_{ij}z_iz_j, \end{aligned} \tag{58}$$

where the a_i,a_{ij} are constants and $a_{ij} = a_{ji}$ for all i,j.

The following lemma is a global version of the Theil (1967, pp. 222–23) and Kloek (1967) local result.

(59) *Quadratic approximation lemma*: if the quadratic function f is defined by (58), then,

$$f(z^1) - f(z^0) = \tfrac{1}{2}[\nabla f(z^1) + \nabla f(z^0)]\cdot(z^1 - z^0), \tag{60}$$

where $\nabla f(z^r)$ is the vector of first-order partial derivatives of f evaluated at z^r.

This result should be contrasted with the usual Taylor series expansion for a quadratic function,

$$\begin{aligned} f(z^1) - f(z^0) = [\nabla f(z^0)]\cdot(z^1 - z^0) + \tfrac{1}{2}(z^1 \\ - z^0)\cdot\nabla^2 f(z^0)(z^1 - z^0), \end{aligned}$$

where $\overline{\nabla}^2 f(z^0)$ is the matrix of second-order partial derivatives of f evaluated at an initial point z^0. In the expansion (60), a knowledge of $\nabla^2 f(z^0)$ is not required, but a knowledge of $\nabla f(z^1)$ is required. Actually, (60) holds as an equality for all z^1,z^0 belonging to an open set if and only if f is a quadratic function, provided f is once continuously differentiable (cf. Lau 1979).

Suppose we are given a homogeneous translog aggregator function (Christensen, Jorgenson, and Lau 1971) defined by

$$\ln f(x) \equiv \beta_0 + \sum_{n=1}^{N} \alpha_n \ln x_n + \tfrac{1}{2} \sum_{j=1}^{N} \sum_{k=1}^{N} \beta_{jk} \ln x_j \ln x_k,$$

where $\sum_{n=1}^{N} \beta_n = 1$, $\beta_{jk} = \beta_{kj}$ and $\sum_{k=1}^{N} \beta_{jk} = 0$ for $j = 1,2, \ldots ,N$.

Recall that Jorgenson and Lau have shown that the homogeneous translog function can provide a second-order approximation to an arbitrary twice continuously differentiable linearly homogeneous function. Let us use the parameters that occur in the translog functional form to define the following function f^*:

(61) $$f^*(z) \equiv \alpha_0 + \sum_{j=1}^{N} \alpha_i z_i + \tfrac{1}{2} \sum_{i=1}^{N} \sum_{j=1}^{N} \gamma_{ij} z_i z_j.$$

Since the function f^* is quadratic, we can apply the quadratic approximation lemma (59), and we obtain

(62) $$f^*(z^1) - f^*(z^0) = \tfrac{1}{2}[\nabla f^*(z^1) + \nabla f^*(z^0)] \cdot (z^1 - z^0).$$

Now we relate f^* to the translog function f. We have

(63) $$\partial f^*(z^r)/\partial z_j = \partial \ln f(x^r)/\partial \ln x_j$$
$$= [\partial f(x^r)/\partial x_j]\,[x^r{}_j/f(x^r)].$$
$$f^*(z^r) = \ln f(x^r),$$
$$z^r{}_j = \ln x^r{}_j, \text{ for } r = 0,1 \text{ and } j = 1,2, \ldots ,N.$$

If we substitute relations (63) into (62) we obtain

(64) $$\ln f(x^1) - \ln f(x^0) = \tfrac{1}{2}\left[\hat{x}^1 \frac{\nabla f(x^1)}{f(x^1)} + \hat{x}^0 \frac{\nabla f(x^0)}{f(x^0)}\right]$$
$$\cdot [\ln x^1 - \ln x^0],$$

where $\ln x^1 \equiv [\ln x^1{}_1, \ln x^1{}_2, \ldots , \ln x^1{}_N]$, $\ln x^0 \equiv [\ln x^0{}_1, \ln x^0{}_2, \ldots , \ln x^0{}_N]$, $\hat{x}^1 \equiv$ the vector x^1 diagonalized into a matrix, and $\hat{x}^0 \equiv$ the vector x^0 diagonalized into a matrix.

Now suppose the firm's variable profit function can be adequately approximated by a translog variable profit function (see section 8.2.1 for a definition), which we will denote as $\Pi^*(x,p)$.

If p^* is fixed, then $\ln \Pi^*(x,p^*)$ is quadratic in $\ln x_1, \ln x_2, \ldots, \ln x_N$, and we can apply the identity (64) to obtain the following equality (define $f(x) \equiv \Pi^*(x,p^*)$):

$$\text{(65)} \qquad \ln \Pi^*(x^1,p^*) - \ln \Pi^*(x^0,p^*) = \tfrac{1}{2}\left[\hat{x}^1 \frac{\nabla_x \Pi^*(x^1,p^*)}{\Pi^*(x^1,p^*)} + \hat{x}^0 \frac{\nabla_x \Pi^*(x^0,p^*)}{\Pi^*(x^0,p^*)}\right] \cdot [\ln x^1 - \ln x^0].$$

To proceed further, we need to make two additional assumptions: (*a*) the technology S is a cone (so that constant returns to scale prevail), and hence $\Pi^*(x,p)$ is linearly homogeneous in x, and (*b*) the producer attempts to minimize input costs, or alternatively to maximize nominal value added (or variable profits) subject to an expenditure constraint on inputs. Thus we assume that $x^r \gg 0_N$ is a solution to the maximization problem

$$\text{(66)} \qquad \max_x\{\Pi^*(x,p^r) : w^r \cdot x \leq w^r \cdot x^r,\ x \geq 0_N\},$$

where $w^r \gg 0_N$ for $r = 0,1$[38] where $w^r \equiv (w^r_1, \ldots, w^r_N)$ and w^r_n is the nth input price in period r. The first-order conditions for the two maximization problems, after elimination of the Lagrange multipliers, yield the relations $w^r/w^r \cdot x^r = \nabla_x \Pi^*(x^r,p^r)/x^r \cdot \nabla_x \Pi^*(x^r,p^r)$ for $r = 0,1$. Since Π^* is linearly homogeneous in $x, x^r \cdot \nabla_x \Pi^*(x^r,p^r)$ can be replaced by $\Pi^*(x^r,p^r)$, and the resulting relations are

$$\text{(67)} \qquad w^r/w^r \cdot x^r = \nabla_x \Pi^*(x^r,p^r)/\Pi^*(x^r,p^r), \quad r = 0,1.$$

Now return to equation (65). Assume that the components of the (constant) output price vector $p^* = (p^*_1, \ldots, p^*_N)$ are defined by

$$\text{(68)} \qquad p^*_n \equiv (p^0_n\, p^1_n)^{1/2}, \quad n = 1,2, \ldots, N.$$

Substitution of (68) into (65) and differentiation of the translog variable profit function evaluated at the points (x^1,p^*) and (x^0,p^*) yields the following equation:

$$\text{(69)} \qquad \ln \Pi^*(x^1,p^*) - \ln \Pi^*(x^0,p^*) = \tfrac{1}{2}\left[\hat{x}^1 \frac{\nabla_x \Pi^*(x^1,p^1)}{\Pi^*(x^1,p^1)} + \hat{x}^0 \frac{\nabla_x \Pi^*(x^0,p^0)}{\Pi^*(x^0,p^0)}\right] \cdot [\ln x^1 - \ln x^0]$$

$$= \tfrac{1}{2}\left[\hat{x}^1 \frac{w^1}{w^1 \cdot x^1} + \hat{x}^0 \frac{w^0}{w^0 \cdot x^0}\right] \cdot [\ln x^1 - \ln x^0]$$

using (67), or

(70) $$X(x^0,x^1;p^*) = \Pi^*(x^1,p^*)/\Pi^*(x^0,p^*) = Q_0(w^0,w^1,x^0,x^1);$$

that is, if the technology can be represented by a constant returns to scale, translog variable profit function and the reference output prices p^*_n are chosen to be the geometric mean of the output prices prevailing during the two periods; then the real input index $X(x^0,x^1;p^*)$ is equal to the Törnqvist quantity index of the inputs x^0 and x^1. Note that this result does *not* require the technology to be separable; that is, we do not require that $\Pi^*(p,x) = r(p)f(x)$. However, the above result did require us to pick a very specific reference vector p^*.

Note that we can associate an *implicit input price deflator* $W(w^0,w^1,x^0,x^1,p^*)$ with the real input index X:

(71) $$W(w^0,w^1,x^0,x^1,p^*) \equiv w^1{\cdot}x^1/w^0{\cdot}x^0\, X(x^0,x^1;p^*).$$

Under the assumptions that justified (70), we can see that the implicit input price deflator $W(w^0,w^1,x^0,x^1;p^*) = \tilde{P}_0(w^0,w^1,x^0,x^1)$, the implicit Törnqvist price index for the inputs (defined as $w^1{\cdot}x^1/w^0{\cdot}x^0\, Q_0(w^0,w^1,x^0,x^1)$).

It is also possible to define an input price deflator directly. To do this, we need to define the *joint cost function*[39] C as

(72) $$C(y,w) \equiv \min_x\{w{\cdot}x\colon (x,y)\epsilon S\}.$$

Now define the *input price deflator* W as

(73) $$W(w^0,w^1;y^*) \equiv C(y^*,w^1)/C(y^*,w^0),$$

where the input price vectors w^0 and w^1 have been defined above and y^* is a reference output vector that is held constant during the two periods. As was the case with the real input index, the input price deflator $W(w^0,w^1;y^*)$ is independent of the reference vector y^* (p^* in the case of the input index) if and only if the technology is separable (i.e., if $C(y,w) = g(y)c(w)$).

To obtain a specific functional form for W, we may proceed in a manner entirely analogous to our earlier treatment for X. First assume that the firm's technology can be adequately approximated by a translog joint cost function[40] that exhibits constant returns to scale. Then, assuming optimizing behavior on the part of the producer, we can repeat equations (65) to (70) with the obvious changes in notation, and we obtain the following equality:

(74) $$W(w^0,w^1;y^*) = C^*(y^*,w^1)/C^*(y^*,w^0) = P_0(w^0,w^1,x^0,x^1),$$

where C^* is a translog joint cost function, $y^* \equiv (y^*_1, y^*_2, \ldots, y^*_M)$ and $y^*_m \equiv (y^0_m y^1_m)^{1/2}$ for $m = 1,2,\ldots,M$, and $P_0(w^0,w^1,x^0,x^1)$ is the Törnqvist price index for the inputs.

An *implicit real input index* X can be defined as

(75) $$X(w^0,w^1,x^0,x^1; y^*) \equiv w^1 \cdot x^1 / w^0 \cdot x^0 \; W(w^0,w^1; y^*).$$

Obviously, if the input price deflator W is defined by (74), then the corresponding implicit real input index X is numerically equal to $\tilde{Q}_0(w^0,w^1,x^0x^1)$, the implicit Törnqvist quantity index of inputs.[41]

We now turn our attention to the output side. Define the producer's *real output index* Y as

(76) $$Y(y^0,y^1; w^*) \equiv C(y^1,w^*)/C(y^0,w^*),$$

where y^0 and y^1 are the output (and intermediate input) vectors are periods 0 and 1, C is the producer's joint cost function defined earlier by (72), and $w^* \gg 0_N$ is a reference input price vector. As usual, $Y(y^0,y^1,w^*)$ is independent of w^* if and only if the technology is separable.

Again, we can assume that the firm's technology is approximated by a translog joint cost function C^* that exhibits constant returns to scale. Assuming optimizing behavior, we can repeat equations (65) to (70), with the obvious changes in notation, and obtain the following equality:

(77) $$Y(y^0,y^1; w^*) = C^*(y^1,w^*)/C^*(y^0,w^*) = Q_0(p^0,p^1,y^0,y^1),$$

where C^* is the firm's translog joint cost function, $y^0 \gg 0_N$ and $y^1 \gg 0_M$ are the output vectors produced by the firm during the two periods, p^0 and p^1 are the corresponding output price vectors,[42] and the reference input price vector $w^* \equiv (w^*_1, \ldots, w^*_N)$ is defined by $w^*_n \equiv (w^0_n w^1_n)^{1/2}$, where $w^0 \equiv (w^0_1, \ldots, w^0_N) \gg 0_N$ and $w^1 \equiv (w^1_1, \ldots, w^1_N) \gg 0_N$ are the input price vectors for the two periods. $Q_0(p^0,p^1,y^0,y^1)$ is the Törnqvist quantity index for the outputs.

Note that we can associate an *implicit output price deflator* $P(p^0,p^1, y^0,y^1; w^*)$ with the real output index Y:

(78) $$P(p^0,p^1,y^0,y^1; w^*) \equiv p^1 \cdot y^1 / p^0 \cdot y^0 \; Y(y^0,y^1; w^*).$$

If the real output index Y is defined by (77), then the corresponding implicit output price deflator defined by (78) is numerically equal to $\tilde{P}_0(p^0,p^1,y^0,y^1)$, the implicit Törnqvist price index of outputs.

However, an output price deflator can be defined directly. Following Fisher and Shell (1972), define the firm's *output price deflator* P as

(79) $$P(p^0,p^1;x^*) \equiv \Pi(x^*,p^1)/\Pi(x^*,p^0),$$

where p^0 and p^1 are the output (and intermediate input) price vectors facing the producer during periods 0 and 1, respectively, Π is the producer's variable profit function defined earlier by (56), and $x^* \gg 0_N$ is a reference input vector. Archibald (1977, p. 61) calls P the fixed input quantity output price index. He also shows that it satisfies certain tests, and he develops some bounds for it (along with two other alternative price indexes), utilizing the techniques developed by Pollak (1971) in his discussion of the cost-of-living index.

As usual, assume that the firm's technology can be approximated by a translog variable profit function Π^* exhibiting constant returns to scale, repeat the analysis inherent in equations (65) to (70) with the obvious changes in notation, and obtain the following equality:

(80) $$P(p^0,p^1;x^*) = \Pi^*(x^*,p^1)/\Pi^*(x^*,p^0) = P_0(p^0,p^1,y^0,y^1),$$

where Π^* is the firm's translog variable profit function, $p^0 \gg 0_M$ and $p^1 \gg 0_M$ are the price vectors for outputs (and intermediate inputs) the firm faces during periods 0 and 1, y^0 and y^1 are the corresponding quantity vectors,[43] and the reference input quantity vector $x^* \equiv (x^*_1, \ldots, x^*_N)$ is defined by $x^*_n \equiv (x^0_n x^1_n)^{1/2}$, where $x^0 \equiv (x^0_1, \ldots, x^0_N) \gg 0_N$ and $x^1 \equiv (x^1_1, \ldots, x^1_N) \gg 0_N$ are the input vectors for the two periods. $P_0(p^0,p^1,y^0,y^1)$ is the Törnqvist price index in output prices.

Note that we can associate an *implicit real output index* Y with the output price deflator P:

(81) $$\tilde{Y}(p^0,p^1,y^0,y^1;x^*) \equiv p^1 \cdot y^1/p^0 \cdot y^0 \, P(p^0,p^1;x^*).$$

If the output price deflator P is defined by (80), then the corresponding implicit real output index Y defined by (81) is numerically equal to $\tilde{Q}_0(p^0,p^1,y^0,y^1)$, the implicit Törnqvist quantity index of outputs.

The astute reader will by now have noticed that the definitions given above for real output (input) and output (input) price deflators are entirely analogous to the Konyus (1939) and Allen (1949) definitions for the real cost of living and real income:[44] instead of holding a scalar constant (utility), a vector (of inputs or outputs) is held constant. The astute reader will also know that an alternative approach to the Konyus-Allen approach to defining quantity indexes has ben provided by Malmquist (1953). Malmquist's approach has been extensively used by Pollak (1971) and Blackorby and Russell (1978) in the context of consumer theory, and by Bergson (1961), Moorsteen (1961), and Fisher and Shell (1972) in the context of producer theory. I outline this approach below.

Define the producer's *input distance function D* as

(82) $$D[y,x] \equiv \max_\lambda\{\lambda: (y,x/\lambda) \in S, \lambda \geq 0\},$$

where S is the firm's technological set, y is a given vector of outputs, and $x \rangle\rangle 0_N$ is a given vector of inputs. The interpretation of $D[y,x]$ is that it is the proportion by which the input vector x can be deflated with the resulting deflated input vector just big enough to produce the output vector y. If S is a nonempty, closed, convex set with certain free disposal properties, then it can be shown that $D[y,x]$ is a positive, increasing, linearly homogeneous, and concave function in x for $x \rangle\rangle 0_N$ and, moreover, the distance function can be used to characterize the technology just as the variable profit function or joint cost function was used.[45] We can use the distance function to define the Malmquist (1953), Moorsteen (1961), Fisher and Shell (1972, p. 51), and Usher *real input index* as

(83) $$X_M(x^0,x^1,y^*) \equiv D[y^*,x^1]/D[y^*,x^0],$$

where y^* is a reference output vector and x^0,x^1 are the vectors of inputs utilized by the firm during the two periods under consideration. The interpretation of X_M is straightforward: pick a reference output vector y^*, deflate x^r by $\lambda^r > 0$ so that $(y^*,x^r/\lambda^r)$ is just on the boundary of the production possibility set S for $r = 0,1$, and then measure the volume of inputs in period 1 relative to period 0 by the ratio λ^1/λ^0. The resulting Malmquist real input index $X_M(x^0,x^1,y^*)$ will in general depend on the reference output vector y^*; it will be independent of y^* if and only if the technology is such that $D[y,x] = h(y)f(x)$, which is a separability property that turns out to be equivalent to the earlier separability of outputs from inputs property discussed earlier in this section.[46]

The Malmquist real input index X_M defined by (83) has at least one major advantage over the (Konyus) real input index X defined earlier by (57): the Malmquist index is defined solely by the technology and does not require any assumption that the producer competitively maximizes profits.

However, to evaluate X_M using observable data, it will be necessary to assume cost-minimizing behavior plus a particular functional form for the firm's distance function.

(84) *Theorem*: Assume that the firm's technology can be represented by a translog distance function D^*, where D^* is defined by

(85) $$\ln D^*[y,x] \equiv \alpha_0 + \sum_{i=1}^{N} \alpha_i \ln x_i + \tfrac{1}{2} \sum_{i=1}^{N} \sum_{h=1}^{N} \alpha_{ih} \ln x_i \ln x_h$$

$$+ \sum_{i=1}^{N} \sum_{j=1}^{M} \beta_{ij} \ln x_i \ln y_j + \sum_{j=1}^{M} \gamma_j \ln y_j$$

$$+ \tfrac{1}{2} \sum_{j=1}^{M} \sum_{k=1}^{M} \gamma_{jk} \ln y_j \ln y_k,$$

where $$\sum_{i=1}^{N} \alpha_i = 1, \alpha_{ih} = \alpha_{hi}, \sum_{h=1}^{N} \alpha_{ih} = 0 \text{ for } i = 1,2, \ldots ,N,$$

$$\sum_{i=1}^{N} \alpha_{ij} = 0 \text{ for}$$

$j = 1,2, \ldots ,M$ and $\gamma_{jk} = \gamma_{kj}$.[47] Suppose that the quantity vector x^0 is a solution to the cost minimization problem, $\min_x\{w^0 \cdot x: (y^0,x) \in S\}$, while x^1 is a solution to the period 1 cost minimization problem, $\min_x\{w^1 \cdot x: (y^1,x) \in S\}$, where y^0,y^1 are the output vectors produced during periods 0 and 1, $w^0 \gg 0_N$ and $w^1 \gg 0_N$ are the input price vectors facing the producer during periods 0 and 1 and S is the firm's technology set. Then

(86) $$X_M(x^0,x^1,y^*) = D^*[y^*,x^1]/D^*[y^*,x^0] = Q_0(w^0,w^1,x^0,x^1),$$

where $y^* \equiv (y^*_1, \ldots ,y^*_M)$, $y^*_m \equiv (y^0_m y^1_m)^{1/2}$ for $m = 1,2, \ldots ,M$, and $Q_0(w^0,w^1,x^0,x^1)$ is the Törnqvist quantity index for the inputs.

Thus the Törnqvist quantity index $Q_0(w^0,w^1,x^0,x^1)$ can be interpreted as either a Malmquist real input index (86) *or* a Konyus real input index (70). However, we note that the Malmquist interpretation requires fewer assumptions: constant returns to scale are not required, nor are producers required to competitively optimize with respect to inputs. Thus the Törnqvist quantity index can be given a strong economic justification.

Obviously, once we have defined the Malmquist real input index X_M, we can define an *implicit (Malmquist) input price deflator* W_M as

(87) $$W_M(w^0,w^1,x^0,x^1,y^*) \equiv w^1 \cdot x^1 / w^0 \cdot x^0 \, X_M(x^0,x^1,y^*).$$

If X_M is defined by (86), then (87) becomes $\tilde{P}_0(w^0,w^1,x^0,x^1)$, the implicit Törnqvist price index for inputs.

With minor modifications, the entire Malmquist procedure from equation (82) to equation (87) can be repeated, except that outputs replace inputs; that is, define the producer's output distance function d as $d[y,x] \equiv \min_\lambda\{\lambda: (y/\lambda,x) \in S\}$, define the Malmquist real output index as $Y_M(y^0,y^1,x^*) \equiv d[y^1,x^*]/d[y^0,x^*]$, assume that the producer's technology can be adequately represented by a translog (output) distance function d^* and that the producer is revenue maximizing with respect to outputs and intermediate inputs only, and finally show that

$$(88) \qquad Y_M(y^0,y^1,x^*) = d^*[y^1,x^*]/d^*[y^0,x^*] = Q_0(p^0,p^1,y^0,y^1),$$

where $Q_0(p^0,p^1,y^0,y^1)$ is the Törnqvist quantity index for the outputs and the nth component of the reference input vector, $x^*_n \equiv (x^0_n x^1_n)^{1/2}$, $n = 1,2, \ldots ,N$.[48] Thus again the Törnqvist index can be given a strong economic justification.

8.3 Methods for Justifying Aggregation over Sectors

8.3.1 Aggregation without Optimizing Behavior

Suppose there are M firms in a sector, each of which produces a single product using N inputs. Let the firm technologies be representable by means of firm production functions f^m, where $y^m = f^m(x^m_1, \ldots ,x^m_N)$ denotes the amount of output producible by firm m using input quantities $x^m_1, \ldots ,x^m_N$ for m $= 1,2, \ldots ,M$. Klein's (1946*a*) aggregation over sectors problem[49] can be phrased as follows: What conditions on the firm production function's f^m will guarantee the existence of: (*a*) an aggregate production function G, (*b*) input aggregator functions $g_1, \ldots ,g_N$, and (*c*) an output aggregator function F such that the following equation holds for a suitable set of inputs x^m_n?

$$(89) \qquad F(y^1, \ldots ,y^M) = G[g_1(x^1_1, \ldots ,x^M_1),g_2(x^1_2, \ldots ,x^M_2), \ldots ,g_N(x^1_N, \ldots ,x^M_N)].$$

Klein (1946*b*) explicitly asked that (89) hold without the assumption of profit-maximizing behavior by producers, since in the real world monopolistic practices may be prevalent and thus it would be preferable to be able to derive an aggregate production function without the assumption of competitive behavior.

Unfortunately, Nataf (1948) demonstrated that the conditions on the micro production functions f^m, $m = 1,2, \ldots ,M$, that are necessary to derive (89) are very stringent: the f^m must be strongly separable; that is, f^m must have the structure $f^m(x^m_1, \ldots ,x^m_N) = h^m[k^m_1(x^m_1) + \ldots + k^m_N(x^m_N)]$, where the h^m and k^m_n are monotonically increasing functions.[50]

The restrictive separability assumptions on the micro production functions[51] required for Klein-Nataf sectoral aggregation seem to limit the usefulness of the method from an empirical point of view. A more promising method is outlined in the following section.

8.3.2 Aggregation with Optimizing Behavior

Bliss (1975, p. 146) notes that if all producers are competitive profit maximizers and face the same prices, then the group of producers can be treated as if they were a single producer subject to the sum[52] of the individual production sets. Thus, if the time period is chosen to be long enough so that all inputs and outputs are variable, there is no problem of aggregation over sectors (provided producers are behaving competitively).

This extremely simple aggregation criterion does not seem to have been stressed very much in the literature, but it is certainly explicit in the contributions of Hotelling (1935), May (1946), Pu (1946) and Cornwall (1973, p. 512), though not stated as elegantly as the above criterion noted by Bliss.

8.3.3 Aggregation with Optimizing Behavior for Some Goods: Vintage Production Functions

Assume we have M sectors in an economy (or M firms in an industry or M plants or processes in a firm) and the production possibilities set for the mth sector is denoted by S^m, $m = 1,2, \ldots ,M$. Define the sectoral variable profit functions Π^m as

$$\Pi^m(p,x^m,z^m) \equiv max_y\{p \cdot y\colon (y,x^m,z^m) \epsilon S^m\}, \quad m = 1,2, \ldots ,M, \tag{90}$$

where $p \rangle\rangle 0_K$ is a vector of output (and or intermediate input) prices each sector faces for the first K goods, $x^m \geq 0_N$ is a vector of "labor" inputs utilized by the mth sector, and z^m is a vector of fixed "capital" inputs that could be specific to the mth sector for $m = 1,2, \ldots ,M$. Following Solow (1964), we could interpret the Π^m as being dual to the "vintage" production functions f^m (of a single firm) that utilize the "vintage" capital inputs z^m in addition to labor inputs x^m. Assume further that the firm has a fixed vector of labor inputs $x \rangle\rangle 0_N$ to allocate across the M processes. The firm will then wish to solve the following vintage or micro labor maximization problem (which defines the aggregate variable profit function Π):

$$\max_{x^1,x^2, \ldots ,x^M} \left\{ \sum_{m=1}^{M} \Pi^m(p,x^m,z^m) \colon \sum_{m=1}^{M} x^m \leq x, x^m \geq 0_N \right\} \tag{91}$$

$$\equiv \Pi(p,x,z^1,z^2, \ldots ,z^M). \tag{92}$$

A generalized[53] Solow (1964), Fisher (1965), and Stigum (1967, 1968) vintage capital aggregation problem is: Under what conditions on the "vintage" technologies S^m (or Π^m) do there exist functions $\hat{\Pi}$ and g such that

(93) $$\Pi(p,x,z^1,z^2,\ldots,z^M) = \Pi[p,x,g(z^1,z^2,\ldots,z^M)],$$

where $g(z^1,z^2,\ldots,z^M)$ can be interpreted as a capital aggregate?

This problem is difficult to solve because the aggregate variable profit function $\Pi(p,x,z^1,\ldots,z^M)$ is not related to the micro variable profit functions $\Pi^m(p,x^m z^m)$ in any very obvious way. However, it is possible to derive a problem that is equivalent to (93) and then apply some results from Gorman (1968*a*) to the equivalent problem. Below, I indicate how this equivalent problem can be derived and solved.

If the firm is given a vector of positive labor prices, $w \rangle\rangle 0_N$, the firm can optimize with respect to the labor inputs. Thus define the following vintage or micro (labor optimized) variable profit functions Π^{*m}:

(94) $$\Pi^{*m}(p,w,z^m) \equiv \max_x\{\Pi^m(p,x,z^m) - w \cdot x: x \geq 0_N\}, \quad m = 1,2,\ldots,M,$$

where $p \rangle\rangle 0_K$ is the vector of output prices each sector faces for the first K goods and z^m is the vector of fixed capital inputs specific to the mth sector. The (labor optimized) variable profit functions Π^{*m} can be used to provide a complete characterization of the sectoral technologies S^m (under appropriate regularity conditions; see Gorman 1968*a* or Diewert 1973*a*) just as the original variable profit functions Π^m can be used.

The firm or macro (labor optimized) variable profit function Π^* dual to Π is defined as

(95) $$\Pi^*(p,w,z^1,\ldots,z^M) \equiv \max_x\{\Pi(p,x,z^1,\ldots,z^M) - w \cdot x: x \geq 0_N\}.$$

We may now state the problem that is equivalent to the original generalized Solow vintage capital aggregation problem (93): Under what conditions on the "vintage" technologies S^m (or equivalently Π^m or Π^{*m}) do there exist functions Π^* and g^* such that

(96) $$\Pi^*(p,w,z^1,\ldots,z^M) = \Pi^*[p,w,g^*(z^1,\ldots,z^M)],$$

where $g^*(z^1,\ldots,z^M)$ can be interpreted as a capital aggregate?

This problem is reasonably easy to solve because the aggregate (labor optimized) variable profit function Π^* is related in a simple manner to the micro (labor optimized) variable profit functions Π^{*m}.

(97) *Theorem*: If the micro variable profit functions $\Pi^m(p,x^m,z^m)$ are concave[54] and increasing in x^m for $m = 1,2,\ldots,M$, then

(98) $$\Pi^*(p,w^*,z^1,\ldots,z^M) = \sum_{m=1}^{M} \Pi^{*m}(p,w^*,z^m),$$

where $w^* \rangle\rangle 0_N$ is a vector of Lagrange multipliers or shadow prices for the maximization problem (91).

The decomposition (98) allows us to immediately prove the following theorem.

(99) *Theorem* (Gorman 1968*a*): If the micro (labor optimized) variable profit functions Π^{*m} can be written as

(100) $$\Pi^{*m}(p,w,z^m) = b(p,w)h^m(z^m) + c^m(p,w),\quad m = 1,2,\ldots,M,$$

then capital aggregation is possible; that is,

(101) $$\begin{aligned}\Pi^*(p,w,z^1,\ldots,z^M) &= \sum_{m=1}^{M} \Pi^{*m}(p,w,z^m)\\ &= b(p,w)\left[\sum_{m=1}^{M} h^m(z^m)\right]\\ &\quad + \sum_{m=1}^{M} c^m(p,w)\\ &\equiv \Pi^*\left[p,w, \sum_{m=1}^{M} h^m(z^m)\right].\end{aligned}$$

Thus the separability restrictions (100) on the micro production possibility sets are sufficient to imply the existence of a capital aggregate; Gorman (1968*a*) shows that these conditions are also necessary under suitable regularity conditions on the technology (which do not involve differentiability restrictions).

How restrictive in practice are the restrictions (100)? They are not very restrictive at all if every z^m is a scalar (i.e., there is only one fixed capital good for each sector), for in this case functions of the form $b(p,w)h^m(z^m) + c^m(p,w)$ can provide a second-order approximation to an arbitrary twice-differentiable variable profit function $\Pi^{*m}(p,w,z^m)$. However, the restrictions (100) become progressively more unrealistic from an empirical point of view as the number of fixed capital goods in each sector increases.

8.3.4 Aggregation with Optimizing Behavior for Some Goods: Putty-Putty Production Functions

In the analysis of the previous section, we did not assume that there was any particular relationship between the sectoral production possibility sets S^m. In this section we will assume that these sets are related in the following manner: before the mth producer chooses a vector of fixed inputs z^m, the set of technological possibilities open to him ex ante is S, a set of feasible input and output combinations open to all producers $m = 1,2,\ldots,M$. However, once the mth producer chooses his vector of fixed inputs z^m, his production possibilities set is $S(z^m)$, a subset of S. If we know the ex ante production possibilities set plus the economy's *distribution of fixed inputs*, then we can readily calculate the economy's ex post production possibilities set for the variable inputs and outputs. Often (see Johansen 1959), the ex ante production function is taken to be Cobb-Douglas (putty), while the ex post production possibility sets $S(z^m)$ are taken to be of the fixed coefficients variety (clay), but this putty-clay model can readily be generalized to a putty-putty model (see the contributions by Fuss and McFadden 1978).

Houthakker (1955–56), Johansen (1959, 1972), Cornwall (1973), Sato (1975), and Fuss and McFadden (1978) have all made substantial contributions to the theory of aggregation sketched above.

To make the above discussion more concrete, I will outline in some detail Johansen's (1972) contribution. Johansen's basic theoretical model is presented in chapter 2, where the various types of production function are defined and related to each other. The *ex ante micro production function* $\emptyset$ gives the maximum output y, given amounts of two variable inputs x_1,x_2 and capital z invested in the sector; that is, $y = \emptyset(x_1,x_2,z)$. The *ex post micro production function* for a particular firm or sector is defined as $y = \emptyset(x_1,x_2,z)$; that is, the capital input is fixed at z. Johansen restricts the functional form for $\emptyset$ to be such that the ex post micro production function is of the fixed coefficients variety; that is, $0 \leq y \leq \bar{y}$, $x_1 = \xi_1 y$, $x_2 = \xi_2 y$, where ξ_1 and ξ_2 depend on z. The short-run macro production function, $F(X_1,X_2)$, is defined as

$$(102) \qquad F(X_1,X_2) \equiv \max_{x^1{}_1,x^1{}_2,\ldots,x^M{}_1,x^M{}_2} \left\{ \sum_{m=1}^{M} \emptyset(x^m{}_1,x^m{}_2,z^m) : \sum_{m=1}^{M} x^m{}_1 \leq X_1; \sum_{m=1}^{M} x^m{}_2 \leq X_2 \right\},$$

where the short-run ex post production function of the mth firm is $\emptyset(x^m{}_1,x^m{}_2,z^m)$ and X_j is the available factor supply for the jth variable input, $j = 1,2$. Thus this maximization problem takes the short-run micro production functions as given and maximizes industry output subject to restrictions on the availability of variable inputs. With Johansen's restrictive a priori assumptions on the functional form for the micro production function $\emptyset$, this maximization problem simplifies to:

$$(103) \qquad \max_{y^1,\ldots,y^M} \left\{ \sum_{m=1}^{M} y^m : \sum_{m=1}^{M} \xi^m{}_1 y^m \leq X_1; \sum_{m=1}^{M} \xi^m{}_2 y^m \leq X_2; 0 \leq y^m \leq \bar{y}^m \right\}.$$

Finally, Johansen defines the long-run macro production function. This function may be constructed from the ex ante micro function $\emptyset$ as follows: given (variable) input-capital ratios u_1 and u_2, choose the optimal scale plant; that is, choose z so as to maximize output per unit of capital, $\emptyset(u_1z,u_2z,z)/z$, along a ray in input space. Denote the solution to this maximization problem as $z = g(u_1,u_2)$. Now, given aggregate amounts of inputs X_1,X_2 and Z, the long-run macro production function ψ is defined as $\psi(X_1,X_2,Z) \equiv Z\emptyset[u_1g(u_1,u_2),u_2g(u_1,u_2), g(u_1,u_2)]/g(u_1,u_2)$, where $u_1 \equiv X_1/Z, u_2 \equiv X_2/Z$. Note that ψ is homogeneous of degree one even though the micro function need not be (if $\emptyset$ is linearly homogeneous, then $\psi = \emptyset$).

All the production functions above can be constructed if (*a*) we know the functional form for the ex ante micro function $\emptyset$ and (*b*) we know the distribution of capital stocks across firms, $\{z^1,z^2, \ldots ,z^M\}$. However, because of Johansen's assumption of no substitution between variable inputs for a fixed capital stock, he is able to combine (*a*) and (*b*) by specifying a capacity distribution $\{\xi^m{}_1,\xi^m{}_2,y^m\}$ $m = 1,2, \ldots ,M$ for the industry, where $\xi^m{}_j$ is the jth input-output coefficient for the mth firm and y^m is the capacity for the mth firm. From a discrete capacity distribution for the input-output coefficients, it is a short step to a continuous capacity distribution, and in Johansen (1972), various functional forms for continuous capacity distributions are assumed (including the case of the Pareto distribution pioneered by Houthakker, 1955–56) and the resulting macro production functions are calculated. The important conclusion that there can be considerable substitution at the macro level (even though there is none at the micro level) is emphasized by Johansen.

However, the putty-clay restrictions Johansen places on the functional form for $\emptyset$ are unduly restrictive. Instead of assuming a distribution of input-output coefficients, an empirically richer and computationally simpler model would result if we assumed a "flexible" functional form for $\emptyset$ (or its dual) and a multivariate distribution of fixed inputs.[55] For example, let us combine output(s) and variable inputs in the vector y (where, as usual, inputs are indexed with a negative sign), let z be a vector of fixed inputs, and write the ex ante micro production function in implicit form as $\emptyset(y,z) = 0$. Let p^0 be a vector of variable output and input prices and define a firm's variable profit function as $\pi(p^0;z^0) \equiv \max_y\{p^0 \cdot y\colon \phi(y;z^0) = 0\}$. Now, if π is differentiable with respect to p, it turns out that the firm's (variable) profit maximizing supply and demand functions, $y(p^0;z^0)$, can be obtained by differentiating π with respect to p;[56] that is, $y(p^0;z^0) = \nabla_p\pi(p^0;z^0)$. Now suppose there are M firms in the industry and let the multivariate distribution of fixed inputs in the industry be represented by the multivariate density function $f(z)$; that is, the number of firms having a combination of fixed factors falling between z_1 and z_2 is approximated by the number $M\int_{z_1}^{z_2} f(z)dz$. The short-run industry variable supply and demand functions $Y(p^0)$ can be obtained by integrating the firm supply and demand functions over the distribution of fixed inputs; that is, $Y(p^0) \equiv M\int_z \nabla_p \pi(p^0;z)\, f(z)dz$, and the industry short-run profit function may be defined as $\Pi(p^0) \equiv M\int_z \pi(p^0; z) f(z)dz$, which has as its dual the industry short-run transformation function $F(Y) = 0$. The Houthakker-Johansen putty-clay assumption could be tested in this framework by assuming an appropriate functional form for $\pi(p;z)$.

Unfortunately, this approach to the problem of aggregation over sectors requires (*a*) information on aggregate variable outputs and inputs, and their prices, and (*b*) detailed information on the distribution of fixed inputs by firm, information that is not generally available.

This completes our discussion of the general problems of aggregation over goods and over sectors. We now turn our attention to some specific problems associated with the aggregation of capital that we have not yet discussed.

8.4 The Aggregation of Capital

8.4.1 Capital: A Stock or a Flow of Services

Jorgenson and Griliches (1967, p. 257) note that: "an almost universal conceptual error in the measurement of capital input is to confuse the aggregation of capital stock with the aggregation of capital service." They go on to note that the aggregation procedure appropriate for measuring real investment is *not* appropriate for measuring real capital:

> In converting estimates of capital stock into estimates of capital services we have disregarded an important conceptual error in the aggregation of capital services. While investment goods output must be aggregated by means of investment goods or asset prices, capital services must be aggregated by means of service prices.
>
> The prices of capital services are related to the prices of the corresponding investment goods; in fact, the asset price is simply the discounted value of all future capital services. Asset prices for different investment goods are not proportional to service prices because of differences in rates of replacement and rates of capital gain or loss among capital goods. [Jorgenson and Griliches 1967, p. 267]

Thus, in the Jorgenson-Griliches framework, the user cost of capital in period t, p_t must be distinguished from the purchase cost Q_t of the capital good. The easiest way of deriving the rental price p_t from the purchase price Q_t is to pretend that firms lease all their capital goods at rental price p_t from the "leasing" firm. Competition presumably forces the "leasing" firm to earn the going rate of return r, after corporate income tax, on its leasing activities; thus we have the following equality: {purchase cost of one unit of the capital good plus corporate and property tax expenses minus rental received during the period} $(1+r) =$ depreciated value of the capital good next period; in symbols we have:

$$\{Q_t + u_t[p_t - v_t\delta Q_t - x_tQ_t] + x_tQ_t - p_t\}(1+r) = (1-\delta)Q_{t+1}, \tag{104}$$

where u_t is corporate income tax rate, v_t is the proportion of depreciation allowable for tax purposes, δ is the one-period combined depreciation and obsolescence rate for the capital good, x_t is the property tax rate, and Q_{t+1} is next period's expected purchase price for one unit of the capital good. Now equation (104) may be solved for p_t:[57]

$$p_t = \{rQ_t + \delta Q_{t+1} - (Q_{t+1} - Q_t) - (1+r)u_tv_t\delta Q_t + (1+r)(1-u_t)x_tQ_t\}/(1+r)(1-u_t). \tag{105}$$

If "leasing" firms do not exist, then the rental formula (105) can also be derived by setting up the firm's profit maximization problem. For example, consider the following specific profit maximization problem:

$$\max_{\substack{w.r.t.\\ Y,W,B,K}} \quad p_yY - w_WW - w_BB - \left\{Q_t - \frac{(1-\delta)}{1+r}Q_{t+1} + x_tQ_t\right\}K - u_t\{p_yY - w_WW - w_BB - v_t\delta Q_tK - x_tQ_tK\}, \tag{106}$$

subject to $Y = f(W,B,K)$, where p_y is the price of one unit of output Y, w_W is the white-collar wage rate, w_B is the blue-collar wage rate, W and B are the inputs of white- and blue-collar labor, and f is the firm's production function. The maximand (106) can be rewritten (after some algebraic manipulations) as:

$$(1-u_t)\{p_yY - w_WW - w_BB - p_tK\}, \tag{107}$$

where p_t is defined by (105). Thus, whether "leasing" firms exist or not, p_t defined by (105) is the appropriate user cost of a unit of (corporate) capital, and it appears to be the price which should be used to weight that particular component of the capital stock K, just as p_y is the appropriate price to weight Y, and so on.

Once rental prices for the various components of the capital stock have been determined, the aggregation techniques discussed in sections

8.2 and 8.3 can be used to form estimates of the aggregate stock of capital services (or components of this aggregate). This is essentially the procedure followed by Jorgenson and Griliches (1967).

Under the assumptions above, rental prices of capital goods can be treated *symmetrically* (in the theory of production and productivity analysis) to output and variable input prices. Thus it seems that the aggregation of capital is no more difficult than the aggregation of anything else, such as labor, intermediate goods, or output. This is the position taken by Bliss (1975, p. 144).

However, even if in *theory* the aggregation of capital does not appear to be any more difficult than the aggregation of say, labor, in *practice* it is very much more difficult to construct a capital aggregate that researchers can agree is appropriate for the purpose at hand.[58]

In the following section we will consider some of the practical difficulties (and points of controversy) involved in the construction of capital aggregates using rental price formulas similar to (105) above. In the present section, I will attempt to relax somewhat the simplifying assumptions that allowed us to construct the rental price formula (105).

Thus far my treatment of the capital aggregation problem has made two fundamental simplifying assumptions: (*a*) a depreciated durable good is measured in units of the undepreciated good (i.e., *vintages* are not distinguished), and (*b*) a durable good is assumed to *evaporate* or depreciate at a rate that is independent of "normal" use (and independent of the vintage of the capital good); specifically I have assumed a *constant evaporation rate model.*

Jorgenson (1965, p. 51) has argued that the assumptions above are not as restrictive as they might first appear from the viewpoint of empirical applications; but, nonetheless, since they are restrictive (cf. Feldstein and Rothschild 1974), I shall indicate how they can be relaxed in a model where capital appears as both an input and an output.

The very general model of producer behavior that I propose to utilize was developed by J. R. Hicks in *Value and Capital* (1946, chap. 15; see also Malinvaud 1953; Bliss 1975).

Hicks (1946, pp. 193–94) assumes that producers make production plans at the beginning of period 1 that will extend to period n. The plan consists of a list of inputs and outputs for each period, where period 1 inputs include the firm's existing stocks of durable equipment, distinguished by physical characteristics and vintages. Hicks thinks of period n as the period when the firm winds up its affairs and sells all its remaining durable equipment, so that the list of period n outputs will include the firm's depreciated capital stock that will be left over at the end of the period (or at the beginning of the following period). Thus, if we assume that $n = 1$, the Hicksian intertemporal production model reduces to the following profit maximization model:[59]

(108) $$\max_{z,y,x}\{(1+r)^{-1}p_z\cdot z + p_y\cdot y - p_x\cdot x : (z,y,-x) \in S\} \equiv \Pi([1+r]^{-1}p_z,p_y,p_x),$$

where $x =$ a nonnegative N_1-dimensional vector of current period inputs, including the firm's beginning of the *current* period stocks of durable equipment.

$y =$ a nonnegative N_2-dimensional vector of *current* period outputs.

$z =$ a nonnegative N_3-dimensional vector whose components represent how much durable equipment the firm will have available to it at the beginning of the *following* period,

$p_x =$ an N_1-dimensional vector of nonnegative *current* period (purchase) prices for inputs.

$p_y =$ an N_2-dimensional vector of nonnegative *current* period prices for outputs,

$p_z =$ an N_3-dimensional vector of nonnegative *expected following* period prices for the firm's (depreciated) durable equipment.

$r =$ the one-period interest rate at which the firm can borrow or lend, and

$S =$ the firm's production possibility set, which is assumed to be convex, nonempty, and closed.

We note that Hicks (1946, p. 230) assumes that S is *smoothly convex* (i.e., that the boundary of the convex set Y can be described by a twice-differentiable surface), while von Neumann (1945–46, p. 2) and Morishima (1969, pp. 29–94) assume that S is a *polyhedral convex* set (i.e., S can be described as the set of all convex combinations of a finite number of activities).

If producer durables evaporate at a constant rate that is independent of the firm's utilization of other inputs, then the shape of the production possibility set S will be restricted, and it is easy to see that the profit maximization model (108) reduces to a profit maximization problem similar to (106). However, in general, a firm can prolong the life (and hence the value) of its durable equipment by spending more on inputs of maintenance labor and on inputs of replacement parts. Thus we should distinguish at least two broad types of labor input: production labor and maintenance labor. Increased inputs of the first type of labor will generally lead to smaller outputs of capital equipment available at the beginning of the following period, and vice versa for maintenance labor.

The model of short-run profit maximization defined by (108) is capable of being interpreted in several ways, depending on how narrowly capital goods are classified.

If capital goods are not distinguished according to vintage, then the dimensionality of the x and z vectors will be relatively small, and (108) reduces to a *variable evaporation rate model.*

If capital goods are distinguished not only according to their vintage but also by their physical condition (e.g., trucks may be classified according to how many miles they have been driven, structures may be distinguished by whether or not they have been painted recently, and so on), then the dimensionality of the x and z vectors will be enormous, and (108) may be termed a *"vintage" variable evaporation rate model.*

Some special cases of the very general Hicksian intertemporal model of production have appeared in the literature: (*a*) Taubman and Wilkinson (1970) assume that the physical amount of depreciation per unit of capital per unit of time depends on an index of capital utilization; (*b*) Schworm (1977) assumes that depreciation depends on an index of capital utilization (miles driven in the case of his empirical example using truck data) *and* units of maintenance; while (*c*) Epstein (1977) actually implements a highly aggregated model based on equation (108) using aggregate United States manufacturing data, but his empirical results are not very favorable to the Hicksian intertemporal model (perhaps owing to aggregation problems). On the other hand, Schworm is able to derive a formula for the rental price of capital that is similar to (105) above, except that utilization and maintenance variables also appear in the formula; but the other output and input variables pertaining to the firm do *not* appear in his formula, which makes the construction of rental prices for components of the capital stock much easier than in the more general Hicksian intertemporal model of production.

How can we in fact construct a capital aggregate based on the Hicksian short-run profit maximization model (108), and how will the resulting aggregate differ from a capital services aggregate constructed by means of an index number formula using rental prices similar to (105) above as weights? In the context of the Hicksian model, it is clear that we can construct several capital aggregates that must be carefully distinguished: (*a*) a current-period capital stock aggregate (an input from the viewpoint of the current period) using current-period capital stock prices as weights in the aggregation procedure; (*b*) a (depreciated) following-period capital stock aggregate (an output from the viewpoint of the current period) using discounted expected following-period capital stock prices as weights; (*c*) a current-period investment aggregate (an output) using current-period investment goods prices as weights in the aggregation procedure; and (*d*) a capital aggregate that is an aggregate of (*a*) and (*b*) where capital as an input and capital as an output are oppositely signed in the index number formula that is used. This "Hicksian" capital services aggregate[60] should be comparable to the Jorgenson-Griliches capital aggregate discussed earlier, except that the assumption of constant evaporation rates is not required.

Although the Hicksian model of producer behavior and the corresponding capital aggregates are more appealing than the constant evaporation rate model and the Jorgenson-Griliches capital aggregate, there is a major problem in implementing the Hicksian model; that is, the necessary data do not exist at present. Data on the market value and condition of the firm's beginning of the period holdings of durables are either: (*a*) nonexistent, (*b*) extremely aggregated, or (*c*) conventionally determined according to depreciation rules used for tax purposes.[61]

I will conclude this section by considering a problem Usher raised in his introduction: Should expenditures on maintenance and repair be lumped with expenditures on capital goods? If we have enough data (and we are willing to make the necessary imputations) to implement the approach to capital aggregation based on the Hicksian model of producer behavior defined by (108), then maintenance and repair should not be lumped with capital expenditures. A similar conclusion should hold if the model is based on the constant evaporation rate model (106), since we would expect maintenance and repair expenditures to change δ, the depreciation rate on the existing capital stock.

8.4.2 Special Problems in the Aggregation of Capital

In the previous section I may have left the impression that from a theoretical point of view constructing a capital aggregate is no more difficult than constructing a labor aggregate.[62] In the present section, I will readjust this impression by cataloging some of the practical difficulties and sources of controversy that occur when researchers attempt to construct capital aggregates that are suitable for estimating production functions or for estimating total factor productivity.

Producer's Expectations of Future Prices

Whether we construct a capital services aggregate using the constant evaporation rate model (equation 106) or the variable evaporation rate model (equation 108), it is necessary to estimate the producer's *expectations* about next period's capital stock prices (recall the price Q_{t+1} in eq. 105 and the expected prices $p_z/(1 + r)$ in eq. 108). These expected prices are generally unobservable, and thus reasonable analysts could differ widely on how to estimate them. For example, Christensen and Jorgenson (1969, 1970) assume that producers perfectly anticipate next period's stock prices, whereas Woodland (1972, 1975) and many others[63] assume that producers expect current stock prices to prevail in the following period (static expectations or Hicks's [1946, p. 205] unitary elasticity of expectations). A third alternative (followed by Epstein 1977) is to use a forecasting model to predict next period's asset prices based on past information about the asset prices. It seems clear that the first two methods (perfect anticipations and static expectations) for forming expected prices are not generally correct, while the third alternative requires extensive econometric modeling expertise, which individual producers and accountants may not possess.

Another related difficulty must be mentioned at this point. We have been constructing aggregates under the assumption that producers are maximizing profits subject to their technological constraints, assuming that they are facing *known* prices for selling their outputs and buying their inputs. We have been assuming that there was no *uncertainty* involved in the individual producer's profit maximization problems, and thus that their attitude toward risk and uncertainty was irrelevant. However, since future-period prices of capital goods are not known with certainty, it is clear that our underlying profit maximization models (e.g., eq. 106 or 108) must be modified to incorporate producers' attitudes toward risk. This leads to a great number of complications[64] whose implications for the construction of aggregates have not been fully worked out.

The problem of modeling uncertainty is related to the problem of modeling the formation of expectations, in the sense that neither problem would exist (at least in theory) if there were sufficient future and insurance markets, for then the appropriate prices could be observed in the market. However, in the absence of these markets, the analyst who wishes to construct a capital services aggregate will be forced to make an *imputation* or assumption about future expected prices.

Jorgenson and Griliches (1967) have been criticized (cf. Denison 1969, pp. 6–12; and Daly 1972, pp. 49–50) for including capital gains terms in their rental price formulas for capital services, which they use as weights in order to aggregate different components of the capital stock into a capital aggregate. However, from our rather narrow viewpoint, which concentrates on the measurement of capital in the context of production function estimation and the measurement of total factor productivity, it seems clear that the capital gains term belongs in the rental price formula—what is not as clear is the validity of the Jorgenson-Griliches perfect anticipations assumption.

Interest Rates

The rental price formula (105) and the profit maximization problems (106) and (108) in the previous section all involve an interest rate r. Which r should be used? If the firm is a net borrower, then r should be the marginal cost of borrowing an additional dollar for one period, while if the firm is a net lender, then r should be the one-period interest rate it receives on its last loan. In practice, r is taken to be either (a) an exogenous bond rate that may or may not apply to the firm under consideration, or (b) an internal rate of return. I tend to use the first alternative, while Woodland (1972, 1975) and Jorgenson and his co-workers[65] use the second. As usual, neither alternative appears to be correct from a theoretical a priori point of view; so, again, reasonable analysts could differ on which r to use in order to construct a capital aggregate.[66]

Note that the appropriate interest rate is a *nominal* (not "real") rate of interest: any (anticipated) inflation should be taken into account by the (anticipated) capital gains term in the user cost formula (105).

Depreciation Rates

The user-cost formula in the previous section involved a depreciation rate δ. I have already commented that, in theory, the assumption of an exogenous evaporation rate δ is not warranted; but suppose that data limitations forced us to estimate a constant δ, or perhaps a series of δs, $\{\delta_s\}$, say, where δ_s would be the one-period evaporation rate applicable to a certain component of the capital stock that was s periods old. The depreciation rates $\{\delta_s\}$ are used not only in constructing rental prices in the Jorgenson-Griliches framework, but also by other analysts in constructing capital stock series from deflated investment series (cf. Kendrick 1961, 1976; Denison 1974).

What depreciation rates $\{\delta_s\}$ are to be used, and how are they to be constructed? There is considerable controversy in this area, much of it being very ably reviewed by Creamer (1972, pp. 62–68). Two relatively extreme positions can be discerned in the literature, one used by Jorgenson and his co-workers (constant evaporation; i.e., $\delta_s = \delta$ for all s) and the other used by Denison and Kendrick (one-horse-shay depreciation; i.e., $\delta_s = 0$ for all s, except $s = T$ when $\delta_T = 1$). Actually, Denison's depreciation assumptions are not quite as extreme as one-horse-shay depreciation, as the following quotations indicate:[67]

> It is not assumed that all of the investment in a category made in a particular year disappears from the gross stock simultaneously, after expiration of the average service life. Instead more realistically, retirements are dispersed around the average service life. The Winfrey S-3 distribution is used to obtain this dispersion. [Denison 1974, pp. 53–54]

> To introduce an allowance for rising maintenance expense and deterioration of capital services with the passage of time, I have adopted the following expedient. To measure input of structures and

equipment I have used a weighted average of indexes of the gross stock and net stock based on straight-line depreciation, with the gross stock weighted three and the net stock one. [Denison 1974, p. 55]

On the other hand, for productivity comparisons, Kendrick prefers to use one-horse-shay depreciation "in order to relate real product to the comparable real capital stock estimates on a gross basis rather than a net basis" (Kendrick 1974, p. 20), but he also constructs estimates of a net capital stock using double declining-balance depreciation.

Two questions arise with respect to assumptions made about the depreciation, deterioration, and length of lives of components of the capital stock: (*a*) Do the assumptions make much difference empirically? and (*b*) What is the empirical evidence on the appropriateness of the various assumptions?

The answer to the first question appears to be an emphatic yes. Capital stocks constructed on the basis of different depreciation assumptions can differ considerably.[68]

Some negative empirical evidence on the validity of the constant evaporation rate form of depreciation (or declining-balance or geometric depreciation, as it is sometimes called) is reviewed by Feldstein and Rothschild (1974). Hulten and Wykoff (1977) utilize the theoretical model developed by Hall (1968) to estimate economic depreciation for various types of structures used in the United States manufacturing sector. They found that, in most cases, a constant geometric rate of depreciation could approximate the "true" rate of depreciation rather well, with the exception of the earliest years of the asset's life.

Overall, one can only conclude that empirical information on depreciation rates and lengths of lives of assets is scanty, and I can only echo the recommendations of others that governments devote more resources in order to obtain more information.

Treatment of Indirect Taxes

Indirect taxes in a national income accounting framework are generally defined as an amalgam of taxes on outputs produced by firms (sales taxes and various excise taxes) plus taxes on various inputs (including customs duties, real and property taxes, social insurance levies, and sometimes universal pension plan levies). There has been some controversy over where these taxes should be allocated when constructing a capital aggregate:

> The treatment of indirect taxes, property taxes, and corporate profits taxes can affect the income share of the capital-land category, and also the distribution to assets within that category. The choices of national income at market prices or factor costs for weights is in-

fluenced by this question. This question had come earlier in a review of Solow's book, *Capital Theory and the Rate of Return*, as Solow had included both indirect taxes and corporate profits taxes in estimating the share of income to property. [Daly 1972, p. 49]

From the point of view that underlies the user-cost formula (eq. 105) (which was based on the assumption that producers competitively maximize profits subject to their technological constraints), the treatment of indirect taxes seems clear: indirect taxes (such as property taxes) that fall on durable inputs *should* be included in the user-cost formula for that input, other indirect taxes (such as Social Security payments) that fall on variable inputs *should* be added to the market price of those inputs, whereas indirect taxes (such as sales taxes) that fall on outputs should *not* be added to the market price of these outputs. The conceptually correct prices in the Jorgenson-Griliches framework are the output prices that reflect the revenue actually received by the firm and the input prices that reflect the actual costs paid by the firm for the use of the inputs involved in the production process.

Thus customs duties and tariffs *should* be added to the prices of various imported goods used by firms, but sales taxes imposed on the outputs of a firm as they are sold to households (or other nonbusiness sectors) should *not* be added to the firm's selling prices. But how should we treat (intermediate good) sales taxes imposed on the outputs of a firm (1, say) as the goods are sold to another firm (2, say)? Obviously the tax should not be added to the selling price of firm 1, but it should be added to the selling price of firm 1 when the good is treated as an input into firm 2.[69]

The Form of Business Organization

The user-cost formula (105) developed in the previous section implicitly assumed that the firm was an incorporated firm and thus faced the appropriate corporate tax rate. However, if the firm is not incorporated, then the appropriate tax rate is the owner's *personal* (marginal) tax rate, which will generally differ from the corporate rate. Thus Christenson and Jorgenson (1969) construct rental prices for the components of real capital input, disaggregated by class of asset and by legal form of organization. This appears to be a worthwhile methodological innovation, although reasonable analysts may find fault with some of the specific details of the Christensen-Jorgenson construction.

Weighting the Components of Capital

To construct real capital input, Kendrick (1972, p. 101) and Denison (1974, p. 51) favor weighting components of the captial stock by the components share of property income[70] while Kendrick (1976) simply adds constant-dollar components of the capital stock. None of these weights appear to agree with the user-cost weights we would obtain using formula (105), except in very restrictive circumstances: using the notation of the previous section, the suggested weights that would replace the Jorgenson-Griliches user cost (105) are rQ_t and Q_t respectively, where Q_t is the current period asset price and r is a (gross or net of depreciation) rate of return.

Since rQ_t and Q_t do not have a depreciation term, these weights tend to be much smaller than the Jorgenson-Griliches user-cost weights, and thus measures of real factor input (see section 8.5 below) using Jorgenson-Griliches weights tend to grow faster than Kendrick-Denison measures of real factor input, since capital typically has grown faster than labor during the past century. Thus the question of which weights to use when constructing a capital services aggregate is not empirically unimportant (cf. Denison 1969 and Jorgenson and Griliches 1972).

From the viewpoint of our restrictive theoretical model of production, it seems clear that the Jorgenson-Griliches weights are to be preferred over the Kendrick-Denison weights.[71]

Leased versus Owned Capital in the National Accounts

There is a problem in using national income accounting data to estimate sectoral capital stocks that must be mentioned here.[72] The problem is that all rented or leased components of a firm's capital stock appear as a primary input in the finance, insurance, and real estate sector and as an intermediate input in the firm's sector. This creates problems when sectoral "value added" production functions are estimated, since the sectoral capital services input will be too low.[73] Thus it would be helpful if official accounts were to provide a breakdown on which sector actually used the services of a leased component of the capital stock.

The Domain of Definition of Capital

Another fundamental problem in constructing a capital aggregate that we have not yet faced is the issue Usher raised in his introduction to this volume: Should capital be defined as an aggregate of produced means of production or as an aggregate of produced and nonproduced (natural resource) factors of production? Obviously, this is a definitional matter that could be decided either way. However, if we opt for the first definition of a capital aggregate and are interested in estimating aggregate production functions or explaining productivity change, then it is *essential* that we construct an aggregate for the noncapital, nonlabor, nonproduced primary inputs (such as land and natural resources), since omitting this latter aggregate ("land") will bias estimates of aggregate production functions as well as estimates of total factor productivity. This point has some applications for the current system of national income accounting in most countries, where land (and natural resources in general) is given a very minor role,[74] partly because of data limitations, but partly because researchers have focused for the most part on reproducible capital and neglected the contribution of nonreproducible resources.

A second problem with the definition of capital is that some national income accounting systems do not include inventories and goods in process as components of the capital stock. The essence of a capital good seems to be that it is a produced good, part of which lasts longer than the period under consideration. Thus, in agriculture, inventories of farm animals and feed and seed are generally large and should be included as components of the capital stock. This neglect of inventories seriously biases downward the contribution of capital in most industries. This point is well recognized, and Denison (1974), Kendrick (1976), and Christensen, Cummings, and Jorgenson (1976) all include inventory stocks as components of their capital stocks. However, when estimating production functions, many researchers (e.g., Woodland 1975) omit inventories as components of their capital stock series.

A final, related definitional problem has been raised by Creamer:

> Capital input is typically restricted to some combination of tangible assets although every analyst knows that an enterprise requires financial assets, (cash and accounts receivable) as well as tangible assets in order to function. . . . However, financial assets lead a double life—one entity's claim is another entity's obligation. Thus, at the level of aggregation of the national economy financial claims and obligations cancel each other, except for the net balance of international claims which have been a relatively small part of U.S. stock of capital. If this is the reason for the exclusion of financial capital, it constitutes, in my view, still another argument in favor of a disaggregative approach. [Creamer 1972, p. 60]

An individual firm will generally hold an "inventory" of financial capital (or working capital, as it is sometimes called) during our Hicksian period, and the cost of holding this "inventory" is just as real a cost to the firm as a payment to labor. Aggregating across firms in the private business sector of an economy will not generally cancel out these financial claims: they will cancel only if we include households, governments, and the rest of the world in the aggregate.

That financial capital is similar to physical inventories in some sense (both represent a real cost to a firm and to the private business sector of an economy) suggests that financial capital be treated like any other durable input in our accounting framework, and that financial capital should be included in any capital services aggregate, particularly since Creamer (1972, p. 60) suggests that there may have been substantial productivity gains in the use of financial capital since 1929, at least in

United States manufacturing. Unfortunately, we *cannot* insert financial capital into our production function as just another argument: the amount of financial capital a firm will require to produce a given output, given a vector of physical inputs, is simply not a well-defined quantity.

One way of proceeding would be to exclude financial capital as an input into the firm's "physical" production function, but to include financial capital as an input (along with labor, office space, etc.) into a "transactions" technology that would have the responsibility for *selling* the physical outputs the firm produces in its "plant" and *purchasing* the inputs the "plant" requires. Normal credit arrangements and payment procedures could be worked into the transactions technology.

We have drifted into the domain of monetary theory, and the reader is referred to Fischer (1974) and Nagatani (1978) for further references and suggestions. At this point we can only conclude that Creamer has pointed out a serious conceptual omission from most capital aggregates and that it is not immediately clear how we can insert financial capital into a capital aggregate using our naive production model.

Another definitional issue with respect to the scope of a capital aggregate has been raised by Christensen and Jorgenson's[75] inclusion of the stock of household consumer durables in their recent estimates of the capital stock. Creamer makes the following comments on their procedure:

> This is a puzzling addition. . . . It is certainly inconsistent with the underlying definition of a capital good—one that is used to produce other goods and services. Moreover, it is inconsistent with their own (Christensen-Jorgenson) statement that "the main analytical use of the production account is in the study of producer behavior. Revenue and outlay must be measured from the producer's point of view." . . . Moreover, the inclusion of consumer's durables in the capital stock understates aggregate total factor productivity since the methodology of estimates is such that this sector makes no contribution to productivity.[76] [Creamer 1972, p. 61]

Some further comments seem warranted. Christensen and Jorgenson have included in the private production sector of an economy the "process" that converts household stocks of consumer durables into service flows. Kendrick (1976) has also added consumer durables to the capital stock, justifying the procedure as follows: "This is merely an extension of the treatment presently accorded owner-occupied residential structures and may be justified by the argument cited above—that shifts in sector ownership patterns should not affect investment, capital, or the associated income estimates" (Kendrick 1976, pp. 5–6).

Thus, for some purposes the inclusion of consumer durables in a capital aggregate can be justified.[77] However, since this discussion of capital aggregation is in the context of the estimation of total factor productivity and production function estimation for the business sector of an economy that is oriented toward maximizing private profit, I would not recommend including consumer durables in a capital aggregate, since a household's conversion of durable stocks into flows is not generally a genuine business activity.

To conclude our discussion about the domain of definition of a capital aggregate, let us examine Kendrick's (1976) rather comprehensive definition of the capital stock. Kendrick includes the following items in his capital stock estimates for the United States:

1. *business nonhuman tangibles*, consisting of structures, land, natural resources, machinery and other durable equipment, and inventory stocks used in the private business sector;
2. *household nonhuman tangibles*, consisting of household residential real estate, automobiles, other durable goods, and household inventories;
3. *government nonhuman tangibles*, consisting of government structures, machinery and equipment, and public capital (such as highway construction);
4. *human tangibles*, which are defined as outlays required to produce mature human beings (rearing costs);
5. *research and development expenditures*;
6. *education and training expenses*;
7. *health and safety expenditures* (one-half of all outlays for health and safety, which reduce mortality and disability are taken as representing investment); and
8. *mobility payments*, which includes portions of unemployment insurance benefits paid, job search and hiring expenses, and moving expenses.[78]

From our narrow viewpoint, concerned with productivity and production function estimation for the private business sector of an economy, we would not recommend the inclusion of any of Kendrick's capital stock components beyond item (1), business nonhuman tangibles, since the main effect of the investments listed in items (3) to (8) is to change the prices and possibly the qualities of the inputs a private firm utilizes; but these price changes are quite consistent with our model of producer behavior and do not require any special treatment. However, we can discern three possible exceptions to the general statement made above.

First, if portions of the government capital stock (item 3 above) are leased to private firms, these rentals could be treated as intermediate inputs into the private sector. It would also make sense to aggregate these rentals of government capital together with the corresponding privately owned components of the business capital stock.

Second, the existence of certain "free" government-provided goods such as highways creates some conceptual difficulties with our basic profit maximization problems listed in section 8.4.1. For example, consider the first profit maximization problem in section 8.4.1, modified to allow for the existence of government public goods:

(109)
$$\max_{\substack{w.r.t.\\ Y,W,B,K}} (1 - u_t)\{p_y Y - w_W W - w_B B - p_t K\}$$
$$\text{subject to } Y = f(W,B,K,R_1,R_2),$$

where all variables have been defined in section 8.4.1 except $R_1 \equiv$ number of miles of nonfreeway road utilized by the firm and $R_2 \equiv$ number of miles of freeway used by the firm. If f is differentiable and an interior solution to the profit maximization problem exists, Y^*, W^*, B^*, K^*, say, then the solution will satisfy the following first-order necessary conditions for (109):

(110) $$p_y \frac{\partial f}{\partial w}(W^*,B^*,K^*,R_1,R_2) = w_W$$

(111) $$p_y \frac{\partial f}{\partial B}(W^*,B^*,K^*,R_1,R_2) = w_B$$

(112) $$p_y \frac{\partial f}{\partial K}(W^*,B^*,K^*,R_1,R_2) = p_t.$$

The value of the marginal products of R_1 and R_2 can be defined as

(113) $$p_y \frac{\partial f}{\partial R_1}(W^*,B^*,K^*,R_1,R_2) \equiv p_1 \geq 0 \text{ and}$$

(114) $$p_y \frac{\partial f}{\partial R_2}(W^*,B^*,K^*,R_1,R_2) \equiv p_2 \geq 0,$$

respectively. Define the optimal output as $Y^* \equiv f(W^*,B^*,K^*,R_1,R_2)$. If the production function exhibits constant returns to scale in all five inputs, then Euler's theorem on homogeneous functions implies

(115) $$p_y Y^* = w_W W^* + w_B B^* + p_t K^* + p_1 R_1 + p_2 R_2.$$

If p_1 or p_2 are positive, then the firm will capture the positive marginal products of the two free inputs R_1 and R_2, thus making excess profits. However, if there is free entry into the industry, new firms will enter the industry and the price of the output, p_y, will tend to fall. In fact, if the production function $f(W,B,K,R_1,R_2)$, with R_1 and R_2 held fixed, exhibits initially increasing returns to scale and eventual decreasing returns to scale in $W,B,K,$[79] then for industry equilibrium the price of output will be close to the average cost of production; that is, the following equation should (almost) hold for an individual firm in the industry:

$$(116) \qquad p_y Y^* = w_W W^* + w_B B^* + p_t K^*.$$

Equations (115) and (116) imply that the shadow prices of the two types of road, p_1 and p_2, should be close to zero.

With this highly simplified model in mind, we can return to our discussion of whether to include certain government capital goods such as highways in a capital aggregate. The answer (from the viewpoint of the economic theory of production) appears to be yes, except that the price weights for these government capital stock components will be shadow prices whose magnitude will not generally be known. However, if we assume competitive producer behavior with free entry into each industry using the public capital goods, then the price weights should be close to zero. In this case government capital goods would not show up in a capital aggregate constructed according to the index number formulas discussed in section 8.2.[80]

The third possible exception to my general statement that items (2) through (8) of Kendrick's capital aggregate should not be included in a capital aggregate based on my naive economic model of producer behavior is item (5), research and development expenditures. However, I am unable to make any concrete recommendations on just how research and development expenditures should be treated when forming a capital aggregate: it depends on how R&D enters the underlying economic model upon which we base our aggregation procedures.[81]

The Time Period

This discussion of capital aggregation based on the Jorgenson-Griliches economic model of producer behavior has thus far proceeded under the assumption that all components of the capital stock are freely variable during the period under consideration. Obviously, as we shorten our Hicksian period from, say, a decade to a week, an increasing number of inputs will become *fixed* rather than variable, and in these cases (observable) market prices should be replaced by (unobservable) shadow prices, which equal the value of the marginal products of the fixed inputs. Since these shadow prices are not generally observable, it will not generally be possible to construct capital aggregates based on our model of producer behavior when the time period becomes short enough to cause components of the capital stock to become fixed.

In view of this, one might think that capital stock aggregates based on annual data would be "better" than ones based on weekly data. This is not the case, however: the annual model of producer behavior assumes that all inputs are freely variable and that the prices the producer faces remain constant throughout the year when neither assumption is actually satisfied in practice, and thus neither annual nor weekly aggregates constructed on the basis of market data will be precisely equal to the "correct" aggregates, constructed using the appropriate shadow prices.

In section 8.7 I will discuss how to build up "annual" aggregates from "weekly" aggregates, assuming that the "weekly" aggregates have been constructed correctly from the viewpoint of our economic model of producer behavior.

Choice of Index Number Formula

> Unfortunately, there is no unique solution to the index number problem. Fisher's "ideal" index number, which employs a geometric mean of the weights from both periods in a binary comparison, is neat, but it has no more fundamental economic rationale than using either first or last period weights! [Kendrick 1972, p. 95]

In section 8.2.4 I argued that there was a strong economic rationale for using Fisher's ideal index number formula, since it is a *superlative* index number formula; that is, it corresponds to a *flexible* functional form, for the underlying production function. Moreover, we indicated that all superlative index number formulas approximate each other to the second order if changes in prices and quantities between the two periods are small, while the more commonly used Paasche or Laspeyres formulas approximate superlative indexes to the first order only.

Given that the economic justification for using a superlative index number formula seems fairly strong, should we use the fixed-base method for forming a capital aggregate, or should we compare each period with the immediately preceding period—that is, use the chain principle? In section 8.2.4 I argued for the use of the chain principle, since, if it is used, price and quantity changes should be small, and all superlative index number formulas should generate virtually the same aggregate series, so that the choice of a specific superlative index number formula becomes empirically irrelevant.

To conclude this section, let me note that the construction of a capital aggregate is fraught with both theoretical and empirical difficulties, even taking it as given that we wish to construct an aggregate that would be used in the context of production function or productivity estimation. It appears to me that the major conceptual problems are in the determination of producer's expectations about future prices and how to deal with the resulting uncertainty, while the major practical difficulties are in the estimation of depreciation rates.

With the above difficulties firmly in mind, let us turn now to a closely related topic: how to construct estimates of total factor productivity in the context of our naive model of producer behavior.

8.5 Capital and the Measurement of Technical Progress

8.5.1 The Measurement of Total Factor Productivity with a Separable Technology

For a brief but useful survey of the literature on the measurement of economic growth and total factor productivity, see Christensen, Cummings, and Jorgenson (1976).

Jorgenson and Griliches (1967, 1972, pp. 83–84) advocated the use of the Törnqvist quantity index number formula Q_0 (recall section 8.2.3 of this chapter) and the corresponding implicit Törnqvist price index P_0 in the context of the measurement of total factor productivity. In this section I repeat Diewert's (1976, pp. 124–27) justification for their procedure.

Jorgenson and Griliches (1972) use the index number formula $Q_0(p^0,p^1;x^0,x^1)$ defined in section 8.2.3 not only to form an index of real input, but also to form an index of real output. Just as the aggregation of inputs into a composite input rests on the duality between unit cost and homogeneous production functions, the aggregation of outputs into a composite output can be based on the duality between unit revenue and homogeneous factor requirements functions.[82] I will briefly outline this latter duality.

Suppose that a producer is producing M outputs, $(y_1,y_2,\ldots,y_M) \equiv y$, and the technology of the producer can be described by a *factor requirements function*, g, where $g(y)$ = the minimum amount of aggregate input required to produce the vector of outputs y.[83] The producer's *unit* (aggregate input) *revenue function*[84] is defined for each price vector $p \geqq 0_M$ by

$$(117) \qquad r(p) \equiv \max_y\{p\cdot y : g(y) \leqq 1, y \geqq 0_M\}.$$

Thus given a factor requirements function g, (117) may be used to define a unit revenue function. On the other hand, given a unit revenue function $r(p)$ that is a positive, linearly homogeneous, convex function for $p \gg 0_M$, a factor requirements function g^* consistent with r may be defined for $y \gg 0_M$ by[85]

$$(118) \qquad g^*(y) \equiv \min_\lambda\{\lambda : p\cdot y \leqq r(p)\lambda \text{ for every } p \geqq 0_M\}$$

$$= \min_\lambda \{\lambda : 1 \leqq r(p)\lambda \text{ for every p} \geqq 0_M \text{ such that } p\cdot y = 1\} = 1/\max_p\{r(p) : p\cdot y = 1, p \geqq 0_M\}.$$

As usual, the translog functional form may be used to provide a second-order approximation to an arbitrary twice-differentiable factor requirements function. Thus, assume that g is defined (at least over the relevant range of ys) by

(119) $$\ln g(y^r) \equiv a_0 + \sum_{m=1}^{M} a_m \ln y^r_m + \tfrac{1}{2} \sum_{j=1}^{M} \sum_{k=1}^{M} c_{jk} \ln y^r_j \ln y^r_k, \text{ for } r = 0, 1,$$

where $$\sum_{m=1}^{M} a_m = 1,\ c_{jk} = c_{kj},\ \sum_{k=1}^{M} c_{jk} = 0, \text{ for } j = 1,2,\ldots,M.$$

Now assume that $y^r \rangle\rangle 0_M$ is a solution to the aggregate input minimization problem $\min_y\{g(y):p^r \cdot y = p^r \cdot y^r, y \geqq 0_M\}$, where $p^r \rangle\rangle 0_M$ for $r = 0,1$, and g is the translog function defined by (119). Then the first-order necessary conditions for the minimization problems along with the linear homogeneity of g yield the relations $p^r/p^r \cdot y^r = \nabla g(y^r)/g(y^r)$, for $r = 0,1$, and using these two relations in lemma (59) applied to (119) yields

(120) $$g(y^1)/g(y^0) = Q_0(p^0, p^1; y^0, y^1)$$

where Q_0 is the Törnqvist quantity index defined by (38).

Thus the Törnqvist formula can again be used to aggregate quantities consistently, provided the underlying aggregator function is homogeneous translog.

Similarly, if the revenue function $r(p)$ is translog over the relevant range of data and if the producer is in fact maximizing revenue, then we can show that $r(p^1)/r(p^0) = P_0(p^0,p^1; y^0,y^1)$, the Törnqvist price index.

Using the material above, we may now justify the Jorgenson and Griliches (1972) method of measuring technical progress. Assume that the production possibilities efficient set can be represented as the set of outputs y and inputs x such that

(121) $$g(y) = f(x),$$

where g is the homogeneous translog factor requirements function defined by (119), and f is the homogeneous translog production function defined in section 8.2.4. Let $p^r \rangle\rangle 0_M$, $w^r \rangle\rangle 0_N$, $r = 0, 1$ be vectors of output and input prices during periods 0 and 1, and assume that $y^0 \rangle\rangle 0_M$ and $x^0 \rangle\rangle 0_N$ is a solution to the period 0 profit-maximization problem,

(122) $$\max_{y,x}\{p^0 \cdot y - w^0 \cdot x : g(y) = f(x)\}.$$

Suppose "technical progress" occurs between periods 0 and 1, which we assume to be a parallel outward shift of the "isoquants" of the aggregator function f; that is, we assume that the equation that defines the efficient set of outputs and inputs in period 1 is $g(y) = (1 + \tau)f(x)$, where τ represents the amount of "technical progress" if $\tau > 0$ or "technical regress" if $\tau < 0$. Finally, assume that $y^1 \rangle\rangle 0_M$ and $x^1 \rangle\rangle 0_N$ is a solution to the period 1 profit-maximization problem,

$$(123) \qquad \max_{y,x}\{p^1 \cdot y - w^1 \cdot x : g(y) = (1+\tau)f(x)\}.$$

Thus we have $g(y^0) = f(x^0)$ and $g(y^1) = (1+\tau)f(x^1)$. It is easy to see that $y^r \rangle\rangle 0_M$ is a solution to the aggregate input minimization problem $\min_y\{g(y) : p^r \cdot y = p^r \cdot y^r, y \geqq 0_M\}$, for $r = 0,1$, and thus (120) holds. Similarly, $x^r \rangle\rangle 0_N$ is a solution to the aggregator maximization problem $\max_x\{f(x) : w^r \cdot x = w^r \cdot x^r, x \geqq 0_N\}$, for $r = 0,1$, and thus (43) holds. Substituting (43) and (120) into the identity $g(y^1)/g(y^0) = (1+\tau)f(x^1)/f(x^0)$ yields the following expression for $(1+\tau)$ in terms of observable prices and quantities:

$$(124) \qquad (1+\tau) = \prod_{m=1}^{M} [y^1_m/y^0_m]^{\frac{1}{2}\left[\frac{p^1_m y^1_m}{p^1 \cdot y^1} + \frac{p^0_m y^0_m}{p^0 \cdot y^0}\right]} \Big/ \prod_{n=1}^{N} [x^1_n/x^0_n]^{\frac{1}{2}\left[\frac{w^1_n x^1_n}{w^1 \cdot x^1} + \frac{w^0_n x^0_n}{w^0 \cdot x^0}\right]}$$

$$= Q_0(p^0,p^1,y^0,y^1)/Q_0(w^0,w^1,x^0,x^1).$$

Thus the Jorgenson-Griliches method of measuring technical progress can be justified if: (*a*) the economy's production possibilities set can be represented by a *separable* transformation surface defined by $g(y) = f(x)$, where the input aggregator function f and the output aggregator function g are both homogeneous translog functions; (*b*) producers are maximizing profits; and (*c*) technical progress takes place in the "*neutral*" manner postulated above.[86]

Since the separability assumption $g(y) = f(x)$ is somewhat restrictive from an a priori theoretical point of view, it would be of some interest to devise a measure of technical progress that did not depend on this separability assumption. This can be done, as we shall see in the next section.

8.5.2 The Measurement of Total Factor Productivity in the General Case

Before analyzing a general M outputs, N inputs case, we warm up with the one output, N inputs case.[87]

Suppose the technology of the producer can be represented by the following (time modified) translog production function f:

$$(125) \qquad \ln f(x,t) \equiv \alpha_0 + \sum_{n=1}^{N} \alpha_n \ln x_n + \tfrac{1}{2} \sum_{i=1}^{N} \sum_{h=1}^{N} \alpha_{ih} \ln x_i \ln x_h + \beta_0 t + \sum_{n=1}^{N} \beta_n t \ln x_n + \gamma t^2,$$

where $y = f(x,t)$ is output produced during period t, and $x \equiv (x_1, x_2, \ldots, x_N)$ is a vector of inputs used by the firm during period t. We note that f defined by (125) can provide a second-order approximation to an arbitrary twice continuously differentiable function of x and t. With the following restrictions on the parameters,

$$(126) \qquad \sum_{n=1}^{N} \alpha_n = 1, \alpha_{ih} = \alpha_{hi}, \sum_{i=1}^{N} \alpha_{ih} = 0 \text{ for } h = 1, 2, \ldots, N \text{ and } \sum_{n=1}^{N} \beta_n = 0,$$

f defined by (125) is linearly homogeneous in x, and the resulting function can provide a second-order approximation to an arbitrary twice continuously differentiable function of (x,t) that is linearly homogeneous in x (see Woodland 1976).

We interpret t as representing the effects of technological change. As t changes, the production function f shifts in the manner postulated by equation (125) above. Our present goal is to show how the *impact effect on output of technological change*, $\tau(x,t) \equiv \partial \ln f(x,t)/\partial t$,[88] can be estimated using only observable price and quantity data.

Assuming that f exhibits constant returns to scale (i.e., that the restrictions [126] above are satisfied), then application of the quadratic approximation lemma (59) or its consequence (64) to f defined by (125) and (126) yields the following identity:

$$(127) \qquad \ln f(x^1, t^1) - \ln f(x^0,t^0) = \tfrac{1}{2}[\hat{x}^1 \nabla_x \ln f(x^1,t^1) + \hat{x}^0 \nabla_x \ln f(x^0,t^0)] \cdot [\ln x^1 - \ln x^0] + \tfrac{1}{2}\left[\frac{\partial \ln}{\partial t} f(x^1,t^1) + \frac{\partial \ln}{\partial t} f(x^0,t^0)\right] \cdot [t^1 - t^0],$$

where the notation is the same as in section 8.2.6. If we now add the assumption that the producer faces the input price vectors $w^0 \gg 0_N$, $w^1 \gg 0_N$ during periods 0, 1 and that he competitively minimizes costs, then we can derive the usual identities (recall equation 23):

$$(128) \qquad \nabla_x \ln f(x^0,t^0) = w^0/w^0 \cdot x^0; \nabla_x \ln f(x^1,t^1) = w^1/w^1 \cdot x^1.$$

Substituting (128) into (127) yields the equation

$$(129) \qquad \ln y^1 - \ln y^0 = \sum_{n=1}^{N} [s^1_n + s^0_n] \ln [x^1_n/x^0_n] + \tfrac{1}{2}\left[\frac{\partial \ln}{\partial t} f(x^1,t^1) + \frac{\partial \ln}{\partial t} f(x^0,t^0)]\right][t^1 - t^0],$$

where $y^r \equiv f(x^r,t^r)$ and $s^r_n \equiv w^r_n x^r_n / w^r \cdot x^r$ for $r = 0,1$ and $n = 1,2, \ldots, N$. Equation (129) can be rearranged and exponentiated to yield the following exact relationship:

$$(130) \qquad \exp \left\{ \tfrac{1}{2} \left[\frac{\partial \ln}{\partial t} f(x^1,t^1) + \frac{\partial \ln}{\partial t} f(x^0,t^0) \right] [t^1 - t^0] \right\}$$

$$= \frac{y^1}{y^0} / Q_0(w^0,w^1,x^0,x^1),$$

where $Q_0(w^0,w^1,x^0,x^1)$ is the Törnqvist quantity index in inputs. The left-hand side of (130) represents a theoretical expression for the cumulative effects of technical progress while the right-hand side of (130) can be calculated using observable data. If we define $\tau^r \equiv \partial \ln f(x^r,t^r)/dt$ for $r = 0,1$, then (130) can be rewritten as

$$(131) \qquad e^{1/2[\tau^1 + \tau^0][t^1 - t^0]} = [y^1/y^0]/Q_0(w^0,w^1,x^0,x^1).$$

The expression (131) simplifies further if we make the additional assumption that $f(x,t) = e^{\beta_0 t} f(x,0)$, which is a strong form of Hicks's neutral technological change.[89] This assumption is equivalent to the additional restrictions on the parameters

$$(132) \qquad \beta_n = 0, \; n = 1, 2, \ldots, N \text{ and } \gamma = 0.$$

With assumption (132), (131) can be rewritten as

$$(133) \qquad e^{\beta_0 [t^1 - t^0]} = [y^1/y^0]/Q_0(w^0,w^1,x^0,x^1),$$

where $\beta_0 \equiv \partial \ln f(x,t)/\partial t$ can be interpreted as a constant impact effect of technological change.

Consider now the multiple output, multiple input case. Recall the definition of the firm's variable profit function in sections 8.2.1 and 8.2.6:

$$(134) \qquad \Pi(x^r,p^r,t^r) \equiv \max_y \{p^r \cdot y : (x^r,y) \in S^{t^r}\},$$

where S^{t^r} is the firm's production possibilities set at time t^r, $(x^r,y) \equiv (x^r_1, \ldots, x^r_N, y_1, \ldots, y_M)$ is a feasible vector of inputs and outputs for the firm at time t^r, and $p \gg 0_M$ is a vector of output prices at time t^r.[90]

Recall that the variable profit function can provide a complete description of the technology of a firm under certain conditions. Now assume that the firm's variable profit function is the following (time modified) translog function:[91]

$$(135) \qquad \ln \Pi^*(x^r,p^r,t^r) \equiv \alpha_0 + \sum_{n=1}^{N} \alpha_n \ln x^r_n + \tfrac{1}{2} \sum_{i=1}^{N} \sum_{h=1}^{N}$$

$$\alpha_{ih} \ln x^r_i \ln x^r_h + \beta_0 t^r + \sum_{n=1}^{N} \beta_n t^r \ln x^r_n + \sum_{m=1}^{M}$$

$$\delta_m \ln p^r_m + \tfrac{1}{2} \sum_{m=1}^{M} \sum_{k=1}^{M} \delta_{mk} \ln p^r_m \ln p^r_k +$$

$$\sum_{n=1}^{N} \sum_{m=1}^{M} \epsilon_{nm} \ln x^r_n \ln p^r_m + \sum_{m=1}^{M} \epsilon_m t^r \ln p^r_m + \gamma (t^r)^2,$$

where $x^r \equiv (x^r_1, \ldots, x^r_N) \rangle\rangle 0_N$ is the vector of inputs utilized by the firm at time t^r, and $p^r \equiv (p^r, \ldots, p^r_M) \rangle\rangle 0_M$ is the vector of output (and intermediate input) prices that the firm is facing at time t^r, $r = 0,1$. The parameters on the right-hand side of (135) satisfy the following restrictions (which ensure that $\Pi(x,p,t)$ is linearly homogeneous in p):

(136) $$\sum_{m=1}^{M} \delta_m = 1, \delta_{mk} = \delta_{km}, \sum_{m=1}^{M} \delta_{mk} = 0 \text{ for } k = 1, \ldots, M$$

$$\sum_{m=1}^{M} \epsilon_{nm} = 0 \text{ for } n = 1, 2, \ldots, N \text{ and } \sum_{m=1}^{M} \epsilon_m = 0.$$

We will also assume that the firm's production is subject to constant returns to scale so that the following restrictions are also satisfied:

(137) $$\sum_{n=1}^{N} \alpha_n = 1, \alpha_{ih} = \alpha_{hi}, \sum_{i=1}^{N} \alpha_{ih} = 0, h = 1, 2, \ldots, N,$$

$$\sum_{n=1}^{N} \beta_n = 0 \text{ and } \sum_{n=1}^{N} \epsilon_{nm} = 0 \text{ for } m = 1, 2, \ldots, M.$$

If the producer is (variable) profit maximizing at time t^r, $r = 0,1$, where y^r denotes the profit-maximizing vector of outputs (and intermediate inputs) and the producer is also cost-minimizing at time t^r, where $w^r \rangle\rangle 0_N$ denotes the vector of input prices that the producer is facing at time t^r, then it can be shown[92] that the following equations hold:

(138) $$y^r / p^r \cdot y^r = \nabla_p \ln \Pi^*(x^r,p^r,t^r);$$

$$w^r / w^r \cdot x^r = \nabla_x \ln \Pi^*(x^r,p^r,t^r); \quad r = 0,1.$$

Note that the right-hand side of (135) is quadratic in the variables $\ln x_n$, $\ln p_m$, and t. Thus we can apply the quadratic approximation lemma (59) to (135) and obtain the following equality, which is analogous to (127) above:

(139) $$\ln \Pi^*(x^1,p^1,t^1) - \ln \Pi^*(x^0,p^0,t^0) = \tfrac{1}{2} [$$

$$\hat{x}^0 \nabla_x \Pi^*(x^0,p^0,t^0) + \hat{x}^1 \nabla_x \ln \Pi^*(x^1,p^1,t^1)]$$

$$\cdot[\ln x^1 - \ln x^0] + \tfrac{1}{2}[\hat{p}^1 \nabla_p \ln \Pi^*(x^1,p^1,t^1) + \hat{p}^0$$

$$\nabla_p \Pi^*(x^0,p^0,t^0)] \cdot [\ln p^1 - \ln p^0]$$

$$+ \tfrac{1}{2} \left[\frac{\partial \ln \Pi^*}{\partial t}(x^1,p^1,t^1) + \frac{\partial \ln \Pi^*}{\partial t}(x^0,p^0,t^0) \right] [t^1 - t^0].$$

Now define the *impact effect on real value added of technological change* as $\tau^*(x,p,t) \equiv \partial \ln \Pi^*(x,p,t)/\partial t$. This simply a convenient way of summarizing the percentage change in real value added due to a small increment of time. In particular, define $\tau^{*1} \equiv \partial \ln \Pi^*(x^1,p^1,t^1)\partial t$ and $\tau^{*0} \equiv \partial \ln \Pi^*(x^0,p^0,t^0)/\partial t$. Substitution of these definitions plus the relations (138) plus the identities $\Pi^*(x^1,p^1,t^1) = p^1 \cdot y^1$ and $\Pi^*(x^0,p^0,t^0) = p^0 \cdot y^0$ into (139) yields

$$\text{(140)} \qquad \tfrac{1}{2}[\tau^{*1} + \tau^{*0}][t^1 - t^0] = \ln\left[\frac{p^1 \cdot y^1}{p^0 \cdot y^0}\right] - \sum_{m=1}^{M} \tfrac{1}{2}\left[\frac{p^1{}_m y^1{}_m}{p^1 \cdot y^1} + \frac{p^0{}_m y^0{}_m}{p^0 \cdot y^0}\right] \ln\left[\frac{p^1{}_m}{p^0{}_m}\right] - \sum_{n=1}^{N} \tfrac{1}{2}\left[\frac{w^1{}_n x^1{}_n}{w^1 \cdot x^1} + \frac{w^0{}_n x^0{}_n}{w^0 \cdot x^0}\right] \ln\left[\frac{x^1{}_m}{x^0{}_m}\right].$$

After exponentiating both sides of (140), we get

$$\text{(141)} \qquad e^{1/2[\tau^{*1}+\tau^{*0}][t^1-t^0]} = \tilde{Q}_0(p^0,p^1,y^0,y^1)/Q_0(w^0,w^1,x^0,x^1),$$

an *implicit* Törnqvist index of outputs divided by the Törnqvist index of inputs. Thus the right-hand side of (141) is almost identical[93] to the right-hand side of (124), and the Jorgenson and Griliches (1967, 1972) measure of technical progress can be (approximately) justified in the context of a general (not necessarily separable) technology.

Finally, suppose Π^* satisfies the additional restrictions:

$$\text{(142)} \qquad \beta_n = 0,\ n = 1,2,\ldots,N,\ \epsilon_m = 0,\ m = 1,2,\ldots,M \text{ and } \gamma = 0.$$

Then $\Pi^*(x,p,t) = e^{\beta_0 t}\,\Pi^*(x,p,0) = \Pi^*(xe^{\beta_0 t},p,0)$; that is, technical change is of the primary factor augmenting strongly Hicks's neutral variety. Then $\tau^{*1} = \tau^{*0} = \beta_0$ and (141) becomes

$$\text{(143)} \qquad e^{\beta_0[t^1-t^0]} = \tilde{Q}_0(p^0,p^1,y^0,y^1)/Q_0(w^0,w^1,x^0,x^1).$$

Usher [1974, p. 278] has criticized the use of the continuous time Divisia index (recall section 8.2.3) in the measurement of total factor productivity. I conclude this section by evaluating my measure of the residual (141) in the light of Usher's objections.

Usher's (1974, pp. 277–82) first objection to the Divisia index is that it will not give the correct answer unless the technology is homothetic[94] and technical change affects the technology in a Hicks neutral manner. In my model the technology is restricted to be homothetic, since I have imposed constant returns to scale on my technology by the restrictions (137) above, and thus this part of Usher's objection applies also to my model. However, we do not require Hicks neutral technological change in my model: isoquants are allowed to twist owing to technical change.

Usher's (1974, p. 278) second objection to the Divisia index is that it is defined using time as a continuous variable but has to be computed using some sort of discrete time approximation, and that this approximation will introduce errors that will possibly cumulate over time. My method of calculating the residual seems free from this defect of the Divisia index, since (141) can be evaluated as an exact equality using discrete time data. However, in reality my method is not entirely free from this criticism, since it is unlikely that my modified translog variable profit function Π^* defined by (135) could provide a very accurate approximation to the actual technology we are modeling for very long periods of time.[95]

Usher's (1974, p. 278) third criticism of the Divisia index also applies to my formula (141): the formula depends on the assumption that there is competitive price-taking behavior on the part of producers. However, the assumption of competitive behavior can readily be relaxed in theory: if there is monopolistic pricing behavior on the part of a producer, all we have to do is replace the observed w, p prices that occur in (141) with the appropriate marginal prices.[96] In practice this is extremely difficult to do.

Usher's (1974, p. 288) final criticism of the Divisia index methodology is more subtle than the criticisms above and deserves to be extensively quoted:

> The 1965 graduate is equally productive in some occupations, more productive in others, and he possesses skills that were unknown in 1940 because they depend on technology developed in the intervening period. The point I am making is that the relative wage of college graduates has been preserved because, and only because, technical advance has brought forth new skills and has made it profitable for people to acquire these skills, so that what we measure as labour input contains a very large component of technical change. Inputs with the same name are not the same inputs at different periods of time. . . . These considerations suggest that the use of the Divisia index coupled with the practice of treating factors of production with identical names as though they were identical factors of production may be leading us to attribute a disproportionate share of observed economic growth to the mere replication of factors of production, and may conceal the vital role of invention.

Obviously the above criticism applies with equal force to my formula (141). Of course, one method of attenuating the force of Usher's criticism would be to treat changed inputs as new inputs. This leads us to consider the new goods problem, a problem that will be considered in section 8.6.

Before studying the new goods problem, we will study one additional issue in the measurement of total factor productivity: the problem of defining an aggregate over sectors (or producers) measure of technical change.

8.5.3 Sectoral Estimates of Total Factor Productivity versus Economywide Measures

Domar (1961), in a classic paper,[97] raised the issue of working out a method of measuring technical progress that would be invariant to the degree of aggregation and integration of processes (at the firm level), firms, industries (aggregates of firms), and sectors (aggregates of industries): "We should be free to take the economy apart, to aggregate one industry with another, to integrate final products with their inputs, and to reassemble the economy once more and possibly over different time units without affecting the magnitude of the Residual. The latter's rate of growth should, therefore, be invariant to the degree of aggregation and integration and to the choice of time unit, be it a year or a decade" (Domar 1961, pp. 713–14).

Suppose we have two time periods, J sectors (or processes, or firms, or industries), and that the constant returns to scale technology of each sector can be represented by a variable profit function (which can be interpreted as a value-added function)[98] Π^j, where

$$(144)\qquad \Pi^j(x^{rj}, p^r, t^r) \equiv \max_y\{p^r \cdot y : (y, x^{rj}) \in S^{jt^r}\} = p^r \cdot y^{rj} = w^{rj} \cdot x^{rj}, \quad r = 0, 1; \quad j = 1,2, \ldots, J,$$

where S^{jt^r} is the jth sector's production possibilities set at time t^r, $x^{rj} \equiv (x^{rj}_1, \ldots, x^{rj}_{N_j}) \rangle\rangle 0_{N_j}$ is an N-dimensional vector of primary inputs used by sector j during period r, $w^{rj} \equiv (w_1^{rj}, \ldots, w^{rj}_{N_j}) \rangle\rangle 0_{N_j}$ is the corresponding vector of primary input prices the jth sector faces during period r, $p^r \equiv (p^r_1, \ldots, p^r_M) \rangle\rangle 0_M$ is the vector of positive final product (and intermediate input) prices all sectors face during period r, and $y^{rj}_1, \ldots, y^{rj}_M)$ is the vector of outputs produced (and intermediate inputs used) by the jth sector during period r. As usual, if $y^{rj}_m > 0$, then the jth sector is producing the mth good during period r while if $y^{rj}_m < 0$, then the mth good is being utilized as an input by the jth sector during period r. Thus the components of y^{rj} are not restricted in sign but $p^r \cdot y^{rj} > 0$, since the value of outputs (minus the value of intermediate inputs used), $p^r \cdot y^{rj}$, equals the value of primary inputs used by the jth sector during period r, $w^{rj} \cdot x^{rj} > 0$. Note also that the primary inputs need not be the same across sectors, but that each sector faces the same output (and intermediate input) prices.

Define the aggregate real value function Π as

$$\text{(145)}\quad \Pi(x^{r1},\ldots,x^{rJ},p^r,t^r) \equiv \max_{y^1,\ldots,y^J}\{p^r\cdot\left(\sum_{j=1}^{J} y^j\right): (y^j,x^{rj}) \in S^{jt^{\bar{r}}}, j=1,\ldots,J\} = \sum_{j=1}^{J} \max_{y^j}\{p^r \cdot y^j : (y^j,x^{rj}) \in S^{jt^r}\}$$

$$\text{(146)}\quad = \sum_{j=1}^{J} \Pi^j(x^{rj},p^r,t^r) = p^r\cdot\left(\sum_{j=1}^{J} y^{rj}\right).$$

Thus aggregate value added is equal to the sum of sectoral value added. Define the aggregate net output vector in period r as

$$\text{(147)}\quad y^r \equiv \sum_{j=1}^{J} y^{rj}, \quad r=0,1,$$

and define the "aggregate" vectors of inputs and input prices as

$$\text{(148)}\quad x^r \equiv (x^{r1}, x^{r2},\ldots,x^{rJ}), \quad r=0,1$$

$$\text{(149)}\quad w^r \equiv (w^{r1}, w^{r2},\ldots,w^{rJ}), \quad r=0,1.$$

Finally, define the *sectoral technical change impact coefficients* during period r (assuming differentiability of the Π^j with respect to time) as

$$\text{(150)}\quad \tau^{rj} \equiv \partial \ln \Pi^j(x^{rj},p^r,t^r)/\partial t, \quad r=0,1; j=1,2,\ldots,J,$$

and define the *aggregate technical change impact coefficients* during period r as

$$\text{(151)}\quad \tau^r \equiv \partial \ln \Pi(x^r,p^r,t^r)/\partial t, \quad r=0,1.$$

Using (146) above, it is easy to show that the following relationship between the sectoral coefficients τ^{rj} and the aggregate technical change impact coefficient τ^r holds:

$$\text{(152)}\quad \tau^r = \sum_{j=1}^{J} \frac{\partial \ln \Pi^j}{\partial t}(x^{rj},p^r,t^r)\,\frac{\Pi^j(x^{rj},p^r,t^r)}{\Pi(x^r,p^r,t^r)} = \sum_{j=1}^{J} \tau^{rj} s^{rj}, \ r=0,1,$$

using the definitions (150) and defining the sectoral value added shares as $s^{rj} \equiv \Pi^j(x^{rj},p^r,t^r)/\Pi(x^r,p^r,t^r) = p^r\cdot y^{rj}/p^r\cdot y^r$.

Recall that in section 8.5.2 I indicated that, under certain conditions, an arithmetic average of the impact coefficients $\frac{1}{2}[\tau^0 + \tau^1]$ could be calculated using only observable price and quantity data. Using (152), we see that the following relationship holds between the sectoral and aggregate average technical change coefficients:

$$(153) \qquad \tfrac{1}{2}[\tau^0 + \tau^1] = \sum_{j=1}^{J} \tfrac{1}{2}[\tau^{0j}s^{0j} + \tau^{1j}s^{1j}].$$

Now suppose that for each sector the technology can be adequately represented by a sectoral translog variable profit function Π^{j*} similar to the function defined by (135), (136), and (137). Then for each sector we can derive an identity similar to (141):

$$(154) \qquad e^{1/2[\tau^{0j}+\tau^{1j}][t^1-t^0]} = \tilde{Q}_0(p^0,p^1,y^{0j},y^{1j})/ Q_0(w^{0j},w^{1j},x^{0j},x^{1j}) \text{ for } j = 1, 2, \ldots, J.$$

Unfortunately, the relations (154) do not enable us to calculate the terms $\tfrac{1}{2}[\tau^{0j}s^{0j} + \tau^{1j}s^{1j}]$, which are needed to calculate the average of the aggregate technical change impact coefficients $\tfrac{1}{2}[\tau^0 + \tau^1]$ via formula (153). However, if we assume that the sectoral translog variable profit functions Π^{j*} satisfy the additional restrictions similar to (142) (so that technical change is strongly Hicks neutral in each sector), then we can show, as in section 8.5.2, that

$$(155) \qquad \tau^{0j} = \tau^{1j} \equiv \tau^j \text{ for } j = 1, 2, \ldots, J,$$

and the relations (154) can be rewritten as

$$(156) \qquad e^{\tau^j[t^1-t^0]} = \tilde{Q}_0(p^0,p^1,y^{0j},y^{1j})/Q_0(w^{0j},w^{1j},x^{0j},x^{1j}), \quad j = 1, \ldots, J,$$

which means that the (constant) sectoral technical change coefficients can be calculated using observable price and quantity data for the two periods. Using (153), (155), and (156), it can be seen that the *correct average aggregate technical change impact coefficient* $\tfrac{1}{2}[\tau^0 + \tau^1]$ can be calculated from observable data using the following equations:

$$(157) \qquad e^{1/2[\tau^0+\tau^1][t^1-t^0]} = e^{\sum_{j=1}^{J} \tau^j \, 1/2[s^{0j}+s^{1j}][t^1-t^0]}$$

$$= \prod_{j=1}^{J} [e^{\tau^j[t^1-t^0]}]^{1/2[s^{0j}+s^{1j}]}$$

$$= \prod_{j=1}^{J} [\tilde{Q}_0(p^0,p^1,y^{0j},y^{1j})/Q_0(w^{0j},w^{1j},x^{0j},x^{1j})]^{1/2[s^{0j}+s^{1j}]}$$

$$(158) \qquad \equiv f(p^0,p^1,y^0,y^1,w^0,w^1,x^0,x^1).$$

Thus the correct aggregate measure of technical change, $e^{1/2[\tau^0+\tau^1][t^1-t^0]}$, is equal to a *geometric average* of the sectoral measures of technical change, $e^{\tau_j[t^1-t^0]}$, with weights equal to the sector's average share of value added, $\frac{1}{2}[s^{0j}+s^{1j}]$ (which sum to unity).

Suppose now that we (incorrectly) assume that the technology of the "economy" (i.e., the aggregate over sectors technology) was represented by a translog variable profit function $\Pi^*(x^r,p^r,t^r)$ similar to that defined by (135), (136), and (137) (except that here $x^r \equiv (x^{r1}, x^{r2}, \ldots, x^{rJ})$ and each $x^{rj} \rangle\rangle 0_{N_j}$ is a vector and we calculated the following *incorrect average aggregate technical change impact coefficient* $\frac{1}{2}[\tau^{*0} + \tau^{*1}]$ from observable data using the following equation that corresponds to formula (141):

$$(159) \qquad e^{1/2[\tau^{*0}+\tau^{*1}][t^1-t^0]} \equiv \tilde{Q}_0(p^0,p^1, \sum_{j=1}^{J} y^{0j}, \sum_{j=1}^{J} y^{1j})/Q_0(w^0,w^1,x^0,x^1)$$

$$(160) \qquad \equiv g(p^0,p^1,y^0,y^1,w^0,w^1,x^0,x^1).$$

The formula (159) is incorrect because we are assuming that each of the sectoral technologies is *precisely* representable by a translog variable profit function satisfying the appropriate restrictions, and thus the aggregate technology is not precisely representable by a translog variable profit function. However, the aggregate technology could be *approximated* to the second order by an aggregate translog variable profit function. Thus we would hope that the two estimates of average aggregate technical progress defined by (157) and (159) would give approximately the same answer when applied to empirical data. This hope turns out to be justified, as the following theorem indicates.

(161) *Theorem*: The functions f and g, defined by (158) and (160), respectively, differentially approximate each other to the second order[99] at any point where $p^0 = p^1$, $w^0 = w^1$, $x^0 = x^1$ and $y^0 = y^1$.

The proof of this theorem is a very tedious series of computations that can be simplified using tricks similar to those used in Diewert (1978*b*).

8.6 The New Goods Problem

8.6.1 New Goods and Index Number Formulas

One of the problems that has troubled index number theorists and practioners is constructing price and quantity indexes that are comparable over a period when new commodities are being introduced into the economy. For example, how can one construct meaningful price and quantity indexes of capital during a period of time when new capital goods are constantly appearing on (and disappearing from) the market?

My solution to the problem is quite conventional:[100] assume that the consumer (or producer) is consistently trying to solve the aggregator maximization subject to an expenditure constraint problem $\max_x\{f(x) : p^r \cdot x \leq p^r \cdot x^r, x \geq 0_N\}$ for $r = 0,1$ except that in period 0, when some goods are not available, the aggregator maximization problem has additional constraints imposed upon it that set the components of $x = (x_1,x_2, \ldots ,x_N)$ that correspond to unavailable goods equal to zero.

For the sake of definiteness, let us suppose the first good is the new good that is introduced into the economy at some stage.

Obviously, if a given price and quantity are always zero, then when calculating a price or quantity index the zero good can simply be omitted from the computations. However, if a good is at a zero level during period 0 and nonzero during period 1, it is clear that the Törnqvist quantity index number formula Q_0 cannot be used, since the logarithm of zero is minus infinity. The Fisher quantity index Q_2 is well defined even if a subset of prices and quantities is zero, but we shall show below that it is not in general correct (from the viewpoint of the theory of exact index numbers) to use Q_2 without some modification.

Suppose that the nonzero prices and quantities in period 0 are $p^0{}_2,p^0{}_3, \ldots, p^0{}_N$ and $x^0{}_2, x^0{}_3, \ldots ,x^0{}_N$, while the nonzero prices and quantities in period 1 are $p^1 \equiv (p^1{}_1, p^1{}_2, \ldots, p^1{}_N)$ and $x^1 \equiv (x^1{}_1, x^1{}_2, \ldots, x^1{}_N)$ respectively. We suppose that the quantity of good 1 in period 0 is $x^0{}_1 = 0$. In some circumstances we will often incorrectly assume that the price of good 1 in period 0 is also zero. However, when a new good enters the domain of our model during period 1, we should attempt to estimate the *reservation price* of the new good for the previous period that would rationalize the zero demand for the new good of the previous period.

Thus the theoretically correct procedure would be to form an estimate of the (reservation) price of good 1 in period 0, $p^0{}_1 > 0$, say, and then apply our usual index number formulas (P_2 and Q_2, say), using $p^0 \equiv (p^0{}_1,p^0{}_2, \ldots ,p^0{}_N)$, $x^0 \equiv (0, x^0{}_2, \ldots, x^0{}_N)$ and the period 1 price and quantity vectors, p^1 and x^1. Let us denote the theoretically correct Fisher price index in the usual manner as:

(162) $$P_2(p^0,p^1; x^0,x^1) = [(p^1 \cdot x^0 p^1 \cdot x^1)/(p^0 \cdot x^0 p^0 \cdot x^1)]^{1/2}.$$

Note that the theoretically correct index depends on the empirically unobservable price $p^0{}_1 > 0$. If we incorrectly set $p^0{}_1 = 0$ and substitute the resulting price vector into (162), we obtain the following incorrect Fisher price index (recall that $x^0{}_1 = 0$):

$$(163)\qquad P^{**}_2(p^0,p^1;x^0,x^1) \equiv P_2([0,p^0_2,\ldots,p^0_N],p^1;$$
$$[0,x^0_2,\ldots,x^0_N],x^1) = \left[\frac{p^1\cdot x^0\; p^1\cdot x^1}{p^0\cdot x^0(p^0\cdot x^1 - p^0_1 x^1_1)}\right]^{1/2}.$$

Another theoretically incorrect Fisher price index could be obtained by simply ignoring good 1 for both periods; that is, set $p^0_1 = p^1_1 = x^0_1 = x^1_1 = 0$ and substitute the resulting price and quantity vectors into (162) to obtain the following index:

$$(164)\qquad P^*_2(p^0,p^1;x^0,x^1) \equiv$$
$$P_2([0,p^0_2,\ldots,p^0_N],[0,p^1_2,\ldots,p^N_2];$$
$$[0,x^0_2,\ldots,x^0_N],[0,x^1_2,\ldots,x^1_N])$$
$$= \left[\frac{p^1\cdot x^0(p^1\cdot x^1 - p^1_1 x^1_1)}{p^0\cdot x^0(p^0\cdot x^1 - p^0_1 x^1_1)}\right]^{1/2}.$$

The virtue of the incorrect indexes P^*_2 and P^{**}_2 is that they may be calculated without a knowledge of the empirically unobservable $p^0_1 > 0$.

We now evaluate the *bias* in each of the incorrect index number formulas; that is, we take the ratio of (163) to (162) and the ratio of (164) to (162):

$$(165)\qquad \frac{P^{**}_2(p^0,p^1;x^0,x^1)}{P_2(p^0,p^1;x^0,x^1)} = [1/(1-s^{01}_1)]^{1/2} > 1$$

$$(166)\qquad \frac{P^*_2(p^0,p^1;x^0,x^1)}{P_2(p^0,p^1;x^0,x^1)} = \left[\frac{1-s^{11}_1}{1-s^{01}_1}\right]^{1/2},$$

where $s^{01}_1 \equiv p^0_1\, x^1_1/p^0\cdot x^1$, the share of good 1 using period 0 prices and period 1 quantities, and
$s^{11}_1 \equiv p^1_1\, x^1_1/p^1\cdot x^1$, the share of good 1 using period 1 prices and period 1 quantities.

Several points immediately become apparent. (*a*) The Fisher price index P_2^{**} that incorrectly sets the price of good 1 equal to zero for period 0 is always biased upward. (*b*) The Fisher price index P^*_2 that incorrectly ignores the existence of good 1 for both periods need not be biased. The bias will be zero if $p^1_1/p^0_1 = p^1\cdot x^1/p^0\cdot x^1 = P_P(p^0, p^1; x^0,x^1)$; that is, the bias will be zero if the relative change in the price of good 1 over the two periods is equal to the general change in prices as measured by a Paasche price index. In general we would expect that the relative price of good 1 would be higher in period 0 when good 1 is not yet being demanded; that is, we would expect that $p^1_1/p^0_1 \leq p^1\cdot x^1/p^0\cdot x^1$, in which case

$$(167) \qquad P_2(p^0,p^1;x^0,x^1) \leq P^*_2(p^0,p^1;x^0,x^1) < P^{**}_2(p^0,p^1;x^0,x^1).$$

Thus, in general P^*_2 will probably have a upward bias, while P^{**}_2 will definitely have a larger upward bias. Hence, in empirical applications where nothing is known about the magnitude of the reservation price, p^0_1, I would recommend the use of P^*_2 rather than P^{**}_2 (which is sometimes used).

The quantity index corresponding to P^*_2 is defined by deflating the actual expenditure ratio (remember $x^0_1 = 0$) by P^*_2:

$$(168) \qquad Q^*_2(p^0,p^1;x^0,x^1) \equiv [p^1\cdot x^1/\left(\sum_{i=2}^{N} p^0_i x^0_i\right)] / P^*_2(p^0,p^1;x^0,x^1) = [p^1\cdot x^1/p^0\cdot x^0]/P^*_2(p^0,p^1;x^0,x^1).$$

Thus the quantity index Q^*_2 can be calculated without a knowledge of p^0_1. Note that P^*_2 and Q^*_2 are consistent with the weak factor reversal test.

In the following section we will consider a method for obtaining empirical estimates of demand reservation prices.

8.6.2 A Simple Econometric Approach to the New Goods Problem

Let us consider a slightly more general situation than the model of the previous section. We now suppose that only the first K goods to be aggregated are available in period 0 where $1 < K < N$ and that N goods are available in period t, $t = 1, 2, \ldots, T$. Then the period 0 aggregator maximization problem is

$$(169) \qquad \max_{x_1,x_2,\ldots,x_K} \{f(x_1,x_2,\ldots,x_K,0,\ldots,0): \sum_{k=1}^{K} p^0_k x_k \leq Y^0, x_k \geq 0, k = 1, 2, \ldots, K\},$$

where $Y^0 > 0$ is period 0 expenditure, and the period t aggregator maximization problems are

$$(170) \qquad \max_{x_1,x_2,\ldots,x_N} \{f(x_1,x_2,\ldots,x_N): \sum_{k=1}^{N} p^t_k x_k \leq Y^t, x_k \geq 0, k = 1,2,\ldots,N\}; t = 1,\ldots,T,$$

where $Y^t > 0$ is period t expenditure. Denote a solution to the period 0 aggregation maximization problem by the K-dimensional vector $\tilde{x}^0 \equiv (x^0_1,x^0_2,\ldots,x^0_K)$ and define the N-dimensional vector $x^0 \equiv (x^0_1,x^0_2,\ldots,x^0_K,0,\ldots,0) = (\tilde{x}^0,0_{N-K})$ and similarly denote period 0 prices by the K-dimensional vector $\tilde{p}^0 \equiv (p^0_1,p^0_2,\ldots,p^0_K)$. Denote a solution to the period t aggregation maximization problem by the N-dimensional vector $x^t \equiv (x^t_1, x^t_2, \ldots, x^t_N)$ and define the period t price vector as $p^t \equiv (p^t_1, p^t_2, \ldots, p^t_N) \rangle\rangle 0_N$.

The "demand reservation prices" $p^0_{k+1}, \ldots, p^0_N$ are defined to be prices that "rationalize" the consumer's or producer's choice of x^0 in period 0, assuming that the new goods were available in period 0; that is, $(p^0_{K+1}, p^0_{K+2}, \ldots, p^0_N)$ is a set of period 0 demand reservation (or shadow) prices if x^0, a solution to (169), is also a solution to:

$$\text{(171)} \qquad \max_x\{f(x) : p^0 \cdot x \leq p^0 \cdot x^0, x \geq 0_N\},$$

where $p^0 \equiv (\tilde{p}^0, p^0_{k+1}, p^0_{k+2}, \ldots, p^0_N)$.

If f were differentiable at x^0 and we knew the functional form for f, p^0 could be defined by using the first-order conditions for the constrained maximization problem (171) (after eliminating the Lagrange multiplier); that is, $p^0/p^0 \cdot x^0 = \nabla_x f(x^0)/x^0 \cdot \nabla f(x^0)$ or, since $p^0 \cdot x^0 = \tilde{p}^0 \cdot \tilde{x}^0$,

$$\text{(172)} \qquad p^0 = (\tilde{p}^0 \cdot \tilde{x}^0) \nabla_x f(x^0)/x^0 \cdot \nabla f(x^0).$$

Thus, if the functional form for the aggregator function f were known, formula (172) could be used to estimate the "shadow" price components $p^0_{k+1}, \ldots, p^0_N$ of $p^0 \equiv (\tilde{p}^0, p^0_{k+1}, \ldots, p^0_N) \equiv (p^0_1, \ldots, p^0_k, p^0_{k+1}, \ldots, p^0_N)$.

Now assume $f = f_r$ for some $r > 0$[101] where the quadratic means of order r aggregator functions f_r were defined in section 8.2.4:

$$\text{(173)} \qquad f_r(x) \equiv \sum_{i=1}^{N} \sum_{j=1}^{N} a_{ij} x^{r}_i{}^{/2} x^{r}_j{}^{/2}{}^{1/r};\ a_{ij} = a_{ji}.$$

Assuming that all components of $\tilde{x}^0$ are nonzero, the Kuhn-Tucker conditions for the period 0 aggregator maximization problem (169) imply:

$$\text{(174)} \qquad \tilde{p}^0/\tilde{p}^0 \cdot \tilde{x}^0 = \nabla_{\tilde{x}} f_r(\tilde{x}^0, 0_{N-K})/f_r(\tilde{x}^0, 0_{N-K}).$$

Similarly, assuming that all components of x^1 are nonzero,[102] the Kuhn-Tucker conditions for the period t aggregator maximization problems (170) imply:

$$\text{(175)} \qquad p^t/p^t \cdot x^t = \nabla_x f_r(x^t)/f_r(x^t), \quad t = 1, 2, \ldots, T.$$

Make the base period normalization:

$$\text{(176)} \qquad f_r(\tilde{x}^0, 0_{N-K}) = 1.$$

Now regard the system of equations defined by (174), (175), and (176) as a system of equations in the unknown a_{ij} parameters occurring in f_r defined by (173); that is, we are back to *method I* (recall section 8.2.2) for the determination of an aggregator function. The equations (174)–(176) are particularly simple if $r = 1$ or $r = 2$. Once the parameters a_{ij} that occur in the definition of f_r have been statistically determined, estimated demand reservation prices for period 0 can be calculated using formula (172). However, in order to estimate econometrically the $N(N+1)/2$ a_{ij} parameters,[103] we will require that the number of observations $T+1$ be large relative to the number of goods N. In many practical situations, this condition is unlikely to be met.

8.6.3 The Hedonic Approach to the New Goods Problem

Many capital goods (e.g., trucks) came in so many varieties that it is possible to think of the good as being indexed by varying amounts $x_1,x_2,\ldots,x_N$ of N continuous characteristics. For example, in Griliches's (1961) classic work,[104] automobiles were indexed by the continuous variables horsepower, weight, and length in addition to some discrete variables. In this section I will attempt to provide a theoretical justification for Griliches's hedonic price index approach.

Let us suppose that the producers of "trucks" can produce a truck indexed by the vector of characteristics $x \equiv (x_1,x_2,\ldots,x_N)$ in period r at a price $P_r(x)$ equal to the minimum cost of production:

$$P_r(x) \equiv C(w^r,x), \tag{177}$$

where C is a "truck" producer's *joint cost function*, w^r is a vector of input prices the truck producer faces during period r, and x is the vector of characteristics that indexes the truck. It can be shown[105] that, under reasonable assumptions on the technology, the joint cost function C will be nondecreasing, linearly homogeneous, and concave in the input prices w, and, assuming that we are measuring characteristics so that more of a characteristic increases the cost of a truck, then C will be nondecreasing and concave in the vector x (assuming that the underlying technology is convex). In addition, we make the not-so-reasonable assumption that the technology is subject to constant returns to scale, so that C is linearly homogeneous with respect to x as well as w.

Another producer who uses "trucks" as an input into his productive process will want to solve the following profit maximization problem:

$$\max_{u_0,u,x}\{p^r\cdot u + P_r(x)u_0 : u_1 = t(\tilde{u}, u_0x)\}, \tag{178}$$

where u_0 is the number of "trucks" with characteristics x purchased[106] during period r at price $P_r(x)$, $u \equiv (u_1,\tilde{u}) \equiv (u_1,u_2,u_3,\ldots,u_M)$ is a vector of nontruck outputs (indexed positively) and inputs (indexed negatively) produced and utilized by the producer, $p^r \equiv (p^r{}_1,p^r{}_2,\ldots,p^r{}_M) \rangle\rangle 0_M$ is the vector of nontruck prices facing the producer during period r, and t is the producer's transformation function.[107] Note that we are assuming that characteristics enter the producer's transformation function as $u_0x = (u_0x_1, u_0x_2, \ldots, u_0x_N)$, the number of "trucks" purchased times the per truck vector of characteristics. This is not an innocuous assumption. Now define the total characteristics purchased vector y as

(179) $$y \equiv u_0 x$$

and substitute (177) and (179) into (178). Making use of the linear homogeneity in x property of C, $C(w^r,x)u_0 = C(w^r,u_0x)$, (178) becomes

(180) $$\max_{u,y}\{p^r \cdot u + C(w^r,y) : u_1 = t(\tilde{u},y), u \equiv (u_1,\tilde{u})\}.$$

If t is differentiable with respect to its arguments and C is differentiable with respect to the components of y, then a solution u^r, y^r to (180) will satisfy the following conditions:

(181) $$p^r \equiv (p^r{}_1, p^r{}_2, \ldots, p^r{}_M) = \lambda^r(1, \partial t(\tilde{u}^r,y^r)/\partial u_2, \ldots,$$
$$\partial t(\tilde{u}^r,y^r/\partial u_M),$$

(182) $$\nabla_y C(w^r,y^r) = \lambda^r \nabla_y t(\tilde{u}^r,y^r), \quad r = 1, 2, \ldots, T,$$

where $\nabla_y C(w^r,y^r) \equiv (\partial C(w^r,y^r)/\partial y_1, \ldots, \partial C(w^r,y^r)/\partial y_M)$, $\nabla_y t(\tilde{u}^r,y^r) \equiv (\partial t(\tilde{u}^r,y^r)/\partial y_1, \ldots, \partial t(\tilde{u}^r,y^r)/\partial y_M)$, $u^r \equiv (u^r{}_1, \tilde{u}^r)$, and λ^r is the Lagrange multiplier for the constrained maximization problem (180).

From (182) it can be seen that the partial derivative $\partial C(w^r,y^r)/\partial y_n$ can be interpreted as the price of one unit of the nth characteristic in period r, $P^r{}_n$; that is, define

(183) $$P^r \equiv \nabla_y C(w^r,y^r),$$

where$P^r \equiv (P^r{}_1,P^r{}_2, \ldots, P^r{}_N)$ is a vector of characteristic prices during period r. The constant returns to scale property of C in y implies that

(184) $$P^r \cdot y^r = C(w^r,y^r) = C(w^r,x^r)u^r{}_0.$$

Thus, if econometric estimates of the "truck" producer's joint cost function are available and if we can observe a purchasing firm's input of "trucks" $u^r{}_0$ with characteristics x^r during period r, then we can calculate the characteristic prices P^r using (183), and we can decompose the purchasing firm's expenditure on "trucks," $P_r(x)u^r{}_0$, into a price component P^r and a quantity component y^r. At this point, standard index number formulas can be used to form a "truck" aggregate for the purchasing firm.

A further useful specification of this model is possible. Suppose the truck-producing technology is separable[108] so that the joint cost function C decomposes in the following manner:

(185) $$C(w,x) = c(w)g(x).$$

The effect of the additional assumption (185) is that a combination of cross-sectional and time-series analysis can be used to estimate the parameters of C; that is, we can econometrically estimate the parameters that occur in the following equation:

$$P_r(x^{rj}) = a_r g(x^{rj}), \quad r = 1, 2, \ldots, T; j = 1, 2, \ldots, J, \tag{186}$$

where $a_r \equiv c(w^r)$ and $P_r(x^{rj}) \equiv C(w^r, x^{rj})$ is the price of a "truck" with characteristics x^{rj} purchased by the jth firm during period r.

If, in addition, the function g in (185) can be approximated by the translog functional form, then (186) can be rewritten as (after taking logarithms of both sides):

$$\ln P_r(x^{rj}) = \ln a_r + \ln \alpha_0 + \sum_{n=1}^{N} \alpha_n \ln x^{rj}{}_n \tag{187}$$
$$+ \tfrac{1}{2} \sum_{n=1}^{N} \sum_{m=1}^{N} \alpha_{nm} \ln x^{rj}{}_n \ln x^{rj}{}_m$$
$$r = 1,2, \ldots ,T; j = 1,2, \ldots ,J,$$

where $\sum_{n=1}^{N} \alpha_n = 1$, $\alpha_{nm} = \alpha_{mn}$ and $\sum_{n=1}^{N} \alpha_{nm} = 0$ for $m = 1,2, \ldots, N$. If we further specify that $\alpha_{nm} = 0$ for all n,m, then the model defined by (187) becomes very close to Griliches's (1961) classic hedonic prices model. However, if $\alpha_{nm} = 0$ for all n,m and $\alpha_n > 0$ with $\sum_{n=1}^{N} \alpha_n = 1$, then the function g[109] reduces to the Cobb-Douglas function that is concave in x instead of being convex in x. Thus the Griliches model cannot be obtained as a special case of our model (187), which is based on the assumption that the "truck" producer's technology is separable. However, if we assumed that the *consumers* of "trucks" all used a concave, linearly homogeneous, weakly separable aggregator function f in the characteristics x in order to form a "truck" aggregate $f(x)$, then instead of (186) we would obtain the model $P_r(x^{rj}) = a_r f(x^{rj})$, where a_r can be interpreted as the price of the "truck" aggregate during period r. If we further specify f to be the translog aggregator function, we would again obtain the system of equations (187), but now the Cobb-Douglas case is perfectly consistent with this second model of producer behavior.

There are many difficulties with these theoretical treatments of the new goods problem in the context of a continuous characteristics model. However, in certain industries it should be possible to modify these models into empirically useful techniques.[110]

We have discussed the problems of aggregation over goods and aggregation over producers, but we have not yet discussed the problem of aggregation over time.

8.7 Aggregation over Time: The Problem of Seasonality

All the analysis thus far has been based on the implicit assumption that the time under consideration is a year, or a decade, or some period where seasonal influences are absent. The questions I address in this section are: (*a*) how should "monthly" (or weekly) indexes be constructed (*b*) how should "annual" indexes be related to the monthly indexes? These questions are relevant to the problem of forming capital aggregates as well as other aggregates.

Zarnowitz (1961) looks at the problem of constructing seasonal index in an excellent paper. I extend his analysis a bit by utilizing some of the results discussed earlier in the present paper.

Suppose x^{rm} is a solution to the following producer (or consumer) aggregator maximization problem[111] in year r and month m:

(188) $$\max_x\{f(y^{rm},x) : p^{rm}\cdot x \leq p^{rm}\cdot x^{rm}, x \geq 0_N\},$$

where $p^{rm} \equiv (p^{rm}{}_1, p^{rm}{}_2, \ldots, p^{rm}{}_N) \rangle\rangle 0_N$ is the vector of goods prices facing the producer (or consumer) during year r, and month m, $y^{rm} \equiv (y^{rm}{}_1, y^{rm}{}_2, \ldots, y^{rm}{}_M) \rangle\rangle 0_M$ is a vector of variables that expresses weather and seasonal taste variations in year r and month m, and f is the producer's production function (or the consumer's subutility function) that is a function of both the goods vector $x \equiv (x_1,x_2, \ldots, x_N)$ and the vector of seasonal variables y^{rm}. Suppose further that the aggregator function f can be closely approximated by a linearly homogeneous in x translog aggregator function $f^*(y,x)$ where f^* is defined exactly in the same manner as D^* was defined equation (85). Then we can prove the following result in exactly the same manner as equation (70) or theorem (84) was proved:

(189) *Theorem*: $$Q_0\,(p^{rm}, p^{sn}, x^{rm}, x^{sn}) = f^*(y^*, x^{sn})/ f^*(y^*, x^{rm}),$$

where Q_0 is the Törnqvist quantity index and the vector of average seasonal variables y^* is defined by $y^* \equiv (y^*{}_1, y^*{}_2, \ldots, y^*{}_M)$ where $y^*{}_j \equiv (y^{rm}{}_j\, y^{sm}{}_j)^{1/2}, j = 1, 2, \ldots, M.$

The proof of this theorem rests on the assumptions of: (*a*) optimizing behavior, (*b*) the translog functional form for the aggregator function, and (*3*) the quadratic approximation lemma (59).

We can now attack the questions that were posed at the beginning of this section. First, should the monthly indexes be computed using the chain principle across months within a year, or should we construct twelve separate monthly indexes, chaining the twelve indexes across years? Thus we could calculate the Törnqvist indexes $Q_0(p^{rm}, p^{r,m+1}, x^{rm},x^{r,m+1})$, or the twelve monthly Törnqvist indexes $Q_0(p^{rm}, p^{r+1,m}, x^{rm}, x^{r+1,m}), m = 1,2, \ldots, 12$. In view of theorem (189) above, it seems that the latter procedure of constructing twelve monthly indexes would be better in normal circumstances, where we would expect the seasonal variables y^{rm} to repeat themselves every twelve months. Thus, if $y^{rm} = y^{r+1,m}$, then theorem (189) tells us that we can calculate precisely the ratio we are interested in, $f^*(y^{r+1,m}, x^{r+1,m})/f^*(y^{rm},x^{rm})$, by evaluating the Törnqvist index, $Q_0(p^{rm}, p^{r+1,m}, x^{rm}, x^{r+1,m})$, using observable price and quantity data. This conclusion agrees with that reached by Hofsten and Zarnowitz, as the following quotations indicate.

> This difficulty is especially obvious if seasonal fluctuations are considered. It is unnatural to accept an index which may after a year give a result different from 1, if the prices have returned to their initial values. . . . Yearly links should then be used. [Hofsten 1952, p. 27]

> Since 1887, when Marshall first advanced the chain system and Edgeworth seconded it, many students of index numbers have come to look upon the chain index as the standard statistical solution to changing weights. But careful consideration must be given to the question of how well chain indexes can be applied to the seasonal weight changes with whose specific features they were surely not designed to cope.
>
> It is easy to demonstrate that a chain index with varying weights does not fulfill the test of proportionality (or identity). . . . Thus, on the identity test, the indexes for the same seasons should be equal, too, but they are so only for the fixed-base, not for the chain, formulae. [Zarnowitz 1961, p. 235]

Second, given that we are going to construct twelve monthly indexes, how should these indexes be related during the base year, $r = 0$? A reasonable procedure would be to use the Törnqvist quantity index formula to construct the following eleven numbers, which could be used to compare the levels of the twelve monthly indexes during the base year: $Q_0(p^{0m}, p^{0,m+1}, x^{0m}, x^{0,m+1})$, $m = 1,2,\ldots,11$. Theorem (189) can then be used to provide an economic interpretation of the resulting indexes. We should also note at this point (as does Zarnowitz 1961, p. 244) that the problem of disappearing goods giving rise to zero prices and quantities is particularly acute when we deal with seasonal indexes, and the reader is reminded of the discussion of the new goods problem in sections 8.6.1 and 8.6.2. The techniques discussed there can also be used in the present context. Summarizing the discussion thus far, I have recommended that the chain principle across months during a base year be used to construct monthly indexes for the base year, and then the chain principle across years be used to construct twelve separate monthly indexes. This procedure is of course not invariant to the choice of the base year, but in practice we would expect deviations from circularity[112] to be rather small.

Finally, there is the question of how an annual index should be related to the monthly indexes. In theory, the most appropriate way of forming annual aggregates would be to treat each good in each month as a separate argument in the index number formula; for example, we should compute $Q_0([p^{0,1}, \ldots, p^{0,12}], [p^{1,1}, \ldots, p^{1,12}], [x^{0,1}], \ldots, x^{0,12}], [x^{1,1}, \ldots, x^{1,12}])$ as representing the ratio of the aggregate in year 1 to year 0. However, we could apply the results on two-stage aggregation outlined in section 8.2.5 to conclude that a close approximation to the above aggregate ratio can be obtained by either (*a*) constructing monthly indexes and then aggregating these indexes over the year, or (*b*) constructing annual indexes for each good and then aggregating over goods. The index number formula Q_0 (or any other superlative quantity index) is to be used whenever an aggregate is calculated in the above two-stage procedures.

8.8 Concluding Comments

It is necessary to reemphasize that this discussion of capital aggregation (and aggregation in general) has taken place in the context of production function and total factor productivity estimation, where we have consistently assumed that producers are competitively profit-maximizing or cost-minimizing or both. However, I have noted that the assumption of competitive or price taking behavior can be easily relaxed in theory: simply replace observed prices with the appropriate marginal or shadow prices.[113] In practice, the assumption of competitive behavior will probably be required for some time yet in order to construct aggregates.

Given the rather narrow competitive optimizing framework, I have discussed two methods for justifying aggregation over goods such as components of the capital stock: (*a*) price proportionality[114] or Hicks's aggregation theorem (section 8.2.1), and (*b*) homogeneous weak separability (section 8.2.2). We have discussed a number of methods for justifying aggregation over sectors, including: (*c*) the method that assumes that all producers face the same prices with all goods (except possibly one) being freely variable during the period under consideration (section 8.3.2) and (*d*) a method due to Gorman (1968*a*) and Fisher (1965) that assumes some goods are fixed but the functional forms for producer's production functions are restricted in a certain manner (section 8.3.3).

In actual practice, we do not expect any of the above justifications for aggregation to hold *exactly*; however, we can hope that both methods (a) and (c) hold *approximately* at least, so that, if aggregates are used in actual applications, there is some hope that microeconomic theory will be at least approximately relevant.

I have argued that *superlative* index number formulas (recall section 8.2.4) should be used when aggregating over goods, assuming that there is a homogeneous weakly separable aggregator function defined over the goods in the aggregate, since superlative index number formulas correspond to *flexible* functional forms for aggregator functions. If the prices of the goods to be aggregated move proportionally, then the use of a superlative index number formula will also lead to the construction of an aggregate that is consistent with Hicks's aggregation theorem, even if there does not exist a homogeneous weakly separable aggregator function defined over the micro goods to be aggregated. Thus the use of a superlative index number formula is consistent with both of the general methods above for justifying aggregation over goods, and thus my first specific recommendation is that *superlative indexes* be used to construct aggregates whenever possible.

My second specific recommendation is that the *chain* principle be used (rather than a fixed base) whenever possible. Theoretical and practical reasons for this recommendation are scattered throughout the chapter and will not be reviewed here.

My third recommendation is that *rental prices* be used to weight the components of the capital stock when constructing a capital aggregate suitable for the measurement of productivity and the estimation of production functions. These rental prices should involve depreciation rates, taxes, and expectations of capital gains, although the last item presents some conceptual and practical difficulties (cf. section 8.4). However, rental prices for capital stock components need not be constructed if one employs the Hicksian view of production, which regards depreciated capital as a separate output.

My fourth specific recommendation is that *new goods* be treated in the manner outlined in section 8.6.1 when resources do not permit the implementation of the theoretically more refined techniques outlined in sections 8.6.2 and 8.6.3.

My fifth specific recommendation is that *seasonal series* be constructed in the manner outlined in section 8.7; that is, roughly speaking, "seasonal weights" must be estimated and utilized in the construction of seasonal series.

My final recommendation is that serious consideration be given to *revising the system of national accounts* used in most Western countries. The basic problem with the current system is that it is not very well suited to estimating production functions or systems of consumer demand and labor supply functions: prices that producers face are not generally distinguished from prices consumers pay. In fact, on primary input markets (labor, capital, land, and natural resources), it is often difficult to determine prices or quantities separately at all: total payments to labor, total payments to capital (including land and natural resources), and certain payments to governments (direct and indirect taxes) are distinguished in the current system of accounts, but there is no systematic decomposition of these highly aggregated payments into detailed price and quantity components for each type of labor, capital, land, and so on.

Finally, it is useful to contrast this chapter on the aggregation of capital with the excellent chapter by Murray Brown in this volume (chap. 7). Our discussions of the theoretical conditions allowing for the construction of capital aggregates have been very similar and we have reached broadly consistent conclusions—no small accomplishment considering that our papers were written completely independently. Some differences in emphasis remain—Brown's chapter has a somewhat broader theoretical coverage (his excellent discussion of the Cambridge controversies and of the general equilibrium approach to aggregation is entirely missing in my chapter), whereas mine has placed a greater emphasis on index number problems. However, taken together, perhaps the two offer a fairly comprehensive survey of the current state of aggregation theory, with particular emphasis on the problems of capital aggregation.

Appendix: Proofs of Theorems

Proof of (6)

$$\Pi(w,p) \equiv \max_{x,y}\{w^T x + p^T y : (x,y) \in S\}$$

(A1) $$= w^T x^* + p^T y^* \quad \text{by assumption}$$

$$= \max_x\{w^T x + p^T y^* : (x,y^*) \in S\}$$

$$= \Pi^*(w,y^*) + p^T y^* \quad \text{by the definition of } \Pi^*$$

$$= \Pi^*(p_0\alpha, y^*) + p^T y^* \quad \text{using (3)}$$

$$= p_0\Pi^*(\alpha,y^*) + p^T y^* \quad \text{by a homogeneity property of } \Pi^*$$

(A2) $$\equiv p_0\, y^*_0 + p^T y^* \quad \text{defining } y^*_0 \equiv \Pi^*(\alpha,y^*)$$

$$\leq \max_{y_0\, y}\{p_0 y_0 + p^T y : (y_0,y) \in S_\alpha\} \quad \text{since } (y^*_0,y^*) \in S_\alpha$$

$$\equiv \hat{\Pi}(p_0,p).$$

Suppose $\hat{\Pi}(w,p) < \Pi(p_0,p) = p_0\bar{y}_0 + p^T\bar{y}$, where $(\bar{y}_0,\bar{y}) \in S_\alpha$. Then $\bar{y}_0 = \Pi^*(\alpha,\bar{y}) = \alpha^T\bar{x}$ for some $\bar{x}$ such that $(\bar{x},\bar{y}) \in S$

$$\begin{aligned}\therefore\ \Pi(w,p) &\equiv \max_{x,y}\{p_0\alpha^T x + p^T y : (x,y) \in S\} \\ &\geq p_0\alpha^T\bar{x} + p^T\bar{y} \\ &= p_0\bar{y}_0 + p^T\bar{y} \\ &> \Pi(w,p),\end{aligned}$$

which is a contradiction, and thus our supposition is false and thus $\Pi(w,p) = \hat{\Pi}(p_0,p)$. Note that (A1) = (A2) implies that $p_0 y^*_0 = w^T x^*$, which is equivalent to (7).

Proof of (84)

The producer's technology S can be completely described by means of a transformation function t (see Diewert 1973*a*): $t(y_2,y_3,\ldots,y_M, x_1,x_2,\ldots,x_N) \equiv \max_{y_1}\{y_1 : (y_1,y_2,\ldots,y_M,x_1,\ldots,x_N) \in S\}$. Furthermore, it is easy to see that if the producer has minimized the cost $w \cdot x$ of producing a given vector of outputs $(y_1,y_2,\ldots,y_N)$, then under the usual monotonicity assumptions, the producer will also be producing the maximal amount of output 1 given that he must also produce $y_2,\ldots,y_M$ and is subject to an expenditure constraint on inputs. Thus we assume that x^0 is a solution to $\max_x\{t^*(y^0{}_2,y^0{}_3,\ldots,y^0{}_M,x) : w^0 \cdot x = w^0 \cdot x^0, x \geq 0_N\} = y^0{}_1$ and that x^1 is a solution to $\max_x\{t^*(y^1{}_2, y^1{}_3,\ldots,y^1{}_M, x) : w^1 \cdot x = w^1 \cdot x^1\} = y^1{}_1$, where t^* is the firm's transformation function that corresponds to the translog distance function D^*. The proof of the rest of the theorem is virtually identical to the proof of theorem (2.17) in Diewert (1976, pp. 139–40), except that the transformation function $t^*(y_2,y_3,\ldots,y_M, x)$ replaces the utility function $f(x)$, and y_1 replaces the utility level u.

Proof of (97)

Let $x^{1*}, x^{2*},\ldots,x^{M*}$ be a solution to the maximization problem (91). Using our assumed regularity conditions on Π^m, (91) becomes a concave programming problem, and we may apply the saddle-point theorem of Karlin (1959, p. 201) and Uzawa (1958) to obtain the existence of shadow prices $w^* \geq 0_N$, such that $x^{1*}, x^{2*},\ldots,x^{M*}$ is a solution to the following unconstrained maximization problem:

$$\text{(A3)} \qquad \max_{x^1,\ldots,x^M}\left\{\sum_{m=1}^{M}\Pi^m(p,x^m,z^m) - w^* \cdot \left(\sum_{m=1}^{M} x^m\right)\right\}.$$

In fact, our strong monotonicity assumptions on Π^m (along with the concavity assumptions) imply that $w^* \gg 0_N$ and that

$$\text{(A4)} \qquad \sum_{m=1}^{M} x^{m*} = x.$$

Now rewrite (A3) as

$$\max_{x^1,\ldots,x^M} \left\{ \sum_{m=1}^{M} \Pi^m(p,x^m,z^m) - w^* \bullet \left(\sum_{m=1}^{M} x^m \right) \right\}$$

$$= \sum_{m=1}^{M} \max_{x^m} \{\Pi^m(p,x^m,z^m) - w^* \bullet x^m\}$$

$$\text{(A5)} \qquad \equiv \sum_{m=1}^{M} \Pi^{*m}(p,w^*,z^m) \qquad \text{using definitions (94).}$$

$$= \max_{x,x^1,\ldots,x^M} \left\{ \sum_{m=1}^{M} \Pi^m(p,x^m,z^m) - w^* \bullet x : \sum_{m=1}^{M} x^m = x \right\},$$

which is equivalent to (A3) upon defining $x \equiv \sum_{m=1}^{M} x^m$

$$= \max_{x,x^1,\ldots,x^M} \left\{ \sum_{m=1}^{M} \Pi^m(p,x^m,z^m) - w^* \bullet x : \sum_{m=1}^{M} x^m \leq x \right\}$$

using the monotonicity properties of Π^m

$$= \max_x \{\Pi(p,x,z^1,\ldots,z^M) - w^* \bullet x\}$$

upon optimizing *w.r.t.* $x^1, \ldots, x^N$ and using the definition of Π, (92)

$$\text{(A6)} \qquad = \Pi^*(p,w^*,z^1,\ldots,z^M)$$

using the definition of Π^*, (95).

Thus (A5) = (A6), the desired result.

Notes

1. Notation: $w \rangle\rangle 0_N$ means that each component of the N-dimensional vector $w \equiv (w_1,w_2,\ldots,w_N)$ is positive where 0_N is a vector of zeros; $w \geq 0_N$ means that each component is nonnegative; $w > 0_N$ means $w \geq 0_N$ but $w \neq 0_N$; $w^T x \equiv \sum_{n=1}^{N} w_n x_n = w \bullet x$ is the inner product of the vectors w and x.

2. The only regularity condition we need impose on S is that a solution to the profit maximization problem (1) exist for the set of prices (w,p) under con-

sideration. This existence will generally be assured if S is a closed nonempty set with an appropriate property of boundedness from above. See McFadden (1978) or Diewert (1973*a*) on this point.

3. Gorman (1968*a*) uses this terminology.

4. McFadden (1978) and Lau (1976) use this terminology.

5. Diewert (1973*a*, 1974*b*) uses this terminology.

6. See Gorman (1968*a*), Diewert (1973*a*), and Lau (1976). A property of Π^* that we require below is the linear homogeneity of Π^* in w; that is, for every $\lambda > 0$, $w \rangle\rangle 0_N$, we have $\Pi^*(\lambda w, y) = \lambda\Pi^*(w,y)$.

7. S is convex if and only if for every scalar such that $0 \leq \lambda \leq 1$ and $(x^1,y^1) \epsilon S$, $(x^2,y^2) \epsilon S$, we have $(\lambda x^1 + (1-\lambda)x^2, \lambda y^1 + (1-\lambda)y^2) \epsilon S$.

8. Let $0 \leq \lambda \leq 1$, $(y^1{}_0, y^1) \epsilon S_\alpha$ and $(y^2{}_0, y^2) \epsilon S_\alpha$. Then $y^1{}_0 \leq \Pi^*(\alpha,y^1)$ and $y^2{}_0 \leq \Pi^*(\alpha,y^2)$. Convexity of S implies that $\Pi^*(\alpha,y)$ is a concave function of y (cf. Gorman 1968*a*) so $\Pi^*(\alpha, \lambda y^1 + (1-\lambda)y^2) \geq \lambda\Pi^*(\alpha,y^1) + (1-\lambda)\Pi^*(\alpha,y^2) \geq \lambda y^1{}_0 + (1-\lambda)y^2{}_0$, which implies $(\lambda y^1{}_0 + (1-\lambda)y^2{}_0, \lambda y^1 + (1-\lambda)y^2) \epsilon S_\alpha$.

9. That is, S is a cone; if $(x,y) \epsilon S$ and $\lambda \geq 0$, then $(\lambda x, \lambda y) \epsilon S$.

10. If S is a cone, then $\Pi^*(\lambda\alpha, y) = \lambda\Pi^*(\alpha,y)$ for every $\lambda \geq 0$, and the proof follows readily.

11. See Diewert (1974*b*, p. 139). It is an obvious modification of the translog function introduced by Jorgenson and Lau (1970).

12. $E\epsilon^r = \frac{1}{2} \sum_{i=1}^{N} \sum_{h=1}^{N} \beta_{ih}\, \sigma_{ih}$, which does not depend on r. If $N = 2$, then the regularity conditions (9) on β_{ih} along with the symmetry conditions $\beta_{ih} = \beta_{hi}$ imply that $\beta = \beta_{11} = -\beta_{12} = -\beta_{21} = \beta_{22}$, so that in this case $E\epsilon^r = \frac{1}{2}\beta[\sigma_{11} - 2\sigma_{12} + \sigma_{22}]$. Note that positive semidefiniteness of the variance covariance matrix $[\sigma_{ij}]$ implies that $\sigma_{11} - 2\sigma_{12} + \sigma_{22} \geq 0$, so that the sign of the bias $E\epsilon^r$ is determined by the sign of β. For a general N, we could expect the bias to be small, since we would not expect a systematic correlation between β_{ih} and σ_{ih}.

13. The assumption of time independence is somewhat unrealistic: if the relative price of the first good is higher than usual during a given period, we would expect this condition to persist for a number of subsequent periods. Thus autocorrelation is to be expected when estimating the parameters of an equation like (11).

14. This terminology follows Geary and Morishima (1973). The concept of weak separability is due to Sono (1961) and Leontief (1947). Note that Shephard actually considered the problem of simultaneously aggregating x and z into two aggregates.

15. See Diewert (1974*b*, p. 112). Similar formulas have been derived by Chipman (1970) and Samuelson (1972).

16. $p^{*T}x^* + w^{*T}z^* = C^*(u^*; p^*,w^*)$

$= \min_{x,z}\{p^{*T}x + w^{*T}z : f^*(x,z) \geq u^*\}$

$= \min_{x,z}\{p^{*T}x + w^{*T}z : \hat{f}[f(x),z] \geq u^*\}$ using (14)

$= \min_{x,z,y}\{p^{*T}x + w^{*T}z : \hat{f}[y,z] \geq u^*, y = f(x)\}$ adding an additional variable and equation

$= \min_{z,y}\{c(p^*)y + w^{*T}z : \hat{f}[y,z] \geq u^*\}$ upon minimizing with respect to x using (17)

$= \hat{C}(u^*; c(p^*),w^*)$ using definition (16)

$= c(p^*)f(x^*) + w^{*T}z^*$ since x^*,z^* is a solution to the first cost-minimization problem.

17. *Proof:* $x^{rT}\nabla f(x^r) = f(x^r)$ by Euler's theorem on homogeneous functions.

18. *Proof*: divide (26) by $p^{rT}x^r = c(p^r)f(x^r)$.

19. If all $\gamma_{jk} = 0$, then we are in the Cobb-Douglas case and the two aggregator functions coincide.

20. Or, alternatively, assume that x^r is a solution to the cost-minimization problem (17): $\min_x\{p^{rT}x : f(x) \geq f(x^r)\}$.

21. Solow (1957) presented his exposition in terms of a single output and two inputs. His argument is readily extended to the case of N inputs, as is done in Richter (1966), Star (1974), and Star and Hall (1976), for example.

22. Note that we do not have to estimate the unknown parameters of the production function.

23. See, for example, the empirical examples worked out in Fisher (1922).

24. See Konyus and Byushgens (1926), Afriat (1972), Pollak (1971), and Samuelson and Swamy (1974).

25. See Shephard (1953) or Diewert (1974*b*), or recall the material presented in section 8.2.2.

26. Actually, we require (43) to hold only for an empirically relevant subset of positive prices and outputs.

27. This theory is perhaps more clearly presented in Shephard (1953) and Solow (1955–56).

28. See also Afriat (1972), Pollak (1971), Samuelson and Swamy (1974), and Diewert (1976).

29. The term is due to Lau (1974): f is a second-order differential approximation to f^* at the point x^0 if and only if $f(x^0) = f^*(x^0)$, $\nabla f(x^0) = \nabla f^*(x^0)$ and $\nabla^2 f(x^0) = \nabla^2 f^*(x^0)$; that is, the levels of the functions coincide as well as their first- and second-order partial derivatives evaluated at x^0. Note that $\nabla f(x^0)$ is the vector of first-order partial derivatives of f evaluated at x^0, while $\nabla^2 f(x^0)$ is the matrix of second-order partial derivatives.

30. Note that ∇Q_2 stands for the vector of first-order partial derivatives of Q_2 with respect to all 4N arguments, etc.

31. The Laspeyres and Paasche quantity indexes give the same answer as the three "better" indexes only to the first order; that is, $\nabla^2 Q_L(p,p;x,x) \neq \nabla^2 Q_P(p,p;x,x) \neq \nabla^2 Q_2(p,p;x,x)$.

32. The functional forms f_r and c_r were studied by Denny (1974).

33. The proofs of theorems (50) and (51) do not rest on any assumption of optimizing behavior: they are simply theorems in numerical analysis rather than economics.

34. When the chain principle is used, the limited empirical evidence in Diewert (1978*b*) suggests that even the Paasche and Laspeyres indexes give virtually the same answer as the superlative indexes.

35. See Shephard (1953, pp. 61–71), Solow (1955–56), Gorman (1959), Blackorby et al. (1970), and Geary and Morishima (1973, pp. 100–103).

36. We consider only the Vartia I indexes, since they are indexes that have the property of consistency in aggregation. Sato (1976*a*) showed that the Vartia II indexes were exact for a CES aggregator function.

37. In fact, any pseudosuperlative index could be used. It is shown in Diewert (1978*b*) that any twice continuously differentiable symmetric mean of the Paasche and Laspeyres price indexes is a pseudosuperlative price index; for example, $\frac{1}{2} P_L(p^0,p^1; x^0,x^1) + \frac{1}{2} P_P(p^0,p^1; x^0,x^1)$ is pseudosuperlative.

38. Actually, some of the components of x^r can be outputs instead of inputs, in which case the corresponding components of w^r are indexed with a minus sign.

39. See McFadden (1978) for the properties of these functions.

40. The translog joint cost function is defined analogously to the translog variable profit function defined in section 8.2.1. However, since the logarithm of a negative number is not defined, we must renormalize the components of $y \equiv (y_1, \ldots, y_M)$ so that each $y_m > 0$. If y_m is an intermediate input, then we renormalize the corresponding price p_m to be minus the initial positive price.

41. Diewert (1978*b*) shows that $\tilde{Q}_0$ differentially approximates Q_0 to the second order if the partial derivatives are evaluated at equal price and quantity vectors. Thus, normally, $\tilde{Q}_0(w^0,w^1,x^0,x^1)$ will be numerically close to $Q_0(w^0,w^1,x^0,x^1)$. Similarly, $\tilde{P}_0$ will normally be close to P_0.

42. We make the same sign conventions as were noted in note 40. Thus, if there are intermediate inputs, the corresponding components of p^0 and p^1 will be negative. However, $Q_0(p^0,p^1,y^0,y^1)$ can still be calculated in the usual way even if some components of p^0 and p^1 are negative.

43. We now revert back to our original sign conventions: output and input prices are all positive, as are inputs x, but components of y can be negative if the corresponding good is an (intermediate) input. Note that even if some components of y^0 or y^1 are negative, we can still calculate P_0 using the usual formula.

44. There is also a close correspondence with consumer surplus concepts. Define the consumer's cost or expenditure function m as $m[f(x),p] \equiv \min_x\{p \cdot x : f(x) \geq f(x)\}$, where f is the consumer's utility function and p is a vector of commodity rental prices that the consumer faces. The (Laspeyres) Allen (1949) quantity index is defined as $Q_A(x^0,x^1,p^0) \equiv m[f(x^1),p^0]/m[f(x^0),p^1]$, while the (Laspeyres) Konyus (1939) cost of living index is defined as $P_K(p^0, p^1, x^0) \equiv m[f(x^0),p^1]/m[f(x^0),p^0]$. The consumer surplus concepts use arithmetic differences rather than ratios. Thus Hicks's (1946, pp. 40–41) *compensating variation* in income can be defined as $m[f(x^0),p^1] - m[f(x^0),p^0]$, while Hicks's (1946, p. 331) *equivalent variation* in income can be defined as $m[f(x^1),p^0] - m[f(x^0),p^0]$.

45. For formal proofs of duality theorems between distance functions and production or utility functions, see Shephard (1970), Hanoch (1978), McFadden (1978), Rockafellar (1970) and Blackorby, Primont, and Russell (1978).

46. See Gorman (1970), McFadden (1978), Hanoch (1975), and Blackorby and Russell (1976) for discussions on the separability properties of distance functions.

47. As usual, we have to change our sign conventions with respect to the components of y: assume that $y \equiv (y_1, y_2, \ldots, y_M) \rangle\rangle 0_M$, but if the mth good is actually an intermediate input, then the corresponding price p_m is taken to be negative. Note that we have not restricted $D^*[y,x]$ to be homogeneous of degree -1 in the components of y, which would be the case if production were subject to constant returns to scale. Finally, we note that the translog distance function can provide a second-order approximation to an arbitrary twice-differentiable distance function.

48. The sign conventions of note 47 are operative here also.

49. Actually, Klein considered the problem of simultaneously aggregating over commodities as well as sectors.

50. For an alternative proof, see Green (1964). Nataf (1948) and Green assumed the f^m were twice differentiable. These regularity conditions were relaxed by Gorman (1968*b*) to continuity and by Pokropp (1972) to monotonicity conditions alone.

51. A strongly separable production function can provide only a first-order approximation to a general production function.

52. If the individual production sets are S^m, $m = 1,2,\ldots,M$, then the aggregate technology S can be defined as the sum of the individual production sets; that is, $S \equiv \{z : z = \sum_{m=1}^{M} z_m$, where $z^m \in S^m$ for $m = 1,2,\ldots,M\}$. If the individual producer profit functions are defined as $\Pi^m(p) \equiv \max_{z^m}\{p \cdot z^m : z^m \in S^m\}$, then $\Pi(p) \equiv \max_z\{p \cdot z : z \in S\} = \sum_{m=1}^{M} \Pi^m(p)$; that is, the aggregate profit function equals the sum of the individual profit functions. There does not appear to be a simple characterization of the aggregate transformation function in terms of the individual transformation or production functions.

53. In the Solow problem, K (the number of outputs) is taken to be 1, and p_1 (the price of the output) is taken to be 1 also.

54. Concavity of $\Pi^m(p,x^m,z^m)$ in x^m is implied by convexity of S^m but is a considerably weaker restriction on the technology than convexity of S^m.

55. This approach was pioneered by Cornwall (1973).

56. This result can be traced back to Hotelling (1932). For modern proofs, see Gorman (1968*a*), McFadden (1978), or Diewert (1973*a*).

57. The rental price formula defined by equation (105) is similar to those derived by Jorgenson and Griliches (1967), except that they derive their formulas on the basis of a continuous-time optimization problem (as opposed to my discrete-time "Hicksian" period formulation), and thus the term $(1 + r)$ is missing from the denominator of their formulas. However, my formula (105) has the property that if $\delta = 1$ (i.e., the good is actually a nondurable), then the rental price equals the purchase price of the good plus associated tax payments (cf. eq. 104).

58. For example, consider the controversy between Jorgenson and his coworkers (Jorgenson and Griliches 1967, 1972; Christensen and Jorgenson 1969, 1970; Christensen, Cummings, and Jorgenson 1976) and Denison 1969, 1974, and Kendrick 1961, 1972, 1976.

59. The tax system that the producer is facing is not explicitly modeled in (108) but is implicit in the definitions of the prices p_z, p_y, and p_x.

60. Generally, if interest rates are positive, this capital aggregate would be an aggregate input. However, if maintenance and renovation expenditures were particularly large for the firm under consideration, it is possible for the capital aggregate to be a net output.

61. Epstein (1977, chap. 7) shows how the data limitations can be overcome in theory by an explicit econometric model.

62. From a theoretical point of view, the "Hicksian" capital services aggregate appears to be more appropriate than the Jorgenson-Griliches aggregate. However, from an empirical point of view, the "Hicksian" aggregate is more difficult to construct.

63. Kendrick (1972, p. 37) notes that official national income accounts in the United States and generally elsewhere exclude capital gains and losses, a comment that also applies to private accounting practices. With the recent upsurge of worldwide inflation, it has become more difficult to ignore capital gains, and a literature on accounting for inflation has sprung up (cf. Shoven and Bulow 1975 and the discussion following their paper).

64. See the analysis and references to the literature in Epstein (1977).

65. See Jorgenson and Griliches (1967), Christensen and Jorgenson (1969, 1970), and Christensen, Cummings, and Jorgenson (1976).

66. The former alternative seems more plausible to me: ex post internal rates of return seem to be too volatile to be an adequate approximation to the firm's actual borrowing or lending rates.

67. Winfrey distributions are widely used in the construction of capital stock aggregates. However, the following quotation from Creamer (1972, p. 68) indicates that their empirical foundation is not strong: "An examination of Winfrey's report discloses that the empirical basis of his distribution is his analysis of a sample of equipment retirements that are heavily weighted with railroad ties, trestles and power generating equipment. Moreover, these retirements occurred over the period 1869 and 1934. Clearly, this is an area that calls for new research."

68. See the examples tabulated in Tice (1967) and Creamer (1972).

69. Taxes on intermediate goods could be treated as follows in a model that aggregated firms 1 and 2: for each intermediate tax, break the corresponding commodity up into two commodities, one of which would be the "untaxed" market where firm 1 would sell its output q at price p. The government is thought of as buying the untaxed commodity at price p and then selling it back to firm 2 on the "taxed" market price $p(1+t)$. Aggregating over the two firms would yield an aggregate "untaxed" output of $q > 0$ selling at price p and an aggregate "taxed" input of $-q$ at price $p(1+t)$, while aggregation over the other goods could proceed as outlined in section 8.3.2. If t remained constant over time, the taxed and untaxed commodities could be aggregated using Hicks's aggregation theorem.

70. Denison (1974) favors estimating property income *net* of depreciation, whereas Kendrick (1972, p. 102) favors the *net* concept if one is interested in real product from a welfare standpoint, but the *gross* concept for production and productivity analysis.

71. The most preferred alternative would be to construct the "Hicksian" measure of capital services mentioned in the previous section.

72. See Denny and Sawyer (1976) for references to the theoretical national income accounting literature, plus a review of current Canadian accounting practices from the viewpoint of a neoclassical as opposed to a Keynesian approach to macroeconomic theory.

73. This would not be a problem if the capital services were included in sectoral estimates of intermediate inputs and gross output sectoral production functions were estimated.

74. Typically, rents to land are included in the accounting system, but asset prices and quantities of the different types of land do not appear.

75. See Christensen and Jorgenson (1969) and Christensen, Cummings, and Jorgenson (1976).

76. Creamer attributes this last point to Denison.

77. Under the appropriate assumptions, we can use the results of section 8.3.2 to justify the aggregation over the private producer sector and the household "processes" that create services out of consumer durable stocks.

78. Kendrick's (1976, p. 15) justification for including this item is given in the following quotation: "The costs of transfering resources are a form of investment, for investment in mobility results in an increase in the future income stream beyond what incomes would be if the shifts were not made."

79. Alternative assumptions giving the same result (item 8) are: f is linearly homogeneous, nondecreasing, and concave in all five inputs and the marginal products $\partial f(0,0,0,R_1,R_2)/\partial W$, $\partial f(0,0,0,R_1,R_2)/\partial K$ exist and are finite. In this case the industry will be made up of many tiny firms each earning tiny excess profits.

80. This does not mean that government public capital is unimportant (consider the massive United States interstate highway system): it means that in the

context of production function estimation, public capital goods should not be aggregated together with private capital but should appear as a separate inputs into the production function. However, in the context of productivity measurement, it does no harm to omit public capital goods, provided the shadow prices are zero, as we shall see in section 8.5.

81. Alternative economic models of R&D have recently been very ably surveyed by Woodland (1976).

82. See Diewert (1974*a*), Fisher and Shell (1972), and Samuelson and Swamy (1974) on this topic.

83. Assume g is defined for $y \geq 0_M$, and has the following properties: (*i*) $g(y) > 0$ for $y \rangle\rangle 0_M$ (positivity) (*ii*) $g(\lambda y) = \lambda g(y)$ for $\lambda \geq 0$, $y \geq 0$ (linear homogeneity), and (*iii*) $g(\lambda y^1 + (1-\lambda)y^2) \leq \lambda g(y^1) + (1-\lambda)g(y^2)$ for $0 \leq \lambda \leq 1$, $y^1 \geq 0_M$, $y^2 \geq 0_M$ (convexity).

84. If g satisfies the three properties listed in note 83, then r also has those three properties.

85. The proof is analogous to the proof of the Samuelson-Shephard duality theorem presented in Diewert (1974*a*); alternatively, see Samuelson and Swamy (1974).

86. A more complete exposition of the material presented in this section, with some additional material on the theory of partial Divisia indexes, can be found in Chinloy (1974).

87. The analysis for this case has been independently developed by Christensen, Cummings, and Jorgenson (1976), who cite Jorgenson and Lau (1979) as their source.

88. Ohta (1974) calls τ the primal rate of technical progress, and he shows that it is equal to the dual rate of technical progress λ defined as $\lambda \equiv -\partial \ln C(y,w,t)/\partial t$ if f exhibits constant returns to scale, where $C(y,w,t) \equiv \min_x\{w \cdot x : y = f(x,t)\}$ is the producer's total cost function.

89. See Blackorby, Lovell, and Thursby (1976) for a discussion of the different definitions of neutral technological change.

90. Make the same sign conventions as were made in the first part of section 8.2.6.

91. As usual, $\Pi^*(x,p,t)$ can provide a second-order approximation to an arbitrary twice continuously differentiable $\Pi(x,p,t)$. A special case of the time-modified translog variable profit function Π^* has been considered by Berndt and Wood (1975): in their model, x is a scalar output and y is a vector of inputs, so that, with appropriate sign changes, Π^* becomes a cost function. They also show under what conditions such a functional form can be consistent with factor-augmenting technical change.

92. See Diewert (1974*b*, pp. 137–40).

93. In Diewert (1978*b*) it is shown that $\tilde{Q}_0(p^0,p^1,y^0,y^1)$ and $Q_0(p^0,p^1,y^0,y^1)$ approximate each other to the second order at any point where $p^0 = p^1$ and $y^0 = y^1$.

94. See Shephard (1953, p. 41). A production function f is homothetic if there exists a monotonically increasing function of one variable g such that $g[f(\lambda x)] = \lambda g[f(x)]$ for every $\lambda > 0$, $x \geq 0_N$; that is, $g[f]$ is linearly homogeneous.

95. The use of the chain principle should minimize this type of error: for any two consecutive time periods, t^r, t^{r+1}, we could approximate accurately the shifting technology of the sector by a Π^{*r} defined by (135), whose parameters depend on r.

96. This point was made by Frisch (1936) forty years ago. For more details, see Diewert (1974*a*, p. 155) and Appelbaum (1979).

97. Other papers on the subject include Star (1974) and Hulten (1978).

98. Recall section 8.2.6.

99. Recall the discussion on this concept in section 8.2.5.

100. See Fisher and Shell (1972, p. 101) or Hofsten (1952, p. 97).

101. We require $r > 0$ so that $f_r(x^0, 0_{N-K})$ is well defined. Thus the translog functional form cannot be used as an aggregator function in this section.

102. If any components of x^0 or x^t are zero, then drop the corresponding equations from (174) or (175). For $r = 2$, we can drop the requirement that all components of the x vectors x^0 and x^t be nonnegative. We require only that $p^0 \cdot x^0 > 0$ and $p^t \cdot x^t > 0$. Thus we can deal with the case where f_2 is a transformation function. A negative component of the x vector indicates an output, a positive component indicates an input.

103. Actually, the base period normalization (176) implies that the number of independent parameters is $(N(N+1)/2) - 1$.

104. This paper is reprinted in Griliches (1971), where several other papers and an extensive bibliography on the hedonic approach to the quality adjustment problem will be found. Additional empirical work can be found in Gordon (1977), King (1976), and Ohta and Griliches (1976).

105. See McFadden (1978) for properties of joint cost functions.

106. If "trucks" are a durable input, then $P_r(x)$ should be the user cost of a "truck" with characteristics x during period r rather than the purchase price. Recall the discussion of rental price formulas in section 8.4.1.

107. See Diewert (1973*a*) for a discussion of the properties of such transformation functions. We do not require constant returns for the technology described by t.

108. See Blackorby, Primont, and Russell (1978) for a comprehensive discussion of separability.

109. Such functions are sometimes called input requirements functions. See Diewert (1974*a*) for a discussion of their properties.

110. An excellent discussion of many of the theoretical and practical difficulties associated with "hedonic" techniques can be found in Triplett (1975, 1976).

111. Recall the discussion about homogeneous weak separability in section 8.2.2. Note that we do not assume that the seasonal variables y^{rm} enter the objective function f in a separable way. Gersovitz and MacKinnon (1977) argue that in this case it is extremely difficult to construct deseasonalized p^{rm} and x^{rm} series that will be consistent with an underlying (nonseasonal) economic model. Thus, in the case of nonseparable seasonal variables interacting with economic variables, they suggest that it may often be appropriate to estimate econometrically completely separate models, one for each season, rather than attempting to estimate econometrically one model using data "seasonally adjusted" by conventional methods.

112. See Fisher (1922) for a discussion of the circular test and some empirical evidence that Q_2 satisfies circularity rather well. Since Q_0 is very close to Q_2 in most empirical situations, we would expect the same conclusion to hold for Q_0.

113. Appelbaum (1979) and Appelbaum and Kohli (1979) have applied this theoretical technique due originally to Frisch (1936).

114. Brown (this volume, chap. 7) calls this the commodity aggregation approach.

References

Afriat, S. N. 1972. The theory of international comparisons of real income and prices. In *International comparisons of prices and outputs*, ed. D. J. Daly, pp. 13–69. New York: National Bureau of Economic Research.

Allen, R. G. D. 1949. The economic theory of index numbers. *Economica*, n.s., 16:197–302.

Appelbaum, E. 1979. Testing price taking behavior. *Journal of Econometrics* 9:283–94.

Appelbaum, E., and Kohli, U. R. 1979. Canada–United States trade: Test for the small-open-economy hypothesis. *Canadian Journal of Economics* 12:1–14.

Archibald, R. B. 1977. On the theory of industrial price measurement: Output price indexes. *Annals of Economic and Social Measurement* 6:57–72.

Arrow, K. J. 1974. The measurement of real value added. In *Nations and households in economic growth: Essays in honor of Moses Abramovitz*, ed. P. David and M. Reder. New York: Academic Press.

Bergson (Burk), A. 1936. Real income, expenditure proportionality and Frisch's "New methods of measuring marginal Utility." *Review of Economic Studies* 4:33–52.

———. 1961. *National income of the Soviet Union since 1928*. Cambridge: Harvard University Press.

Berndt, E. R., and Christensen, L. R. 1973. The translog function and the substitution of equipment, structures and labor in U.S. manufacturing, 1929–68. *Journal of Econometrics* 1:81–113.

Berndt, E. R., and Wood, D. O. 1975. Technical change, tax policy, and the derived demand for energy. Mimeographed. Department of Economics, University of British Columbia.

Blackorby, C.; Lady, G.; Nissen, D.; and Russell, R. R. 1970. Homothetic separability and consumer budgeting. *Econometrica* 38:468–72.

Blackorby, C.; Lovell, D.; and Thursby, M. 1976. Extended Hicks neutral technical progress. *Economic Journal* 86:845–52.

Blackorby, C.; Primont, D.; and Russell, R. R. 1978. *Duality separability and functional structure: Theory and economic applications*. New York: American Elsevier.

Blackorby, C., and Russell, R. R. 1976. Conjugate implicit separability. Submitted to the *Review of Economic Studies*.

———. 1978. Indices and subindices of the cost of living and the standard of living. *International Economic Review* 19:229–40.

Bliss, C. J. 1975. *Capital theory and the distribution of income*. Amsterdam: North-Holland.

Bowley, A. L. 1928. Notes on index numbers. *Economic Journal* 38: 216–37.

Bruno, M. 1978. Duality, intermediate inputs and value-added. In *Produciton economics: A dual approach to theory and applications,* vol. 2, ed. M. Fuss and D. McFadden. Amsterdam: North-Holland.

Chinloy, P. 1974. Issues in the measurement of labor input. Ph.D. diss., Harvard University.

Chipman, J. S. 1970. Lectures on the mathematical foundations of international trade theory. I. Duality of cost and production functions. Mimeographed. Vienna: Institute of Advanced Studies.

Christensen, L. R.; Cummings, D.; and Jorgenson, D. W. 1976. Economic growth, 1947–1973: An international comparison. Harvard Institute of Economic Research Discussion Paper 521, Harvard University.

Christensen, L. R., and Jorgenson, D. W. 1969. The measurement of U.S. real capital input, 1929–1967. *Review of Income and Wealth,* ser. 15, no. 4, pp. 293–320.

———. 1970. U.S. real product and real factor input, 1929–1967. *Review of Income and Wealth* 16, no. 1:19–50.

Christensen, L. R.; Jorgenson, D. W.; and Lau, L. J. 1971. Conjugate duality and the transcendental logarithmic production function. *Econometrica* 39, no. 4:255–56.

Cornwall, R. R. 1973. A note on using profit functions to aggregate production functions. *International Economic Review* 14:511–19.

Creamer, D. 1972. Measuring capital input for total factor productivity analysis: Comments by a sometime estimator. *Review of Income and Wealth,* 18, pp. 55–78.

Daly, D. J. 1972. Combining inputs to secure a measure of total factor input. *Review of Income and Wealth,* ser. 18, pp. 27–53.

Denison, E. F. 1969. Some major issues in productivity analysis: An examination of estimates by Jorgenson and Griliches. *Survey of Current Business* 49, no. 5, part 2:1–27.

———. 1974. *Accounting for United States economic growth 1929–1969.* Washington, D.C.: Brookings Institution.

Denny, M. 1974. The relationship between functional forms for the production system. *Canadian Journal of Economics* 7:21–31.

Denny, M. G. S., and Sawyer, J. A. 1976. Revising the national accounts. *Canadian Journal of Economics* 9:720–32.

Diewert, W. E. 1971. An application of the Shephard duality theorem: A generalized Leontief production function. *Journal of Political Economy* 79:481–507.

———. 1973*a*. Functional forms for profit and transformation functions. *Journal of Economic Theory* 6:284–316.

———. 1973*b*. Afriat and revealed preference theory. *Review of Economic Studies* 40:419–26.

———. 1974*a*. Functional forms for revenue and factor requirements functions. *International Economic Review* 15:119–30.

———. 1974*b*. Applications of duality theory. In *Frontiers of quantitative economics*, vol. 2, ed. M. D. Intriligator and D. A. Kendrick. Amsterdam: North-Holland.

———. 1976. Exact and superlative index numbers. *Journal of Econometrics* 4:115–45.

———. 1978*a*. Hicks' aggregation theorem and the existence of a real value added function. In *Production economics: A dual approach to theory and applications*, ed. M. Fuss and D. McFadden, pp. 17–51. Amsterdam: North Holland.

———. 1978*b*. Superlative index numbers and consistency in aggregation. *Econometrica* 46:883–900.

Divisia, F. 1926. *L'indice monétaire et la théorie de la monnaie*. Paris: Société Anonyme du Recueil Sirey.

Domar, E. D. 1961. On the measurement of technological change. *Economic Journal* 71:709–29.

Epstein, L. E. 1977. Essays in the economics of uncertainty. Ph.D. diss. University of British Columbia, Vancouver.

Feldstein, M. S., and Rothschild, M. 1974. Towards an economic theory of replacement investment. *Econometrica* 42:393–424.

Fischer, S. 1974. Money and the production function. *Economic Inquiry* 12:517–33.

Fisher, F. M. 1965. Embodied technical change and the existence of an aggregate capital stock. *Review of Economic Studies* 32:263–88.

Fisher, F. M., and Shell, K. *The economic theory of price indices*. New York: Academic Press.

Fisher, I. 1922. *The making of index numbers*. Boston: Houghton Mifflin.

Frisch, R. 1936. Annual survey of general economic theory: The problem of index numbers. *Econometrica* 4:1–39.

Fuss, M., and McFadden, D. eds. 1978. *Production economics: A dual approach to theory and applications*. Amsterdam: North-Holland.

Geary, P. T., and Morishima, M. 1973. Demand and supply under separability. In *Theory of demand: Real and monetary*, ed. M. Morishima and others. Oxford: Clarendon Press.

Gersovitz, M., and MacKinnon, J. G. 1977. Seasonality in regression: Economic theory and econometric practice. Discussion Paper 257, Queen's University, Kingston, Canada.

Gordon, R. J. 1977. *The measurement of durable goods prices*. New York: National Bureau of Economic Research. Forthcoming.

Gorman, W. M. 1953. Community preference fields. *Econometrica* 21:63–80.

———. 1959. Separable utility and aggregation. *Econometrica* 27:469–81.

———. 1968*a*. Measuring the quantities of fixed factors. In *Value, capital and growth: Papers in honour of Sir John Hicks*, ed. J. N. Wolfe, pp. 141–72. Chicago: Aldine.

———. 1968*b*. The structure of utility functions. *Review of Economic Studies* 35:367–90.

———. 1970. Quasi-separable preferences, costs and technologies. Mimeographed. London School of Economics and Political Science.

Green, H. A. J. 1964. *Aggregation in economic analysis: An introductory survey*. Princeton, N.J.: Princeton University Press.

Griliches, Z. 1961. Hedonic price indexes for automobiles: An econometric analysis of quality change. In *The price statistics of the federal government*. New York: National Bureau of Economic Research.

———, *Price indexes and quality change: Studies in new methods of measurement*. Cambridge, Mass.: Harvard University Press.

Hall, R. 1968. Technical change and capital from the point of view of the dual. *Review of Economic Studies* 35:35–46.

Hanoch, G. 1975. Production or demand models with direct or indirect implicit additivity. *Econometrica* 43:395–420.

———. 1978. Symmetric duality and polar production functions. In *Production economics: A dual approach to theory and applications*, ed. M. Fuss and D. McFadden, 1:113–31. Amsterdam: North Holland.

Hardy, G. H.; Littlewood, J. E.; and Polya, G. 1934. *Inequalities*. Cambridge: Cambridge University Press.

Hicks, John R. 1946. *Value and capital*. 2d ed. Oxford: Clarendon Press.

———. 1965. *Capital and growth*. Oxford: Oxford University Press.

Hofsten, E. v. 1952. *Price indexes and quality changes*. London: George Allen and Unwin.

Hotelling, H. 1932. Edgeworth's taxation paradox and the nature of demand and supply functions. *Journal of Political Economy* 40:577–616.

———. 1935. Demand functions with limited budgets. *Econometrica* 3:66–78.

Houthakker, H. S. 1955–56. The Pareto distribution and the Cobb-Douglas production function in activity analysis. *Review of Economic Studies* 23:27–31.

Hulten, C. R. 1973. Divisia index numbers. *Econometrica* 41:1017–26.

———. 1978. Growth accounting with intermediate inputs. *Review of Economic Studies* 45:511–18.

Hulten, C. R., and Wykoff, F. C. Economic depreciation and the taxation of structures in U.S. manufacturing industries: An empirical analysis. Discussion Paper 77–02, Department of Economics, University of British Columbia.

Johansen, L. 1959. Substitution vs. fixed production coefficients in the theory of economic growth: A synthesis. *Econometrica* 27:157–76.

———. 1972. *Production functions*. Amsterdam: North-Holland.

Jorgenson, D. W. 1965. Anticipations and investment behavior. In *The Brookings Quarterly econometric model of the United States*, ed. James S. Duesenberry and others, pp. 35–94. Chicago: Rand McNally.

———. 1966. The embodiment hypothesis. *Journal of Political Economy* 74:1–17.

Jorgenson, D. W., and Griliches, Z. 1967. The explanation of productivity change. *Review of Economic Studies* 34:249–83.

———. 1972. Issues in growth accounting: A reply to Edward F. Denison. *Survey of Current Business* 52, no. 5, part 2: 65–94.

Jorgenson, D. W., and Lau, L. J. 1970. The transcendental logarithmic utility function and demand analysis. Department of Economics, Harvard University.

———. 1979. *Duality and technology*. Amsterdam: North-Holland. Forthcoming.

Karlin, S. 1959. *Mathematical methods and theory in games, programming and economics*. vol. 1, Palo Alto: Addison-Wesley.

Kendrick, J. W. 1961. *Productivity trends in the United States*. Princeton: Princeton University Press.

———. 1972. *Economic accounts and their uses*. New York: McGraw-Hill.

———. 1976. *The formation and stocks of total capital*. New York: National Bureau of Economic Research.

Khang, C. 1971. An isovalue locus involving intermediate goods and its applications to the pure theory of international trade. *Journal of International Economies* 1:315–25.

King, A. T. 1976. The demand for housing: Integrating the roles of journey-to-work, neighborhood quality and prices. In *Household production and consumption*, ed. N. E. Terleckyj, pp. 451–83. New York: National Bureau of Economic Research.

Klein, L. R. 1946*a*. Macroeconomics and the theory of rational behavior. *Econometrica* 14:93–108.

———. 1946*b*. Remarks on the theory of aggregation. *Econometrica* 14:303–12.

Kloek, T. 1967. On quadratic approximations of cost of living and real income index numbers. Report 6710, Econometric Institute, Netherlands School of Economics. Mimeographed.

Könus [Konyus], A. A. 1939. The problem of the true index of the cost of living. *Econometrica* 7:10–29. (Translation of a paper first published in *Ekonomicheskii Byulleten Konyunkturnovo Instituta* 3 [1924]:64–71.)

Konyus, A. A., and Byushgens, S. S. 1926. K probleme pokupatelnoi cili deneg. *Voprosi Konyunkturi* 2:151–72.

Lau, L. J. 1974. Comments on applications of duality theory. In *Frontiers of quantitative economics*, ed. M. D. Intriligator and D. A. Kendrick, 2:176–99. Amsterdam: North-Holland.

———. 1976. A characterization of the normalized restricted profit function. *Journal of Economic Theory* 12:131–63.

———. 1979. On exact index numbers. *Review of Economics and Statistics* 61:73–82.

Leontief, W. W. 1947. Introduction to a theory of the internal structure of functional relationships. *Econometrica* 15:361–73.

McFadden, D. 1978. Cost, revenue and profit functions. In *Production economics: a dual approach to theory and applications.* eds. M. Fuss and D. McFadden, 1:3–109. Amsterdam-North-Holland.

Malinvaud, E. 1953. Capital accumulation and the efficient allocation of resources. *Econometrica* 21:233–68.

Malmquist, S. 1953. Index numbers and indifference surfaces. *Trabajos de Estadistica* 4:209–42.

May, K. 1946. The aggregation problem for a one-industry model. *Econometrica* 14:285–98.

Moorsteen, R. H. 1961. On measuring productive potential and relative efficiency. *Quarterly Journal of Economics* 75:451–67.

Morishima, M. 1969. *Theory of economic growth.* London: Oxford University Press.

Nagatani, K. 1978. *Monetary theory*, Amsterdam: North-Holland.

Nataf, A. 1948. Sur la possibilité de construction de certains macromodèles. *Econometrica* 16:232–44.

Neumann, J. von. 1945–46. A model of general economic equilibrium. *Review of Economic Studies* 12:1–9.

Ohta, M. 1974. A note on duality between production and cost functions: Rate of returns to scale and rate of technical progress. *Economic Studies Quarterly* 25:63–65.

Ohta, M., and Griliches, Z. 1976. Automobile prices revisited: Extensions of the hedonic hypothesis. In *Household production and consumption*, ed. N. E. Terleckyj, pp. 325–90 New York: National Bureau of Economic Research.

Parkan, C. 1975. Nonparametric index numbers and tests for the consistency of consumer data. Department of Manpower and Immigration, Ottawa, Research Projects Group.

Pokropp, F. 1972. A note on the problem of aggregation. *Review of Economic Studies* 39:221–30.

Pollak, R. A. 1971. The theory of the cost of living index. Research Discussion Paper no. 11, Office of Prices and Living Conditions, U.S. Bureau of Labor Statistics.

Pu, S. S. 1946. A note on macroeconomics. *Econometrica* 14:299–302.

Richter, M. K. 1966. Invariance axioms and economic indexes. *Econometrica* 34:739–55.

Rockafellar, R. T. 1970. *Convex analysis.* Princeton, N.J.: Princeton University Press.

Ruggles, R. 1967. Price indexes and international price comparisons. In *Ten economic studies in the tradition of Irving Fisher*, ed. W. Fellner and others, pp. 171–205. New York: John Wiley

Samuelson, P. A. 1953–54. Prices of factors and goods in general equilibrium. *Review of Economic Studies* 21:1–20.

———. 1972. Unification theorem for the two basic dualities of homothetic demand theory. *Proceedings of the National Academy of Sciences, U.S.A.* 69:2673–74.

Samuelson, P. A., and Swamy, S. 1974. Invariant economic index numbers and canonical duality: Survey and synthesis. *American Economic Review* 64:566–93.

Sato, K. 1975. *Production functions and aggregation.* Amsterdam: North-Holland.

———. 1976*a*. The ideal log-change index number. *Review of Economics and Statistics* 58:223–28.

———. 1976*b*. The meaning and measurement of the real value added index. *Review of Economics and Statistics* 58:434–42.

Schworm, W. 1977. *User cost and investment theory.* Ph.D. diss., University of Washington, Seattle.

Shephard, R. W. 1953. *Cost and production functions.* Princeton: Princeton University Press.

———. 1970. *Theory of cost and production functions.* Princeton: Princeton University Press.

Shoven, J. B., and Bulow, J. I. 1975. Inflation accounting and nonfinancial corporate profits: Physical assets. *Brookings Papers on Economic Activity* pp. 557–98.

Solow, R. M. 1955–56. The production function and the theory of capital. *Review of Economic Studies* 23:101–8.

———. 1957. Technical change and the aggregate production function. *Review of Economics and Statistics* 39:312–20.

———. 1964. Capital, labor and income in manufacturing. In *The behavior of income shares*, pp. 101–28. Studies in Income and Wealth no. 26, Princeton: Princeton University Press.

Sono, M. 1961. The effect of price changes on the demand and supply of separable goods. *International Economic Review* 2:239–75.

Star, S. 1974. Accounting for the growth of output. *American Economic Review* 64:123–35.

Star, S., and Hall, R. E. 1976. An approximate divisia index of total factor productivity. *Econometrica* 44:257–64.

Stigum, B. P. 1967. On certain problems of aggregation. *International Economic Review* 8:349–67.

———. 1968. On a property of concave functions. *Review of Economic Studies* 35:413–16.

Taubman, P., and Wilkinson, M. 1970. User cost, capital utilization and investment theory. *International Economic Review* 11:209–15.

Theil, H. 1967. *Economics and information theory.* Amsterdam: North-Holland.

———. 1968. On the geometry and the numerical approximation of cost of living and real income indices. *De Economist* 116:677–89.

Tice, H. S. 1967. Depreciation, obsolescence, and the measurement of the aggregate capital stock of the United States, 1900–1962. *Review of Income and Wealth* 13:119–54.

Törnqvist, L. 1936. The Bank of Finland's consumption price index. *Bank of Finland Monthly Bulletin*, no. 10, pp. 1–8.

Triplett, J. E. 1975. The measurement of inflation: A survey of research on the accuracy of price indexes. In *Analysis of Inflation*, ed. P. H. Earl, pp. 19–82 Lexington, Mass.: D. C. Heath.

———. 1976. Consumer demand and characteristics of consumption goods. In *Household production and consumption*, ed. N.'E. Terleckyj, pp. 305–24. New York: National Bureau of Economic Research.

Usher, D. 1974. The suitability of the Divisia index for the measurement of economic aggregates. *Review of Income and Wealth* 20:273–88.

———. 1958. The Kuhn Tucker theorem in concave programming. In *Studies in linear and nonlinear programming*, ed. K. J. Arrow, L. Hurwicz, and H. Uzawa. Stanford: Stanford University Press.

Uzawa, H. 1964. Duality principles in the theory of cost and production. *International Economic Review* 5:216–20.

Vartia, Y. O. 1974. Relative changes and economic indices. Licensiate thesis in Statistics, University of Helsinki.

———. 1976. Ideal log change index numbers. *Scandanavian Journal of Statistics* 3:121–26.

Wold, H. 1944. A synthesis of pure demand analysis. *Skandinavisk Aktuarietidskift* 27:69–120.

Wold, H., in association with L. Juréen. 1953. *Demand analysis.* New York: John Wiley.

Woodland, A. D. 1972. The construction of price and quantity components of inputs for Canadian industries, 1927–1969. Department of Manpower and Immigration, Ottawa.
———. 1975. Substitution of structures, equipment and labor in Canadian production. *International Economic Review* 16:171–87.
———. 1976. Modelling the production sector of an economy: A selective survey and analysis. Discussion Paper 76-21, Department of Economics, University of British Columbia.
Zarnowitz, V. 1961. Index numbers and the seasonality of quantities and prices. In *The price statistics of the federal government*. New York: National Bureau of Economic Research.

Comment Michael Denny

The analysis of capital aggregation given at this conference may appear technically complex, but it is possible to summarize the results in a simpler, though not rigorous, manner. Before turning to the details of Professor Diewert's paper, let me consider some implications of the basic results that underlie and motivate both his paper and Professor Brown's. As theorists, both Brown and Diewert are arguing that the conditions required for aggregation are stringent. So stringent that perhaps we should not publish or use aggregated data in the unassuming manner that is our current practice.

We are all familiar with the necessity to aggregate quantities of different goods or services. It is impossible to imagine economic data without aggregation: thus we should seriously consider the losses involved in our current techniques. Fundamentally, aggregation in practice involves weighting the elements according to some formula that produces an aggregate of the elements. One must remember that it is *not* the voluminous literature on index numbers that is relevant. Our authors are asking a prior question: When may we aggregate by any method and not suffer losses because of the information suppressed by aggregation? The aggregate provides less information, and in the loose framework that I am currently using there is a loss that will result in errors. Consider a specific example in which two types of capital, K_1 and K_2, and labor, L, are used to produce output (fig. C8.1). We can characterize this process abstractly as a production function, $Q = f(K_1,$

Michael Denny is associated with the Institute for Policy Analysis and the Department of Political Economy, University of Toronto.

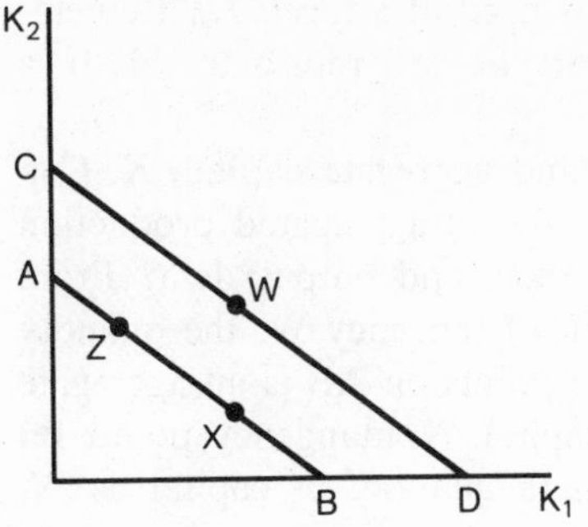

Fig. C8.1

K_2, L). Although I have chosen a production function, the argument would be similar for any other technical or behavioral function, for example, supply, demand, or cost function.

Suppose we consider the aggregation of the two types of capital. In general we will have, $K = g(K_1, K_2)$, where K is the aggregate quantity of capital and g is the function or rule that describes how we aggregate. In figure C8.1, the line "AB" represents a specific value of aggregate capital using a particular aggregation rule. Similarly, the line "CD" represents a greater value of aggregate capital using the same aggregation rule or formula. The loss of information is obvious. Any point Z, on line AB, represents particular quantities of the two capital services. Once we aggregate we can not distinguish Z from any other point X on the same line AB. We can distinguish Z (and X) from W on line CD.

We wish to know how this loss of information will affect our ability to investigate our production process. In figure C8.2, the line AB represents an aggregate quantity of capital. An isoquant, labeled (Q_o, L_o), has also been drawn tangent to AB at point W. The isoquant shows the alternative combinations of the two types of capital that can be used

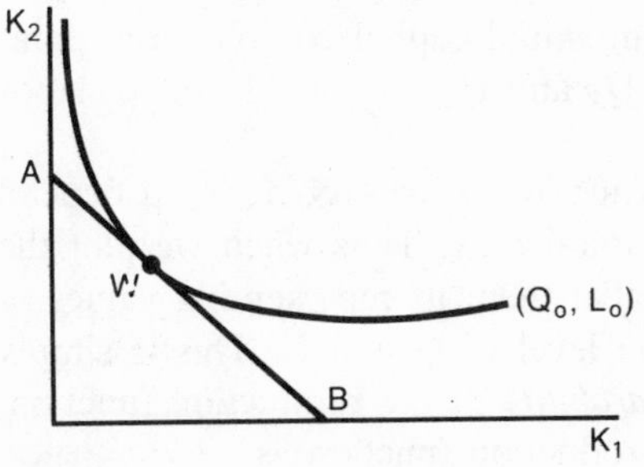

Fig. C8.2

to produce output *level*, Q_o, when labor is used at a *level*, L_o. Remember that we have to fix the level of labor; we will return to this in a moment.

Suppose we have data only on Q, L, and aggregate capital, K. Can we adequately acquire information about the disaggregated production technology from the aggregate capital, labor, and output data? From figure C8.2, we can state that at the point of tangency W, the quantity of aggregate capital represented by all the points on AB is an aggregate of the true disaggregated quantities of capital. Nontangency points on AB, while they present the same aggregate quantity of capital as W, must represent capital input combinations that lie on different isoquants.

Holding labor constant, the same aggregate quantity of capital will produce smaller and smaller quantities of output as we move away from W along AB in either direction. The use of aggregate capital will imply that the same quantities of aggregate capital and labor are capable of producing a wide variety of output levels. This is inconsistent with the production function that assumes that only one output level is associated with the efficient use of a given input bundle.

A very special linear aggregation function was used in figure C8.1. Consider bending the line AB so that it coincides precisely with isoquant (Q_o,L_o). Now this will mean that the single aggregate quantity of capital corresponds to all disaggregated input quantities that produce output Q_o in conjunction with a labor input, L_o. This seems hopeful, since now we have a measure of aggregate capital that corresponds to a particular unique input-output combination.

We have made a different but special assumption about the aggregation formula when we require that it correspond to the isoquant. However, this assertion is required if we are to eliminate aggregation errors.

Our special aggregator function that corresponds to a unique isoquant in figure C8.2 must be generalized to cover situations in which the level of output or labor do not equal (Q_o,L_o). The set of isoquants in figure C8.3 represents three different levels of output and the *same* quantity of labor input. However, these labels are not necessarily unique: any point on an isoquant could be consistent with a large number of output-labor combinations. For example, our initial capital combination, point A, could also produce output levels Q_1 and Q_2 for some levels of labor greater than L_0.

We have defined our aggregator function, $K = g(K_1,K_2)$, to depend on the disaggregated quantities of capital only. Thus when we plot the level sets of this function, we can label them as representing values of aggregate capital, independent of the level of Q and L. This is simply the condition required for *weak separability* of the production function, and in this case, we can write our production function as

$$(1) \qquad Q = f(g(K_1,K_2),L).$$

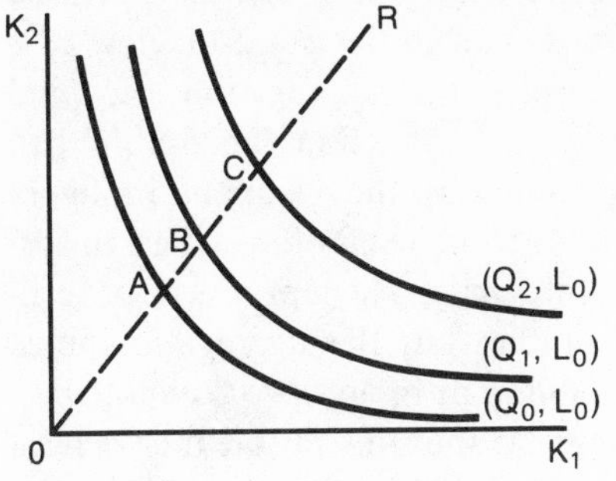

Fig. C8.3

Our aggregator function *g* is the first argument of the production function in this case. It turns out that the micro capital inputs, K_1 and K_2, must be weakly separable from all other inputs and output in order for a capital aggregate to exist; that is, we must be able to write the production function in the form (1) in order for a capital aggregate to exist (*unless* the rental prices of K_1 and K_2 happen to vary proportionally, in which case an aggregate can be constructed using Hicks's aggregation theorem even if the technology is not weakly separable in the micro capital inputs). Moreover, to actually *measure* the capital aggregate using just market data, we require an additional assumption in addition to (1): we require that the aggregator function *g* be *homothetic*, that is, we require that *g* be a monotonically increasing function of a linearly homogeneous function. In fact, it turns out that there is no real loss of generality in assuming that *g* is actually linearly homogeneous once we have made the initial assumption of homotheticity.

In figure C8.3, the ray OR through the origin cuts the isoquants at points A, B, and C. It was mentioned above that, to measure the capital aggregate, we required homotheticity in addition to weak separability. This property requires that the slopes of the isoquants at A, B, and C are equal. Why is this property or the (equivalent in the present context) property of linear homogeneity needed? The link between aggregation theory and index number theory requires the homogeneity property. Index numbers almost always have the property that they are linear homogeneous in their elements. If you double all the components, then you double the aggregate. If we are to have an aggregate quantity calculated by a rule that is consistent with an index number formula, then the isoquants in figure C8.3 must be homothetic (except when one uses a Malmquist index number formula, which does not require homotheticity). However, there are other reasons for assuming homotheticity. Consistent two-stage maximization will require this property, and this is the primary theoretical rationale.

The other major conditions that permit aggregation can be discussed in relation to the first case. Remember that from the point of view of a national statistics office, our first case implies that aggregation of capital must be done *separately* for each *different* production function. When the aggregation function was "bent" to match the isoquant in figure C8.2, this was done for a specific production technology. The unfortunate conclusion must be that not only must *each* production technology be homothetically weakly separable, but the aggregation must be done separately if the isoquants are different in any two technologies. Practically, this is impossible, and it may be that this problem is at least as important in practice as the assumption of separability.

For a single aggregate capital to be useful in two different production sectors, it turns out that each sector, i, must have a production function, $Q_i = f_i(g(K_1,K_2),L)$, $i = 1,2$. The idea of aggregating across sectors is only an extension of using the same aggregate in different sectors. Although the details will not be included here, the nonmathematical reader should be able to understand the following argument.

Consider the following special case of intersectoral aggregation. The disaggregated problem is to maximize the value of one output given the value of the other output and a fixed total amount of our three inputs. This problem will have a solution of the form $\emptyset\ (Q_1,Q_2,K_1,K_2,L) = 0$, where Q_i is the ith output and K_j and L are the simple aggregates of each input. Suppose we wish to have aggregate production technology of the form,

$$Q = H(Q_1,Q_2) = f(K_1,K_2,L), \quad (2)$$

or

$$Q = H(Q_1,Q_2) = F(K,L), \quad (3)$$

where $K = g(K_1,K_2)$ is an aggregate of the different types of capital.

Without rigorous proof we can link this type of problem to our earlier case. If we are to shift from the disaggregated function $\emptyset$ to the aggregation involved in (2) we are already severely constraining the technologies of the sectors. For (2) to be a valid representation of $\emptyset$, the production technologies for the individual sectors must have *almost* identical isoquants. The *almost* has to be put in because the isoquants can be numbered differently for each sector. Notice that in (2) we have not aggregated capital of *different types*. Even without capital aggregation, the aggregation of output will force the isoquants of the two sectors to be almost identical. If we now aggregate the different *types* of capital, the restrictive assumptions on the already similar isoquants of the two sectors will be increased. This movement from equation (2) to equation (3) is nothing more than the simultaneous application of our earlier argument to both sectors. Aggregation of outputs and capital requires a more complex and restrictive set of assumptions.

Should we throw up our hands? No, the requirements of both policy and science rule against that reaction. Economic theory without empirical confirmation will not be science. *Both* theorists and empirical investigators must accept the stringent conditions of aggregating. However, while more disaggregated data is desirable and is becoming available, the high costs of high-quality disaggregated data will preclude the elimination of aggregation. The notion of a *totally disaggregated* production function as a technical constraint is an abstraction. There is no room for an extensive catalog of possibilities, but I will state a rough guide. Both empirical and theoretical economists must continue attempts to reorient the theory to bring the "level" of abstraction closer to the "level" of observations.

At the most general level, one can approach Diewert's paper in the following manner. There is a large body of literature on aggregation and index numbers. What Diewert has done is to focus and link the powerful theoretical tools of duality theory and the recent work on flexible functional forms with this traditional literature. While there are no startling new results, the paper does integrate a scattered literature and provide some interesting insights on the interface between these areas.

Diewert has broken down the problems of aggregation into (*a*) aggregation over goods, (*b*) aggregation over sectors, and (*c*) aggregation over time. The aggregation of capital is initially treated as a special case of these types of aggregation. However, in the final three sections the special problems of technical progress, new goods, and seasonality are investigated. These are all problems that are intimately related to the special nature of capital goods and their production.

There are two sets of conditions that permit aggregation of goods. These are price proportionality and homogeneous weak separability (which is equivalent to the homothetic weak separability assumption we discussed above). The first condition states that if the prices of a group of goods varies proportionally, then it is possible to define an aggregate quantity of the goods. Provided the micro price proportionality holds, then the aggregate quantity can be used in place of the micro quantities. Many empirical price series seem to move with approximate proportionality. Diewert opens the investigation of an area that could have wide application. For a particular model of how prices deviate from proportionality, Diewert shows how the absence of strict price proportionality will affect the results. In this example as well as several others, Diewert does not clearly indicate the possibilities of generalizing his special case. It may be possible to aggregate with relatively small errors in a wide variety of situations if the very particular model can be expanded.

The second set of conditions, homogeneous weak separability, imposes restrictions on the production, demand, or utility function. Diewert concentrates on investigating the alternative methods of finding the most suitable aggregate under the assumption that homogeneous weak separability is acceptable. This problem provides the core of a very large section of the paper. If micro data are available and the second set of aggregation conditions is acceptable, then one can proceed by two methods. Using the micro data, the investigator may either estimate a functional form for an aggregator function or else choose an index number formula. Diewert defines the concepts of exact and superlative index numbers to provide a link between these two methods. If we choose an index number, then what assumptions about the underlying technology are we making? For a number of well-known index formulas, Diewert shows that they are equivalent to the use of a particular functional form. This work provides a link to the recent development of flexible functional forms. Essentially, the following proposition is being suggested. Flexible functional forms such as the Translog can approximate to the second order any functional form. Consequently, if we do not know the true functional form for an index, we should choose a *superlative* index, that is, one that is *exact* for a flexible functional form. This will ensure that we can approximate the true form, and we do not need to estimate the true function. This also suggests that the choice of a particular index formula from those that are superlative is not important. All the formulas will provide a second-order approximation to the true function, and it will not matter which formula is chosen.

If one uses one of the superlative indexes, then the following problem will arise. If one aggregates over some group of commodities and then uses the calculated aggregates in a second-state aggregation, will the results be consistent with single-stage aggregation? The answer in general is no. For consistency in two-stage aggregation, the function must be Cobb-Douglas. What Diewert does is to show that, provided one uses a superlative index or a Vartia index, the results will be approximately consistent. Basically, as one would expect, the underlying rationale is that if observations in adjacent periods are chained, then for small changes between adjacent periods, no problem will arise with multistage aggregates.

Let me provide one concrete example of the type of specific problem that is being considered. A *true index of inputs* between two periods $X(X^0,X^1;p^*)$ must equal the ratio of the variable profit functions in the two periods: $\pi(X^1,p^*)/\pi(X^0,p^*)$.

It is shown that if there are:

(*a*) constant returns to scale,

(*b*) profit-maximizing behavior with respect to inputs X and outputs Y for periods 0 and 1 given output price vectors p^0, p^1 and input price vectors w^0,w^1,

(*c*) a translog function for π, and

(*d*) the reference price p^* equals the geometric mean of p^0 and p^1,

then $Q_0(w^0,w^1,X^0\,X^1)$ — a Törnqvist index of inputs will be correct.

An alternative approach to index numbers has been developed by Malmquist and extended by Pollak and by Blackorby and Russell. What Diewert is able to show is that the Törnqvist index defined above can be interpreted as a Malmquist index provided the distance function is translog and producers minimize with respect to the inputs. The point is that the Malmquist interpretation requires fewer restrictions. Neither constant returns to scale nor profit maximization is required.

Diewert has developed a very useful set of procedures for choosing an aggregation function. We must remember that he has accepted the weak separability conditions required for aggregation. While this may seem like a very weak second-best procedure, I believe this type of two-stage investigation will become very common. This topic is beyond the concern of this conference, but it is one of the links of index numbers and aggregation theory with a growing empirical literature.

The section on aggregation over sectors is brief and, as expected, the results do not suggest much optimism. I believe Diewert is correct in focusing on the possibilities of models, such as Johansen's, that attempt to link micro and macro observations. Further empirical investigations of these models is needed.

Capital aggregation suffers from all the problems of goods aggregation in general. While Diewert does suggest a more general intertemporal Hicksian model for a capital-using firm, he backs away from any serious suggestion of its implementation owing to the difficulties of obtaining the required data. This section should be extended to clarify the possibilities of measurement. If capital aggregation is viewed as equivalent to noncapital aggregation, as Diewert states in section 8.4.1, then the problems of aggregation over time must be solved. Better data on depreciation, discards, and used capital market prices could mean that capital aggregation is similar to noncapital aggregation. However, at present this is not true. The durability of capital creates difficulties in constructing a capital aggregate from an empirical point of view, *additional* to the theoretical difficulties inherent in constructing any kind of an aggregate.

The rest of the chapter turns to a number of special problems that are closely connected with capital goods. The latter are generally thought to be durable, heterogeneous in design, and subject to rapid design changes. This description may be biased toward problems with equipment, although structures are by no means homogeneous even if design changes may be less relevant.

The measurement of technical change has been fraught with all the problems of capital goods measurement. It has also been an emotional area where prior beliefs often determine one's evaluation of particular studies. Using the work of Jorgenson and Griliches as an example, several points are made. Provided all variables are measured correctly the Jorgenson-Griliches technique requires: (*a*) separability of outputs and inputs; (*b*) competitive profit-maximizing behavior; (*c*) neutral technical progress. Diewert develops a more general case in which (*a*) and (*c*) are weakened. His results, which are mildly surprising, are that the measure of technical change is approximately equal in both cases. The only difference is the use of an implicit rather than explicit index. This is encouraging.

In attempting to extend this result to technical progress over a number of sectors, some difficulties arise. To obtain an answer, further restrictions on technical change within a sector are required. They must all be strongly Hicks neutral. In this case, the geometric mean of the sectoral measures of technical change provides the correct answer.

Having assessed the present status of measures of technical change, Diewert turns to perhaps the most serious and frustrating problem of all. New goods are continually being developed, and our capability of analyzing problems is limited by the complexity of measurement and theory in the presence of new goods.

In examining the new-goods problem, two approaches are considered. An attempt to evaluate the errors associated with (*a*) setting the price of a good equal to zero in the period in which a new good is unavailable and (*b*) setting the price equal to zero in both periods. The first is always biased upward. The second is biased upward if the new good has a relative price change less than the relative price change of a Paasche price index of all goods. It is shown that the upward bias in (*a*) is smaller than in (*b*), which suggests a method for measuring prices not commonly used in these cases.

The second approach uses duality theory and flexible functional forms to suggest a possible method for estimating the "reservation" prices of the new good in the first period. I cannot explain the details here. However, I think it is clear as the author states that the data requirements for implementation are severe.

I would like to see some suggestions made from the floor over the course of this conference on how we proceed under conditions that I believe we can roughly agree upon. If our theoretical understanding of measurement and aggregation problems in capital requires vastly improved data, then how are we to proceed on either generating that data or evaluating the net benefits of alternative data collection systems? The distance in Canada and the United States between the designers and implementers of data-collection systems and the users in economics is large. While my appeal is not original, I believe we need to and can provide assistance in improving the data. I will go no further here, but I hope that some mechanism for more serious consultation will arise in both the United States and Canada.

Although he has not pursued it intensively enough, in my opinion, Diewert does begin the investigation of the problems of specifying and estimating a hedonic model in which goods have characteristics. Unfortunately, the problem of aggregating the qualities of characteristics is simplified by assuming that only one type of trade is purchased and that the total quantity of a given characteristic is simply the product of the number of trades, times the per trade quantity of that characteristic. Diewert is aware of this limitation, and within a limited space he does provide the beginnings of a useful model for estimating hedonic models.

I have omitted several topics such as aggregation of seasonal variables and vintage capital models. It is very difficult to provide an evaluation of a very long and detailed paper. I will restrict myself to some quite general remarks. The theory of index numbers has predominantly been developed in terms of homogeneous functions. This appears perfectly reasonable when you think of an aggregate quantity index as independent of any behavioral or technical function. However, if you pursue the links between economic theory, index numbers, and flexible forms, then this assumption becomes suspect. If you double a subset of the micro inputs of a production function, you need not expect the aggregate input to double unless you want the production technology to be homogeneous. The problem is that, though weak separability does not require homotheticity or homogeneity, consistent two-stage optimization and consequently consistent aggregation does require one of these assumptions. It would be pleasant to hope some work could be done on considering weaker forms of homotheticity and errors associated with approximate homotheticity. The latter, of course, should be contrasted with the possibility of approximate price proportionality.

I would like to emphasize a few points of danger. First, the detailed concrete results in many portions of the paper are derived using particular cases of flexible functional forms. I have urged Diewert to attempt to clarify the following issue. In what cases is it true that the results can be obtained for any or many flexible forms, and in what case are the results highly specific to a particular form?

Empirical studies in economics are slowly recognizing the necessity of a more direct recognition of the approximations involved in both the data and the functional forms. The pure theory of aggregation is never going to comfort the empirical economists. The gap must be closed with more explicit models of the errors of approximation and aggregation that are bound to arise. Diewert's paper is a contribution to this very broad question, although it is only a beginning.

Reply by Diewert

A brief response to a number of specific points raised by Professor Denny seems in order. Section 8.4 of my paper has been totally revised to reflect Denny's comment that "the durability of capital creates difficulties in constructing a capital aggregate from an empirical point of view, *additional* to the theoretical difficulties inherent in constructing any kind of an aggregate."

Second, Professor Denny astutely observes that the many concrete results in the paper have been derived under the assumption that the underlying functional form is translog, and he asks whether similar concrete results can be generated by using other flexible functional forms instead of the translog. My answer is that it may be possible, but I have not been able to do it. It appears to be difficult to obtain functional forms that are linearly homogeneous, flexible, and quadratic in logarithms so that the quadratic approximation lemma (59) yields the very useful identity (64), upon which my concrete results are built.

Third, Professor Denny notes that the theory of index numbers has predominantly been developed in terms of homogeneous functions, and he wonders to what extent this assumption could be relaxed. I have certainly made liberal use of the assumption of constant returns to scale in my paper. However, the reader should note that all of my results involving the Malmquist quantity index did *not* require the linear homogeneity assumption (but they *did* require the choice of a very specific reference vector). I further note that although I have assumed homogeneous weak separability in order to justify two-stage optimization and aggregation, the *theoretical* literature on two-stage budgeting and decentralization does not require homogeneous weak separability. The main theorems in this area are due to Gorman (1959) and the extensive literature on the subject is reviewed and extended by Blackorby, Primont, and Russell (1978, chap. 5). On the other hand, the index number implications of this literature have not yet been completely worked out, although Afriat's (1972) theory of marginal price indexes makes a start in this direction. This appears to be a fruitful area for further research, as Denny notes.

Contributors

Martin J. Bailey
Economics Department
University of Maryland
College Park, Maryland 20742

Murray Brown
Department of Economics
State University of New York
at Buffalo
608 O'Brian Hall
Buffalo, New York 14260

Edwin Burmeister
Department of Economics
114 Rouss Hall
University of Virginia
Charlottesville, Virginia 22901

Robert M. Coen
Department of Economics
Northwestern University
Evanston, Illinois 60201

Michael Denny
Institute for Policy Analysis
University of Toronto
150 St. George Street
Toronto, Ontario M5S 1A1

W. E. Diewert
Department of Economics
University of British Columbia
Vancouver, British Columbia
V6T 1W5

Robert Eisner
Department of Economics
Northwestern University
Evanston, Illinois 60201

Stanley Engerman
Department of Economics
University of Rochester
College of Arts and Science
Rochester, New York 14627

Solomon Fabricant
National Bureau of Economic
Research
15–19 West Fourth Street
Washington Square
New York, New York 10012

Jack G. Faucett
Jack Faucett Associates
5454 Wisconsin Avenue
Suite 1150
Chevy Chase, Maryland 20015

Charles R. Hulten
The Urban Institute
2100 M Street, N.W.
Washington, D.C. 20037

John W. Kendrick
Department of Economics
George Washington University
Building C, Room 624
Washington, D.C. 20052

John C. Musgrave
National Income and Wealth Division
United States Department of Commerce
Bureau of Economic Analysis
Washington, D.C. 20230

Sherwin Rosen
Department of Economics
University of Chicago
1126 East 59th Street
Chicago, Illinois 60637

Thomas K. Rymes
Economics Department
Carleton University
Ottawa, Ontario K1S 5B6

John J. Soladay
Exxon Corporation
1251 Avenue of the Americas
New York, New York 10020

Paul Taubman
Department of Economics
University of Pennsylvania
3718 Locust Walk CR
Philadelphia, Pennsylvania 19104

Dan Usher
Department of Economics
Queen's University
Kingston, Ontario K7L 3N6

J. W. S. Walton
Cabinet Office
Central Statistical Office
George Street
London, United Kingdom SW1P 3AQ

Frank C. Wykoff
Department of Economics
Pomona College and the Claremont Graduate School
Claremont, California 91711

Allan H. Young
United States Department of Commerce
Bureau of Economic Analysis
Washington, D.C. 20230

Author Index

Subject Index